Lecture Notes in Artificial Intelligence 3661

Edited by J. G. Carbonell and J. Siekmann

Subseries of Lecture Notes in Computer Science

Themis Panayiotopoulos   Jonathan Gratch
Ruth Aylett   Daniel Ballin
Patrick Olivier   Thomas Rist (Eds.)

Intelligent
Virtual Agents

5th International Working Conference, IVA 2005
Kos, Greece, September 12-14, 2005
Proceedings

 Springer

Series Editors

Jaime G. Carbonell, Carnegie Mellon University, Pittsburgh, PA, USA
Jörg Siekmann, University of Saarland, Saarbrücken, Germany

Volume Editors

Themis Panayiotopoulos
University of Piraeus, Department of Informatics
80 Karaoli & Dimitriou str., Piraeus, 18534, Greece
E-mail: themisp@unipi.gr

Jonathan Gratch
University of Southern California, Institute for Creative Technologies
13274 Fiji Way, Marina del Rey, CA 90292, USA
E-mail: gratch@ict.usc.edu

Ruth Aylett
Heriot-Watt University, Mathematics and Computer Science
Edinburgh EH14 4AS, UK
E-mail: ruth@macs.hw.ac.uk

Daniel Ballin
Chief Technology Office
BT Group, Room 66, B54, Adastral Park, Ipswich IP5 3RE, UK
E-mail: daniel.ballin@bt.com

Patrick Olivier
University of Newcastle upon Tyne, Informatics Research Institute
Newcastle upon Tyne NE1 7RU, UK
E-mail: p.l.olivier@ncl.ac.uk

Thomas Rist
University of Applied Sciences Augsburg
Friedberger Str. 2a, 86161 Augsburg, Germany
E-mail: tr@rz.fh-augsburg.de

Library of Congress Control Number: 2005931803

CR Subject Classification (1998): I.2.11, I.2, H.5, H.4, K.3

ISSN   0302-9743
ISBN-10   3-540-28738-8 Springer Berlin Heidelberg New York
ISBN-13   978-3-540-28738-4 Springer Berlin Heidelberg New York

This work is subject to copyright. All rights are reserved, whether the whole or part of the material is
concerned, specifically the rights of translation, reprinting, re-use of illustrations, recitation, broadcasting,
reproduction on microfilms or in any other way, and storage in data banks. Duplication of this publication
or parts thereof is permitted only under the provisions of the German Copyright Law of September 9, 1965,
in its current version, and permission for use must always be obtained from Springer. Violations are liable
to prosecution under the German Copyright Law.

Springer is a part of Springer Science+Business Media

springeronline.com

© Springer-Verlag Berlin Heidelberg 2005
Printed in Germany

Typesetting: Camera-ready by author, data conversion by Scientific Publishing Services, Chennai, India
Printed on acid-free paper   SPIN: 11550617   06/3142   5 4 3 2 1 0

Preface

The origin of the Intelligent Virtual Agents conference dates from a successful workshop on Intelligent Virtual Environments held in Brighton at the 13th European Conference on Artificial Intelligence (ECAI'98). This workshop was followed by a second one held in Salford in Manchester in 1999. Subsequent events took place in Madrid, Spain in 2001 and Irsee, Germany in 2003 and attracted participants from both sides of the Atlantic as well as Asia.

This volume contains the proceedings of the 5th International Working Conference on Intelligent Virtual Agents, IVA 2005, held on Kos Island, Greece, September 12–14, 2005, which highlighted once again the importance and vigor of the research field. A half-day workshop under the title "Socially Competent IVA's: We are not alone in this (virtual) world!" also took place as part of this event. IVA 2005 received 69 submissions from Europe, North and South America, Africa and Asia. The papers published here are the 26 full papers and 14 short papers presented at the conference, as well as one-page descriptions of the 15 posters and the descriptions of the featured invited talks by Prof. Justine Cassell, of Northwestern University and Prof. Kerstin Dautenhahn, of the University of Hertfordshire.

We would like to thank a number of people that have contributed to the success of this conference. First of all, we thank the authors for their high-quality work and their willingness to share their ideas. We thank the Program Committee, consisting of the editors and 74 distinguished researchers, who worked hard to review the submissions and to select the best of them for presentation. A special thanks goes to the Local Organizing Committee for their efficient work on preparing and running the event. We would like to thank our sponsors for their financial support and, last but not least, we thank all those who attended the conference.

We invite readers to enjoy the papers in this book and look forward to the next Intelligent Virtual Agents conference.

July 2005

Themis Panayiotopoulos
Jonathan Gratch
Ruth Aylett
Daniel Ballin
Patrick Olivier
Thomas Rist

Committee Listings

Conference Chairs

Jonathan Gratch (USC Institute for Creative Technologies, USA)
Ruth Aylett (Heriot-Watt University, UK)
Daniel Ballin (Chief Technology Office, BT Group, UK)
Patrick Olivier (University of Newcastle Upon Tyne, UK)
Thomas Rist (University of Applied Sciences Augsburg, Germany)

Local Conference Chair

Themis Panayiotopoulos (Department of Informatics, University of Piraeus, Greece)

Organizing Committee

Nikos Avradinis (University of Piraeus, Greece)
George Anastassakis (University of Piraeus, Greece)
Spyros Vosinakis (University of Piraeus, Greece)
Aris Belesiotis (University of Piraeus, Greece)
Aris Koutsiamanis (University of Piraeus, Greece)
John Giannakas (University of Piraeus, Greece)
Kostas Tilelis (University of Piraeus, Greece)

Invited Speakers

Justine Cassell (Northwestern University, USA)
Kerstin Dautenhahn (University of Hertfordshire, UK)

Program Committee

Jan Albeck
George Anastassakis
Elisabeth André
Norman Badler
Paulo Barthelmess
Josep Blat
Joanna Bryson
Lola Canamero
Justine Cassell
Marc Cavazza
Nicolas Ech Chafai

Elizabeth Churchill
Toni Conde
Kerstin Dautenhahn
Betsy van Dijk
Patrick Doyle
Angelica de Antonio
Fiorella de Rosis
Patrick Gebhard
Marco Gillies
Erdan Gu
Bruno Herbelin

Randy Hill
Adrian Hilton
Kristina Hook
Xiao Huang
Katherine Isbister
Mitsuru Ishizuka
Ido Iurgel
Sverker Janson
Lewis Johnson
Natasa Jovanovic
Martin Klesen
Stefan Kopp
John Laird
James Lester
Craig Lindley
Zhen Liu
Brian Loyall
Nadia Magnenat-Thalmann
Andrew Marriot
Stacy Marsella
Michael Mateus
Alexander Nareyek
Anton Nijholt
Magalie Ochs
Gregory O'Hare
Sharon Oviatt

Martijn van Otterlo
Ana Paiva
Zhigeng Pan
Catherine Pelachaud
Chris Pennock
Paolo Petta
Tony Polichroniadis
Helmut Prendinger
Jaime Ramírez
Matthias Rehm
Daniela Romano
Alejandra Garcia Rojas
Zsofia Ruttkay
Wei Shao
Anthony Steed
Matthew Stone
Paul Tepper
Daniel Thalmann
Kris Thorisson
Demetri Terzopoulos
David Traum
Ana Vaz
Hannes Vilhjalmsson
John Vince
Spyros Vosinakis
Michael Young

Sponsoring Institutions

University of Piraeus Research Center
AgentLink
Hellenic Artificial Intelligence Society
Medicon SA
Focus Magazine

Table of Contents

Cognition, Reasoning and Behaviour

NonVerbal Communication

Storytelling/Interactive Narrative

Social Intelligence

Emotions/Affect/Personality

Evaluation and Methodology

Poster Session

Training Agents: An Architecture for Reusability

Gonzalo Mendez and Angelica de Antonio

Computer Science School,
Technical University of Madrid,
Campus de Montegancedo s/n, 28660 Boadilla del Monte (Madrid), Spain
gonzalo@gordini.ls.fi.upm.es, angelica@fi.upm.es

Abstract. During the last years, Intelligent Virtual Environments for Training have become a quite popular application of computer science to education. These systems involve very different technologies, ranging from computer graphics to artificial intelligence. However, little attention has been paid to software engineering issues, and most of these systems are developed in an ad-hoc way that does not allow the reuse of their components or even an easy modification of the application. We describe an agent-based software architecture that is intended to be easily extended and modified. Also, some experiments to test the suitability of the architecture are shown.

1   Introduction

Many of the advances in the application of intelligent agents to the field of Intelligent Virtual Environments for Training (IVET) have come from the Artificial Intelligence community, such as Herman the Bug [1], Cosmo [2] or Steve [3,4].

However, little effort has been devoted to software engineering issues, and in the few cases where some attention has been paid to design methods, such as in Jacob [5], they have focused in object oriented design rather than agent oriented design.

The MAEVIF (*Model for the Application of Intelligent Virtual Environments to Education*) project is the result of several experiences integrating virtual environments and intelligent tutors [6,7] that served to point out the problems that commonly arise in such integrations. The objective of the MAEVIF project was to define a model for the application of intelligent virtual environments to education and training, which involved:

- The definition of a generic model for intelligent learning environments based on the use of virtual worlds.
- The definition of an open and flexible agent-based software architecture to support the generic model of an IVET.
- The design and implementation of a prototype authoring tool that simplifies the development of IVETs, based on the defined architecture.
- The definition of a set of methodological recommendations for the development of IVETs.

T. Panayiotopoulos et al. (Eds.): IVA 2005, LNCS 3661, pp. 1–14, 2005.
© Springer-Verlag Berlin Heidelberg 2005

In the remainder of this paper it will be described how the traditional architecture of Intelligent Tutoring Systems (ITS) [8,9] has been extended to support Virtual Environments (section 2) and how it has been transformed into an agent-based architecture (section 3). In section 4, an explanation of the functionality of the authoring tool will be given. Section 5 will present a discussion of the results that have been achieved with the MAEVIF project. Then, the basic functioning of the system will be described (section 6), and finally, in section 7, some future work lines will be shown.

2   An Extension to the Architecture of Intelligent Tutoring Systems

The development of three dimensional Virtual Environments (VEs) has a quite short history, dating from the beginning of the 90s. The youth of the field, together with the complexity and variety of the technologies involved, have led to a situation in which neither the architectures nor the development processes have been standardized yet. Therefore, almost every new system is developed from scratch, in an ad-hoc way, with very specific solutions and monolithic architectures, and in many cases forgetting the principles and techniques of the Software Engineering discipline [10]. Some of the proposed architectures deal only partially with the problem, since they are centered on a specific aspect like the visualization of the VE [11,12] or the interaction devices and hardware [13].

Our approach to the definition of an architecture for IVETs is based on the agent paradigm. The rationale behind this choice is our belief that the design of highly interactive IVETs populated by intelligent and autonomous or semi-autonomous entities, in addition to one or more avatars controlled by users, requires higher level software abstractions. Objects and components are passive software entities which are not able to exhibit the kind of proactivity and reactivity that is required in highly interactive environments. Agents, moreover, are less dependent on other components than objects. An agent that provides a given service can be replaced by any other agent providing the same service, or they can even coexist. New agents can be added dynamically providing new functionalities. Extensibility is one of the most powerful features of agent-based systems. The way in which agents are designed make them also easier to be reused than objects.

Since an IVET can be seen as a special kind of ITS, and the pedagogical agent in an IVET can be seen as an embodiment of the tutoring module of an ITS, our first approach towards defining an standard architecture for IVETs was to define an agent for each of the four modules of the generic architecture of an ITS [9] (see Fig. 1).

The ITS architecture, however, does not fit well with the requirements of IVETs in several aspects:

- IVETs are usually populated by more than one student, and they are frequently used for team training. An ITS is intended to adapt the teaching

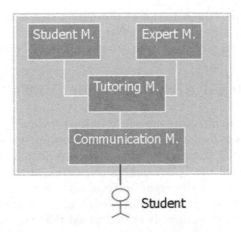

Fig. 1. Architecture of an ITS

and learning process to the needs of every individual student, but they are supposed to interact with the system one at a time. However, in a multi-student IVET, the system has to adapt both to the characteristics of each individual student and to the characteristics of the team. Consequently, the student module should model the knowledge of each individual student but also the collective knowledge of the team.

– The student is not really out of the limits of the ITS, but immersed in it. The student interacts with the IVET by manipulating an avatar within the IVET, possibly using complex virtual reality devices. Furthermore, each student has a different view of the VE depending on their location within it.
– The communication module in an ITS is usually realized by means of a GUI or a natural language interface that allows the student to communicate with the system. It would be quite intuitive to consider that the 3D graphical model is the communication module of an IVET. However, there is a fundamental difference among them: in an IVET, the learning goals are directly related to the manipulation and interaction with the 3D environment, while the communication module of a classical ITS is just a means, not an end. Therefore, the ITS needs to have explicit knowledge about the 3D VE, its state, and the possibilities of interaction within it.

As a first step we decided to modify and extend the ITS architecture by considering some additional modules. First of all, we split the communication module into a set of different views for all the students with a particular communication thread for each student, and a centralized communication module to integrate the different communication threads. Then, we added a world module, which contains geometrical and semantic information about the 3D graphical representation of the VE and its inhabitants, as well as information about the interaction possibilities. The tutoring module is unique to be able to make decisions that affect all the students, as well as specific tutoring decisions for a certain student. The expert module contains all the necessary data and inference rules to maintain a simulation of the behavior of the system that is represented through the VE (e.g. the behavior of a nuclear power plant). The student module, finally, maintains an individual model for each student as well as a model of the team.

3   An Agent-Based Architecture for IVETs

Taking the extended architecture described in the previous section as a starting point, the next step is to decide which software agents are necessary to transform this component-oriented architecture into an agent-oriented architecture, which has been designed using the GAIA methodology [14]. In this methodology, the authors suggest the use of the *organizational metaphor* to design the system architecture, which basically consists of analyzing the real-world organization in order to emulate its structure. It is mentioned that this approach does not always work (depending on particular organization conditions), but in this case, considering the extended architecture of an ITS as the real world, it seems quite appropriate to imitate its structure to develop the system architecture.

Figure 2 shows how the extended ITS architecture is transformed, from a modular point of view, into an agent-based architecture. It has five agents corresponding to the five key modules of the extended ITS architecture:

- A Communication Agent
- A Student Modelling Agent
- A World Agent
- An Expert Agent
- A Tutoring Agent

Analyzing the responsibilities of these agents, some additional roles can be identified that point to the creation of new, subordinate agents that can carry them out, subsequently giving rise to a hierarchical multi-agent architecture.

3.1   Central Communication Agent

The Central Communication Agent is responsible for the communication between the Virtual Environment and the Tutoring System. It delegates part of its responsibilities to a set of Individual Communication Agents dedicated to each student. There is also a Connection Manager Agent, which is responsible for coordinating the connections of the students to the system, and a set of Device Agents in charge of managing the data provided by the devices the students use to interact with the Virtual Environment.

3.2   Student Modelling Agent

This agent is in charge of maintaining a model of each student, including personal information, their actions in training sessions, and a model of the students' knowledge.

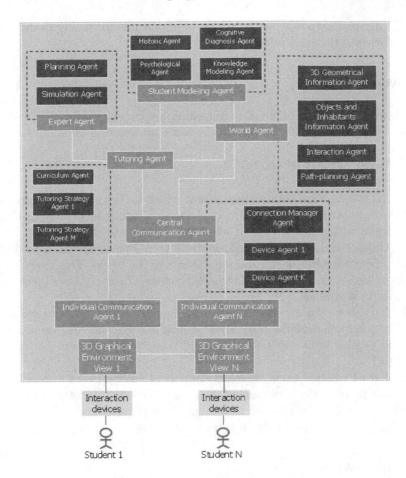

Fig. 2. Agent-based architecture

Figuring out the student's abilities and beliefs/knowledge is usually not a trivial issue. To better individualize training and appropriately understand the student's behavior, a representation of some of its personal features (personality traits, mood, attitudes,...) is defined and maintained. To do this, the Student Modelling Agent is assisted by:

- A Historic Agent, which is responsible for registering the history of interactions among the students and the system.
- A Psychological Agent, which is responsible for building a psychological profile of each student including their learning style, attentiveness, and other personality traits, moods and emotions that may be interesting for adapting the teaching process.
- A Knowledge Modelling Agent, which is responsible for building a model of the student's current knowledge and its evolution.

- A Cognitive Diagnostic Agent, which is responsible for trying to determine the causes of the student's mistakes.

3.3   World Agent

The World Agent is in charge of maintaining a coherent model of the VE, so that all the agents and students have the same information about the state of the world.

The World Agent is related to:

- The 3D Geometrical Information Agent which has geometrical information on the objects and the inhabitants of the world. Among other responsibilities, this agent will answer questions about the location of the objects.
- The Objects and Inhabitants Information Agent, which has semantic knowledge about the objects and the inhabitants of the world. This agent will be able to answer questions about the utility of the objects or the objects being carried by a student.
- The Interaction Agent, which has knowledge about the possible actions that the students can perform in the environment and the effects of these actions. It will be able to answer questions like "What will it happen if I push this button?"
- The Path-Planning Agent, which is capable of finding paths to reach a destination point in the environment avoiding collisions with other inhabitants and objects. For the purpose of finding these paths, the A* algorithm will be applied to a graph model of the environment.

3.4   Expert Agent

The expert agent contains the expert knowledge about the environment that is being simulated, as well as the expert knowledge necessary to solve the problems posed to the student and to reach the desired goals. Most of the activities to be executed by the students consist of finding an appropriate sequence of actions, or plan, to go from an initial state of the environment to a desired final state. These actions have to be executed by the team of students. The Expert Agent delegates some of its responsibilities to a Simulation Agent, that contains the knowledge about the simulated system, and a Planning Agent, that is able to find the best sequence of actions to solve different activities.

The plan for an activity is worked out by the Planning Agent with the collaboration of three other agents:

- The Path-Planning Agent can determine whether there is a trajectory from a certain point of the world to another one.
- The Interaction Agent provides information about the actions that a student can directly execute in the environment.

– The Simulation Agent provides information about some high-level actions that can be executed over the simulated system (e.g., a nuclear power plant). One of these high-level actions will typically require the execution of one or more student's actions; therefore, a hierarchical planning will be performed. In the nuclear power plant domain, an example of a high-level action may be to raise the reactor's temperature. This high-level action would be decomposed into two student actions, go to the control panel and press the button that closes the input water valve.

3.5 Tutoring Agent

It is responsible for proposing activities to the students, monitoring their actions in the virtual environment, checking if they are valid or not with respect to the plan worked out by the Expert Agent, and making tutoring decisions. The activities that can be proposed by the Tutoring Agent are dependent on the particular environment that is being simulated in the IVET, and they can be defined by means of an authoring tool. Some XML files will define the activities in the IVET, the characters that should take part in them and the role to be performed by each character.

The adaptation of the tutoring strategy to every particular student may also encompass how the virtual tutor will behave: a student may need a tutor with a particular character (e.g., training children may require a funny, enthusiastic tutor, while for training nuclear power plant operators a more serious one will be more convenient), or with a specific mood (e.g., if a student does not pay much attention to the procedure for long, a disgusted tutor may be effective). Poor or upsetting tutor behaviors will lead to a lack of believability, possibly reducing the student's feeling of presence and therefore the effectiveness of the training.

The Tutoring Agent is assisted by a Curriculum Agent, which has knowledge of the curricular structure of the subject matter, and several Tutoring Strategy Agents, which implement different tutoring strategies.

3.6 Communication with the Virtual Environment

Currently, the proposed architecture has been implemented using JADE (*Java Agent DEvelopment Framework*), while the VE has been built using C++ and OpenGL. The communication between the agents and the VE is made using a CORBA middleware, which has allowed us to distribute the different elements of the training application in different machines (see Fig. 3).

When the application is started, a few general-purpose objects are created that allow the communication of events that affect all users. In addition, when a student connects to a training session, some specific objects are created, too, so that the communication that only affects that student can be carried out. Every time a message has to be sent from the VE to JADE, the appropriate object receives the information that has to be transmitted.

Some information has to be exchanged between the different VE clients that correspond to each student, such as changes in the positions of the avatars and objects. Microsoft's DirectPlay library has been used with this purpose.

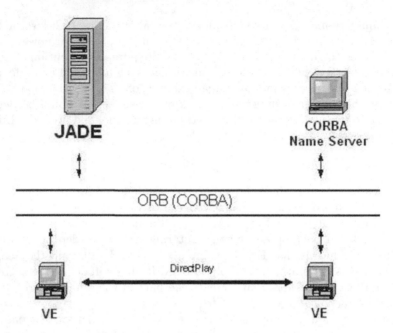

Fig. 3. CORBA communication architecture

4   Authoring Tool

The architecture that has been described in the previous sections has allowed us to build a basic infrastructure of agents that work as a runtime engine. One of the main goals of this architecture is for it to be flexible enough, so it can be used for different kinds of training in heterogeneous environments without having to extensively modify it.

This can be done by changing the knowledge and goals that the agents have according to the different training needs. To ease this task, an authoring tool has been developed to help human tutors to design new training courses.

The authoring tool allows the human tutor to load an existing 3D environment in which the training process will take place. This environment is typically created using 3DStudio Max or a similar application, and is then exported to the format that has been created for the MAEVIF system. A script has been created to be used with 3DStudio with this purpose.

The human tutor can then select the objects with which the students will be able to interact, and he can define the different actions that can be carried out with each object (e.g. take, drop, use, open, put on...) and all the aspects related to those actions (e.g. pre-conditions, post-conditions, parameters, animations that must be triggered...). These actions are stored in an xml file that is read by the appropriate agents when a training scenario of the MAEVIF system is started.

Subsequently, the author can create new training activities. To do this, he has to decide how many students have to take part in the activity, what their initial positions are in the virtual environment, what goals they must achieve, and the initial state of the world. This information is also stored in an xml file that is read by the Tutoring agent when a training scenario is started.

In turn, some variables of the initial state will be generated randomly every time the students have to train the activity, so that they can solve the same problem starting from different situations.

The authoring tool also generates the world map that is used by the A* algorithm for the path-planning task. To do this, all the objects that are present in the VE are projected on the floor of the scenario, which is divided in cells. All the cells are marked as occupied by an object or free, and these free cells are used by the A* algorithm to calculate the best route between two points.

As a prototype application of our tool we have developed a training system for Nuclear Power Plants operators. We had previously developed this system from scratch in 1999, during a one year period. The re-development using our infrastructure has just taken a few weeks, and the achieved functionality is superior. For instance, the previous implementation was for a single user, the tutor was not embodied, and the communication tutor-student was restricted to correction feedback.

5   Discussion

All along the design and development of the described architecture, one of the aspects that has had a bigger impact on it has been the planning process, since, due to the fact that it is a collaborative process, a change in the planning method or in the way that knowledge is represented may imply changes in all the agents that take part in it. At the beginning, a simple STRIPS (*STanford Research Institute Problem Solver*) planner [15] was implemented, but we are currently working on the utilization of a new planner based on SHOP2 (*Simple Hierarchical Ordered Planner 2*) [16] or LPG (*Local search in Planning Graphs*) [17]. This change involves the substitution of the planning agent, but it may cause changes in the Interaction, Simulation and Path-Planning agents, which also take part in the planning task.

However, there are two factors that suggest that collaborative planning is the adequate solution. The first one is the fact that, given a planning algorithm, our solution allows for the real-time inclusion of new agents with different knowledge that can help to solve a problem. In addition, a careful design of the operators and their responsibilities can minimize the impact of a change in the planning algorithm or in the knowledge representation.

Another aspect we have tested is how easy it is to add new functionality to the IVET. To do this, we have added an embodied tutor whose goal is to observe what happens in the VE and follow the student to supervise him. It has been necessary to add two new agents, namely the Virtual Tutor agent, whose responsibility is to control the 3D representation of the tutor (its embodiment), and the Perception agent, who is in charge of monitoring the events of the virtual world. Both of them are under the supervision of the World agent.

It has been quite easy to make these changes, since the Perception agent can ask the World agent for the information it needs and, according to this information, the Virtual Tutor agent can decide how to follow the student and send commands to its 3D representation through the communication agents. Neither the World agent nor the Communication agent have needed further changes.

Finally, we have tested the difficulty of using the described system in a completely different environment, and even with a different purpose. We have designed an experiment where a group of zebras have to drink water in a river, trying to avoid being eaten by a lion, but also trying not to die of thirst. In this case, the Perception and Virtual Tutor agents are in charge of controlling the zebras and lions, and the Tutoring agent is responsible for deciding what to do according to their state of thirst and hunger, assisted by the Planning agent. Some of the existing agents, such as the Simulation agent, have been removed, since their functionality was not required. However, some of the agents play a role that is significantly different than the one they were originally thought to play, so if they are to be used in such a way, the architecture will probably have to be modified.

As a result, we can conclude that the architecture has successfully supported the experiments, and has proven to be flexible and extensible enough to allow changes and extensions without having to be redesigned.

5.1   Performance Issues

Performance is always an important issue in applications where real-time execution is needed, and agent-based architectures tend to easily raise concerns about this matter. Using an individual agent for each high-level responsibility may seem an unnecessary waste of processing capacity.

Even though our main concern were the software engineering issues, such as extensibility and reusability, we have devoted some effort to identify bottlenecks in terms of performance, given that the architecture will be useless if it can be used due to performance issues.

Three potential sources of problems have been identified: rendering, communications and agent platform, and they have been tested using different configurations (vg. agent platform running in one machine, one VE running in one machine, agent platform and one VE running in one machine, agent platform running in one machine and several VEs running in different machines). The results we have obtained show that the architecture does not influence much the performance of the system.

In contrast, it seems to be the network communication what lowers the execution speed, and the more students there are, the slower the application runs. This effect can be appreciated since the first student connects to the training session, which is leading us to redesign the communication mechanism to improve this aspect.

6   How the System Works

In this section, a sample training session with one student will be presented. The student is a maintenance operator in a Nuclear Power Plant who has to learn how to change a filter that divides two sections of a pipe.

During the training, when an activity is posed to the student, the Planning agent builds the plan that leads to the resolution of the activity, given the initial state at that moment and the desired final state of the world. Moreover, during the planning process, the Path-Planning agent computes the ideal trajectories through the geometric representation of the environment that the students must follow to accomplish the plan.

In order to learn this activity, the student must carry it out in the virtual environment. Not knowing what to do, the student uses a voice recognition system to ask the tutor *"What should I do now?"* (the student can ask some other questions, such as *"What is this for?"*, *"What happens if I...?"*, *"What should I have done?"*). The question is sent to the tutoring system, and the Tutoring agent identifies it is a question he is in charge to answer. He asks the Planning agent for the next action in the plan, builds the answer and sends it to the student who, through a text-to-speech application, hears the tutor saying *"You have to remove the filter"*.

The student tries to carry out the action *remove filter*. To do it, using a data glove, he touches the filter to select it and says *"remove"*. When this happens, the Individual Communication agent associated with the student receives a message and informs about this attempt to the Central Communication agent; eventually, the message is delivered to the Tutoring agent.

Now, the Tutoring agent needs to find out whether the action can be executed under the current conditions in the virtual world, that is, if the preconditions of the action hold. For that, the Tutoring agent resorts to the Interaction agent, since *remove filter* is an action in this level of abstraction. The Interaction Agent determines that he needs to check whether the student's avatar is close enough to the filter and if he is carrying the appropriate tools in order to remove it. To check these preconditions, the Interaction agent writes them in a blackboard that is used as a communication mechanism between agents. The 3D Geometrical Information agent and the Objects and Inhabitants Information agent read the blackboard and see there are preconditions they are able to check. Each precondition corresponds to one and only one of the aforementioned agents.

If all the preconditions of the action hold, the Interaction agent must guarantee the execution of the consequences of the action. For that, it may need to delegate some responsibilities on other agents, such as the World agent and the Simulation agent, using the blackboard again as a communication mechanism. One of the consequences, managed by the Interaction Agent itself, will be launching a 3D animation in the virtual world that represents the student removing the filter. The command is sent to the VE via the Communication agents (in case there are several students, this message is sent to all the students, since all the students should see the animation).

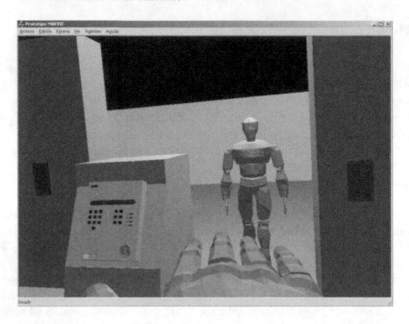

Fig. 4. The MAEVIF system

When the Tutoring agent receives the result of verifying the preconditions of the action from the Interaction agent, it asks the Student Modelling agent to register the action and the result of the verification, and it checks whether the executed action is valid with respect to the plan associated with the activity. If this action is the next correct action according to the plan, the Tutoring Agent asks the Student Modelling agent to register that the student has carried out the correct action. Otherwise, the Tutoring agent allows the student to go on in spite of having executed an incorrect action. This strategy poses a new problem, since the Tutoring Agent needs to know whether the desired final state is reachable from the current state of the world. To find this out, the Planning agent must be endowed with the capacity of re-planning.

The movements of the student in the virtual world are considered a special kind of action that is managed in a different manner to the one explained above. As the student moves through the environment, the Central Communication agent informs the 3D Geometrical Information Agent of the new student's positions. At the same time, the Tutoring agent asks the 3D Geometrical Information agent for these positions, in order to compare them with the trajectory provided by the Path-Planning agent, and to inform the Student Modelling agent so that it can store the trajectory followed by the student during the training session. As a result of the comparison between the ideal trajectory and the student's trajectory, a quality measure of the student's trajectory is calculated by the Path-Planning agent and then stored by the Student Modelling agent.

All through the training, the virtual tutor, controlled by the Virtual Tutor agent, follows the student in order to supervise his actions and correct them.

7   Future Work

As it has been mentioned previously, one of the elements that can affect more deeply the system architecture is the planning process. In addition, the STRIPS planning algorithm has been used as a testbed for the Planning Agent, but it lacks a lot of features that would be desirable in an IVET, such as arithmetic operations or concurrent actions. Therefore, other planning algorithms are being evaluated, because of their improved functionality, but also to test their impact in the system architecture.

Another research is being carried out in parallel to design an architecture for the cognition of intelligent agents, with reactive, deliberative and social capabilities, and it is planned to use that architecture for the Virtual Tutor and any other cognitive agents that may be required (such as zebras, lions or simulated students).

It is mainly in the context of nuclear power plants where we have been applying our prototypes. Up to now, the Simulation agent hasn't played a very active role. Therefore, we are in the process of applying the system to other environments where the simulation agent is more complex, so that it can be tested whether its design is adequate or it needs to be modified.

Finally, the Student Modelling group of agents have been subject to less experimentation than the rest, since its behaviour is quite complex from the pedagogical point of view. Therefore, a research line has been established to fully understand its implications and to modify the architecture where needed.

Acknowledgements. This research has been funded by the Spanish Ministry of Science and Technology through the MAEVIF project under contract TIC2000-1346.

References

1. Lester, J.C., Stone, B.A.: Increasing believability in animated pedagogical agents. In: Proceedings of the First International Conference on Autonomous Agents, ACM Press (1997) 16–21
2. Lester, J.C., Voerman, J.L., Towns, S.G., Callaway, C.B.: Deictic believability: Co-ordinating gesture, locomotion, and speech in lifelike pedagogical agents. Applied Artificial Intelligence **13** (1999) 383–414
3. Rickel, J., Johnson, W.L.: Animated agents for procedural training in virtual reality: Perception, cognition, and motor control. Applied Artificial Intelligence **13** (1999) 343–382
4. Rickel, J., Johnson, W.L.: Virtual humans for team training in virtual reality. In: Proceedings of the Ninth International Conference on Artificial Intelligence in Education, IOS Press (1999) 578–585
5. Evers, M., Nijholt, A.: Jacob - an animated instruction agent for virtual reality. In: Advances in Multimodal Interfaces - ICMI 2000, Third International Conference. Volume 1948 of LNCS., Beijing, China, Springer-Verlag (2000) 526–532

6. Mendez, G., Rickel, J., de Antonio, A.: Steve meets jack: the integration of an intelligent tutor and a virtual environment with planning capabilities. In: 4th International Working Conference on Intelligent Virtual Agents (IVA03). Volume 2792 of LNCS-LNAI., Kloster Irsee, Germany, Springer-Verlag (2003) 325–332

7. Mendez, G., Herrero, P., de Antonio, A.: Intelligent virtual environments for training in nuclear power plants. In: Proceedings of the 6th International Conference on Enterprise Information Systems (ICEIS 2004), Porto, Portugal (2004)

8. Sleeman, D., Brown, J., eds.: Intelligent Tutoring Systems. Academic Press, London (1982)

9. Wenger, E.: Artificial Intelligence and Tutoring Systems. Computational and Cognitive Approaches to the Communication of Knowledge. Morgan Kaufmann Publishers, Los Altos, California (1987)

10. Munro, A., Surmon, D., Johnson, M., Pizzini, Q., Walker, J.: An open architecture for simulation-centered tutors. In: Artificial Intelligence in Education. Open Learning Environments: New Compu-tational Technologies to Support Learning, Exploration and Collaboration. (Proceedings of AIED99: 9th Con-ference on Artificial Intelligence in Education), Le Mans, France (1999) 360–67

11. Alpdemir, M., Zobel, R.: A component-based animation framework for devs-based simulation environments. In: Simulation: Past, Present and Future. 12th European Simulation Multiconference. (1998)

12. Demyunck, K., Broeckhove, J., Arickx, F.: Real-time visualization of complex simulations using veplatform software. In: Simulation in Industry'99. 11th European Simulation Symposium (ESS'99). (1999) 329–33

13. Darken, R., Tonessen, C., Passarella, J.: The bridge between developers and virtual environments: a robust virtual environment system architecture. In: Proceedings of the SPIE - The International Society for Optical Engineering. Volume 2409. (1995) 234–40

14. Zambonelli, F., Jennings, N.R., Wooldridge, M.: Developing multiagent systems: The gaia methodology. ACM Transactions on Software Engineering and Methodology (TOSEM) **12** (2003) 317–370

15. Fikes, R.E., Nilsson, N.J.: Strips: a new approach to the application of theorem proving to problem solving. Artificial Intelligence **2** (1971) 189–208

16. Nau, D., Au, T., Ilghami, O., Kuter, U., Murdock, W., Wu, D., F.Yaman: Shop2: An htn planning system. Journal of Artificial Intelligence Research (JAIR) **20** (2003) 379–404

17. Gerevini, A., Saetti, A., Serina, I.: Planning through stochastic local search and temporal action graphs. Journal of Artificial Intelligence Research (JAIR) **20** (2003) 239–290

Ask&Answer: An Educational Game Where It Pays to Endear Your Capricious Virtual Companion

Ido A. Iurgel and Manuel Ziegler

ZGDV, (Computer Graphics Center), Fraunhoferstr. 5,
64283 Darmstadt, Germany
Ido.Iurgel@zgdv.de, mziegler@gmx.de
http://www.zgdv.de/zgdv/departments/z5

Abstract. This paper presents a competitive, educational, novel multi-user game that involves two groups of human users and a single virtual character. Within this game, it pays for the users to create social bounds with the virtual character, and to adapt the natural language, typed input to the limited natural language processing faculties of the agent. We expect that the socially complex scenario will enhance learning pleasure and efficiency. The game also aims at clarifying educational, technological and conceptual problems related to the creation of social bounds with virtual agents, and to the use of natural language in this context. Specifically, this game is an environment where the concept of a rationally profitable social relationship with a virtual agent can be examined.

1 Introduction

This paper presents a competitive, educational, novel multi-user edutainment game that involves two groups of human users and a single virtual character[1]. Within this game, it pays off for the users to create social bounds with the single virtual character, and to adapt the natural language, typed input to the limited NLP faculties of the virtual agent. We expect that this socially complex scenario involving team cooperation, competition and game will enhance learning pleasure, motivation and efficiency. In particular, we expect that the presence of a virtual character with which it is profitable to create social bounds and that needs care will trigger positive learning effects.

The proposed scenario delivers clear reasons for human/human and human/virtual-human collaboration – both collaboration types are useful in order to win the game. The human/virtual-human collaboration shall be motivating, engaging and funny, but it also enables to dwell with an additional channel on the learning content.

The game also aims at clarifying educational, technological and conceptual problems related to the creation of social bounds with virtual human-like agents, and to the use of natural language in this context. More specifically, we want to study the concept of profit in interactions with a virtual character. The application presented in this paper shall foster our understanding of intelligent virtual characters in situations where there are strategically rational reasons for the user to pay attention to the moods and wants of the intelligent agent. We expect that fun and motivation will last longer

---

[1] "Virtual character" and "intelligent agent" are used synonymously in this paper.

T. Panayiotopoulos et al. (Eds.): IVA 2005, LNCS 3661, pp. 15–24, 2005.
© Springer-Verlag Berlin Heidelberg 2005

if they are grounded in utility, even if artificially as part of a game. Coping with the virtual character's peculiarities and establishing social bounds with it thus become part of the challenge of the game. Many edutainment and entertainment applications could be conceived from this starting point: The focus need not be in human-like behavior of virtual characters; rather, the focus can be *on the human-like situation where it is profitable to adapt to the social expectancies and emotional peculiarities of the (virtual) other.*

This is the central interaction concept of the game, concerning the communication with the virtual agent, which we call Capricious Non-Player Character, or CNPC: The efforts of emotional, social and linguistic interaction with a virtual character shall remunerate. This much differs from the concept of a virtual character as assistant, which won't normally deny its help on personal reasons, and from virtual characters as actors that try to be believable – the CNPC must be understandable, rather than believable, in order for the player to be able to endear and manipulate it. A real life analogy is provided by obvious rationality that lies in the establishment of an agreeable emotional atmosphere in a business meeting that shall result in a profitable contract.

This implies that a virtual character must

1. possess resources that it controls and also retains;
2. that these resources are desirable to the user, and
3. that through skilful social and emotional interaction, the user can obtain these resources.

Thus, interaction with a virtual character is most entertaining and most useful not necessarily if its psychological model or its NLP is accurate, but if it pays off for the user to maintain a successful interaction. This much simplifies the Herculean tasks of NLP and psychological and cognitive modeling:

In short, we expect that

1. the creation of social bounds with Intelligent Virtual Agents as learning companions can foster the learning experience;
2. interaction through (typed) natural language is useful, provided that it is possible and pays for the user to adapt his language use to the limited faculties of the system;
3. emotional expressions and models of virtual characters need not necessarily be psychologically accurate, as long as the behavior patterns are understandable, and as long as it pays for the user to understand those patterns and to stay tuned to the emotions of the virtual companion.

The paragraphs that follow will explain the game and its technical and conceptual starting points in more detail, and elaborate on these theses.

2   Related Work

The creation of social bounds with intelligent virtual agents was examined e.g. by Cassell and Bickmore [1], with focus on small talk and increase in credibility through it. Prendinger and Ishizuka [2], [3] have developed emotional agents and scripting languages for believable virtual agents with autonomous faculties. Paiva et al. [4] have studied the context of empathy with agents and bullying, presenting concepts that would allow for the creation of emphatic relations. Stonks et al. [5] have elaborated on the prerequisites that would be necessary for the establishment of a friendship between a human and a virtual human. These works did not address social bounds and emotion from the game oriented, strategic point of view addressed in this paper.

The effects of virtual characters on learning have been widely studied; a final conclusion is not possible yet. Vassileva's and Okonkwo's [6] studies suggest that the effect on the direct influence of learning efficiency is small, but that effects on motivation and enjoyment are very clear. A fierce advocate of games as the most natural way of learning for young "digital natives" is Marc Prensky [7].

Chris Crawford [8] has already extensively elaborated on the idea that it is up to the user to learn the language of the virtual character, and not the other way round, in interactive storytelling. Iurgel [9] has examined the context of interactive storytelling and social bounds, but without entering into language issues.

3   The Rules of the Game

3.1   Idea of the Game

Ask&Answer is an educational, competitive game. Two teams of 2-8 participants play over the network. A team scores when it knows the right answer to a question asked by the system. Each participant has its own speech enabled avatar.

The answer is usually typed in with the keyboard. Any participant may post an answer, but he risks negative scores for his team if the answer is wrong. Therefore, in order to coordinate the answers, the participants can communicate through their avatars. Avatars that are within a specific area, the territory of the group, can only be heard by members of the group that are located within this area. The players are allowed to use other material to find out the answers, e.g. textbooks. The exemplary current domains of learning are history and geography.

Fig. 1. Two teams confront each other, the CNPC is in-between. The right inner screen contains a question (Java3D version).

A most important participant in the game is the single CNPC. It knows every answer to any question of the game – but it is capricious, and a team has to endear and take care of this character to tease the knowledge out of it. If the team does not succeed, the character might refrain from cooperating, or even worse, it might leave the neglecting team and change to the other team. The CNPC can only be heard by the team it is near to.

Fig. 2. "Girlish" design of the Flash version of Ask&Answer, with Elvis playing the role of CNPC

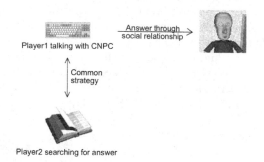

Fig. 3. Acquiring the right answer implies team collaboration. Player1 and Player2 have assumed separate roles to acquire the correct answers. Here, Player1 is responsible for endearing the CNPC.

Thus, this game involves social elements in a complex way:

1. members of a team have to cooperate to acquire knowledge and coordinate answers, in order to defeat the other team;
2. a team has to develop a common strategy on how to endear the CNPC, for example by nominating a CNPC-officer to exploit this source of knowledge, and
3. the relationship to the CNPC is a social relation it pays off to maintain.

3.2 The Peculiarities of the CNPC

The CNPC evaluates, based on the technical framework described below, whether it "likes" the team it is interacting with. The current CNPC wants

- to talk constantly;
- to be praised for its vast knowledge;
- not to be insulted;
- to talk about certain themes, and not about others, and
- to understand the user.

The emotions of the CNPC towards a team – its sympathy for this team– depends on the fulfillment of these wants. If it is dissatisfied, it may leave the team he was talking to.

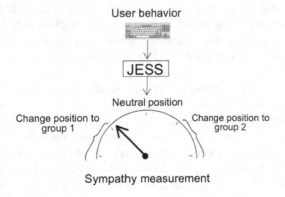

Fig. 4. The CNPC has the tendency to move to the adversary team, if it does not feel enough sympathy

Now, using adapted social and linguistic skills when interacting with the virtual characters is clearly beneficial for the player:

- The CNPC possesses resources that the user wants, namely the right answers.
- The user can access those resources through social interaction.
- Attentiveness to the emotional state of the CNPC pays off, because its emotions are indicators of how successful the user is being in acquiring the resource – a dissatisfied character may even change the team, causing the loss of the resource.
- It is beneficial for the user to adapt its language to the limited faculties of the CNPC, because it tends to become dissatisfied when it does not understand.

If the themes the CNPC wants to speak about are chosen by the author to be those relevant for the curriculum, important additional learning effects can be achieved, since the conversation with the CNPC will be about things that have to be learnt.

Heuristics sum up the interaction and assign numeric values that are directly mapped to the valence of the emotional state of the CNPC (i.e. positive or negative;

the first version of *Ask&Answer* won't consider directional aspects that would allow to discriminate between e.g. "angry" and "sad").

Further rules express

- that the CNPC will tend to join the team which promises the better emotional outcome;
- that the CNPC will try out, more frequently at the beginning of the game than later on, which team is the most agreeable for it, and
- that the CNPC prefers the company of the loosing team (this shall diminish a bit its influence on the final outcome).

3.3 Playing the Game

Ask&Answer is a network game that starts with a registration of the players. Every player sees the same, on his own screen, but only hears what his team members say (they speak through their avatars and TTS). The team members only hear the CNPC if it is in the territory of the group. Questions appear on a separate window. The CNPC is aware of the question, but is reluctant to manipulate the game and has to be persuaded.

The teams now will start the quest for the correct answer, possibly employing the internet. Any player of the team near the CNPC can talk to it. Currently, it only distinguishes between its sympathy to one of the two teams, not to particular players. If a team has the correct answer – either by prior knowledge, through a hint of the CNPC, or with the help of external material –, it may type it into the Q&A window. A correct answer scores with 1 point, a wrong answer with -2 points. Thus, it is better to be sure. In the current version of the game, the avatars of the users do not move around, and are animated autonomously, without neither a deep linguistic nor an emotional model.

The game ends after a fixed number of questions. It is a matter of difficult and still ongoing balance to regulate the game such as that the best strategy for the players consists in both consulting external knowledge sources and in endearing the CNPC.

4 Technology

Ask&Answer employs a client-server architecture. All of the AI, the TTS, and the animation directions to the virtual environment lie on server-side. The main server component is the *Narrator*. The client basically only translates XML directions from the server into rendering.

The most important component of the game is the module which controls the behavior of the CNPC, the *VirtualCharacter-Manager (VC-Manager)*. It is based on rules expressed in the production system JESS[2], and on some faculties of the chatterbot ALICE[3] (the so called "reduction" functions) to process text input. Additionally, a hierarchic transition network can be combined, in the same framework.

---

[2] Cf. http://herzberg.ca.sandia.gov/jess/
[3] Cf. http://www.alicebot.org/

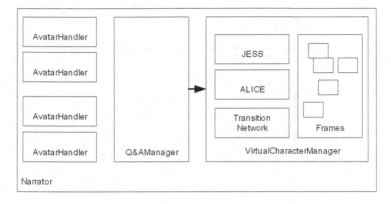

Fig. 5. The main modules on the server side, forming the *Narrator*

The main requirement was that the system should remain fairly easy to author and allow for a visual authoring tool, because thematic experts and educators shall be able to feed it. The current stage does not perform linguistically "deep" processing. Current "deep" dialogue management systems produce either results that aren't funny enough, too restricted to goal-oriented dialogues, or too difficult to author for a non-expert. But the system presented here also contrasts with Mateas and Stern's equally "shallow" methods, because their orientation on the pragmatic dimension of speech acts is not appropriate to cover educational themes, apart from the authoring complexity of *Façade* (cf. [11]).

The goal here is not as ambitious as to create "realistic" conversations, which is impossible with current technology. As stated in the introduction, this is happily no prerequisite here. It suffices that the results of the dialogue management are sensible enough for a player to learn to maintain a successful conversation, but not so simplistic that no efforts are necessary and no mistakes can be made. The basic technological concept consists in allowing the assignment of a separate JESS-production system (in fact, of a separate engine of any kind that would decide on the activation of a state) to any composite state S, and metadata to any composite or simple state inside state S; the metadata then allows the rules to be applied to those inner states. The very same composite or simple states can be connected to form a directed graph of a Harel State Chart, a transition with Boolean value "true" having priority over any rule that could apply to the currently active state.

The encapsulation of the production system into the composite state allows creating different behaviors for different thematic frames, e.g. the virtual character tries to employ conciliation strategies if the user is insulting it, but attempts at a broad exploration of the theme if it is chatting about the French Revolution with the user. When located within the scope of a rule set, a composite state may be viewed as an arbitrary hierarchical data structure that contains e.g. behavior directions for different situations. For example, a composite state C may be assigned to a certain question, a composite state D inside C may contain a set of utterances to be used when the user asks the same question repeatedly, and another composite state E inside C may contain utterances that are employed to guide the user pro-actively to ask the right question.

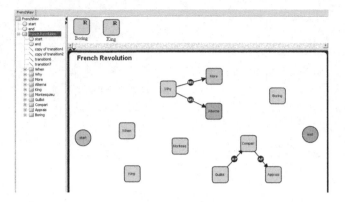

Fig. 6. Screenshot of the authoring tool "Cyranus". Composite states are squares, simple states circles. Note that only some states are connected by arrows. The screenshot represents part of a composite state that defines the scope of the rules of a production system.

JESS is also responsible for other pro-active behavior and for controlling thematic changes, i.e. it may allow or disallow that a behavior element of another thematic frame be addressed by user input, or may initialize such a thematic change. For thematic orientation, a set of generic dialogue control phrases ("Let's change the theme!") are available. User input, e.g. "I want to hear more about the French revolution", can also be used to cause JESS rules to fire, employing the Q&A pattern scheme described above (cf. [10] for some more details on the dialogue management of the system).

The combination of the production system with the transition network allows to model short predicable dialogue moves, e.g. "yes-no"-questions ("Are you sure that I shall tell you again the year of the French Revolution?"), greetings, etc. Educators are not expected to program; they use fixed rule sets, adapt parameters, and create the composite states and short directed graph sequences, partly using prefabricated patterns.

The Virtual Character-Manager allows to employ a main achievement of the freely available chatterbot ALICE, namely the "reduction" mechanism, which groups utterances into equivalence classes; thus, different text input can be easily recognized as equivalent, with respect to the reaction of the system. Though ALICE's approach is "shallow", both theoretically and in its NLP-processing accuracy, it is efficient and able to produce funny and witty results and allows extending the data base gradually, adapting to concrete interaction logs.

ALICE could not be used directly, because some essential features are missing:

- there is no serious mechanism to create pro-active behavior of the attached virtual character; thus, with ALICE, the normal pattern consists of a single utterance responding to a single input;
- there is little dialogue management in a more strict sense, i.e. management of thematic changes, of utterance dependencies, repetitions, etc.;
- it is quite difficult to author ALICE (respectively AIML).

The VC-Manager used for the first prototype of Ask&Answer aims at alleviating those weaknesses of ALICE while reusing its reduction functions and obtaning the means for funny and mostly sensible dialogues.

5   Implementation

Ask&Answer is completely implemented in Java1.4. As TTS, ATT Natural Voices is employed. The complete AI and speech technology resides on server side, the client being merely responsible for displaying. A Java3D viewer is already available, based on Sun's *Webstart*. A Flash version of the viewer is under development. The software basis was partly developed within the EC-project *art-E-fact*[4](cf. [10]).

6   Conclusion

We have presented an edutainment game with a complex social setting. A player of this game has a clear profit from maintaining a social relation with the virtual character; this includes adapting the language to its limited faculties and paying attention to its wants and its emotions. This will allow us to understand the design and the properties of social and emotional virtual agents that do not have their focus on believability or human-likeness, but that are mainly disposers of resources that a user wants to acquire through the social relation, in an edutainment or entertainment application.

Ask&Answer shall later become a single chapter (or level) of a more complex story that exploits the ideas of creating social bounds and mutual dependencies of humans and virtual humans within an educational, narrative game. The move of assigning parts to other dramatic persons, e.g. to an antagonist, is currently being considered.

Certainly, CNPCs are first of all designed for applications which take entertainment aspects seriously. The lessons learnt with CNPCs in *Ask&Answer* shall also meet in novel interactive, purely narrative systems that do not possess similar, secondary educational goals (cf. [12] for more details). These systems shall emphasize on a "capricious" virtual protagonist that the user has to console and assist, when it is exposed to dramatic stakes; this constellation is expected to deepen the user's experience and psychological understanding of the situation of the dramatic persons of a narration.

References

1. Cassell, J., Bickmore. T.: Negotiated collusion: Modeling social language and its relationship effects in intelligent agents. In: User Modeling and Adaptive Interfaces (2002) 12:1, 44
2. Prendinger,H., Ishizuka, M.: Designing and Evaluating Animated Agents as Social Actors. In: IEICE Transactions on Information and Systems, Vol.E86-D, No.8 (2003) 1378-1385

---

[4]   Cf. http://www.art-e-fact.org/

3. Prendinger,H., Ishizuka, M.: Evolving Social Relationships with Animate Characters. In: Proceedings of the AISB-02 Symposium on Animating Expressive Characters for Social Interactions (2002) 73-78

4. Paiva, A., Dias, J., Sobral, D., Aylett, R., Sobreperez, P., Woods, S., Zoll, C., Hall, L.: Caring for Agents and Agents that Care: Building Empathic Relations with Synthetic Agents. Third International Joint Conference on Autonomous Agents and Multiagent Systems - Volume 1 (AAMAS'04) 07 19 - 07, New York City, New York (2004) 194-201

5. Stonks, B., Nijholt, A, van der Vet, P., Heylen, D.: Designing for Friendship: Becoming Friends with Your ECA. Workshop on Embodied conversational agents - let's specify and evaluate them! 16 July, 2002. Bologna, Italy. In conjunction with The First International Joint Conference on Autonomous Agents & Multi-Agent Systems 91-97

6. Vassileva, J., Okonkwo, C.: Affective Pedagogical Agents and User Persuasion. In: Proc. Universal Access in Human-Computer Interaction (UAHCI), held jointly with the 9th International Conference on Human-Computer Interaction. New Orleans, USA (2001) 397-401

7. Prensky, M.: Digital Game-Based Learning, Paragon House 2005

8. Crawford, Ch.: On Interactive Storytelling. New Riders, Berkley 2005

9. Iurgel, I.: Automated Emotional Immersion in Interactive Storytelling. In: TIDSE 2003. 24-26 March, 2003. Darmstadt, Germany. (Computer Graphik Edition 09) (2003) 351-356

10. Iurgel, I.: Narrative Dialogues for Educational Installations. NILE 2004, Edinburgh, 10th - 13th August (2004)

11. Mateas, M, Stern, A: Natural Language Understanding in Façade: Surface-text Processing. In: TIDSE 2004, 24-26 June 2004. Darmstadt, Germany. (LNCS 3105)

12. Iurgel, I.: Virtual Actors in Interactivated Storytelling. *IVA 2003*, September, 2003, Kloster Irsee, Germany. 254-258

Natural Behavior of a Listening Agent

R.M. Maatman[1], Jonathan Gratch[2], and Stacy Marsella[3]

[1] University of Twente,
Drienerlolaan 5, 7522 NB, Enschede, The Netherlands
[2] University of Southern California, Institute for Creative Technologies,
13274 Fiji Way, Marina del Rey, CA 90292, USA
[3] University of Southern California Information Sciences Institute,
4676 Admiralty Way, Marina del Rey, CA 90292, USA

Abstract. In contrast to the variety of listening behaviors produced in human-to-human interaction, most virtual agents sit or stand passively when a user speaks. This is a reflection of the fact that although the correct responsive behavior of a listener during a conversation is often related to the semantics, the state of current speech understanding technology is such that semantic information is unavailable until after an utterance is complete. This paper will illustrate that appropriate listening behavior can also be generated by other features of a speaker's behavior that are available in real time such as speech quality, posture shifts and head movements. This paper presents a mapping from these real-time obtainable features of a human speaker to agent listening behaviors.

1 Introduction

Have you ever presented in front of an unresponsive audience? Audiences that fail to react during a speech can negatively impact a speaker's performance, increasing cognitive load, raising doubts and breaking the speaker's rhythm. Not surprisingly, public speaking instructors often recommend that a speaker ignore unresponsive listeners. Listener behavior also has a critical impact in dyadic conversations (Warner 1996; Bernieri 1999; Lakin, Jefferis et al. 2003).

Similar effects have been demonstrated when people speak to virtual humans or avatars. As with human listeners, unresponsive virtual listeners can interfere with a speaker's cognitive processes. Worse, static characters can lead to a host of negative effects: Observers are more likely to criticize the quality of the graphics, they may feel less immersed, and they frequently form incorrect interpretations of the situation. For example, the authors of this paper have found in their own work that, in the context of highly emotional virtual scenarios, the lack of listener behavior can lead observers to read emotions into the virtual human's static behavior ("He must be really pissed.").

In the face of the important role that listener behavior plays, virtual human designers are faced with a basic dilemma. Most automated speech recognition (ASR) technologies used in virtual human systems do not give an interpretation of the speaker's utterance until the speaker is finished. There are no ongoing partial interpretations. Therefore a listening virtual human cannot respond to what the speaker is saying as

T. Panayiotopoulos et al. (Eds.): IVA 2005, LNCS 3661, pp. 25–36, 2005.
© Springer-Verlag Berlin Heidelberg 2005

they speak. Rather, designers are forced to use simple behaviors at the start and end of an utterance (e.g., gaze or head nods), incorporate random (or "idle-time") listening behaviors, or more commonly have often ignored modeling listening behavior completely, instead focusing more on behavior of the agent while talking. Unfortunately, such design choices can be distracting or misread by the human participants.

The situation is not, however, as bleak as it may seem. The literature on human-human communication makes clear that there are solid correlations of listener behavior with various physical properties of the speaker's behavior, such as the speaker's nonverbal movement, the amplitude and pitch of the speech signal and key utterances. This suggests an approach to listening behavior that works in parallel with speech recognition. Namely, extracting information from the speech signal and physical movements of the human speaker that informs listener behavior as ASR is still processing the signal.

In this paper, we present such a system. After reviewing related work, we start by discussing the literature on listening behavior and how that literature informs our rules to drive virtual human listening behavior. The system we implemented is then detailed. Finally, we discuss our thoughts on evaluating the approach and present a preliminary evaluation.

2   Related ECA Research

The creation of human-appearing intelligent agents is an active area of computer science research. Known as *embodied conversational agents* (ECAs) or *virtual humans,* such systems allow humans to engage in face-to-face conversation with synthetic people, and attempt to model the full richness of such interactions including natural language communication, gestures, emotional expression, as well as the cognitive apparatus that underlies these capabilities (Cassell, Sullivan et al. 2000; Gratch, Rickel et al. 2002).

When it comes to conversational gestures, most virtual human research has focused on gestures related to speech production. Rea, for example, acts as a real estate agent (Cassell, Bickmore et al. 2000) and incorporates the Behavior Expression Animation Toolkit (BEAT) to automatically annotate virtual human speech with hand gestures, eye gaze, eyebrow movement, and intonation.

Some work has attempted to extract extra-linguistic features of a speakers' behavior, but not for the purpose of informing listening behaviors. For example, Brand's voice puppetry work attempts to learn a mapping between acoustic features and facial configurations to drive a virtual puppet with the speaker's voice. Several systems have attempted to recognize speaker gestures, though typically to help disambiguate speaker intent, as in "go that way [pointing left]". Such techniques could be repurposed to inform the present work.

Most virtual human systems have rudimentary listening behaviors triggered by the start and end of user speech. For example, the Mission Rehearsal Exercise system detects when a user begins speaking and orients its gaze towards the user for the duration of their speech, then looks away as it prepares to respond (Marsella, Gratch et al. 2003). These behaviors are typically fixed, however, and are not sensitive to the user's behavior during his or her utterance.

A few systems can condition their listening responses to features of the user's speech, though typically this feedback occurs only after an utterance is complete. For example, Neurobaby analyzes speech intonation and uses the extracted features to trigger emotional displays (Tosa 1993). More recently, Breazeal's Kismet system extracts emotional qualities in the user's speech (Breazeal and Aryananda 2002). Whenever the speech recognizer detects a pause in the speech, the previous utterance is classified (within one or two seconds) as indicating approval, an attentional bid, a prohibition, soothing or neutral. This is combined with Kismet's current emotional state to determine a facial expression and head posture. People who interact with Kismet often produce several utterances in succession, thus this approach is sufficient to provide a convincing illusion of real-time feedback.

Only a small number of systems have attempted to provide listening feedback *during* a user's utterance, and these methods have used only simple features of the speaker's behavior. For example, REA will execute a head nod or paraverbal (e.g. say "mm-hum") if the user pauses in mid-utterance for less than 500 milliseconds (Cassell, Bickmore et al. 1999). In contrast, a review of the psycholinguistic literature suggests that many other speaker behaviors are correlated with listener feedback and could be readily exploited by virtual characters.

3 Behavior of Human Listeners

The psycholinguistic literature has identified a variety of behaviors that listeners perform when in a conversation. Of course, many listener behaviors provide feedback about the semantic content the speaker's speech, but a large class of behaviors appear unrelated to specific meaning. Rather, these behaviors seem to trigger off of non-semantic features of the speaker's presentation, may precede complete understanding of the speech content, and are often generated without the listener or speaker's conscious awareness. Nonetheless, such behaviors can significantly influence the flow of a conversation and the impressions and feelings of the participants.

Here we review some of these behaviors, the circumstances that trigger their production and their hypothesized influence on the interaction. From this literature we extract a small number of simple rules that a listening agent could possibly utilize to drive its behavior.

3.1 Backchannel Continuers

Listeners frequently nod and utter paraverbals such as "uh-huh" and "mm-hmm" as someone is speaking. Within the psycholinguistic literature, such behaviors are referred to as *backchannel continuers* and are considered as a signal to the speaker that the communication is working and that they should continue speaking (Yngve 1970). Several researchers have developed models to predict when such feedback occurs. Cathcart, Carletta et al. (2003) propose a model based on pause duration and trigram part-of-speech frequency. According to the model of Ward and Tsukahara (2000), backchannel continuers are associated with a lowering of pitch over some interval. Cassell (2000) argues that head nod's could result from the raised voice of the speaker. The approaches of Ward and Cassell are more amenable to a real-time treatment as they are based purely on simple properties of the audio signal, so we will adopt these methods for developing behavior mapping rules:

Rule-1: Lowering of pitch in speech signal → head nod
Rule-2: Raised loudness in speech signal → head nod

3.2 Disfluency

Spoken language often contains repetition, spurious words, pauses and filled pauses (e.g., ehm, um, un). Such disfluency is viewed as a signal to the listener that the speaker is experiencing processing problems or experiencing high cognitive load (Clark and Wasow 1998) and frequently elicit "take your time" feedback from the listener (Ward and Tsukahara 2000). According to own video analysis, rather than nodding or uttering sounds as in backchannel continuers, listeners tended to perform posture shifts, gaze shifts or frowns in response to disfluency. The presumed meaning of such a posture shift is the listener is telling the speaker to take his time (Cassell 2000). It should be possible to detect disfluency in the audio signal and this leads to the following behavior mapping rule:

Rule-3: Disfluency in speech signal → Posture Shift / Gaze shift / Frown

3.3 Mimicry

Listeners often mimic behavior of a speaker during a conversation. Although they are not necessarily aware of doing it, people in a conversation will adjust the rhythm of speech, their body posture and even their breathing to each other (Warner 1996; McFarland 2001; Lakin, Jefferis et al. 2003). Mimicry, when not exaggerated to the point of mocking, has a variety of positive influences on the interactants. Speakers who are mimicked are more helpful and generous toward the listener (Van baaren, Holland et al. 2004). Mimicry can result in the perception of a pleasant, natural conversation (Warner, Malloy et al. 1987). It may also be important in synchronizing conversational flow, for example, by providing expectations on when a speaker can be interrupted. Given such influences, many of the agent's listening behaviors should mimic aspects of the speaker's behavior.

One salient speaker behavior is shifts in posture. When a speaker shifts her posture, for example by changing her weight distribution from one leg to another, or by folding her arms, this is often mirrored by the listener. Such posture shifts, both for speakers and listeners, tend to occur at discourse segment boundaries and may function to help manage such transitions (Cassell, Nakano et al. 2001). When present, such mimicry has been shown to positively influence the emotional state of the speaker (Van baaren, Holland et al. 2004). This suggests that a listening agent should detect posture shifts and mimic the resulting posture:

Rule-4: Speaker shifts posture → Mimic Posture

Gaze is also an important aspect of a speaker's behavior. Speakers will often gaze away from the listener, for example, when mentioning a concrete object within his vicinity, he will often look at it. When this lasts for a certain amount time, the listener could mimic this by looking in the same direction.

Rule-5: Speaker gazes away for longer period → Mimic Gaze

Listeners will frequently mimic the head gestures of a speaker. If a speaker shakes or nods his head, listeners may repeat this gesture. Although this may simply reflect an understanding and agreement with the speaker's utterance, many of us have probably been in conversations where such gestures were produced without any real understanding. In any event, an agent can easily mimic such gestures without explicit understanding. This leads to the following mimicry rule:

Rule-6: Speaker nods or shakes head → Mimic Head Gesture

3.4 Other External Influences

Obviously, such rules are an oversimplification of the factors that mediate human behavior. Many factors influence the occurrence of gestures during a conversation. For example, listeners frequently mimic the facial expression of speakers and this apparently plays an important role in the perception of empathy (Sonnby-Borgstrom, Jonsson et al. 2003). Individuals also differ in their response to the same speech based on a variety of dispositional and situational factors. There are people who almost do not gesture at all and there are people who gesture like it is a workout. Often, this is related to the speaker's emotions during the conversation. For example, people tend to gesture more when excited and less when sad. Also, the relation of the two people is of importance. People tend to gesture remarkably more when they talk to a friend then when they are talking to a complete stranger (Welji and Duncan 2004).

Thus, the mapping presented here is not a complete coverage of all gestures that at all times are accompanied by the certain speech features, but could be sufficient to increase the perceived authenticity of the conversation.

4   Real-Time Classification of Speaker Behavior

We implement the behavior rules listed above by detecting the various implicated aspects of the speaker's behavior. As such listening behaviors occur within utterances, this imposes strong real-time requirements on what features can be reasonably extracted given the limits of current technology. Here we describe the implementation of feature detectors that support the behavioral rules listed above.

There are two ways to determine physical features from a human in real time: image analysis or using 3d-trackers. Image analysis consists of recording the human with a camera and analyzing the data from the camera. The advantage of this method is that the complete human is visible and thus in theory all information could be extracted (with two or more cameras it might even be possible to get a 3D-image from the human). The disadvantages however are that it is computationally intensive and it is much work to create such a system from scratch.

In contrast to the image analysis method, there are tracker devices that can detect position and orientation with a high degree of accuracy. The advantage of using trackers is that they are fast and are not as computationally intensive as image analysis. The major drawback is that the trackers need to be set up and are only operational

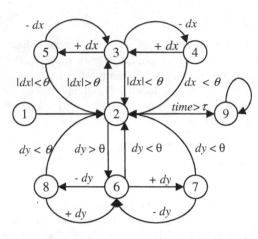

1: Calibration state.

2: Head stationary.

3: Horizontal rotation. If follows state 4 or 5, report a shake.

4: Head looks right

5: Head looks left

6: Vertical rotation. If follows state 7 or 8, report a nod.

7: Head looks up

8: Head looks down

9: No move for τ seconds. Report a gaze.

Fig. 1. State machine for detecting head gestures. dx (dy) denotes horizontal (vertical) rotation, θ is a distance and τ a time threshold.

in a limited area. In addition to this, when using a tracker, only the point of the tracker is known and no other parts of the human body.

For this research however, a space was available where a tracker device was already operational and thus this device has been used to extract the physical features of the human. With this tracker it was possible to extract both head gestures (such as gazes, nodding and shaking) and posture shifts.

From the speech signal, we can extract certain features that are not directly related to the semantics of the speech. These features could then be calculated instantly from the input from a microphone. Only the basic features are considered here, because although the computational speed of the current computers is rapidly increasing, it should be kept relatively simple.

According to Milewski (1996), it is possible to extract frequency and intensity information from a speech signal in real time using a Fourier transformation. When these two aspects of the speech signal are known, many useful derivatives can be calculated, such as silences, monotone sounds, et cetera. Thus, when using this transformation, there can be much information available in real time concerning the features of the speech signal.

4.1 Detecting and Classifying Body Movements

4.1.1 Head Gestures

Certain head gestures and body posture are readily detected in real time through the use of a six-degree-of-freedom tracking sensor attached to the speakers head.

The speaker's head shakes, nods and gazes can be detected by attending to the orientation of the head over time. When the orientation of the head rotates back and forth along some axis, this indicates either a nod or a shake. It would be a shake it the movement is a horizontal rotation would be a nod if the movement is a vertical rotation. In contrast, if the head rotates to some orientation and holds this position for some time, it must mean that the speaker is staring in a certain direction. We implemented a finite state machine to recognize such speaker gestures (Figure 1).

This state diagram allows the system to extract the different gestures from the human head and thus let the agent perform some mimicking according to the mapping rules that have been specified in the gesture theory chapter. The relevant rules for the head gestures are numbers 5 and 6.

4.1.2 Posture Shifts

Certain posture shifts are obtained by using the tracker information. For example, if a speaker shifts her weight from one foot to the other, this is typically accompanied by the translation of the head with respect to a static position between the feet (see Figure Y). This way, a weight shift could be detected with just one tracker placed on top of the head of the speaker assuming they do not move their feet.

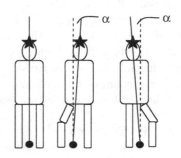

In our current system, we detect certain posture shifts in this way by measuring the angle α between the origin (dotted line in Figure Y) and the position of the tracker, placed on the head of the human. If this angle is greater than a certain threshold, this must mean the human is slouch-

Fig. 2. We detect posture shifts involving a weight shift by measuring angle α

ing. We use a restraining device to ensure that the speaker's feet remain stationary (this restriction could be eliminated be incorporating an additional tracker at the speaker's waist).

More specifically, posture shifts can be detected with just the angle between the head and the position between the legs and the height of the tracker (the length of the human), both obtainable from the tracker. With this, the angle α can be computed as follows:

$$\alpha = atan(dx / height\_of\_tracker)$$

Where dx is the relative position of the tracker with respect to the initial position where the human is standing straight. The current angle is compared to the threshold in order to get the type of slouch (left, right or neutral).

4.2 Detecting and Classifying Acoustic Features

Besides the different gestures from the trackers, we also extract features from the speaker's audio signal such as pitch and loudness. Given the real-time requirements of the system, all audio feature detectors utilize the Fast Fourier Transform (FFT) which is not described here, but can be found in various sources of literature (e.g. Milewski, 1996). FFT can separate an audio signal into an arbitrary number of frequency-intensity pairs and these pairs can be used in the computation of several features of the speech signal. This means, that when the continuous speech signal is sampled in parts of a certain length, from each sample the FFT could be computed and compared.

4.2.1 Intensity Detection

With some minor adjustments, the algorithm by Arons (1994) is used to perform the intensity detection. After determining the average (normal) intensity of a speaker during an initialization phase, the real time intensity can be compared to a pre-computed threshold. This threshold would be the top one percent value of the initial intensity value computed during initialization. When the real time intensity value exceeds the threshold it must mean that there is a raise in intensity. With this information, mapping rule number 2 can be implemented.

Besides this approach to the computation of the intensity of a speech signal, another approach is proposed by Fernandez (2004). His model uses the computation of certain loudness features, which could improve the previously described method. The code to perform these loudness computations in Matlab has been available to us, but unfortunately this proved too slow to be useful for real time computations. Due to the limited amount of time available for this research, no optimizations could be made and thus the loudness detection model was discarded.

4.2.2 Pitch Detection

Pitch detection is done in a similar fashion as the intensity detection. For each sample, from the resulting frequency/intensity pairs of the FFT, the frequency is chosen that has the highest intensity and this is compared to the previous highest frequencies. This way, a significant drop or raise in the frequency of the speech can be detected.

We re-implemented the backchannel-algorithm by (Ward and Tsukahara 2000) within Matlab, using a pitch detection algorithm is available from the Matlab User Community. To actually implement this algorithm, the pitch values of the last 120 milliseconds have to be stored. Then, if all these values are below the 23rd percentile pitch level, an output can be performed after 700 milliseconds when all the other conditions are met. With this algorithm, mapping rule number 1 can be implemented.

4.2.3 Disfluency Detection

The final mapping rule depends on the detection of stuttering of disfluency in the speech signal. An example of this would be the expression 'uhhhh' for a longer period of time. To detect this, the frequency of the signal could be used. If a certain frequency holds for a longer period of time and does not vary much, this could mean disfluency.

This method of detecting disfluency was proposed by Shriberg (1999), and concerns different types of disfluency, like filled/unfilled pauses, false starts and repetition of words. For this research, only the filled and unfilled pauses shall be considered, because these types do not depend on semantic information and thus can be detected using frequency and intensity respectively.

Specifically, Shriberg argues that a filled pause in an audio signal is accompanied by a relatively low frequency region for a period of at least 200 milliseconds. Thus, to extract this from the audio signal, the frequencies over 200 milliseconds have to be stored and evaluated. When the standard deviation of these frequencies is smaller than approximately one hertz, the module reports the detection of a disfluency.

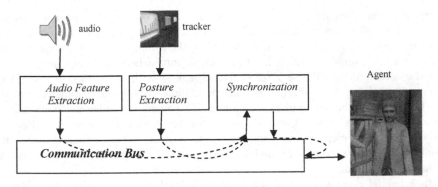

Fig 3. Overall system architecture

5   Behavior of a Listening Agent

Through recognizing features of the speaker's behavior and applying these features to the behavior rules in Section 3, we can generate listening behaviors. The final issue is how to integrate these behaviors into an overall performance. As we are simultaneously recognizing features from multiple channels (head, body, ands speech), and listening behaviors have some duration, it is possible that a listening behavior will be proposed that overlaps with a currently executing behavior. This could easily result in unnatural behavior.

We use a synchronization module to solve this problem. This module parses messages on the communication bus and determines if the message is intended for the agent and which type of gesture is contained in the command. Once this parsing has been done, the function accompanying that type of gesture can be called. This function determines whether a previous gesture is still performing, and when this is not the case, a message is created which is to be sent to the agent. The module also incorporates a flexible behavior mapping allowing designers to easily experiment with alternative mappings between classes of listening behaviors and their physical manifestation.

6   Evaluation

This listening module could be integrated into a variety of embodied conversational agent applications, potentially improving the naturalness and subjective impressions of the interaction. In assessing the suitability of such an integration, we must consider several factors. Does the system correctly detect features of the speaker's behavior? Do the behavior mapping rules suggest appropriate feedback? Is the performed behavior judged natural at the time it is performed? Finally, do agent listening behaviors have the predicted influence on the human speaker's perceptions? Here we discuss the results of informal evaluations. Formal evaluations are planned for later this year.

In evaluating the system we adapt the "McNeill lab" paradigm (McNeill 1992) for studying gesture research. In this research, one participant, the Speaker, has previously observed some incident (e.g., a Sylvester and Tweety cartoon clip), and describes it to another participant, the Listener. Here, we replace the Listener with our agent system. Speakers see a life-sized animated character projected in a room. They stand in a foot restraining device in the middle of the room, wear a Intersense acoustic motion tracking sensor on their head and speak into a headset microphone. In the formal evaluation, we will use a 2x2 design. Speakers will be assigned to one of two priming conditions: they will be told that the Listener's behavior is either controlled by a human in another room or by a computer. The agent will either use our mapping rules or random behavior. Currently, we have performed preliminary evaluations using several staff members associated with the project. Notable findings from this initial feedback are reported here and will be used to adjust system parameters prior to the formal evaluations.

Backchannel continuers suggested by Ward's Pitch Detection Algorithm seem to occur in the appropriate location and thus Ward's algorithm does work fairly well. The only drawback here is that this algorithm is dependant of the initial recorded pitch threshold and thus when this initial recording would be modified, the results would be different.

The detection of disfluency consists of two parts, which are silences and filled pauses. The detection of silences worked very well although they tended to occur too soon. This can be resolved by extending the buffer which is an easy adaptation. The detection of filled pauses however did not work as well as predicted. The allowed variation in frequency of 0.05 Hertz proved too small and this has to be increased.

Observers reported the listening agent appeared more autonomous and natural. In particular, the occurrence of head nods and gazes seemed to contribute to this effect. Naturalness and autonomy does not necessarily translate into a feeling of engagement and our initial tests identified several factors that appeared to detract from engagement. For example, if the agent gazes away from the speaker too frequently, one is left with the impression that the agent is uninterested in the conversation. This led us to adjust downward the frequency of gaze shifts. We also decided the delay of 700 milliseconds in the algorithm by Ward was too long. This has been changed to 200 milliseconds and this led to more reasonable head nods. Some speakers systematically vary the intensity of the speech across utterances which can confuse our feature detectors. This could be resolved by re-computing the thresholds when the voice of the speaker undergoes a big change.

Although definitive testing has not been completed to date, the results of the informal tests seem promising. Especially the performing of head nods and the behavior when the human is silent seem to result in more natural behavior. Even though the speech signal was quite noisy, the responsive behavior improved the natural behavior of the agent.

7 Conclusions

Although they have not been a strong focus in the virtual human community, listening behaviors play an important role in promoting effective communication. A challenge in generating real-time listening behaviors is that the semantic content of a user's speech is typically available only after they are done speaking. Indeed, this information is sometimes only available a second or two after an utterance. This paper has reviewed the psycholinguistic literature to show that many listening behaviors are also correlated with physical behaviors that are easier to detect in real time. In other words, not only the meaning of the words is of importance, but also features as the intonation and the loudness of the speech signal.

Using this knowledge, we tried to find a mapping between these certain features and the accompanying gestures. The suggested mapping in this chapter is however not complete because there are many external factors that influence the occurrence of gestures, like the emotional state and relation of the persons involved. The suggested mapping can however be used to perform these gestures for example with a virtual human in order to let the virtual human react in a more natural way.

Acknowledgements

Stacy Marsella suggested the initial idea underlying this work – that some information in the speech signal could drive back channeling behaviors of a virtual character. Sue Duncan pointed us to several references on this literature and provided feedback on drafts. Roz Picard, Shri Narayanan and David Traum suggested several approaches for extracting information from the speech signal and Raul Galt provided us Matlab code that helped inform our work. Regina Cabrera provided valuable editorial feedback. This work was sponsored by the U. S. Army Research, Development, and Engineering Command (RDECOM), and the content does not necessarily reflect the position or the policy of the Government, and no official endorsement should be inferred.

References

Arons, B. (1994). Pitch-Based Emphasis Detection For Segmenting Speech Recordings. International Conference on Spoken Language Processing.

Bernieri, J. E. G. a. F. J. (1999). "The Importance of Nonverbal Cues in Judging Rapport." Journal of Nonverbal Behavior 23(4): 253-269.

Breazeal, C. and L. Aryananda (2002). "Recognition of Affective Communicative Intent in Robot-Directed Speech." Autonomous Robots 12: 83-104.

Cassell, J. (2000). Nudge Nudge Wink Wink: Elements of Face-to-Face Conversation for Embodied Conversational Agents. Embodied Conversational Agents. J. Cassell, J. Sullivan, S. Prevost and E. Churchill. Cambridge, MA, MIT Press: 1-27.

Cassell, J., T. Bickmore, et al. (1999). Embodiment in Conversational Interfaces: Rea. Conference on Human Factors in Computing Systems, Pittsburgh, PA.

Cassell, J., T. Bickmore, et al. (2000). Human conversation as a system framework: Designing embodied conversational agents. Embodied Conversational Agents. J. Cassell, J. Sullivan, S. Prevost and E. Churchill. Boston, MIT Press: 29-63.

Cassell, J., Y. I. Nakano, et al. (2001). Non-verbal cues for discourse structure. Association for Computational Linguistics Joint EACL - ACL Conference.

Cassell, J., J. Sullivan, et al., Eds. (2000). Embodied Conversational Agents. Cambridge, MA, MIT Press.

Cathcart, N., J. Carletta, et al. (2003). A shallow model of backchannel continuers in spoken dialogue. 10th Conference of the European Chapter of the Association for Computational Linguistics, Budapest.

Clark, H. H. and T. Wasow (1998). "Repeating words in Spontaneous Speech." Cognitive Psychology.**37**: 204-242.

E., S. (1999). Phonetic Consequences of Speech Disfluency. International Congress of Phonetic Sciences, San Francisco, CA.

Fernandez, R. (2004). A Computational Model for the Automatic Recognition of Affect in Speech. Cambridge, MA, Ph.D. Thesis, MIT Media Arts and Science.

Gratch, J., J. Rickel, et al. (2002). Creating Interactive Virtual Humans: Some Assembly Required. IEEE Intelligent Systems. **July/August:** 54-61.

Lakin, J. L., V. A. Jefferis, et al. (2003). "Chameleon Effect as Social Glue: Evidence for the Evolutionary Significance of Nonconsious Mimicry." Journal of Nonverbal Behavior **27**(3): 145-162.

Marsella, S., J. Gratch, et al. (2003). Expressive Behaviors for Virtual Worlds. Life-like Characters Tools, Affective Functions and Applications. H. Prendinger and M. Ishizuka. Berlin, Springer-Verlag: 317-360.

McFarland, D. H. (2001). "Respiratory Markers of Conversational Interaction." Journal of Speech, Language, and Hearing Research **44**: 128-143.

McNeill, D. (1992). Hand and mind: What gestures reveal about thought. Chicago, IL, The University of Chicago Press.

Milewski, B. (1996). The Fourier Transform, Reliable Software, Relisoft.com.

Sonnby-Borgstrom, M., P. Jonsson, et al. (2003). "Emotional Empathy as Related to Mimicry Reactions at Different Levels of Information Processing." Journal of Nonverbal Behavior **27**(1): 3-23.

Tosa, N. (1993). "Neurobaby." ACM SIGGRAPH: 212-213.

Van baaren, R. B., R. W. Holland, et al. (2004). "Mimicry and Prosocial Behavior." Psychological Science **15**(1): 71-74.

Ward, N. and W. Tsukahara (2000). "Prosodic features which cue back-channel responses in English and Japanese." Journal of Pragmatics **23**: 1177-1207.

Warner, R. (1996). Coordinated cycles in behavior and physiology during face-to-face social interactions. Dynamic patterns in communication processes. J. H. Watt and C. A. VanLear. Thousand Oaks, CA, SAGE publications.

Warner, R. M., D. Malloy, et al. (1987). "Rhythmic organization of social interaction and observer ratings of positive affect and involvement." Journal of Nonverbal Behavior **11**(2): 57-74.

Welji, H. and S. Duncan (2004). Characteristics of face-to-face interactions, with and without rapport: Friends vs. strangers. Symposium on Cognitive Processing Effects of 'Social Resonance' in Interaction, 26th Annual Meeting of the Cognitive Science Society.

Yngve, V. H. (1970). On getting a word in edgewise. Sixth regional Meeting of the Chicago Linguistic Society.

Providing Computer Game Characters
with Conversational Abilities

Joakim Gustafson[1], Johan Boye[1],
Morgan Fredriksson[2], Lasse Johanneson[2], and Jürgen Königsmann[2]

[1] Voice Technologies, TeliaSonera, Rudsjöterrassen 5, 136 80 Haninge, Sweden
{joakim.gustafson, johan.boye}@teliasonera.com
[2] Liquid Media, Skånegatan 101, 116 32, Stockholm, Sweden
{morgan, lasse, jurgen}@liquid.se

Abstract. This paper presents the NICE fairy-tale game system, which enables adults and children to engage in conversation with animated characters in a 3D world. In this paper we argue that spoken dialogue technology have the potential to greatly enrichen the user's experience in future computer games. We also present some requirements that have to be fulfilled to successfully integrate spoken dialogue technology with a computer game application. Finally, we briefly describe an implemented system that has provided computer game characters with some conversational abilities that kids have interacted with in studies.

1 Introduction

The text adventure games of the 70's could achieve a limited sense of omniscience, since their goal-oriented users wanted to be immersed into the adventure, which refrained them from trying to deceive the system. The immersion was limited, due to the systems' limited understanding capabilities. Paradoxically, today's commercial 3D adventure games have even more limited input understanding capabilities – only allowing its users to navigate in the 3D world, selecting objects via mouse input and selecting what their avatar should do or say next from predefined menus. These computer games provide an excellent application area for research in spoken dialogue technology. Speech input is already used in some commercial computer games (e.g. Lifeline, 2004), but these do not support conversational interaction. More advanced spoken dialogue have the potential to greatly enrichen computer games. For example, it would allow players to refer to past events and to objects currently not visible on the screen, as well as interacting socially and negotiating solutions with the game characters.

The NICE project aims at to providing users with an immersive dialogue experience in a 3D fairy-tale game, engaging in multi-party dialogue with animated conversational characters. Spoken and multimodal dialogue is the user's primary vehicle of progressing through the story, and it is by verbal and non-verbal communication that the user can gain access to the goals and desires of the fairy-tale characters. This is critical as the characters ask the users to help them in solving problems. These problems either relate to objects that have to be manipulated or information that has to be retrieved from other fairy-tale characters.

T. Panayiotopoulos et al. (Eds.): IVA 2005, LNAI 3661, pp. 37–51, 2005.
© Springer-Verlag Berlin Heidelberg 2005

2 Background

Spoken dialogue systems have so far mostly been designed with an overall goal to carry out a specific task, e.g. accessing timetable information or ordering tickets [4, 35]. With task-oriented systems, it is possible to build domain models that can be used to predefine the language models and dialogue rules. The existence of predefined tasks makes it rather straightforward to evaluate the performance of the dialogue system. Some dialogue systems have aimed to present its users with an engaging and entertaining experience, without the presence of an external predetermined task. Conversational kiosks, such as August [22] and MACK [12], encourage users to engage in social dialogues with embodied characters. Some spoken dialogue systems have addresses the problem of managing conversational speech with animated characters that reside in a 3D-world, e.g. the Mission Rehearsal Exercise system from the USC Institute of Creative Technologies, a system that also allow for multi-party dialogue [32].

Over the recent years interactive story-telling research systems have been developed that in some cases allow linguistic input. Hayes-Roth [24] lists a number of principles that are important for interactive story-telling systems. The user has to be given an illusion of immersion by participating in an interesting story where they feel that they are actively participating by interacting with the characters in a meaningful and natural way. Young [34] suggests that the drama manager of the system should put a limit to the user's actions by not allowing interference that violates the overall narrative plan. Most interactive games developed so far allow users to intervene in the storytelling by acting on physical objects on the screen using direct manipulation [10, 34]. Moreover, some systems allow users to interact with characters by means of written text input [28], while others explored using a speech interface [10].

3 Conversational Skills

Humans who engage in face-to-face dialogues use non-verbal communication such as body gestures, gaze, facial expressions and lip movements to transmit information, attitudes and emotions. If computers are to engage in spoken dialogue with humans it would seem natural to give them the possibility to use both verbal and non-verbal communication. Verbally, they have to be able to communicate their goals and plans to the user, and they should be able to cooperate with the user to solve problems. In order to convey personality and to build a collaborative trusting relationship with the users, the characters also have to be able to engage in socializing small talk. In order to be able to coordinate their action towards a goal that is shared with the user, the characters have to be able to collaborate with the user [15, 21]. The characters also have to be able to engage in grounding dialogue with the users to be able to certify that they have understood what the user wants them to do. In conversation the coordination of turns is crucial, and it is regulated by a number of turn management subfunctions that can be expressed verbally or non-verbally [3]. There are two simultaneous information channels in a dialogue: the information channel from the speaker, and the back-channel feedback from the listener. The back-channel feedback indicates attention, feelings and understanding, and its purpose is to support the interaction. It has been argued that dialogue systems should be able to provide positive feedback in successful contexts and negative feedback when problems have been detected [8]. Initial cue words can be used to facilitate grounding by providing information on the speaker's orientation towards the content of the previous turn [9]. Disfluencies like filled pauses may be indicators of problems in dialogue, but initial fillers are used to manage turn taking and both filled and silent pauses are used to indicate feeling-of-knowing [7].

Animating the face brings the embodied character to life, making it more believable as a dialogue partner. Facial actions can be clustered according to their communicative functions in three different channels: the phonemic, the intonational and the emotional [18]. *The phonemic channel* is used to communicate redundant and complementary information in what is being said. *The intonational channel* is used to facilitate a smooth interaction. Facial expressions, eyebrow raising and head nods can be used to communicate the information structure of an utterance [11, 30]. *The emotional channel* is used to increase the animated character's social believability. There are *display rules* that regulate when speakers show emotions. These rules depend on the meaning the speaker wants to convey, the mood of the speaker, the relationship between speaker and listener and the dialogue situation [17]. Gaze indicates three types of mental processes: spontaneous looking, task-relevant looking and looking as a function of orientation of thought [25]. Thus, in conversation gaze carries information about what the interlocutors are focusing on, the degree of attention and interest during a conversation, to regulate the turn-taking, to refer to visible objects and to display emotions or to define power and status. Pelachaud et al. [31] described a facial animation system that among other things could display different gaze patterns, and the BEAT system uses gaze, head nods and eyebrow-raising for turn-handling [11]. Finally, turn-handling gaze can be used to indicate who is talking in multi-party dialogues such as virtual conferencing [16].

4 The NICE Fairy-Tale Game Scenario

The fairy-tale domain was chosen because of its classic themes and stereotypical characters, are well known to most adults as well as children. So far two scenes have been implemented, see Fig. 1. There are two main characters in the system: the helper Cloddy Hans, who has been introduced to facilitate progression through the story and gatekeeper Karen, who is introduced as an obstacle in the story. Personality traits are not explicitly modeled, but they are rather used as guidance in the design of the characters to ensure that their behaviors are perceived by the users as compatible with their intended personalities. Personality is conveyed by modes of appearance, actions, wording, speaking styles, voice quality, and non-verbal behavior. In order to match the characters' different roles in the game, the output behavior of the two characters have been designed to display these quite different OCEAN personality traits[29]: Cloddy Hans is *Dunce, Uncertain, Friendly, Polite, Calm* and *Even tempered*, while Karin *is Intellectual, Frivolous, Self-confident, Unfriendly, Touchy* and *Anxious*.

Cloddy Hans and the fairy-tale machine

The user meets Cloddy Hans in H. C. Andersen's study, where there is fairy-tale machine and a shelf with fairy-tale objects. The objects have to be put in one of several icon-labeled slots in the machine in order to construct a new story and thereby get transferred into the fairy-tale world. This introduction scene thus develops into a straightforward "put-that-there" game, where the system is able to anticipate what the user will have to say to solve it. The real purpose of the first scene is not to solve the task, but to engage in a collaborative conversation where the player familiarises himself with the possibilities and limitations of the spoken input capabilities.

Karen and Cloddy Hans at the drawbridge

The fairy-tale world is a large 3D virtual world, where the user and Cloddy Hans land on a small island, where they are trapped. A deep gape separates them from the rest of the world. There is a drawbridge in the gap, operated by Karin, who has the gatekeeper role in the scene. She will only lower the drawbridge when offered something she finds acceptable in return, which she never does until the user's third attempt, thereby encouraging negotiative behavior. Furthermore, both Cloddy Hans and Karen openly show some amount of grudge against each other, with both characters occasionally prompting the user to choose sides.

Fig. 1. The first two scenes in the fairy-tale game

Narrative Progression

The two scenes described above contain certain key moments, *story-functional events*. The passing of such an event means that there has been a progression in the story (thus it is important that a story-functional event can not be undone). The first scene contains the following story-functional events: *Cloddy Hans introduces himself; Cloddy Hans introduces the plot; Cloddy Hans picks up an object for the first time; Cloddy Hans puts object number X in the fairy-tale machine; Cloddy Hans pulls the lever so that he and the user can enter the fairy-tale world.* Since it is impossible to retrieve an object from the machine, all put-object-in-machine events are story-functional. The second scene contains the following types of story-functional events: *Cloddy Hans introduces the fairy-tale world; Karin introduces herself; Cloddy Hans gives his opinion of Karin; Karin gives her opinion of Cloddy Hans; Karin informs the user that she demands payment in order to lower the drawbridge; Karin accepts an object and lowers the drawbridge; Cloddy Hans crosses the drawbridge and gives Karin the payment.* The knowledge about these story functional events are encoded into the scene descriptions that all character loads when a scene is initialized. This means that they can add goals on their agenda that leads to the realization of all story functional events in a scene. This also makes it possible for the helper character Cloddy Hans to guide the user when she gets stuck in a scene. Some of events involve more than one action or the exchange multiple pieces of information. In order for the introduction to be complete Cloddy Hans has to talk about his and the users name, age and health. There are also default objects and corresponding destination slots in the scene description that could be used by the system to suggest a possible next object to pick up and then where it could be placed.

5   The Output Capabilities of the Fairy-Tale Characters

The fairy-tale characters in the NICE system are able to generate both verbal and non-verbal behaviour. They have different roles in the game and consequently they have to be able to convey different personalities that match their respective roles. Charles and Cavazza [13] distinguish between two types of characters in their character-based story telling system - *feature characters* and *supporting characters*. In the Nice fairy-tale game a third kind of character have been added - a *helper character*. This means that there are these three types of characters in the fairy-tale world, that require different levels of conversational abilities:

Helper Character - A character that guides and helps the user throughout the whole fairy-tale game. *Cloddy Hans* is a friendly character with no long-term goals for himself, other than doing what the user asks him to. Helper characters need conversational capabilities allowing both for grounding and cooperation, and for dialogue regulation and error handling. They need to have knowledge of all plots and subtasks in the game. Finally they need simple visual perception so that they can suggest actions that involves objects in the scene that the user have not noticed yet, and they have to be aware of the other characters actions as well as their verbal output.

Feature Characters - Characters that has a key function in the plots. *Karen* is a feature character that has a *Gatekeeper* function in the second scene. She is a selfish character with goals of her own. She will not help the user unless she gets a reward. Feature characters need less cooperative and grounding conversational abilities, since they have goals of their own that they simply want to convey to the user. However, they need dialogue regulation and error handling capabilities. They only need knowledge about the plots and subtasks they appear in, and they have to be aware of the other characters actions as well as their verbal output.

Supporting Characters - Characters that only tell the pieces of information needed for the plot, but that are not willing to engage in conversation with the user. Supporting characters only need to be provided with the verbal capabilities needed to convey the information they are supposed to communicate to the user. Apart from these they only need to be provided with verbal utterances like "I don't want to chat with you". They only need knowledge about the subtasks they are supposed to comment on, and they may be aware of the other characters actions as well as their verbal output. *Thumbelina* is added as a non-verbal supporting character that uses the default objects and destinations in the first scene in order to be able to point at the slot where she thinks a certain object should be placed. If the user gets Cloddy Hans to put it in another slot she shows her discontent with large emotional body gestures.

The fairy-tale characters are able to talk about the plots and scenes, as well as their own plans and to goals that relate to these. When characters first meet the user they are able to engage in formalized socializing small talk. In later phases they are still able to respond to social initiatives from the users, but without goals of their own to pursue the social topic. The characters are also provided with general dialogue regulating speech acts that they can use in all scenes: *Plan Regulating* (e.g. agree, ask for request), *Error Handling* (e.g. report not hearing, asking for clarification), *Turn Han-*

dling (e.g. floor holders), *Attitudal Feedback* (positive or negative feedback), *Discourse Markers* (respond to unexpected info), and *Extralinguistic sounds* (clear throat, exhalation, laughter, sigh). In order to be able to talk about the plot, their goals and plans, the fairy-tale characters have also been provided with a number of task oriented plot dependent speech acts: *Introduction and explanation of the plot, Initiatives that serve to fulfill the characters' plan or long-term goals, Requests for instructions, Responses to instructions from the user, Stating intentions, plans and goals*.

The main characters are able to perform the actions needed to progress through the plots of the game. In order to be reactive they are also able to generate gestures as a result of user input and events in their environment. These reactions are either displays of attitude, state of mind, turn regulation gestures or attention gestures. The characters can also look at and point at interactive objects, non-interactive objects and landmarks in the 3D-world. They are able to walk between locations that are far apart. If the user has not engaged in interaction with the characters for a while they enter an idle state where they start off with small encouraging gestures, then after a while they indicate impatience by gazing around in the environment or displaying various idle gestures. All characters have been provided with a number of communicative gestures, as well as a number of simple, single body part animations that can be used to generate more complex multi body part gestures. This makes it possible to either play ready animations for communicative gestures or to generate animation lists consisting animation tracks on the individual body parts. Fig 2. below shows the different types of non-verbal behavior the characters are able to display.

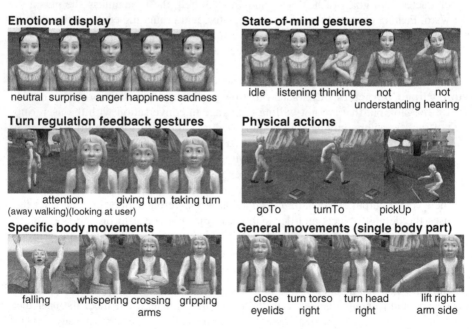

Emotional display

neutral surprise anger happiness sadness

State-of-mind gestures

idle   listening thinking   not   not
                          understanding hearing

Turn regulation feedback gestures

attention   giving turn taking turn
(away walking)(looking at user)

Physical actions

goTo   turnTo   pickUp

Specific body movements

falling   whispering crossing gripping
                        arms

General movements (single body part)

close   turn torso   turn head   lift right
eyelids   right   right   arm side

Fig. 2. The characters' different types of non-verbal behavior

The gestures, movements and actions of the different characters are used to convey their respective personalities. To make the characters' output behavior consistent, the body gestures, actions and idle behaviors of the two characters have been designed with their respective personality traits in mind. The manner in which characters move conveys their different personalities in the same way as their different speaking styles does. Chi et al [14] has developed a parametrisized system, EMOTE, that describes the manner of movements and Allbeck and Badler [2] describes an initial attempt to link the EMOTE parameters with the OCEAN personality parameters. If this linkage is applied to the two characters, they get the following EMOTE parameters with accompanying non-verbal behavior:

	Space	Weight	Time	Flow
	*Direct:* Single focus, e.g. he either looks bluntly at the user, or glances at the object that he or the user is referring to.	*Strong:* Powerful, having impact, e.g. he walks with determined steps.	*Sudden:* Hurried, e.g. he performs the actions asked for immediately	*Bound:* Controlled, restrained, e.g. he walks the shortest way to a location, and then he turns to the user, looking encouraging.
	*Indirect:* Multi-focus, e.g. doesn't look at the user for a very long time, before breaking their mutual gaze, letting her gaze wonder into the surroundings.	*Light:* Delicate, easily overcoming gravity, e.g. she walks about with light steps.	*Sustained:* Lingering, indulging in time, e.g. she tries to avoid to do what the users asks her	*Free:* Uncontrolled movement, e.g. she wanders about on her way to an location, looking as she doesn't quite know where she is heading

Fig. 3. The impact of the derived EMOTE parameters on the characters' non-verbal behaviors

To support the intended personalities of these characters, Cloddy Hans displays small, but slow and deliberate body gestures while Karen displays larger, and faster body gestures. The characters' different personalities are also conveyed by their different idle behaviors: Karin is not patient which is reflected by the fact that she enters her idle phase faster, and she lets her attention wander away from the user to the environment, and after a while she even walks away from the user. Cloddy is more calm and keeps his attention at the user. Finally, to give the characters basic simple perceptual abilities a number of reactive behaviors have also been added in the system:

Auditory Perception - is simulated by generating attention gestures that for example involve turning to the speaker. When user speech is detected the characters will turn to the active camera, and when there are multiple character speaking in a scene the other characters will turn towards the speaking character

Visual Perception - is simulated by generating attention gestures when the users starts gesturing or glancing at the object that the user has encircled. It is also simulated by adding triggers nearby interesting objects, and generating an appropriate attention gesture towards an object that the character walks by. It is also possible for the system to request a list of all objects that are visible (either on the screen or from a characters field of vision), and then request the character to turn to or talk about a found object.

Perception of Time - is simulated by letting a central server time-stamp all messages from both input and output modules, and by letting it generate timeouts that are used to manage the characters' idle behavior. The Animation system keeps track of all characters' current actions, in order to be able to change a certain character's behavior dependent on the current situation and to be able to coordinate different characters' simultaneous actions.

6 System Architecture

To make the animated fairytale characters appear lifelike, they have to be autonomous, i.e. they must do things even when the user is not interacting with them. At the same time they have to be reactive and show conversational abilities when the user is interacting with them. This means that the characters have to be able to generate carefully planned goal-oriented actions as well as very fast, less planned actions. In order to be able to build a system that can harness all these functionalities, an event driven, asynchronous, modular hub architecture was chosen, where a set of processes that communicate via message-passing over TCP/IP. Events from all servers are sent to a central hub, the Message Dispatcher server, (similar but simpler than OAA [27] or Communicator [1]). The central Message Dispatcher is responsible for coordinating input and output events in the system, by time-stamping all messages from the various modules. The behavior of the Message Dispatcher is controlled by a set of simple rules, specifying how to react when receiving a message of a certain type from one the modules. Since the Message Dispatcher is connected both to the input channels and the output modalities, it can increase the system's responsiveness by giving fast but simple feedback on input events. Timeouts from the Message Dispatcher are used to allow the system to have a perception of time, which is used to control the characters' idle behavior, and to let the dialogue managers take the imitative and generate suggestions of actions in cases where the users has not answered a request for the next action.

The spoken input is handled by a speech recognizer with statistical language models trained on 5600 user utterances from 57 users that interacted with a semi-automated version of the system (the wizard could correct the ASR-string if needed). A robust natural language understanding module has also been developed using this data[6]. To be able to provide the animated character with Swedish voices with natural voice quality and prosody, a unit selection synthesizer was developed in cooperation with KTH [23]. An important role of the synthesis component in the fairy-tale system is to convey the personality of the characters. To get to the different speaking styles, the voice talents were told to read the utterances in manners that matched the targeted personalities. This resulted in two voices with speaking styles that, among other things, differed in frequency range. They also differed in speaking rate and voice pitch. In order to accentuate these last two differences, all utterances were re-sampled changing speaking rate and voice pitch at the same time. All Cloddy's utterances were slowed down and all Karen's utterances were speeded up. This simple procedure had desired side-effects: apart from making Cloddy's voice slower it made him sound larger, and, apart from making Karen's voice faster, it made her sound younger. The personalities of the two characters were deliberately chosen so that this simple voice transformation would also make their voices more matching with the visual appearance of the two animated characters.

6.1 Dialogue Management

There are two dialogue managers in the NICE fairy-tale game system, one per fairy-tale character. The functionality of these two dialogue managers are somewhat different, reflecting the fairy-tale characters' different personalities. Moreover, the functionality of any dialogue manager varies over time, reflecting supposed changes in the characters' knowledge, attitudes and state of mind. However, when considered at an appropriate level of abstraction, most of the functions any dialogue manager needs to be able to carry out remain constant regardless of the character or the situation at hand. As a consequence, the dialogue management software in the NICE fairy-tale system consists of a *kernel* laying down the common functionality, and *scripting code* modifying the dialogue behavior as to be suitable for different characters and different situations[5]. This model of code organization is common in computer games[33].

The dialogue management kernel issues dialogue events at important points in the processing. Some kinds of dialogue events, the so-called external events, are triggered from an event in a module outside the dialogue manager (for instance, a recognition failure in the speech recognizer), whereas for others, the internal events, an internal event takes place within the dialogue kernel. There are e number of external dialogue event that the dialogue manager can receive: *BroadcastEvent* (some other character has said and done something), *GestureEvent* (the Gesture Interpreter has recognized a gesture), *ParserEvent* (the natural language parser has arrived at an analysis of the latest utterance), *PerformedEvent* (the animation system has completed an operation), *RecognitionFailureEvent* (the speech recognizer has detected that the user has said something, but failed to recognize it), *WorldEvent* (an event has occurred in the 3D world), and *TriggerEvent* (the animation system has detected that the character has moved into a trigger). There are also a number of internal dialogue events: *AlreadySatisfiedEvent* (a goal which already is satisfied has been added to the character's agenda), *CannotSolveEvent* (an unsolvable goal has been added to the character's agenda), *IntentionEvent* (the character has an intention to say or do something), *NoReactionEvent* (the character has nothing on the agenda), *PossibleGoalConflictEvent* (a goal is added to the agenda, but the agenda contains a possibly conflicting goal), and *TimeOutEvent* (a timeout has expired). The kernel provides a number of operations through which the scripting code can influence the dialogue behaviour of the character. These are: *interpret an utterance* in its context; *convey* a dialogue act; *perform* an action; *add a goal* to the character's agenda; *remove a goal* from the character's agenda; *find the next goal* on the agenda, and *pursue a goal* on the agenda.

6.2   The Animation System

The *Animation System,* (see Fig. 4) is responsible for generating the character animations and actions. It is divided into two modules: The *Animation Handler* and the *Animation Renderer.*

6.2.1   The Animation Handler

The Animation Handler deconstructs action requests from the dialogue managers into sequences of more fine-grained animation instructions. For instance, a "go to the fairy-tale machine" request is translated into (1) change camera (2) walk to the machine (3) change camera again, and (4) turn to camera. These animation instructions are queued (there is one queue per fairy-tale character) and sent one at a time to the Animation Renderer. After successful execution of an instruction, the Renderer sends back a receipt, after which the next instruction is sent, and so on. Upon receipt of a speech-synthesis request from a dialogue manager, the Animation Handler instructs

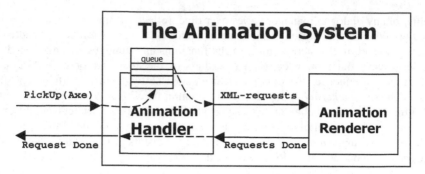

Fig. 4. The internal handling of requests to the Animation System and its place in the system

the speech synthesizer to generate a sound file with corresponding *lip-synchronization track*. The latter is a sequence of time-stamped animation instructions for the different facial movements needed to achieve lip-synchronization. If the character is walking or otherwise moving when the lip-synchronization instructions are rendered, the facial animations are blended with the bodily movements.

Within the Animation Handler, there is one synthesis queue per fairy-tale character. Each speech-synthesis request comes with a priority, needed to determine the correct action to take if the character is already talking (due to the event-based dialogue management method, this happens occasionally). If the priority of the incoming request is lower than that of the utterance currently being produced, the incoming request is ignored. If the priority of the incoming request is higher, the ongoing utterance is interrupted, and the new utterance is produced instead. If the two requests have equal priority, the incoming request is enqueued and produced after the ongoing utterance has finished. Synthesis requests with high priority typically concern replies to the user's utterance, requests with medium-high priority typically concern suggestions to the user on how to proceed (generated when the user has been silent for a while), and requests with low priority concern chit-chat.

6.1.2 The Animation Rendering System

The subsystems of the rendering system communicate with each other through façade classes with virtual interfaces [19]. The use of virtual facades makes it easy to switch between different implementations of a specific subsystem without affecting the other systems or applications using the game engine. The *Resource System* is a responsible for keeping track of all resources (like e.g. graphical meshes and animated models). All resources have been given a type and a name in order to make them unique and distinguishable from each other. The *Animation System* is responsible for creating and updating animated models. An *Animated Model* is a deformable graphical object built upon a hierarchy of frames. Each frame has a 3D-space transformation matrix representing its rotation and position relative the parent frame. An *Animation* is a named data set containing rotation, position, and scale values for a given frame and point in time. Animations can contain values for all of the frames in the hierarchy or just a single one. The graphical artist creating the animation decides which frames that are included in an animation. To be able to move different parts of the hierarchy simultaneously and independently, animated models can be ordered to play animations at separate *tracks*. Currently each model has 8 tracks, but this could easily be changed if there is a need for it. If animations played at different tracks affects the same set of frames, the resulting movement will be decided by the animation played at the track with the highest index.

It is the physics and collision systems that are responsible for real time simulation of the movement of walking characters, falling objects etc. The collision system is also responsible for handling some of the game logic controlling duties, such as triggering events when an object enters a specific area or picking out objects selected by the user mouse input. The animation system uses an externally developed collision and a physics system called Tokamak [26]. To speed up the complex calculations involved in realistically simulating collisions between objects, 3-dimensional mathematical shapes are used as simple collision primitives. Objects and characters are provided with one or more simple collision primitive. In addition to collision between these simple collision primitives, the system also supports collisions between primitives and arbitrary shaped geometries. For performance reasons only one complex collision object is allowed to be active at the time. This single complex collision geometry is normally used for the static game world environment. The complex collision geometry is automatically generated from the files that describe the visual appearance of the game world. The graphics designer has however the opportunity to exclude some parts of the visual geometry from the resulting collidable geometry. He can also add geometry that only will be collidable and not visible.

The XML interface to the rendering system includes the following actor commands: *ResetAnimController, ClearAnimationTrack, GetPostition, GoTo, turnTo, play*(single animation, a sound or Animation list with parameters for start percentage and speed*), PickUp, releaseHeldObject, Jump*. There are also a number of object commands: *GetPostition, SetPosition, Highlight, Render, PutInPlace, TogglePhysicalState*. The camera commands include: *setActiveCamera, InterpolateToCamera, SetTargetEntity*. Finally there are a number of other commands: *GetOnScreenObjects, SetInputReceiver, ExecuteCommandLine* (commands to the renderers built in Python-based script interpreter), *GetCurrentLevelName, SetCurrentLevel*.

7   User Evaluations

During 2004–2005, data was collected on several occasions using the NICE system at different stages during its development. The system could be run either in fully automatic mode or in supervised mode, in which a human operator had the possibility to intervene and modify the ASR result or select an appropriate output speech act or action for a character to perform next. This made it possible to develop the system in a data-driven, iterative fashion. 57 children (aged 8 to 15) interacted with the system, resulting in a human–computer dialogue corpus containing about 5,800 system turns and 5,600 user turns. The usability study showed that the addition of spoken and multimodal dialogue creates a positive user experience, and that it is possible to use spoken language as the main device for story progression. In the interviews, users unanimously reported that Cloddy Hans was a bit stupid, but kind, while Karen being rather the opposite. Personality differences were also found in analyses of the post-experiment questionnaires, where the user judged the how well different personality traits described the characters. Differences between Cloddy Hans and Karen were tested for significance using Wilcoxon Signed Ranks Test ($p<0.05$). It was found that users rated Cloddy Hans as more *Kind, Stupid, Lazy, Calm, Polite* and *Distressed*, while Karin was found to be more *Smart, Quick* and *Self-confident*.

The analysis of the users' interaction showed that there were significant differences in speaking rate were observed between the User-Cloddy dialogues and the User-Karin(-Cloddy) dialogues. In the first repetitive scene the users took more and more initiative and needed fewer and fewer turns for each object they put into the machine, but at the same time they talked slower and slower, to make sure that the sluggish Cloddy Hans would understand them. In the second scene, they started of speaking faster, but then they slowly began to talk slower again with Cloddy Hans for each turn during their exploration of the island. As soon as they started talking to Karin, they talked faster, but this time the actually increasing their speech rate for each turn. This could be because the interaction was faster, and because it felt more lively when Cloddy Hans came with side-comments during the negotiation between the user and Karin. It was probably also because Karin appeared to be smarter when she drove the dialogue, without showing any problems in understanding the user. Actually, she did not always have to understand what the user said since she could "see" that Cloddy had brought a certain object that she then simply could reject regardless of how the user presented it.

To conclude, the user study showed that it was possible to design characters, which were perceived as having fundamentally different personalities and conversational abilities, and that in three-party dialogue with several animated figures each character was regarded as a separate entity who did not always hear or understand the others. This made it possible to decrease the shortcomings of the speech recognizer by letting the system tell the users (via Karen) what they should say to Cloddy Hans in the next turn. That this seemingly simple trick "worked" is indicated by the fact that users rated Cloddy Hans as stupid and Karen as smart even though the trick was used in both directions. Finally, several users explicitly perceived shortcomings of the natural language interface as part of the game, constituting a new kind of interesting and engaging obstacle to overcome. They thought it could be an interesting mind puzzle to figure out how to talk and what to say in order to get Cloddy Hans to do what the wanted.

Acknowledgements

This research was carried out within the EU 5th framework project NICE (IST-2001-35293). The NICE homepage can be found at http://www.niceproject.com.

References

1. Aberdeen, J., Bayer, S., Caskey, S., Daminos, L., Goldschen, A., Hirschman, L., Loehr, D. and Trappe, H. (1999) Implementing practical dialogue systems with the DARPA Communicator architecture. Proc. IJCAI'99 workshop on knowledge and reasoning in practical dialogue systems,pp 81-88.

2. Allbeck, J. and Badler, N. "Representing and Parameterizing Agent Behaviours" In Life-Like Characters: Tools, Affective Functions, and Applications, Prendinger, H. and Ishizuka, M, Eds. Springer, Germany, 2004.
3. Allwood, J. "Reasons for management in dialog", in Beun, R.J., Baker, M. and Reiner, M. (eds.) Dialogue and Instruction. Springer-Verlag.pp 241-50, 1995.
4. Aust, H., M. Oerder, F. Seide and V. Steinbiss (1995). The Philips automatic train timetable information system. Speech Communication 17(3-4): 249-262.
5. Boye, J., and Gustafson, J. (forthcoming) "How to do dialogue in a fairy-tale world", a demo session paper at the sixth SIGdial Workshop on Discourse and Dialogue, Lisabon, 2005.
6. Boye, J, Gustafson, J. & Wirén, M. (Forthcoming) "Robust spoken language understanding in a computer game",J. of Speech Communication,forthcoming special issue on spoken language understanding.
7. Brennan, S. "Processes that shape conversation and their implications for computational linguistics," Proceedings, 38th Annual Meeting of the ACL. Hong Kong, 2000.
8. Brennan, S. and Hulteen, E. "Interaction and feedback in a spoken language system: a theoretical framework," Knowledge-Based Systems(8): 143-151, 1995.
9. Byron, D. and Heeman, P. "Discourse Marker Use in Spoken Dialog", In Proceedings of the 5th Eurospean Conference On Speech Communication and Technology, Rhodes, Greece, September 1997.
10. Cavazza, M., Charles, F. and Mead S. J. (2002). Character-based interactive storytelling. IEEE Intelligent Systems, Special issue on AI in Interactive Entertainment,, pp. 17-24.
11. Cassell, J., Vilhjálmsson, H. & Bickmore, T. "BEAT: The Behavior Expression Animation Toolkit". Proceedings of SIGGRAPH '01, Los Angeles, CA, 2001, pp. 477–486, 2001
12. Cassell, J., T. Stocky, T. Bickmore, Y. Gao, Y. Nakano, K. Ryokai, D. Tversky, C. Vaucelle and H. Vilhjlmsson (2002). MACK: Media lab Autonomous Conversational Kiosk. Imagina 02. Monte Carlo.
13. Charles, F. and Cavazza, M. (2004) Exploring the scalability of character-based storytelling. Proc. ACM Joint conference on autonomous agents and multi-agent systems, New York, USA.
14. Chi, D., Costa, M., Zhao, L. and Badler, N. "The EMOTE Model for Effort and Shape," Proceedings of SIGGRAPH 2000, ACM Computer Graphics Annual Conference, New Orleans, Louisiana, 23-28 July, 2000, pp. 173-182.
15. Clark, H. "Managing problems in speaking", Speech Communication, 15:243-250, 1994.
16. Colburn, A., Cohen, M. & Drucker, S. (2000) "The Role of Eye Gaze in Avatar Mediated Conversational Interfaces". MSR-TR-2000-81. Microsoft Research, 2000.
17. Ekman, P. *Emotion in the human face*. New York: Cambridge University Press, 1982.
18. Ekman, P. "About brows: Emotional and conversational signals". In: Cranach, M. von, Foppa, K., Lepenies, W. & Ploog, D. (eds.), Human Ethology: Claims and Limits of a New Discipline: Contributions to the Colloquium, Cambridge, Cambridge University Press, pp. 169–202, 1979
19. Gamma E., Helm R., Design patterns: elements of reusable object-oriented software, Addison-Wesley Longman Publishing Co., Inc., Boston, MA, 1995.
20. Goodwin, C. "Conversational Organization: interaction between speakers and hearers," New York/London, Academic Press, 1981.
21. Grosz, B. and Sidner, C. "Attention, Intention, and the Structure of Discourse," Computational Linguistics 12(3), pp. 175–204, 1986.
22. Gustafson, J. and L. Bell (2000). Speech technology on trial - Experiences from the August system. Natural Language Engineering 6(3-4): 273-286.

23. Gustafson, J. and Sjölander, K., (2004). "Voice creation for conversational fairy-tale characters." In Proceedings of the 5th ISCA Speech Synthesis Workshop. Pittsburgh.

24. Hayes-Roth, B. "Character-based Interactive Story Systems," IEEE Intelligent Systems and Their Applications 13.6: pp 12-15, 1998.

25. Kahneman, D. *Attention and Effort.* Prentice–Hall, Englewood–Cliffs, New Jersey, 1973.

26. Lam D, "Tokamak Game Physics SDK", http://www.tokamakphysics.com/, 2004.

27. Martin, D. and Cheyer, A. and Moran, D. (1999) The Open Agent Architecture: a framework for building distributed software systems. Applied Artificial Intelligence, vol. 13, no. 1-2, pp. 91-128, January-March 1999.

28. Mateas, M. and A. Stern (2002). Architecture, authorial idioms and early observations of the interactive drama Facade. Technical report CM-CS-02-198.

29. McCrae, R. and Costa, P. "Toward a new generation of personality theories: Theoretical contexts for the five-factor model," In J. S. Wiggins (Ed.), The five-factor model of personality: Theoretical perspectives (pp. 51-87). New York: Guilford, 1996.

30. Pelachaud, C. & Prevost, S. "Sight and Sound: Generating Facial Expressions and Spoken Intonation from Context". Proceedings of the second ESCA Workshop on Speech Synthesis, New Paltz, NY, USA, September 1994, pp. 216–219, 1994.

31. Pelachaud, C., Badler, N. & Steedman, M. "Generating Facial Expressions for Speech". Cognitive Science 20(1), pp. 1–46, 1996.

32. Traum, D. (2004) Issues in multi-party dialogues. In Dignum (ed), Advances in agent communication, Lecture notes in artificial intelligence 2922, pp. 201-211, Springer-Verlag.

33. Varanese A. and LaMothe, A. (2003) Game scripting mastery. Premier Press.

34. Young, R. M. (2001). An overview of the Mimesis architecture: Integrating intelligent narrative control into an existing gaming environment. Working notes of the AAAI spring symposium on Artificial intelligence and interactive entertainment.

35. Zue, V., J. Glass, D. Goodline, H. Leung, M. Phillips, J. Polifroni and S. Seneff (1991). Integration of speech recognition and natural language processing in the MIT voyager system. Proc. ICASSP'91. Toronto.

An example dialogue in the second scene with actual dialogue excerpts from three children's interactions	
user	where are we?
cloddy	now we are in the fairy-tale world...what should we do?
user	please walk over and pick up the sword
cloddy	good idea *[cloddy walks over to the sword]*
user	walk over to the girl over there
cloddy	her name is Karin *[cloddy walks over to the bridge where Karen stands on the other side]*
user	could you please talk with Karin
cloddy	why don't you talk with her instead … she usually is a bit ill-tempered
user	okey *[the camera moves from Cloddy to Karin]*
karin	who are you?
user	Johanna .. and you
karin	my name is Karin...how are you?
user	fine how are you
karin	well so so ... I'm an orphean and I hardly have any friends
user	would you like to become my friend?
karin	yes!
user	could you please lower the drawbridge for us?
karin	if I am to lower the drawbridge i want something in return
cloddy	she is easily bribed *[from the side, without camera turning away from Karin]*
user	how about this sword?

karin	you can keep that old junk for yourself, that's nothing for me
cloddy	she's so grumpy *[from the side, without camera turning away from Karin]*
user	but what do you want then?
karin	I thought I saw something shining falling down at the same time as the schmuck
user	you can have a ruby .. I'll return with something nice for you
karin	why do you keep dragging along that Cloddy Hans figure, by the way
user	he refuse to leave
cloddy	mmm (with negative prosody) *[the camera turns to Cloddy]*
user	drop the sword *[cloddy drops the sword]*
user	could you please pick up the emerald
cloddy	ok I'll walk over to the jewels *[walks over to the emerald and picks it up]*
user	go back to Karin *[cloddy walks to Karin where the camera swings over to Karin]*
karin	what do you have for me?
user	an emerald
karin	now you're talking
user	could you lower the bridge now?
karin	okey *[Karin lowers the drawbridge]*
cloddy	Hurray
user	walk over the bridge *[Cloddy walks over the bridge]*
user	now give her the emerald, after all she did lower the bridge
cloddy	should we really give it to her - shouldn't we keep it?
user	give it to her even though she was rude to you
cloddy	but she is only a little runt
user	yeah..but she DID lower the bridge
karin	well if only you had asked nicely I would have let you over anyway
user	but you said that you needed the something nice for you to be able to lower the bridge!?!
karin	I don't care!
user	if you want the emerald then you'll have to apologize!

Fight, Flight, or Negotiate: Believable Strategies for Conversing Under Crisis

David Traum[1], William Swartout[1], Stacy Marsella[2], and Jonathan Gratch[1]

[1] Institute for Creative Technologies,
University of Southern California,
Marina del Rey, CA, USA
traum@ict.usc.edu
[2] Information Sciences Institute,
University of Southern California,
Marina del Rey, CA, USA

Abstract. This paper describes a model of conversation strategies implemented in virtual humans designed to help people learn negotiation skills. We motivate and discuss these strategies and their use to allow a virtual human to engage in complex adversarial negotiation with a human trainee. Choice of strategy depends on both the personality of the agent and assessment of the likelihood that the negotiation can be beneficial. Execution of strategies can be performed by choosing specific dialogue behaviors such as whether and how to respond to a proposal. Current assessment of the value of the topic, the utility of the strategy, and affiliation toward the other conversants can be used to dynamically change strategies throughout the course of a conversation. Examples will be given from the SASO-ST project, in which a trainee learns to negotiate by interacting with virtual humans who employ these strategies.

1 Introduction

How can we teach negotiating skills effectively? Effective negotiating skills are critical for many fields, such as commerce, diplomacy and the military. While general principles for effective negotiation can be taught in a classroom setting, becoming an effective negotiator requires practice, usually in a role-playing situation where a teacher or mentor plays the part of one of the opposing party in the negotiation. While this approach can be very effective, it is also expensive in terms of the human resources it requires. In this paper, we describe advances we have made in the technology of virtual humans with the aim of allowing them to act as role-players in a negotiation practice. While a negotiation can be viewed as a rational process of weighing costs and benefits, anyone who has haggled with a salesman over the purchase price of a new car knows that there are significant emotional and non-rational aspects. If virtual humans are to be effective role-players, they must incorporate these aspects as well.

Our work on virtual humans is part of the overall research agenda of creating embodied conversational agents (see collected papers in [1]) that can engage in

T. Panayiotopoulos et al. (Eds.): IVA 2005, LNCS 3661, pp. 52–64, 2005.
© Springer-Verlag Berlin Heidelberg 2005

spoken language interaction with humans, although our emphasis in this paper on modeling human-like negotiation behavior is unique. This emphasis also sets us apart from the efforts in the multi-agent community on negotiation where the emphasis is in modeling largely agent-agent negotiations as a means to achieve better or more profitable coordination and cooperation (e.g., [2]). The research we describe here extends virtual human models such as those deployed in the MRE project [3,4] by endowing the virtual humans with strategies for negotiation, endowing them with the ability to model the emotions that arise during a negotiation, and providing facilities for them to communicate verbally and non-verbally during a negotiation dialogue.

The next section describes the initial domain we have chosen to illustrate this research. Section 3 discusses an approach to adversarial communication based on analyses of negotiation in social sciences. Section 4 presents a first synthesis of this work in terms of strategies for virtual humans. Section 5 describes the extensions we have made to the virtual humans from the MRE project to incorporate these strategies and support adversarial negotiation. Section 6 concludes with a discussion of future work.

2 Domain Testbed: Stabilization and Support Operations

Whether it is Kosovo, East Timor, or Iraq, one lesson that has emerged from attempts at "peacemaking" is that negotiation skills are needed across all levels of civilian and government organizations involved. To be successful in these operations, a local military commander must be able to interact with the local populace to find out information, negotiate solutions, and resolve minor problems before they become major. To have a lasting positive effect, interactions

Fig. 1. SASO-ST VR clinic and virtual human doctor

between military and locals must be carried out in a way that generates goodwill and trust. We have selected this general class of operations as a testbed for our work on negotiation.

More specifically, we are developing a training scenario in which a local military commander (who has a rank of captain) must negotiate with a medical relief organization. A virtual human plays the role of a doctor running a clinic. A human trainee plays the role of the captain, and is supposed to negotiate with the doctor to get him to move the clinic, which could be damaged by a planned military operation. Ideally, the captain will convince the doctor without resorting to force or threats and without revealing information about the planned operation. Figure 1 shows the trainee's view of the doctor in his office inside the clinic. The success of the negotiation will depend on the trainee's ability to follow good negotiating techniques, when confronted with different types of behavior from the virtual doctor.

3   Adversarial Negotiation

One of the central ways to characterize negotiation under adversarial conditions is with respect to the tension between competition and cooperation. Negotiators may have different goals, perceive themselves in conflict over those goals but may also perceive the need to cooperate to some degree to achieve their goals. In this view, one can characterize the state of a negotiation process from the perspective of the competitive/cooperative orientation of the parties to the negotiation and the strategies they employ in light of those orientations. Specifically, one oft-made distinction is between integrative and distributive [5] situations. If a negotiation is a win-lose game where there is a fixed value to be distributed, then it is called distributive. There will be a winner and a loser. In contrast, an integrative situation is one where both sides can potentially win, a win-win situation where negotiation could add value and be of benefit to both sides. These basic distinctions presume some commitment to engage in negotiation. However, an individual may simply believe that there is no possible benefit or even need to negotiate. This individual may have an orientation to simply avoid the negotiation or deny the need for it, what is termed avoidance (e.g., [6]). We thus start with three basic orientations toward a negotiation: avoidance, distributive, and integrative. Whenever an agent seriously considers a negotiation situation it will choose one of these three orientations.

Negotiators may perceive a situation as one to be avoided, or as a distributive or integrative situation regardless of whether this reflects the true situation. Changing the perceptions of other agents is often one of the main tasks in a successful negotiation. Based on current perceptions, people tend to use a range of dialog tactics consistent with their orientations [7,6]. Avoidance tactics include shifting the focus of conversation and delays. Distributive tactics can include various defensive moves such as stating prior commitments that bind the negotiator or arguments that support the negotiator's position. Distributive tactics can also be more offensive, such as threats, criticisms, insults, etc. Integrative tactics are more cooperative with negotiators actually attempting to see issues from the other's perspective. Tactics can be arguments that support the other's position, acceptances of offers, offers of support, etc. Note at a finer grain of analysis, the tactics employed have both instrumental and affective components. For example, distributive tactics, besides trying to gain competitive advantage, tend to be associated with angry or intimidating behavior whereas the integrative tactics try to promote a positive affective climate [7].

Negotiators will often shift orientations during the course of a negotiation. Several factors have been identified as being critical to moving towards an integrative orientation, including acts of reciprocity, establishing trust, reinforcing shared goals, etc. (e.g., [8]).

4   Negotiation Strategies for Virtual Humans

One of our first steps toward implementing a virtual doctor character was to analyze how people act in that role. To this end, we have been conducting a series of role-play sessions, in which one person plays the role of the captain while another plays the role of doctor. Each is given a short set of instructions with different background information, goals, and resources for the negotiation, but given freedom as to how to conduct the negotiation and react to their partner. In these dialogues we can see examples of each of the orientations described in the previous section. For example in (1), the doctor displays an avoidance orientation, and is able to divert the topic of the conversation from the move to the military's role in upcoming operations for over 10 turns (only the first few are shown here). In (2), we see a doctor illustrating the distributive orientation, contesting the basic facts and goals rather than working together on common issues. In (3), we see an example of integrative orientation, the doctor having accepted the danger of the current location and willing to meet the captain's goals if his own are also addressed.

(1) C: it's a temporary move, once the battle is over, you will be moved back.
    D: Why don't you cancel your battle? Why don't you not kill these people.
    C: We're not the ones deciding the battle.
    D: You're the ones here. You're telling me this.

(2) C: We need to move as soon as possible. There are insurgents in the area. This is very unsafe, you're putting yourself and your patients in danger.
    D: Why? I don't want to move. I have all these patients here. They won't move, if I move who would who could save them?
    C: Sir, Everyone is in danger! If we stay here there's ...
    D: I'm not in danger

(3) C: insurgents will not hesitate to harm civilians if that's their path that they need to take. They won't hesitate to harm doctors, a doctor or even injured patients if they feel that's the the means to their end.
    D: well
    C: this is why you need to come to us.

D: I think we can make a deal. You can give me medical supply, and then we can go with you. I need supplies as soon as possible. As you can see, we are running out of supplies.

We have developed *strategies* for each of these orientations. Our virtual humans can use the strategies to adjust their behavior toward the orientations described above. A strategy consists of several aspects including: **entry conditions**, which indicate when adoption is appropriate; **exit conditions**, which indicate when the strategy should be dropped (often in favor of more appropriate strategies); **associated moves**, which can be performed as tactics to implement the strategy; and **influences** of the strategy on behavior and reasoning. These aspects result from the underlying emotion and dialogue models of the virtual humans.

The EMA (**EM**otion and **A**daptation) model of emotion [9] describes how coping strategies arise as cognitive and physical responses to important events, based on the appraisal [10] of perceptions related to goals and beliefs. Appraisal characterizes events in terms of variables that guide the selection of an appropriate response (e.g., is this desirable? can it be avoided?), but the event need not be physical. Negotiation strategies can thus be seen as types of coping strategies in which the event in question is the negotiation itself, and moves are the types of dialogue actions an agent will perform as part of a negotiation.

The avoidance orientation arises from an appraisal that the negotiation is undesirable but avoidable. The main motivation is to try to escape from the negotiation. When this appraisal is active, the agent chooses an **avoidance** strategy. Exit conditions will be the negation of either of the entry conditions — when the agent believes either that the negotiation has some utility or that it is not avoidable, the agent will abandon the avoidance strategy. The avoidance strategy involves attempts to change the topic of a conversation or get out of it entirely. When applying the avoidance strategy an agent will refrain from commenting on the object of negotiation, even to refute claims.

When in distributive mode, the agent will attempt to "win" rather than "lose" the negotiation. This can be associated with several strategies, depending on the type of decisions to be made and the range of possible alternatives. An *attack* strategy is appropriate when the appraisal is that a negotiation is not avoidable and the proposal is undesirable. Other strategies are also appropriate for a distributive orientation, including defense against a threat rather than attack, or making unreasonable demands in the hope the other party will drop the negotiation. We defer this for future work. One should drop an attack strategy when either the negotiation becomes desirable, or it becomes more profitable to avoid (or defend) than attack. The attack strategy involves pointing out the reasons why a proposal is flawed, or ad hominem attacks on the negotiator.

An integrative orientation leads to attempts to satisfy the goals of each of the participants. The **negotiate** strategy is appropriate when an agent thinks there is a possible value to the negotiation — e.g., there is a higher expected utility from the expected outcomes than would be the case without the negotiation. This strategy is dropped either when the perceived utility of continuing to negotiate drops below a threshold, or when the negotiation has been completed. Moves in the negotiation strategy involve problem solving and bargaining, much in the manner of the team negotiation in [4].

The success of a negotiation is also mediated by factors that influence the perceived trust between parties, including a belief in shared goals, credibility and interdependence. The doctor is unlikely to be swayed by an offer of aid if he does not believe the captain can and will fulfill his commitments. Trust issues are pervasive throughout the strategies, though building trust will be crucial in allowing the adoption of integrative strategies, since there can be little point in negotiating with someone you expect to lie, be ill-disposed toward you, or not keep their side of a bargain.

Implementing the strategies in a virtual human leads to much more realistic negotiation behavior, allowing our virtual human to engage in many of the types of behavior seen in the role play exercises. For example, the dialogue in Figure 2 shows a sample interaction with our virtual doctor. This is just one of many possible interactions, depending on the choices of the human captain, as well as several aspects (some probabilistic) influencing the choice of moves and strategy transitions of the virtual human doctor. We can see several distinct phases of this dialogue, relating to different negotiation strategies. The initial segment (turns 1-7) includes initial greetings and establishing the topic for the conversation - the captain wants to move the clinic. In turns 8-12, the doctor engages in the avoidance strategy, trying to avoid this topic by bringing up other issues, such as his need for supplies, and the general problems of conflict. In turns 14-20, the doctor has adopted the attack strategy, and points out problems with the proposed move. In turns 22-25, the doctor is in the negotiate strategy, and an actual bargain is struck. Finally, turns 26-30 show a closing phase in which the doctor disengages from the conversation, while the captain tries to establish good relations for future interaction. Application of these strategies influences not just the choice of dialogue move, but the whole body posture of the doctor and use of gestures and expressions as well. In the next section we give more details on how these strategies are implemented in virtual humans.

5   Virtual Human Negotiation Implementation

We take as our starting point the virtual humans implemented as part of the MRE project [3]. These virtual humans are embedded in a dynamic virtual world, in which events can happen, agents can perform actions, and humans and virtual humans can speak to each other and communicate using verbal and non-verbal means. The virtual humans include sophisticated models of emotion reasoning [9], dialogue reasoning [11] and a model of team negotiation [4]. Agents use a rich model of dialogue closely linked with a task model and emotional appraisals and coping strategies for both interpretation of utterances as well as for decisions about when the agent should speak and what to say.

To negotiate and collaborate with humans and artificial agents, virtual humans must understand not only the task under discussion but also the under-

1   C Hello Doctor Perez.
2   D Hello.
3.1   C I am Captain Kirk.
3.2   C Very nice to meet you! [+FAMILIARITY]
4   D What do you want?
5   C I have orders to assist you in moving this clinic to a safer location.
6   D You want to move the clinic?
7   C Yes [-SOLIDARITY]

Strategy shift: Avoid negotiating about move

8.1   D This conflict is madness, it is killing people!
8.2   D We need proper supplies here!
9   C It is not safe here we can't protect you. [-CREDIBILITY]
10.1 D Protect me? Protect me from what?
10.2 D Are you going to attack?
11   C I can not disclose more information but it will be a problem to stay here.
12   D You are the problem your bombs are killing these people!
13   C Sir, we are trying to help these people too. [-CONTROL +SOLIDARITY]

Strategy shift: Disrupt negotiation about move

14.1 D The patients are here,
14.2 D to move the clinic is not possible we have many patients in critical condition.
15   C We can move you to a safer location.
16   D I can't move all these patients.
17   C We can organize transportation and assist you with moving. [+SOLIDARITY]
18   D I can't move all these patients.
19   C We can have locals move you. [+SOLIDARITY]
20   D There are no supplies there.
21   C We can provide you with supplies to help your patients. [+SOLIDARITY]

Strategy shift: Willingly negotiate about move

22.1 D I think I understand what you say.
22.2 D Well perhaps we can reach an agreement,
22.3 D but before we can think about moving, we need you to bring antibiotics and
         plasma to stabilize the patients. [+INTERDEPENDENCE]
23   C We can do that! [+SOLIDARITY]
24.1 D Well,...
24.2 D Very well Captain contact my assistant to make further arrangements.
25   C I'll see to it personally. [+SOLIDARITY]
26.1 D I understand your position.
26.2 D My patients need my attention now.
27   C Thank you Doctor!
28.1 D Well,....
28.2 D I must go now
29   C Goodbye.
30   D Good bye.

Fig. 2. Example negotiation dialogue between C, a captain (human trainee) and D, a doctor (virtual Human), showing strategy shifts and positive and negative effects on trust

lying motivations, beliefs and even emotions of other agents. The virtual human models build on the causal representations developed for decision-theoretic planning and augment them with methods that explicitly model commitments to beliefs and intentions. Plan representations provide a concise representation of the causal relationship between events and states, key for assessing the relevance of events to an agent's goals and for assessing causal attributions. Plan representations also lie at the heart of many reasoning techniques (e.g., planning, explanation, natural language processing) and facilitate their integration. The decision-theoretic concepts of utility and probability are key for modeling non-determinism and for assessing the value of alternative negotiation choices. Explicit representations of intentions and beliefs are critical for negotiation and for assessing blame when negotiations fail [12].

These virtual humans thus provided a good starting point for implementation of the negotiation strategies described in the previous section. In the rest of this section we describe the enhancements to these virtual humans which were necessary to allow adversarial negotiations such as that shown in Figure 2. First, we talk about aspects of the task and emotion model, including meta-actions for negotiation itself, which allows explicit calculation of the costs and benefits of negotiating, and serves to inform the decisions for entering and exiting strategies. Next, we talk about the trust model, which is both dynamic through the course of a dialogue and influences cognitive and expressive behavior. Then we examine extensions to the dialogue model to use strategies in choice of move and body posture. Finally we briefly describe a tool to look inside the mind of the virtual human and see the effects of specific utterances.

5.1 Appraising the Negotiation

The EMA model of emotion incorporates general procedures that recast the notion of emotional appraisal into an analysis of the causal relationship between actions and goals in an agent's working memory. For example, if an action of the Captain threatens one of the doctor's goals, this is undesirable and deserving of blame, resulting in a response of anger. Depending on if the Doctor can take actions to confront the threat, he may feel in control and engage in problem-focused coping, or resign himself to the threat.

Our view of negotiation orientation as a form of appraisal and coping can be represented within this existing model by simply encoding the negotiation process as just another plan (albeit a meta-plan [13]) within the task representation described above. The potential outcomes of this plan are appraised alongside the rest of the task network by the existing appraisal mechanisms, and coping strategies applied to this task are mapped into different dialogue moves. Thus, the negotiation about moving the clinic is represented as a single "negotiate(move-clinic)" action that is automatically added to the task model in response to the user opening a negotiation. This action has two meta-effects, "cost" and "benefit" which represent the potential costs and benefits of moving the clinic to another location.

Two extensions are needed to derive the utility of these meta-effects and their likelihood of attainment. One extension to the model is that the utilities of these meta-effects are dynamically computed based on the current task and dialogue state. In particular, the costs and benefits are derived by appraising the individual sub-actions of the "move-clinic" plan. Any desirable effects with high intensity are viewed as benefits and any undesirable effects with high intensity are costs. Currently, these are simply added to compute an overall cost and benefit. The perceived cost and benefit may change through the course of the negotiation. For example, the doctor may believe there are no supplies in the new location (a necessary precondition of the important goal of treating victims), but the trainee may offer to provide supplies, and if believed, this commitment would negate this threat to the move-clinic plan. A second extension is to base the likelihood that the negotiation will succeed on properties of the dialogue state. Currently, we adopt a simple heuristic. If the trainee persists in discussing the negotiation, its likelihood of success increases, though the costs and benefits of that success will depend on what concessions. the trainee has made.

Appraisal and coping operate directly on this meta-action. If the costs exceed the benefits (appraised as undesirable) but the negotiation is unlikely to succeed (leading to an appraisal of high changeability), the doctor will respond with mild fear and copes through avoidance. If the trainee persists in discussing the move (leading to an appraisal of low changeability), without addressing the underlying costs and benefits, the doctor will respond with anger and cope by working against the negotiation (corresponding to the distributive orientation). If the trainee makes concessions that raise the perceived benefits of the move, the doctor will respond with hope and work towards the negotiation (corresponding to the integrative orientation).

5.2   Modeling Trust

According to the dialogue model in [14], the direct effect of an assertion is the introduction of a commitment, whether or not either party believes in the assertion. While this is sufficient for reasoning about the claims and responsibility for information, we need to go further and potentially change beliefs and intentions based on communicated information. Trust is used to decide whether to adopt a new belief based on the commitments of another.

Similar to [15] and [16] , trust is modeled as function of underling variables that are easily derived from our task and dialogue representations. *Solidarity* is a measure of the extent to which parties have shared goals. Solidarity is positively updated when the trainee makes assertions or demands that are congruent with the agent's goals. *Credibility* is a measure of the extent to which a party makes believable claims. It is positively updated when the trainee makes assertions that are consistent with the agent's beliefs. Finally, *familiarity* is a measure of the extent to which a party obeys norms of politeness. Currently, an overall measure of trust is derived as a linear combination of these three factors.

5.3   Acting on Negotiation Strategies

We extended the dialogue model of [3,4] to take explicit account of strategies and their influence on dialogue behavior. This model already allowed both reactive responses (e.g., to answer a question, to ground an utterance, to respond to a proposal) or speaker initiatives (e.g., to suggest a necessary or desired action, to bring the dialogue back on track, according to an agenda of "to be discussed" items). This model did not address non-team negotiation; the integrative approach was assumed and there was no possibility of avoiding a negotiation or trying for an outcome other than what was good for the whole team. We have extended the model to include explicit strategies, as described above, which govern how agenda items will be discussed. Strategies govern choice of topic and dialogue acts, base body posture, and verbal and non-verbal (e.g. words and gestures) realizations of acts.

The avoidance strategy is implemented by reversing the usual topical coherence guidelines of sticking with one topic until it is resolved before bringing up a new agenda item. When avoiding a topic, rather than direct grounding or negotiation, agenda items which are not central to the topic itself are raised. The doctor's nonverbal behavior also changes, including a posture shift to a crossed arm stance, as shown in Figure 1.

The attack strategy does focus on the topic itself, but only on the reasons why it might be bad. Each of these (potential) reasons, as calculated by the task model, are added to the agenda, prioritized by the importance of the objection. When the speaker no longer thinks they are objections, they will be removed from the agenda. There is also a preference to bring up new objections rather than repeat old ones (subject to the relative importance). If the attack strategy is used when there are no objections in the task model, the speaker will instead question the motivations for the action. When applying the attack strategy, the doctor assumes an aggressive stance, with arms on hips at rest position.

The negotiate strategy follows the model from [4], with the focus of negotiation to make sure that subactions of a plan to achieve a shared goal are committed to by the relevant agents, and maximizing utility for the speaker, perhaps through bargaining. When following the negotiate strategy, the doctor's posture is more open, with arms casually to the side, when at rest.

Some of the same topics may be brought up in both the attack and negotiate strategies, for example, the deficiencies of a plan. Generally there will be a difference in focus, however — in the attack strategy the focus is on why this is a reason not to act, while in the negotiate strategy, the focus is on the concern as a mutual problem to be addressed and solved.

5.4   Explaining Agent Negotiating Behavior

For really learning about negotiation it is very helpful to know not just what the other party did, but why. In real negotiations it is usually not possible to get "inside the head" of the negotiating partner, and even subsequent questions can sometimes damage the nature of the interaction itself. In this respect, virtual

9   C it is not safe here we cant protect you
DECREASES CREDIBILITY: captain asserted unbelieved state 'patients-unsafe-here'
10.1 D protect me protect me from what
'patients-unsafe-here' could be established by captain's act of 'planned-attack'
10.2 D are you going to attack
11   C i can not disclose more information but it will be a problem to stay here
12   D you are the problem your bombs are killing these people
13   C sir we are trying to help these people too
DECREASES CONTROL:captain persists in negotiating 'run-clinic-there'
INCREASES SOLIDARITY: captain committed to achieve desired state 'help-victims'
Strategy shift: Disrupt negotiation about run-clinic-there
(outcome seems negative but negotiation seems unavoidable)

Fig. 3. example trace from AAR tool

humans present a real opportunity to improve on training. We have implemented
a trace facility that provides an annotated transcript of the dialogue, showing not
just what the virtual human thought was said, but how it influenced his trust,
beliefs, and strategy choice. This tool can be used in an "after action review"
(AAR) to look in detail at the specific effects the trainee's negotiation tactics
had. Figure 2 shows a very abbreviated version of this (for both space and clarity
reasons). In Figure 3 we show the full trace for a small section of the dialogue.
Here we can see the reason for decreases in credibility and control and increases
in solidarity at these points as effects of the commitments the captain makes in
relation to desires and beliefs of the doctor. Initially the doctor does not believe
the assertion made in 9. However, he realizes that if the captain attacks, that
would establish the unsafe condition, leading to the provocative question. Later
on, we see that the captain's persistence in talking about moving leads to the
abandonment of the avoidance strategy.

6   Current Directions and Future Work

Our current implementation allows a human to interact with the virtual doctor using speech and have many different negotiations of the sort illustrated in
Figure 2. The success or failure of the negotiation depends on the use of good
negotiating tactics. We are expanding the coverage in several directions to be
able to handle fully spontaneous dialogue such as those from which (1),(2), and
(3) were taken from. We also plan to evaluate the performance of the doctor
virtual agent, in a manner similar to the evaluation done for the MRE system
[17].

Negotiation is a complex human interaction. Although we have made significant progress in modeling negotiation, much work remains and there are several
directions we plan to take our research next in order to extend our models. The
social science literature has identified a wide range of dialog moves/tactics that
negotiators use and we are interested in extending our work to incorporate these

moves. We also want to extend the reasoning capabilities to handle other issues in constructing arguments and conflict resolution, e.g. [18]. Another key interest for us is the role that cultural factors play in negotiation, specifically, the role that culture plays in the concerns of the negotiators, their tactics and nonverbal behavior.

Acknowledgments

We would like to thank other members of the SASO-ST project. The project described here has been sponsored by the U.S. Army Research, Development, and Engineering Command (RDECOM). Statements and opinions expressed do not necessarily reflect the position or the policy of the United States Government, and no official endorsement should be inferred.

References

1. Cassell, J., Sullivan, J., Prevost, S., Churchill, E., eds.: Embodied Conversational Agents. MIT Press, Cambridge, MA (2000)
2. Rosenschein, J.S., Zlotkin, G.: Rules of Encounter: Designing Conventions for Automated Negotiation among Computers. MIT Press (1994)
3. Rickel, J., Marsella, S., Gratch, J., Hill, R., Traum, D., Swartout, W.: Toward a new generation of virtual humans for interactive experiences. IEEE Intelligent Systems **17** (2002)
4. Traum, D., Rickel, J., Marsella, S., Gratch, J.: Negotiation over tasks in hybrid human-agent teams for simulation-based training. In: In proceedings of AAMAS 2003: Second International Joint Conference on Autonomous Agents and Multi-Agent Systems. (2003) 441–448
5. Walton, R.E., Mckersie, R.B.: A behavioral theory of labor negotiations: An analysis of a social interaction system. McGraw-Hill (1965)
6. Sillars, A.L., Coletti, S.F., Parry, D., Rogers, M.A.: Coding verbal conflict tactics: Nonverbal and perceptual correlates of the avoidance-distributive- integrative distinction. Human Communication Research **9** (1982) 83–95
7. Putnam, L.L., Jones, T.S.: Reciprocity in negotiations: An analysis of bargaining interaction. Communications Monograph (1982)
8. Wilson, S.R., Putnam, L.L.: Interaction goals in negotiation. Communication Yearbook **13** (1990) 374–406
9. Gratch, J., Marsella, S.: A domain-independent framework for modeling emotion. Journal of Cognitive Systems Research (2004)
10. Scherer, K.R., Schorr, A., Jonstone, T., eds.: Appraisal Processes in Emotion. Oxford University Press (2001) Series in Affective Science.
11. Traum, D.R., Rickel, J.: Embodied agents for multi-party dialogue in immersive virtual worlds. In: Proceedings of the first International Joint conference on Autonomous Agents and Multiagent systems. (2002) 766–773
12. Mao, W., Gratch, J.: Social judgment in multiagent interactions. In: In proceedings of AAMAS 2004: Third International Joint Conference on Autonomous Agents and Multi-Agent Systems. (2004) 210–217
13. Litman, D.J., Allen, J.F.: A plan recognition model for subdialogues in conversation. Cognitive Science **11** (1987) 163–200

14. Matheson, C., Poesio, M., Traum, D.: Modelling grounding and discourse obligations using update rules. In: Proceedings of the First Conference of the North American Chapter of the Association for Computational Linguistics. (2000)
15. Marsella, S., Pynadath, D., Read, S.: Psychsim: Agent-based modeling of social interactions and influence. In: In proceedings of International Conference on Cognitive Modeling. (2004) 243–248
16. Cassell, J., Bickmore, T.: A relational agent: A model and implementation of building user trust. In: Proceedings of ACM CHI conference, New York, ACM Press (2001) 396–403
17. Traum, D.R., Robinson, S., Stephan, J.: Evaluation of multi-party virtual reality dialogue interaction. In: Proceedings of Fourth International Conference on Language Resources and Evaluation (LREC 2004). (2004) 1699–1702
18. de Rosis, F., Grasso, F., Castelfranchi, C., Poggi, I.: Modelling conflict resolution dialogues. In Müller, H., Dieng, R., eds.: Computational Conflicts - Conflict Modeling for Distributed Intelligent Systems. Springer (2000)

Dialog Simulation for Background Characters

Dušan Jan and David R. Traum

USC Institute for Creative Technologies, 13274 Fiji Way, Marina del Rey, CA 90292

Abstract. Background characters in virtual environments do not require the same amount of processing that is usually required by main characters, however we still want simulation that is more believable than random behavior. We describe an algorithm that generates behavior for background characters involved in conversation that supports dynamic changes to conversation group structure. We present an evaluation of this algorithm and make suggestions on how to further improve believability of the simulation.

1   Introduction

When we are dealing with virtual environments with a large number of virtual characters we encounter the problem when it is no longer feasible to simulate each character as a fully animated conversational agent. It is acceptable and desirable to provide main characters with speech recognition, speech synthesis, high-fidelity gestures and lipsynch, analysis of input and an AI agent capable of making informed decisions. On the other hand we would have to spend too many resources to support this for many characters.

While we can ignore characters that are too far away from action, we need at least some form of scripting to control the behavior of background characters in view, to maintain the illusion [6]. Such scripting in form of hand animating all motions is labor intensive and, if the simulation goes on for longer than the amount of hand-animated material, usually provides repetitive behavior which detracts from realism. One solution to this problem is use of simulation algorithms to generate dynamic behavior for background characters. In our case [2] we were mainly interested in behavior of agents involved in conversation. While [8] bases its multimodal conversation model on information structure, a model based on visual perception of the scene rather than on speech is more appropriate for our domain. Therefore we decided to use the algorithm [1] proposed by Padilha and Carletta as a starting point for our simulation.

We have extended the work in [2], adapting to characters in the unreal tournament game engine, and allowing more dynamic starting, ending, and joining of conversation flow. One of the limitations of the simulation algorithms in [1] and [2] was the fact that it only supported one dialog going on at a time, meaning that all characters participated in the same conversation. While we could run multiple conversation simulations and explicitly assign different characters to different conversations, this is still not realistic for many situations in which characters move around and join or leave conversations. Likewise, even when

T. Panayiotopoulos et al. (Eds.): IVA 2005, LNCS 3661, pp. 65–74, 2005.
© Springer-Verlag Berlin Heidelberg 2005

people stay in the same position (e.g., at a meal or meeting), there are often dynamic splits and realignments into sub-conversations. Adapting a simulation that can handle dynamic creation and entry to conversations will allow more realism as well as scaling to situations with larger numbers of characters than would be supported by a single conversation.

2   Background

Since the conversation simulation is meant for background characters, who are too far away from the main action to hear the content, we focus on the appearance of conversation and the patterns of interaction, rather than actual information exchange or communication of internal state. To achieve realistic behavior we use behavior observed in real human conversations, as synthesized in [1]. Participants in conversation take turns at talk. During the turn they monitor others to see if the others follow the conversations and to react to feedback given by other participants. When the speaker is speaking there are natural points where others can begin their turn. These are called transition relevance points (TRPs). If the speaker addresses a particular participant with a question then that person will usually take a turn at the TRP. On the other hand if the speaker leaves a free TRP anyone can select to speak or the speaker may choose to continue to talk.

At a free TRP we can have more than one participant deciding to start to talk. In such cases we may have overlapped speech and there are various factors that influence who keeps speaking. Another case that involves simultaneous speech are interruptions. These can have several outcomes. The interrupter may stop after a false start, the original speaker may be cut off or the original speaker could decide to ignore the interrupter if he perceives the interruption as side talk and is not bothered by it.

Most transitions however will happen at TRPs with only a small gap or no gap at all. This is possible since the participants can anticipate the time TRP will occur based on speech characteristics and also other non-verbal behavior. Since we do not generate actual content of conversation speakers have to provide explicit pre-TRP cues to give participants the level of information required to behave realistically such as changing postures and similar non-verbal behavior that indicates the intention of taking the turn at the next TRP.

3   Aspects of Conversational Simulation

In our test scenario we connected our algorithm to virtual characters within the Unreal Tournament game engine. These characters had a small set of animations available to indicate different modalities of conversations we were simulating. These animations could be triggered by calling Unreal Tournament commands from an external character controller. Besides the outputs that trigger animations we also have messages between characters (such as TRP signals, selection

speech
- begin speaking
- end speaking
- pre-TRP signal
- TRP signal
- selection of addressee
- positive or negative feedback

non-verbal
- nodding
- gestures
- posture shifts
- gaze

Fig. 1. Conversation Agent Message types

of addressee) that do not result in any direct visible outcome in the simulation. Message types are shown in Figure 1.

The implementation in [2] used a blackboard where all participants of the conversation would exchange their messages and also had a fixed conversation cycle synchronized between all participants. We found this setting limiting in making the algorithm suitable for large number of agents with several ongoing conversations so we implemented a distributed solution in which each character implements its own decisions independently from other characters. To facilitate this we have each character controller running in a separate thread, communicating with other characters using messages. When a character receives a new message it can react to it immediately or just update its internal state and make a decision during normally scheduled processing.

In the algorithms in [1] and [2] every character was in conversation all the time. Our extensions, however, allow situations when a character is not involved in a conversation at all. From this arises the need to have some higher order planning involved which decides when the character should join an existing conversation, when it should start a new conversation and also when to leave conversation because of the reasons external to the dialog simulation itself. In a real virtual environment simulation this would also include planning for walking around and performing other activities, but in this simple scenario we started with conversation activities only.

Behavior of characters is controlled by a set of properties in a probabilistic manner as in the previous algorithms. Each of these properties has a value from 0 to 1. Whenever one of these properties is tested, a random number is selected and compared to the property value (possibly scaled based on contingent factors of the conversation). The properties currently used are shown in Figure 2.

Each character also keeps track of information about other characters. Each character tracks the gaze of each other, and whether they are speaking, and how long since that character has interacted in the conversation group of the tracker. Characters also track the composition of their conversation group — conversation groups are not defined externally but interpreted on the basis of perceived actions. Characters can also mis-interpret the actions of others, and

talkativeness likelihood of wanting to talk

transparency likelihood of producing explicit positive and negative feedback, and turn-claiming signals

confidence likelihood of interrupting and continuing to speak during simultaneous talk

interactivity the mean length of turn segments between TRPs

verbosity likelihood of continuing the turn after a TRP at which no one is self selected

Fig. 2. Conversational Agent Properties

can have different ideas about the composition of a conversation group. In future work, we will use more realistic approaches to perception (e.g., [7]), so that agents will only observe gaze and speech within their focus of attention.

4   Conversational Participation Algorithm

Each character runs a separate instance of the algorithm in its own thread, with its own setting for the attributes, and its own internal representation of the behaviors of others and group composition. The algorithm mainly consists of a series of event handlers. We briefly describe the major events and behaviors.

4.1   High-Level Planning

This part of the code is external to the main conversation algorithm. It represents the high order planning of the character and in our case makes characters join or leave conversation.

```
every planning cycle (approx. every 5 sec)
    if in conversation
        test to leave conversation
    else if talkativeness test successful
        decide to join existing conversation
        or start a new conversation
```

4.2   Claiming a Turn

Characters decide (using the talkativeness parameter) whether or not to take a turn when they receive pre-TRP signal. If they decide they will speak, they will also decide (using the transparency parameter) whether to signal their intention to speak with turn claiming signals if appropriate.

```
when receiving pre-TRP signal
    test talkativeness to decide to speak
    if so, test transparency to make turn claiming signal
```

4.3   Starting to Speak

Whenever the character starts to speak it determines the timing of its turn, including when to send a pre-TRP signal.

```
when starting to speak
    if at TRP and someone already started speaking
        test confidence to continue speaking
    select segment length based on interactivity
```

4.4   Continuing Speaking

Sometimes when one finishes a segment, no one else takes over. In this case the agent has the option to continue his own speech beyond what was initially planned.

```
when you end segment and no one takes turn
    test verbosity to continue speaking
```

4.5   Tracking Others Participation

Whenever an agent speaks or gives feedback to someone in a conversation group, they will be an active participant as well. This section maintains the conversational group and activity of its members.

```
when receiving input from other characters
    if they are signalling to someone in my group
        then add them to group (if not already there)
    if they are in my group and addressing someone in my group
        update last time they were active
```

4.6   Responding to Others

This section calculates how an agent should respond to the initiation of speech by another. Reaction will depend on whether the agent is also speaking and who started first, whether the agent is part of the same conversation as the speaker, and parameters of confidence (whether to continue speaking or not), talkativeness (whether to join a conversation), and transparency (whether to show feedback behavior). Decisions about leaving one conversation for another are also made if a character is addressed by someone who is not in the same conversation.

```
when someone starts to speak
    if in conversation with me
        if at TRP and I already started speaking
            test confidence to continue speaking
        if not speaking
            test transparency to gaze at speaker
    if I am not in conversation and they are speaking to me
        test talkativeness to join conversation
        test transparency to give signals of joining
```

4.7   Main Loop

Below is the main loop that agents go through, as modified by the above events.

```
every conversation cycle (approx. every 0.5 sec)
    remove characters that were inactive for too long
    if no one is speaking
        test talkativeness to start to speak
        if so, start with random interval
            select addressee
            test transparency to shift posture
        if no one was speaking for some time
            if talkativeness test fails leave conversation
    if listening to someone
        if there is more than one speaker for some time
            group was split into two or more conversations
                keep speaker that I am listening to
                remove participants that are  attending to others
        test talkativeness and confidence to interrupt
    if speaking simultaneously
        if there is only one additional speaker
            and their addressee attends to them
                then treat this as a side talk
                    remove both from conversation
        otherwise test confidence to continue speaking
    if speaking alone in a turn
        decide when to gesture and gaze away
        if no one is paying attention to me
            if confidence test fails stop speaking
```

5   Evaluation

There are many possible ways to evaluate the simulation. One can try to fit the model to observed conversations, as suggested by [1]. One could also test the differences in simulation that would result from different sets of characters with different sets of parameter values, e.g., whether it leads to domination of the conversation by a single character or small set of characters. As suggested in [2], we decided to test if the simulation "looks like a conversation" to the viewer.

In our test scenario we used for our characters 6 Iraqi civilians that initially are not involved in conversation. We recorded several simulations with different character attributes and stored videos and internal logs of each agent to later analyze and compare their internal states with responses from the viewers. A snapshot from a conversation simulation is shown in Figure 3. We balanced selection of attributes with the physical bodies to control for surface characteristics of the bodies and the effect of positioning. We also made one simulation where characters decided randomly when to start speaking and who to gaze to in order to have a baseline for comparison with our algorithm.

Fig. 3. Iraqi civilians engaged in conversation

We created 3 different tests for the viewers. In the first part they were asked to view several 30 second clips of simulations and decide how believable they think each simulation was on a 7-point Likert scale. We also asked them to provide any information about what factors they thought made the conversation less believable. In the instructions we also made clear to viewers that when judging believability of the simulation they were to pay most attention the appropriateness of behavior, particularly gaze and dialogue rather than animation quality of the characters.

In the second part we asked viewers to view multiple 2 minute clips of simulations. We instructed them to pay attention to only one of the characters (different characters for different clips) and analyze their behavior. Since the attributes used in the algorithm are not all very visible in such a short dialog we decided to ask viewers about the perceived properties of the characters rather than about underlying attributes. We asked viewers to judge the following properties on scale from 1 to 7:

talkative how often is he talking:
  1 – almost never talks
  4 – talks about as much as everyone else
  7 – talks almost all the time

predictive does he give any signals before speaking:
  1 – never gives any hints that he is about to speak
  7 – always indicates that he wants to speak
transparent is he giving any signals that he is attending to the speaker:
  1 – seems oblivious to others
  7 – always signals understanding of others
interruptive is he interrupting when others are speaking:
  1 – always waits for others to finish
  7 – jumps into conversation all the time
confident is he likely to keep talking if others speak at the same time:
  1 – gives up his turn if someone else starts to speak,
  7 – never shuts up when others speak

How talkative a character is is influenced by talkativeness attribute, predictive and transparent are both influenced by transparency. Confident characters have high confidence attribute and interruptiveness is determined by combination of both talkativeness and confidence. We have not asked about verbosity or interactivity because that would require observation of longer segments to get significant results.

In the last part we asked viewers to track who they think is speaking with whom, again for clips of 2 minutes in length. We used this data to compare how the internal state of each character correlates to what is perceived by the viewer.

6   Results and Future Work

Eight people of various ages and cultural background anonymously participated in our web-based evaluation. The average believability score for our algorithm was 5.3 compared to score of 3.3 for random behavior. The difference is statistically significant which indicates that most viewers were able to identify the random behavior. We found that the highest scores were received by simulations where either all characters participate in the same conversation or where the conversation groups correspond to positioning of the characters in the setting. Since our algorithm does not take positioning of characters into effect when deciding about creating new conversations and allowing conversations to split it is not able to prevent this kind of undesirable behavior from happening. We propose to make modifications to the algorithm that will take positioning into account and will also control character movement to achieve positioning where characters in the same conversation group separate themselves from other characters. We plan to achieve this by tracking noise level for each character. Each speaking character that is speaking, but not in the conversation group of this character, would contribute to the noise level based on their distance. If the noise level would get too high characters would either decide to break their conversations or move away from characters that bother them in their conversation.

Part 2 proved to be a lot more difficult than we expected. Not only were there differences between the values predicted by underlying attributes and results from viewers, but also the values varied widely between viewers. This would suggest that it is hard for humans to judge what the personality of a virtual character is, probably because of the lack of expressiveness when we compare virtual characters to real humans. We guess that it would be hard to grasp the personality of a background character anyway. However, we still think that having parameterized algorithm has its benefits since the structure of dialog changes with different attribute settings. Since it is hard to evaluate personality of a single character we propose to evaluate how different personality compositions influence believability of simulation.

Results from part 3 showed that what viewers perceived roughly agreed with the internal state of the characters. When a certain group composition was held for a longer time most of the characters and viewers agreed with what the current group composition was. Most of them correctly differentiated between normal transitions, interruptions and side conversations. However when the side conversations do not last long the results vary between characters and also between viewers.

We have not yet tested the algorithm with large numbers of virtual characters, but as Ulicny reports in [9] the limiting part in large scale crowd simulations is usually in rendering and not in the behavior generation. From our work so far we can see that it is beneficial to dynamically create behavior for background characters as it both removes labor intensive work of creating scripts and also improves believability of the simulations. However, we have seen from the evaluation results that we have a lot of room for improvements, especially in incorporating character movement in the simulations.

Acknowledgements

We would like to thank Patrick Kenny, Richard Almodovar, and Kurosh Valenejad for help with unreal tournament animations. We would also like to thank the anonymous reviewers for helpful comments on this paper. The project described here has been sponsored by the U.S. Army Research, Development, and Engineering Command (RDECOM). Statements and opinions expressed do not necessarily reflect the position or the policy of the United States Government, and no official endorsement should be inferred.

References

1. Padilha, E., Carletta, J.: A simulation of small group discussion. Proceedings of EDILOG 2002: Sixth Workshop on the Semantics and Pragmatics of Dialogue. (2002) 117–124
2. Patel, J., Parker, R., Traum, D.R.: Simulation of Small Group Discussions for Middle Level of Detail Crowds. Army Science Conference (Orlando, November 2004)
3. Padilha, E., Carletta, J.: Nonverbal behaviours improving a simulation of small group discussion. Proc. 1st Nordic Symp. on Multimodal Comm. (2003) 93–105
4. O'Sullivan, C., Cassell, J., Vilhjalmsson, H., Dingliana, J., Dobbyn, S., McNamee, B., Peters, C., Giang, T.: Levels of detail for crowds and groups. Computer Graphics Forum. 21(4) 2002

5. Rickel, J., Marsella, S., Gratch, J., Hill, R., Traum, D., Swartout, W.: Toward a new generation of virtual humans for interactive experiences. IEEE Intelligent Systems. **17** (2002)
6. Swartout, W., Hill, R., Gratch, J., Johnson, W.L., Kyriakakis, C., Labore, K., Lindheim, R., Marsella, S., Miraglia, D., Moore, B., Morie, J., Rickel, J., Thiebaux, M., Tuch, L., Whitney, R., Douglas, J.: Toward the holodeck: Integrating graphics, sound, character and story. Proceedings of 5th International Conference on Autonomous Agents. (2001)
7. Hill, R. Perceptual Attention in Virtual Humans: Toward Realistic and Believable Gaze Behaviors. In Proceedings of the AAAI Fall Symposium on Simulating Human Agents, pp.46-52, AAAI Press, Menlo Park, Calif., 2000.
8. Cassell, J., Torres, O., Prevost, S.: Turn taking vs. Discourse Structure: How Best to Model Multimodal Conversation
9. Ulicny, B., Thalmann, D.: Crowd simulation for interactive virtual environments and VR training systems

INTERFACE Toolkit: A New Tool for Building IVAs

Piero Cosi, Carlo Drioli, Fabio Tesser, and Graziano Tisato

Istituto di Scienze e Tecnologie della Cognizione,
Sezione di Padova "Fonetica e Dialettologia",
Consiglio Nazionale delle Ricerche,
Via G Anginoni, 10 - 35121 Padova, Italy
{cosi, drioli, tesser, tisato}@pd.istc.cnr.it
http://www.pd.istc.cnr.it

Abstract. INTERFACE is an integrated software implemented in Matlab© and created to speed-up the procedure for building an emotive/expressive talking head. Various processing tools, working on dynamic articulatory data physically extracted by an optotracking 3D movement analyzer called ELITE, were implemented to build the animation engine and also to create the correct WAV and FAP files needed for the animation. By the use of INTERFACE, LUCIA, our animated MPEG-4 talking face, can copy a real human by reproducing the movements of passive markers positioned on his face and recorded by an opto-electronic device, or can be directly driven by an emotional XML tagged input text, thus realizing a true audio/visual emotive/expressive synthesis. LUCIA's voice is based on an Italian version of FESTIVAL - MBROLA packages, modified for expressive/emotive synthesis by means of an appropriate APML/VSML tagged language.

1 Introduction

Emotions are quite important in human interpersonal relations and individual development. Linguistic, paralinguistic and emotional transmission are inherently multimodal, and different types of information in the acoustic channel integrate with information from various other channels facilitating communicative processes. The transmission of emotions in speech communication is a topic that has recently received considerable attention, and automatic speech recognition (ASR) and multimodal or audio-visual (AV) speech synthesis are examples of fields, in which the processing of emotions can have a great impact and can improve the effectiveness and naturalness of man-machine interaction.

Viewing the face improves significantly the intelligibility of both natural and synthetic speech, especially under degraded acoustic conditions. Facial expressions signal emotions, add emphasis to the speech and facilitate the interaction in a dialogue situation. From these considerations, it is evident that, in order to create more natural talking heads, it is essential that their capability comprises the emotional behavior.

In our TTS (text-to-speech) framework, AV speech synthesis, that is the automatic generation of voice and facial animation from arbitrary text, is based on parametric descriptions of both the acoustic and visual speech modalities. The visual speech synthesis uses 3D polygon models, that are parametrically articulated and deformed,

T. Panayiotopoulos et al. (Eds.): IVA 2005, LNCS 3661, pp. 75–87, 2005.
© Springer-Verlag Berlin Heidelberg 2005

while the acoustic speech synthesis uses an Italian version of the FESTIVAL diphone TTS synthesizer [1] now modified with emotive/expressive capabilities.

Various applications can be conceived by the use of animated characters, spanning from research on human communication and perception, via tools for the hearing impaired, to spoken and multimodal agent-based user interfaces.

The aim of this work was that of implementing INTERFACE a flexible architecture that allows us to easily develop and test a new animated face speaking in Italian.

2   A/V Acquisition Environment

INTERFACE is an integrated software designed and implemented in Matlab© in order to simplify and automate many of the operation needed for building-up a talking head. INTERFACE is mainly focused on articulatory data collected by ELITE, a fully automatic movement analyzer for 3D kinematics data acquisition [2].

ELITE provides for 3D coordinate reconstruction (see Fig. 1), starting from 2D perspective projections, by means of a stereophotogrammetric procedure which allows a free positioning of the TV cameras.

The 3D data dynamic coordinates of passive markers such as those illustrated in Fig.2 are then used to create our lips articulatory model and to drive directly, copying human facial movements, our talking face.

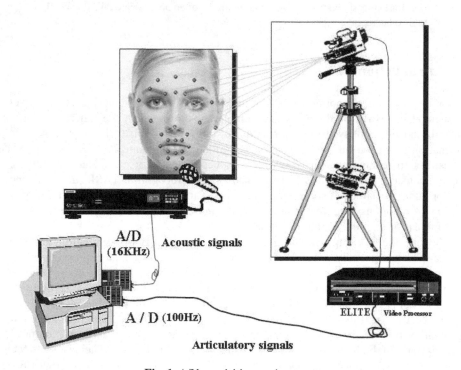

Fig. 1. A/V acquisition environment

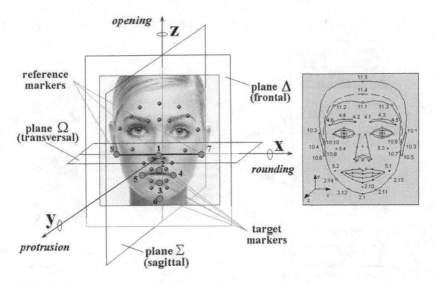

Fig. 2. Position of reflecting markers and reference planes for the articulatory movement data collection (on the left), and the MPEG-4 standard facial reference points (on the right)

Two different configurations have been adopted for articulatory data collection: the first one, specifically designed for the analysis of labial movements, considers a simple scheme with only 8 reflecting markers (bigger grey markers in Fig. 2) while the second, adapted to the analysis of expressive and emotive speech, utilizes the full and complete set of 28 markers. All the movements of the 8 or 28 markers, depending on the adopted acquisition pattern, are recorded and collected, together with their velocity and acceleration, simultaneously with the co-produced speech which is usually segmented and analyzed by means of PRAAT [3], that computes also intensity, duration, spectrograms, formants, pitch synchronous F0, and various voice quality parameters in the case of emotive and expressive speech [4-5].

3 INTERFACE

INTERFACE, whose block diagram is given in Fig. 3, was created mainly to develop LUCIA [6] our graphic MPEG-4 [7] compatible Facial Animation Engine (FAE). In MPEG-4 FDPs (Facial Definition Parameters) define the shape of the model, while FAPs (Facial Animation Parameters), define the facial actions [8]. In our case, the model uses a pseudo-muscular approach, in which muscle contractions are obtained through the deformation of the polygonal mesh around feature points that correspond to skin muscle attachments. A particular facial action sequence is generated by deforming the face model, in its neutral state, according to the specified FAP values, indicating the magnitude of the corresponding action, for the corresponding time instant.

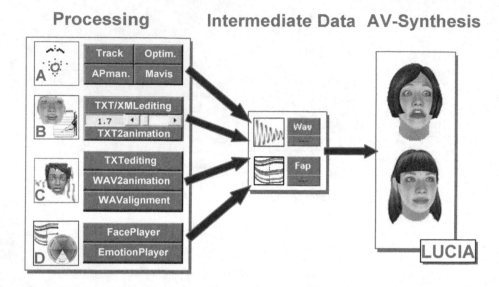

Fig. 3. Block diagram of INTERFACE (see text for details)

For a complete description of all the features and characteristics of INTERFACE, a full detailed PDF manual is being prepared and it is available at the official LUCIA web site: http://www.pd.istc.cnr.it/LUCIA/docs/InterFace20.pdf .

INTERFACE handles four types of input data from which the corresponding MPEG-4 compliant FAP-stream could be created:

⚫ **Articulatory data**, represented by the marker trajectories captured by ELITE; these data are processed by 4 programs:

- "*Track*", which defines the pattern utilized for acquisition and implements a new 3D trajectories reconstruction procedure;
- "*Optimize*", that trains the modified coarticulation model [9] utilized to move the lips of LUCIA, our current talking head under development;
- "*APmanager*", that allows the definition of the articulatory parameters in relation with marker positions, and that is also a DB manager for all the files used in the optimization stages;
- "*Mavis*" (Multiple Articulator VISualizer, written by Mark Tiede of ATR Research Laboratories [10]) that allows different visualizations of articulatory signals;

⚫ **Symbolic high-level TXT/XML text data**, processed by:

- "*TXT/XMLediting*", an emotional specific XML editor for emotion tagged text to be used in TTS and Facial Animation output;
- "*TXT2animation*", the main core animation tool that transforms the tagged input text into corresponding WAV and FAP files, where the first are synthesized by emotive/expressive FESTIVAL module, and the last, which are needed to animate MPEG-4 engines such as LUCIA, by the optimized animation model (designed by the use of Optimize);

- "TXTediting", a simple text editor for unemotional text to be used in TTS and Facial Animation output;
- **WAV data**, processed by:
  - "*WAV2animation*", a tool that builds animations on the basis of input wav files after automatically segmenting them by an automatic ASR alignment system [11];
  - "*WAValignment*", a simple segmentation editor to manipulate segmentation boundaries created by WAV2animation;
- **manual graphic** low-level data , created by:
  - "*FacePlayer*", a direct low-level manual/graphic control of a single (or group of) FAP parameter; in other words, *FacePlayer* renders LUCIA's animation, while acting on MPEG-4 FAP points, for a useful immediate feedback;
  - "*EmotionPlayer*", a direct low-level manual/graphic control of multi level emotional facial configurations for a useful immediate feedback.

3.1 "Track"

MatLab© *Track* was developed with the aim of avoiding marker tracking errors that force a long manual post-processing stage and also a compulsory stage of marker identification in the initial frame for each used camera. *Track* is quite effective in terms of trajectories reconstruction and processing speed, obtaining a very high score in marker identification and reconstruction by means of a reliable adaptive processing. Moreover only a single manual intervention for creating the reference tracking model (pattern of markers) is needed for all the files acquired in the same working session. *Track*, in fact, tries to guess the possible target pattern of markers and the user must only accept a proposed association or modify a wrong one if needed, then it runs automatically on all files acquired in the same session. Moreover, we let the user the possibility to independently configure the markers and also the FAP-MPEG correspondence. The actual configuration of the FAPs is described in an initialization file and can be easily changed. The markers assignment to the MPEG standard points is realized with a context menu as illustrated in Fig. 4. By *Track* the articulatory movements can also be separated from the head roto-translation, thus allowing to realize a correct data driven articulatory synthesis.

The main innovations introduced with the *Track* software can be here summarized:

- the reference model (see Fig. 4) remains the same for the entire working session, that is for all the acquisition files for which the configuration model is not modified; in other words, once the valid mask for a particular session is defined, the process of tracking the trajectories could be automatically started for the whole set of files;
- the marker identification and the reference space deformation problem have been exceeded with an algorithm based on the Singular Value Decomposition (SVD)[12]; this procedure has the intrinsic advantage to operate an error minimization while calculating the roto-translation, even independently from using a perfect undeformable reference space;

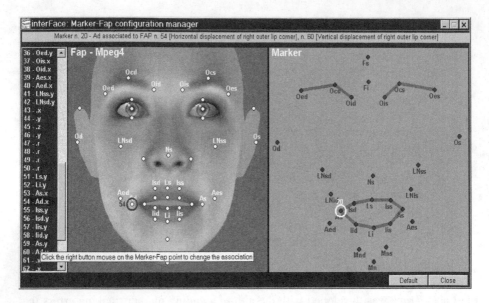

Fig. 4. Marker MPEG-FAP association with the *Track*'s reference model. The MPEG reference points (on the left) are associated with the *Track*'s marker positions (on the right).

- almost all the processing stages have been automated; *Track* can work on a single file or on an entire directory, without manual intervention; a manual error correction phase can always be obviously set at the end of the processing;
- in the generation of the necessary FAP-stream for the animation, the correspondence between the acquisition marker points and standard MPEG-4 points is completely reconfigurable, this implying the possibility to adopt whichever other protocol to be used for the animation;
- the produced FAP-stream takes into account the roto-translation and the scale factors of the head that has to be animated, thus allowing a correct data-driven synthesis of whichever MPEG-4 compatible agent.

The *Track* interface is illustrated in Fig. 5. The area on the left regards operations on single files that is the 3D reconstruction, the MPEG-4 compatible data conversion, the visualization and editing of 2D and 3d marker trajectories, and the setting of the reference model (see Fig. 4).

The central *Directory Operation* buttons do the same processing with directories instead of single files, while the bottom area shows the correspondence between the FAP animation parameters and the trajectories of the markers that are currently under control. The presence of more than a single identification number for each FAP means that the control can be executed along the three different Cartesian axes. As an example, the first cell on the left (Mn), relative to the chin, contains the movements on all the three reference axes. With a simple click on the relative push-buttons it is possible to redefine the marker-FAP correspondence. Processing and Synthesis buttons refers to other INTERFACE programs which can be directly called within T*rack* itself other than within the main interface.

In summary, as illustrated in the examples shown in Fig. 6, for LUCIA, *Track* allows 3D real data driven animation of a talking face, converting the ELITE trajectories into standard MPEG-4 data and eventually it allows, if necessary, an easy editing of bad trajectories. Different MPEG-4 Facial Animation Engines (FAEs) could obviously be animated with the same FAP-stream allowing for an interesting comparison among their different renderings.

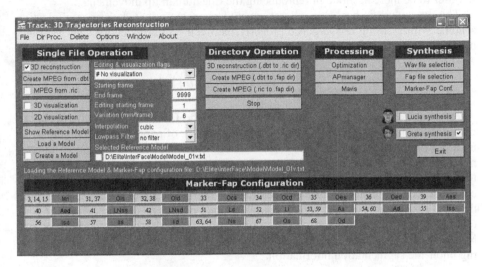

Fig. 5. "Track" interface

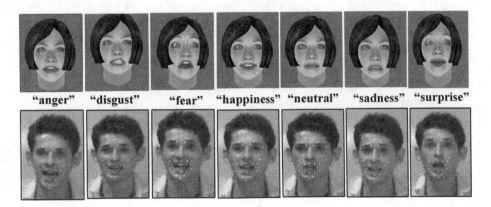

Fig. 6. Examples of a single-frame LUCIA's emotive expressions. These were obtained by acquiring real human movements with ELITE, by automatically tracking and reconstructing them with "Track", and by reproducing them with LUCIA.

3.2 *"Optimize"*

The *Optimize* module implements the parameter estimation procedure for LUCIA's lip articulation model. For generating realistic facial animation is necessary to reproduce the contextual variability due to the reciprocal influence of articulatory move-ments for the production of following phonemes. This phenomenon, defined coarticu-lation is extremely complex and difficult to model. A modified version of the Cohen-Massaro coarticulation model [6] has been adopted for LUCIA and a semi-automatic minimization technique, working on real cinematic data acquired by the ELITE opto-electronic system [2], was used for training the dynamic characteristics of the model, in order to be more accurate in reproducing the true human lip movements .

This procedure is based on a least squared phoneme-oriented error minimization scheme with a strong convergence property, between real articulatory data Y(n) and modeled curves F(n) for the whole set of R stimuli belonging to the same phoneme set:

$$e = \sum_{r=1}^{R} \left(\sum_{n=1}^{N} \left(Y_r(n) - F_r(n) \right)^2 \right) \tag{1}$$

where F(n) is generated by a modified version of the Cohen-Massaro coarticulation model [6] as introduced in [13-14]. Even if the number of parameters to be optimized is rather high, the size of the data corpus is large enough to allow a meaningful esti-mation, but, due to the presence of several local minima, the optimization process has to be manually controlled in order to assist the algorithm convergence. The mean total error between real and simulated trajectories for the whole set of parameters is lower than 0.3 mm in the case of bilabial and labiodental consonants in the /a/ and /i/ con-texts [15, p. 63]. At the end of the optimization stage the lip movements of our MPEG-4 LUCIA can be obtained simply starting from a wav file and its correspond-ing phoneme segmentation information.

3.3 "TXT/XMLediting"

This is an emotional specific XML editor explicitly designed for emotional tagged text such as that shown in Fig.7.

```
<?xml version="1.0"  encoding="iso-8859-1"?>
<!DOCTYPE APML SYSTEM "apml.dtd">
<apml>
Ciao sono LUCIA.
<affective type="anger"> Sono proprio arrabbiata.</affective>
<affective type="fear"> Ma anche molto impaurita.</affective>
<affective type="sadness"> Sono molto triste,</affective>
</apml>
```

Fig. 7. Example of a text tagged with APML mark-up language extensions for emotive au-dio/visual synthesis

The APML mark up language [16] for behavior specification permits to specify how to markup the verbal part of a dialog move so as to add to it the "meanings" that the graphical and the speech generation components of an animated agent need, to produce the required expressions (see Fig. 8).

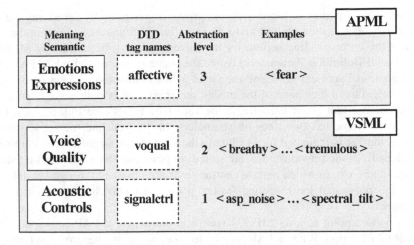

Fig. 8. APML/VSML mark-up language extensions for emotive audio/visual synthesis

So far, the language defines the components that may be useful to drive a face animation through the facial description language (FAP) and facial display functions. The extension of such language is intended to support voice specific controls. An extended version of the APML language has been included in the FESTIVAL speech synthesis environment, allowing the automatic generation of the extended ".pho" file from an APML tagged text with emotive tags. This module implements a three-level hierarchy in which the affective high level attributes (e.g. <anger>, <joy>, <fear>, etc.) are described in terms of medium-level voice quality attributes defining the phonation type (e.g., <modal>, <soft>, <pressed>, <breathy>, <whispery>, <creaky>, etc.). These medium-level attributes are in turn described by a set of low-level acoustic attributes defining the perceptual correlates of the sound (e.g., <spectral tilt>, <shimmer>, <jitter>, etc.). The low-level acoustic attributes correspond to the acoustic controls that the extended MROLA synthesizer can render through the sound processing procedure described above. This descriptive scheme has been implemented within FESTIVAL as a set of mappings between high-level and low-level descriptors. The implementation includes the use of envelope generators to produce time curves of each parameter.

3.4 *"TXT2animation" ("AVengine")*

This represents the main core animation module. *TXT2animation* (also called *"AVengine"*) transforms the emotional tagged input text into corresponding WAV and FAP files, where the first are synthesized by the Italian emotive version of FESTIVAL, and the last by the optimized coarticulation model, as for the lip movements, and by specific facial action sequences obtained for each emotion by knowledge-based rules.

Anger, for example, can be activated using knowledge-based rules acting on action units AU2 + AU4 + AU5 + AU10 + AU20 + AU24, where Action Units correspond to various facial action (i.e. AU1: "inner brow raiser", AU2: "outer brow raiser", etc.) [8].

In summary, a particular facial action sequence is generated by deforming the face model, in its neutral state, according to the specified FAP values, indicating the magnitude of the corresponding action, for the corresponding time instant. In MPEG-4, FDPs (Facial Definition Parameters) define the shape of the model while FAPs (Facial Animation Parameters), define the facial actions deforming a face model in its neutral state. Given the shape of the model, the animation is obtained by specifying the FAP-stream that is for each frame the values of FAPs (see Fig. 9). In a FAP-stream, each frame has two lines of parameters. In the first line the activation of a particular marker is indicated (0, 1) while in the second, the target values, in terms of differences from the previous ones, are stored. In our case, the model uses a pseudo-muscular approach, in which muscle contrac-tions are obtained through the deformation of the polygonal mesh around feature points that correspond to skin muscle attachments.

Each feature point follows MPEG4 specifications where a FAP corresponds to a minimal facial action. When a FAP is activated (i.e. when its intensity is not null) the feature point on which the FAP acts is moved in the direction signaled by the FAP itself (up, down, left, right, etc.).

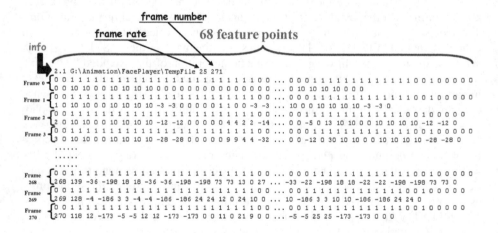

Fig. 9. Example of a FAP stream

Using the pseudo-muscular approach, the facial model's points within the region of this particular feature point get deformed. A facial expression is characterized not only by the muscular contraction that gives rise to it, but also by an intensity and a duration. The intensity factor is rendered by specifying an intensity for every FAP. The temporal factor is modeled by three parameters: onset, apex and offset [8].

The FAP-stream needed to animate a FAE (Facial Animation Engine) could be completely synthesized by using a specific animation model, such as the coarticulation one used in LUCIA, or it could be reconstructed on the basis of real data captured by an optotracking hardware, such as ELITE.

3.5 "WAV2animation" and "WAVsegmentation"

WAV2animation is essentially similar to the previous TXT2animation module, but in this case an audio/visual animation is obtained starting from a WAV file instead that from a text file. An automatic segmentation algorithm based on a very effective Italian ASR system [11] extracts the phoneme boundaries. These data could be also verified and edited by the use of the *WAVsegmentation* module, and finally processed by the final visual only animation module of TXT2animation. At the present time the animation is neutral because the data do not correspond to a tagged emotional text, but in the future this option will be made available.

3.6 "FacePlayer" and "EmotionPlayer"

The first module *FacePlayer* (see Fig. 10) lets the user verify immediately through the use of a direct low-level manual/graphic control of a single (or group of) FAP (acting on MPEG4 FAP points) how LUCIA or another FAP Player renders the corresponding animation for a useful immediate feedback.

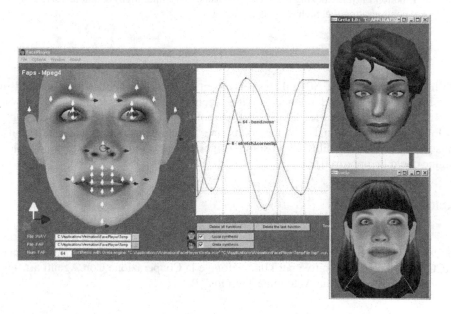

Fig. 10. *FacePlayer*. A simple graphic tool for the facial rendering of a FAP Player such as LUCIA or GRETA [17] by the dynamic manipulation of single markers.

EmotionPlayer, which was strongly inspired by the EmotionDisc of Zofia Rutkay [18]), is instead a direct low-level manual/graphic control of multi level emotional facial configurations for a useful immediate feedback, as exemplified in Fig. 11.

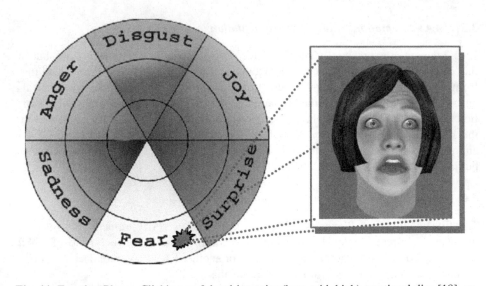

Fig. 11. Emotion Player. Clicking on 3-level intensity (low, mid, high) emotional disc [18], an emotional configuration (i.e. high -fear) is activated.

4 Conclusions

With the use of INTERFACE, the development of Facial Animation Engines and in general of expressive and emotive Talking Agents could be made, and indeed it was for LUCIA, much more friendly. Evaluation tools will be included in the future such, as for example, perceptual tests for comparing human and talking head animations, thus giving us the possibility to get some insights about where and how the animation engine could be improved.

Acknowledgements

Part of this work has been sponsored by PF-STAR (Preparing Future multiSensorial inTerAction Research, European Project IST-2001-37599, http://pfstar.itc.it) and TICCA (Tecnologie cognitive per l'Interazione e la Cooperazione Con Agenti artificiali, joint "CNR - Provincia Autonoma Trentina" Project).

References

1. Cosi P., Tesser F., Gretter R., Avesani, C., "Festival Speaks Italian!", Proc. Eurospeech 2001, Aalborg, Denmark, September 3-7, 509-512, 2001.
2. Ferrigno G., Pedotti A., "ELITE: A Digital Dedicated Hardware System for Movement Analysis via Real-Time TV Signal Processing", IEEE Trans. on Biomedical Engineering, BME-32, 943-950, 1985.
3. Boersma P., "PRAAT, a system for doing phonetics by computer", Glot International, 5 (9/10), 341-345, 1996.

4. Magno Caldognetto E., Cosi P., Drioli C., Tisato G., Cavicchio F., "Coproduction of Speech and Emotions: Visual and Acoustic Modifications of Some Phonetic Labial Targets", Proc. AVSP 2003, Audio Visual Speech Processing, ISCA Workshop, St Jorioz, France, September 4-7, 209-214, 2003.
5. Drioli C., Tisato G., Cosi P., Tesser F., "Emotions and Voice Quality: Experiments with Sinusoidal Modeling", Proceedings of Voqual 2003, Voice Quality: Functions, Analysis and Synthesis, ISCA Workshop, Geneva, Switzerland, August 27-29, 127-132, 2003.
6. Cosi P., Fusaro A., Tisato G., "LUCIA a New Italian Talking-Head Based on a Modified Cohen-Massaro's Labial Coarticulation Model", Proc. Eurospeech 2003, Geneva, Switzerland, 127-132, 2003.
7. MPEG-4 standard. Home page: http://www.chiariglione.org/mpeg/index.htm
8. Ekman P. and Friesen W., Facial Action Coding System, Consulting Psychologist Press Inc., Palo Alto (CA) (USA), 1978.
9. Cohen M., Massaro D., "Modeling Coarticulation in Synthetic Visual Speech", in Magnenat-Thalmann N., Thalmann D. (Editors), Models and Techniques in Computer Animation, Springer Verlag, Tokyo, 139-156, 1993.
10. Tiede, M.K., Vatikiotis-Bateson, E., Hoole, P. and Yehia, H, "Magnetometer data acquisition and analysis software for speech production research", ATR Technical Report TRH 1999, ATR Human Information Processing Labs, Japan, 1999.
11. Cosi P. and Hosom J.P., "High Performance 'General Purpose' Phonetic Recognition for Italian", Proc. of ICSLP 2000, Beijing, Cina, Vol. II, 527-530, 2000.
12. Soderkvist I. and Wedin P., Determining the movements of the skeleton using well-configured markers, Journal of Biomechanics, 26:1473-1477, 1993.
13. Pelachaud C., Magno Caldognetto E., Zmarich C., Cosi P., "Modelling an Italian Talking Head", Proc. AVSP 2001, Aalborg, Denmark, September 7-9, 2001, 72-77.
14. Cosi P., Magno Caldognetto E., Perin G., Zmarich C., "Labial Coarticulation Modeling for Realistic Facial Animation", Proc. 4th IEEE International Conference on Multimodal Interfaces ICMI 2002, Pittsburgh, PA, USA, 505-510, 2000.
15. Perin G., Facce parlanti: sviluppo di un modello coarticolatorio labiale per un sistema di sintesi bimodale, MThesis, Univ. of Padova, Italy, 2000-1.
16. De Carolis, B., Pelachaud, C., Poggi I., and Steedman M., "APML, a Mark-up Language for Believable Behavior Generation", in Prendinger H., Ishizuka M. (eds.), Life-Like Characters, Springer, 65-85, 2004.
17. Pasquariello S., Pelachaud C., "Greta: A Simple Facial Animation Engine", 6th Online World Conference on Soft Computing in Industrial Appications, Session on Soft Computing for Intelligent 3D Agents, September, 2001.
18. Ruttkay Zs., Noot H., ten Hagen P., "Emotion Disc and Emotion Squares: tools to explore the facial expression space", Computer Graphics Forum, 22(1), 49-53, 2003.

Autonomous Virtual Agents Learning a Cognitive Model and Evolving

Toni Conde and Daniel Thalmann

Ecole Polytechnique Fédérale de Lausanne (EPFL), Virtual Reality Lab,
CH-1015 Lausanne, Switzerland
{Toni.Conde, Daniel.Thalmann}@epfl.ch
http://vrlab.epfl.ch

Abstract. In this paper, we propose a new integration approach to simulate an Autonomous Virtual Agent's cognitive learning of a task for interactive Virtual Environment applications. Our research focuses on the behavioural animation of virtual humans capable of acting independently. Our contribution is important because we present a solution for fast learning with evolution. We propose the concept of a Learning Unit Architecture that functions as a control unit of the Autonomous Virtual Agent's brain. Although our technique has proved to be effective in our case study, there is no guarantee that it will work for every imaginable Autonomous Virtual Agent and Virtual Environment. The results are illustrated in a domain that requires effective coordination of behaviours, such as driving a car inside a virtual city.

1 Introduction

The production of believable Autonomous Virtual Agents (AVAs) that are outfitted with learning abilities in a Virtual Environment (VE) is very helpful in many areas. In computer games, the use of AVAs capable of learning a specific task and evolving their skills for that task can greatly improve both the enjoyment and the strategy of the game-play.

An AVA driving a car inside a virtual city is an example of this feature. By adjusting its internal "memory" to match the level of difficulty, the AVA is able to accomplish the task. This process of problem solving can be referred to as task learning. In real life, human learning involves many complex cognitive processes. Realistically, the simulation of AVAs exhibiting behaviours that reflect those of humans demands efficient simulation algorithms. This is especially true for the interactive systems such as computer games.

A number of challenges are raised in developing a system incorporating learning AVAs. From a behavioural animation point of view, there are several areas to consider, such as:

1. The design of a learning control structure,
2. The internal storage of the learning information and
3. The efficient evaluation and calculation of feedbacks and reactions from the environment.

T. Panayiotopoulos et al. (Eds.): IVA 2005, LNCS 3661, pp. 88–98, 2005.
© Springer-Verlag Berlin Heidelberg 2005

Learning involves adaptation and evolution in which modifications made by internal subunits of the adaptive system, like the human brain, mirror external environmental changes. Up to a certain degree of complexity, many Artificial Intelligence (AI) models are able to simulate human learning behaviour [1].

The simulation of human behaviour is achieved through the use of a complex "cognitive map" and the application of a hierarchy of behavioural strategies [2]. The overall cognitive mapping process involves acquisition, coding, storage, recall and decoding [3] of the environmental information. In fact, an individual "cognitive map" will often contain numerous inaccuracies or distortions [4]. Many of these are due to the fact that humans predominantly use a visual perception system and they are unable to process everything they see because of the vast amount of incoming information [5]. Other errors result from the way the information is processed and stored within the "cognitive map" structure itself. Therefore, to simulate human-like behaviour more closely, we separate the AVA from its environment and provide it with perception and effector systems only.

We have developed [6] new methodologies to map all the information coming from the VE and from the virtual sensors of vision, audition and touch in the form of a "cognitive map". They enable the partial re-mapping of the cognitive and semantic information at a behavioural level. For example, when spatial attention is primed with tactile stimulation, the location of the attention spotlight is only partially re-mapped in visual coordinates. With the aid of this framework, we can prepare multi-sensory information for *cognitive learning*.

Unlike mechanical memory that can permanently store information, human memory is imperfect and information can be forgotten. Humans and animals selectively process only the information that is important to them whilst actively searching for new information. Similarly, we can have two types of learning in an intelligent system:

1. *Active learning* where the system selects filters and searches for relevant information.
2. *Passive learning* where the system accepts all incoming data.

In this paper we are presenting research work in the domain of behavioural animation using a high learning approach combined with an active learning approach. This is accomplished through the use of a *cognitive model* defining how the AVA should react to stimuli from its environment. In summary, this paper presents a novel approach that allows an AVA to learn a "cognitive model" by itself.

Document Organisation: Section 2 – State of the Art; Section 3 – Methodology; Section 4 - Realisation and Integration; Section 5 – Experimental and Results; Section 6 – Discussion and Improvement Proposals.

2 State of the Art

A great deal of research has been performed on the control of animated autonomous characters [7-10]. These techniques have produced impressive results, but are limited in two aspects. Firstly, they have no learning ability and are thus limited to explicit pre-specified behaviours. Secondly, they only perform behavioural, not cognitive, control (where *behavioural* means reactive decision making and *cognitive* means reasoning and planning to accomplish long-term tasks).

On-line behavioural learning has begun to be explored in computer graphics [11] and [12]. A notable example is [13], where a virtual dog can be interactively taught by the user to exhibit a desired behaviour. This technique is based on *reinforcement learning* and has been shown to work well in [14]. However, it has no support in long-term reasoning to accomplish complex tasks. Also, since these learning techniques are all designed to be used on-line, they are, for the sake of interactive speed, limited in terms of how much can be learned.

3 Methodology

In this section we introduce AVA learning in which an AVA automatically learns an unknown *cognitive model*. We have developed a novel technique to achieve AVA learning using a tree search with a *k-nearest neighbours* (k-NN) method.

3.1 Human Adaptability to Learn

In order to simulate the AVA's learning behaviour, a learning model has to be adapted. Learning by experience is one of the most well known principles of human task learning behaviour [15]. Indeed, most of the time we learn by direct experience in performing a task. Learning is an intricate process which involves many aspects of cognitive activities including knowledge acquisition, observing and thinking.

Since each person has his/her own motivations and method of learning, the learning process is affected by the learning pattern. To perform a specific task, a person's

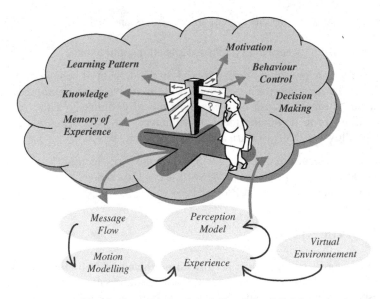

Fig. 1. General behavioural Simulation Model

skills and abilities for the task can be developed during practice [16]. This concept is summarised in Fig. 1 and is used to make up the basis of our learning *cognitive model* for the AVA simulation. Fig. 1 shows the key elements of the human learning process such as: background knowledge of a specific task, motivations to accomplish the task, memory of the past experiences, individual learning pattern and finally trial and error. The learning process is a process of adaptation, evolution and decision making as a whole. Another key issue of learning is the environmental feedback.

3.2 AVA Learning a Cognitive Model and Control Structure

For any given AVA and VE the state space must be continuous. This is because in a stimulating environment where an agent and a human are competing or cooperating intimately, a small difference in state can lead to a large difference in behaviour. A continuous state space can also help achieve a realistic VE. For example, in our car driving case study, a discrete state space would be very unnatural for a car driving simulator. Therefore, our technique uses a continuous internal representation of states and actions.

Most machine-learning algorithms make general and weak assumptions about the nature of the training data. As a result, they typically require large amounts of data to learn accurate classifiers. Normally, the performance improves as the algorithm exploits more information. It generally performs better at recognition than at generalization. This problem can be solved by taking advantage of prior knowledge to eliminate the inconsistent classifiers. Hence, the resulting learning algorithms may be able to learn from very few training examples. To recognise a point, the k-NN method implicitly makes a comparative estimate of all the densities of class probabilities appearing in its vicinity and chooses the most probable. In fact, it approximates the Bayesian decision. Finally, a vector of quantification is introduced. The technique consists of replacing a completed combination of points by a limited number of prototypes representative of the training set.

However, there is a risk involved in incorporating prior knowledge, since this can add a bias to the learning process. If the knowledge is incorrect, it will then eliminate all the accurate classifiers. As a result, learning algorithms tend to perform fairly well on small training sets but, as the amount of data increases, as in our driving context, their performance suffers because they under fit the data.

In most real-world problems all of these approaches are limited by the very large space of the possible states. These algorithms typically require time that is scaled in terms of the cube of the number of states. Hence, [17] and other researchers have focused on methods to construct computationally manageable approximations of the policy, the value function and the model.

The k-NN algorithm was chosen as it provides a local approximation of the target function and can be used automatically without the designer selecting the inputs. It is guaranteed to learn the target function based on the quality of the examples provided and to memorize the decisions made by planning through a *cognitive model*. The decision-making of a *cognitive model* is a very important piece of information. The mapping is likely to be smoother if the information is presented as a separate input to the k-NN algorithm.

Generally with the *k-NN* approach, decreasing the number of points reduces the search space and the storage problem. This also leads to a diminution of the computation time. We used a pre-computed phase before the search phase to reorganize the learning space.

The *k-NN* method does not require the separation of the various classes of learning. Instead, we selected a sub-domain of learning points. However, the method necessitates the explicit storage of many examples of the target function. It can also automatically discover the inputs necessary to approximate the target function like in our car driving *cognitive model*. The choice of the *k-NN* metric influences the rate of error and rejection.

Our technique is quite scalable since, if a global approximation is needed, the *cognitive model* can be approximated by several separate machine learners: *k-NN, DSM (Decision Surface Mapping), LVQ (Learning Vector Quantization)* and *SVM (Support Vector Machine)*. Each of them learns a distinct subset of the state to action mapping (see Fig. 2). Decision-making in different regions of the state space may rely on different state information and therefore these machine learners can use different state formulations to reduce the dimensionality.

Our new approach uses a methodology adapted from the data mining domain [18] which computes a locally flexible metric by means of *SVM*. The maximum margin boundary is used to determine the most discriminated direction over the query's neighbourhood. Such direction provides a local weighting scheme for the input features.

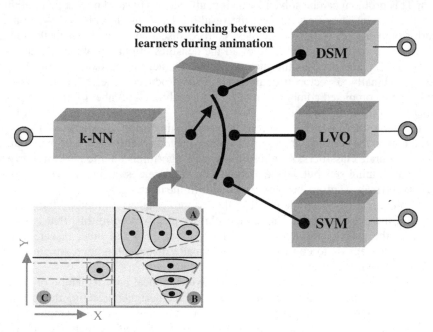

Fig. 2. Cognitive Model with smooth blending. For query A, dimension X is more relevant because a slight move along axis X may change the class label, while for query B, dimension Y is more relevant. For query C, however, both dimensions are equally relevant.

To allow for smooth switching between learners during animation, the actions recommended by each one can be blended for a period of time (see Fig. 2). Traditionally, *cognitive models* are very slow to execute. Performing our smooth blending technique accelerates this cognitive learning process.

3.2 Evolving Process

Each individual's learning pattern and knowledge about the task are represented by predefined motion patterns that may be motion capture data.

Taking the example of high jump, an AVA is assumed to have previously acquired the knowledge of how to jump by making full body movement. However, the AVA has to improve its performance in order to achieve a target. A high jump athlete may have to make several attempts before he/she can jump over a horizontal bar. Similarly, simulating this kind of task requires an evolution model that approximates the evolving learning process during which the ability of the virtual athlete evolves as it improves.

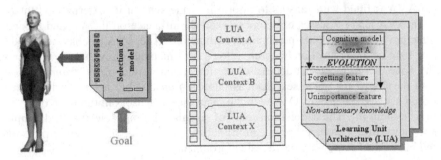

Fig. 3. AVA High Learning (AVAhighLEARN) with our Learning Unit Architecture (LUA)

Our proposal of an approach for the evolving process involves "behaviour capture" and a *Learning Unit Architecture (LUA)*. Supplying a different cognitive model for each context is a simple method of learning context-sensitive policies. These policies are then placed in the AVA's brain and the selection of the suitable *k-NN* to use is determined by the AVA's current internal state (see Fig. 3).

For the evolving process, we introduce features such as forgetting and unimportance. If a state to action case was recorded long ago and/or is very similar to a new one being added, it is likely to be removed. Thus the AVA has the ability to "forget", which is very important in learning something as dynamic as a human behaviour.

4   Realisation and Integration

The realisation and integration of our AVA High Learning (*AVAhighLEARN*) methodology which combines different machine-learning techniques with several novel improvements could be more useful to the computer graphics community than techniques based purely on machine-learning approaches (see Fig. 4).

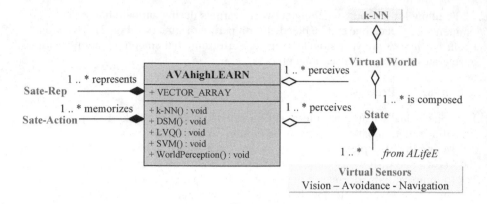

Fig. 4. Comprehensive UML design of *AVAhighLEARN* including virtual sensors from our *AlifeE framework*

An AVA is fitted with sensors to inform it of the state of its external and internal VE. An AVA also possesses effectors to exert an influence on the VE and a control architecture to coordinate its perceptions and actions. The AVA's behaviour is adaptive as long as the control architecture allows it to maintain its variables in their viability zone. All of these characteristics are integrated in our *ALifeE framework* (see Fig. 4) developed for our research. It is based on an original approach inspired by neuroscience and equips an AVA with the main virtual sensors in the form of a small nervous system [6]. The acquisition steps of signals, filtering, selection and simplification intervening before proprioception, active and predictive perception are integrated into virtual sensors and a virtual environment.

5   Experimental and Results

With our approach it is not necessary to program an explicit *cognitive model*. Studying how a task is accomplished is usually necessary before an explicit AI model can be programmed. Thus, in this experiment, our technique for AVA learning relieved us of this burden and therefore reduced the animation workload.

We implemented our *cognitive model* learning approach to the driving simulation of a car inside a virtual city (see Fig. 5a and b). The AVA is a pilot driving a car inside the virtual city. The pilot and his/her co-pilot, have dual control over the acceleration and the wheel of the car (see Fig. 6). The controls are real-value (e.g. the action space is continuous) and the car can move to any location or take any orientation. The continuous action is then quantified to achieve real-time performance. Consequently, the possible actions of the pilot and the virtual instructor become limited.

The experiment is performed with an approximate cognitive model with the *ALifeE framework* [6] but with pseudo-perception features. The characteristics of pseudo-perception are used to compare the performances obtained with case study including our *ALifeE framework*. Indeed, in most of the AVA's simulation environments, sensorial modalities and perception are not integrated in a way faithful to reality. In this experiment visual pseudo-perception is provided by the AVA pilot's field of view which is in the shape of a circular zone (see Fig. 7a and b). Dynamic (e.g. cars) and static (e.g. road signals, traffic lights) objects are represented by rectangular graphic symbols. To test the recognition of the road signals and traffic lights, we integrated this visual pseudo-perception method so that it could determine which object is the closest to a given ray "r" of the circular zone (see Fig. 7b).

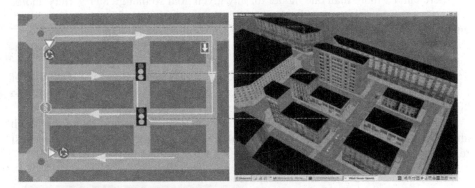

Fig. 5a and b. Car driving simulation inside a virtual city. Semantic information such as road signals and traffic lights are included.

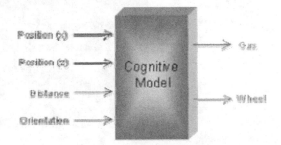

Fig. 6. Explicit cognitive model with inputs and outputs

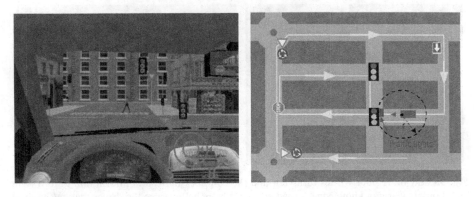

Fig. 7a and b. An AVA learning to drive a car inside a virtual city with visual pseudo-perception. The car "sees" the traffic lights inside a circular zone.

The k-NN algorithm was trained to approximate a single policy. It is only useful for one cognitive model and one goal at a time (see Fig. 3). Fig. 8a and b show the training of the approximate cognitive model for driving and the path of a car inside the virtual city, respectively. Subsequently, the information is used to simulate the behaviour of the AVA pilot.

There can be more than one model for any given goal so that greater variety and/or robustness can be achieved. It is also possible to use the k-NN algorithm with different explicit cognitive models of the same AVA's "brain" (see Fig. 3).

In this experiment we improved the planning of our cognitive model taking advantage of the pseudo-perception features.

We tested our methodology with a *LUA* concept, mainly to encourage evolution of push the behaviours of the pedestrians to evolve and to verify the car pilot's ability to "forget", which is essential in learning dynamic human behaviours.

The final result was good driving behaviour, since the pilot could plan far enough ahead to adequately manoeuvre the car inside the virtual city. We achieved our best results by performing low-level learning method for 40 iterations (see Table 10).

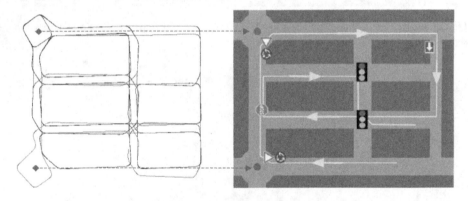

Fig. 8a and b. Snapshot of the car path with approximate cognitive model

Fig. 9a and b. A pilot wishes turns left and the co-pilot's indicators inform him to turn right based on his learning knowledge – road signals. The panel informs the driver that he/she must turn right (Arrow in red at bottom right corner of fig. 9b). The co-pilot, steering wheel is indicated by a red circle.

Table 10. Results of our cognitive model with AVAhighLEARN method, using Learning Unit Architecture (LUA). All animations were rendered in real time using OpenGL on a 3.0 GHz PC with an nVIDIA GeForce FX Go5350 video card.

	k-NN	DSM	LVQ	SVM
Execution time	15 µs	9 µs	8 µs	6 µs
Storage	1.4 MB	1.4MB	1.2 MB	24 KB

6 Discussion and Improvement Proposals

In this paper we presented a novel approach to simulate an AVA's task learning behaviour for interactive VE applications. Our contribution is to propose the concept of a *Learning Unit Architecture* (LUA) that works as a control unit of the AVA's brain. The *LUA* model is based on a human learning model. It is not a true simulation of the real human brain's learning activities, but rather a simulation system that models its numerous aspects. This *LUA* can also be extended to represent different types of learning behaviours.

Through this general and reusable technique, an AVA automatically learns to mimic the intelligent decision making process of a human. This is carried out by a human animator who has interactive control over the actions and decisions of the AVA. The designer constructs the *cognitive model* in an intuitive manner thus making this process simpler and quicker.

Future work should continue to improve the current simulation system in order to simulate more complex human learning behaviours. The challenges that need to be addressed concern the efficiency, the realism and the control of the simulation.

Through this *AVAhighLEARN* method, an AVA can independently and automatically learn a *cognitive model*. For the animator, this alleviates the workload of designing an explicit model. It also permits the creation of tasks for which it would be difficult, or virtually impossible, to develop an explicit model.

However, there are some weaknesses in our approach. For instance, when performing on-line AVA learning, it can be hard to design the expected behaviour of the *cognitive model* with exactitude.

Simulating automatically learning behaviours is a not an easy and appealing task. Our approach could take interactive computer graphics to a completely new level, especially in the entertainment market. It would also be very useful if an animator could interactively train an AVA for *cognitive learning*.

The approach presented here is part of a more complex model that is the object of our research. The goal is to realize a Virtual Life environment for an AVA including different interfaces and sensorial modalities coupled with different evolving learning methodologies.

Acknowledgments. This research has been partially funded by the Swiss National Science Foundation.

References

1. Flake, G. W.: *The Computational Beauty of Nature.* The MIT Press, 2000.
2. Larkin, P.: Achieving human style navigation for synthetic characters. A survey. In *Proceedings of Neural Networks and Computational Intelligence*, 2003.
3. Downs, R., Stea, D.: Cognitive maps and spatial behavior. *Image and Environment.* R. Downs and D. Stea, Eds. Chicago: Adline Publishing, 8-26, 1973.
4. Griffin, D.: Topographical Orientation. *Image and Environment.* R. Downs and D. Stea, Eds. Chicago: Adline Publishing, 296-299, 1973.
5. Kamwisher, N., Downing P.: Separating the wheat from the chaff. *Science*, vol. 282, 57-58, 1998.
6. Conde, T., Thalmann, D.: An Artificial Life Environment for Autonomous Virtual Agents with multi-sensorial and multi-perceptive features. *Computer Animation and Virtual Worlds*, 15(3-4), 311-318, John Wiley, 2004.
7. Reynolds, C.: Flocks, herds, and schools: A distributed behavioural model. In *Proceedings of ACM SIGGRAPH*, 25-34, 1987.
8. Tu, X., Terzopoulos, D.: Artificial fishes: Physics, locomotion, perception, behaviour. In *Proceedings of ACM SIGGRAPH*, 43-50, 1994.
9. Blumberg, B., Galyean, T.: Multi-level direction of autonomous creatures for real-time virtual environments. In *Proceedings of ACM SIGGRAPH*, 47-54, 1996.
10. Perlin, K., Golberg, A.: A improv: a system for scripting interactive actors in virtual worlds. In *Proceedings of ACM SIGGRAPH*, 205-216, 1996.
11. Burke, R., Isla, D., Downie, M., Ivanov, Y., Blumberg, B.: Creature smarts: The art and architecture of a virtual brain. In *Proceedings of the Computer Game Developers Conference*, 2001.
12. Tomlinson, B., Blumberg, B.: Alphawolf: Social learning, emotion and development in autonomous virtual agents. In *Proceedings of First GSFC/JPL Workshop on Radical Agent Concepts*, 2002.
13. Blumberg, B., Downie, M., Ivanov, Y., Berlin, M., Johnson, M., Tomlinson, B.: Integrated learning for interactive synthetic characters. In *Proceedings of ACM SIGGRAPH*, 417-426, 2002.
14. Conde, T., Tambellini, W., Thalmann, D.: Behavioral Animation of Autonomous Virtual Agents helped by Reinforcement Learning. In *Lecture Notes in Computer Science*, vol. 272, Springer-Verlag: Berlin, 175-180, 2003.
15. Jordan, M.I., Rumelhart, D.E.: Supervised Learning with a distal Teacher, In *Cognitive Science*, 16, 307-354, 1992.
16. Bransford J.D., Brown A.L.: Cocking R.R. Brain, Mind, Experience, and School, National Academy Press, Washington, 1999.
17. Mitchell, T.: *Machine Learning,* McGraw Hill, 1997.
18. Domeniconi, C., Gunopulos, D.: Adaptive Nearest Neighbor Classification using SupportVector Machines. In *Advances in Neural Information Processing Systems 14*, MIT Press, 223-229, 2001.

Using Real Objects to Communicate with Virtual Characters

Patrick Gebhard and Martin Klesen

German Research Center for Artificial Intelligence,
DFKI GmbH, Stuhlsatzenhausweg 3, D-66123 Saarbrücken
{patrick.gebhard, martin.klesen}@dfki.de

Abstract. We present an interactive installation with life-size virtual agents that inform, entertain, encourage, and assist visitors during the process of building a car. It will be installed as an exhibit in an automobile theme park. Visitors can take car elements from a shelf and put them on a workbench. The virtual agents continually comment the visitor's actions and the current state of the construction. We use Radio Frequency Identification (RFID) devices to monitor the location of the car elements. This tsechnology allows us to design a natural, unobtrusive and robust interaction by letting the visitors using real objects to communicate with our virtual characters. We show how such an interactive presentation can be created with our SceneMaker authoring tool. We address the problem of authoring content for a large number of combinations and we explain how to design the interaction for an installation where visitors can do anything at anytime.

1 Introduction

Intelligent virtual agents live – by definition – in a virtual world. The human user however lives and acts in the real world. This raises some fundamental questions. How can we bridge the gap between the real and the virtual world and how can we create common bonds between them? How do the virtual characters "know" what's going on out there? How can we establish a kind of co-presence in a shared environment? Depending on the kind of application, the available input and output devices and the target audience these questions can be addressed quite differently.

The environment for our installation is a theme park where visitors can experience and interactively explore past, present, and future trends in automobile construction and design. The exhibits address different aspects like, for example, safety features and environmental issues and are used by dozens and sometimes hundreds of visitors per day. The target audience is not restricted to a specific age or user group. Installations usually run 24 hours a day over a period of several weeks and sometimes month and require a minimum of supervision by members of the staff.

Looking for new attractions, we have been asked to build an interactive installation with life-size virtual characters that inform, entertain, encourage, and assist the visitors in the task of building a car. Using a small set of front, cockpit, middle and rear elements, visitors can build different car types (a convertible, a limousine, a SUV, etc.) and different versions of each type (e.g. with two, four, or six seats). However,

T. Panayiotopoulos et al. (Eds.): IVA 2005, LNCS 3661, pp. 99–110, 2005.
© Springer-Verlag Berlin Heidelberg 2005

the objective is not to show the visitors how to build a car – that should be fairly obvious – but to provide them with interesting bits and pieces of information about automotive engineering during the construction process. We therefore allow visitors to build unusual and even nonsensical constructions like, for example, a two-seater with the rear of a SUV. Actually this is considered to be part of the fun as it challenges our characters – trying to continually comment the construction process – to make an appropriate statement. In this case it could be a humorous remark about why they think that this construction will probably not become a big commercial success.

For this installation we were looking for new kinds of interaction modalities that would allow us to design a natural, unobtrusive and robust interaction with our intelligent virtual agents. In this theme park, we cannot use facilities for speech and gesture input and the direct manipulation of the virtual world (e.g. data gloves), because they only work reliably under controlled conditions. Looking for alternatives, we had the idea to let the visitors use real objects to communicate with our virtual characters. We consider this to be a natural way for humans to interact with the exhibit because taking objects and putting them together is something we do since childhood. To monitor the user's actions and the state of the construction process we use Radio Frequency Identification (RFID) devices. This technology allows us to determine the position of the car elements wirelessly using radio waves if the elements are equipped with RFID tags. Visitors can build their car by taking elements from a shelf and by putting them on a workbench. Depending on how these actions are classified and interpreted by the system, the virtual characters will alter their behavior and show an appropriate reaction. They are designed to be mainly reactive, but they will take the initiative if the user is (too) passive.

As a future exhibit in the automobile theme park, our installation meets some additional requirements. It needs no personnel – it is self-explaining and runs in an endless loop. It is both entertaining and informative by embedding the relevant comments and pieces of information into a narrative context. Based on our experience with animated presentation teams [1, 2] we decided to use two virtual characters instead of a single one as this bears a number of advantages: We can use simulated dialogs between these two characters to convey information in a less obtrusive way. It is also a means of attracting nearby visitors and it can reduce interaction inhibitions because the user is not directly addressed and therefore not under constant pressure to do something in order to elicit a reaction of the agents. To create a feeling of co-presence with the visitors in the context of the installation and to come across as believable and life-like, our virtual characters use context knowledge (e.g. about the current car element, state of construction, weather, upcoming events) in their comments and conversations.

2 Installation

The installation consists of the following main components: a shelf and a workbench equipped with RFID readers (see Sect. 4) to determine the presence and the location of the elements. The set of RFID-tagged elements on the scale 1:5 used to build a car. A data projector and a screen for displaying our two virtual characters Adrian and Carina in life-size. A virtual screen within their 3D environment that can be used to display images and videos during their presentation. A camera to detect the presence and absence of visitors. Figure 1 shows a prototype of the exhibit.

The workbench has five adjacent areas where elements can be placed. Each area can hold exactly one element and the elements can be placed in either direction, i.e. the user can build the car with the front on the left and the rear on the right hand side or the other way around. We distinguish four different categories of pieces or building blocks. The front element with bumper, engine hood, and front tyres, the cockpit with windscreen, front doors, steering wheel, driver and passenger seat, the middle element with additional doors and back seats, and the rear element with trunk and back tyres. The elements are abstractions and simplifications of their real-life counterparts. A complete car consists of three, four, or five elements. A front element, a cockpit, and a rear element are mandatory while the

Fig. 1. Main components and spatial layout of the installation

middle elements are optional. The car type is defined by the number of elements and by the rear element used. A roadster, for example, consists of a front element, a cockpit, and the rear of a convertible; whereas a limousine can be build using a front element, a cockpit, two middle elements, and a fastback. Elements that are currently not required can be stored in the shelf.

The installation runs in two modes. The OFF mode is assumed when no user is present. A visitor entering the installation is being detected by the camera and lets the system switch to ON mode. The idea behind these two modes is based on our experiences with CrossTalk – a self-explaining virtual character exhibition for public spaces [3]. In OFF mode Adrian and Carina perform idle time actions like looking around or shifting posture. They talk to each other about their job and their hobbies while making occasional references to the situational context, i.e. the current time of day, the weather outside, upcoming events, and so on. Making references to the real world creates an illusion of life and establishes common bonds with the user's world. Their activities in OFF mode are supposed to attract the attention of passers-by and to invite them to enter the installation. In case this happens the characters switch to their ON mode behavior. They welcome the visitor and briefly explain the purpose of this installation, i.e. that visitors can build their own car using the set of available elements. In the construction phase visitors can remove elements from the shelf and put them on the workbench and they can modify their construction by removing elements from the workbench, by rearranging them or by replacing them with other elements. Adrian and Carina continually comment the user's actions and the current state of the construction. They provide information about individual elements, their interrelation with other elements and they talk about the various valid and invalid (partial) combinations. They can use the virtual screen between them to display images and short video sequences, e.g. to highlight certain aspects by showing a close-up of the relevant parts or to clarify technical terms by showing a drawing or a picture. This feature makes their presentation livelier and enhances their believability because it creates the illusion that they have full control over the system. If there is no user action detected within a certain period of time, they will try to motivate the visitor by encouraging him or her to do something or by giving hints how the current construction could be modified or completed. If the user has intentionally or unintentionally produced an invalid configuration (e.g. by adjoining a front and a middle element) they will point out that the car cannot be completed this way and they give hints how to correct this error. Once a complete car has been built, the closing phase is initiated. Adrian and Carina make some final comments before pointing out that the visitor can continue the construction process simply by removing an element from the car. If the user doesn't follow this suggestion, the two characters will say thank you and goodbye and after a while they will resume their private conversations. However, as soon as someone removes a piece from the finished car, they interrupt their conversation and start commenting on the new construction. The ON mode ends if there are no more visitors at the installation.

The realisation of this exhibit confronts us with a number of problems and challenges. Visitors can pick up elements and put them on the shelf or the workbench at any time. Since we have no control over the pieces, the system must be able to cope with the fact that multiple users move elements simultaneously. These actions must be reliably detected by the system and adequately commented by the two virtual characters. They should react instantly (e.g. by interrupting their current remarks) and according to the current state of the construction. At the same time we must avoid that their comments and conversations become too fragmented because they jump from one piece of explanation to the next. Last but not least, we have to find a way to handle the large number of possible valid and invalid combinations of elements on the workbench. With one front element, one cockpit, two identical middle elements, and a rear element there are already 15480 different combinations on the workbench! It is obvious that we cannot address each configuration individually. On the other hand we need to be careful not to over-generalize. If the characters just point out that "This configuration is invalid." without being able to explain why or without giving a hint how this could be rectified, their believability is immediately destroyed and they are perceived as rather unintelligent virtual agents.

3 Authoring

Our authoring approach relies on the concept of the separation of content and narrative structure, which we have introduced in [2, 4]. The content is organized with *scenes*, whereas the narrative structure is represented by a *sceneflow*. Scenes are pieces of user-edited contiguous dialog. Additionally, they can contain commands for controlling the characters' non-verbal behavior and for the presentation of media objects (e.g. showing pictures or videos). Authors usually refer to a scene as a coherent and closed unit regarding a message, agent characterization, or a humorous punch line. Authors can define the narrative structure by linking the scenes in a graph called sceneflow. Transitions in a sceneflow are triggered by transition events. These events represent the user's actions and the current state of the construction. Transition events are produced by *transition event rules* that map signals produced by the installations input devices onto transition events.

The content for our interactive presentation is created by human authors with the help of the SceneMaker authoring suite. As described above, the presentation relies on three distinct types of content: scenes, a sceneflow, and transition events. According to this, the authoring steps are:

- *The writing of the dialog content.*
  This is done using a screenplay-like language.
- *The creation of the sceneflow.*
  This is done with the help of a graphical user interface, that is part of the SceneMaker tool.
- *The definition of the transition event rules.*
  This is done by an XML-based rule language.

Compared to the authoring of the scenes and the sceneflow that can be done by non-computer experts, the definition of transition event rules is done by programmers. In a final step the SceneMaker tool is used to compile the scenes and the sceneflow into an executable program.

Scenes

The use of context information in scenes helps authors to create the impression that characters are fully aware of what is going on by reflecting the actual situation in their comments, e.g. by talking about the current weather conditions. Beginning with our first system CrossTalk [2] that uses context data in scenes and in the sceneflow, we constantly extended the underlying software by adding new dynamic context types. At this stage of the implementation, we provide the authors with the following additional context functions:

- *Current (car) element* (current_piece).
  Returns the inflected form or the pronoun for the currently used element based on a small dictionary containing German words and their inflections.
- *Weather conditions* (weather).
  Relying on the data of an Internet weather channel, descriptions for the current meteorological conditions are generated, such as temperature, high or low-pressure area, forecast of the next day, weather of the last day.
- *Part of day* (part-of-day) and *fuzzy time* (time-fuzzy).
  Taking the current time as input, many commonly used time descriptions are generated. These are the part of day, e.g. morning, afternoon, evening, or a fuzzy time description like near four o'clock.
- *Visitor Counter* (all-visitors, daily-visitor).
  This kind of information reflects the overall number of visitors that have visited this installation and the number of the daily visitors.
- *Piece Counter* (pieces-on-shelf, pieces-on-workbench).
  They reflect the number of pieces on the shelf and on the workbench. They are used for motivation comments; in the case the visitor has no clue how to go

on with the construction. For example, the characters can encourage the visitor take a piece from the shelf, when the `piece-on-shelf` counter is greater than zero.

Authors can insert the content of theses context variables (e.g. `weather`) in scenes by using the common access function `GET`. If needed, they can provide additional parameters (e.g. `adj`). The following dialog line: "This [`GET part-of-day`] the weather is [`GET weather adj`]" will be resolved at run-time to: "This afternoon the weather is bad."

All context information can also be used to model the branching in a sceneflow by using them in conditional transitions. Refer to [2, 4] for a comprehensive overview. Beside the context access commands, scenes can contain gesture or posture tags and emotion tags for letting a character perform a gesture (e.g. [`progress`]) or express an emotion (e.g. [`happy`]), as well as media tags for displaying pictures and video [`picture roadster`]. Some gestures (e.g. nodding or shaking the head) can be combined with other gestures. In this case the virtual characters execute the two motions simultaneously. To signal that a gesture should be played on top of another one, the author simply puts a "+" in front of the gesture name, e.g. [`+nod`]. We use this overlay technique extensively for feedback-channel gestures, like nodding, shaking the head, and looking at somebody when he starts speaking. The following example shows a scene that is played, when a visitor has finished the construction of a roadster:

Carina: [`progress`][`+turn2visitor`] The car you've build is called a roadster.
[`picture car1.jpg`] [`happy`] It's a very sportive car with two doors.
Adrian: Well, [`happy`] this car is stylish!
Carina: [`+nod`]

There are pre-scripted scenes for the topics small talk, welcoming visitors, as well as comments regarding the current state of the car construction and the different car types. Currently, there are more than 260 scenes, covering the above topics. To minimize the repetition of scenes, most scenes are available in multiple versions.

Sceneflow

The sceneflow represents the narrative structure of an interactive presentation by defining transitions between scenes in a scene flow graph. Technically we use cascaded Finite State Machines (FSMs) to represent the sceneflow. A cascaded FSM consists of nodes and edges (transitions). So-called *supernodes* contain a sub-graph. Scenes can be attached to both nodes and edges. Transitions are used to model reactions of user actions or to model variations of a presentation. A detailed description on how we use sceneflow elements to model a presentation in given in [4].

While in previous versions the sceneflow had to be manually created in a XML style language, we are now introducing a new version of SceneMaker with a graphical user interface for creating the sceneflow (see Fig. 2). It provides authors with Drag&Drop facilities to "draw" the sceneflow, to attach scenes, and to define conditions for the transitions between scenes. It also checks the integrity of the actual sceneflow before compiling it to an executable program.

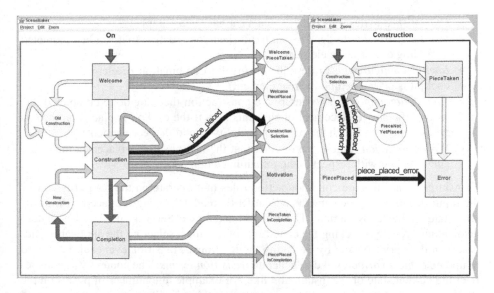

Fig. 2. The SceneMaker tool displaying the ON mode and the Construction supernode

Figure 2 displays a part of the sceneflow of this presentation. The left side shows the ON mode with its supernodes Welcome, Construction, and Completion. These reflect the major phases in ON mode. The right side shows the expanded Construction phase with its supernodes (phases) PieceTaken, PiecePlaced, and Error. As the names might suggest, PieceTaken and PiecePlaced contain nodes with scenes attached that let the characters comment a piece taken/placed action. Afterwards, if an error has occurred, this is commented by scenes of the Error phase.

As mentioned above, we use the generated transition events to trigger sceneflow transitions and to activate corresponding scenes. Starting in the Construction phase, there are various possibilities how the presentation can continue. If nothing happens, the transition that leads to the Motivation phase (left side) is activated by a time-out event. Being in the Motivation phase, the user gets help on how to continue with the construction. If the user is placing a piece on the workbench thereby creating an error, the following transition events are generated: `piece_placed`, `piece_placed_on_-workbench`, and `piece_placed_error`.

As shown in Figure 2, the `piece_placed` event activates the transition leading to the node ConstructionSelection. Any active node or transition (and any active scene) inside of the Construction supernode gets terminated. Afterwards, the piece placed action will be commented in the PiecePlaced phase. Then, the error is explained in the Error phase.

Transition Events Rules

The authoring process for this installation focuses on the different states that can occur during the car construction. As described in Sect. 2 visitors can put the pieces in either direction on one of the five areas of the workbench. To classify the various constructions, we use the following states:

- *Car finished* to describe the fact that a car has been completed.
- *Valid construction* to describe an unfinished construction that can be completed by adding one or more elements.
- *Invalid configuration* to describe an invalid combination of elements (e.g. the cockpit is placed behind the rear element).
- *Completion impossible* to describe a construction that cannot be completed due to an unfavorable placement of elements (e.g. if the cockpit is placed on the last area on the workbench there is no possibility to add the rear element)
- *Wrong direction* to describe the fact that the last piece was placed in the opposite direction with respect to the remaining elements.

Transition event rules are condition-action rules that operate on the data provided by the input devices (e.g. the camera and the RFID readers) taking into account the current state of the construction. The EventManger (see Sect. 4) performs a match-resolve-act cycle by checking the conditions of all rules, selecting the applicable ones based on their priority, and by executing their actions. Transition event rules are used to update *context variables* and to generate *transition events*. The context variables reflect the current state of the installation like, for example, the number of pieces on the shelf or the type and location of pieces on the workbench. Transition events are used to enable transitions in the sceneflow.

As pointed out before (see Sect. 2), we have to deal somehow with the large number of valid and invalid car configurations that visitors can build. Therefore, we focus on the local context of the last placed piece on the workbench. Based on this, we generate transition events describing the above-mentioned states that can occur during a car construction. For example, if the user places a cockpit in front of the front element, the analysis of the local context results in an *invalid configuration* error.

Another problem mentioned in Section 2 is that fact that we must be able to cope with many (concurrent) actions of the visitor(s) and that the current state of the construction can be interpreted in different ways. We deal with this problem by assigning priorities to the transition event rules. For example, if the visitor puts an element on the workbench thereby completing the construction of a car, two transition event rules are applicable: one representing a `piece_placed` event and another one representing a `car_finished` event. Since the latter rule has a higher priority only the `car_finished` transition event will be generated.

In general, for each action performed by the visitor a set of transition events is generated. This approach follows the idea that actions (or situations as a result of these actions) can be described at different levels of details. The generated set of events includes both detailed and general information about the action. This provides the authors of the scenes and the sceneflow with a maximum of flexibility in designing the virtual characters' reactions. Actions like taking, moving, or placing elements can generate the transition events `piece_placed`, `piece_taken`, or `car_finished`. These events are followed by an event that describes the location where the piece was taken or placed (e.g. `piece_placed_workbench`). In case the car construction is valid, an event describing the current car configuration is triggered (e.g. `construction_code_fc` meaning a front and a cockpit are placed on the workbench next to each other). This event is also generated, after a `car_finished` event, followed by an event describing the car type (e.g. `construction_type_roadster`). In case the car construction is invalid, an error event (`piece_placed_error`) and an event describing the error are generated (e.g. `invalid_configuration_cf` meaning a cockpit is placed in front of the front element). If the error can be corrected, an error correction event is generated (e.g. `error_correction_shift_to_right` suggesting that the last piece should be shifted to the right).

The generated sets of transition events are used to trigger consecutive scenes in which the characters make more and more specific comments to the state of the construction. This is done by enabling the corresponding transitions in the sceneflow. Transition events are therefore a means to define a path through the sceneflow.

4 Architecture

This interactive installation should react instantly and appropriately to changes in the environment. To avoid hardware delays we run the system on three computers using a distributed software architecture (Fig. 3). One computer controls the input devices: the camera, the user detection mat, and the RIFD readers. A Text-To-Speech-System runs on a second computer because it needs 4 GB of main memory and a fast (3 GHz) processor. A third computer runs the main modules including the Charamel CharaVirld™ 3D[1] presentation system.

Visitors and their actions must be reliably detected by the system. Visitors are detected by a camera and a detection mat. The software for optical user detection was developed in the department of Multimedia Concepts and their Applications at the University of Augsburg. It is able to detect people based on their skin color. In combination the two systems guarantee that the presence and absence of visitors is reported

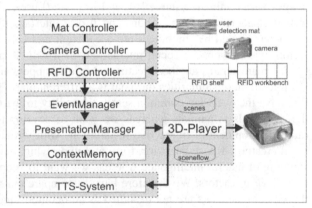

Fig. 3. System modules and architecture

correctly. Car elements and their locations are reliably and robustly detected by using current RFID technology. The overall goal is to provide a mostly unobtrusive detection of the presence and orientation at specific areas. In our opinion, the RFID technology fulfills perfectly these requirements.

Based on the output of the various input devices the system modules (see Fig. 3) are operating. These are the EventManager, the ContextManger, the Charamel CharaVirld™ 3D-Player, and the PresentationManager. The latter is the central module. It is responsible for selecting and executing scenes based on the defined sceneflow. Executing scenes consists of forwarding commands for character and screen

---

[1] http://www.charamel.de

control to the 3D-Player on the one hand, and handling transitions events generated from the EventManager on the other.

The EventManager processes the input data from the various input devices. Its task is to interpret these data and to elicit transition events. Transition events are passed on to the PresentationManager. Depending on the actual state of the sceneflow, transition events can trigger transitions between scenes. The ContextMemory module stores the discourse history (e.g. user and system actions, scenes played, etc.) and situational context (e.g., part of day) and as an addition to previous versions, it includes a simple dictionary. The 3D-Player implements the graphical front end of the installation. It renders the 3D scene with the virtual characters.

5 Related Work

Our work is inspired by the interactive installations created by Bruce Blumberg's Synthetic Characters Group[2] and by Justine Cassell's Gesture and Narrative Language Group[3] at the MIT Media Lab. Both groups used a variety of tangible interfaces to interact with their synthetic characters. In *Swamped!* a plush toy is used to control a virtual version of a chicken as it runs around a barn yard scenario [5], in *sand:stone* visitors could move stones around on a surface of sand causing changes in a projected display of an animated statue [6], and in *(*void)* users could communicate with the virtual characters through a "buns and forks" interface [7]. We share their view that characters should be combined into a coherent and cohesive installation, e.g. by designing installations for social interactions in which "A participant is [...] being seen by the characters as another creature who just happens to be 'outside the box'." [8]. Despite all these similarities our goal is a different one. They want to build characters that have the everyday common sense, the ability to learn, and the sense of empathy that one finds in animals whereas we want to develop tools and techniques for the rapid development of interactive installations with virtual actors. Their mission is to build creatures whose behavior, form and underlying architecture informs our understanding of natural intelligence whereas we want to support the human author in directing virtual actors. We therefore have to compare our work with systems in which the virtual characters are not designed as autonomous agents but rather as virtual actors following a script written by an author. A detailed comparison of our authoring approach relying on a strict separation of narrative structure and content with other tools and scripting languages can be found in [2]. A comprehensive collection of the latest developments in scripting and representation languages for life-like characters is given in [9].

The system that probably comes closest to our approach of using real objects to communicate with virtual characters is *Sam*, a collaborative story listening system for children [10]. Sam is a life-sized virtual child and projected on a screen behind a toy castle with a figurine. The figurine has a RFID tag attached to track its location within the castle by RFID readers embedded in the rooms. It has a virtual counterpart and it

---

[2] http://characters.media.mit.edu/
[3] http://www.media.mit.edu/gnl/

is passed back and forth between Sam and the child as a token during the collaborative construction of stories. This is similar to our installation in which the car elements are used to elicit comments by the virtual actors. However, Sam is designed to act as a peer playmate to children that can engage in a face-to-face conversation, whereas the virtual characters in our system are talking most of the time to each other about the construction that is being built by the visitor. These simulated dialogs are supposed to convey information in an unobtrusive and enjoyable way.

6 Summary

In this paper we have presented an interactive installation with virtual characters that will entertain, inform, and assist visitors of an automotive theme park during the task of building cars. A special feature of this installation is the fact that it uses real objects as a communication interface. Looking for new interaction modalities we decided to use RFID technology to reliably detect the car pieces. This allows us to monitor actions of visitors unobtrusively.

Using real objects as an intuitive communication interface is a great challenge for the interaction design and for scripting the characters' behavior. We have shown how we deal with several thousands of possible combinations of car elements, and how we handle different types of errors during the car construction phase. The most critical aspect is however, how to react instantly and appropriately to changes in the environment. We introduced the concept of transition events reflecting a user's actions and the current state of the construction. Combining them with our authoring approach that separates narrative structure and content, we created scenes, and a sceneflow that lets the virtual characters give a lively interactive performance.

In addition, we have presented enhancements of the SceneMaker technology that facilitate the creation of interactive presentations and that provide better support for scripting the verbal and non-verbal behavior of virtual characters. Firstly, these are overlay gesture commands for our screenplay like language. They allow us to combine often-used conversational gestures with backchanneling gestures (e.g. nodding, shaking the head, ...). This increases the expressiveness of the characters. Secondly, a dictionary and new dynamic context functions let authors use utterance templates to produce more variations in scenes by inserting content dynamically and by computing it's correct inflected form. This has the advantage that less pre-scripted scenes are needed. Thirdly, our new graphical user interface of the SceneMaker tool reduces the development time for this interactive installation dramatically. It enables a fast redesign and it provides a visual representation of the narrative structure. The current state of the car construction process is associated with a unique position in the sceneflow graph. This makes the system's behavior more transparent for authors and developers and helps in debugging and refining the sceneflow. Using the SceneMaker authoring tool and additional software components such as the EventManger and the ContextManger it took us three weeks to write more than 260 scenes, to model the sceneflow, and to define the transition event rules. All in all, seven people including the project manager have been involved in the whole process.

Acknowledgements

The work presented in this paper is a joint effort with contributions from our colleagues Michael Kipp, Gernot Gebhard, Thomas Schleiff, Michael Schneider, and Alassane Ndiaye. We thank the people from Charamel for their continuous support and for providing us with the two virtual characters Adrian and Carina. We also thank our colleagues from the department of Multimedia Concepts and their Applications at the University of Augsburg for the vision detection software.

References

[1] André, E. and Rist, T. (2000). Presenting through performing: On the use of multiple life-like characters in knowledge-based presentation systems. In Proc. of the 5th International Conference on Intelligent User Interfaces (IUI 2000), pages 1–8, New York. ACM Press.

[2] Klesen, M., Kipp, M., Gebhard, P., and Rist, T. (2003). Staging exhibitions: methods and tools for modelling narrative structure to produce interactive performances with virtual actors. Virtual Reality, 7(1):17–29.

[3] Rist, T., Baldes, S., Gebhard, P., Kipp, M., Klesen, M., Rist, P., and Schmitt, M. (2002). Crosstalk: An interactive installation with animated presentation agents. In Proc. of the Second Conference on Computational Semiotics for Games and New Media (COSIGN'02), Augsburg.

[4] Gebhard, P., Kipp, M., Klesen, M., and Rist, T. (2003). Authoring scenes for adaptive, interactive performances. In Proc. of the Second International Joint Conference on Autonomous Agents and Multi-Agent Systems, Melbourne, Australia. ACM Press.

[5] Blumberg, B. (1998) Swamped! Using plush toys to direct autonomous animated characters. In Visual Proceedings of SIGGRAPH 1998, New York. ACM Press.

[6] Downie, M., Benbasat, A., Wahl, J., Stiehl, D., and Blumberg, B. (1999) sand:stone. Leonardo, 32(5): 462-463.

[7] Blumberg, B. (1999) (void*): A Cast of Characters. In Visual Proceedings of SIGGRAPH 1999, New York. ACM Press.

[8] Blumberg, B., Tomlinson, B., and Downie, M. (2001). Multiple conceptions of character-based interactive installations. Computer Graphics International, pages 5–11.

[9] Prendinger, H. and Ishizuka, M., editors (2004). Life-Like Characters: Tools, Affective Functions, and Applications. Cognitive Technologies. Springer-Verlag.

[10] Ryokai, K., Vaucelle, C., and Cassell, J. (2002). Literacy Learning by Storytelling with a Virtual Peer. In Proc. of Computer Support for Collaborative Learning.

A Software Engineering Approach Combining Rational and Conversational Agents for the Design of Assistance Applications

Jean-Paul Sansonnet, Jean-Claude Martin, and Karl Leguern

LIMSI-CNRS, BP 133, 91403 Orsay Cedex, France
{jps, martin}@limsi.fr

Abstract. A Conversational Agent can be useful for providing assistance to naïve users on how to use a graphical interface. Such an assistant requires three
features: understanding users' requests, reasoning, and intuitive output. In this
paper we introduce the DAFT-LEA architecture for enabling assistant agents to
reply to questions asked by naive users about the structure and functioning of
graphical interfaces. This architecture integrates via a unified software engineering approach a linguistic parser for the understanding the user's requests, a
rational agent for the reasoning about the graphical application, and a 2D cartoon like agent for the multimodal output. We describe how it has been applied
to three different assistance application contexts, and how it was incrementally
defined via the collection of a corpus of users' requests for assistance. Such an
approach can be useful for the design of other assistance applications since it
enables a clear separation between the original graphical application, its abstract
DAFT model and the linguistic processing of users' requests.

1 Introduction

Embodied Conversational Agents (ECAs) can be useful in the relation between users
and web services. As assistants, they might welcome naïve users and help them to
understand the structure and the functions of a new graphical application. This leads
to several requirements on such an assistant agent, mainly regarding dialogue and
reasoning. Indeed, this assistant should be able to interact with the user via Natural
Language Understanding (NLU) in order to answer her questions on the state or on
the control of the graphical application. It should also be able of reasoning upon the
structure and the functioning of the graphical application it is in charge of. This requires that it should be able to browse the internal state of the application at runtime.

From a software engineering point of view, such assistants should be easily defined
for existing or new graphical applications. The design of full-fledge dialog systems
requires huge efforts in terms of Natural Language Processing expertise and implementation time. Allen [2] declared that the *genericity* of dialogue systems would be
the key to their success. A *generic* dialogue system can be defined as a framework
that is not designed for a particular application but a) can be *plugged* to various appli-

T. Panayiotopoulos et al. (Eds.): IVA 2005, LNCS 3661, pp. 111–119, 2005.
© Springer-Verlag Berlin Heidelberg 2005

cations and b) with minimal linguistic knowledge and minimal adaptation effort for the developers. Theoretically, this derives into two genericity criteria that we will refer to as: a) the embedding criterion, b) the knowledge separation criterion. We introduced the notion of *active mediating symbolic representation* hereafter called *model* (as in the classical Model View Component model used in Graphical User Interfaces) since it is an intermediary between the NLU module and the application to extend with dialog capacities [8]. We do not aim at a complete genericity over language but rather, a genericity restricted to calls for assistance in simple graphical applications.

Enabling an agent to control a GUI is a well known problem in the application testing and application integration domains (see [6] for reusing GUI-driven applications and [3] for a discussion about middleware solutions such as *connectors* and *mediators*). Our primary goal is not software *reuse*, but software *introspection by agents on behalf of human users*. Thus, we need to be able to scan the runtime of a software/hardware component in order to answer questions about its current state. As mentioned in [6], this is obviously an open question if we seek for a 100% browsing of the 'insides' of the instructions (Java byte code for example). Moreover, we need to deal with a complete representation of the component: a) its GUI (the view) but also b) its *internal algorithm* (the controller). This is why we chose to 'mirror' the component with a symbolic representation (hereafter called the *model*) that is easy to browse and update because of its S-expressions based structure; we need to maintain a *dynamic* semantic homogeneity between the runtime and the model: this issue is the key point of this paper.

Section 2 describes three assistance applications. Section 3 describes the DAFT-LEA framework that was used for their specification and implementation. Section 4 concludes by a description of the corpus of users' requests that we collected during evaluation.

2 Studying the Design of Assistant Agents

A graphical interface might change according to three possible operating modes. *Modal operating mode*: the user operates directly on the graphical interface. *Modeless operating mode*: the internal processing of the graphical application modifies its internal state variables independently from the user. *Dialogical operating mode*: the user operates on the internal state of the application through a natural language request. We have selected three examples covering these dimensions in different application contexts (Fig. 1). The 2D cartoon-like characters which are used for embodying the assistant are the LIMSI Embodied Agents (LEA) enabled to display various postures, facial expressions and gesture functions such as deictics or iconics [1]. These agents have already been used in a simulation of a conversational game application [5] and for evaluating various multimodal output strategies during technical presentations [4].

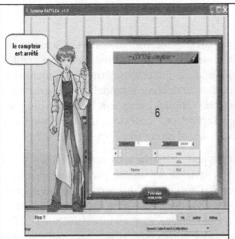

A simple counting application. The user can either directly act on a graphical button in a *modal* operating mode (e.g. *stop* button in order to stop the counting thread), or ask the agent to do it in a dialogical operating mode (by typing *stop it* in the text field below). The user can also ask questions to the agent (e.g. "*is it possible to stop the counting?*", "*Show me the cursor controlling the speed of the counting*"). The assistant displays non-verbal and verbal (Elan Speech© synthesis) behaviors ("*the counter has been stopped*"). The graphical interface also changes independently of the user when counting is going on (*modeless operating mode*).

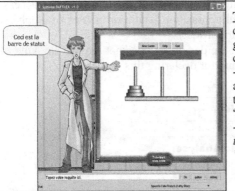

The towers of Hanoi game. The user can directly move the graphical elements of the game on the application area itself, or he/she can use natural language for:
- direct commands: on the left, one can see an illustration of the deictic capabilities of the agent responding to the direct command "*show me the status bar*"
- asking for information or help: "*what are the rules?*", "*can I revert*", "*play for me*", "*can we play with more disks?*",...

A web page browser. The user can browse and *edit* the 130 dynamic web pages via direct natural input:

"*modify the 22nd June*",
"*go to the project DAFT web page*",
"*please, who is Sansonnet?*".

Fig. 1. Three applications illustrating the versatility of the design of assistance tasks: a simple counting application (*top*), the towers of Hanoi game (*middle*) and a web page browser (*bottom*)

3 The DAFT-LEA Framework

DAFT (**D**ialogical **A**gent **F**ormal **T**alk) is the name of the formal language we defined
for managing dialogue with the user about the structure and functioning of the graphical interface (Fig. 2). Regarding the "embedding genericity criterion" identified
above, the graphical interface developer first has to declare a model of this graphical
application using the DAFT language. Then, the rational agent can be easily plugged
into this model. Regarding the "knowledge separation" criterion, the mediation between the user and the graphical interface is achieved along three levels (Fig. 2):

1. The linguistic analyzer receives questions typed in by the user and translates them
   into DAFT formal requests. This parser is specialized in the processing of questions asked by users when they encounter difficulties in the control and the operating of the components. It has been incrementally defined with a corpus collection.
2. The rational Agent is able of reasoning about the structure and the functions of the
   application that it can access only via its model. It receives as input formal requests
   defined in the DAFT language. The rational agent solves these requests by accessing values in the model of the graphical application (static properties of graphical
   components, dynamic values of state variables…).
3. The model of the graphical application: the developer does not require any kind of
   specific expertise in dialogue or reasoning for declaring this model.

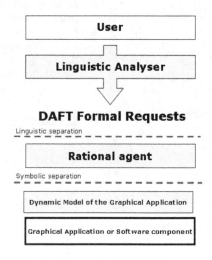

Fig. 2. Architecture for processing user's utterances about the structure and the functioning of a
graphical application. User's questions are parsed into the DAFT formal language, processed
by a rational agent who has access to the application via its dynamic model.

For an existing software component such as a Java applet, it is indeed first of all
necessary to define the symbolic model of this component, using the formalism provided by DAFT. It is a language of symbolic descriptions based on a classical S-
expressions formalism. The description can be viewed, at each step of the functioning,

as an *evolving tree structure* [7]. It is an object-oriented programming language which facilitates the translation between the structure of object oriented graphical components and the structure of the model.

In the three operating modes described above, the state of the component changes over time. Therefore, it must be the same for the state of the model if one wants to keep a semantic consistency in order to enable the rational agent to reason about the proper representation of the component and to answer user's questions. Maintaining this kind of semantic synchronicity between the component and its model is a main feature of the DAFT framework (Fig. 3).

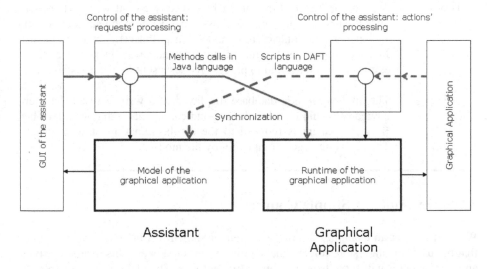

Fig. 3. The user can interact with the application via Natural Language utterances typed in the graphical user interface of the *assistant* (*left*) or via direct manipulation on the ordinary *graphical interface of the component* itself (*right*). Semantic consistency is maintained between the runtime of the component and the model the assistant has of the component (*bottom*). This enables the assistant to answer questions about the current state of the application

The semantic synchronicity at runtime is ensured in our model for the three possible operating modes (modal, modeless and dialogical). When the state of the effective graphical application evolves (modal or modeless cases), it is necessary to send an update event to the model (Fig. 3, dashed arrow). This is implemented by overloading the methods of the related actual objects. In our implementation, where we use components developed in the Java programming language, this process is carried out in a transparent way for the developer during the post-compilation phase of the code of the component. It then remains the responsibility of the model to recover these events and to interpret them in the model so as to update it. When the model evolves (dialogical case), we are in the opposite case: the operations altering the model must be mirrored by sending update events to the component (Fig. 3, plain arrow). In our implementation, it is achieved by remote invocation of Java objects methods. The designing process for the three illustrative applications is described in Table 1.

Table 1. Applying the DAFT framework to several illustrative application with different design processes

Application	Description of the design process
Simple counter	A Java component provided with autonomous processes (threads). The counting process is controlled by an on/off switch and a speed controller. The assistant and the graphical application are designed and coded at the same time.
Towers of Hanoi game	A Java component functioning in a strictly modal way: if the user does not interact, nothing happens. The Java component is coded in an independent context then modeled a posteriori. The code of the Java component is filtered in an automatic way in order to send events to the model and to process requests sent by the assistant.
Web page	The application is a database displayed as a web service. The user navigates within the base/the site and can update it dialogically. The Java component is reduced to the display function of web pages. The site is managed completely by the model.

4   An Example: A Simple Counter

We will take as an example, the first component shown in Fig. 1: a simple counter that the user can start, stop, reset or make going faster or slower. This is quite a trivial application but it will serve here our illustrative purpose. The main developing phases are:

i.   First the Java applet of the counter was developed ;
ii.   Then a Symbolic Model of this applet was developed (it was easy because here it was the same developer that created the applet and the model – note that in the Hanoi example (second example in Fig. 1.) *that is not the case*: the developer of the Hanoi applet never knew that its component had been 'dialogized') and the sub-objects of the model where carefully mapped *by-hand* towards the sub objects of the applet ; hence when an event occurs in the model (following a user's request), it is reported to the applet;
iii.   The code of the applet was filtered by a Java tool we have developped in order to automatically install the reverse mapping, i.e. from the sub objects of the applet towards the sub objects of the model; hence when an event occurs in the applet (the user operates the applet's GUI or internal functions change the state of the variables), it is reported in the model;
iv.   Finally the applet is embedded into the agent framework (see the GUI of the agent encompassing the applet GUI in Fig. 1.) and the agent is active.

Here is an excerpt of the scripting of the generic class $switch. This class defines an abstract model of a boolean value on which four operations can be done: on, off, switch (the not operator), and reset. An instance of the switch class is created in the counter in order to support a symbolic representation of the start/stop/reset functions of the counter.

```
// $switch is the name of the model class
// The Mathematica instructions below define an abstract
// representation of both the attributes and the perceptual features
// of the Java object

// referenceToJavaObject is the corresponding Java object
NEW[$switch, referenceToJavaObject, initialValueOfBoolean]:=

// Local variables are created
            Module[{run,buttonOn,buttonOff,buttonReset},

 (** instanciation of the subparts of the switch **)
// bool and button are names of generic classes
// start and stop are the names that are displayed
// on the buttons in the GUI
    NEW[$bool,run,"_status","running",initialValueOfBoolean];
    NEW[$button,buttonOn,"_bStart","start",DO[run,ON]&];
    NEW[$button,buttonOff,"_bStop","stop",DO[run,OFF]&];
    NEW[$button,buttonReset,"_bReset","reset",DO[run,RESET]&];

 (** attributes **)
    (* this maps the model-switch to the Java-switch *)
    $[JREF]=referenceToJavaObject;
    $[ISA]     = {SWITCH};
    $[PARTS]   = {run,buttonOn,buttonOff,buttonReset};
    $[BKGCOLOR]= "pinkColor";
    $[LAYOUT]  = FRAME[DOWN[run,buttonOn,buttonReset,buttonOff]];

 (** methods **)
    $[START,SCRIPT]  = DO[run,ON]&;
    $[STOP,SCRIPT]   = DO[run,OFF]&;
    $[SWITCH,SCRIPT] = DO[run,SWITCH]&;
    $[RESET,SCRIPT]  = DO[run,RESET]&;
    $]
```

This snippet of code illustrate the following features of our model:

- We use as an S-Expression language (Mathematica from Wolfram Research[®]). It is a powerful, completely dynamic, symbolic computing environment useful for rational agent introspection.
- In order to make easier for the developers the 'alignment' between the component and its symbolic model we used an object-oriented *notation* (one can recognize the notions of: class, inheritance, instantiations, attributes, methods);
- the classes are a library of predefined objects so that building the model of a component consists mainly in calling the constructors of the library with the appropriate arguments;
- the mapping of an instance of the class **$switch** to its Java counterpart is just implemented by the single line **$[JREF]=referenceToJavaObject**.
- No explicit linguistic information is filled in by the developer of the model in order to provide the Natural Language Unit with clues about the component: actually

this knowledge lays in the symbols of the attributes and methods (ISA, PARTS, LAYOUT, ...) that, contrary to object oriented programming conventions, cannot be chosen arbitrarily by the model designer but must be chosen from the Daft Model Ontology (DMO) that proposes a static list of concepts together with their lexical semantic (à la *Wordnet*). The same policy is applied to the right-part expressions where 'heads' are also to be chosen with care by the developer in the DMO (SCOPE, FRAME, ON, ...).

Suppose that the user enters the question "please could you tell what I can do with the switch on the right?", it will be analyzed and the main semantic parts of this question will be extracted as:

1. the speech act part: <ASK>
2. the predicate part : <USAGE>
3. the associative extensional reference part: <REF[Sbest, Mright, Qswitch]>

which would result in the complete DAFT formal request:

DAFT[<ASK>, <USAGE>, {<REF[Sbest, Mright, Qswitch]>}]

This formal request will be handled by the rational agent which will:

- First check for the existence of a non empty and not ambiguous referential domain (here there is only one switch, but in case there are several the Mright observatory would be convenient);
- then interpret the speech act (<ASK>) and call the usage-observer which in turn will browse the switch instance for methods returning {START, STOP, SWITCH, RESET};
- Finally, the result will be wrapped as a reply by the natural language production module, so that the answer to that question could be "*Well, you can do: start, stop, switch or reset operations with this switch.*"

We emphasize here, and it is our claim, that the Natural Language Unit does not have to be involved with the actual runtime. It just has to browse the dynamic symbolic model. However, this is not going without some drawbacks, since writing models are an extra effort of software development.

5   Conclusion and Future Research

We have presented a software engineering approach for the design of conversational agents for assistance tasks. Describing the graphical application via an abstract model enables to reason about it and hence provide assistance to the user. The three presented examples of applications were used to collect a corpus of 4300 user's requests (52 users between 22 and 43 years old, gender balanced). This corpus has been used to incrementally define the ontology used by the linguistic analyzer. 200 semantic classes have been identified involving requests, meta-communication, and perceptual properties of the components of the graphical interface.

In the future, we also intend to process indirect acts such as for the web page example: "Today a new member entered the team", "I cannot give my seminar on Monday", "the DAFT project has been cancelled".

We also plan to compare different non-verbal behaviors for providing assistance and evaluate the usefulness of the 2D embodied agent in such tasks.

References

1. Abrilian, S., Buisine, S., Rendu, C., Martin, J.-C.: Specifying Cooperation between Modalities in Lifelike Animated Agents. International Workshop on "Lifelike Animated Agents: Tools, Functions, and Applications", held in conjunction with the 7th Pacific Rim International Conference on Artificial Intelligence (PRICAI'02) (2002) Tokyo, Japan 3-8
2. Allen, J. F., Byron, D. K., Dzikosvska, M. O., Fergusson, G., Galescu L., Stent, A.: Towards conversational Human-Computer Interaction. AI magazine (2001)
3. Balzer, R., N., G.: Mediating Connectors. 19th IEEE Int Conf on Distributed Computing Systems Workshop (1999) Austin, Texas 73-77
4. Buisine, S., Abrilian, S., Martin, J.-C.: Evaluation of Individual Multimodal Behavior of 2D Embodied Agents in Presentation Tasks. From Brows to Trust. Evaluating Embodied Conversational Agents. Kluwer (2004)
5. Buisine, S., Martin, J.-C.: Children's and Adults' Multimodal Interaction with 2D Conversational Agents. CHI'2005 (2005) Portland, Oregon
6. Grechanik, M., Batory, D., Perry, D. E.: Integrating and reusing GUI-Driven applications. International conference on software reuse (2002) Austin, Texas
7. Sabouret, N., Sansonnet, J.-P.: Automated Answers to Questions about a Running Process. CommonSense'2001 (2001) New York 217-227
8. Sansonnet, J.-P., Sabouret, N., Pitel, G.: An Agent Design and Query Language dedicated to Natural Language Interaction. Poster session at AAMAS (2002) Bologna, Italy

Marve: A Prototype Virtual Human Interface Framework for Studying Human-Virtual Human Interaction

Sabarish Babu, Stephen Schmugge, Raj Inugala, Srinivasa Rao,
Tiffany Barnes, and Larry F. Hodges

Department of Computer Science, University of North Carolina at Charlotte,
Charlotte, NC 28223
{sbabu, sjschmug, rkinugal, srao3, tbarnes2, lfhodges}@uncc.edu

Abstract. Human to virtual human interaction is the next frontier in interface design, particularly for tasks that are social or collaborative in nature. Several embodied interface agents have been developed for specific social, place-related tasks, but empirical evaluations of these systems have been rare. In this work, we present Marve (Messaging And Recognition Virtual Entity), our general purpose Virtual Human Interface Framework, which integrates cutting-edge interface technologies into a seamless real-time system, to study human to virtual human interaction. Marve is a prototype of a real-time embodied, interactive, autonomous, virtual human interface agent framework. Marve "lives" next to the primary entrance of the Future Computing Lab. His primary tasks are to greet everyone who enters or leaves the lab, and to take and deliver messages to the students and faculty who work there. Marve uses computer vision techniques for passer-by detection, gaze tracking, and face recognition, and communicates via natural language. We present a preliminary empirical study of the basic elements of Marve, including interaction response times, recognition of friends, and ability to learn to recognize new people.

1 Introduction

Human to virtual human interfaces, while challenging to develop and evaluate, have the potential to revolutionize the accessibility, usability, and applicability of computers in everyday life. Since virtual humans are modeled after humans, these interfaces can use several modalities for communicating information, such as gestures and facial expression, which are "transparent" to the user [5]. Furthermore, research evidence suggests that people can achieve tasks effectively when the behavior and attitude of an interface agent is similar to a real human [18]. These benefits come from the strength of the virtual human interface metaphor and leverage people's experience with real social interaction to enrich the human-computer interaction.

Research has shown that humans often interact with computers as they do with other people, according to social rules and stereotypes, even when the interface is not a virtual human [3]. These studies suggest that the social factors governing human-human interaction may also apply to human-computer interactions. Some of these factors, including voice, appearance, behavior, and personality, may have particular

T. Panayiotopoulos et al. (Eds.): IVA 2005, LNCS 3661, pp. 120–133, 2005.
© Springer-Verlag Berlin Heidelberg 2005

importance in social or collaborative tasks, such as those performed by virtual computer aided assistants, virtual information experts, and virtual tutors [6]. However, research suggests that decisions regarding what qualities are necessary in effective human-virtual human interaction such as appearance, personality, and behaviors are frequently based on introspection rather than careful consideration of the tasks and users of these systems [1, 6].

Human-virtual human interaction research is challenging in several ways. Until recently, the technology to create multimodal, embodied interface agents was developed individually, and methods to evaluate such interfaces have not been standardized or uniformly applied [1]. In addition, research in this area is scattered among a variety of fields, including agent systems, animated characters, user emotions, graphics and animation, conversational interface agents, animated pedagogical agents, and human factors involving agent interaction from a socio-psychology perspective [1].

As Thalmann, et al. point out in their work on integrating rendering, animation, and action selection to simulate virtual human behavior [9, 10], it is a challenge to build a multimodal system that works in real time. A working virtual human interface framework requires the integration of techniques from a variety of disciplines, including speech recognition, animation and rendering, planning and discourse modeling, unobtrusive forms of human identification, and real-time speech synthesis. To effectively study human-virtual human interaction, an extensible application framework that supports all of these aspects of a virtual human interface agent is needed.

We present Marve, our Virtual Human Interface Framework that incorporates the existing relevant technologies to create real-time virtual human interface agents. Using Marve, researchers can begin to understand the relevance and importance of these technologies in human-virtual human interaction. We believe that Marve will facilitate the systematic study of both the tasks for which virtual human interfaces are particularly suited, and the aspects of these interfaces that are most important to the effective accomplishment of these tasks.

Currently, Marve is a working system that combines cutting edge speech, graphics, and vision technologies with an extensible discourse model to:

- Detect the presence of people as they pass by or stop to interact.
- Unobtrusively recognize people to personalize behavior.
- Interact using a combination of spoken natural language with non-verbal cues that include appropriate eye contact, facial expressions, and gestures.
- Support turn-taking, feedback, and repair mechanisms, as well as task-specific planning and execution.

Marve performs the tasks of a virtual receptionist, and mimics human-to-human interaction using *face-to-face conversation* as a metaphor. Marve is able to take and deliver messages, announcements, and reminders to his friends, and to greet passers-by. However, since Marve is designed to be extensible, we may continue to add additional behaviors and capabilities to Marve's repertoire.

1.1 Related Work

As Justine Cassell [5] pointed out in 2000, "To date, empirical evaluations of any kind of embodied interfaces have been few, and their results have been equivocal." In

2002, Isbester and Doyle identified the need for consensus, and developed a taxonomy of embodied conversational agent research. As part of this work, Isbester and Doyle defined a set of common expectations and criteria for describing and evaluating research and design advances in each category of research in conversational characters [1]. In particular, they point out that, for social interfaces, quantitative measures of speed and evaluation of agent's achievement of tasks are significant [1].

In 2002, Catrambone et al. created a rudimentary experimental framework for studying anthropomorphic agents [3]. Their framework employed Wizard of Oz techniques to interact with users doing a particular task in three separate conditions: 1) voice, 2) voice and a picture, and 3) voice and an animated head. Their experimental results using this framework suggested that a user's perception of the agent was strongly influenced by the user's task and the agent's role in the task. They also noted that user performance and satisfaction were not significantly affected by the appearance of the agent.

These studies highlight the need for a framework that supports autonomous embodied agents for the express purpose of studying human-virtual human interaction. Marve is built to include many of the aspects of existing embodied agent systems, including Gandalf [4], Rea [5], Valerie [14], and Jacob [8], providing a general purpose framework for investigating human-virtual human interaction without having to build embodied agents from scratch each time.

In 1998 researchers at MIT built Gandalf, a communicative humanoid agent to guide planetary exploration [4]. Users see Gandalf as a hand and face on a small monitor, and interact with Gandalf using natural speech and gesture. User gaze and gesture are tracked using ocular tracking and a body suit, respectively. Gandalf's behavior rules for face-to-face conduct are derived from psychology literature on human-human interaction.

Rea, built in 2000 at MIT, is a virtual real estate agent [5]. Rea's head and torso are visible on a projected screen as she displays pictures and layouts of properties for sale, and points out and discusses their features. Rea uses background subtraction to detect the presence of users but does not use any face recognition or gaze tracking. Rea uses complex conversational models to engage in subtle human-like conversational patterns, and also exhibits several nonverbal behaviors.

Valerie from CMU is a virtual receptionist who gives directions, answers the phone, and even gossips [14]. Valerie's face is displayed on a flat-screen monitor and users interact with her using keyboard input. Jacob is a virtual instruction agent for the Tower of Hanoi problem [8]. Jacob's head and torso are displayed on a monitor and he uses natural speech for interaction.

Each of these interface agents include characteristics that are important for both perception and conveying information. Brave and Nass have suggested that any interface that ignores a user's emotional state or fails to manifest the appropriate emotion can dramatically impede performance and risk being perceived as cold, socially inept, untrustworthy, and incompetent [11]. Catrambone, et al. suggest that a multimodal interface that includes voice, face, and body can manifest a wider range of emotions than is possible in purely textual interfaces [3]. Using both speech and gesture also contributes to making embodied agents seem more lifelike and believable [6].

Non-verbal cues are important in the perception of the agent, but they can also be used to convey important information. For example, gaze gives cues in conversational turn taking [5], a nod conveys understanding, and propositional hand gestures and facial expressions can direct the user's attention [6].

Marve also incorporates these features, using natural speech for communication, and displaying both the head and torso to enable non-verbal cues and gestures. Like Rea, Marve uses background subtraction to detect passers-by, but also learns to recognize frequent users, using computer vision techniques similar to those in Argus [15]. Computer vision is also used for gaze tracking. Gandalf, on the other hand, uses wired devices to track human gaze and gesture, which can be both cumbersome and costly, and difficult to upgrade as technologies improve. With vision-based tracking, when the software for gesture and/or gaze tracking improves, the vision component of Marve can simply be interchanged.

2 Marve Software and Hardware Framework

Marve provides the infrastructure for both natural language and visual input for human-virtual human interaction. Marve utilizes best-existing, widely available components and agent technologies to ensure high quality graphics, speech recognition and generation, animation, vision, and virtual human representation.

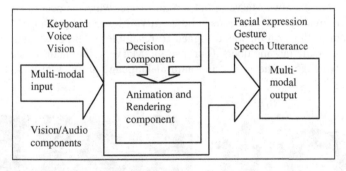

Fig. 1. Marve's Software and Hardware Framework

Marve consists of four major components: vision, audio, rendering and animation, and decision. In order to provide the processing capability necessary to run the system for long periods of time at high frame rates (approximately 40 FPS), the four components are distributed on three PCs. The vision and audio components each run on separate PCs, and the third PC is used for the rendering and animation, and decision. As seen in Fig. 1, the vision and audio components communicate with the decision component over a network using UDP protocol and the VRPN library [12]. The decision component processes the messages sent by the audio and vision components and decides a course of action based on the current state. The decided event is executed by the rendering and animation component.

The vision component of Marve consists of a camera, algorithms from the OpenCV library for face recognition and for detecting gaze direction, and a custom adaptive background subtraction algorithm to detect passers-by. Gaze direction is determined using Haar Face detection. The Hidden Markov Model (HMM) method, trained using images taken of "friends" at random times of day, is used for face recognition [13]. A Sony DFW-VL500 camera, placed on top of the screen, is used for video capture. The viewing extent of the camera was marked on the floor and a line on the floor indicated how far from Marve a user should stand in order for his face to be detected by the vision component. This provided visual cues to the user regarding Marve's perceptual ability to detect the presence of and recognize a user. A wooden wall was placed on the other side of the door opposite Marve to serve as a consistent background for the vision component. Users were told that in order to interact with Marve they needed to stand in the marked floor area.

The speech recognition module was built using Microsoft SAPI and SpeechStudio library [16]. An Audio-technica ATR-20 cardioid unidirectional microphone captures audio input. An interactive 3D character from Haptek Corp. [17] was used to create and animate Marve, and openGL was used to render the graphics.

3 Overview of Marve

Marve's prototype tasks resemble that of a virtual lab receptionist. Marve is presented on a 21-inch monitor next to our lab entrance, an ideal location for his main tasks: greeting lab members and taking and delivering messages, reminders, and announcements. Figure 2 shows Marve in his virtual office, which is decorated to convey Marve's individuality, and hence his believability. Marve's appearance, a quality that can be varied in the system, was designed to resemble a college student to promote camaraderie with lab members (our users). Marve's interactions are multimodal, taking advantage of the visual and natural language abilities provided in his framework.

Fig. 2. Screenshots of Marve greeting a user, and interacting with a user

4 Exploring Sample Interaction Scenarios

In this section we describe typical interactions with Marve. Currently, Marve's role is to greet people as they enter or leave the Future Computing Lab, and to take and deliver messages to students and faculty who work in the lab. Greeting people, message taking, and message delivery were chosen as a proof-of-concept tasks that resembled socially interactive tasks that a lab receptionist might carry out. For friends (people whose faces Marve recognizes) there are three scenarios of interaction; (i) they can leave messages, (ii) they can listen to the messages that another friend has left for them, or (iii) they can get acknowledgment that their message to another friend has been picked up. For users that Marve doesn't recognize (strangers) there is a different interaction scenario. During all his interactions with users, Marve maintains gaze with the users as they move within the viewing extent of the camera.

Table 1 lists an excerpt from an example interaction with Marve. In this excerpt, a user, Sab, wants to leave a message for Amy with Marve.

Table 1. Message scenario: Sab, a user, wishes to leave a message for Amy

Person	Verbal Output	Non-Verbal Output
Marve	*Good Morning! (Greeting based on time of day)*	*Marve waves at Sab.*
Sab	*Hi Marve.*	
Marve	*Hello Sab. Hope you are doing well today.*	*Marve lifts his hand up.*
Marve	*You have no messages. If you would like to leave messages please say "record message" or press the dash key!*	
Sab	*Record message.*	
Marve shows a menu on his left with list of names that the user could choose from (Figure 3).		
Marve	*Please choose from the menu on the left, and say the name of the person.*	*Marve gestures to his left to show the menu.*
Marve	*Please speak into the microphone and say "Conclude" when you are done leaving a message!*	
Sab	*Amy.*	
Marve	*Do you want to leave a message for Amy?*	
Sab	*Yes.*	
Marve nods his head to convey understand and displays text "Recording Message" to indicate to the user that audio recording has been initiated. As observed above, Marve also verifies to make sure he has understood the right command.		
Sab says the message for Amy to Marve, which is recorded as an audio file by Marve. Sab ends his message by saying...		
Sab	*Conclude.*	
Marve	*Thank You. If you would like to leave another message please say your choice from the menu.*	*Marve gestures left to show the menu (see Figure 3).*
Sab	*Thank you.*	*Sab walks away from Marve.*
Marve	*Goodbye Sab, I will see you around!*	*Marve smiles and waves.*
After Sab walks away, Marve turns around to the computer behind him in the virtual environment and sends a message to Amy, notifying her that she has a message with Marve from Sab. During this time he also displays a text on the screen "Marve is Busy", to notify users that he is currently busy working on his computer.		

As mentioned in the preceding interaction scenario, if a friend wishes to leave a message for another friend, Marve asks the friend to say "record message". If the friend gives the command, Marve displays a menu with the names of all the friends that Marve can take messages for. Messages are recorded as an audio file and an email notification is sent to the recipient informing them that they have a message from the friend with Marve. Friends can also leave reminders or memos for themselves, or announcements for the lab, with Marve.

After the interaction scenario mentioned above, the next instance Marve encounters Amy he notifies her that she has a message from Sab and plays the message upon her request. He then asks her if she wants to leave messages as in scenario 1. After Amy has picked up her message from Marve, the next instance Marve encounters Sab he provides visual acknowledgment to Sab by showing the picture of Amy taken when she picked up her message from Marve (Figure 4). Marve makes a hand gesture at the picture, and tells Sab that his message to Amy has been delivered.

Fig. 3. Screen shot of Marve showing the menu from which the user can choose who to leave a message for

Fig. 4. Screen shot of Marve showing the user an image of the person to whom a message was delivered

When Marve interacts with someone he is not trained to recognize (stranger), or if Marve identifies a known friend as a stranger, he asks the stranger to say his/her name, records the name of the stranger, and sends an email containing an image of the unknown person to the administrator of the system. The administrator, a human, can choose to create a user profile in the system for the stranger.

5   Interaction Discourse Planning and Cognitive Modeling

Marve's decision component is implemented using behavior states, as have been proposed for other conversational systems [4, 6]. Each behavior state, which corresponds to a particular conversational function such as greeting a user, is modeled as a combination of synchronized events consisting of gestures, body movements, posture, facial expression based on emotion, and speech utterance. They are parameterized, allowing the interface agent to customize behavior based on context and user. The decision component maintains a user model for each user, which contains user specific meta-data such as the status of the person, conversational content such as personalized greetings for each user, and task-based information such as the number of messages a user has. These behavior states are interchangeable, since the semantic information and temporal aspects can be modeled based on the contextual information. An example formulation of the behavior state structure for greeting users is provided below;

```
behavior_state_ID greetingUser(user_name, status){
   IF status(student) : interaction_behavior = informal;
   ELSE IF status(professor | staff) : interaction_behavior = formal;
   Say("Hello "+user_name);
   IF interaction_behavior = informal
   EvokeGestures_and_FacialExpressions(Happy1,Laugh1,HandGesture1);
      ELSE
      EvokeGestures_and_FacialExpressions(Happy2,Smile1,HandGesture2);
   Say("How are you doing today?");
}
```

Rules pertaining to the interaction are also encapsulated within the behavior state structure, which are used to define interaction behavior and emotions of the interface agent. The rules defined within the behavior state structure also help in associating emotions and other non-verbal conversational signals with the social role of the interface agent.

The basic building blocks of the non-verbal cues evoked in the behavior states are pre-scripted using key-framing techniques afforded by the Haptek [17] agent animation coding tool. The gesture space consists of deictic, propositional, beat, and interactional gestures pertaining to initiation of conversation, and signoff. The facial expression space consists of nods, smiles, frowns, and gaze (to direct user's attention). Animations for blinking and breathing are continuously evoked by the Haptek motion generation engine. Speech utterance is implemented using Microsoft text-to-speech to generate Marve's voice, and the motion generation engine deciphers the appropriate viseme for the current phoneme for lip synchronization from the content. Speech utterance is tailored to provide appropriate intonation and pitch. Emotions are expressed through facial expression, verbal output, and gestures, all of which are encapsulated within the behavior states.

| *Cough* | *Clears Throat* | *Yawn* |

Fig. 5. Sample passive behaviors exhibited by Marve

Marve's framework provides the capability to define and execute pre-scripted passive behaviors. When Marve is not busy interacting with a user, he performs a series of non-verbal and verbal behaviors that resemble those of a human waiting for someone. These behaviors provide users with a sense of behavioral fidelity that is necessary when interface agents are deployed in ever-present, socially interactive systems, such as virtual receptionists and virtual exhibitors. These passive non-interactive behaviors were scripted as a state-machine of behavior states and are looped to play back every 20 minutes. These baseline behaviors include coughing, sniffing, clearing throat, yawning, smiling, glancing around, and humming a tune (see Figure 5).

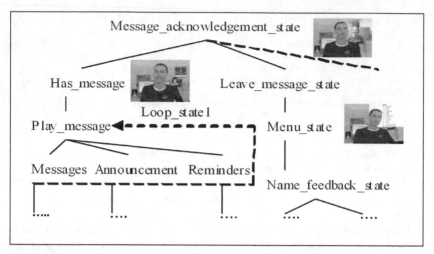

Fig. 6. Tree showing a snippet of the cognitive model of Marve's knowledge base used for discourse planning including the behavior states that encapsulate gesture, facial expression, speech utterance, and emotion

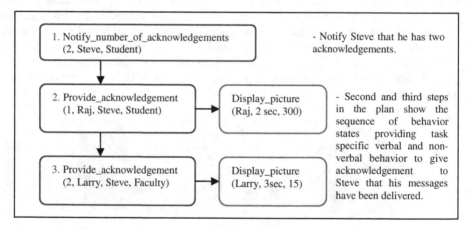

Fig. 7. Segment of the discourse plan instance formulated by the planner using the cognitive model showing the sequence of behavior states parameterized with context specific information towards the goal of providing acknowledgement to a user (Steve) that his messages were delivered

Marve's decision component includes a higher level cognitive model for user interaction, which is represented as a tree of linked behavior states. The tree based cognitive model for discourse planning is tailored to be interchangeable depending on the choice of tasks performed by the embodied agent. The cognitive model could also be layered to accomplish sub-goals of a particular task. The decision component keeps track of the state of the interaction and execution of the appropriate behavior state upon action choice and user input. The cognitive model discourse tree structure serves as a rich task-based knowledge base using which a discourse plan can be initias a rich task-based knowledge base using which a discourse plan can be initiated. The decision component of Marve employs a planner which utilizes the cognitive model to devise a plan of interaction which consists of a task-specific and context-specific tree instance towards realizing a specific goal or a sub-goal. An action scheduler processes the task specific behavior state as dictated by the plan. In order to ensure that global status of interaction is maintained by the decision component, the action scheduler notifies the decision component as to the current status of the interaction such as what behavior state is currently being processed and changes in context specific primitives. These context specific primitives include data such as message ID of the message currently being played or the duration of the message. Based on the plan instance the action scheduler then evokes the rendering and animation component to execute the state-specific visual animation and audio output to the user. Upon execution the animation and rendering component sends a message back to the action scheduler that multi-modal output is complete. During the time when the rendering and animation component is realizing the behavioral actions, the decision component has the ability to asynchronously process the next interaction event or user input. However, if an agent is waiting for user input, baseline human-like pre-scripted behaviors are initiated in order to maintain visual and behavioral fidelity.

One of the advantages of the cognitive model tree structure is that it enables Marve to perform context specific grammar switching, which helps in increasing speech recognition accuracy. The grammar file is modified based on interaction-specific behavior states defined within the cognitive model. Behavior states can also be repeated within the plan instance as devised by the planner such that the same behavior can be performed consecutively, for example; if the user has multiple messages that need to be played the verbal and non-verbal behavioral actions associated with playing a message for the user must be executed for each instance upon request. A snippet of the tree representing a part of Marve's cognitive model knowledge base is shown in Figure 6. Figure 7 shows an example of a goal oriented plan instance devised by the planner.

If a user decides to walk away and disengage in conversation with the interface agent, Marve is robust enough to save all the interaction specific information about the user, terminate the current behavior state, and initiate the next appropriate behavior state. For example; if a friend walks away in the middle of leaving a message for another friend, Marve stops recording, saves the message, and says goodbye with the appropriate termination behavior state being animated. In the case above, within the system framework the action scheduler is notified to skip the rest of the queue of behavior states within the plan instance and process the conversation termination state with the user. The rendering and animation component executes verbal and non-verbal signals from its current behavior to the end of dialogue termination.

6 Initial Evaluation

Isbester and Doyle point out that, for social interfaces, quantitative measures of speed and evaluation of an agent's achievement of tasks are significant [1]. For example, if Marve takes too long to recognize a user and respond to them by name, he will probably not be an effective interface agent. In this section we present quantitative measures of Marve's performance with respect to recognition accuracy, response times, and ability to learn to recognize new friends.

6.1 Recognition Accuracy

The vision component of an embodied agent framework must recognize users accurately in order to initiate personalized behavior and to carry out user specific subgoals of the task. Marve has to be able to recognize his friends correctly and consistently in order to accurately carry out the task of taking and delivering messages between friends. We used the following protocol for evaluating recognition accuracy of Marve's vision component. We defined two sets of people, known (friends) and unknown (strangers). Friends are members of the lab whom Marve is trained to recognize. Strangers are unknown to Marve and each was chosen to match a friend in terms of ethnicity, gender, and approximate similarity of physical features. Recognition of each friend and stranger was tested ten times. Friends and strangers attended five sessions, during which they interacted with Marve twice at each session. In order to test the accuracy of recognition at various times of the day, the sessions were held at 11am, 2pm, 5pm, 7pm, and 9pm. Marve recognized his friends 97% of the time (s.d. = 6.7), as shown in Table 2. Marve accurately identified strangers as people he did not know 72.4% of the time (s.d. = 23.3), also shown in Table 2.

Table 2. Accuracy rates for recognizing friends and for recognizing someone is a stranger. Interaction event response times in milliseconds (ms) for greeting passers-by, recognition, and saying goodbye are also reported for friends and strangers.

Friends	Recognition Accuracy(%)	Response times (ms)			Strangers	Recognition Accuracy(%)	Response times (ms)		
		Greet Passerby	Recognize User	Say Goodbye			Greet Passerby	Recognize User	Say Goodbye
Aditya	100	83.8	3101.33	78.8	Karthik	100	85.7	2991.8	75.8
Amy	100	86	2795.11	77	Ellen	100	85.9	2387	74.6
Caroline	100	79.75	2847.2	75.2	Jeff	100	85.7	2852.5	75.3
Dong	100	79.9	2925.4	78.7	James	80	85.7	4061	78.9
Jonathan	100	82.4	2616.8	72.5	David	80	85.75	2802.75	71
Larry	100	73	2619.3	76.6	Santosh	70	83.9	2976.2	78.6
Sab	100	83.57	3004	76.6	Dongwan	56	79.4	3369.8	70
Steve	100	85.3	3621.7	80.3	Jen	50	85.5	2632.7	85.75
Jenny	90	82.4	2843.3	83.3	Prasanna	50	92	2926.4	77.75
Raj	80	77.8	3468.3	80.3	Pratiba	37.5	76.6	2846.9	76.9
Mean	97.0	81.4	2984.2	77.9		72.4	84.6	2984.7	76.5
S.D.	6.7	3.9	333.5	3.0		23.3	4.1	454.7	4.4

6.2 Response Time

Marve should respond to input events and to unexpected changes in users' interactions immediately and appropriately in order to facilitate continuous human-virtual human interaction. One of our design goals was for Marve to respond to events within a time frame similar to that of a real human's response. We evaluated the verbal and non-verbal response times of Marve in milliseconds for major events in the system such as greeting a passerby, recognizing a friend or a stranger, and saying goodbye when someone walks away. In each of the categories the response time is measured from the time the user walks up to Marve and is detected, to the time when Marve initiates an appropriate verbal and/or non-verbal response. The response times for greeting passers-by, recognition, and saying goodbye for both friends and strangers are shown, respectively, in Table 2.

The mean response times for greeting a passerby and saying goodbye as someone walks away are under a tenth of a second. The mean response time for recognizing a friend or recognizing that someone is a stranger is less than three seconds. To keep this recognition processing delay from being noticeable, a design choice was made to initiate an immediate greeting based on time of day. By the time this initial greeting is concluded, Marve has completed the recognition task and can respond appropriately.

6.3 Learning New Friends

Real humans are capable of meeting and remembering the names of new friends. Marve also has this capability. When Marve recognizes someone as a stranger, he captures an image of that person and an audio file with the name of the stranger. The image captured is used for training the system to recognize the new person. Typically it takes more than a single image for the system to recognize a new friend consistently. To determine the number of times a stranger must introduce himself to Marve before Marve begins recognizing him consistently as a friend, we devised the following protocol.

1. A single random image of the new person is used to train the vision component.
2. That person is asked to interact with Marve twice to see if Marve recognizes him.
3. If that person is not recognized both times, then another random image of that person is added to the system and the experiment is repeated starting at step 2.
4. If the person is recognized in both trials, then eight more trials are performed and accuracy of recognition is noted.
5. If recognition accuracy is less than 100% for those ten trials, then another image is added to the system, and the experiment is repeated starting from step 2.
6. If the recognition accuracy is 100% then another image is added to the system, and the experiment is repeated from step 2 till 100% accuracy is obtained in three consecutive iterations starting from step 2.

A friend was defined as anyone for whom Marve could maintain 100% recognition accuracy over three iterations. The minimum number of images needed to recognize a friend was defined as the number of images needed to do the first group of ten correct recognitions in a row.

The mean number of visits necessary before Marve recognized a user was eight, although this varied highly (s.d. 4.16). We noticed that recognition accuracy can be affected by shadows that fall on a user's face due to the light source position relative to the user's position.

7 Summary and Future Work

We have described Marve, a prototype Virtual Human Interface Framework for studying human-virtual human interaction. Whereas most virtual human interface agents are specifically designed to cater to a specific contextual need, our extensible framework is designed to support a variety of tasks facilitated through a conversational interface. Our current framework provides an extensible and detailed infrastructure, including a rich task based discourse model that enables researchers to build and deploy virtual human interface agents and study interactions between the virtual human and his human interlocutor. Currently Marve's perceptual capabilities include vision and speech recognition. Marve's framework handles input modalities as distributed components facilitating ease of adding new input modalities when necessary. Marve's proof-of-concept tasks are similar to a real-time ever-present virtual receptionist. Marve detects the presence of people as they pass by or stop to interact, recognizes his friends, and is capable of learning to recognize new friends gradually. Marve can interact with users using a combination of verbal and non-verbal cues that include a natural language interface, maintaining eye contact with the user, facial expressions and gestures. When conversing with users, Marve employs key conversational functions such as turn-taking feedback, and repair mechanisms, which are built into Marve's decision component. Marve's response times for interacting with someone who walks up to or away from him are on the order of less than one tenth of a second for greeting someone or saying good-by. Marve recognizes his friends consistently (97% recognition rate) and calls them by name within three seconds. Marve is not as good at recognizing that he does not know someone (72.4% recognition rate).

Currently we are conducting user studies to determine which tasks are engaging or interesting for users to stop by and interact with Marve. Marve's task capabilities are being extended to include a useful task (messaging), an entertaining task (jokes), and small-talk (talk about movies and weather). In future work we plan to extend Marve's capabilities to include more meaningful or truly interactive tasks that will be designed and tested using this framework. Future work will also include conducting user studies that measure the effectiveness of and user satisfaction with embodied interface agents.

Acknowledgments

The authors wish to thank the members and friends of the Future Computing Lab for taking time to interact with Marve and Amy C. Ulinski for producing the demonstration video.

References

1. Isbester, K., and Doyle, P.: Design and Evaluation of Embodied Conversational Agents: A Proposed Taxonomy. AAMAS Workshop: Embodied Conversatinal Agents (2002).
2. Nass, C., Steuer, J., and Tauber, E.: Computers are social actors. Proceedings of CHI `94, Boston MA (1994).

3. Catrambone, R., Stasko, J., and Xiao, J.: Anthropomorphic Agents as a User Interface Paradigm: Experimental Findings and a Framework for Research. Proceedings of CogSci 2002, (2002) 166-171.
4. Thorisson, K.: Real-time decision making in multimodal face-to-face communication. Proceedings of the Second International Conference on Autonomous Agents, Minneapolis, MN (1998) 16-23.
5. Cassell, J.: Embodied conversational interface agents. Communications of ACM 43 (2000) 70-78.
6. Cassell, J., Sullivan, J., Prevost, S., and Churchill, E.: *Embodied Conversational Agents.* MIT Press, Cambridge, MA (2000).
7. Badler, N., Bindiganavale, R., Allbeck, J., Schuler, W., Zhao, L., Lee, S., Shin, H., and Palmer, M.: Parameterized action representation and natural language instructions for dynamic behavior modification of embodied agents. AAAI (1999).
8. Evers, M., and Nijholt, A.: Jacob – An animated instruction agent in virtual reality. Proceedings 3rd International Conference on Multimodal Interfaces (ICMI 2000), (2000) 526-533.
9. Thalmann, D.: The Virtual Human as a Multimodal Interface. Proceedings of Advanced visual interfaces, (2000) 14-20.
10. Ulicny, B., and Thalmann, D.: Crowd simulation for virtual heritage. Proceedings of the First International Workshop on 3D Virtual Heritage, (2002) 28-32.
11. Brave, S., and Nass, C.: Emotion in human-computer interaction. The Human-Computer Interaction Handbook: Fundamentals, Evolving Technologies and Emerging Applications (chap. 4). Hillside, NJ, (2002).
12. Taylor, R. M., II, Hudson, T. C., Seeger, A., Webber, H., Juliano, J., and Helser, A. T.: VRPN: a device-independent, network-transparent VR peripheral system. Proceedings of ACM symposium on Virtual reality software and technology, ACM Press, (2001) 55-61.
13. Nefian, A. V., Hayes, M. H.: An Embedded HMM-Based Approach for Face Detection and Recognition. Proceedings of IEEE International Conference on Acoustics, Speech, and Signal Processing, 6 (1999) 3553-3556.
14. http://www.roboceptionist.com
15. 15 Sukthankar, R., Stockton, R.: Argus: The Digital Doorman. Proceedings of IEEE International Conference on Intelligent Systems, (2001) 14-19.
16. http://www.speechstudio.com
17. http://www.haptek.com
18. Takeuchi, Y. and Katagiri, Y.: Social Character Design for Animated Agents. RO-MAN99 (1999).

A Knowledge-Based Scenario Framework to Support Intelligent Planning Characters

Paul Hsueh-Min Chang[1], Yu-Hung Chien[1], Edward Chao-Chun Kao[2], and Von-Wun Soo[1,2,3]

[1] Department of Computer Science,
[2] Institute of Information Systems and Applications,
Nation Tsing Hua University,
101, Section 2, Guangfu Rd., 300 Hsinchu, Taiwan
[3] Department of Computer Science, National University of Kaohsiung,
700, Kaohsiung University Rd., 811 Kaohsiung, Taiwan
{pchang, sot, edkao, soo}@cs.nthu.edu.tw

Abstract. Agent technologies have been successfully applied to craft believable characters in interactive scenarios. However, intelligent characters specialized for a controlled scenario with a predefined story are inadequate for open-ended scenarios. The key to deal with the open-endedness problem lies in the characters' ability to understand and analyze unexpected situations. Thus, an explicit representation of the environment is crucial. We found ontologies in the form of interconnected concepts to be an appropriate high-level representation because it enables character agents to reason about the world through inference. This paper proposes a knowledge-based framework for the construction of agent-based scenarios. The physical properties of the environment are dynamically converted to instances of concepts. We also show how an intelligent planning character, without any implicit knowledge about the scenario, can exploit the resources in the environment to make plans. With ontology support, characters show better adaptability and utilize the environment more creatively.

1 Introduction

Many approaches to agent-based virtual scenarios exist, featuring virtual characters playing roles in a story. Although they all share cosmetic resemblances, in essence these approaches often have very different goals in mind. Some systems aim to present a drama to the audience [5], while others focus on user participation [13][18]. Some systems aim to preserve the storyline and to deal with exceptions [5][15], while others allow the user to somewhat influence the progress of the story. Some work on modeling a sophisticated short scenario [13], while others try to enhance the liveliness of a long journey [9]. These different goals influence design decisions on range of potential outcomes of the scenarios.

However, few works to date have allowed the scenario to evolve in ways the system designer do not foresee. Usually the story progresses either linearly or

T. Panayiotopoulos et al. (Eds.): IVA 2005, LNCS 3661, pp. 134–145, 2005.
© Springer-Verlag Berlin Heidelberg 2005

along many possible but still predefined directions. In a very short scenario, the system designer may conceive and write down all possible outcomes of each decision made by either agent-based characters or human players, so that each action brings about reasonable consequences. However when the scenario becomes longer and larger in scale, or when the characters become more autonomous, the human designer loses control of the direction of story development unless she restrict the actions and their outcomes. Nevertheless, stories with restricted possibilities often leave human players wondering what the result would differ if they could act otherwise. Such "what-ifs" are central to a player's experience about a story, especially in an open-ended scenarios (such as in open-ended role-playing games) where empowered players act and take responsibility of the consequences. As the consequence of the emphasis on the autonomy of *both* users and virtual agents, players, non-player characters and the environment collaborate to create a story rather than follow one that a system designer has predefineed.

The major challenge of this approach, thus, lies in the requirement that characters and the environment must respond reasonably to a broad range of actions. As a result, if one decides to build such a multiagent system where software agents represents characters in the story, these agents will have to reason about the world and make plans dynamically rather than follow predefined scripts. Planning agents can show better adaptability than script-following agents because the former do not need to know in advance everything in the environment in order to exhibit reasonable behaviors; instead, they retrieve information from the environment, generate intentions and emotions, and employ objects in the environment for their plans. The ability to utilize the environment, however, requires the character agents to first understand the meaning and functionality of environment objects and relate them to their plans. Thus, the planner of a character agent must interact with the environment model to operate in virtual scenarios.

This paper presents a layered framework for scenario construction, emphasizing the concept layer that provides character agents with ontology-based environmental information to support planning and inference. A character agent equipped with a planner can use ontological inference to associate objects in the world with his goal and build a plan from the objects as soon as he enters the environment. Thus, the design of characters does not depend on a specific scenario. Instead, characters can function in different scenarios with little or no modification. The concept layer, supporting the planning agents, provides flexibility of design, because it decouples the development of character agents from that of the environment. It also provides the adaptability of characters, because it describes objects and actions in terms of instances of concepts that make situations understandable to character agents. The conceptual model includes physical concepts that reflects the physical circumstances and social concepts that reflect the social situation of the scenario, but the scope of this paper covers only the former.

The remaining sections of this paper describe the framework in detail. The next section introduces the layered architecture which separates decouples the agent mind from physical reality with the help of the middle layer of concepts. Section 3 presents the ontology schema based on Web Ontology Language (OWL) [16] as a format to represent commonsense knowledge in the environment. With this ontology support, a traditional backward-search planner can deal with a wide variety of situations. Section 4 illustrates with an example how a the planner works with the concept layer. Section 5 concludes this paper.

2   Overview of the Framework

Our framework for scenario construction consists of three pluggable layers. The reality layer at the bottom models the physical environment. The concept layer in the middle maps aspects of the environment to concepts in the ontology. The minds of character agents, comprising the top layer, can use the concepts to reason about the world. Fig. 1 illustrates the framework with a simple example about overcoming fear in a dark room. The following subsections briefly describes each layer. We implemented a prototype of this framework based on Java Agent Development Framework (JADE) [2]; the reader is referred to [6] for detailed information about the design and implementation this cognitive architecture.

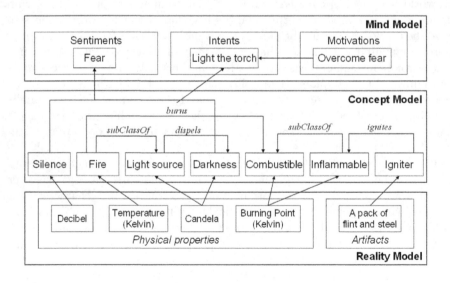

Fig. 1. Overview of the three-layer scenario framework

2.1   The Reality Layer

Unless the scenario is reduced to merely conversation between characters, it will need a model of physical environment in which character agents are situated. The complexity of the model depends on how realistic an environment the scenario requires. For example, the reality layer can model the environment as physical attributes, such as sound in decibels, temperature in kelvins, and hardness, luminance, etc., and employ approximations of physical laws to model the change of these physical properties. A set of mapping functions map these physical aspects, often in numerical form, to discrete concepts in the concept layer. For example, a mapping function can accept a low luminance value in the atmosphere as input and return an instance of the concept Darkness. The mapping function also returns a similarity value, indicating how much the thing resembles an ideal instance of the concept. However, some artificial objects, such as a pack of flint and steel, have delicate design and would not fit in a concept using simple physical properties. Thus, the reality layer models such things as *artifacts* that directly map to a concept without need to go through numerical calculations. Note that a designer of the reality layer can model environments in any way she desires to, as long as her model can correspond to the concepts.

2.2 The Concept Layer

The concept layer contains a copy of the concept model which specifies the relations among physical concepts, or between physical concepts and actions. The connections among concepts essentially comprises knowledge, for the mind cannot reason over isolated concepts, as psychologists and educationalists suggested [3][14]. The connections between concepts fall into two types: ontological relations and causal rules. Ontological relations include both the hierarchy of concepts and the causal relations between instances of concepts. Concept hierarchy defines the subclass relations among concepts, while causal relations describe the effect a specific instance can cause on another instance. "Key k unlocks Lock l" exemplifies such a causal relation. Causal rules, on the other hand, represent the effect that *all* instances of a concept can cause on *all* instances of another. "Fire burns Combustible" exemplifies a causal rule. Causal relations rules also come with a triggering action and an effect. Through the concept model, character agents can infer what they need to achieve a goal. For example, the character knows through the concept layer in Fig. 1 that to dispel darkness, he need to produce a light source, and that he can also produce a fire since all fires are light sources. He also knows that he can use an igniter on an inflammable thing to produce fire. He can then start looking for a pack of flint and stone (an instance of Igniter) and a torch (an instance of Inflammable). Such concept structure effectively organizes knowledge, allowing developers to classify things in a structured fashion rather than describing each of them individually. Section 3 will offer a detailed account of the concept structure and how it supports planning.

Although encoding the concept model in the mind of character agents may suffice to enable agents to reason about the world, a separate concept layer has several merits. In [9], Doyle proposes the "knowledge-in-the-world" approach to create intelligent characters, arguing that annotating the environment with knowledge allows independent development of characters and the environment, and saves unnecessary duplication of knowledge. In addition, agents can always correctly interpret the the environment no matter how the authors change it. As an example in a similar vein, Thalmann et al [17] supports virtual humans populating a large city by embedding semantic notions in the environment. We accept Doyle's view, and intend to point out that an independent concept layer also serves as a common basis of understanding and communication. A character agent can perform an action and expect other characters to interpret the result of the action using a common ontology, which also provides vocabulary for exchange of messages. Such design avoids confusion that may arise if every agent has a different concept model.

However, static annotations does not suffice for a dynamic environment, because they become invalid when the environment changes. For example, the annotation "romantic room" will appear inappropriate when too many characters enter the room and make a lot of noise. The concept layer overcomes this problem by working with the reality layer to annotate the environment on the fly. It works as follows: When a character agent enters the world, the concept layer passes a copy of the concept model to the agent. The concept layer then monitors the reality layer to retrieve instances of concepts within the line of sight of each character. It then reports the instances to the characters, who process the information and generate sentiments and intentions.

2.3   The Mind Layer

While the concept layer implements what an agent can perceive and act, the emotions, intentions, planning and decision-making capabilities belongs to the mind of the character agent. Certain instances that the concept layer reports to the character agent triggers emotions, while some instances become a part of the agent's plan. For example, the character represented in Fig. 1 feels afraid for he senses darkness and silence. To overcome fear, he then reasons about the concept model and the objects around him and generate an intention of lighting a torch. The agent then uses a planner to generate further intentions that constitute a plan for the original intention.

Coddington and Luck [7] state that despite AI research continues working on developing efficient planners, such efforts have largely ignored the environment and its interaction with the planning system. They argue for an autonomous situated planning agent that generates goals from motivations (meta-goals) and uses context information to evaluate plans and improve the planning process. In a similar vein, this paper focuses on the interface between concepts and planning, an essential part of the mind of an intelligent character, and leaves the design of a versatile agent mind for future investigation.

3   Combining Planning and Inference in Scenarios

Planning techniques play various roles in the creation of a storyline for multiagent scenarios depending on how developers apply the techniques [5][15][11]. Most systems create plans as story elements offline and incorporate the elements during the performance of the story. For example, Riedl and Young [15] use an intent-driven planner to generate coherent stories for characters to follow. On a more individual level, Cavazza et al [5] allow virtual characters to find plans for their goals by searching a hierarchical task network (HTN), but the scenario designer must manually specify the HTN beforehand. In contrast, this paper addresses the issue of enabling characters to handle unforeseeable situations and changing environments, and therefore demands that character agents make plans on the fly. In the rest of this section, we will describe the structure of the concept model based on OWL, and how the concept model help intelligent planning agents achieve flexible behavior through ontological inference.

3.1   Introduction to OWL

Many consider W3C's Web Ontology Language (OWL) the prospective standard for creating ontologies on the Semantic Web. OWL has three species: OWL Lite, OWL DL and OWL Full, in ascending order according to expressiveness. Our scenario framework adopts OWL Full as the language to specify the concept model for several reasons, despite that OWL is designed primarily for Semantic Web development. First, public interest in OWL results in API toolkits (e.g. [4]) and editors (e.g. [12]) that facilitate the development of the concept layer. Second, OWL DL, based on Description Logic [1], has desirable properties for inference. The decidability of DL is a major reason why we choose OWL as the language for the concept model, and several reasoners for OWL already exist at this time.

OWL features two core elements: classes and properties. A class represent a set of individuals, all of which also belongs to any superclass of the class. A property specifies the relation between an instance of the domain class to an instance of the target class. OWL DL also specifies the disjointness, union, intersection, complement of classes, and reflexivity, transitivity of properties. Although the schema of the concept model requires OWL Full the part of the schema that falls outside OWL DL fortunately does not present additional difficulty of inference. In brief, the rich expressiveness of OWL provides a solid foundation for concept modeling and knowledge-based agent architectures such as [8].

3.2   Schema of the Concept Model

The concept model follows the OWL-based schema that facilitates automatic interpretation of the world. Fig. 2 depicts this schema where concepts denote classes of things with something in common, such as keys, locks, and fires. The linking word connects two concepts, pointing out the relationship between a source concept and a target concept. A linking word can denote a causal relation such as "the key *unlocks* the lock" where "unlocks" is the linking word, or a causal rule[1] such as "a fire *burns* an combustible thing". A linking word is also associated with action classes that trigger the causal rule relation and an effect

---

[1] Although causal rules in a strict sense do not belong to ontologies for they do not describe the relation between individuals, we nevertheless include them into the OWL-based schema for convenience.

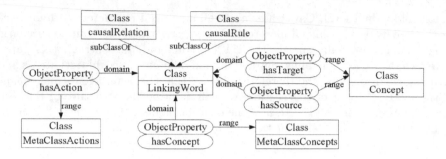

Fig. 2. OWL-based schema of the concept model

on the target instance. The schema defines the effect as a concept, meaning that the causal rule/relation turn the target into an instance of that concept. For example, an attempt of the action Touch triggers the causal rule that a fire burns a combustible thing, and causes the effect of turning the target into an instance of Fire. Since the schema associates a linking word with classes of actions and effects, we need to define two meta-classes: **MetaClassActions**, which contains action classes as instances, and **MetaClassConcepts**, which has concept classes as instances. Given the schema, designers of the scenario can subclass the concepts, causal relations/rules and actions to create a concept model for a scenario.

3.3   Inferring One Plan Step

Classical representation of planning knowledge relies on the notion of states and actions [10]. An action causes the world to change from one state to another. The planner then use a search algorithm to find a sequence of actions that will eventually lead to the goal state. The planner should also adapt to any change of the environment. For example, after the agent touches a wooden stick with a torch, resulting in the postcondition that the stick burns, the planner must know that the agent can light another stick with the lit stick. Although enumerating the effects of an action can be difficult due to the frame problem, we believe virtual environments deserve a more flexible representation than simply linking specific states with specific actions.

Serving as a format of planning knowledge, the schema of the concept model offers better flexibility than unstructured representations, reducing the effort of environment modeling. The inference capability also helps characters find more possible actions to achieve the same goal and allow them to make use of the environment more creatively. Fig. 3 illustrates an example of the concept model that deals the case of fire. This concept model follows the OWL-based schema, although here we use a simplified representation for the sake of readability.

Now we explain how to infer one plan step using Fig. 3 as an example. Planning starts with a goal, which has the format: Concept(item), meaning that item must be an instance of Concept in the goal state. Leaving the item as

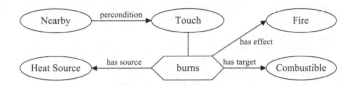

Fig. 3. A small concept model describing the rule of burning

null means that the item can be an arbitrary one. In Fig. 3, suppose that the character intends to create a light source and has a goal LightSource(null). The character agent first looks for causal rules whose linking word has an effect that is *either Concept or a subclass of Concept.* The inference engine for OWL automatically performs such subsumption reasoning. In this case, the agent finds the rule: "HeatSource burns Combustible" because its effect Fire is a subclass of LightSource. The actions associated with the linking word are then the candidate actions for one plan step. The presence of an instance of the source concept and an instance (which must be the item if it is non-null) of the target concept, and the inherent preconditions of the action, constitute the preconditions of the plan step. In the above case, the agent infers that to create a light source, he can touch an instance of Combustible with an instance of HeatSource. If he happen to have these these instances, a one-step plan is done. Evidently, a simple concept model can allow agents to discover many possible actions to satisfy many types of goals because of the inference capability regarding relations between classes. The planning example in section 4 features more complex DL reasoning. Frequently recurring one-step plans, which are learned by or statically recorded in agents constitute the reactive behaviors of agents.

Although a character agent can infer potential actions for one plan step, the current state does not always fulfill all preconditions of any of the actions. In such cases, the agent must use a planner to find ways to satisfy these preconditions.

3.4   Situated Backward-Search Planning

We have shown how an agent can generate a one-step plan with the help of the concept model. By connecting multiple steps, the agent can create complex plans that require more than one action. Fig. 4 presents an augmented version of the backward-search planning algorithm in [10] that obtains necessary knowledge from the environment. This algorithm serves as a simple example showing the feasibility of developing such a situated planner, and provides a hint about how to make more sophisticated planners to work with the environment.

In Fig. 4, C denotes the concept model including the concept ontology and action ontology, s_0 denotes the initial state and g denotes the goal of the agent. The part of world state not explicitly declared in g is left as don't-care. This algorithm first finds all relevant causal rules for the goal using the inference procedure stated in the previous subsection. Then it retrieves all possible actions

```
set π to an empty plan
set search level limit n
Backward-search (C, sₒ, g, n)
    if InfiniteLoopCheck(π) = true then return failure
    ruleSet ← findRelevantRules(g)
    if ruleSet = Ø then return failure
    actionSet ← { a | a is linked to a rule r in ruleSet }
    if actionSet = Ø then return failure
    evaluate and choose an action a from actionSet
    for each precondition p of a
        if p.item is not null and p ∈ sₒ then continue
        if p.item is null and ∃i, i is an instance of p.concept then continue
        if Backward-search(C, sₒ, p, n-1) = failure
            remove a from actionSet and choose another action a
    update π by adding link a→g
    return success
```

Fig. 4. Situated backward-search planning algorithm

associated with the rules. Since the concept model may associate one action with multiple causal rules, this algorithm can discover side effects that an action brings about in addition to the intended goal. The algorithm then allows the agent to evaluate the actions and choose the one with minimal undesirable side effects. Some other criteria not covered by this paper, such as personality, emotion states and so on, can also influence the decision making process. After selecting the action a, the algorithm expands all of its preconditions, which also have the format Concept(item) as a goal does. The algorithm then checks whether the current world state reported by the concept layer satisfies these preconditions. More specifically, a precondition is satisfied if one of these two conditions holds: (a) the item is non-null, and it is already an instance of Concept, and (b) the item is null, and an instance of Concept exists in the environment. The algorithm treats all open preconditions as sub-goals, and recursively calls itself to plan for them. If eventually it finds no way to achieve all preconditions, it removes action a from the action set and chooses another one. The algorithm will terminate with success when no open preconditions remain, or with failure when it fails to find any plan for the goal. A successful planning attempt generates only a partial-order plan, which cannot be executed directly. To convert a partial-order plan to a solution plan is a traditional problem of planning. If the plan has unresolvable flaws, the algorithm is executed again to nondeterministically produce another plan, until a solution plan is produced or time has run out.

The execution of a plan, however, may fail halfway because of unexpected changes in the environment, since a scenario contains multiple characters influencing the environment simultaneously. Re-planning from scratch would take unnecessary amounts of time. To avoid this, the algorithm keeps track of the action sets for each sub-goal. If an action to achieve a sub-goal fails, the planner chooses a substitute from the action set, and call the backward-search algorithm again to plan for the sub-goal. The planner backtracks if all actions for the sub-goal fail, until it finds an alternative plan or terminates with failure.

4   Illustration

This section presents a short scenario about how an agent plans upon the concept layer. Edward the chemist designed the robot R1 to assist him in experiments in his chemical laboratory. Unfortunately, Edward, being a prolific chemist, was not an AI researcher, and he gave R1 an unbalanced mind. The flawed R1 eventually went crazy and started destroying everything he saw. Fig. 5 depicts the concept model of this lab, which contained lots of chemicals as well as bottles strong acids, and a fire axe. The concept layer reports these inferences to the Edward agent.

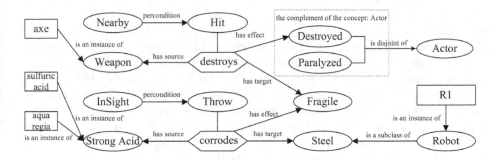

Fig. 5. Concept model for the robot mini-scenario

Edward, having analyzed the situation, immediately generated the emotion of fear and subsequently the intention to remove the source of his fear. His goal to disable the robot is represented as ‾Actor(R1), which means that R1 is an instance of the complement of the class Actor. Intuitively, a paralyzed or destroyed robot does not act. The concept model reflects this intuition by describing the classes Paralyzed and Destroyed as disjoint classes from Actor. The reasoner then infers that they are also subclasses of Actor's complement class. Thus, Edward could apply the causal rule "Weapon destroys Fragile" because it has the effect Destroyed, and he thought about hitting R1 with a weapon.

However, R1, being mentally ill but physically robust, is not an instance of Fragile. Thus Fragile(R1) is an open precondition and a hence sub-goal of the goal Destroyed(R1). Edward looked into the concept model for ways to make R1 fragile, and found the rule "strong acid corrodes steel" is applicable. Fortunately, the laboratory could provide necessary resources for this rule, for R1 was a robot and thus an instance of Steel, and bottles of strong acid exist. Since aqua regia has a higher similarity value to ideal strong acid than sulfuric acid, Edward chose to use it.

Having satisfied Fragile(R1), Edward checked whether the another precondition, Weapon(null) holds, and discovered that he could use the fire axe as a weapon. Finally, Edward completed the partial-order plan, which is to throw the bottle of aqua regia at R1 and then hit R1 with a fire axe. He would then transform the partial-order plan to a total-order plan. Note that if the system designer throws Edward to another scenario where he would have to break the steel gate to escape the laboratory, Edward would still function correctly by constructing a plan to corrode the door and than hack it. In fact, the planner of Edward works in any scenario constructed upon the three-layer framework.

5   Conclusion

In an open-ended scenario or role-playing game, virtual characters constantly face unexpected situations caused by user participation and other characters' reactions. Scripting the behaviors of agents suffers scalability problems because as the world becomes large and complex, the number of scripts proliferates. By separating the agent mind from the environment, our scenario framework enables agents of the same design to function in different situations. The middle layer of concepts in our framework mediates between the physical reality and the agent mind. It maps the environment to ontologies, through which characters understand the world as instances of interconnected concepts rather than as numerical values, allowing them to infer the relation between objects. Planning agents build on top of the concept layer are adaptable because of the interoperability of the environment. They are also more creative, being able to find more ways to achieve the same goal than traditional planning agents thanks to automated inference.

We have implemented the concept layer as a pluggable toolkit based on tools for the Semantic Web and multi-agent systems. As a first step towards creating a evolving scenario, this paper only covers the physical aspect of the environment. In the future we aim to extend the framework to cover social aspects of a scenario by modeling communication and social relations among characters as ontologies.

Acknowledgement

This work is supported by National Science Council of ROC under grant number NSC 93-2213-E-007-061.

References

1. Baader, F., Calvanese, D., McGuinness, D., Nardi, D., Patel-Schneider, P. (eds): The Description Logic Handbook. Cambridge University Press (2002)
2. Bellifemine, F., Poggi, A., Rimassa, G.: Jade, A FIPA-compliant Agent Framework. 4th International Conference on Practical Application of Intelligent Agents and Multi-Agent Technology. (1999)
3. Cantor, N., Kihlstrom, J. F.: Personality and Social Intelligence. Prentice-Hall. Englewood Cliffs, NJ (1987)
4. Carroll, J. J., Dickinson, I., Dollin, C., Reynolds, D., Seaborne, A., Wilkinson, K.: Jena: Implementing the Semantic Web Recommendations. Proceedings of the 13th International World Wide Web Conference. ACM Press, New York (2004) 74-83

5. Cavazza, M., Charles, F., Mead, S. J.: Interacting with Virtual Characters In Interactive Storytelling. Proc. of the First International Joint Conference on Autonomous Agents and Multiagent Systems. ACM Press, New York (2002) 318-325

6. Chang, P. H.-M., Chen, K.-T., Chien, Y.-H., Kao, E., Soo, V.-W.: From Reality to Mind: A Cognitive Middle Layer of Environment Concepts for Believable Agents. In Weyns, D., Parunak, H. V. D., Michel, F. (eds): Environments for Multi-Agent Systems. Lecture Notes in Artificial Intelligence, Vol. 3374. Springer-Verlag, Berlin Heidelberg New York (2005) 57-73

7. Coddington, A. M., Luck, M.: A Motivation-based Planning and Execution Framework. International Journal on Artificial Intelligence Tools 13(1) (2004) 5-25

8. Dickinson, I., Wooldridge, M.: Towards Practical Reasoning Agents for the Semantic Web. Proceedings of the Second International Joint Conference on Autonomous Agents and Multiagent Systems. ACM Press, New York (2003) 827-834

9. Doyle, P.: Believability through Context: Using "Knowledge in the World" to Create Intelligent Characters. Proc. of the First International Joint Conference on Autonomous Agents and Multiagent Systems. ACM Press, New York (2002) 342-349

10. Ghallab, M., Nau, D., Traverso, P.: Automated Planning: Theory and Practice. Morgan Kaufmann Publishers (2004)

11. Gratch, J.: Socially Situated Planning. AAAI Fall Symposium on Socially Intelligent Agents - The Human in the Loop, North Falmouth, MA (2000) 61-64

12. Knublauch, H., Musen, M. A., Rector, A. L.: Editing Description Logic Ontologies with Protégé OWL Plugin. Proceedings of the 2004 International Workshop on Description Logics, Whistler, British Columbia, Canada (2004)

13. Marsella S., Johnson, W. L., LaBore, C: Interactive Pedagogical Drama for Health Interventions. Proceedings of the Eleventh International Conference on Artificial Intelligence in Education. Australia (2003)

14. Novak, J. D.: The Theory Underlying Concept Maps and How to Construct Them. Available on http://cmap.coginst.uwf.edu/info/printer.html. (2001)

15. Riedl, M. O., Young, R. M.: An Intent-Driven Planner for Multi-Agent Story Generation. Proc. of the Third International Joint Conference on Autonomous Agents and Multiagent Systems. IEEE Computer Society, Washington, DC (2004) 186-193

16. Smith, M. K., Welty, C., McGuinnes, D. L (eds).: OWL Web Ontology Language Guide. W3C Recommendation. http://www.w3.org/TR/owl-guide/ (2004)

17. Thalmann, D., Farenc, N., Boulic, R.: Virtual Human Life Simulation and Database: Why and How. 1999 International Symposium on Database Applications in Non-Traditional Environments. IEEE Computer Society, Washington, DC (1999) 471-479

18. Traum, D., Rickel, J., Gratch, J., Marsella, S.: Negotiation over Tasks in Hybrid Human-Agent Teams for Simulation-Based Training. Proceedings of the Second International Joint Conference on Autonomous Agents and Multiagent Systems. ACM Press, New York (2003) 441-448

CAA: A Context-Sensitive Agent Architecture for Dynamic Virtual Environments

In-Cheol Kim

Department of Computer Science, Kyonggi University,
Suwon-si, Kyonggi-do, 442-760, South Korea
kic@kyonggi.ac.kr

Abstract. In this paper, we introduce the Context-Sensitive Agent Architecture (CAA). The CAA is a generic agent architecture developed for use with pure Java programming language. The CAA can support complex long-term behaviors as well as reactive short-term behaviors. It also realizes high context-sensitivity of behaviors. It adopts other relevant behaviors depending on the changing context, rather than blindly follows a prearranged long-term behavior. By instantiating the CAA, any intelligent virtual agent can be implemented. The CAA UTBot is an intelligent virtual agent built on our CAA for the Unreal Tournament games. We explain the implementation of the CAA UTBot.

1 Introduction

There are several major stumbling blocks that one faces when trying to implement an intelligent virtual agent for a dynamic environment.

1. We need a way to easily implement complex long-term behaviors as well as reactive short-term behaviors. Reactive short-term behaviors do not usually maintain or use any internal state, and have difficulties in accomplishing coherently goal-directed tasks. On the other hand, complex long-term behaviors may not usually respond promptly the dynamic changes of the environment.
2. We need a behavior representation and an execution mechanism to support context-sensitive behaviors. The subsumption architecture and the Belief Desires Intentions (BDI) architecture provide some support for this but they are not explicit enough [2].
3. We need a pure object-oriented implementation tool or programming environment. Existing subsumption implementations are usually hardware-based, while BDI implementations are usually based on logic and rule-based programming, or implement a new language and its interpreter [3].

In this paper, we introduce the Context-Sensitive Agent architecture (CAA) along with an intelligent virtual agent (UTBot) built on our CAA for the Unreal Tournament games [1]. The CAA is a generic agent architecture developed for use with the Java programming language. The CAA can support complex long-term behaviors as well as reactive short-term behaviors. It also realizes high context-sensitivity of behaviors.

T. Panayiotopoulos et al. (Eds.): IVA 2005, LNCS 3661, pp. 146–151, 2005.
© Springer-Verlag Berlin Heidelberg 2005

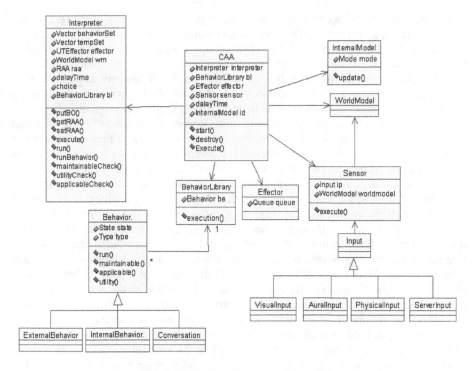

Fig. 1. UML Class Diagram of the CAA

2 Context-Sensitive Agent Architecture

Our CAA (Context-Sensitive Agent Architecture) consists of (1) a world model; (2) an internal model; (3) a behavior library; (4) an interpreter; and (5) a set of sensors and effectors. Fig. 1 shows the UML class diagram of the CAA including these major components. The world model contains a set of objects representing current beliefs or facts about the world. The world model is defined as an abstract class to be implemented as a domain-specific world model for a certain kind of application. The world model is constantly updated upon the sensor information. On the other hand, the internal model contains a set of objects representing internal modes, or intentions. Each internal mode can be viewed as an implicit goal to be pursued. Depending on the changes of the world model, the internal model may be updated accordingly. Transitions between distinct internal modes can be modeled and designed as a finite-state machine. The behavior library contains a set of pre-defined behavior objects. The behavior class has three sub-classes: external behavior, internal behavior and conversational behavior. While external behaviors change the state of the environment through effectors, internal behaviors change the internal state – namely, the internal mode and parameters- without any change of the environment. Conversational behaviors can be used to communicate with other agents in a certain agent communication language or protocol. Conversational behaviors can be also viewed as a special kind of external behaviors.

The behavior class has five main member methods: applicable(), utility(), maintainable(), run(), and failure(). The applicable() method checks if the preconditions of a behavior can be satisfied with the state of the world model and/or the internal model. The utility() method computes the relative utility of an applicable behavior by considering the current world model and internal model. Whenever multiple behaviors are applicable for a given situation, the highest-utility behavior is automatically selected and executed from them. The maintainable() method continually checks the context of a behavior during the execution once it starts execution, to make sure that the behavior is still applicable to the intended situation. The run() method is the main body of a behavior. It gets called when the selected behavior starts execution. This method usually generates one or more atomic actions, sets some member variables, and returns. Finally, the failure() method is a procedural specification of what the agent should do when a behavior fails. In the CAA, a behavior lifecycle consists of the behavior states: *create, waiting, executing, interrupt, fail, resume,* and *finish.*

The interpreter controls the execution of the entire CAA system. Whenever there is new or changed information in the world model or internal model, the interpreter determines a set of applicable behaviors by calling the applicable() method of each behavior. From this set of applicable behaviors, it selects the highest-utility behavior by using the utility() methods. By invoking the run() method of the selected behavior, the interpreter starts the execution of the behavior. Once the selected behavior starts execution, the interpreter continually checks the behavior's context by calling the maintainable() method periodically. If the context of the behavior gets unsatisfied with either the current state of the world model or the internal model, the interpreter immediately stops the execution of the behavior, and then replaces it with a new behavior appropriate to the changed situation.

Sensors continually perceive the surrounding environment and update the world model. The inputs to sensors are classified into several sub-types: visual input, aural input, physical input, and server input. Effectors execute the atomic actions requested by the run() method of the current external behavior and, as a result, affect the environment. Each sensor and effector has its own thread and work concurrently with the interpreter. An intelligent virtual agent based on the CAA can have multiple domain-specific sensors and effectors.

3 Dynamic Virtual Environment

Unreal Tournament (UT) is a category of video games known as first-person shooters, where all real time players exist in a 3D virtual world with simulated physics. Every player's senses are limited by their location, bearings, and occlusion within the virtual world. Fig. 2 shows a screenshot of the UT Domination game. The Gamebots [1] is a multi-agent system infrastructure derived from Unreal Tournament. The Gamebots allows UT characters to be controlled over client-server network connections by feeding sensory information to client agents and delivering action commands issued from client agents back to the game server.

In a dynamic virtual environment built on the Gamebots system and the UT game engine, agents must display human-level capabilities to play successfully, such as planning paths, learning a map of their 3D environment, using resources available to them, coordinating with their teammates, and engaging in strategic planning which takes their adversaries into account.

Fig. 2. A Screenshot of the Unreal Tournament Game

4   UTBot

In order to investigate the potential power of the CAA, we implemented an intelligent agent to play in the 3D virtual environment of the UT Domination game. The CAA UTBot adopts the CAA as its brain to decide and execute the proper behaviors in response to the changing environment. Fig. 3 shows the UML class diagram of the CAA UTBot. The UT world model class contains various domain-specific objects. This world model should contain both static and dynamic information. Static information does not change during the course of a game. Static information includes, for example, the agent's name and ID, the team number, the number of team members, the maximum team score, and the address of the game server. In contrast, dynamic information continually changes during the game. Dynamic information includes, for example, the agent's position and direction, the health and skill information, the current weapons and armors, a partial world map, and the discovered domination points. The UT internal model contains an internal mode and the related parameters. There are five distinct internal modes: *Explore, Dominate, Collect, Died*, and *Healed*. In cases of Explore, Dominate, and Collect modes, some internal parameters such as the starting position and the target object may be given together.

Table 1. The Internal Modes and the Associated External Behaviors

Internal Mode	External Behaviors
Explore	MoveTo, Explore, Attack, Chase, Retreat
Dominate	MoveTo, Attack_Point, Defend_Point
Collect	MoveTo, Collect_Powerup, Collect_Weapon, Collect_Armor, Retreat, Attack
Died	No Behaviors
Healed	No Behaviors

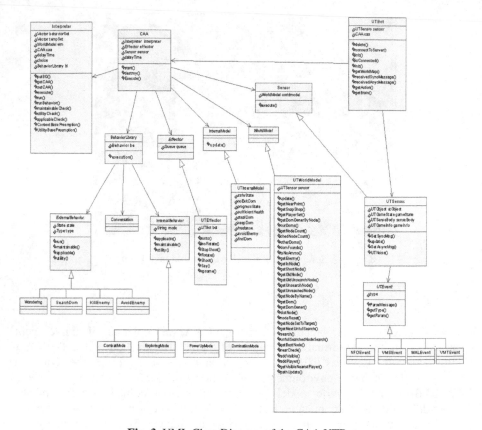

Fig. 3. UML Class Diagram of the CAA UTBot

The CAA UTBot has a variety of external behaviors such as *Explore, Attack_Point, Defend_Point, Collect_Powerup, Collect_Weapon, Collect_Armor, Chase, Attack, Retreat,* and *MoveTo.*

The applicable() and maintainable() methods of each external behavior may contain conditions against the UT world model, the UT internal model, or both. However, most of applicable external behaviors of the CAA UTBot are primarily categorized depending on its internal mode. During the game, therefore, the set of applicable external behaviors is first restricted by the current internal mode of the agent. Table 1 lists the internal modes and the associated external behaviors. Although more than one external behavior is applicable at a certain internal mode, the utility values may be different among them. To realize transitions between internal modes, the CAA UTBot has a specific set of internal behaviors such as *ExploreToDominate, DominateToCollect,* and *CollectToDominate.*

This set of internal behaviors forms a unique strategy of the CAA UTBot for determining the external behaviors. Fig. 4 shows the UTBot Launcher and the deploying UTBots. Our UTBot Launcher also provides functionalities of the graphic viewer and the behavior analyzer.

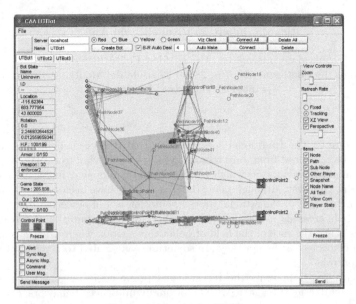

Fig. 4. The Deploying UTBots

5 Conclusions

We introduced a Context-sensitive Agent Architecture (CAA), along with an intelligent virtual agent (UTBot) built on our CAA for the Unreal Tournament games. The CAA can support complex long-term behaviors as well as reactive short-term behaviors. It also realizes high context-sensitivity of behaviors.

Acknowledgement. This research was supported by Kyonggi University Overseas Research Grant 2003.

References

1. Adobbati, R., Marshall, A.N., Scholer, A., Tejada, S., Kaminka, G.A., Schaffer, S., Sollitto, C.: GameBots: A 3D Virtual World Test Bed for Multiagent Research. Proceedings of the 2nd International Workshop on Infrastructure for Agents, MAS, and Scable MAS (2001)
2. Howden, N., Ronnquist, R., Hodgson A., Lucas, A.: JACK Intelligent Agents^{TM} – Summary of an Agent Infrastructure, Proceedings of the 5th International Conference on Autonomous Agents (2001)
3. Pokahr, A., Braubach, L., Lamersdorf, W.: Jadex: Implementing a BDI-Infrastructure for JADE Agents, EXP - In Search of Innovation (Special Issue on JADE), Vol 3, No. 3, Telecom Italia Lab, Turin, Italy (2003) 76-85

When Emotion Does Not Mean Loss of Control

Ricardo Imbert and Angélica de Antonio

Facultad de Informática, Universidad Politécnica de Madrid,
Campus de Montegancedo, s/n, 28660 Boadilla del Monte, Madrid, Spain
{rimbert, angelica}@fi.upm.es

Abstract. The traditional consideration that intelligent behaviors can only be produced from pure reasoning fails when trying to explain most of human behaviors, in which the emotional component has a decisive weight. However, although many different efforts have been made to consider emotions in the rational process, emotion is still perceived by many research areas as a non-desirable quality for a computational system. This is not the case of the field of believable agents, where emotions are well respected, although they are sometimes associated to a certain loss of control.

This paper presents the mechanisms proposed by a generic cognitive architecture for agents with emotionally influenced behaviors, called COGNITIVA, to maintain behaviors control without giving up the richness provided by emotions. This architecture, together with a progressive specification process for its application, have been used successfully to model 3D intelligent virtual agents.

1 Reconsidering the Role of Emotions in the Rational Process

Intelligent behavior and decision making have been traditionally related to the —complex— modeling of pure rational process. The consideration of emotion as an influent factor, sometimes decisive, has been systematically pushed aside —even nowadays— in many research areas. In fact, emotion has been observed as something rather irrational that plays down value to human rationality [1], something "non scientific" [2]. At best, in some fields such as that of believable agents, emotion, mood, personality or attitudes are perceived as useful qualities, although sometimes have been also considered synonyms of a certain loss of control and entropy growth, emphasizing only their passional perspective.

The consequence is that most of the behaviors produced following this classical conception are far away from those observable, for instance, in human beings. The influence of emotions should not be understood as a distorting and purely passional element. It should be incorporated, based on a precise and well defined model. Reason and emotion are not antagonistic and irreconciliable concepts, but complementary strengths that act upon mental processes.

Not in vain, recent theories [3] [4] suggest that emotions are an essential part of human intelligence, and are of paramount importance in processes such

T. Panayiotopoulos et al. (Eds.): IVA 2005, LNCS 3661, pp. 152–165, 2005.
© Springer-Verlag Berlin Heidelberg 2005

as perception, learning, attention, memory, rational decision-making and other skills associated to intelligent behaviors.

Even more, it has been stated that an excessive deficit of emotion may be harmful to decision-making [5]. Emotion is essential to understand human cognition.

2   Related Work

The search for architectures combining rational and emotional behaviors has been a frequent challenge in the last two decades.

Most of the solutions proposed hitherto follow one of two main emotional computational models, generally, the appraisal model (cf. [6], [7], [8], [9], [10]) or the motivational model (cf. [11], [12], [13], [14]). However, although all these models present many interesting virtues, they also suffer from some well-known drawbacks.

Besides, the structure underlaying emotional architectures is, actually, very complex. Sometimes, emotional elements and mechanisms are interwoven with the restrictions and particularities of the application context and with the problem faced, making them very hard to be reused in a different context. (cf. [15], [16]).

In other situations, emotional architectures are very generic, independent from any specific problem (cf. [13], [11]). The lack of adaptation to the particular necessities of the problem originates less-efficient, computationally demanding mechanisms. Frequently, to produce feasible solutions, their structure must be reconsidered, and some of their inherent characteristics simplified, losing some of their properties, and demanding a lot of effort.

Current solutions are not as satisfactory as they should be because they: (1) do not detail mechanisms to control instinctive behaviors at will; or (2) do not detail the way in which perceptions must be considered to behave coherently with regards to the past action; or (3) fail, precisely, in the "attitude" with which they cope with complexity: they bet on *specificity* for better efficiency or *generality* for wider applicability.

3   A Cognitive Architecture to Manage Emotions

Our proposal is to model individuals using, not a conventional architecture with an addition resembling emotions, but a truly emotionally-oriented architecture. Emotions must not be understood only as an influential part on the behavior of the individual. In our opinion, explainable and elaborated emotion-based behaviors can only emerge when the whole architecture has an emotional vocation.

The architecture that we propose is an agent-based one, called COGNITIVA. Agents are a common choice to model this kind of systems, since they present an structure and operation suitable to their needs.

Considering an agent as a continuous *perception-cognition-action* cycle, we have restricted the scope of our proposal to the "cognitive" activity, although no constraint on the other two modules (perceptual and actuation) is imposed. This is the reason why this architecture will be sometimes referred to as "cognitive".

In COGNITIVA, emotions are not considered just as a component that provides the system with some "emotional" attributes, but all the components and processes of the architecture have been designed to deal naturally with emotions.

COGNITIVA is a multilayered architecture: it offers three possible layers to the agent designer, each one corresponding to a different kind of behavior, viz reactive, deliberative and social (see Fig. 1). The interaction of these three layers with the other two modules of the agent, the sensors (perceptual module) and the effectors (actuation module), is made through two specific components, the interpreter and the scheduler, respectively.

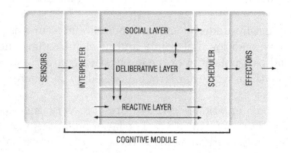

Fig. 1. General structure of COGNITIVA

One of the main characteristics of COGNITIVA—and one of its strengths— is that, having been conceived as a generic, domain-independent architecture, not restricted to any emotional theory or model, it is accompanied by a progressive specification process to be applied for the design and adaptation of the abstract structures and functions proposed to the particular needs of the application context.

Along this paper, we will analyze how COGNITIVA deals with emotions to provide both instinctive and conscious behaviors. Every component and function will be exemplified with the results obtained from an application of the architecture to the modeling of the characters in a particular domain (following the progressive application process commented above), a virtual environment called the *3D Virtual Savannah.*

The 3D Virtual Savannah represents an African savannah inhabited by two kinds of individuals, zebras and lions, whose behavior is controlled by intelligent virtual agents (IVAs), derived from COGNITIVA. The ultimate scope of this environment is to simulate the behavior of these virtual animals, restricting their actuation to a reduced set of actions, related to their movement (*walking, running, fleeing*) or to some minimal necessities to be satisfied (*drinking, eating, hunting*). This simple scenario has been used as test bed for COGNITIVA.

4   Representing the State of the Agent

4.1   Management of the Current State: Beliefs

Beliefs represent the information managed by the agent about the most probable state of the environment, considering all the places, objects and individuals in it. Emotional information about itself and about others is part of an IVA's beliefs.

The amount of the agent's beliefs and their accuracy are of paramount importance to perform appropriate decision-making processes. However, a good representation and structure for beliefs is also fundamental. COGNITIVA defines a taxonomy of beliefs, depending on their object and their nature. On one hand, a belief may refer to a *place* in the environment, to *objects* located in the environment, and to other *individuals*. Besides, the agent maintains beliefs concerning the *current situation*, for instance, a belief of a zebra about the current situation in the 3D Virtual Savannah scenario may be the fact that it is being pursued by a lion. That is not information about the lion, nor about the zebra, but about the situation that is taking place.

On the other hand, beliefs about places, objects and individuals may describe:

- **Defining characteristics (DCs)**, traits that mark out the fundamental features of places, objects or individuals. DCs will hardly change in time, and if they do, it will happen very slowly.
  For instance, the (x, y, z) *dimensions* of the savannah are DCs about this place; the *position* in the scenario of the lion's den is a DC for an object; a DC about a lion (individual) is its *personality*.
  Among all the DCs that an IVA can manage, most of them will be strictly related to the context of application, but COGNITIVA prescribes the existence of a set of *personality traits* (P) for individuals. Personality traits define the general lines for the IVA behavior. For instance, zebras in the 3D Virtual Savannah have been provided with two personality traits, *courage* and *endurance*.
- **Transitory states (TSs)**, characteristics whose values represent the current state of the environment places, objects or individuals. Unlike the DCs, whose values are, practically, static in time, the TSs values have a much more dynamic nature.
  Some examples of TSs could be the *number of inhabitants* (TS of a place), the *flow* of the river (TS of an object), or the *position* in the scenario of a lion (TSs of an individual).
  COGNITIVA considers essential two kinds of TSs for individuals: their *moods* (M), which reflect the emotional internal state of the IVAs; and their *physical states* (F), which represent the external state of the IVAs (the state of their *bodies* or representations in the virtual environment).
  In the 3D Virtual Savannah, zebras have as moods *happiness*, *fear* and *surprise*, and as physical states, *thirst*, *hunger* and *fatigue*.
- **Attitudes (As)**, which determine the predisposition of the agent towards the environment's components (places, objects and individuals). Attitudes are less variable in time than TSs, but more than DCs.

Examples of attitudes selected for our scenario are the *apprehension* of an IVA about another.

Attitudes are important to help the IVA's decision making, action selection and, above all, to keep coherence and consistency in the agent's behavior.

4.2   Management of the Past State: History

Behaviors that do not take into account past events are specially disappointing to human observers. COGNITIVA considers two mechanisms to maintain the agent's past history information:

- **Accumulative effect of the past:** this is an implicit mechanism, related to the way in which beliefs are managed. External changes in the environment or internal modifications in the agent's internal state may produce an update of the agent's beliefs. However, in the case of transitory states, this update is performed as a variation —on higher or lower intensity— on the previous value of the belief, avoiding abrupt alterations in the individual's state.
- **Explicit management of the past state:** an accumulative effect of the past events may not be enough to manage efficiently the past state, because it does not consider information related to the events themselves or to the temporal instant in which they took place.

  COGNITIVA maintains explicit propositions related to any significant event —to the IVA— that happened. Past history allows the agent to reason considering facts occurred in past moments.

  For instance, an inverse delta based mechanism has been developed to manage past events for the zebras, such as *saw another animal, drank, grazed...*

4.3   Management of the Desirable State: Concerns

Beliefs represent information about what the IVA thinks is the most probable state of the environment, including itself and the rest of the IVAs. However, they do not give any significant clue about the IVA's preferences on those beliefs.

For instance, a belief about a zebra's current *fear* does not tell if that is an acceptable value for that zebra in that moment or not.

COGNITIVA proposes the use of *concerns* (C) as a tool to express the desirable/acceptable values for the TSs of an IVA anytime, in particular, for **emotions** and **physical states**. Concerns restrict the range of values of the TSs of the agent, expressing the acceptable limits in a certain moment. With this aim, concerns provide two *thresholds*, *lower* and *upper*, for every TS. All the values among them will be considered as desired by the agent; those values out of this range will be unpleasant, and the IVA will be inclined to act to avoid them and let them move to the desired range.

4.4   The Personal Model. Relationships Among Beliefs

Among all the beliefs managed by the IVA, there is a small group specially related to the emotional behavior. This set, that has been called the agent's *personal model*, is composed by the beliefs that the agent has about itself, and that are related to the emotions. More precisely, this personal model consists on personality traits, moods, physical states, attitudes and concerns.

The elements of the personal model in the context of the 3D Virtual Savannah have been modeled with a fuzzy logic representation. Fuzzy logic linguistic labels are nearer to the way in which humans qualify these kind of concepts (it is usual to hear "I am *very* happy", instead of "My happiness is *0.8*"). Besides, fuzzy logic is a good approach to manage imprecision.

As the rest of components of COGNITIVA deal with the elements of the personal model, the whole design and implementation generated follows a fuzzy logic approach, including relationships among personal model elements.

Relationships among personal model elements are a key point in COGNITIVA. Many of these beliefs are conceptually closely related, and have a direct influence on each other, as it is shown in Fig. 2:

- Personality traits exert an important influence determining emotions. For instance, in a similar situation, the value of the mood *fear* will be different for a *courageous* IVA than for a *pusillanimous* one.
- The set of attitudes of an IVA has some influence on the emotions that it experiences. For instance, the presence of a lion in the surroundings will produce an increment on a zebra's *fear*, because of its attitude of *apprehension* towards lions.
- Personality traits, in turn, have influence on attitudes. The value of a zebra's attitude *apprehension* towards a lion is different depending on its value for the personality trait *courage*: a cowardly zebra will feel absolute rejection towards a lion, whereas a courageous one just will not like it.
- Physical states have also influence on emotions. For instance, when a zebra is very *thirsty*, its *happiness* will decrease.
- Finally, personality traits exert some influence on concerns. Thus, although an IVA may want to have, in a certain moment, a very high upper threshold for its mood fear (the IVA wants to risk more for a while and be more fear-resistant), in fact, and depending on its personality traits, that value will be more or less high.

All these relationships have been designed and implemented for the 3D Virtual Savannah through special fuzzy rules and fuzzy operators. The result is a set of fuzzy relationships, including the following:

```
courage DECREASES ⟨much⟩ fear

courage DECREASES ⟨few⟩ apprehension

apprehension DECREASES ⟨some⟩ happiness

apprehension INCREASES ⟨much⟩ fear

...
```

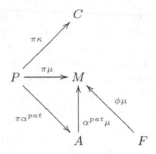

Fig. 2. Generic relationships among beliefs of the IVA personal model, together with the dependency functions determined in COGNITIVA. P = Personality traits; C = Concerns; M = Moods; A = Attitudes; F = Physical states

5   Controlling the State of the Agent

Emotions, in particular moods, may be a strong force to drive the IVA's behavior, but does not mean that an agent's behavior must be necessarily subjugated to their changing values. Emotions are part of the state of the agent. If their values are properly updated and their effects are justified, the outcomes of the emotionally based behavior will not be unpredictable, but coherent responses.

COGNITIVA provides some mechanisms to update and control the internal state of the agent —current, past and desirable— and, in particular, to control the values of the components of the personal model. The dynamics of the architecture follow a continuous cycle, represented in the Fig. 3, that leaves no room for chaotic behaviors.

The following sections describe how beliefs, past history and concerns are updated to maintain coherence, and how their values are handled to provide proper actions.

5.1   Updating the State of the Agent as a Consequence of Perceptions

The cognitive module described by COGNITIVA receives from the perceptual module (the agent's sensors) *perceptions* of the environment. This input may not be directly manipulable by most of the processes of the cognitive module and must be interpreted (for instance, sensors might provide measures about light wavelengths, but the cognitive module could only be able to manage directly colors). In other situations, many inputs may be irrelevant for the IVA, and should be filtered (when a lion is chasing a zebra, the zebra does not mind anything but the lion and the escape route).

COGNITIVA provides a component, called **interpreter**, which acts as an interface between sensors and the rest of the cognitive module, receiving the perceptions coming from the perceptual module, filtering and discarding those non-

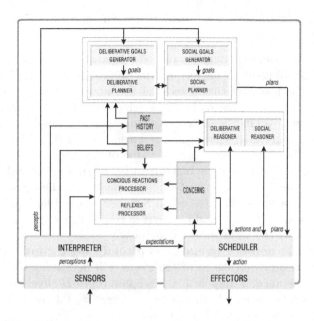

Fig. 3. Internal components and processes of COGNITIVA

interesting to the agent, and translating them into *percepts*[1], inteligible by the rest of the components and processes of the cognitive module.

On one hand, the interpreter directs the interpreted percepts to the convenient processes in every layer of the architecture, to be managed reactively, guided by goals, or guided by interactions with other agents. On the other hand, the interpreter also updates the value of past history events and beliefs. Most of that updating may be more or less automatic, and needs no further processing. For instance, if a zebra perceives that the lion has moved, the interpreter will update automatically the new position of the lion.

However, that is not the case for moods. And moods are the core of emotional behavior. The new value of moods depends on their old value and on the perceptions, but also on what was expected to happen and to which degree that occurrence was desired.

Moods need a new factor to be conveniently generated. With this aim, COGNITIVA includes the mechanism of the **expectations**, inspired on the proposal of Seif El-Nasr [18], which has been adapted, in turn, from the OCC Model [19].

Expectations capture the predisposition of the agent toward the events — confirmed or potential. In COGNITIVA, expectations are valuated on:

– Their *expectancy:* Expressing how probably the occurrence of the event is expected.
– Their *desire:* Indicating the degree of desirability of the event.

---

[1] Name proposed by Pierce [17], in the context of visual perception, to design the initial interpretative hypothesis of what is being perceived.

Through expectations, the interpreter has enough information to update moods from perception:

- When the event **occurrence has not yet been confirmed**. Moods will be updated depending on the degrees of expectancy and desire for the event. For example, if the last time that a zebra A saw another zebra B, this one was being chased by a lion, the zebra A may elaborate the expectation "zebra B has been hunted". That is an expected undesirable event, whose occurrence has not been confirmed, what produces a sensation of *distress*, increasing the value of its "fear" and decreasing the value of its "happiness".
- When the event **occurrence has already been confirmed**. Again, depending on the degrees of expectancy and desire for the event, moods will be updated. For instance, if the zebra A finds the dead body of zebra B, its fears have been confirmed, and its *distress* transforms into *sadness*, decreasing considerably the value of its "happiness".
- When the event **non-occurrence has already been confirmed**. The degree of expectancy and desire of the event will determine the updating of moods. For instance, if the zebra A sees again zebra B alive, the expectation about zebra B being hunted vanish, and *distress* would give way to *relief* by increasing "happiness" and "surprise".

This is how expectations are used to update moods, but, what is the origin of those expectations? Each time some internal reasoning process, in any of the three layers of the architecture, proposes an action to be executed, it must be properly sequenced with other previous and simultaneous action proposals. This should not be a responsibility of the actuation module (effectors), since this module should not need to have any information about the origin and final goal of the actions it receives.

COGNITIVA proposes a component, the **scheduler**, to act as interface between the cognitive module and the effectors, managing an internal agenda in which action proposal are conveniently sequenced and ordered. Once it has decided which is/are the most adequate action/s to be executed, it sends it/them to the effectors. Every action will have a set of associated expectations. The scheduler takes them and informs the interpreter about what is expected to occur in the future, according to the action that is being executed.

Expectations provide coherence to the IVA's behavior since they close its internal reasoning cycle, maintaining a reference for future perceptions according to its current actuation.

5.2   Updating the Desired State of the Agent to Control Actuation

The scheduler organizes the actions according to the only information it has about them: their priority, established by the reasoning process that generated them, and their concurrence restrictions, which allow the scheduler to send simultaneously compatible actions.

It is reasonable that actions proposed by the reactive layer have a higher priority in the queue of actions to be executed than those coming from the deliberative o social layers. Even more, it makes sense that deliberative or social action executions are interrupted when a reactive action emerges. Then, does not that mean that reactive, instinctive, passional actions will always take the control of the actuation, leaving out higher level behaviors? Is not that, in fact, losing control?

Tito Livio relates in its famous work *Ab Urbe Condita* the story of the ancient Roman hero Mucius Scaevola, who preferred to introduce voluntarily his arm inside the pyre for sacrifices, before betraying Rome. How is it possible to hold back the reaction of retiring the arm from fire, to avoid the pain (a reactive, more prioritized action), and execute instead a goal-based behavior (to assure the survival of Rome)?

The mechanism proposed in COGNITIVA is the use of concerns to control the IVA's actuation. A reaction, besides some triggering conditions, the operator to be executed, the consequences of its execution, and some other parameters, such as its priority or its expiry time, has to be provided with *justifiers*, i.e., emotional restrictions that must be satisfied to execute the action.

Justifiers are expressed in terms of restrictions related to the value of the IVA's concerns, that is, restrictions on the desirable state of the agent. For instance, a justifier to trigger a reaction to retire the arm because of the pain produced by the fire will be:

$$pain > upper\_threshold\_concern(pain) \tag{1}$$

Whenever some agent wants to be able to stand a bit more pain, it first must raise the value of the upper threshold of this concern. If pain does not surpass the value of the upper threshold, the reaction will not be justified and it will not be triggered.

Depending on the personality traits of the individual, which have some influence on concerns (see Fig. 2), the real new value for that upper threshold will be higher or lower. That is why a normal person will not resist for long with the arm on the fire, while a hero as Mucius Scaevola was able to stand without resign.

Thus, higher processes of the architecture (deliberative and social) can adjust the value of the thresholds of the agent's concerns to control the instinctive actuation whenever it is not desirable.

Coming back to the scenario of the 3D Virtual Savannah, if two zebras, one courageous (in the Fig. 4, the black striped one, the farthest one from the user point of view), and another one easily frightened (in the Fig. 4, the red striped one, the closest to the viewer), feel thirsty and they are not near any source of water, their deliberative layer will produce a plan to arrive to the only river they know (Fig. 4 (1)). However, if arriving near the river, they perceive a lion, their fear will raise and a reaction of escape will be triggered (Fig. 4 (2)).

Once they are far enough and their fear has descended under the value of the upper threshold of its corresponding concern, still they will need to quench their thirst. However, the new information included in their beliefs, the position of the lion, prevents them from generating a potentially successful plan if they do not consider assuming some risk. As far as thirst has increased after the running, they decide to increase their fear tolerance (the upper threshold of their concern about fear), each one according to their possibilities (their personality traits).

They come back to the surroundings of the river, perceive the lion and, again, their fear raises. But, this time, the level of the fear of the brave zebra (the black one) does not surpass its fear tolerance upper threshold, and it advances cautiously in the presence of the lion (Fig. 4 (3)) and gets to drink (Fig. 4 (4)). The other zebra, less courageous, cannot raise enough its fear tolerance upper threshold, and, every time the fear surpasses it, the red zebra escapes frightened, without attaining its goal.

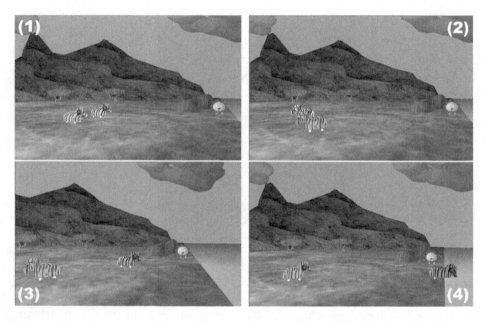

Fig. 4. Snapshots of the use of the concerns to control reactions in the 3D Virtual Savannah scenario

6   Adapting the Generic Architecture to an Specific Context

COGNITIVA has been generically conceived, without restrictions about its internal emotional and reasoning models, the format of its components, the specific design of its functionalities or the application context.

However, this architecture is provided with a progressive specification process, which allows to apply it in a variety of problems and contexts, reusing designs and implementations, without loss of efficiency.

As a general outline, this process consists on two phases of specification. The first one is a *funcional specification phase*, in which the developer details the particular structure and format of every component of the architecture, specifying also the design of all the functions proposed by COGNITIVA. For instance, it was in this phase where we selected and designed a fuzzy logic representation for beliefs and their relationships.

As a result of this functional specification phase, a full operative, context independent *module* of the abstract architecture is obtained.

The second phase of this process, *the contextual specification phase*, deals with the particularization of the concrete values needed for every architectural element, according to the application context. In this phase, for instance, we decided that we needed an agent of the kind "zebra", whose behavior would be influenced by two personality traits: *courage* and *endurance*.

The advantage of this systematical adaption approach, against the traditional architectures (too specific or too general) is that:

1. The major effort is devoted to the development of the functional specification, which is context independent. A functional specification may be the basis for many different contextual specifications, whose development is far less expensive, in terms of effort (in our case, the development of the contextual specification of the 3D Virtual Savannah meant an effort seven times lower than that of the functional specification).
2. It differentiates the technical and the domain designs, allowing to separate both kinds of designer roles.

7 Conclusions

Human behaviors are rarely exclusively explainable through pure reasoning. There exist other emotional factors that influence decisively on them, that must also be considered. However, the efforts until today to build architectures including those emotional factors have not yet succeeded, and emotion is still frequently observed as an undesirable quality to be included in computational systems.

This paper presents some of the mechanisms proposed in COGNITIVA, an architecture with generic mechanisms and structures to build agents with emotionally influenced behaviors, dealing with the problem of the loss of control in the emotionally based behavior generation.

In particular, COGNITIVA deals with the control of instinctive behaviors through the use of *concerns*. Concerns, not explicitly considered by appraisal models, are, in a certain way, conceptually present in most of the motivational models, under the name of "drives" [20] or, just, "concerns" [21]. However, concerns have been extended in COGNITIVA to allow, not only to control the IVA's reactive behaviors, but also to justify and explain them.

Moreover, the feedback mechanism proposed by the motivational models to link the behaviors produced by the agent to those drives is intricate, and does not allow a clear, understandable management of the emotions produced by future events. The proposal of some appraisal models, such as the OCC model [19], is more intuitive and explainable, including *expectations* with this aim. COGNITIVA particularizes the OCC model's expectations, considering not only a degree of *expectancy* of the perceived events, but also their *desirability*.

Finally, together with the architecture, a progressive process of specification is proposed, which allows facing particular contexts of application without giving up any of the architecture's properties and at a reasonable cost. COGNITIVA places the key in a controlled *adaptivity* to achieve the efficiency of the specific architectures together with the applicability of the general ones. This is a common development strategy in both software and knowledge engineering that, however, has not been considered by any previous emotional architecture to fight against the complexity of this kind of systems.

References

1. Darryl N. Davis and Suzanne J. Lewis. Computational models of emotion for autonomy and reasoning. *Informatica (Special Edition on Perception and Emotion Based Reasoning)*, 27(2):159–165, 2003.
2. Rosalind W. Picard. Affective computing. Technical Report 321, MIT Media Laboratory, Perceptual Computing Section, November 1995.
3. Joseph LeDoux. *The Emotional Brain*. Simon and Schuster, New York, 1996.
4. R. Adolphs, D. Tranel, A. Bechara, H. Damasio, and Antonio R. Damasio. *Neurobiology of Decision-Making*, chapter Neuropsychological Approaches to Reasoning and Decision-Making, pages 157–179. Springer-Verlag, Berlin, Germany, 1996.
5. Antonio R. Damasio. *Descartes' Error. Emotion, Reason, and the Human Brain*. Gosset/Putnam Press, New York, 1994.
6. Clark Elliott. I picked up catapia and other stories: A multimodal approach to expressivity for "emotionally intelligent" agents. In W. Lewis Johnson and Barbara Hayes-Roth, editors, *Proceedings of the First International Conference on Autonomous Agents (Agents'97)*, pages 451–457, New York, 5–8, 1997. ACM Press.
7. Daniel Rousseau and Barbara Hayes-Roth. Improvisational synthetic actors with flexible personalities. Technical Report KSL 97-10, Knowledge Systems Laboratory, Computer Science Dept., Stanford University, Stanford, CA, 1997.
8. Alexander Staller and Paolo Petta. Introducing emotions in the computational study of norms. In *Proceedings of the AISB'00 Sympoisum on Starting from Society -The Application of Social Analogies to Computational Systems*, pages 101–112, Birmingham, UK, 2000.
9. Helmut Prendinger and Mitsuru Ishizuka. Designing and evaluating animated agents as social actors. *IEICE Transactions on Information and Systems*, Vol.E86-D(8):1378–1385, 2003.
10. Jonathan Gratch and Stacy Marsella. Evaluating the modeling and use of emotion in virtual humans. In Nicholas R. Jennings, Carles Sierra, Liz Sonenberg, and Milind Tambe, editors, *Proceedings of the Third International Joint Conference on Autonomous Agents and Multi Agent Systems (AAMAS 2004)*, pages 320–327, New York, 2004. ACM Press.
11. Dolores Cañamero. Modeling motivations and emotions as a basis for intelligent behavior. In W. Lewis Johnson and Barbara Hayes-Roth, editors, *Proceedings of the First International Symposium on Autonomous Agents (Agents'97)*, pages 148–155, New York, 1997. ACM Press.

12. Hirohide Ushida, Yuji Hirayama, and Hiroshi Nakajima. Emotion model for life-like agent and its evaluation. In *Proceedings of the Fifteenth National Conference on Artificial Intelligence and Tenth Innovative Applications of Artificial Intelligence Conference (AAAI'98/ IAAI'98)*, pages 8–37, Madison, Wisconsin, United States, 1998.

13. Steve Richard Allen. *Concern Processing in Autonomous Agents*. PhD thesis, Faculty of Science of The University of Birmingham, School of Computer Science. Cognitive Science Research Centre. The University of Birmingham, UK, 2001.

14. Carlos Delgado-Mata and Ruth Aylett. Emotion and action selection: Regulating the collective behaviour of agents in virtual environments. In Nicholas R. Jennings, Carles Sierra, Liz Sonenberg, and Milind Tambe, editors, *Proceedings of the Third International Joint Conference on Autonomous Agents and Multi Agent Systems (AAMAS 2004)*, pages 1302–1303, New York, 2004. ACM Press.

15. Sandra Clara Gadanho. Learning behavior-selection by emotions and cognition in a multi-goal robot task. *Journal of Machine Learning Research*, 4:385–412, 2003.

16. Etienne de Sevin and Daniel Thalmann. An affective model of action selection for virtual humans. In *Proceedings of Agents that Want and Like: Motivational and Emotional Roots of Cognition and Action Symposium at the Artificial Intelligence and Social Behaviors 2005 Conference (AISB'05)*, University of Hertfordshire, Hatfield, UK, 2005.

17. Charles Sanders Pierce. *Collected Papers*. The Belknap Press of Harvard University Press, Cambridge, 1965.

18. Magy Seif El-Nasr, John Yen, and Thomas R. Ioerger. FLAME — a fuzzy logic adaptive model of emotions. *Autonomous Agents and Multi-Agent Systems*, 3(3):219–257, 2000.

19. Andrew Ortony, Gerald Clore, and Allen Collins. *The Cognitive Structure of Emotions*. Cambridge University Press, Cambridge, UK, 1988.

20. Juan D. Velásquez. When robots weep: Emotional memories and decision-making. In *Proceedings of the Fifteenth National Conference on Artificial Intelligence and Tenth Innovative Applications of Artificial Intelligence Conference (AAAI'98/ IAAI'98)*, Madison, Wisconsin, United States, 1998. American Association for Artificial Intelligence.

21. Ian Paul Wright. *Emotional Agents*. PhD thesis, Faculty of Science of The University of Birmingham, School of Computer Science. Cognitive Science Research Centre. The University of Birmingham, UK, 1997.

Social Situated Agents in Virtual, Real and Mixed Reality Environments

M. Dragone[1], T. Holz[1], B.R. Duffy[2], and G.M.P. O'Hare[1]

[1] Department of Computer Science,
University College Dublin, Belfield, Dublin 4, Ireland
{Mauro.Dragone, Thomas.Holz, Gregory.OHare}@ucd.ie
http://prism.cs.ucd.ie
[2] Institut Eurécom, 2229 Route des Crêtes, BP 193 - F 06904,
Sophia-Antipolis, France,
Brian.Duffy@eurecom.fr

Abstract. This paper details a framework for explicit deliberative control of socially and physically situated agents in virtual, real and mixed reality environments. The objective is to blur the traditional boundaries between the real and the virtual and provide a standardized methodology for intelligent agent control specifically designed for social interaction. The architecture presented in this paper embraces the fusion between deliberative social reasoning mechanisms and explicit tangible behavioural mechanisms for human-agent social interaction.

1 Introduction

To date, research in intelligent virtual agents can be placed along a spectrum with two differing perspectives [1]: research focusing on the physical aspects, where the aim is to try reproduce the physical attributes of natural agents (such as modelling artificial fish [2] or virtual humans [3]); and research focusing on deliberation, user modelling and, in general, more abstract high level capabilities. Such classification effectively draws an arguable distinction between mind, body and behavioural context. This work, in addition, blurs the boundaries in a third direction, between the real and the virtual (often viewed as delineated) and aims to facilitate the integration of situated real and virtual agents in social deliberative interaction with humans.

We consider social deliberative interaction as encompassing all levels of social interaction between agents which utilize deliberative mechanisms, and in keeping with [4] we believe that current models, such as Belief-Desire-Intention (BDI), are sufficiently sophisticated to facilitate this.

In developing sophisticated control paradigms, robotics research has also provided a rich arena for intelligent reasoning systems as applied to real world contexts, with the field of intelligent agent research providing numerous strategies. While an obvious synergy exists between the two often viewed as disparate domains, few have strongly embraced the inherent advantages of achieving a coherent synthesis between the fields of intelligent agents, virtual characters, and intelligent robot control.

In order to develop a coherent framework for socially situated agents in multi-reality environments, this work draws on previous research in the field of autonomous

T. Panayiotopoulos et al. (Eds.): IVA 2005, LNCS 3661, pp. 166–177, 2005.
© Springer-Verlag Berlin Heidelberg 2005

social robotics, an arena where considerable research has been undertaken in recent years in developing the social deliberative capabilities of artificial systems [5,6]. One of the core methodologies employed in this paper is that of behaviour-based synthesis between perception-acting and deliberation as found in recent robotic research. Instrumental in the development of mobile agent technologies and cross-reality migration, is the work undertaken by the Agent Chameleons project [7].

In order to situate this work within the current state of the art, section 2 briefly discusses relevant control strategies as applied to virtual and real agents. This sets the stage for the Social Situated Agent Architecture (SoSAA) introduced in section 3.

2   Related Work

Over the years, different control strategies for virtual agents have been proposed and implemented. Isla et al. [8], for example, propose a layered model for an artificial brain, where different layers communicate via a shared blackboard, allowing high-level functions to control lower ones (*subsumption*, cf. [9]) and vice versa (*supersumption*). They distinguish between sensing (noticing a stimulus) and perceiving (assigning meaning to a stimulus), allowing different perceptors to extract meaning from the same sensor. The agent's action selection mechanism is governed by a function that looks for the highest expected reward among the possible actions. Egges et al. [10] employ Finite State Machines to control the behaviour of a virtual, conversational agent that takes into account the perceived emotion of the user (via face recognition techniques) and the personality and emotional state of the agent. Chittaro and Serra [11] use a similar approach in the decision process of their agents, applying personality factors to Finite State Machines, but the influence is modelled probabilistically to further the realism of the agent by making it less predictable.

Although some of these systems use personality and emotion to promote agent believability, they are generally based on *reactive behaviour*, i.e. directly mapping perception to action. Cognitive agents, on the other hand, are inspired by models of human-like cognition, allowing the agent to deliberate about, and reflect upon these perceptions and actions before taking an action. De Rosis et al. [12], for example, use Dynamic Belief Networks [13] to model the mind of their conversational agent Greta.

One of the most popular and most widely researched cognitive models is that of BDI agents [14]. BDI theory has proven a particularly apt methodology for autonomous agents in modelling human practical reasoning and grounding traditional symbolic reasoning in situations requiring real-time reactivity.

This work adopts the stance that the future lies in the central area of the spectrum between reactive agents and cognitive agents, where a fusion of the two is necessary. The framework and its implementation presented in the following sections aims to achieve a coherent synthesis between grounded perception-acting and BDI agent-based deliberation.

3   Social Situated Agent Architecture (SoSAA)

The Social Situated Agent Architecture (SoSAA) is a design methodology originally emerging from ongoing research with autonomous social robotic systems [15,5]. The

SoSAA seeks to develop autonomous, rational, resource bounded, social and intentional agents, which can demonstrate an ability to perceive their environment, deliberate about their future and directed actions, and opportunistically form collaborative alliances with other agents (robots or humans) situated within their multi-reality environment. In investigating numerous control strategies capable of dealing with time and resource constraints, and uncertain and partial perceptions in typically noisy and dynamic environments, this work has embraced the synthesis between reactive and deliberative methodologies in order to achieve a coherent integration of representational and non-representational approaches.

The SoSAA can be conceptually decomposed into a number of fundamental levels; reactive, deliberative, and social, as outlined in the following sections. It is important to note that there is a strong interplay between these levels in order to achieve a structured integration of the system's functionality and its subsequent robustness.

3.1 Reactive-Behavioural Level

As in [16], in designing the SoSAA reactive level, a *divide-and-conquer* strategy was adopted, breaking down complex actions into primitive control units called behaviours. Each behavioural unit performs a mapping between sensorial inputs, internal states and a robot's actions in an attempt to accomplish a specific goal (i.e. keeping a constant distance to the wall).

The SoSAA includes a behavioural suite which is the result of the ongoing effort in identifying a set of navigational and behavioural primitives for autonomous mobile robots. These primitives implement both reflex robot responses to unexpected or dangerous events (i.e. *stop on collision*) as well as more complex actions (i.e. *find goal*).

The reactive level functionality is organized into a reactive controller component, which is responsible for the management of every activity (i.e. sensor drivers) and aforementioned behaviour functions (for a more accurate description see [15]. The reactive controller performs a tight closed loop between sensing and acting. At each cycle, the sensor's outputs are routed to the set of active behaviours and the resulting commands redirected to the relevant effectors.

Some behavioural systems (i.e. the Fuzzy Control of the Saphira Architecture [16] implement blending mechanisms that merge behaviour outputs in order to handle more complex situations while still relying on simple behavioural modules. This work argues that there are few cases that justify supporting behavioural blending in general.

In contrast, this work instead on a specific assemblage of behaviours obtained through traditional object-oriented methodology and the possibility of having more than one behaviour active at any given time covering different effectors or devices (i.e. arm grip, wheels). The navigational capabilities of the robots used, for instance, are based upon seminal methods for real time mobile robot obstacle avoidance like the Vector Field Histogram Plus [VFH+] [17] and the Dynamic Window algorithm [18]. The basic obstacle avoidance behaviours consider the disposition of the obstacle in the vicinity of the robot – found, for example, by examining the output of the 2-D range-finder – to deduce a *set of feasible directions*. These are obtained by examining all the manoeuvres available to the robotic platform and excluding those leading to a collision within a pre-determined timeframe. The set of feasible directions may then be used to trade between different objective components. For example, each direction can be evaluated in relation to different aspects like a measure of the control effort (i.e. the acceleration required), the position of reference targets (i.e. for way-point navigation), or the distance from obstacles. The resulting manoeuvre is finally selected by maximizing a weighted sum of these evaluations. By balancing the weights of the components in different ways, different behaviours emerge (see section 4.2).

3.2 Behavioural – Cognitive Synthesis

BDI reasoning is based upon mental attitudes representing the informational (*beliefs*), motivational (*desires* and *goals*), and deliberative (*commitments*) states of the agents. These attributes provide the agent with a usable description of the present and future states of the agent's environment. This description may not necessarily be a faithful representation of the true state of the system, nor of the consequences of the agent's actions, as it would normally be expected of a traditional logic planning systems. A BDI agent's belief is instead a subjective statement of what the agent believes to be true at the current moment, with regard to its own state, the state of the environment, or the state of other agents in its environs.

Consequently, in order to account for incomplete and incorrect information, BDI agents generally employ temporal epistemic logic to deliberate upon their beliefs and find a suitable agent conduct. The BDI methodology decomposes the latter problem into primarily two stages. Firstly, certain facts are included in a set of agent desires (the statements representing states that the agent wishes to be true); secondly, suitable courses of actions are identified as a set of commitments of the agent (each commitment representing a state that the agent is committed to achieve). The second stage usually takes the form of means-end reasoning mechanisms.

SoSAA adopts a constructional approach to bridge the gap between BDI theory and practice (see [19]). In this work, the practical logic reasoner and planner is delivered through Agent Factory [20], an integrated environment for the rapid prototyping of social intentional agents. This system, while simplifying certain aspects of the BDI methodology, provides clear constraints on the agent computational model through the definition of the strategies controlling, for example, the selection of goals or the reconsideration of commitments. SoSAA complements the architectural constraints embedded in Agent Factory with a number of design tools [21] and guidelines, which facilitates the design of BDI style agents and their instantiation in a number of different domains.

Core to the architecture is the Object Tracking subsystem. This subsystem implements an anchoring mechanism, which is similar to the *Artefacts* in the Saphira architecture or to *Sensorial Anchoring* in [22]. The subsystem creates and maintains the connection between symbols and physical objects over time (even if they temporarily disappear from the field of view), identified through the robot's sensorial apparatus. The subsystem also manages to notify the cognitive layer of meaningful events in conjunction with significant changes in the state of the perceptual space of the robot (i.e. start_tracking(object), close(object)).

A soccer player robot, for instance, will be able to reason about objects not directly sensed, without attempting inappropriate activities such as kicking when not in control of the ball, or avoidance of nonexistent objects or, even worse, cancelling pursuit of the ball when it becomes occluded.

A key issue of the interface between the behavioural and the cognitive layer is the interplay between reactive and cognitive control. The deliberation process should not be inundated with requests to deduce new facts and commitments based on every numeric change in the reactive layer (i.e. the position of a tracked object). The agent instead should be able to describe – based on the context of the current task - meaningful geometric relationships between objects to which it intends to respond. For this purpose, the Object Tracking subsystem extracts basic qualitative representation of the situation surrounding the robot. The mechanism is based upon the *Constraints Ontology for Qualitative Reasoning* [23]. In it simplest form, the value space for the variables residing inside behavioural modules is partitioned, defining meaningful landmark values, and subsequently used to create qualitative representations. In addition to the interplay problem, with an increasing number of events computational issues may arise. SoSAA addresses these issues with functional partitioning of the reasoning process. The sensor information at the physical level, for example, is abstracted and organized into intermediate representations following a hierarchical organisation based upon increasing levels of persistence. As in [24] these intermediate representations form the basis of partitioning the deliberative process, defining regions of competences and dependencies among functional areas.

Consequently, the SoSAA cognitive level follows a Multi-Agent-System (MAS) organization with several agents supervising the different functional levels of the robot. At any given time, a number of agents share the control of the robotic platform. These agents vary in complexity from simple procedural knowledge modules that deal with lower level capabilities of the platform (i.e. sensorial organization, configuration and behavioural sequencing) to means-end reasoning (i.e. path-planning).

An important domain-specific issue for autonomous agents sensing and acting in the real world is the creation of beliefs from uncertain and noisy information. The SoSAA Behavioural Level incorporates perception units in association with its behavioural modes. In observing that sensory-motor primitive constrains the dynamic of the interactions between the robot and its environment, this constitutes an effective motivation to perception structuring and attention focusing. In earlier work [25], it has been shown how behavioural modes simplify the perceptual space and how feature detection (i.e. identifying signatures in the values returned from the sonar ring during wall following) can be used to create perception hypothesis and expectations in order to channel future structured sensing strategies, leading to the formation of perceptual evidence.

3.3 Social Intentional Agents

A distinguishing feature of the Agent Factory-developed deliberative level of SoSAA is its support for explicit social interaction in the form of a social level implanted in each of its agents. This social level is charged with maintaining a model for every agent acquaintance so that their behaviour can be accounted and influence the reasoning process. To facilitate collaboration among agents, Agent Factory agents make use of Speech Act Theory [26], a formalism for accurate and expressive communication mechanisms in Multi-Agent Systems. This is undertaken by performing a speech act (such as *requesting, ordering, informing* or *promising*) that sends a message to one or more of their socially capable acquaintances in order to affect their mental states. In this work, the robotic agents interact via Agent Communication Language (ACL) directives with semantic corresponding to the specifications outlined within FIPA (Foundations of Intelligent Physical Agents, see http://www.fipa.org). At a simple level, the messages received may trigger specific commitment rules governing the reaction of the receiving agent. The following example (in pseudocode) illustrates how a robot playing soccer, when asked to move to its home position (`reset`) on the football pitch, adopts the appropriate commitment.

```
BELIEF(requested_achieve(reset) & BELIEF(role(?R)) &
BELIEF(Home (?R,?X,?Y)
=> Commit(Self, Now, ActivateBehav-
iour(MoveTo(x,?X,y,?Y)))
```

In addition to FIPA "`inform`" and "`request`" directives, a number of more sophisticated interaction protocols have also been implemented, among them, the Contract-Net-Protocol, which is used in group formation or task allocation for example.

4   The Social Situated Agent Architecture in Action

The Social Situated Agent Architecture provides for multi-reality implementations. As the SoSAA employs embodiment abstraction strategies implemented across its multi-layered architecture, it facilitates instantiations within virtual, physical and mixed reality environments. At the cognitive layer, SoSAA makes use of the embodiment mechanism of Agent Factory. This defines `Actuator` and `Perceptor` modules for interfacing to diverse applicative domains and provides a framework for reasoning about embodiment forms in terms of agent capabilities and constraints [14]. The reactive-behavioural layer achieves a degree of abstraction from the sensor and actuator modalities by individually tailoring to each hardware platform. `Behaviour` implementations do not address the specifics of what body they are controlling, thus enabling easy portability of code from simulated to physical robots of differing platforms. The following examples illustrate how the system has been instantiated with a view to demonstrating the systems flexibility and versatility.

4.1   Physical Agents

Figure 1 illustrates a section of the specifications for a single robotic agent (a Nomad Scout robot) fetching a coloured ball and bringing it to its home position.

SoSAA Agent specifications are stored in ASCII files containing Agent Factory Agent Programming Language (AF-APL [19]) scripts. AF-APL scripts contain initial beliefs; the declaration of actuators and perceptors in use by the robotic agent and commitment rules governing behavioural transitions, plan activation, and goal decomposition. A Platform Manager Agent constitutes the main script, which describes the robotic agent and supervises its initialisation. This script can also contain a list of references to additional AF-APL scripts (i.e. roles and plans), each specifying the BDI design for a different functional area.

```
DEFINE close(Ball) RobotCtrl.Tracking.ObjectTrracked.distance < 1000   // close if less than 1m
DEFINE distant(Ball) RobotCtrl.Tracking.ObjectTracked.distance >= 100  // distant otherwise
DEFINE touching(Ball) RobotCtrl.Tracking.ObjectTracked.distance < 50   // touching if closer than 5cm
...
BELIEF(start) ⇒ COMMIT(Self, Now, ActivateBehaviour(Stop))
BELIEF(start_tracking(ball)) & (BELIEF(distant(ball))
       ⇒ COMMIT(Self, Now, ActivateBehaviour(MoveTo(Object,ball,MaxV,100))
BELIEF(end_tracking(ball)) ⇒ COMMIT(Self, Now, ActivateBehaviour(Scan, timeout, 5000)))
BELIEF(timeout_Scan) ⇒ COMMIT(Self, Now, ActivateBehaviour(MoveFree, timeout, 20000)))
BELIEF(timeout_MoveFree) ⇒ COMMIT(Self, Now, ActivateBehaviour(Scan, timeout, 5000)))
BELIEF(close(ball)) & BELIEF(sensing(ball)) &
!BELIEF(current(FaceObject)) & !BELIEF(touching(ball))
       ⇒ COMMIT(Self, Now, ActivateBehaviour (FaceObject (Object
       ,ball,MaxV,40,w,450,aw,300,PID,1000,0.2,0)))
BELIEF(start_touching(ball))
       ⇒ COMMIT(Self, Now, ActivateBehaviour(TurnToward(X,0,Y,0,MaxV,200)))
BELIEF(turned) ⇒ COMMIT(Self, Now, ActivateBehaviour(MoveTo(X,0,Y,0,MaxV,100)))
```

Fig. 1. AF-APL Script controlling the fetch-ball task

Fig. 2. A Nomad Scout robot fetching a coloured ball

Figure 2 shows key snapshots from the execution of the *fetch ball* task. The robot can be seen approaching the ball using its estimated coordinates - as deduced by the camera activity that performs colour-segmentation on the image captured from the on-board camera - as way-point targets for its obstacle avoidance behaviour. Thereafter, when the ball is judged sufficiently close, a PID (Proportional Integrative Derivative) controller is selected as the behaviour of choice to control the gaze of the robot and direct the acquisition of the ball. Once the robot is in control of the ball, it turns and returns to its home position, reactivating the obstacle avoidance behaviour.

The DEFINE macros in the first part of the script describe simple landmark values for a qualitative description (*close/distant/touching*) of the distance of the ball.

4.2 Virtual Agents

Using Virtual Environments for simulation, prototyping, and testing of robotic control architectures is an obvious and widely employed approach, as experimenting in the real world can prove both, complicated and costly. SoSAA comprises of a set of simulated sensors and effectors interchangeable with the real world counterparts. Figure 3 shows a simulated robot performing the fetch-ball task in a virtual space. The simulated robot is under control of the same AF-APL script as the real robot (see Figure 1). The only difference is that all sensor drivers and actuators have been replaced with simulated objects. The emphasis in this work is on the faithful replication of real behaviours. By mirroring simple behaviours in virtual space (i.e. emulating noises and timing of the sensorial apparatus), all layers of the SoSAA architecture can be subsequently exercised.

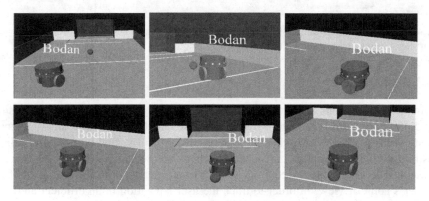

Fig. 3. A simulated Scout robot fetching a coloured ball

While the degree of complexities existing in real world environments is not found in artificial virtual spaces, there are advantages in transferring robotic architectures to virtual agents. Real-world robotic architectures are usually more robust, as they have to cope with a more complex, a more unpredictable, and a more uncertain world.

BDI agents are particularly well suited for the creation of believable characters as their cognitive framework facilitates the implementation of subjective behaviours.

Figure 4 shows three different views of a virtual environment populated by a group of virtual robots and other artificial characters animated using AF-APL scripts. In the example each agent is under the control of a different behaviour obtained with different weights of the components in the SoSAA obstacle avoidance module.

Figure 4 (left) shows the different trajectories followed by each agent. The set of weights for the behaviour of the robot "Bodan" (in the corridor) are set to maximize the speed of the robot. The agent "Bunny" is instead performing the *wall following* behaviour, favouring manoeuvres that approach the closer obstacle on the left of the robot. The robot "Bui" (in the right-lower room) is using an *Escape* behaviour which brings it to prefer to stay clear of obstacles. Finally, the agent "Snowman" is static, permanently located in the corridor. Its script controls an animation effector which makes him salute the user (by waving its hat) when the avatar of the user gets in its proximity. The right picture exposes the perceptual state of the robot "Bodan", showing in the example the detection of a door and other objects through its range and vision sensors. The virtual world in the example has been implemented with the Virtual Robotic Workbench [27], our Multimedia Collaborative Virtual Environment framework for communities of intentional agents.

Fig. 4. Views from a Virtual Test Environment. Left: Agent trajectories. Middle: User view. Right: Perspective and tracked objects from Robot Bodan.

4.3 Mixed Agents

Having previously considered our physical and virtual agent cousins we now consider how SoSAA can accommodate a hybrid of these capabilities within an Augmented Reality scenario. We believe that the synergy of real and virtual worlds offer unique possibilities that each realms independently cannot provide. One of the challenges of Augmented Reality is to correctly align the virtual images with the real scene from the user's point of view. In order to track the user's position in an efficient and cost-effective way, we employ ARToolkit [28], a system that facilitates the recognition and pose estimation of physical markers within a camera image. We arranged five markers in a cube (Figure 5 (a)) to make the robot traceable from all angles. The SoSAA makes the user's point of view known to the robot, which then turns its physical body to the user and greets him via its virtual avatar. The agent thus makes a combined use of its physical and virtual embodiment. Figure 5 (b) shows a snapshot of the robot fetching the ball on the user's request. Since the robot knows the position of the observer, it can bring the ball to the user's location.

Fig. 5. (a) The agent turns to the user to greet him. (b) The agent fetches the ball for the user.

The agent is able to manipulate the physical world, e.g. by passing the ball to the user, as well as the virtual, e.g. moving a virtual object. The virtual avatar provides a powerful interaction modality for the user, supporting a rich set of body forms, gestures and facial expressions. As the agents are aware of the user's gaze, he can identify and directly address the member of a team of agents by looking at it. In turn, the robot can try to get the attention of the user by moving into the user's field of view.

5   Future Work and Conclusions

Prior research [27] incorporates strong notions of perceptual identity in artificial systems through the use of stereotypes, character (perceived identity) and roles [27]. We intend to integrate this work into the SoSAA framework to provide a flexible mechanism where users can customise both the agent's virtual persona and how this is managed through explicit mechanisms for artificial identity. While each agent's representation is fundamentally grounded on a unique identity, these personalisation mechanisms allow users to select their own preferred avatars in both virtual and augmented reality applications. In such a personalized mixed reality environment, the SoSAA supports not only different users seeing different avatars, but also facilitates users with no equipment such as a Head Mounted Display (HMD). Such participants would merely see the robot's physical body and as such would only interact at the physical level, while HMD users could avail of the visual representation and the richer interaction it affords.

By making the agent aware of its own embodiment, its capabilities and those of its acquaintances, both humans and agents, it is able to use both worlds to their full potential. The agent could, for example, offer a virtual object to the user if it thinks he is capable of grabbing it, e.g. with a data glove.

Furthermore, migration mechanisms empower the agent, for example, it may move to a user's desktop PC in order to download a different outfit for the avatar, and then take control of the robot again.

The primary objective of the work presented in this paper has been to introduce a framework for explicit social interaction between people and a situated deliberative agent. This agent can manifest itself through a virtual avatar or an augmented reality agent in conjunction with a physical robot. The concept of artificial identity is specifically addressed to augment persistent social grounding between people and artificial systems. The result is a flexible infrastructure which allows for the rapid prototyping of social situated agents.

Numerous different implementations of the SoSAA have been undertaken which clearly fuses the notion that a physical robot is in fact a physically embodied agent. The system's context and environmental situatedness simply provides a different data set for deliberation and reactive behaviour. While it is argued that physical embodiment is a necessary criterion for the development of artificial intelligence, this work adopts the stance that an inherently artificial system is fundamentally constrained by its artificiality and as such can exploit quite different frames of reference.

While the work presented in this paper describes relatively weak forms of social interaction involving communication via Speech Act Theory and rudimentary acquaintance models, it does however offer a framework within which much richer social interactions can be accommodated incorporating a tapestry of human, physical and virtual entities.

The research presented herein envisages a community of interacting agent entities that are either human, or physical or virtual. The SoSAA architecture provides the necessary infrastructure upon which effective demonstrators of this vision can be realized.

Acknowledgments

This research is based upon works supported by the Science Foundation Ireland under Grant No. 03/IN.3/1361.

References

[1] Aylett, R. and Luck, M.: Applying Artificial Intelligence to Virtual Reality: Intelligent Virtual Environments. Applied Artificial Intelligence 14 (2000) 3-32

[2] Terzopoulos, D., Tu, X. and Grzeszczuk, R.: Artificial Fishes: Autonomous Locomotion, Perception, Behavior, and Learning in a Simulated Physical World. Artificial Life 1 (1994) 327-351

[3] Thalmann, D.: Challenges for the Research in Virtual Humans. In: Proceedings of the Workshop on Achieving Human-Like Behavior in Interactive Animated Agents, Barcelona, Spain (2000)

[4] Smit, R. and Verhagen, H.: On being social: degrees of sociality and models of rationality in relation to multiagent systems. In: Proceedings of the 1995 AAAI Fall Symposium: Concepts, Theories, Models and Applications (1995)

[5] Duffy, B.R.: The Social Robot. Ph.D. Thesis, University College Dublin, Department of Computer Science (2000)

[6] Dragone, M.: The Virtual Robotic Workbench. Technical Report No. UCD-PRISM-05-11. University College Dublin, Department of Computer Science (2005)

[7] Duffy, B.R., O'Hare, G.M.P., Martin, A.N., Bradley, J.F. and Schön, B.: Agent Chameleons: Agent Minds and Bodies. In: Proceedings of the 16th International Conference on Computer Animation and Social Agents (CASA '03), New-Brunswick, USA (2003)

[8] Isla, D.A., Burke, R.C., Downie, M. and Blumberg, B.: A Layered Brain Architecture for Synthetic Creatures. In: Proceedings of the 17th International Joint Conference on Artificial Intelligence (IJCAI '01), Seattle, USA (2001)

[9] Brooks, R.A.: Intelligence without Reason. In: Proceedings of the 12th International Joint Conference on Artificial Intelligence (IJCAI '91), Sydney, Australia (1991)

[10] Egges, A., Kshirsagar, S., Zhang, X. and Magnenat-Thalmann, N.: Emotional Communication with Virtual Humans. In: Proceedings of the 9th International Multimedia Modeling Conference (MMM '03), Taiwan (2003)

[11] Chittaro, L. and Serra, M.: Behavioural programming of autonomous characters based on probabilistic automata and personality. Computer Animation and Virtual Worlds 15 (2004) 319-326

[12] de Rosis, F., Pelachaud, C., Poggi, I., Carofiglio, V. and De Carolis, B.: From Greta's mind to her face: modelling the dynamics of affective states in a conversational embodied agent. International Journal of Human-Computer Studies 59 (2003) 81-118

[13] Nicholson, A. and Brady, J.: Dynamic belief networks for discrete monitoring. IEEE Transactions on Systems, Man, and Cybernetics 24 (1994) 1593-1610

[14] Rao, A.S. and Georgeff, M.P.: BDI-agents: from theory to practice. In: Proc. of the 1st International Conference on Multiagent Systems (ICMAS '95), San Francisco, USA (1995)

[15] Duffy, B.R., Dragone, M., O'Hare, G.M.P: Social Robot Architecture: A Framework for Explicit Social Interaction. Android Science: Towards Social Mechanisms, CogSci 2005 Workshop, Stresa, Italy (2005)

[16] Konolige, K., Myers, K., Saffiotti A. and Ruspini, E.: The Saphira architecture: a design for autonomy. Journal of Experimental and Theoretical Artificial Intelligence 9 (1997) 215-235

[17] Ulrich I. and Borenstein, J.: VFH+: Reliable Obstacle Avoidance for Fast Mobile Robots. IEEE International Conference on Robotics and Automation, Leuven, Belgium (1998)

[18] Fox, D., Burgard, W. and Thrun, S.: The dynamic window approach to collision avoidance. IEEE Robotics and Automation Magazine 4/1 (1997)

[19] Ross, R., Collier, R., and O'Hare, G.M.P.: AF-APL: Bridging Principles & Practice in Agent-Oriented Languages. In: Proceedings of the 2nd International Workshop on Programming Multi-Agent Systems Languages and Tools (PROMAS-2004) at the 3rd International Joint Conference on Autonomous Agents and Multi Agent Systems (AAMAS04), Columbia University, New York, USA (2004). Lecture Notes in Computer Science (LNCS), Springer Verlag Publishers (2004)

[20] Collier, R.W.: Agent Factory: A Framework for the Engineering of Agent-Oriented Applications, Ph.D. Thesis, University College Dublin, Ireland (2001)

[21] Rooney, C F.B., Collier, R.W. and O'Hare, G.M.P.: VIPER: VIsual Protocol EditoR. In: Proceedings of the 6th International Conference on Coordination Languages and Models (COORDINATION 2004), Pisa, Italy (2004). Lecture Notes in Computer Science (LNCS), Springer Verlag Publishers (2004)

[22] Coradeschi S. and Saffiotti, A: Perceptual Anchoring of Symbols for Action. In: Proceedings of the 17th IJCAI Conference, Seattle, USA (2001)

[23] Kuipers , B.: Qualitative Simulation. Artificial Intelligence 29 (1986) 289-338

[24] Sheshagiri M. and des Jardins, M.: Data Persistence: A Design Principle for Hybrid Robot Control Architectures. Proceedings of the International Conference On Knowledge Based Computer Systems, Mumbai, India (2002)

[25] Duffy, B.R., Garcia, C., Rooney, C.F. and O'Hare, G.M.: Sensor Fusion for Social Robotics In: Proceedings of the 31st International Symposium on Robotics (ISR '00), Montreal, Canada (2000)

[26] Searle, J.: Speech Acts: An essay in the philosophy of language. London, Cambridge University Press (1969)

[27] Duffy, B.R.: Social Embodiment in Autonomous Mobile Robotics. International Journal of Advanced Robotic Systems 1/3 (2004) 155-170

[28] Kato, H., Billinghurst, M. and Poupyrev I.: ARToolKit. Technical report, Hiroshima City University (2000)

Do You See What Eyes See? Implementing Inattentional Blindness

Erdan Gu[1], Catherine Stocker[2], and Norman I. Badler[1]

[1] Department of Computer and Information Science, University of Pennsylvania,
Philadelphia PA, 19104-6389
{erdan, badler}@seas.upenn.edu
[2] Department of Psychology, University of Pennsylvania, Philadelphia PA, 19104
cstocker@sas.upenn.edu

Abstract. This paper presents a computational model of visual attention incorporating a cognitive imperfection known as inattentional blindness. We begin by presenting four factors that determine successful attention allocation: conspicuity, mental workload, expectation and capacity. We then propose a framework to study the effects of those factors on an unexpected object and conduct an experiment to measure the corresponding subjective awareness level. Finally, we discuss the application of a visual attention model for conversational agents.

1 Introduction

If an embodied (virtual) agent is expected to interact with humans in a shared real or virtual environment, it must have the cognitive ability to understand human visual attention and its limitations. Likewise, an embodied agent should possess human attention attributes so that its eyes and resultant body movements convey appropriate and humanly understandable behaviors. Suppressed or inappropriate eye movements can by themselves damage the communicative effectiveness of an embodied agent. Thus, in order to build convincing computational models of human behavior, one should have a thorough understanding of communication and interaction patterns of real people. Attention models may be the key to leading animated agents out of the "uncanny valley" where increasing visual accuracy, combined with lifeless eyes, results in a "ghoulish" appearance when animated.

As a first step to making the appearance of virtual agents more realistic, we are creating a model of human visual attention. The visual attention system has been proposed to employ two filters − bottom-up [10] [18] and top-down [9][4] − to limit visual processing to the most important information of the world. In our early work [7], we suggested a computational model that was unique because not only did it integrate both of these filters, but also combined 2D snapshots of the scene with 3D structural information. However, after extensive examination of the Psychology literature, we became aware of the many intricate shortcomings of human cognition, and recognized the importance of incorporating *inadequacies* in processing as a means of making a simulated human agent more realistic.

T. Panayiotopoulos et al. (Eds.): IVA 2005, LNCS 3661, pp. 178–190, 2005.
© Springer-Verlag Berlin Heidelberg 2005

Inattentional blindness [21], as the name implies, occurs when objects that are physically capable of being seen in fact go unnoticed. Inattentional blindness was chosen as the primary phenomenon to include in our framework for two reasons. First, evidence suggests that it mainly involves the attention system, rather than other cognitive structures such as memory or language [1]. Other prominent attentional deficits, such as change blindness, appear to be tied much closer to these additional cognitive structures [17]. Second, inattentional blindness is a robust feature of multimodal attention and analogous paradigms, such as the "cocktail party effect", have been well documented in auditory attention [19]. Therefore, once this model is complete its future applications will not be restricted to the visual system, but can be extended into other realms of cognitive processing.

While it is commonly believed that an object requires only perceptible physical properties to be noticed in a scene, recent studies have found that people often miss very visible objects when they are preoccupied with an attentionally demanding task [20]. Mack and Rock coined the term inattentional blindness, and concluded that conscious perception is not possible without attention [12]. Green [6] attempted to classify all of the prominent features of the phenomenon, and suggested that there are four categories that these features fall into: *conspicuity*, *mental workload*, *expectation* and *capacity*. Through experimental testing, Most *et al.* [13] forged a link between attention capture and inattentional blindness, and revealed the single most important factor affecting the phenomenon, the attentional set. They also introduced the concept of different levels of attentional processing, which, in our work, is categorized as four stages of subject awareness [22]: *unnoticed*, *subliminal*, *non-reflective* and *semantic*.

In order to formulate a realistic attentional framework, we will examine attentional deficiency and inattentional blindness, while attempting to answer three questions:

1. What kinds of stimulus properties will influence the likelihood of missing the unexpected object or event?
2. What kinds of perceiver-controlled mechanisms decide what should be permitted into consciousness and what should be rejected?
3. How much, if any, of a scene do we perceive when we are not attending to it?

2 Theories and Experiment

First we define the four factors critical to inattentional blindness and describe how they are used in our experiment to study their effects on subjective awareness level. By questioning subjects who participated in our experiment, we hoped to determine quantitative descriptions of each parameter's individual and combined importance in attention allocation.

The Four Factors Model

Because cognitive resources are limited, attention acts as a filter to quickly examine sensory input and allow only a small subset of it through for complete processing. The rest of the input never reaches consciousness, so is left unnoticed and unremembered. It has been suggested that the attentional filter is affected by four factors [6]: conspicuity, mental workload, expectation and capacity.

Conspicuity
Conspicuity refers to an object's ability to grab attention, and can be divided into two distinct groups: sensory and cognitive conspicuity [20]. Sensory conspicuity refers to the physical or bottom-up properties of an object, such as contrast, size, location and movement. Cognitive conspicuity, on the other hand, reflects the personal and social relevance that an object contains. Face pop-out – the phenomenon where faces that are meaningful to a person are more likely to capture attention – is an example of cognitive conspicuity in visual attention capture.

Mental Workload
There is only a finite amount of attention available to be rationed to objects and events. Thus, items that require more attention decrease one's ability to allocate this limited resource to other objects. As tasks become more difficult they increase the mental workload of the subject and require more attention, increasing the likelihood that an unexpected event will go unnoticed. Similarly, as tasks become less difficult, they require less attention. An object requiring less mental processing with time is said to be habituated [6]. This will cause workload to decrease and allow for other objects in the scene to be attended to more readily. An example of habituation is learning to drive a car. While driving may begin as a very difficult task, as it becomes more ingrained in one's repertoire of abilities, it becomes less mentally taxing.

Expectation
While the habituation process slowly decreases workload levels for the entire scene with time, expectation quickly causes specific stimuli to gain more weight over time and trials. According to the Contingent-Capture Hypothesis [20], as items and properties of items become more expected they become part of an attentional set. This attentional set then informs a person what is important and relevant in a scene. Inattentional blindness occurs when certain items are expected so much that people ignore any others. The Contingent-Capture Hypothesis, and the attentional set's involvement in inattentional blindness, will be described in detail in the next section.

Capacity
Attentional capacity refers to the number of items and information that a person can attend to at a time. Variations in capacity are a result of the individual differences between people, but are also affected by a person's current mental state (fatigue), cognitive processes (habituation), and physiological state (drugs and alcohol) [6].

Our Experiment and Its Parameters

Our study was based on a famous demonstration of inattentional blindness, "Gorillas in our midst" [16], which asked participants to count the number of times a basketball was passed among a group of people. During this activity, a individual in a gorilla costume walked into and through the scene. Rather remarkably, many subjects do not recall seeing anything unusual! In our variation (Fig. 1), subjects were assigned the task of counting the number of ball passes between images of human-like characters that we created in a virtual environment. During this time, an unexpected image passed through the scene and the event continued, undisturbed.

Fig. 1. Example Frame of Animation Demo in the Experiment: Eight players (four in black T-shirts, four in white) move around the screen randomly while two 'balls': (one white, one black) bounce between them. Subjects were responsible for counting the number of passes made to the black T-shirt team using the black ball. A pass was considered to be completed when the ball hit the image, and the image 'jumped' Fifty seconds into the task an unexpected, face-forward, gray boxed character (the unexpected object) passed through the scene, but the players continued as normal. The task lasted a total of 90 seconds.

The four factors of inattentional blindness were measured by adjusting various parameters during the experiment. The appearance and movement of the objects contained in the scene, as well as the scene itself, were varied in order to affect the cognitive workload, sensory conspicuity and attentional set.

The first variation, the mental workload of the subject, could be high, medium, or low, determined by the speed that the balls moved and the amount of background clutter. A subject in a high mental workload group observed very fast moving balls and a cluttered (green and white checkered) background; the medium mental workload group saw medium speed moving balls and a cluttered background; the low mental workload group watched a slow moving ball and an uncluttered (all gray) background.

The sensory conspicuity of the unexpected object could also be varied: high, medium, or low, determined by the inherent physical salience of the unexpected object. Here, the saliency was dependent on the speed, as well as the trajectory that the unexpected object took. High sensory conspicuity groups were presented with an unexpected image that appeared and disappeared while moving quickly along the background of the scene. The unexpected object of the medium sensory conspicuity group moved at a medium speed, in an irregular manner (beginning in the background, moving back-and-forth towards the foreground) across the screen. The low sensory conspicuity group received an unexpected object that moved at a slow speed in a straight line across the background of the scene.

Finally, the attentional set held by our subjects always contained the color black because they were attending to the black T-shirt group and tracking a black ball. What varied in the attentional set parameter is how similar the unexpected object's features were to the attentional set held by the subject, so the values were: matched, neither matched nor unmatched, or unmatched, according to the color of the unexpected object's T-shirt (black, maroon or white respectively). In Table 1, we list the variables in the experiment and their corresponding factors.

Table 1. Summary of the relationship between the four factors and the experimental parameters. It shows how the four factors interact with shown the attentional set and object properties.

Factors		Definition	Parameters
Conspicuity	Sensory	Pop-out due to an object's inherent physical saliency in a scene.	Color & Intensity ·Contrast ·Opaqueness ·Environment ·Clutter ·Illumination Size Movement ·Velocity ·Trajectory
	Cognitive	Pop-out due to the perceiver's mental state and task relevance.	Personal Relevance ·Meaningful Face Pop-Out ·Familiarity
Workload		The amount of attention that the current item requires. Reduces probability of attention shift.	Difficulty Environment Habituation ·Time ·Trial
Expectation		The amount of attention an object receives varies according to a perceiver's beliefs about its relevance in the scene, due to past experience.	Attentional Set ·Task-specific features
Capacity		The total amount of attention available varies by individual	Individual differences Mental State

3   Computational Framework

Green's four-factor model specifies a theoretical set of parameters involved in inattentional blindness, while Most *et al.* provide the evidence for a detailed progression from "ignored" to "part of consciousness." Our model integrates the two theories – attempting to retain the individual contribution of each – into a comprehensive theory of attention allocation (Fig. 2).

Dynamic Internal Representation of the World

Our attention capture framework relies on the cooperation of an internally-driven top-down setting and external bottom-up input. The bottom-up setting uses the "saliency" (sensory conspicuity features) of objects in the scene to filter perceptual information and compute an objective saliency map. Primary visual features such as color, contrast and motion are the features examined by this filter. Simultaneously, top-down settings, such as expectation and face pop-out determine the set of items that are contextually important, such as the attentional set, which is a subjective feature pool of task-prominent properties maintained in memory. At any moment, focused attention only provides a spatio-temporal coherence map for one object [15]. This coherence map highlights the object that has been calculated to be the most important at that moment in the scene, and can thus be used to drive the gaze of an embodied agent.

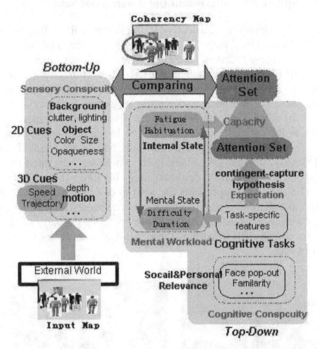

Fig. 2. Block Diagram for computational framework. It illustrates the computational model of visual attention incorporating the four factors model and the contingent capture hypothesis.

The final coherency map is created in three steps. First, a spatial coherency map is created, then it is augmented by temporal coherency and finally moderated by the attentional set. The spatial coherency map is computed by transforming a snapshot of the scene to the retinal field by a retinal filter. It is generally believed that the internal mental image is built through non-uniform coding of the scene image. This coding is determined by the anatomical structure of the human retina, causing the image to appear very clear wherever the center of the retina is located, and increasingly blurry as distance from the center increases. In other words, whatever a person looks directly at will appear the most clear in their mental image, and objects will appear less clear the further they are from the in-focus object. Log-polar sampling [2] is employed as an approximation to the foveated representation of the visual system. The processing occurs rapidly (i.e., within a few hundred milliseconds) and in parallel across a 2D snapshot image of the scene. To allow real-time computation, interpolation between the partitions of receptive fields is implemented [8]. For each trial of our experiment, the size of the fixation field (the patch with the highest resolution) remained approximately constant since the distance from the subject to the screen, as well as the resolution of the animated demo, were fixed.

Once the spatial map is created, a temporal mapping highlights the direction of important movement. A final coherency map is generated by integrating these two maps and filtering the objects of interest using the attentional set.

The Contingent-Capture Hypothesis and the Attentional Set

The attentional set, determined by subjective expectation, will further tune the generated spatio-temporal coherency map. The Contingent-Capture Hypothesis states that the only time that an object receives attention is when it, or properties of it, is contained in the attentional set held by the subject [5]. Most *et al.* expand on this theory, revealing that before an object can even be considered for attention, and thus compared to the attentional set, a transient orienting response to the object must occur. Consequently, the likelihood of noticing an unexpected object increases with the object's similarity to the currently attended object. In our animation demo, since the task was to count the number of times that the black ball hit the black T-shirt players, attentional set={black T-shirt people, black ball} would be warranted by the Contingent-Capture Hypothesis. Fig. 3(a), demonstrates the three influences on the final coherency map. The red circle represents the spatial coherency map, the green circle denotes the temporal coherency, and the blue square reveals the object that matches the black color as well as the black T-shirt people held as a property of the attentional set. The red ellipse in Fig. 3(b) illustrates the readjusted coherency map that incorporates all three influences.

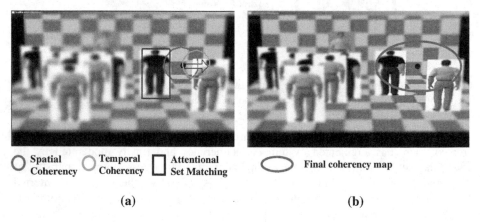

○ Spatial Coherency   ○ Temporal Coherency   ☐ Attentional Set Matching   ○ Final coherency map

(a)   (b)

Fig. 3. Generation of Coherency Map. **(a):** Three influences of attention capture: spatial, temporal and attentional set. **(b):** The final coherency map, resulting from the combined effect of the three influences.

Subjective Awareness Level

Following completion of the task, participants filled out a questionnaire to determine if they noticed an unexpected object. To discover the level of processing that the object received, questions probed how well they perceived the object. Questions began by vaguely asking about anything unusual, and increased in specificity until subjects were asked to choose the unexpected image out of a line-up of eight.

We now introduce the concept of awareness level to describe the degrees of perceptual organization achieved by the visual system. At the lowest extreme is complete inattentional blindness – attentional resources failed to be allocated to the object resulting in a failure to notice it. At the opposite end is the highest level of consciousness, the semantic level, where the object is perceived as a figure-ground discrimination with meaning. In between the two extremes are the subliminal level and the non-reflective level. The subliminal level is represented by a subject's acknowledgement of the presence of the unexpected object, but no conscious awareness of any of its physical characteristics. Hence, important subliminal messages were transmitted for further processing because they were salient enough to cause a transient orienting response, but were prevented from reaching higher levels. With a little more attentional investment, objects could have been processed at the non-reflective level. At the non-reflective level the object receives enough attention to allow the subject to retain some, but not all, of its features in memory. At this level, the subject has not yet developed a figure or ground structure. Thus, a partial description of the object can be expected, but some details will be missed. Fig. 4 shows a block diagram of these processing levels.

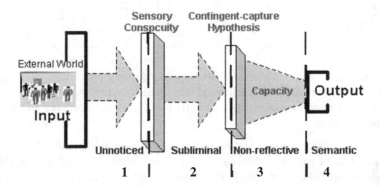

Fig. 4. Workflow of three filters. It demonstrates how three filters work to determine different level of process.

The amount of attention devoted to the processing of an object can also be explained by how several filters work. When an object is not physically salient enough to catch attention, it is discarded by the sensory conspicuity filter, resulting in no processing and, consequently, no conscious awareness of it. An object has passed the sensory conspicuity comparison when it was eye-catching enough to induce an unconscious transient shift of attention. If the properties of this object do not match those held in the attentional set, it falls out of current coherence map, having received only minimal attention. But even if the object was physically salient and held many properties that matched the attentional set, it can still be discarded due to the capacity bottleneck. At this level, the object has been processed quite a bit, but not completely, so a subject's description of the object would contain some partial or even incorrect details. Finally, the object approaches the semantic level and is fully processed in conscious perception. For people who allowed the unexpected item to be sustained in attention, a detailed description is not difficult.

4 Experiment Results and Discussion

Thirty-six participants were randomly assigned to one of 27 groups that varied according to three parameters: mental workload, sensory conspicuity and attentional set. The data from six participants was discarded because of previous experience with inattentional blindness, or incorrect performance on the task. The results are summarized in Table 2 and illustrated in Fig. 5. The awareness level is assigned as a score from 1 to 4, corresponding to the processing levels from unnoticed to semantic, respectively. Each group included 10 subjects. The average score for the matched, unmatched, and neither matched nor unmatched attentional set groups was 2.5, 2.1 and 3.0, respectively.

Table 2. Summary of the levels of processing averaged by the subjects in each group

Attentional set	Average	Workload			Conspicuity		
		Low	Med	High	Low	Med	High
Match (subj : 10)	2.5	2.7	2.0	2.2	2.0	2.3	3.3
Unmatch (subj: 10)	2.1	3.3	1.7	1.7	2.0	2.5	2.0
Neither (subj: 10)	3.0	3.5	3.0	2.7	1.7	3.7	3.7
Average		3.2	2.2	2.2	1.9	2.8	3.0

Thus, we can consider the results favorable since they agree with the four-factor model and our computational framework. This validates our model's assumption on these three very important factors of inattentional blindness. There are a few interesting findings to note.

1. We found the neither matched nor unmatched object is generally the most easily noticed one of the three attentional set groups. While counterintuitive, this finding is supported by our model. The model allows for the possibility that objects that perfectly match the attentional set will be discarded in level one if they are not physically salient enough. It would be reasonable to believe that the black and white T-shirt unexpected images (matched and unmatched, respectively) were not physically salient in the scene, and could have been discarded in level one. The maroon T-shirt unexpected object (neither matched nor unmatched), could have been inherently salient enough to pass through the first bottom-up filter and then made its way into awareness because of its similarity to the attentional set in pant color and body shape as well as the T-shirt which is darker than it is light. (That is, it was more black than white – so more likely to be in the attentional set than in the inhibition set). More work should be done to illuminate the causal features in this situation.

2. Additionally, there are two interesting findings about workload. Not only does it show the largest difference between its largest variations, suggesting that workload is the most important feature of attention capture and inattention blindness, but it also shows its largest variation between its *medium* and *low* settings (as opposed to the expected high and low settings). The only difference between the high and medium setting is the ball speed, but the ball with high speed was ex-

tremely fast. It is possible that the high setting was too difficult, and that people were more easily distracted because they had actually given up on the task. The medium speed may have been just difficult enough. This is another important parameter to investigate.

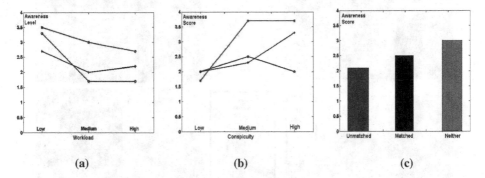

         (a)   (b)   (c)

Fig. 5. For all charts, red corresponds to the neither matched nor unmatched attentional set, black corresponds to the matched set and blue corresponds to the unmatched set. (a) Awareness Score vs. Workload. The unexpected object becomes more noticeable as the workload is reduced for all three attentional set groups. (b) Awareness Score vs. Conspicuity. The unexpected object receives greater processing when sensory conspicuity increases though there is some noise in the unmatched group. (c) Awareness Scores vs. Attentional set. The unexpected object receives the most processing when it is neither matched nor unmatched and the least when it is unmatched.

5   Application

The importance of a flawed attention model is considerable. Communication, especially face-to-face conversational interaction [3], is affected not only by the individuals involved, but also by what is taking place in the external environment [14]. To improve the naturalness of conversations, we are attempting to use the attentional framework to create embodied agents that are aware of a perceived world. While attention to the conversational partner is the most basic form of signaling understanding by the agent, a listener whose eyes never waver from her partner, despite background events, appears lifeless.

An agent with a realistic attentional system also has the ability to use the perceptual information it gains from the external world to enhance its engagement during a conversation. Engagement is defined here as the process by which two (or more) participants establish and maintain their perceived connection during interactions they jointly undertake [19][20]. Three types of engagement cues are categorized: those with oneself, those with a conversational partner, and those with the environment. Our inattention blindness framework can improve the engagement behaviors of an embodied agent, particularly for the transition from self/partner to the environment. Therefore, in conjunction with an eye-movement model [11], the attentional model will increase the realism of an agent's engagement behaviors, as demonstrated in Fig. 6.

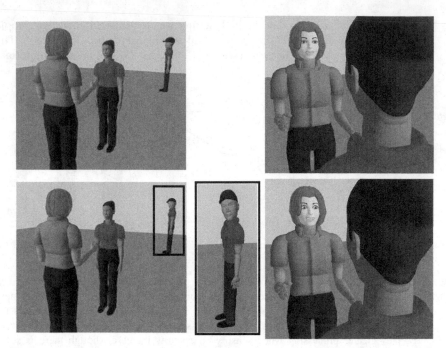

Fig. 6. Snapshots of two conversational agents interacting. During the conversation, a man with red eyes walks through the background. In the first case (top), the red T-shirt man walks off and does not turn his face towards the speaker. Thus, the speaker continues to talk, paying no attention to the man, even though he has fallen into her line of vision. In this situation, the perceptual information of the man is discarded by the visual attention model of the speaker. In the second case (bottom), when the man turns his head and shows his red eyes, the speaker is shocked. The face pop-out and physical saliency of the man causes the engagement of the speaker to shift from the listener to the external world stimuli.

6   Future Work and Conclusion

As embodied agents become more commonplace elements of interpersonal interactions, adequate computational frameworks for cognitive processes are essential. Not only must the framework replicate normal human functioning, it should also demonstrate abnormal and imperfect human functioning, or else the agent will never be able to assimilate into a human-interactive environment. We have presented current theories of inattentional blindness and demonstrated how to integrate them into one model of visual attention. We attempted to justify our model with an experiment that examined three of the most important parameters, and discovered that the results agree with our proposed computational framework.

Future work for the model will include: further exploration of the parameters of habituation and capacity level, as well as more experimentally supported quantification. In addition, it is important to have models that can predict attention failure in order to decide how to compensate for, as well as reduce, human errors in perception in critical situations such as operating machinery or security monitoring. We hope that future work on our model can help contribute to these challenging problems.

Acknowledgements

This work is partially supported by the ONR VITRE project under grant N000140410259, and NSF IIS-0200983. Opinions expressed here are those of the authors and not of the sponsoring agencies. The authors are deeply grateful to Jan M. Allbeck for the human model. Also the authors thank all the participants in our IRB-approved experiments.

References

1. Becklen, R. and Cervone, D. (1983). Selective looking and the noticing of unexpected events. *Memory and Cognition, 11*, 601-608.
2. Bernardino, A. and Santos-Victor, J. (2002). A binocular stereo algorithm for log-polar foveated systems. *In Proc. 2nd International Workshop on Biologically Motivated Computer Vision*, pages 127–136. Springer-Verlag.
3. Cassell, J., Bickmore, T., Campbell, L., Vilhjalmsson, H. and Yan, H. (2001). More Than Just a Pretty Face: Conversational Protocols and the Affordances of Embodiment. *Knowledge-Based Systems, 14 (2001)*, pp. 55-64.
4. Chopra-Khullar, S. and Badler, N. (2001) Where to look? Automating attending behaviors of virtual human characters. *Autonomous Agents and Multi-agent Systems 4*, 9-23.
5. Folk, C. L., Remington, R. W. and Johnston, J. C. (1992). Involuntary covert orienting is contingent on attentional control settings. *Journal of Experimental Psychology*: *Human Perception and Performance*, 18, 1030-1044.
6. Green, G. (2004), Inattentional blindness and conspicuity. Retrieved November 10, http://www.visualexpert.com/Resources/inattentionalblindness.html
7. Gu, E. (2004), Attention Model in Autonomous Agents, Technical Report, CIS, University of Pennsylvania.
8. Gu, E., Wang, J. and Badler, N. (2005). Generating Sequence of Eye Fixations Using Decision Theoretic Bottom-Up Attention Model. *3rd International Workshop on Attention and Performance in Computational Vision*..
9. Itti, L. (2003), Visual attention. *The Handbook of Brain Theory and Neural Networks*, pages 1196–1201.
10. Itti, L., Koch, C. and Niebur, E. (1998), A model of saliency-based visual attention for rapid scene analysis. *IEEE Transactions on Pattern Analysis and Machine Intelligence*, 20(11):1254–1259.
11. Lee, S. P., Badler, J. and Badler, N. (2002). Eyes Alive. ACM Transactions on Graphics 21(3):637-644.
12. Mack, A. and Rock, I. (1998). *In Inattentional Blindness*. 1998. Cambridge, MA: MIT Press.
13. Most, S. B., Scholl, B. J., Clifford, E. R. and Simons, D. J. (2005). What you see is what you set: Sustained inattentional blindness and the capture of awareness. *Psychological Review*, 112, 217-242.
14. Nakano, Y. I. and Nishida, T. (2005). Awareness of Perceived World and Conversational Engagement by Conversational Agents, AISB 2005 Symposium: Conversational Informatics for Supporting Social Intelligence & Interaction, England.
15. Rensink, R. (2002). Internal vs. external information in visual perception. *Proceedings of the 2nd International Symposium on Smart Graphics*.

16. Simons, D. J. and Chabris, C. F. (1999). Gorillas in our midst: Sustained inattentional blindness for dynamic events. *Perception, 28,* 1059-1074.

17. Simons, D. J. and Rensink, R. A. (2005). Change blindness: past, present, and future. *Trends in Cognitive Sciences*, 9, 16-20.

18. Sun, Y. and Fisher, R. (2003). Object-based visual attention for computer vision. *Artificial Intelligent*, 146:77–123.

19. Treisman, A. (1964). Monitoring and storage of irrelevant messages in selective attention. *Journal of Verbal Learning and Verbal Behavior*, 3, 449-459.

20. Ward, T. A., An Overview and Some Applications of Inattentional Blindness Research, research paper for PSY 440 (Perception), Stephen F. Austin State University.http://hubel.sfasu.edu/courseinfo/SL03/inattentional_blindness.htm

21. Wolfe J. M. (1999). "Inattentional amnesia", in Fleeting Memories. *In Cognition of Brief Visual Stimuli*. Cambridge, MA: MIT Press. 71-94.

22. Woodman, G. F. and Luck, S. J. (2003). Dissociations among attention, perception, and awareness during object-substitution masking. *Psychological Science*, 14, 605–611.

Social Causality and Responsibility: Modeling and Evaluation

Wenji Mao and Jonathan Gratch

Institute for Creative Technologies, University of Southern California,
13274 Fiji Way, Marina del Rey, CA 90292, U.S.A.
{mao, gratch}@ict.usc.edu

Abstract. Intelligent virtual agents are typically embedded in a social environment and must reason about social cause and effect. Social causal reasoning is qualitatively different from physical causal reasoning that underlies most current intelligent systems. Besides physical causality, the assessments of social cause emphasize epistemic variables including intentions, foreknowledge and perceived coercion. Modeling the process and inferences of social causality can enrich the believability and the cognitive capabilities of social intelligent agents. In this paper, we present a general computational model of social causality and responsibility, and empirically evaluate and compare the model with several other approaches.

1 Introduction

Research in intelligent virtual agents has emphasized human-like qualities in the physical manifestation of agents, but such realism is typically skin-deep. Although agents can interact in naturalistic ways with human users and can successfully mimic speech, body language and even, the core reasoning techniques that drive such behaviors have not fundamentally changed. Most intelligent systems incorporate planning and reasoning techniques designed to reason about *physical* causality. Unfortunately, physical causes and effects are simply inadequate for exploiting and explaining social phenomena. In contrast, *social causality*, both in theory and as practiced in everyday folk judgments and in the legal system, emphasizes multiple causal dimensions, incorporates epistemic variables, and distinguishes between cause, responsibility and blame.

Recent approaches to social causality have addressed these differences by extending causal models [Halpern & Pearl, 2001; Chockler & Halpern, 2004], although it is unclear whether a full accounting of social causality will (or even should) result from such extensions. In contrast, we start with social causality theory and consider how this could be formalized in a computational model. This allows intelligent entities to reason about aspects of social causality not addressed by extended causal models and provides a complementary perspective to the enterprise of causal reasoning about social events.

Psychological and philosophical theories identify key variables that mediate determinations of social causality. In these theories, social causality involves not only physical causality, with an emphasis on human agency, but also people's freedom of choice (e.g., coercion [Shaver, 1985] and controllability [Weiner, 1995]), intentions

T. Panayiotopoulos et al. (Eds.): IVA 2005, LNCS 3661, pp. 191–204, 2005.
© Springer-Verlag Berlin Heidelberg 2005

and foreknowledge [Shaver, 1985; Zimmerman, 1988]. Using these variables, social causality makes several distinctions not present in the determinations of physical cause. For example, an actor may physically cause an event, but be absolved of responsibility and blame. Or a person may be held responsible and blameworthy for what she did not physically cause.

Our goal is to model the underlying process and inferences of social causality to enrich the cognitive and social functionality of intelligent agents. Such a model can help an agent to explain the observed social behavior of others, which is crucial for successful interactions among social entities. It can enrich the design components of human-like agents, guide strategies of natural language conversation and model social emotions [Gratch & Marsella, 2004]. To achieve this end, we base our work on the broad variables people use in determining social causality and responsibility. Psychological and philosophical theories largely agree on these basic variables though they differ in terminology. In this paper, we adopt the terminology of Shaver [1985]. In Shaver's model, the judgment process proceeds by assessing several key variables: who *caused* the event; Did the actor *foresee* the consequence; Did she *intend* to bring the consequence about; Did she have *choices* or act under *coercion* (e.g., by an authority)?

Though the theory identifies the conceptual variables for social causality and responsibility judgment, in modeling social behavior of intelligent agents, we cannot assume that an agent has privileged access to the mental states of other agents, but rather, an agent can only make inferences and judgment based on the evidence accessible in the computational system it situates. Current intelligent systems are increasingly sophisticated, usually involving natural language conversation, interactions of multiple agents and a planning module to plan for sequence of actions, with methods that explicitly model beliefs, desires and intentions of agents. All these should play a role in evaluating the conceptual variables underlying social causality and responsibility judgment.

In order to bridge the conceptual descriptions of the variables and the computational realization in application systems, we need to model the inferential mechanism that derives the variable values needed for the judgment from information and context available in practical systems. This paper presents a domain-independent computational model of social causality and responsibility by inferring the key variables from plan knowledge and communication. To assess the veracity of the approach in modeling human social inference, we conduct empirical studies to evaluate and compare the model with several other models of responsibility and blame.

In this paper, we first introduce the judgment process and how the key variables are utilized in the process, and then present the computational model. We finally evaluate the model using empirical data and compare our approach with the related work.

2 Judgment Process and Key Variables

We base our work on the most influential attributional models of Shaver [1985] and Weiner [1995] for social causality and responsibility. Their models suggest that physical causality and coercion identify *who* is responsible for some outcome under evaluation, whereas mental factors, intention and foreseeability, determine *how much* responsibility and blame/credit are assigned.

The evaluations of physical causality and coercion identify the responsibility party. *Physical causality* refers to the connection between actions and the effects they produce. In the absence of external coercion, the actor whose action directly produces the outcome is regarded as responsible. However, in social situations, an agent may cause an outcome because she could not have done otherwise. *Coercion* occurs when some external force, such as a more powerful individual or a socially sanctioned authority, limits an agent's freedom of choice. The presence of coercion can deflect some or all of the responsibility to the coercive force, depending on the perceived degree of coercion.

Intention and foreseeability determine the degree of responsibility and blame. *Intention* is generally conceived as the commitment to work towards a certain act or outcome. Most theories view intention as the major determinant of the degree of responsibility. If an agent intends an action to achieve an outcome, then the agent must have the foreknowledge that the action brings about the outcome. *Foreseeability* refers to an agent's foreknowledge about actions and their consequences. The higher the degree of intention, the greater the responsibility assigned. The lower the degree of foreseeability, the less the responsibility assigned.

An agent may intentionally perform an action, but may not intend all the action effects. It is *outcome intent* (i.e., intentional action effect), rather than *act intentionality* (i.e., intentional action) that are key in responsibility judgment [Weiner, 2001]. Similar difference exists in *outcome coercion* (i.e., coerced action effect) and *act coercion* (i.e., coerced action). An agent's intentional action and action effect may succeed or fail. However, as long as it manifests intentions, a *failed attempt* can be blamed or credited almost the same as a successful one [Zimmerman, 1988].

The result of the judgment process is the assignment of certain blame or credit to the responsible agent(s). The intensity of blame or credit is determined by the degree of responsibility as well as the severity or positivity of the outcome. The degree of responsibility is based on the assessed values of attribution variables.

3 The Social Inference Model

We build a computational model of this social judgment process, showing how automated methods for causal and dialogue reasoning can provide a mechanistic explanation of how people arrive at judgments of blame and responsibility. Here we briefly summarize the model. The reader may refer to [Mao & Gratch, 2003a, 2003b, 2004a, 2004b] for details.

3.1 Modular Structure

The judgment of social causality and responsibility is a subjective process. It is from the perspective of a perceiving agent (i.e., the agent who makes the judgment), and based on the perceiver's interpretation of the significance of events. The perceiver uses her own knowledge about the observed agents' behavior to infer certain beliefs (in terms of the key variables). The inferred variable values are then applied to the judgment process to form an overall result.

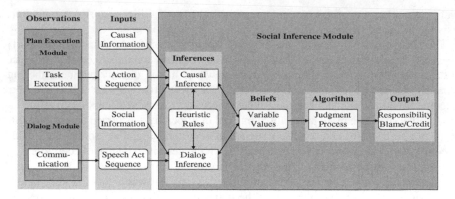

Fig. 1. Structure of the Social Inference Module

Two important *sources* of information contribute to the inference of key variables. One source is general beliefs about actions and their effects. The other is observations of the actions performed by the observed agents, including physical and communicative acts (e.g., in a conversational dialogue). The inference process acquires beliefs from communicative events (i.e., dialogue inference) and from the causal information about the observed action execution (i.e., causal inference). To construct a computational model, we need to represent such information and make inferences over it. We also need an algorithm to describe the overall judgment process.

We have designed a modular structure for evaluating social causality and responsibility (i.e., a social inference module), and its interface with other system components. *Figure 1* illustrates the structure of the module. It takes the observed communicative events and executed actions as inputs. *Causal information* and *social information* are also important inputs. Causal information includes an action theory and a plan library (discussed below). Social information specifies social roles and the power relationship of the roles. The *inference* process first applies dialogue inference, and then causal inference. Both make use of the commonsense heuristics, and derive beliefs about the variable values. The values are then served as inputs of the *algorithm*, which determines responsibility, and assigns certain blame or credit to the responsible agents.

3.2 Computational Representation

To represent an agent's causal knowledge, we have adopted a hierarchical plan representation used in many intelligent agent systems. This representation provides a concise description of the physical causal relationship between events and world states. It also provides a clear structure for exploring alternative courses of actions and detecting plan interactions.

Actions and Plans. Physical causality is encoded via a hierarchical plan representation. *Actions* consist of a set of propositional preconditions and effects (including conditional effects). Each action step is either a *primitive* action (i.e., an action directly executable by some agent) or an *abstract* action. An abstract action may be decomposed in alternative ways and the effects of an abstract action depend on these alternatives. For example, if there are two alternatives for performing an abstract action, only those effects that occur in each alternative are necessarily the effects of the abstract act. The desirability of action effects is represented by utility values [Blythe, 1999].

A *plan* is a set of actions to achieve certain intended goal(s). As a plan may contain abstract actions (i.e., an abstract plan), each abstract plan indicates a *plan structure* of decomposition. Decomposing the abstract actions into primitive ones in an abstract plan results in a set of primitive plans (i.e., plans with only primitive actions), which is directly executable by agents. In addition, each action in the plan structure is associated with the *performer* (i.e., agents capable of performing the action) and the *authority* (i.e., agent who authorizes the action execution). The performer cannot execute the action until authorization is given by the authority. This represents the hierarchical organizational structure of social agents.

Communicative Events. Natural language communication is a rich information source for inferring attribution variables. We assume conversations between agents are *grounded* and they conform to Grice's maxims of *Quality* and *Relevance* (i.e., true and relevant information exchange in conversation). We represent communicative events as *speech act* [Austin, 1962] sequence, and analyze the following acts that are typical in negotiation dialogues [Traum *et al*, 2003], *inform, order, request, accept, reject*, and *counter-propose*.

3.3 Inferences

The inference of physical causality, coercion, intentions and foreknowledge is informed by dialogue and causal evidence in social interactions. We introduce commonsense heuristics that allow an agent to make inferences based on this evidence.

Agency. A first step in attributing responsibility and blame is to identify which actors' actions contribute to the occurrence of an outcome under evaluation. In a multi-agent plan execution environment, an actor can produce an outcome through the assistance of other agents. These other agents are viewed as indirect agency. Given a specific outcome p and the observed action set S, the following actions in S are relevant to achieving p:

- The primitive action A that has p as its effect.
- The actions that establish a precondition of a relevant action to achieving p.
- If p or a precondition of a relevant action is enabled by the consequent of a conditional effect, the actions that establish the antecedent of the conditional effect are relevant.

These relevant actions are the possible causes of the outcome p. Therefore, their performers are potentially responsible for p.

Coercion. An actor could be absolved of responsibility if she was coerced by other forces, but just because an agent applies coercive force does not mean coercion actually occurs. What matters is whether this force truly constrains the actor's freedom to avoid the outcome. Causal inference helps evaluate outcome coercion from evidence of act coercion.

Two concepts are important in understanding coercion. One concept is social *obligation*, created by utterance, role assigned, etc. The other is *(un)willingness*. For example, if some authorizing agent commands another agent to perform a certain action, then the latter agent has an obligation to do so. But if the agent is actually willing to, this is a voluntary act rather than a coercive one.

If there is no clear evidence that an agent intends beforehand, and the agent accepts her obligation, there is evidence of coercion. In this inference rule, intend(x, p, $t1$) represents that agent x intends that proposition p at time $t1$, obligation(x, p, y, $t2$) represents that x has an obligation p by agent y at time $t2$, accept(x, p, $t3$) represents that x accepts that p at time $t3$, and coerce(y, x, p, $t4$) represents that y coerces x that p at time $t4$.

$$\neg(\exists t1)(t1<t3 \wedge \text{intend}(x, p, t1)) \wedge \text{obligation}(x, p, y, t2) \wedge \text{accept}(x, p, t3) \wedge t2<t3<t4 \Rightarrow \text{coerce}(y, x, p, t4)$$

In another case, when there is clear evidence of the unwillingness (i.e., intend(x, p, $t1$) is false), there is *strong* evidence of coercion.

Given the action preconditions are initially true or enabled by other agents (these other agents are viewed as indirect coercers if outcome coercion is true), if an agent is coerced to execute a primitive action, the agent is also coerced to achieve all the action effects. If being coerced to execute an abstract action and the action has only one decomposition, then the agent is also coerced to execute the sub-actions and achieve all the sub-action effects. If the coerced action has multiple decompositions, then the agent has options: only the effects appear in all alternatives are unavoidable, and thus these effects are coerced; Since other effects that only appear in some (but not all) alternatives are avoidable, they are not coerced. If some agents block other action alternatives (by disabling action preconditions), the only alternative left as well as its effects are coerced. These blocking agents are also viewed as coercers.

If a conditional effect is coerced and its antecedent is true or enabled by other agents (these other agents are viewed as indirect coercers if outcome coercion is true), then its consequent is coerced; Otherwise, if the antecedent is false or enabled by the performing agent (i.e., by self), the consequent is not coerced.

Intentions. Intentions play a central role in determining the degree of responsibility and blame assignments. Act and outcome intentions can be inferred from conversation communication between agents. For example, an *order* or a *request* shows the speaker's *intent*. The two speech acts have different implications on the social status between the speaker and the hearer. If an order is successfully issued to a subordinate, it creates a social *obligation* for the subordinate to perform the content of the act. The hearer may *accept, reject* or *counter-propose*. Various inferences can be made depending on the response of the hearer and the power relationship between the speaker and the hearer. For example, if the hearer counters the order, and proposes another alternative, it can be inferred that both the speaker and the hearer *know* the alternatives. It is also believed that the hearer does not *intend* what is ordered, but *want* the alternative. If the speaker has known the alternatives yet still orders one, infer that the speaker *intends* the chosen action but *not* the alternative. The reader may refer to [Mao & Gratch, 2003b] for the complete rules.

$$\text{intend}(s, p, t1) \wedge \neg\text{obligation}(h, p, s, t2) \wedge \text{accept}(h, p, t3) \wedge t1<t3 \wedge t2<t3<t4 \Rightarrow \text{intend}(h, p, t4)$$

Outcome intent can also be partially inferred from evidence of act intentionality. For example, if an agent intends an action voluntarily, the agent must intend at least one action effect. If there is only one action effect (significant to the agent), we can exactly infer which effect the agent intends. As plans provide context in evaluating intention, with association to the goals and reasons of an agent's behavior, in the absence of clear evidence from dialogue inference, we employ a general plan-based algorithm to recognize intentions [Mao & Gratch, 2004b].

Foreknowledge. Since foreknowledge refers to an agent's epistemic state, it is mainly derived from dialogue inference. For example, *inform* gives evidence that the conversants know the content of the act. Besides, intention recognition also helps infer an agent's foreknowledge, as intentions entail foreknowledge (*Axiom 4* in [Mao & Gratch, 2004a]).

3.4 Algorithm

The judgment process begins with some specific outcome that is under evaluation, and the judgment result is based on the inferences of variable values introduced above. The acquired values for agency and coercion contribute to the evaluation of responsible agents. We have developed an algorithm for tracing the responsible agents [Mao & Gratch, 2003b]. The algorithm starts with the primitive action that directly causes the evaluated outcome and works up the plan hierarchy. During each loop, it applies inference rules and intention recognition method to reason about attribution variables. If outcome coercion is true, the algorithm proceeds until reaching the root of the plan hierarchy. In the meantime, the application of inference rules and intention recognition algorithm acquires beliefs for foreknowledge and act/outcome intentions, which determine the intensity of responsibility and blame/credit.

4 Evaluation and Comparison

Our *claim* of evaluation is that this model will approximate human judgments of blame and perform better than other potential approaches. Here, we report the results of an experiment comparing our model and three computational alternatives to human data.

4.1 Alternative Models

It is not uncommon to use physical causality as a substitute for modeling social causality. This was the approach used, for example, in the *MRE* team training system [Rickel *et al*, 2002]. A *simple causal model* always assigns responsibility and blame to the actor whose action directly produces the outcome.

Instead of always picking up the actor, a slightly more sophisticated model can choose the highest authority (if there is one) as the responsible and blameworthy agent. We call such model *simple authority model*.

Chockler and Halpern [2004] propose a structural-model approach to responsibility and blame (abbreviated to *C&H model* below). They give a definition of responsibility, which extends the definition of causality introduced by Halpern and Pearl [2001].

For example, if a person wins an election 11-0, then each voter who votes for her is a cause for the victory, but each voter is less responsible for the victory than if she had won 6-5. Based on this notion of responsibility, they then defined the degree of blame, using the expected degree of responsibility weighed by the epistemic state of an agent.

4.2 Method

Our model argues that people will view blame differently based on their perception of key variables such as intentions and coercion. Thus a good test is to see how the models perform when such variables are systematically manipulated. We compare attributions of blame by the four models with human judgments using four variants of the "firing squad" scenario in [Chockler & Halpern, 2004]. *Scenario 1* is the original example: There is a ten-man firing squad. Only one marksman has live bullets in his rifle; the rest have blanks. The marksmen do not know who has the live bullets. They shoot at the prisoner and the death occurs. *Scenario 2* extends the example to include an authority - the commander, who orders the squad to shoot. *Scenario 3* further extends the example by presenting a negotiation dialogue between the commander and the marksmen. The marksmen first reject the commander's order. The commander insists and orders again. Finally the squad accepts the order and shoot. In *Scenario 4*, the commander still orders. However, each marksman has freedom to choose either using blanks or live bullets before shooting.

In each scenario, we query 27 subjects (mostly university staffs including graduates, with ages ranging from 20 to 45 and evenly distributed genders) to assess their judgments of responsibility, blame and coercion.

4.3 Results

Figure 2 shows proportions of the subjects that attribute blame and responsibility to different categories of agents in the scenarios, and corresponding confidence intervals for large population ($\alpha=0.05$) [Rice, 1994]. For example, in *scenario 1*, 3 subjects blame the marksman with live bullets in his rifle, 19 blames all the marksmen and the rest do not blame any of them. The analysis of the sample data and their confidence intervals show that a small percentage of the population will blame the marksman with live bullets, a significant majority will blame all the marksmen, and a small percentage won't blame any, with 0.95 confidence.

Table 1 shows the results on blapme generated by different models. All the results are compared with the dominant proportions (i.e. majority) of people's agreement (though in *Scenario 4*, there is an overlap between two categories. That's why we note our model as a partial fit). The simple causal model always chooses physical causality. It only partially matches the human agreement in *Scenario 4*, but is inconsistent with the data in *Scenarios 1-3*. Simple authority model always picks up the highest authority. It matches the human data in *Scenario 2 and 3*, but is inconsistent with the data in other scenarios. In general, simple models are insensitive to the changing situation specified in each scenario.

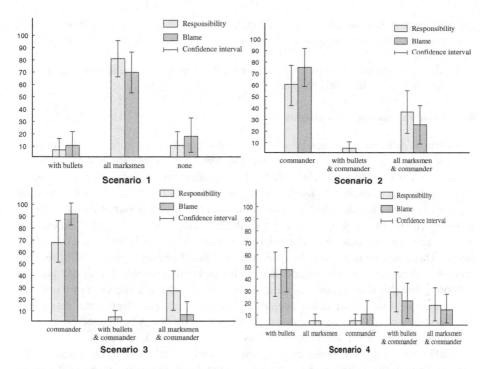

Fig. 2. Proportions of the Population Agreement on Responsibility/Blame in Sample Scenarios

Table 1. Comparison of Results by Different Models with Human Data

B L A M E	Simple Cause Model		Simple Authority Model		C&H Model		Social Inference Model		Human Majority Agreement
	Results	Match	Results	Match	Results	Match	Results	Match	
S 1	with bullets	no	N/A	N/A	all marksmen	yes	all marksmen	yes	**all marksmen**
S 2	with bullets	no	commander	yes	all marksmen& commander	no	commander	yes	**commander**
S 3	with bullets	no	commander	yes	all marksmen& commander	no	commander	yes	**commander**
S 4	with bullets	yes (partial)	commander	no	N/A	N/A	with bullets	yes (partial)	**with bullets/ w. bullets & commander**

C&H model does not perform well either. It matches human judgments only in *Scenario 1*. In the remaining scenarios, its results are incompatible with the data. Like other work in causality research, the underlying causal reasoning in C&H model is based on *philosophical* principles (i.e., counterfactual dependencies). Though their extended definition of responsibility accounts better for the extent to which a cause contributes to the occurrence of an outcome, the results show that their blame model does not match the human data well. These empirical findings generally support our hypothesis.

In the next section, we discuss how our model appraises each scenario and compare our approach with C&H model.

4.4 Comparison and Discussions

Scenario 1. Actions and plans are explicitly represented in our approach. In *Scenario 1*, each marksman performs a primitive action, *shooting*. The action has a conditional effect, with the antecedent *live bullets* and the consequent *death*. All marksmen's shooting actions constitute a team plan *squad firing*, with outcome *death*. The team plan is observed executed, and plan outcome occurs. Applying our intention recognition algorithm[1] [Mao & Gratch, 2004b], the marksmen are believed to intend the actions and the only outcome. The marksman with the bullets is the sole cause of the death. This marksman intends the outcome, and thus deserves high degree of responsibility and blame. As other marksmen with blanks also intend the actions and the outcome, and shooting actions are observed executed but the antecedent of the conditional effect is false, their failed attempt can be detected. Therefore, other marksmen are also blameworthy for their attempt (recall that an agent can be blamed/credited for a successfully produced outcome as well as for an unsuccessful attempt).

C&H model judges responsibility according to the actual cause of the event. As the marksman with the bullets is the only cause of the death, this marksman has degree of responsibility 1 for the death and others have degree of responsibility 0. This result is inconsistent with human data. In determining blame, C&H model draws the same conclusion as ours, but their approach is different. They consider each marksman's epistemic state before action performance (corresponding to foreknowledge). There are 10 situations possible, depending on who has the bullets. Each marksman is responsible for one situation with degree of responsibility 1. Given that each situation is equally likely to happen (1/10 possibility), each marksman has degree of blame 1/10.

As there is no notion of intention in their model, C&H model uses foreknowledge as the only determinant for blame assignment. This is fine when there is no foreknowledge, as no foreknowledge entails no intention. However, when there is foreknowledge, the blame assigned is high, even if there might be no intentions in the case. For example, if a marksman fires the gun by mistake, without any intention of shooting or attempting the death, in C&H model, still he will be blamed just the same as those who intend.

Scenarios 2 & 3. In our model, we take different forms of social interactions into account. The inference process reasons about the beliefs from both causal and dialogue evidence. *Figure 3* illustrates the team plan of the squad in *Scenarios 2* and *3*, where a commander acts as an authority of the squad (*AND* denotes that the action has only one decomposition).

---

[1] Note that our intention recognition algorithm is generally applied to a plan library with multiple plans and sequences of actions, which is typical in intelligent agent applications. In this oversimplified example, intention recognition becomes trivial.

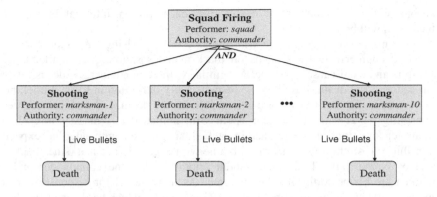

Fig. 3. Team Plan of the Squad in Scenarios 2 and 3

The intermediate inference results for *Scenario 2* are given below (*cmd*, *sqd* and *mkn* stand for the commander, the squad and the marksman, respectively. Beliefs are ordered by time).

(1) intend(*cmd*, *do*(*sqd*, *firing*))	(Act *order*)
(2) obligation(*sqd*, *firing*, *cmd*)	(Act *order*)
(3) intend(*cmd*, *death*)	(Rule for *intention* & Result *1*)
(4) coerce(*cmd*, *sqd*, *firing*)	(Act *accept* & Result *2*)
(5) coerce(*cmd*, *mkn*, *shooting*)	(Rule for *coercion*)
(6) coerce(*cmd*, *mkn*, *death*)	(Rule for *coercion*)

So in *Scenario 2*, the marksmen cause/attempt the death due to coercion. The commander is responsible for the death. As the commander intends the outcome, the commander is to blame with high intensity.

Scenario 3 includes a sequence of negotiation acts. The above beliefs 4-6 thus change to the following:

(4) ¬intend(*sqd*, *firing*)	(Act *reject* and Result *1*)
(5) coerce(*cmd*, *sqd*, *firing*)	(Act *accept* and Results *2* & *4*)
(6) coerce(*cmd*, *mkn*, *shooting*)	(Rule for *coercion*)
(7) coerce(*cmd*, *mkn*, *death*)	(Rule for *coercion*)

Clearly the marksmen do not intend firing. *Scenario 3* shows strong coercion. This is also reflected in the data. More proportions of people regard the commander as responsible and blameworthy in *Scenario 3* than in *Scenario 2*.

C&H model represents all the relevant events in the scenarios as random variables. So if we want to model the communicative acts in *Scenarios 2* and *3*, each act would be a separate variable in their model. This is problematic when conversational dialogue is involved in a scenario. As the approach uses the structural equations to represent the relationships between variables, and each equation in the model must be deterministic, it is difficult to come up with such equations for a dialogue sequence. For example, if we want to model communicative acts in *Scenario 3*, we will have to give deterministic relationship between them (e.g., if the commander orders, the squad will accept). Such strict equations simply do not exist in a natural conversation.

If we ignore some communicative acts in between, important information conveyed by these acts will be lost.

Assume marksman-1 is the one with the live bullets. Using C&H approach, the outcome is counterfactually depends on marksman-1's shooting, so marksman-1's shooting is an actual cause of the death. Similarly, the commander's order is also an actual cause of the death. Based on the responsibility definition in C&H model, both the commander and marksman-1 are responsible for the death, and each has degree of responsibility 1. This result is inconsistent with human data. In assigning blame, there are ten situations altogether, and in each situation, the commander has expected responsibility 1, so the commander is to blame with degree 1. The marksmen each has degree of blame 1/10. Thus C&H model appraises that the commander and all marksmen are blameworthy for the outcome. As their model for responsibility and blame is the extension of counterfactual causal reasoning, which has been criticized as far too permissive [Hopkins & Pearl, 2003], the same problem is also reflected in their model of responsibility and blame.

Scenario 4. Different from the previous scenarios, in *Scenario 4*, the bullets are not initially set before the scenario starts. The marksmen can choose to use either bullets or blanks before shooting. Firing is still the joint action of the squad, but there is no team plan or common goal for the squad. As the commander orders the joint action, act coercion is true. However, based on the rules of inferring outcome coercion from act coercion, the marksmen are not coerced the outcome. So in this case, the commander is not responsible for the outcome, but rather, the marksmen who choose to use bullets and cause the death are responsible and blameworthy. *Figure 2* shows that in *Scenario 4*, people's judgments somehow diffuse. There is an overlap between blaming the marksmen with bullets and blaming both the commander and the marksmen with bullets. Nonetheless, the category our model falls into is clearly better than the rest three.

C&H model requires all the structural equations to be deterministic. In essence, their model could not handle alternative courses of actions, which inherently have nondeterministic property. One way to compensate for this is to push the nondetrminism into the setting of the context. For example, in *Scenario 4*, they could build a causal model to let the context determine whether the bullets are live or blank for each marksman, and then have a probability distribution over contexts. After that, they can compute the probability of an actual cause. However, since these contexts are only background variables, their probabilities could not actually impact the reasoning process per se

5 Summary

Intelligent virtual agents are typically embedded in a social environment and must reason about social cause and effect. Social causal reasoning is qualitatively different from physical causal reasoning that underlies most current intelligent systems. In this paper, we present a general computational model of social causality and responsibility. Our approach bases on the broad features people use in behavior judgment, including physical cause, intentions, foreknowledge and coercion. We present how our model reasons about beliefs about attribution variables for the judgment process, and empirically evaluate and compare the model with several other approaches.

The initial results show that our model approximates human judgment of blame and responsibility and performs better than other potential approaches. Our future work needs to further refine the model and conduct more experiments to systematically evaluate the veracity of the approach.

Acknowledgements

The project or effort described here has been sponsored by the U.S. Army Research, Development, and Engineering Command (RDECOM). We would like to thank Joseph Halpern and Andrew Gordon for the helpful discussions. Statements and opinions expressed do not necessarily reflect the position or the policy of the United States Government, and no official endorsement should be inferred.

References

1. Austin, J. 1962. *How to Do Things with Words*. Harvard University Press, 1962.
2. Blythe, J. 1999. Decision-Theoretic Planning. *AI Magazine* 20(2):37-54.
3. Chockler, H. and Halpern, J. Y. 2004. Responsibility and Blame: A Structural-Model Approach. *Journal of Artificial Intelligence Research* 22:93-115.
4. Gratch, J. and Marsella, S. 2004. A Domain-Independent Framework for Modeling Emotion. *Journal of Cognitive Systems Research* 5(4):269-306.
5. Halpern, J. Y. and Pearl, J. 2001. Causes and Explanations: A Structural-Model Approach – Part I: Causes. *Proceedings of the Seventeenth Conference in Uncertainty in Artificial Intelligence*.
6. Hopkins, M. and Pearl, J. 2003. Clarifying the Usage of Structural Models for Commonsense Causal Reasoning. *Proceedings of AAAI Spring Symposium on Logic Formulizations of Commonsense Reasoning*.
7. Mao, W. and Gratch, J. 2003a. The Social Credit Assignment Problem. *Proceedings of the Fourth International Working Conference on Intelligent Virtual Agents*.
8. Mao, W. and Gratch, J. 2003b. The Social Credit Assignment Problem (Extended Version). *ICT Technical Report ICT-TR-02-2003*.
9. Mao, W. and Gratch, J. 2004a. Social Judgment in Multiagent Interactions. *Proceedings of the Third International Joint Conference on Autonomous Agents and Multiagent Systems*.
10. Mao, W. and Gratch, J. 2004b. Utility-Based Approach to Intention Recognition. *AAMAS 2004 Workshop on Agent Tracking: Modeling Other Agents from Observations*.
11. Rice, J. A. 1994. *Mathematical Statistics and Data Analysis (Second Edition)*. Duxbury Press.
12. Rickel, J., Marsella, S., Gratch, J., Hill, R., Traum, D. and Swartout, W. 2002. Toward a New Generation of Virtual Humans for Interactive Experiences. *IEEE Intelligent Systems*, 17(4):32-38.
13. Shaver, K. G. 1985. *The Attribution of Blame: Causality, Responsibility and Blameworthiness*. Springer-Verlag.
14. Traum, D., Rickel, J., Gratch, J. and Marsella, S. 2003. Negotiation over Tasks in Hybrid Human-Agent Teams for Simulation-Based Training. *Proceedings of the Second International Joint Conference on Autonomous Agents and Multiagent Systems*.

15. Weiner, B. 1995. *Judgments of Responsibility: A Foundation for a Theory of Social Conduct*. The Guilford Press.
16. Weiner, B. 2001. Responsibility for Social Transgressions: An Attributional Analysis. In: B. F. Malle, L. J. Moses and D. A. Baldwin (Ed.). *Intentions and Intentionality: Foundations of Social Cognition*, pp. 331-344. The MIT Press.
17. Zimmerman, M. J. 1988. *An Essay on Moral Responsibility*. Rowman & Littlefield.

Teaching Virtual Characters How to Use Body Language

Doron Friedman and Marco Gillies

Virtual Environment and Computer Graphics Lab,
Department of Computer Science,
University College of London
{d.friedman, m.gillies}@cs.ucl.ac.uk

Abstract. Non-verbal communication, or "body language", is a critical component in constructing believable virtual characters. Most often, body language is implemented by a set of ad-hoc rules. We propose a new method for authors to specify and refine their character's body-language responses. Using our method, the author watches the character acting in a situation, and provides simple feedback on-line. The character then learns to use its body language to maximize the rewards, based on a reinforcement learning algorithm.

1 Introduction

Social interaction is a core part of human life, and social behavior has become a key research area in Intelligent Virtual Agents (IVAs). Non-Verbal Communication (NVC) is vital to social interaction; it consists of all the signals sent between people that are not contained in language utterances. NVC is responsible for many aspects of social interaction: expressing emotion; regulating turn taking in conversation, and defining and expressing social relationships. These signals are often picked up subconsciously, without being explicitly noticed or understood. NVC varies greatly between people and can be an extremely useful method of making virtual agents that have their own individuality and personality. In addition, there is a large variation in NVC across cultures. For these reasons the generation of NVC has become one of the main challenges and one of the most active areas of IVA research. In this paper we suggest a new approach based on the ability of humans to judge NVC, and we present first results from our work in progress.

The typical approach for constructing characters with NVC relies on results from psychology, complemented by empirical data. This approach has been extremely fruitful, a prime example being the work of Cassell and her group [1,2], and was also used by one of the present authors [3,4]. However, there are limitations to this approach. First, our theoretical understanding of NVC is still incomplete. Second, and possibly more important, obtaining and analyzing data can be extremely time consuming and costly. We thus propose a new approach that tries to leverage the human capacity for evaluating NVC, without explicitly

T. Panayiotopoulos et al. (Eds.): IVA 2005, LNCS 3661, pp. 205–214, 2005.
© Springer-Verlag Berlin Heidelberg 2005

being able to define it. This is done by allowing humans to watch a character act in a specific context and provide a simple feedback, every few seconds: whether the character's NVC is appropriate to the situation or not.

In this paper we discuss the first steps in this work in progress. First, we devised a method that combines exploration and generalization to allow the user to quickly prune and evaluate a large space of states and actions. Next, we have adapted a reinforcement learning (RL) [5,6] algorithm that allows the character to acquire a policy for making the right NVC actions to achieve a long-term reward.

Our focus in this paper is on the adaptation of RL to the domain of virtual characters with NVC-related behavior. We provide a description of our methods and the insights we have gained throughout their construction and initial evaluation.

2   Related Work

Machine learning has been adopted to train believable agents in virtual environments. Blumberg et al. [7] have trained an autonomous animated dog based on a real dog trianing technique called "clicker training". They demonstrate that the autonomous dogs can recognize and use acoustic patterns as cues for actions, as well as synthesize new actions from novel paths through its motion space. Isbell et al. [8] report on a software agent with RL capabilities inhabiting a multi-user text-based virtual environment. The agent was trained to proactively take actions in a social context by receiving rewards from other users in the VE. Conde, Tambellini, and Thalmann [9] demonstrate how agents can learn, using RL, to explore a virtual environment in an efficient yet flexible way.

Our research is aimed at using RL to learn non-verbal communication. There have been a number of general computational models of NVC. These include: Cassell et al.'s various systems, and particularly their virtual real-estate agent, Rea [1]. Guye-Vuillème et al. [10] have demonstrated avatars with a wide range of controllable expressive behavior. The Affective Presentation Markup Language (APML) is an XML-based language for defining the expressive behavior of characters [11].

Non-verbal behavior is generally divided into a number of modalities, many of which have been studied by virtual characters researchers. These include: facial expression(Pelachaud and Poggi [12]), eye gaze (Cassel et. al. [1], Rickel and Johnson [13], Garau et al. [14], and Gillies and Dodgson [3]), and style of motion (Chi et. al. [15]). In this paper we use the modalities of proxemics (or personal distance[1]), which has been little studied for virtual characters, in addition to posture and gesture.

Among research on posture, Cassell et al. [17] have investigated shifts of postures and their relationship to speech. Bécheiraz and Thalmann [18] use posture to display social closeness or distance between characters.

---

[1] The term "proxemics" was coined by the researcher E.T. Hall [16] when he investigated people's use of personal space.

The generation of gestures has been studied by a number of researchers. For example, Cassell *et al.* [1] have produced a character capable of extensive non-verbal behavior including sophisticated gestures. Chi *et al.* [15] present a way of generating expressive movements, similar to gestures using Laban notation. Gestures are closely related to speech and should be closely synchronized with it. Cassell, Vilhjálmsson, and Bickmore [2] present a system that parse text and suggests appropriate gestures to accompany it.

3   The Approach: Training Characters

NVC includes eye gaze, head motion, whole body movement, arm gestures, facial expressions, etc. A character acting in a virtual environment can have any combination (Cartesian product) of these elements in every moment. This allows for a rich possibility of expression. The question is: what combination of body-language elements should the character display at any given moment?

For simplicity we assume that the character's behavior occurs in discrete steps. In each such step the system needs to select a combination of body-language elements. This combination will typically be different from the previous one, so every step will typically involve a combination of basic animations. We will refer to such set of body-language elements, or to the set of basic animations, as an *action*; this use is also consistent with RL terminology.

Our experience indicates that the most difficult problem is context dependence, i.e., how to choose the right action *in a given situation*. Our idea is to allow the author of a virtual character to introduce the character into a situation, observe its behavior, and train it in real-time, by giving it a simple feedback. The author may provide feedback at any moment during watching the scenario. The feedback is a grade on a five point scale ranging from "very good" to "very bad". Figure 1 displays our simple interface and a scenario involving two characters.

We have by now implemented a basic system and have evaluated it with a simple scenario. Assume we want to train Alice who is in conversation with Bob[2]. Bob, whom we call the partner, uses NVC based on a pre-defined behavior mapping. Alice performs NVC behavior based on inputs from the learning component.

3.1   Animation Generation

We use the Demeanour architecture [19] to generate the non-verbal behavior of our characters. Demeanour is a general toolkit for creating character behavior. It is based around mappings from a number of inputs to output behaviors. A declarative language is provided for defining these mappings. In Bob's case the input is the state of the character and the output behavior consists of body movement (posture and gesture) and proxemics. The body movement engine uses a set of 33 pre-existing base motions (posture changes and gestures) to generate the behavior of the character. A number of these base motions are

---

[2] The conversation did not include actual speech.

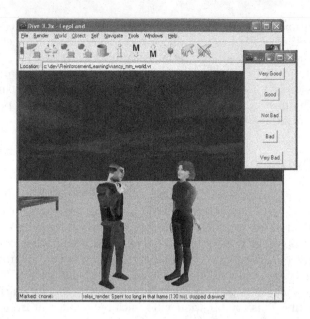

Fig. 1. A snapshot: the users watch the Dive window with the interacting characters, and are encouraged to hit one of the five rating buttons whenever they have an opinion on the recent NVC action performed by the female character.

chosen based on the output of Demeanour and these are blended together to create a new motion. The proxemics engine works by choosing one of a set of simple motions (step forward/backard, turn left/right) to control the distance to another character to that character.

For the learning character, Demeanor divides the NVC components into five classes depending on the part of the body used and the type of motion:

Arm gestures: conversational (beat) gestures, crossing arms, scratching head
Body postures: e.g., leaning forward or backward, being hunched over
Head postures: holding the head high, low or to the side
Head gestures: nodding or shaking the head
Distance: moving forward or backward

At each time step, one of each class is chosen (an empty motion can be chosen for each class), and the resulting animation is performed simultaneously.

Demeanor was implemented on top of Dive [20,21]. The RL component was implemented in Matlab[3]; this allows rapid prototyping. Our configuration allows running the animation and the learning components on different machines, which communicate using the network protocol VRPN[4]. This, together with the fact that we use Dive, will allow us to evaluate the system in immersive virtual reality (VR), and in multi-user settings.

---

[3] http://www.mathworks.com
[4] http://www.cs.unc.edu/Research/vrpn

3.2   Defining the Learning Problem

In RL, problems of decision-making by agents interacting with uncertain environments are usually modelled as Markov decision processes (MDPs). In the MDP framework, at each time step the agent senses the state of the environment, and chooses and executes an action from the set of actions available to it in that state. The agent's action (and perhaps other uncontrolled external events) cause a stochastic change in the state of the environment. The agent receives a scalar reward from the environment. The agent's goal is to choose actions so as to maximize the expected sum of rewards over some time horizon. An optimal policy is a mapping from states to actions that achieves the agent's goal.

In our case, the state space is comprised of a combination of four factors that we call *classes*:

1. partner conversation state — speaking, listening, or none,
2. partner mood — neutral or unhappy,
3. learning character conversation state — speaking, listening, or none; and
4. proximity — five categories from very near to very far.

If the classes are denoted by C_1, C_2, C_3, and C_4, then each state is a tuple $< c_1, c_2, c_3, c_4 >$ such that $c_1 \in C_1$, $c_2 \in C_2$, $c_3 \in C_3$, and $c_4 \in C_4$.

The actions are similarly arranged in five classes, which correspond to the animations as described in Section 3.1. The reward, in our case, is an integer number between 1 (negative reward) and 5 (positive reward).

We have started with a simple approach for quickly exploring the space, and have then extended it to use policy learning; the next two sections describe these two approaches.

3.3   Exploration with Generalization

First, we recognize that we rely on human feedback to learn the space, and in such context the space is quite large.[5] We want to quickly explore it and find the right actions, or the right NVC behavior, for every state.

In the first instance we are only concerned with immediate reward, and we assume a stationary environment. Thus, we assume there is an optimal value function that assigns a value to each state-action pair, $Q :: S \times A \rightarrow R$, where S is the set of all states, A is the set of all actions, and R denotes the real numbers.

Fortunately, our space is a combinatoric product of what we have called classes. Given a reward for an action, which is a combination of gestures and postures in different classes, we want to reward each class accordingly. This is sometimes referred to as the structural credit-assignment problem.

Our method is based on two principles. Given the n-dimensional space of state and action classes[6], we want to sample it in a smart way, and then generalize from our samples, using assumptions from our domain.

---

[5] The number of states is 120, the number of actions is 4275, so the space is comprised of 513,000 values.

[6] In our case $n = 9$.

Sampling may be done in several ways. A greedy approach would always pick the action with the highest Q value for the current state. In order to encourage some exploration of the space, it is possible to use an ε-greedy approach; this selects the optimal action with probability $1 - \varepsilon$ and a random action with probability ε. The parameter ε can be tuned to balance exploration versus exploitation. We have also tested Boltzmann exploration [5], which is popular in the context of RL. Using simulations we have found the ε-greedy exploration to work best, when ε is small and is gradually decreased. Since, in this stage, we are only interested in exploring the space, we do not repeat a combination of space-action more than once.

The second principle involves generalizing from the samples. The underlying assumption is that we can generalize a specific instance by extrapolating into the different dimensions of the space.

Typically, RL uses function approximation for generalization. This is necessary in the case of continuous or very large spaces. In our case we want to generalize because the space is large relative to the sample size, but it is discrete, and is not large in terms of the number of computations required. In addition, we want to take advantage of our knowledge about the combinatoric nature of the space. Note that we cannot assume that the space is continuous; our generalization principle is weaker. This will become clear below as we explain our method for generalization.

We define a and a' to be similar if a and a' have equal value for at least four out of five classes, or, more generally, we say that a and a' are $k - similar$ if they are equal in at least $n - k$ out of the total n number of classes.

For generalization, we assume that similar actions have similar value, or that there is some small enough K for which:

if a and a' are similar then $\forall s \in S : |Q(s,a) - Q(s,a')| < K$

We expect that this correlation might have exceptions, but we use it as a heuristic to try to find good candidate actions, which will then be rated by the user.

The same similarity heuristic holds for states. We define s and s' to be $k - similar$ if they are equal in at least $n - k$ out of the total n number of classes.

if s and s' are similar then $\forall a \in A : |Q(s,a) - Q(s',a)| < K$

Generalizing for states, in our domain, is more risky than generalizing for actions. For example, if the character is required to be submissive we would prefer her head to be low, regardless of whether she is speaking or listening. However, it is quite possible that we would want our character to respond to a happy partner in a very different way than to an unhappy character.

Such distinctions are much easier handled by knowledge-based approaches than by statical approaches such as RL. Although it is not impossible to introduce such domain knowledge into the RL algorithm, we have used an easier resort: we assigned a smaller weight to state similarity.

Our algorithm is as follows. First we initialize $Q(s, a)$ to be the average reward for all s, a. The training includes a continuous iteration where we sample actions as explained earlier. The parameter ε is slowly decreased to slightly reduce exploration. Q is updated as follows: If the user provides a reward r to action a when in state s, then:

$$Q(s, a) = r$$
$$\forall s' \text{ similar to } s \text{ and } a' \text{ similar to } a : Q(s', a') = Q(s', a') + \alpha[r - Q(s', a')]$$

The constant α determines the rate of generalization[7]. In our case, we found that the update described above, together with a $2 - similar$ generalization for actions only, result in covering 0.5% of the space per each user rate. This is enough to ensure learning with a reasonable feedback of a few hundred feedback data points. We can terminate the learning process when most of the space is covered.[8]

By the end of the training phase, we are left with a table that is assumed to be a good approximation of the value function Q. Based on this table a policy may be defined and used in real-time to drive the virtual characters. Such a policy would pick up, for each state, from the actions with a relatively high Q value.

3.4   Learning a Behavior Policy

In our initial evaluation of the exploration and generalization method we have found that it is possible to quickly learn that some gestures are better than others, in a given situation. However, we realized one of the limitations of this method: very often the facts that the agent needs to learn are reflected in the states rather than in the actions.

The main reason that this happens is that our domain requires learning with delayed reward. For example, say we want to encourage Alice to keep her head low. Assume Alice lowered down her head, and kept it low for a while. In this case she will probably get a relatively high reward for the whole duration that her head was lowered, and not only for the action that included lowering the head. Another example involves encouraging Alice to get farther away from the partner. Getting farther away might result in a large reward when she is far away, rather than an immediate reward for every backwards step.

This leads us to the more general problem involving IVAs that need to learn a behavior policy with delayed rewards. While some mappings can be learned using traditional supervised learning, such as immediate rewards and state transitions,

---

[7] We actually use different values for state generalization and for action generalization; since we want to be more careful with state generalization we use smaller values of α.

[8] If the space has larger dimensionality, we can update for $k - similar$ actions and states with higher k values.

policies cannot be learned this way. The RL framework is specifically intended for learning good policies in such conditions. While feedback is given by the user to the last state-action, it is "backed-up" to other state-action pairs by the RL algorithm.

RL may be best regarded as a framework of problems and approaches, and includes many specific techniques. We have selected Sarsa [5,6], which allows learning directly from raw experience, without having a model of the environment's state dynamics.

In this section we are interested in learning a policy: $\Pi :: S \times A \rightarrow [0, 1]$, i.e., we want to learn to choose the right actions in a given state with higher probabilities. In Sarsa we look at quintuple of events $(s_t, a_t, r_{t+1}, s_{t+1}, a_{t+1})$, which makes up a transition from one state-action pair to the next. The update rule is:

$$Q(s_t, a_t) \leftarrow Q(s_t, a_t) + \alpha[r_t + 1 + \gamma Q(s_{t+1}, a_{t+1}) - Q(s_t, a_t)]$$

We use generalization, similar to the exploration and generalization as explained in Section 3.3. For the generalization to similar states and actions, we use the same formula, but instead of r_t we use $\frac{r_t}{k}$ where $k > 1$ reflects the rate of generalization.

We terminate the training phase when the user is satisfied with the learned policy. This policy may then be used in real time to control the character's behavior.

4   Discussion and Future Work

Using simulations we have validated the methods and found out the optimal values for the learning parameters. At this stage we are evaluating our approach using empirical experiments; we let users train characters and evaluate their perceived NVC capabilities, as compared with characters with random NVC, and with characters with hard-coded NVC behavior. This will eventually be done in a highly-immersive Cave-like [22] system, as part of our research on the sense of presence [23]. The results will be reported in a full paper.

Body language is, we believe, a good starting point to evaluate our method. Our animation platform includes other aspects of body language, which we intend to incorporate into the framework described here; this includes gaze direction and facial expressions. A more ambitious extension that we hope to explore is learning blending parameters for fine tuning of motions. This will entail learning in a continuous space, rather than a discrete combinatoric space.

Clearly, we need to train the characters and evaluate our system in the context of more complex scenarios. We see this as gradually leading to the construction of tools for authoring characters for non-linear narratives. Eventually, our method needs to be evaluated in the context of a complete application. This means we will need to extend our method to much larger state-action spaces, which means that our methods will need to be refined. Specifically, we intend to further investigate our generalization principle and base it on more formal grounds.

While our work is in its early stages we can already draw some conclusions. We believe the general approach, that of letting humans provide high-level feedback to train character NVC, to be promising. We believe our approach as described here can be extended to cover a wide variety of situations and scenarios.

A second conclusion is that standard machine-learning algorithms need to be carefully adapted to the problem. We explained why purely symbolic approaches are not adequate for NVC, but we have still learned that domain knowledge should be integrated into the algorithm. This calls for the development of specialized algorithms, and for an approach that relies more heavily on empirical evaluation. In general, there is interest in the RL research community in knowledge-based methods for using domain knowledge in the learning process; such research needs to be adapted to our domain.

Acknowledgements

This work has been supported by the European Union FET project PRESEN-CIA, IST-2001-37927. The development of the Demeanour behavior engine was supported by BT, plc. We would also like to thank Mel Slater and the UCL Department of Computer Science Virtual Environments and Graphics group for their help and support.

References

1. Cassell, J., Bickmore, T., Campbell, L., Chang, K., Vilhjálmsson, H., Yan, H.: Embodiment in conversational interfaces: Rea. In: ACM SIGCHI, ACM Press (1999) 520–527
2. Cassell, J., Vilhjálmsson, H.H., Bickmore, T.: BEAT: the behavior expression animation toolkit. In: ACM SIGGRAPH. (2001) 477–486
3. Gillies, M., Dodgson, N.: Eye movements and attention for behavioural animation. Journal of Visualization and Computer Animation **13** (2002) 287–300
4. Gillies, M., Ballin, D.: A model of interpersonal attitude and posture generation. In Rist, T., Aylett, R., Ballin, D., Rickel, J., eds.: Fourth Workshop on Intelligent Virtual Agents, Kloster Irsee, Germany (2003)
5. Sutton, R.S., Barto, A.G.: Reinforcement Learning: An Introduction. MIT Press, Cambridge, MA (1998)
6. Kaelbling, L.P., Littman, M.L., Moore, A.W.: Reinforcement learning: A survey. Journal of Artificial Intelligence Research **4** (1996) 237–285
7. Blumberg, B., Downie, M., Ivanov, Y., Berlin, M., Johnson, M.P., Tomlinson, B.: Integrated learning for interactive synthetic characters. In: SIGGRAPH '02: Proceedings of the 29th annual conference on Computer graphics and interactive techniques, New York, NY, USA, ACM Press (2002) 417–426
8. Isbell, C., Shelton, C.R., Kearns, M., Singh, S., Stone, P.: A social reinforcement learning agent. In: AGENTS '01: Proceedings of the fifth international conference on Autonomous agents, New York, NY, USA, ACM Press (2001) 377–384

9. Conde, T., Tambellini, W., Thalmann, D.: Behavioral animation of autonomous virtual agents helped by reinforcement learning. In Rist, T., Aylett, R., Ballin, D., Rickel, J., eds.: 4th International Workshop on Intelligent Virtual Agents (IVA'03). Volume 272., Springer-Verlag: Berlin (2003) 175–180

10. Guye-Vuilléme, A., T.K.Capin, I.S.Pandzic, Magnenat-Thalmann, N., D.Thalmann: Non-verbal communication interface for collaborative virtual environments. The Virtual Reality Journal **4** (1999) 49–59

11. DeCarolis, B., Pelachaud, C., Poggi, I., Steedman, M.: APML, a markup language for believable behaviour generation. In Prendiger, H., Ishizuka, M., eds.: Life-like characters: tools, affective functions and applications. Springer (2004) 65–87

12. Pelachaud, C., Poggi, I.: Subtleties of facial expressions in embodied agents. Journal of Visualization and Computer Animation. **13** (2002) 287–300

13. Rickel, J., Johnson, W.L.: Animated agents for procedural training in virtual reality: Perception, cognition, and motor control. Applied Artificial Intelligence **13** (1999) 343–382

14. Garau, M., Slater, M., Bee, S., Sasse, M.A.: The impact of eye gaze on communication using humaniod avatars. In: ACM SIGCHI. (2001) 309–316

15. Chi, D., Costa, M., Zhao, L., Badler, N.: The emote model for effort and shape. In: ACM SIGGRAPH, ACM Press/Addison-Wesley Publishing Co. (2000) 173–182

16. Hall, E.T.: The Hidden Dimension. New York: Doubleday (1966)

17. Cassell, J., Nakano, Y., Bickmore, T., Sidner, C., Rich, C.: Annotating and generating posture from discourse structure in embodied conversational agents. In: Workshop on Representing, Annotating, and Evaluating Non-Verbal and Verbal Communicative Acts to Achieve Contextual Embodied Agents, Autonomous Agents 2001 Conference, Montreal, Canada (2001)

18. Bécheiraz, P., Thalmann, D.: A model of nonverbal communication and interpersonal relationship between virtual actors. In: Proceedings of the Computer Animation '96, IEEE Computer Society Press (1996) 58–67

19. Gillies, M., Ballin, D.: Integrating autonomous behavior and user control for believable agents. In: Third international joint conference on Autonomous Agents and Multi-Agent Systems, Columbia University, New York City (2004)

20. Steed, A., Mortensen, J., Frecon, E.: Spelunking: Experiences using the DIVE System on CAVE-like Platforms. In: Immersive Projection Technologies and Virtual Environments. Volume 2. Springer-Verlag/Wien (2001) 153–164

21. Frecon, E., Smith, G., Steed, A., Stenius, M., Stahl, O.: An overview of the COVEN platform. Presence: Teleoperators and Virtual Environments **10** (2001) 109–127

22. Cruz-Neira, C., Sandin, D.J., DeFanti, T.A., Kenyon, R.V., Hart, J.C.: The CAVE: Audio visual experience automatic virtual environment. Comm. ACM **35** (1992) 65–72

23. Slater, M., Usoh, M.: Presence in immersive virtual environments. In: Proc. IEEE Virtual Reality 1993, Seattle, WA (1993) 33–40

Direction of Attention Perception for Conversation Initiation in Virtual Environments

Christopher Peters

IUT de Montreuil,
Université Paris8,
c.peters@iut.univ-paris8.fr
http://www.iut.univ-paris8.fr/

Abstract. We consider the role of gaze and direction of attention for providing embodied agents with the capability of visually perceiving the attention of others in a virtual environment. Such a capability is of importance in social environments where the directions in which others orient themselves provides information necessary for detecting important social cues and serving as a basis for inferring information about their possible motives, desires and intentions. Our real-time model uses synthetic vision and memory to implement a perceptually-based theory of mind that considers the direction of the eyes, head, body and locomotion of others. These contribute to metrics that describe the awareness and amount of interest that another is deemed to have in the self. We apply this capability to an automated conversation initiation scenario where an agent who encounters a potential interaction partner considers not only its own interaction goal, but also its theory of the goal of the other. Our aim is to improve the plausibility of animated social interaction and is inspired by human social behaviour, where one generally wishes to avoid the embarrassing situation of committing to a conversation with an unwilling participant.

1   Introduction

Social interaction among embodied agents usually considers scenarios where all of the agents are in close proximity to each other and have started interacting. An important question in relation to such scenarios is "how did the conversation start in the first place?". In an analysis of human greetings, Kendon [10] describes a sequence of cues in the opening of a meeting interaction and notes that the participants must first sight each other and identify the other as someone they wish to greet. Furthermore, as Goffman notes in his study of human social behaviour [8], we seek to avoid the social embarrassment of engaging in interaction with an unwilling participant. In this way, even if we have identified another as one we wish to interact with, if we are to limit the possibility of social embarrassment, we may first establish some degree of confidence that they will reciprocate in the interaction before we become explicit.

T. Panayiotopoulos et al. (Eds.): IVA 2005, LNCS 3661, pp. 215–228, 2005.
© Springer-Verlag Berlin Heidelberg 2005

In this paper, we are interested in creating a model that allows us to explore the notion that, in the early stages of the opening phase of an engagement, explicit requests for communication may be preceded by a more subtle negotiation between the potential participants. This may serve to provide cues to the other of ones openness in engaging with them, while also limiting their explicitness so as to minimise the potential social repercussions of failure. We are particularly interested in studying the role of direction of attention as a key underlying factor in this process, although we are careful to point out that this is only one among a large number of factors that must ultimately be considered for a complete model; not only do direction of attention behaviours support vital visual monitoring and cuing, but they also allow them to take place in a discreet manner over distance, minimising the risks and potential for social embarrassment. Our model perceives direction of attention of another through synthetic vision, processes it through and the early stages of a theory of mind model and stores percepts in memory. Percepts are integrated over a time period to provide a key concept in our model: *level of interest*. This is the term we use to refer to the amount of interest that another agent is perceived to have in the self; it is an indicator of their intention or openness towards interaction. These theories are stored in a theory of mind module and are a key part in driving the behaviours of the agent during conversation initiation: the perception of the other is used, in conjunction with the goals of the agent, to determine how the interaction opening proceeds.

2   Related Work

Vertegaal et al. [21] considered the significance of gaze and eye contact in the design of GAZE-2, a video conferencing system that ensures parallax-free transmission of eye-contact during multiparty mediated conversation. Previously, they had concluded that gaze was an excellent predictor of conversational attention in multiparty situations [20]. In the domain of social robotics, Scassellati [17] is constructing a humanoid robot as a test bed for the evaluation of models of human social development. The robot, Cog, has been endowed with social abilities based on a merger of two models of theory of mind. The movement of environmental stimuli is used to distinguish between animate and inanimate objects. Animate stimuli are then further processed by Baron-Cohen's model. More recently, Sidner et al. [18] have studied rules of looking behaviour that allow robots to maintain engagement with humans in a collaborative environment.

In relation to embodied agents, there has been a large amount of research conducted on animating conversation (see for example [3]) and the role of gaze behaviours in this process. Vilhjálmsson [22] outlined the importance of flexible conversation initialisation protocols and related gaze behaviours for creating social encounters for embodied autonomous agents who have not been positioned *a priori* in their environment. Colburn et al. [5] have studied the effects of eye gaze in virtual human characters and found avatars that use a natural gaze model elicit changes in viewers' eye gaze patterns. Poggi and Pelachaud [16] have studied the different communicative functions of gaze during conversations. Garau et al. [7] studied the effects of different gaze models and avatar realism settings on the perceived quality of communication in virtual environments.

3   Theoretical Basis

Our work draws from two important areas of research that, thus far, have not received a great deal of attention for application to embodied agents in virtual environments: direction of attention perception and theory of mind.

In relation to direction of attention, gaze is a vital social cue which is employed for social purposes not only by humans [1], but also in the animal kingdom where, for example, studies of gorillas have shown visual attention to play an important role in social cohesion and dominance hierarchy structuring [4]. In what is the most striking aspect of gaze, it allows a mutual bidirectional channel of communication between two living entities. Coupled with its relationship to attention, a mechanism that has been referred to as "the gateway to consciousness" [19], it is perhaps from this last example that the well known phrase "the eyes are the windows to the soul" arises and the high regard for the eyes of others as social indicators, which *Cicero* regarded "like sentinels, hold the highest place in the body". Following from this, it is not surprising to find that the directing of attention may be treated by others as a salient behaviour. In humans, privileged processing in brain areas related to emotion and attention takes place when the eye gaze of another is directed at oneself as opposed to averted [23]. Furthermore, as with explicit verbal signals, calling ones name for example, the direction of an others gaze has been found to be important in activating brain regions concerning the self, something that is important for initiating social contact [9].

Theory of mind research is concerned with the mechanisms involved in creating theories of the beliefs, goals and intentions of others. Baron-Cohen [2] has proposed an influential model that emphasises the evolutionary importance of gaze detection. It consists of a series of specialised modules, including an *Eye-direction detector* (EDD) which functions by detecting the presence of eyes or eye-like stimuli in the environment and computing the direction of gaze, an *Intentionality detector* (ID) which attributes the possibility of an object having goals and desires based on self propulsion and a *Theory of Mind Module* (ToMM), which stores the attribution of mental states to the other agent based on results from the other modules. The ToMM contains working theories that may not necessarily be correct, but are nonetheless vital for forming an internal representation of the possible motives behind the actions of other living entities. Perrett and Emery [12] have evaluated the model from a neurophysiological perspective and have proposed further modules. The *Direction of attention detector* (DAD) is a more general form of Baron-Cohens EDD, that combines information from separate detectors to also consider body and locomotion direction. The *Mutual attention mechanism* (MAM) represents a dyadic relationship involving mutual gaze. The research undertaken by Baron-Cohen and Perrett and Emery serves as a basis for our perceptually-based theory of mind model applied to autonomous agents in virtual environments.

4 Our Model

Our model is based on the theory as described in Section 3. The key components are a synthetic vision module, short-term sensory storage (STSS) and short-term memory (STM) modules, and direction of attention detector (DAD), mutual attention (MAM) and theory of mind (ToMM) modules. An overview of the process is summarised as follows (see Figure 1):

The vision system takes frequent snapshots of the environment to provide basic visibility information about what the agent can see, which is stored as false-colour percepts in the STSS (Section 4.1). At each visual update, these percepts are processed by the ID module, which filters agents and agent subparts into a *person percepts list*. Entries in the person percepts list are resolved and elaborated before being processed by the DAD (Section 4.2), which measures the orientation of subparts with respect to the self and produces an attention level metric; this metric represents the amount of attention that another agent is perceived to be paying in the current visual snapshot. Information from the DAD is used by the MAM to establish if there is eye-contact or if agents are paying attention to each other. This information, along with the output of the DAD are time-stamped and stored as a record in the STM.

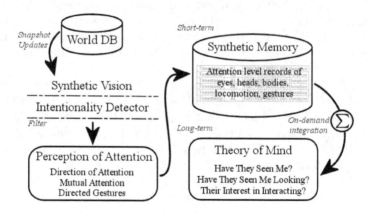

Fig. 1. An overview of the main stages in the model. In the diagram, the flow of processing proceeds from top to bottom, left to right. Representations become more explicit as processing progresses: a large amount of information must be processed at the level of the synthetic vision system, while only a few high-level values are stored at the level of the theory of mind module.

The consideration of all of the entries in memory for a single agent provides a record of their attention behaviours towards the self: a profile of these behaviours (called the *attention profile* - see Section 4.3) provides a better basis for inferring overall interest than only a single perceptual snapshot. Once this profile has been integrated over a time-interval, with gestures also accounted for (Section 4.3), high-level theories regarding other agents behaviour are updated in the ToM module (Section 4.3). Our implementation stores theories as numeric values that indicate other agents awareness of the self ($HTSM$), if the other agent is thought to be aware of ones awareness of them ($HTSML$) and an *interest level*, representing the theory of how much interest another agent has in the self. We describe in Section 5 how these theories and the information from the perceptual stages of theory of mind can be used to provide a basis for more elaborate conversation initialisation behaviour.

4.1   Synthetic Vision

We endow agents with a synthetic vision capability (see [11]) that provides the necessary information for the perceptually-based theory of mind modules (Section 4.2). Unlike robotics systems, we deal with virtual environments and use virtual sensors: this approach is easier to implement as complex and time-consuming issues such as segmentation and recognition are avoided. We have previously demonstrated the use of synthetic vision systems for a bottom-up model of a computer agent's attention that can be directed in both an object-and spatially-based view-dependent manner, something that would not be feasible using ray-casting approaches alone (see [14] and [15]). Our visual sensing model in this work is similar and utilises a monocular, multi-resolution vision system that provides input to higher-level processing systems.

The synthetic vision system operates in a snapshot manner by taking frequent updates of the visible portions of the scene. Objects in the scene are assigned unique false-colours, with which they are rendered in simplified scenes. Each false-colour corresponds to a scene element, where an element is at a granularity defined by the scene creator: we assign agents different false-colours for their eyes, heads and the remainder of their bodies, in order to differentiate between the visibility of these parts. The resulting renderings are then scanned to provide lists of false-colours in the agents field of view: these are stored in the Short-Term Sensory Storage, STSS. Our ID module is implemented as a filter that processes the list of percepts in the STSS and extracts those false-colours relating to agents into a separate person percepts list. The person percepts list is then processed further by the theory of mind modules (Section 4.2): other objects are thus considered as being incapable of goal-directed behaviour.

4.2   Perception of Attentive Behaviours

In this Section, we are primarily concerned with modelling the direction of attention detector, or DAD which measures the amount of attention directed towards the self at a certain instant of time. The purpose of the DAD is to attribute an *attention level* to another agent based on the direction of their eyes, head, body and locomotion with respect to the self, as perceived by synthetic vision module for a single visual perception update. Although there are a number of ways to

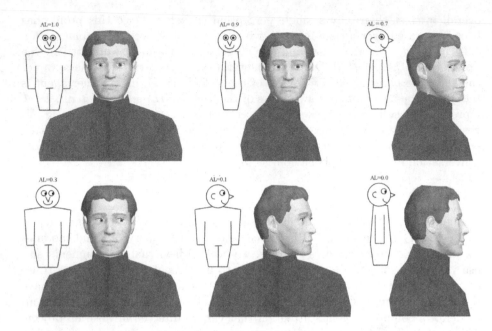

Fig. 2. Examples of the *attention level* metric for some key postures of another agent. The contribution of the eye, head and body directions are weighted, where eye direction is deemed to be the main determinant of the attention level paid by another agent.

infer the directed attention of others, such as hearing ones name being called, in this paper we infer direction of attention primarily on the basis of body orientation and locomotion direction, while also accommodating directed gestures (see Section 4.3).

Eye, Head and Body Direction Detectors. The *eye, head* and *body direction detectors* (EDD, HDD and BDD respectively) have the tasks of locating eyes, heads or bodies in the environment and determining if they are currently directing attention towards *me*. As mentioned in Section 4.1, the synthetic vision module handles the first part of this step, in a fast way, by filtering agents from the environment and storing their uniquely colour-coded subparts in a person percept list in the STSS (Algorithm 1).

The second task is then achieved by directly querying the agent database for the orientations and locations of the eyes, heads and bodies of the other agents and comparing them with position of the self in the environment: each subpart of the other agent (eyes, head, body) is attributed a *direction* value between 0 and 1, where 1 represents that the subpart is directed towards the self with intermediate values relating to the orientation of the part with respect to the perceiving agent. We adopt this approach as opposed to trying to calculate these values directly from the visual image to ensure real-time performance of the system.

Algorithm 1. Updates **perceived gaze information and attention levels**

UPDATEVISUALPERCEPTION*(database,STSS, STM)*

    VisualSnapshot(STSS) //capture visual snapshot
    STSS.ExtractAgentPercepts(personPerceptList) //Detect intentionality
    Resolve(personPerceptList,database) //Resolve person percepts list
    for each person in *personPerceptList* **do**
        //calculate Direction of Attention and Attention Level
        $eyeDir \leftarrow Dir(eye, me)$, $headDir \leftarrow Dir(head, me)$, $bodyDir \leftarrow Dir(body, me)$
        CalculateAttentionLevel(eyeDir, headDir, bodyDir)
        $eyeContact \leftarrow Direction(eyeDir, myEyeDir)$ //detect Mutual Attention
        STM.AddEntry(personPercept, AL, eyeContact) //store in short term memory
    end for

The final task of this module is to establish an overall attention level based on the direction of the subparts. Research from neuroscience [13] suggests a hierarchy of importance exists when all cues are available for processing, whereby the eyes act as a more important cue than the head, and the head provides a more important cue than the body. We therefore weight the direction of subparts to produce the *attention level* as follows:

$$AL = F_{Eye} * C_{Eye} + F_{Head} * C_{Head} + F_{Body} * C_{Body}$$

where F is the facing of a subpart and C is the weight of its contribution to the attention level, AL. In our implementation, we have weights set to 0.7, 0.2 and 0.1 for F_{Eye}, F_{Head} and F_{Body} respectively (see Figure 2).

Mutual Attention Mechanism (MAM). The mutual attention mechanism is connected to the output of the EDD. It is activated when two conditions are simultaneously satisfied: (1) the eyes of the other are deemed to be directed towards the eyes of the self and (2) ones own eyes are directed at the eyes of the other.

Distance and Occlusion. Our model also includes the ability to detect when certain parts of an other agent's body are not visible due to being occluded or too distant to discern; in the latter case, such objects are too small to occupy a single pixel in the false-colour map generated by the synthetic vision module (see Section 4.1). Our model uses a heuristic proposed by Emery [6] to handle the weighting process described in 4.2 when various parts are not visible. Essentially, if the eyes are not visible, then only the head and body are weighted towards the attention level. In the case where neither the eyes or the head are visible, the body orientation is used.

Locomotion Direction Detector (LDD). In Kendon's observations of human greeting rituals [10], he notes that a common behaviour when two people meet and close to converse involves at least one participant looking away from the other while changing direction and walking towards them in order to start talking. We therefore include a locomotion direction detector to allow for the perception and storage of the movement of another. As with the other detectors, locomotion information is read directly from the environmental database as opposed to deriving it from vision through optical flow methods, which would be too time consuming for our purposes.

During each perceptual "snapshot", each of these modules is activated for each entry in the current person percepts list, which is stored in the STSS. The output of the DAD is a memory record containing a timestamp, attention level, velocity information and the facing value of each subpart, which is then added to the person percepts history in the STM, as well as visibility information and MAM activation.

4.3   Interpretation of Another's Attention

The early perception modules discussed in Sections 4.1 and 4.2 provide both current information and a profile of the history of direction of attention behaviours made by visible agents. Here, we discuss how this information may be used to form high-level theories which we store in a Theory of Mind module. In particular, we store an *interest level* which represents an agents theory of the amount of interest that another agent has in it, as inferred from visual perceived attention behaviours. Here, we regard interest as being inferred from an others attention direction over a time-period - such information is intended as a basis for later combination with other factors of importance to interaction, such as facial expression, speech and context. We have begun to consider how one of these factors, gesture, can be integrated with the system.

Directed Gestures. A number of other cues, such as verbal communication, facial expressions and gestures, may have the effect of modulating ones perception of the interest of an other. Our system currently supports gesture modulation (we intend to also look at facial expression and speech in future work - see Section 6) in particular, what we refer to as *directed gestures*. These are the gestures that one perceives to be directed towards them due to the coinciding fixation of the gaze of the other on the perceiver. We use the MAM to establish if a gesture is directed and if it is, the magnitude and communicative intent of the gesture is read from the gesticulating agent.

Short-Term Memory. The memory system contains a history of the attentive behaviours of each agent and their relevance to the self. It is important for obtaining a clearer picture of the behaviours of an other; consider an agent that gave a small wave upon passing by, but didn't intend to stop to converse. If the attention level at the time of the gesture was interpreted in isolation, it could indicate a highly interested agent that wanted to interact. However, put in the context of the other behaviours of the agent, it would be more properly identified as mannerly signal from an otherwise disinterested agent. Each record stored in memory contains a timestamp, attention level, velocity information, visibility and facing value of each agent subpart and activation of the MAM. The memory system also stores records of directed gestures. Of key importance here is the ability to concatenate multiple separate memory entries, each with a separate attention level, into a coherent indicator of an agents attentive actions over a period of time. We achieve this by constructing and analysing an *attention profile*, which is a curve that intersects attention levels over a specified time period. Analysis of the profile in terms of magnitude, slope and duration of MAM activation provides important high level information on the behaviours and intentions of an other: For example, peaks in an otherwise low magnitude curve are interpreted as 'social inattention' or salutation behaviours without the intention to escalate the interaction. A profile that is of high magnitude and increasing is indicative of an agent that has more than a passing curiosity in an other and possibly an intention to interact. Entries regarding locomotion towards the self actively maintain the level of attention in cases where the profile would otherwise drop due to the eyes or head being oriented away.

Theory of Mind Module. The theory of mind module stores some high level variables that are set according to the perception and interpretation of behaviours as described in the previous Sections.

	Abbreviation	Theory	Represents
1.	HTSM	Have they seen me	*Other* has seen *S1*
2.	HTSML	Have they seen me looking	*Other* thinks (*S1* has seen *other*)
3.	IL	Interest level	*Other* has intention for *S1*

1. *HTSM* Have they seen me: Does S1 think the other agent is aware of it. This theory is based on the consideration of eye gaze directions from memory and the DAD and MAM.
2. *HTSML* Have they seen me looking: Does S1 think the other agent is aware that S1 is aware of it. This theory is also based on the consideration of eye gaze directions from memory, particularly MAM activation.
3. *IL* Interest level: How much interest has the other agent being paying to S1. This value is based on the *attention profile* integrated over a time interval, as queried from attention levels in memory (see Algorithm 2).

These theories, although not as sophisticated as those in humans, are important, explicit high-level representations that encapsulate a large amount of perceived information over a time interval. They are vital even for trivial situations where an agent is signalling to an other agent; in such cases, the signalling agent must have some knowledge that the other agent is actually paying attention to it, or else the attempt will be in vain. The perception of an others interest over a time period is important, not only for gaining feedback, but possibly also for interpreting the intention to interact as we will consider in the next Section.

5   Application and Evaluation

In this Section, we show how the direction of attention and theory of mind systems presented can be applied to the generation of autonomous interaction

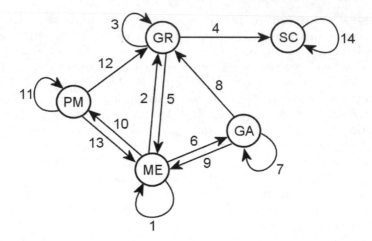

Fig. 3. Substates contained in the initialise conversation state of our HFSM. The same type of HFSM is executed on each agent. Permissable state transitions are numbered from 1 to 13. The *Grab Attention* (GA) and *Gauge Reaction* (GR) states are of high importance to this work: Gauge Reaction refers to the process by which an agent perceives the behaviour of another in order to interpret interest in conversation and decide to either commit to conversation (transition 4) or to return to monitoring the environment (transition 5).

initiation behaviours for agents. We detail a design that we are in the final stages of implementing and also describe how we plan to use it to evaluate the role of gaze in conversation initiation scenarios.

5.1   Conversation Initialisation

We use a hierarchical finite state machine to represent conversation initialisation (see Figure 3). There are five high level states in the HFSM: *Monitor Environment* (ME), in which the agent attends to the environment looking for other agents, *Grab Attention* (GA) in which the agent attempts to elicit the attention of another agent, *Passive Monitoring*(PM) which represents a discrete monitoring of another agent without trying to attract their attention, and *Gauge Reaction* (GR) where an agent is actively sends signals and interprets received signals to decide whether it should commit to conversation. The final state is *Starting Conversation* (SC) which is presumed to be the terminating state and handles the situation where both participants have successfully engaged in conversation.

State transitions in the HFSM take place as determined by not only the goals of an agent, as represented by a *conversational stance* variable (values: *avoid, interact, don't care*), but also according to their perception and theories of the state and intentions of the other agent (see Section 4.3) as well as their *relationship* (values: *good, bad, stranger, neutral*). We will detail some key states in the HFSM and how this process takes place:

Algorithm 2. Calculate **interest level and start conversation**

CALCULATEINTERESTLEVEL *(agent, timeInterval)*
    //get interest level over time interval
    $IL \leftarrow STM.Integrate(agent,$ all AL's over *timeInterval*)

STARTCONVERSATION *(agent, timeInterval, interestThreshold)*
    if $myGoal == interact$ **and** $eyeContact == TRUE$
    and $CalculateInterestLevel(agent, timeInterval) > interestThreshold)$
    and $STM[agent].AttentionProfile(timeInterval) == RISING$ **then**
        Signal explicit conversation request
    end if

In the *grab attention* state, an agent tries to explicitly attract the attention of an agent, by directing its attention and gesturing, if its goal is to *interact*. The HTSM and HTSML theories are used to establish when this attempt has (Figure 3, transition 8) or has not (Figure 3, transition 9) been successful.

The *passive monitoring* state will allow an agent to monitor the other in a discreet manner, for example, when the relationship is *good* but the goal is not set to interact; this might be the case when an agent is in a hurry and does not have time to converse. As long as they think the other is not aware of them through the HTSML flag, they continue unnoticed. If the HTSML flag becomes activate though, then they move to the gauge reaction state (Figure 3, transition 12) to see if the other wishes to interact. On the other hand, if only HTSM is active, then the agent may choose to be deceptive and simply ignore the other, since the other is not aware that mutual awareness has occurred and the behaviour may not be considered as bad mannered. Although this case has not yet been implemented, it has been included in our design so as to demonstrate how our model may act as a basis for supporting complex social behaviours based on perception.

The *gauge reaction* state is critical in our application; it encapsulates the sending of multiple signals between agents and interpretation of feedback when mutual awareness has been established (Figure 3, transition 3). In particular, it is the attempt by the agent to reach a conclusive theory as to the intention of the other to converse; it thus results in either a close to conversation (Figure 3, transition 4) or a return to monitoring the environment (Figure 3, transition 5). It is in this state that salutations, sustained gaze and/or locomotion changes occur depending on the goals of the agent and the perception of the other is integrated to infer interest. Agents that have their conversational stance set to *avoid* either ignore the other agent or only provide brief salutations and limited looking behaviour, depending on their relationship. Those that have their conversational stance set to *don't care* base their commitment to conversation solely on the feedback that they receive from the other agent and tend to mimic the other, while an agent actively seeking conversation provides cues to the other that attempt to maximise the others perception of their interest in them. An agent commits to conversation by making an explicit conversation request when a number of conditions have been met (see Algorithm 2). In particular, the other agent must have shown a high interest and the attention profile should be stable or rising over a time interval: this corresponds to an escalation in the level of attention and cues being exchanged by both agents. If the other agent previously showed interest but its profile is now low, then the opportunity to establish conversation with it is deemed to have passed.

5.2   Evaluation

Our evaluation of the model will consist of a number of studies where the user is presented with a view of a mobile agent enacting a number of scenarios in a virtual environment. At predefined times in each scenario, the simulation will pause and prompt the user to rate the agent's behaviour up to that point in a number of categories:

Have they seen you	Yes, No, Don't Know
How interested are they in you	Very, Somewhat, Not Very, Not At All
Do they want to interact	Definitely, Probably, Don't Know, Probably Not, Definitely Not

The behaviours of the agent will consist initially of direction of attention behaviours (e.g. locomotion changes, gaze direction, etc) and four types of 'wave' greeting gesture. At a later stage, the user can be replaced with an agent running the model described in Section 4 and the short-term memory of the agent queried at each simulation pause for comparison with the corresponding user data. Simulation pauses will be an important aspect of the evaluation: agents will be scripted so that after each pause, one or more aspects of the agents behaviour will change and can be later correlated with changes in user ratings. For example, previous to a pause, an agent may walk perpendicular to the user, but after the pause, may change locomotion direction towards the user. The effect of this change can be compared with any change in the users perception of interest and intention to interact.

6   Conclusions

We have presented a model that endows agents with a number of social perception capabilities by combining agent gaze perception with theory of mind models, something not yet considered for graphical agents in virtual environments. We are in the final stages of the implementation of the model using the *Torque* game engine (http:\\www.garagegames.com) and will shortly conduct an evaluation study as described in Section 5.

We hope to use the model to highlight important factors relating to the interplay of attention and emotion that may be crucial to understanding conversation initiation and engagement. Our immediate future work will focus on implementing facial expression capabilities into the current engine and considering the role of emotional expression and verbal cues, as well as visual attention behaviours, in establishing interaction. In the longer term, we would like to improve our evaluation methodology by considering more appropriate approaches and equipment, as our current experimental set-up is limited in accuracy and scope. Annotation of real-world conversation initiation situations is one option, although obtaining the required accuracy for detecting body part direction may be difficult, especially for mutual gaze situations, as individuals are mobile in the environment. Another option involves gaze tracking in an immersive virtual reality environment, although the level of similarity between conversation initiation situations in such environments and their real-life counterparts is not clear. We would also like to consider the role of context in our theory of mind model, which currently relies heavily on perception.

Acknowledgements

Thanks to Catherine Pelachaud for her invaluable advice throughout this work. This work has been funded by the Network of Excellence Humaine (Human-Machine Interaction Network on Emotion) IST-2002-2.3.1.6 / Contract no. 507422 (http:\\emotion-research.net\).

References

1. M. Argyle and M. Cook. *Gaze and mutual gaze.* Cambridge University Press, Cambridge, 1976.
2. S. Baron-Cohen. How to build a baby that can read minds: cognitive mechanisms in mind reading. *Cahiers de Psychologie Cognitive*, 13:513–552, 1994.
3. J. Cassell, C. Pelachaud, N. Badler, M. Steedman, B. Achorn, T. Becket, B. Douville, S. Prevost, and M. Stone. Animated conversation: rule-based generation of facial expression, gesture, spoken intonation for multiple conversational agents. *Computer Graphics*, 28(Annual Conference Series):413–420, 1994.
4. M.R.A. Chance. Attention structure as a basis of primate rank orders. *Man*, 2:503–518, 1976.
5. A. Colburn, M. Cohen, and S. Drucker. The role of eye gaze in avatar mediated conversational interfaces, 2000.
6. N.J. Emery. The eyes have it: The neuroethology, function and evolution of social gaze. *Neuroscience and biobehavioural reviews*, 24:581–604, 2000.
7. M. Garau, M. Slater, V. Vinayagamoorthy, A. Brogni, A. Steed, and M.A. Sasse. The impact of avatar realism and eye gaze control on perceived quality of communication in a shared immersive virtual environment. In *Proceedings of the conference on Human factors in computing systems*, pages 529–536. ACM Press, 2003.
8. E. Goffman. *Behaviour in public places: notes on the social order of gatherings.* The Free Press, New York, 1963.
9. K.K.W. Kampe, C.D. Frith, and U. Frith. "hey john": signals conveying communicative intention toward the self activate brain regions associated with "mentalizing," regardless of modality. *Journal of Neuroscience*, 23(12):5258–5263, 2003.

10. A. Kendon. *Conducting interaction: patterns of behaviour in focused encounters.* Cambridge University Press, New York, 1990.
11. H. Noser and D. Thalmann. Synthetic vision and audition for digital actors. *Computer Graphics Journal*, 14(3):325–336, 1995.
12. D.I. Perrett and N.J. Emery. Understanding the intentions of others from visual signals: neurophysiological evidence. *Current Psychology of Cognition*, 13:683–694, 1994.
13. D.I. Perrett, J.K. Hietanen, M.W. Oram, and P.J. Benson. Organisation and functions of cells responsive to faces in the temporal cortex. *Philosophical Transactions of the Royal Society of London: Biological Sciences*, 335:23–30, 1992.
14. C. Peters and C. O' Sullivan. Synthetic vision and memory for autonomous virtual humans. *Computer Graphics Forum*, 21(4):743–753, 2002.
15. C. Peters and C. O' Sullivan. Bottom-up visual attention for virtual human animation. In *Proceedings of Computer Animation and Social Agents (CASA)*, pages 111–117, New York, 2003.
16. I. Poggi and C. Pelachaud. Gaze and its meaning in animated faces. In P. McKevitt, editor, *Language, vision and music*. Amsterdam: John Benjamins, 2000.
17. B. Scassellati. Investigating models of social development using a humanoid robot. In Barbara Webb and Thomas Consi, editors, *Biorobotics*. M.I.T. Press, 2000.
18. C.L. Sidner, C.H. Lee, and N.B. Lesh. Engagement by looking: Behaviors for robots when collaborating with people. In Kruiff-Korbayova and Kosny (eds.), editors, *Diabruck: Workshop on the Semantics and Pragmatics of Dialogue*, pages 123–130, 2003.
19. J.G. Taylor. Paying attention to consciousness. *Progress in Neurobiology*, 71:305–335, 2003.
20. R. Vertegaal, R. Slagter, G. van der Veer, and A. Nijholt. Eye gaze patterns in conversations: there is more to conversational agents than meets the eyes. In *CHI '01: Proceedings of the SIGCHI conference on Human factors in computing systems*, pages 301–308, New York, NY, USA, 2001. ACM Press.
21. R. Vertegaal, I. Weevers, C. Sohn, and C. Cheung. Gaze-2: conveying eye contact in group video conferencing using eye-controlled camera direction. In *CHI '03: Proceedings of the SIGCHI conference on Human factors in computing systems*, pages 521–528, New York, NY, USA, 2003. ACM Press.
22. H.H. Vilhjálmsson. Autonomous communicative behaviors in avatars. Master's thesis, Media Arts and Sciences, M.I.T. Media Lab, Cambridge M.A., 1997.
23. B. Wicker, D.I. Perrett, S. Baron-Cohen, and J. Decety. Being the target of another's emotion: a pet study. *Neuropsychologia*, 41:139–146, 2003.

A Model of Attention and Interest Using Gaze Behavior

Christopher Peters[1], Catherine Pelachaud[1], Elisabetta Bevacqua[1],
Maurizio Mancini[1], and Isabella Poggi[2]

[1] IUT de Montreuil, Université de Paris 8
{c.peters, c.pelachaud, e.bevacqua,
m.mancini}@iut-univ.paris8.fr
[2] Università di Roma
poggi@univroma3.it

Abstract. One of the major problems of user's interaction with Embodied Conversational Agents (ECAs) is to have the conversation last more than few second: after being amused and intrigued by the ECAs, users may find rapidly the restrictions and limitations of the dialog systems, they may perceive the repetition of the ECAs animation, they may find the behaviors of ECAs to be inconsistent and implausible, etc. We believe that some special links, or bonds, have to be established between users and ECAs during interaction. It is our view that showing and/or perceiving interest is the necessary premise to establish a relationship. In this paper we present a model of an ECA able to establish, maintain and end the conversation based on its perception of the level of interest of its interlocutor.

1 Introduction

Embodied Conversational Agents (ECAs) are being used more and more in applications involving interactions with users. One of the major problems these applications face is to have the conversation last more than few second between the users and the ECAs. The reasons for such a short duration may be manifold: after being amused and intrigued by the ECAs, users may find rapidly the restrictions and limitations of the dialog systems, they may perceive the repetition of the ECAs animation, they may find the behaviors of ECAs to be inconsistent and implausible, etc. Research in several areas has been undertaken to overcome these shortcomings. But we believe that another aspect to consider is the creation of special links, or bonds, that could be established between users and ECAs. Building a relationship is linked to the notion of engagement in the conversation.

Our view is that cognitive and emotional involvement and commitment are key factors that underlie the notion of engagement. If this is the case, then for an ECA to be able to establish, maintain and end interactions, it must be endowed with mechanisms that allow it to perceive, adapt to and generate behaviors relating to attention and emotion. In this paper, we will discuss some important capabilities that we have been working on: we do not present a full Speaker/Listener model, but rather illustrate how the concepts may group together to form the core of such a model. We will also focus on two important aspects of human communication, that is interest and attention during conversation. These factors have not been considered in previous studies in the same research field.

T. Panayiotopoulos et al. (Eds.): IVA 2005, LNCS 3661, pp. 229–240, 2005.
© Springer-Verlag Berlin Heidelberg 2005

In the next Section we will present an overview of the state of the art of studies on gaze behavior. In Section 3 we will give some definitions of engagement and we will describe its importance in Human communication. In Section 4 we will then present the steps involved in engagement detection and discuss some algorithms that can be used to detect engagement at the beginning of conversation and during interaction with ECAs.

2   State of the Art

A number of studies have underlined the importance of gaze behavior in the communication process. Vertegaal et al. [26] found that gaze was an excellent predictor of conversational attention in multiparty situations and placed special consideration on eye contact in the design of video conferencing systems [27]. Colburn et al. [8] have studied the effects of eye gaze in virtual human characters and found avatars that use a natural gaze model elicit changes in viewers' eye gaze patterns. Garau et al. [12] found that when avatars used gaze behaviors related to turn-taking during conversation, they consistently and significantly outperforming random-gaze conditions in terms of participants' subjective responses. Several researches [3,25] have been undertaken to study the effects of manipulated eye gaze on persuasion in a small group. Three users, in three remote rooms, entered in a common virtual environment where their visual representations could interact. Their gaze behavior was modified in order to augment or diminish eye interactions with the other participants.

Another research area related to our work is backchannel modelling. K.R. Thòrisson developed a multi-layer multimodal architecture able to generate the animation of the virtual agent Gandalf during a conversation with an user [24]. Gandalf recognizes information like head movements or short statements, using it to generate backchannel feedback. The Rea system [6] generates backchannel feedback each time the user makes a pause shorter than 500 msec. The feedback consists in paraverbals (e.g. "mmhmm") or head nods or short statements such as "I see". Models have also been developed for controlling gaze behavior of ECAs conversing with other ECAs. For example the models of Colburn et al. [8] and Fukayama et al. [11] are based on state machines. The first one uses hierarchical state machines to compute gaze for both one-on-one conversation than multiparty interactions while the second uses a two-state Markov model which outputs gaze points in the space derived from three gaze parameters (amount of gaze, mean duration of gaze and gaze points while averted).

3   From Engagement to Interaction

Engagement is viewed, by Sidner et al. [23], as "the process by which two (or more) participants establish, maintain and end their perceived connection during interactions they jointly undertake". In our terms [9,19], it could be defined as "the value that a participant in an interaction attributes to the goal of being together with the other participant(s) and of continuing the interaction". Engagement is generally linked to (possibly caused by) interest, which could be defined as an emotional state linked to the participant's goal of receiving and elaborating new and potentially useful knowledge. Engagement and interest in their turn are a cause of attention: if I am interested in the topic or the

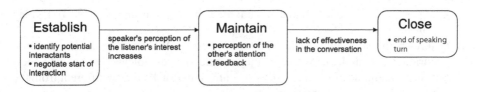

Fig. 1. Diagram of interaction phases

persons involved in an interaction, I engage in the interaction and pay attention to its topics and participants.

Actually, communication is an activity involving two (or multiple) partners. A Sender wants an Addressee to receive some information, and to do so he produces communicative signals; the Addressee, in his turn, must use his resources of attention, perception and intelligence to understand what the Sender is trying to communicate: communication is not worthwhile without the Addressee's engagement. In at least two stages it is important for the Sender to assess the Addressee's interest and engagement in conversation: first, at the moment of starting a communicative interaction; second, when the interaction is going on, just to see whether the Addressee is following, understanding, concerned in, agreeing with what the Sender is saying. sIn case of lack of Addressee's engagement the Sender might decide to close the conversation (see Figure 1).

3.1 Addressee's Capabilities

In the construction of intelligent interactional human-like Agents, both these stages can be reproduced and the capacities held by Human conversationalists should be implemented in ECAs. When a Sender produces communicative signals, for communicative interaction to go on, the Addressee must go through a number of steps:

Attention. The Addressee must pay attention to the signals produced to perceive, process and memorise them. Attention (at least intentional attention) is made possible by engagement: if for the Addressee the goal of interacting with the Sender has a very low value, he will not pay much attention to what the Sender is communicating. In the same vein, attention is a pre-condition of all subsequent steps, which are, thus, all dependent on initial engagement.

Perception. The Addressee must be able to perceive the signals produced by the Sender, while not being impaired either by permanent perceptual handicaps or by transitory noise.

Comprehension. The Addressee must have the cognitive capacities for literal and non-literal comprehension: to understand the meaning of the Sender's each signal he must master the linguistic (lexical and semantic) rules of his language; moreover, he must have the inferential capacities to understand the indirect meanings implied by the Sender.

Internal reaction. Once the Addressee has processed the signal and extracted the Sender's meaning, he might have internal reactions of a cognitive and emotional kind: for example, he may find that what the Sender said is unbelievable, or he may feel upset or amused by it.

Decision whether to communicate the internal reaction. Whatever the internal reaction occurred in his mind, the Addressee may decide to communicate how he really feels (sincere communication), or to communicate an internal reaction different from the real one (deceptive communication [10,7]), or not to manifest his reactions at all (omission). This decision whether to communicate internal reactions may be driven by a number of factors, among which the consequences of this communication, the social relationship with the Sender, his capability to comprehend and/or accept the Addressee's reaction (see [21]).

Generation. Once he decided to communicate (either sincerely or deceptively) his internal reaction, the Addressee should be able to display expressive synchronized visual and acoustic behaviors.

All of these processes, however, must not necessarily occur at a completely aware level: in some cases the Addressee may be aware of the fact and the ways of their occurrence, but in many cases they are quite automatic. For example, both the decision to exhibit a signal of comprehension and its generation may be quite unreflected. In any case, though, the occurrence of these processes is quite necessary for one to conclude that the Addressee is engaged in the conversation.

4 Detecting Engagement Before and During Interaction

As we mentioned, the issue of detecting engagement in a prospective or actual Addressee is mainly relevant in two stages of an interaction:

1. **establish phase**: at the start, when the Sender must decide if it is worthwhile to start an interaction, and does so on the basis of how possibly engaged/engageable he sees a prospective Addressee;
2. **maintain phase**: in the course of interaction, to monitor the level of engagement of the Addressee and the effectiveness of the interaction.

In the establish phase the prospective Sender must decide by himself whether to engage in conversation, by assessing the prospective Addressee's level of interest and attention; in the maintain phase, the Sender can be helped in doing so by the Addressee's backchannel. During conversation, in fact, the interlocutors generally produce some signals in order to make the Speaker aware if they are really paying attention, listening to, understanding and agreeing with what is being said. That is, the interlocutors often inform the Sender about their engagement and about the smooth flowing of the processes necessary to communicative interaction: attention, perception, comprehension and internal reactions. The signals providing such information, when performed by the interlocutor without a speaking turn, are called backchannel [1], and they are performed in different modalities: by paraverbals (like mmhmm, oh), facial expression, head movements, gaze [18].

In this work we focus our efforts on both moments of the check for the Addressee's interest and attention. First we propose an algorithm for the establish phase through which the Sender can detect the Addressee's attention in order to decide whetheror not to engage in a conversation. Second, we propose an algorithm for the maintain phase aimed at detecting and interpreting those backchannel signals of the Addressee that are provided through eye-gaze.

4.1 Perception of Attention

Attention is a vital, if not fundamental, aspect of engagement. Indeed, it is doubtful that one could be considered to be engaged to any great extent in the absence of the deployment of attention. There are many facets of attention that are of relevance to engagement. Attention primarily acts as the control process for orienting the senses towards stimuli of relevance to the engagement, such as the Speaker or an object of discussion, in order to allow enhanced perceptual processing to take place. In social terms, the volitional deployment of attention, manifested as overt behaviors such as gaze and eye contact, may also be used for signalling one's desires, such as to become or remain engaged [22]. Therefore, the perception and interpretation of the attentive behaviors of others is also an important factor for managing ECA engagements in a manner consistent with human social behavior.

This capability focuses on social perception and attention in the visual modality geared towards the opening of an engagement. We model engagement opening as something that may start at a distance and may not initially involve an explicit commitment to engage, such as the use of a greeting utterance. In this way, the opening of the engagement may consist of a subtle negotiation between the potential participants. This negotiation phase serves as a way to communicate the intention to engage without commitment to the engagement and has the purpose of reducing the social risk of engaging in conversation with an unwilling participant [13].

4.2 Establish Phase

In our model, a synthetic vision system allows our agent to visually sense the environment in a snapshot manner. Sensed information is filtered by social attention mechanism that only allows continued processing of other agents in the environment. This mechanism acts as an agency or intentionality detector [15], so that only the behaviors of other agents are considered in later processing. Perception then consists of the segmentation of perceived agents into eye, head and body regions and the retrieval of associated direction information, as well as locomotion data, from an object database. Direction information is then weighted based on region, so that the eyes and regions oriented towards the viewer receive a higher weighting. This results in an attention level metric for an instant of time that is stored in a short-term memory system. Percepts from the memory system may then be integrated on demand to provide an attention profile spanning a time segment. Such a profile is useful for the interpretation of the attention behaviors of others: we link it, along with a gesture detection, to a theory of mind module [2] in order to establish the intention of the other to interact. Explicit commitments to interaction are only made when an agent wants to interact and theorises that there is a high probability that the other also wants to interact (see Algorithm 1 for an overview of the process).

Algorithm 1. Updates **perceived gaze information and calculates interest level**
Input:
    World database *database*
    Sensory memory $STSS$
    Short-term Memory STM

UPDATEVISUALPERCEPTION(*database, STSS, STM*)

    $VisualSnapshot(STSS)$ //capture visual snapshot percepts into sensory memory
    $STSS.ExtractAgentPercepts(personPerceptList)$ //Detect intentionality
    $Resolve(personPerceptList, database)$ //Resolve person percepts list with database
    for each person in $personPerceptList$ **do**
        //calculate Direction of Attention
        $eyeDir \leftarrow Direction(eye, me)$
        $headDir \leftarrow Direction(head, me)$
        $bodyDir \leftarrow Direction(body, me)$
        $CalculateAttentionLevel(eyeDir, headDir, bodyDir)$ //calculate Attention level
        $eyeContact \leftarrow Direction(eyeDir, myEyeDir)$ //detect Mutual Attention
        $STM.AddEntry(personPercept, AL, eyeContact)$ //add information to short term memory

---

CALCULATEINTERESTLEVEL(*agent, timeInterval*)

    //get interest level over time interval
    $IL \leftarrow STM.Integrate(agent,$all AL's over $timeInterval)$

STARTCONVERSATION(*agent, timeInterval, interestThreshold*)

    if $myGoal == interact$ **and**
    $CalculateInterestLevel(agent, timeInterval) > interestThreshold)$ **and**
    $STM[agent].AttentionProfile(timeInterval) == RISING$ **and**
    $eyeContact == TRUE$ **then**
        Signal start of conversation

4.3 Maintain Phase

Now we want to focus our research on the attention and the interest of the Listener during conversation and how they affect the Speaker. Through the evaluation of the level of interest, the Speaker can perceive the effectiveness of the conversation and decide if it is high enough to maintain the interaction with the Listener or if he should close it. Regarding the assessment of the Listener's attention, in this paper we focus above all on gaze. Gaze is an especially important way of providing feedback and subtle signaling. Through it a Listener can show his level of interest and engagement. For example, a Listener that needs to disengage from a conversation may start to avert his gaze more frequently. Moreover, the more people share looking behaviors, the more they are involved and coordinate in the conversation. This may not necessarily involve mutual eye contact with the Speaker: during shared attention situations involving another object or entity, the Listener may actually signal their interest in the situation by directing their attention away from the Speaker and at the object in question [23].

Gaze Behavior Dynamism for Speaker and Listener

In a previous version of gaze model we used Bayesian Belief Networks [16] to determine the gaze behavior of a virtual agent. This model was based on statistical data reported in [5], corresponding to the annotation of body behaviors (gaze direction, head nods, back channels) of two subjects having a conversation. It was able to generate gaze from an input file containing both text and some tags taken from an XML-style language called APML [17]. An APML text contains what the Speaker will say and the meaning he aims at conveying, that is it does not specify which signals (i.e. facial expressions, gestures) have to be used.

A weakness of the model is the impossibility of simulating multi-party conversations without having to redefine transition tables needed by the Belief Network model. The tables increase exponentially in their complexity. Our current model is based on both APML input and two state machines defined using HPTS++ [14]. HPTS++ is a

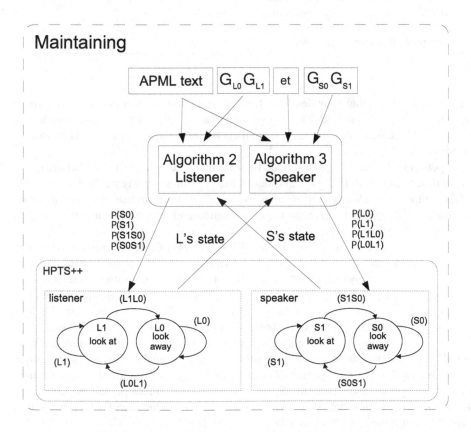

Fig. 2. Diagram of the maintaining state of the conversation

Algorithm 2. Computes **probabilities for HPTS++ Listener's state machine**
Input:

    APML text $apml$

    Max duration of Listener's look-atG_{L1} Max duration of Listener's look-away
G_{L0}

---

  while $t \leq turn\_duration$ **do**

    $L_t \leftarrow Gaze\_of\_Listener(t)$ //compute expected Listener's gaze direction

    if $L_t == L0$ **then**

      $incr(P(L0)), incr(P(L1L0))$ //incr the proba to remain or to transit to state L0

      $decr(P(L1)), decr(P(L0L1))$ //decr the proba to remain or to transit to state L1

    if $L_t == L1$ **then**

      $incr(P(L1)), incr(P(L0L1))$ //incr the proba to remain or to transit to state L1

      $decr(P(L0)), decr(P(L1L0))$ //decrease the proba to remain or to transit to state L0

    //if the Listener has been in a state L0 for too long (i.e. for a duration longer than G_{L0}) then
    incr the proba that it will change state

    if $Time\_Listener\_in\_L0 \geq G_{L0}$ **then**

      $incr(P(L0L1))$

    //if the Listener has been in a state L1 for too long (i.e. for a duration longer than G_{L1}) then
    incr the proba that it will change state

    if $Time\_Listener\_in\_L1 \geq G_{L1}$ **then**

      $incr(P(L1L0))$

  compute gaze state of the Listener

---

definition language that provides tools for describing multi-agent systems using finite state machines. It also provides an environment to automatically manage the parallel execution of these machines and resolve conflicts between the allocation of the resources needed by each machine.

Speaker and listeners are described by state machines and their gaze behavior at a given time corresponds to the current state of the machines (see Figure 2). So, for example, to simulate multiparty conversations we need just to instantiate one state machine for each one of the participants to the conversation and let the system elaborate gaze behavior through time.

In the lower part of the diagram (the HPTS++ levels of implementation) the nodes of the state machines represent the possible gaze states of Speaker and Listener: gaze at (S1, L1) and gaze away (S0, L0). On the arcs there are the probabilities to either remain in the same state or to change state. At each time step (phoneme level) the probabilities on the arcs may vary (see Algorithms 2 and 3). Based on these values the HPTS++ system decides if a given gaze state should hold or should transit to another one.

Algorithm 2 computes Listener's gaze behavior. It takes 2 inputs, an input text with APML tags and two numbers which represent the maximum duration the Listener may consecutively look at the Speaker G_{L1} and the maximum duration the Listener may consecutively look away from the Speaker G_{L0}. Actually these parameters characterize the Listener's gaze behavior and they have been introduced in [16]. Algorithm 2, starting from APML, determines when the Listener is expected to look at the Speaker (such as on emphasis, boundary markers, change of speaking turn, etc. see [17]). These

---

Algorithm 3. Computes **probabilities for HPTS++ Speaker's state machine**
Input:
    Effectiveness threshold et APML text $apml$
    Max duration of Speaker's look-at G_{S1}
    Max duration of Speaker's look-away G_{S0}

---

  while $t \leq turn\_duration$ **do**
    $L_t \leftarrow Gaze\_of\_Listener(t)$
    $S_t \leftarrow Gaze\_of\_Speaker(t)$
    $L_a \leftarrow Listener\_attention$ from L_t and S_t
    $L_i \leftarrow Listener\_interest$ from L_a
    if L_i is low **then**
      $incr(P(S1)),incr(P(S0S1))$ //incr the proba to remain or to pass to state S1
      $decr(P(S0)),decr(P(S1S0))$ //decr the proba to remain or to pass to state S0
    else
      $incr(P(S1S0)),incr(P(S0))$ //incr the proba to remain or to pass to state S0
      $decr(P(S0S1)),decr(P(S1))$ //decr the proba to remain or to pass to state S1
    //if the Speaker has been in a state S0 for too long (i.e. for a duration longer than G_{S0}) then
    incr the proba that it will change state
    if $Time\_Speaker\_in\_S0 \geq G_{S0}$ **then**
      $incr(P(S0S1))$
    //if the Speaker has been in a state S1 for too long (i.e. for a duration longer than G_{S1}) then
    incr the proba that it will change state
    if $Time\_Speaker\_in\_S1 \geq G_{S1}$ **then**
      $incr(P(S1S0))$
    //if Speaker is looking at the Listener
    if $S_t ==$ S1 **then**
      if L_i is low **then**
        $decr(effectiveness)$
      else
        $incr(effectiveness)$
    if $effectiveness \leq et$ **then**
      end of the conversation, quit the algorithm
    compute gaze state of the Listener

---

pre-calculated behaviors are used at each time step t to determine the four probabilities for the Listener's gaze states. The algorithm considers also if a given gaze state of the Listener has not last too long (determined by G_{L1} and G_{L0} values). This allows us to avoid the state machine to remain in a deadlock state.

Algorithm 3 computes Speaker's gaze behavior. It takes as input the APML text, a threshold value and two maximum duration values for gaze direction G_{S1} and G_{S0} that work similarly as for the Listener (see description of Algorithm 2) . At first the algorithm computes the expected Speaker's gaze based on APML tags (see [20]). Then the Listener's level of attention L_a is computed as a function of Listener's gaze state L_t. Then the Listener's level of interest L_i is computed as an integration over time of the attention level. At this point it is possible to look at L_i and decide to modify or not the Speaker's HPTS++ probabilities and the *effectiveness* of conversation accordingly.

This computation is done only when the Speaker is gazing at the Listener. The level of *effectiveness* of conversation is compared with the threshold *et*. If it is lower the Speaker ends the conversation. Otherwise the next Speaker's and Listener's gaze state are decided based on the probabilities just computed. Since they use different parameters ($G_{S0}, G_{S1}, G_{L0}, G_{L1}$) and algorithms, the Speaker and Listener behaviors will be different if their roles are exchanged.

5   Conclusion and Future Works

In this paper, we have presented capabilities that an ECA requires to be able to start, maintain and end a conversation. We addressed in particular the notion of engagement from the point of view of the Speaker and Listener. We have also presented our preliminary developments toward such a model.

In the future we aim at considering other modalities than gaze in our algorithms. HPTS++ allows one to have a common component for all the communicative modalities of the agent and easily define relations of coordination and synchronization between them. So it will be possible to create some new state machines for hand gestures for example or for facial expressions and let them run in parallel to generate consistent multimodal agent's behavior.

In the current state of our model, we do not consider the agents' mental and emotive states in consideration. But an effect of Listener's lower level of interest for the conversation may be to make the Speaker in a negative emotional state. Our model should not consider simply behavior information but also cognitive and emotional information of the agents.

Finally we will like to try out different ways for the Speaker to get the attention of the Listener by transgressing some communicative and social rules. Distractors could be applied such as making a strange noise, not gazing in a direction when expected [4].

Acknowledgements

We thank Stéphane Donikian and Fabrice Lamarche for letting us use the HTPS++ toolkit. We are grateful to Nicolas Ech Chafaï for discussing with us on this paper. This work has been partially funded by the Network of Excellence Humaine (Human-Machine Interaction Network on Emotion) IST-2002-2.3.1.6 / Contract no. 507422 (http://emotion-research.net/).

References

1. J. Allwood. Bodily communication dimensions of expression and content. In I. Karlsson B. Granstrm, D. House, editor, *Multimodality in Language and Speech Systems*, pages 7–26. Kluwer Academic Publishers, 2002.
2. S. Baron-Cohen. How to build a baby that can read minds: cognitive mechanisms in mind reading. *Cahiers de Psychologie Cognitive*, 13:513–552, 1994.
3. A.C. Beall, J. Bailenson, J. Loomis, J. Blascovich, and C. Rex. Non-zero-sum gaze in immersive virtual environments. In *Proceedings of HCI International*, Crete, 2003.

4. Diane M. Beck and Nilli Lavie. Look here but ignore what you see: effects of distractors at fixation. *Journal of Experimental Psychology: Human Perception and Performance*, September 2004.
5. J. Cappella and C. Pelachaud. Rules for responsive robots: using human interaction to build virtual interaction. In Reis, Fitzpatrick, and Evangelisti, editors, *Stability and change in relationships*. Cambridge University Press, New York, 2001.
6. J. Cassell, T. Bickmore, M. Billinghurst, L. Campbell, K. Chang, H. Vilhjlmsson, and H. Yan. Embodiment in conversational interfaces: Rea. In *CHI*, Pittsburgh, PA, April 15-20 1999.
7. C. Castelfranchi and I. Poggi. Bugie finsioni sotterfugi. In *Per una scienza dell'inganno*. Carocci, Roma, 1998.
8. M. F. Cohen, R. A. Colburn, and S. M. Drucker. The role of eye gaze in avatar mediated conversational interfaces. In *Technical Report MSR-TR-2000-81*. Microsoft Corporation, 2000.
9. R. Conte and C. Castelfranchi. *Cognitive and Social Action*. University College, London, 1995.
10. P. Ekman. *Telling lies*. New York: Norton, 1985.
11. A. Fukayama, T. Ohno, N. Mukawa, M. Sawaki, and N. Hagita. Messages embedded in gaze of interface agents — impression management with agent's gaze. In *CHI '02: Proceedings of the SIGCHI conference on Human factors in computing systems*, pages 41–48, New York, USA, 2002. ACM Press.
12. M. Garau, M. Slater, V. Vinayagamoorthy, A. Brogni, A. Steed, and M.A. Sasse. The impact of avatar realism and eye gaze control on perceived quality of communication in a shared immersive virtual environment. In *Proceedings of the conference on Human factors in computing systems*, pages 529–536. ACM Press, 2003.
13. E. Goffman. *Forms of Talk*. Oxford: Blackwell, 1981.
14. F. Lamarche and S. Donikian. Automatic orchestration of behaviours through the management of resources and priority levels. In *Proceedings of Autonomous Agents and Multiagent Systems (AAMAS'02)*, Bologna, Italy, July 15-19 2002. ACM.
15. A.M. Leslie. The perception of causality in infants. *Perception*, 11(2):173–186, 1982.
16. C. Pelachaud and M. Bilvi. Modelling gaze behavior for conversational agents. In *proceedings of the IVA 2003 conference*. Springer LINAI Series, 2003.
17. C. Pelachaud, V. Carofiglio, B. De Carolis, and F. de Rosis. Embodied contextual agent in information delivering application. In *First International Joint Conference on Autonomous Agents & Multi-Agent Systems (AAMAS)*, Bologna, Italy, July 2002.
18. C. Peters, C. Pelachaud, E. Bevacqua, M. Mancini, and I. Poggi. Engagement capabilities for ecas. In *AAMAS'05 workshop Creating Bonds with ECAs*, 2005.
19. I. Poggi. *Mind, hands, face and body. A goal and belief view of multimodal communication*. To be published, Forth.
20. I. Poggi and C. Pelachaud. Signals and meanings of gaze in animated faces. In P.McKevitt, S.Nuállain, and C.Muhlvihill, editors, *Language, Vision and Music*. John Benjamins, Amsterdam, 2001.
21. I. Poggi, C. Pelachaud, and B. De Carolis. To display or not to display? towards the architecture of a reflexive agent. In *Proceedings of the 2nd Workshop on Attitude, Personality and Emotions in User-adapted Interaction. User Modeling 2001*, Sonthofen (Germany), 13-17 July 2001.
22. I. Poggi, C. Pelachaud, and F. De Rosis. Eye communication in a conversational 3d synthetic agent. In *AI Communications*, volume 13, pages 169–181. IOS Press, 12 2000.
23. C. L. Sidner, C. D. Kidd, C. Lee, and N. Lesh. Where to look: A study of human-robot interaction. In *Intelligent User Interfaces Conference*, pages 78–84. ACM Press, 2004.
24. K.R. Thórisson. Layered modular action control for communicative humanoids. In *Computer Animation'97*, Geneva, Switzerland, 1997. IEEE Computer Society Press.

25. M. Turk, J. Bailenson, J. Blascovich, and R. Guadagno. Multimodal transformed social interaction. In *Proceedings of the 6th International Conference on Multimodal Interfaces*, 2004.

26. R. Vertegaal, R. Slagter, G. van der Veer, and A. Nijholt. Eye gaze patterns in conversations: there is more to conversational agents than meets the eyes. In *CHI '01: Proceedings of the SIGCHI conference on Human factors in computing systems*, pages 301–308, New York, NY, USA, 2001. ACM Press.

27. R. Vertegaal, I. Weevers, C. Sohn, and C. Cheung. Gaze-2: conveying eye contact in group video conferencing using eye-controlled camera direction. In *CHI '03: Proceedings of the SIGCHI conference on Human factors in computing systems*, pages 521–528, New York, NY, USA, 2003. ACM Press.

Where Do They Look? Gaze Behaviors of Multiple Users Interacting with an Embodied Conversational Agent

Matthias Rehm and Elisabeth André

Multimedia Concepts and Applications,
University of Augsburg, Germany
{rehm, andre}@informatik.uni-augsburg.de

Abstract. In this paper, we describe an experiment we conducted to determine the user's level of engagement in a multi-party scenario consisting of human and synthetic interlocutors. In particular, we were interested in the question of whether humans accept a synthetic agent as a genuine conversational partner that is worthy of being attended to in the same way as the human interlocutors. We concentrated on gaze behaviors as one of the most important predictors of conversational attention. Surprisingly, humans paid more attention to an agent that talked to them than to a human conversational partner. No such effect was observed in the reciprocal case, namely when humans addressed an agent as opposed to a human interlocutor.

1 Introduction

In face-to-face communication, humans employ a number of verbal and non-verbal signals to show their level of engagement in a dialogue. According to Sidner and colleagues [15] engagement "is the process by which two (or more) participants establish, maintain and end their perceived connection during interactions they jointly undertake". The appropriate use and correct interpretation of engagement signals is a necessary prerequisite for the success of an interaction. In particular, gaze has been recognized as an important means to show engagement in a dialogue. While the listener employs gaze to indicate that s/he is paying attention to the speaker, the speaker monitors the listener's gaze to find out whether s/he is still interested in continuing the conversation.

According to Kendon [9], we can distinguish between at least four functions of seeking or avoiding to look at the partner in dyadic interactions: (i) to provide visual feedback, (ii) to regulate the flow of conversation, (iii) to communicate emotions and relationships, (iv) to improve concentration by restriction of visual input. Kendon showed that speakers tend to look away at the beginning of an utterance and turn their attention towards the conversational partner at the end of an utterance. Regarding the listener, Argyle and Cook [1] show that people look nearly twice as much while listening (75%) than while speaking (41%).

Compared to dyadic conversations, we know little about gaze behavior in multiparty interactions. Vertegaal and colleagues [16] describe a study of the gaze behavior in a four-party interaction. Subjects looked about 7 times more at the individual they listened

T. Panayiotopoulos et al. (Eds.): IVA 2005, LNCS 3661, pp. 241–252, 2005.
© Springer-Verlag Berlin Heidelberg 2005

to (62%) than at others (9%). They looked about three times more at the individual they spoke to (40%) than at others (12%). In accordance with Sidner et al. [15] or Nakano et al. [12], they conclude that gaze, or looking at faces, is an excellent predictor of conversational attention in multiparty conversations. Vertegaal et al. also showed that

1. People look more at the person they speak or listen to than at others.
2. Listeners in a group can still see they are being addressed. Each person still receives 1.7 times more gaze than could be expected had s/he not been addressed.
3. Speakers compensate for divided visual attention by increasing the total amount of their gazes.
4. Listeners gaze more than speakers (1.6 times).

The question arises of whether the attentive behaviors of humans change when they interact with a synthetic agent instead of another human. Most studies conducted on gaze behaviors in human-agent conversation focus on humanoid avatars representing people engaged in a conversation. This research is driven by the objective to provide the participants of video-based tele conferences with a means to establish a connection via gaze.

Colburn and colleagues [5] investigated whether natural eye gaze behaviors of an avatar that are informed by studies of human-human conversation elicit more natural eye gaze behaviors in users communicating with it. When an avatar was present, subjects spent more time looking at the screen. Even more attention was directed to the avatar when the agent relied on an eye gaze model that was informed by psychological studies on human-human conversation. Colburn and colleagues hypothesize that humans feel less shy when talking to a monitor than when talking to a real human. The effect occurred, however, only in the user-as-speaker condition which Colburn and colleagues attribute to the bad quality of the employed lip-synch mechanism.

While Colburn and colleagues concentrate on the behavioral response to avatars employing an informed eye gaze model, Garau and colleagues [7] as well as Lee and colleagues [11] investigate the effect of informed gaze models on the perceived quality of communication by means of questionnaires. Both research teams observed a superiority of informed eye gaze behaviors over randomized eye gaze behaviors. A follow-up study by Vinayagamoorthy and colleagues [17] focused on the correlation between visual realism and behavioral realism. They found that the model-based eye gaze model improved the quality of communication when a realistic avatar was used. For cartoonish avatars, no such effect was observed.

Another line of research focuses on how humans respond to the gaze behaviors of autonomous conversational agents. Nakano and colleagues [12] developed a model of grounding for the kiosk agent Mack that provides route descriptions for a paper map. The agent uses gaze as a deictic device as well as a feedback and turn taking mechaninsm to establish a common understanding between user and agent of what is being said and meant. A preliminary study revealed that a system with a grounding mechanism seems to encourage more non-verbal feedback from the user than a system without any grounding mechanism.

Based on an analysis of human-human conversation, Sidner and colleagues [15] developed a model of engagement for a conversational robot that is able to track the user's face and adjusts its gaze accordingly. Even though the set of communicative behaviors of the robot was strongly limited, an empirical study revealed that users indeed seem to be sensitive to a robot's conversational gestures and establish mutual gaze with it.

Summing up, it can be said that the studies found a positive effect of natural gaze behaviors on the communication between humans and synthetic agents. While the studies above focused on dyadic interactions between humans and agents, we will investigate how humans behave in a multi-party dialogue scenario with human and synthetic participants. In particular, we are interested in the following questions:

1. Do people apply different attentive behavior patterns in multi-party scenarios when *talking to an agent* as opposed to *talking to a human*?
2. Do people apply different attentive behavior patterns in multi-party scenarios when *listening to an agent* as opposed to *listening to a human*?

To investigate such behaviors, we recorded users interacting with a human and a synthetic game partner in a game of dice called Mexicali. The scenario allows us to directly compare gaze behaviors in human-human with gaze behaviors in human-agent interaction.

We suppose that humans interact with an agent in a way that roughly ressembles interaction with a human. Based on [1] and [16], we assume that humans spend more time on looking at the agent when listening to it than when talking to it. Following [9], we expect similar behaviors at sentence boundaries as in human-human communication. Nevertheless, the user will probably pay more attention to the other human conversational partner since the communicative skills of the agent are strongly limited. For instance, the user might not establish frequent gaze contact with the agent since s/he does not expect it to notice it anyway. Furthermore, there is empirical evidence that humans tend to avoid computer-controlled agents when navigating through a virtual 3D environment (see a study by Bailenson and colleagues [2] on social group dynamics in virtual realities which seems, however, to be in conflict with the observations by Colburn and colleagues [5] who assume that humans might feel less shy to address an agent).

2   Testbed for Our Research

As a testbed for our research, we used Gamble, a small game of dice (known as Mexicali) where one of the game partners is substituted by a synthetic agent (see Fig. 1). To win the game, it is indispensible to lie to the other players and to catch them lying to you.

The traditional (not computer-based) version of the game is played with two dice that are shaken in a cup. Let's assume player 1 casts the dice. He inspects the dice without permitting the other players to have a look. The cast is interpreted in the following way: the higher digit always represents the first part of the cast. Thus, a 5 and a 2 correspond to a 52. Two equal digits (11, ..., 66) have a higher value than the other casts, the highest cast is a 21. Player 1 has to announce his cast with the constraint that he has to say a higher number than the previous player. For instance, if he casts a 52, but the previous player already announced a 61, player 1 has to say at least 62. Now player 2

Fig. 1. The setting

has to decide whether to believe the other player's claim. In this case, she has to cast next. Otherwise, the dice are shown and if player 1 has lied he has lost this round and has to start a new one. For the experiment, each player was equipped with a PDA which replaced the cup with the dice in the original game.

The implementation of the synthetic game partner is based on the Greta agent system developed by Catherine Pelachaud and colleagues [13,8]. The Greta system is compliant with the MPEG-4 standard which allows to control the facial expressions and body gestures by so-called facial animation parameters (FAPs) and body animation parameters (BAPs).

In the game, Greta tries to mislead the other players by portraying facial expressions that do not correspond to her actual emotional state. For instance, she might express false joy to make her game partners believe that she achieved a high score. Nevertheless, Greta does not lie in a perfect manner, but still reveals her deceptive behaviors by subtle facial cues. Based on Ekman [6], we modeled 32 facial expressions that convey such deceptive cues by combining different degrees of masking with different degrees of asymmetry. For instance, humans involuntarily reveal information regarding a deceptive expression of joy often by an asymmetric smile (see [14] for a more detailed description of our implementation of the deceptive behaviors).

To make the interaction more natural and to enhance the entertaining factor of the Gamble system, we dubbed the animations of the Greta agent with a human voice. Moreover, a full body agent was used and a number of emblematic german gestures were modelled relying on the descriptions in the Berlin dictionary of everyday gestures ("Berliner Lexikon der Alltagsgesten", [4]).

We consider Gamble as a useful testbed for our studies since it allows us to study attentive behaviors to a synthetic agent as well as attentive behaviors to another human player in a multi-party setting. Furthermore, both the synthetic agent and the human players may be in the role of a speaker (when announcing casts or believing/disbelieving other players) or in the role of an addressee (when listening to announcements of casts or belief statements). Finally, the rules of the game determine who gets the next turn. At least in the case of announcements and belief statements, there is usually no doubt who is addressed by whom.

3   Experimental Method

3.1   Subjects and Design

Subjects were 24 students, all native speakers of German, recruited from the computer science and philosophy faculties at Augsburg University. 12 students from each faculty in their second and third year of study participated, 14 male and 10 female.

As independent variables, we defined the type of interlocutor (ToI) with the levels Human vs. Agent and the user's role in the dialogue (RoU) with the levels Speaker vs. Addressee. Both variables were manipulated between-subjects.

The value of the independent variables depends on the position of the single players. If the subject is standing on the right-hand side in Fig. 1, s/he has to listen to the agent's announcements and to make announcements to the human player on his/her left. If the subject is standing on the left-hand side in Fig. 1, s/he has to listen to the announcements of the human player on his/her right and to make announcements to the agent.

As dependent variables, we defined the length and number of attentive behaviors directed to the conversational partner.

3.2   Procedure

The subjects were randomly divided into 12 teams. At the beginning of the experiment, the subjects were presented with a three minute video of the Gamble system. In addition, they had to participate in a test round to get acquainted with the game, the handling of the PDA and the Greta agent. After the test round, each team played two rounds of 12 minutes. The participants changed positions after the first round so that each participant came to play before and after the agent. We told the subjects that the agent might not be able to conceal her emotions perfectly, but left it open how deceptive behaviours might be detected. Consequently, the subjects had no idea which channel of expression to concentrate on or whether it would be easier to recognize deceptive clues from the behaviors of the agent than from the behaviors of the other human player. To increase interest in the game, the winner was paid five Euros. We videotaped the interactions, and we logged the game progress for the analysis.

3.3   Coding Scheme

The videos are coded for utterances, gaze, role in the game, and laughing. Following [15], gaze is interpreted as indicators for the level of attention. Moreover, we coded who was the current player and because subjects sometimes although rarely addressed the experimenter, a track was introduced for his utterances. Coding is done in Anvil [10] and Fig. 2 gives an impression of the annotation board. It contains the following tracks:

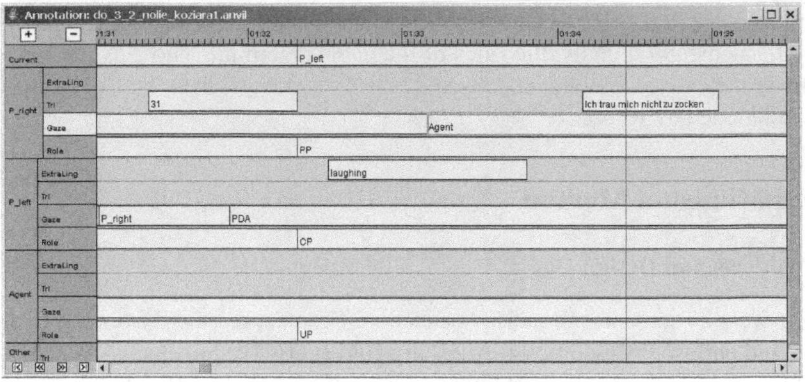

Fig. 2. The annotation board

- *Current:* Indicates the current player, i.e., the player that has to announce her belief/disbelief and that has to cast the dice. Possible elements are Agent, P_right, and P_left.
- *P_right:* Group of tracks for the right player[1] who plays after the agent. The group consists of
  - *ExtraLing:* For annotating if the player is laughing. This information will be used to test automatic recognition of emotions from speech.
  - *Trl:* In this track the utterance of the player is annotated. Utterances are coded per sentence to minimize the coding effort.
  - *Gaze:* The head movements of the player are given in this track. They are interpreted as gaze towards different entities in the environment.[2] Possible elements are Agent, P_right, P_left, PDA, Camera, and Elsewhere. Coding of gaze behaviors was adopted from Nakano et al. ([12]). A gaze is defined in the following way. The gaze ends and a new one starts in the moment the head starts moving. The direction of the gaze is determined at the end of the head movement.
  - *Role:* This is a secondary track that is bound to the Track *Current*. It specifies the role of the player at the moment in the game. Possible elements are Current, Previous, and Unaffected. Current duplicates the information present in the primary track. Previous indicates that the player is judged by the current player in this turn, and Unaffected indicates that it is the player who is on turn next.
- *P_left:* see P_right
- *Agent:* see P_right
- *Other*
  - *Trl:* The utterances of other people like the experimenter. This track is very rarely used.

---

[1] The right player seen from the perspective of the coder, not from the agent. This minimizes problems with left/right distinctions, because no cognitive transformations are necessary.

[2] This method is of course not nearly as accurate as using an eye tracker but has the obvious advantage of unobstrusiveness for the user during the interaction. Due to the spatial setting of the interaction (see Fig. 1), it is moreover necessary to move the head to look at the agent, the other human player, or the PDA thus allowing for a good reliability in coding.

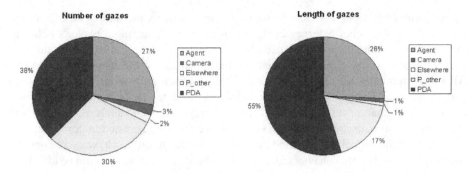

Fig. 3. Number of gazes and length of gazes

Until now, half of the material has been coded by 24 coders. Each video sequence is coded by two people. The interrater reliability has been calculated for gaze and is very good with a kappa value of around 0.9 for each pair. At the moment, the corpus contains 2200 utterances of which 645 are done by the agent, 675 by the right player, and 700 by the left player. Moreover, we have 5398 head movements which are interpreted as gaze behavior of the users.

4 Results of the Analysis

The goal of the annotation work was twofold. On the one hand, we were interested in collecting information to develop an appropriate gaze model for agents in multi-party scenarios. On the other hand, analyzing the users' gaze behavior should reveal to what extent they regard the agent as a real game partner worthy of communication.

Starting with some basic statistics, Figure 3 (left) shows the number of gazes towards each of the given directions. The total number of gazes is 5398. The players looked roughly as often towards the synthetic agent (27%) as towards the other human player (30%). Just considering the number of the gazes, the agent seems to be as attractive as the other player. The fact that people look slightly more often at the PDA (38%) could be attributed to its use as the interface for casting the dice and indicating belief or disbelief.

If we examine instead the length of the gazes towards each of the given directions (Fig. 3 right), this interpretation no longer holds. More than half of the time the players look at the PDA (55%), which seems to bind a lot of their attention. Noteworthy is the fact that players spend considerably more time (1.5) looking at the agent (26%) than looking at the other player (17%). Obviously, the type of interlocutor (human or agent) influences the users' gaze behavior.

The total number of gazes and the length of gazes during the game provide a rough impression of the users' attention towards human and synthetic interlocutors. In addition, we are interested in the question of whether the users' gaze behaviors depends on their role as a speaker or as an addressee. Because Gamble is a strictly round-based game, the utterances can be categorized into three main categories: announcement, belief, and comment. During announcements, the current player announces his cast or what he pretends to be his cast to the next player who is the addressee of this announcement. The belief category comprises utterances indicating a player's belief or disbelief of an announcement. Hence, the addressee of such an utterance is the previous player who made the announcement that is subject to the speaker's evaluation. All other utterances are categorized as comments which are - strictly speaking - not game-relevant. Among other things, utterances in this category comprise general comments on the game or on the behavior of other players. For the analysis conducted in this paper, comments are disregarded since we are mostly interested in conversational utterances with uniquely determined addressees. In our future work, we will consider comments to study gaze behaviors in situations where the addressee cannot be identified with certainty or where several conversational partners are addressed simultaneously.

Table 1. Gaze behavior of speaker towards addressee and vice versa

User's Role in the Dialogue (RoU)					
Speaker			Addressee		
Interlocutor (ToI)			Interlocutor (ToI)		
Agent	Human	Result	Agent	Human	Result
9.33	8.75	F(1,23)=0.77	31.75	20.17	F(1,23)=23.87

Table 1 compares the gaze behaviors of human interlocutors in the role of a speaker and an addressee for game-relevant utterances. A comparison of the speakers' and addressees' gaze behaviors only makes sense for human interlocutors because the agent is driven by a gaze model (which is not the subject of our investigations). We further distinguish whether their interlocutor is an agent or another human user.

No significant difference was observed in the gaze behavior of the speaker in the two conditions (i) agent (as interlocutor) and (ii) human (as interlocutor). That is people did not apply different gaze behaviors when talking to an agent. Interestingly, similarities in gaze behaviors towards human and artificial addressees could also be observed when humans were lying about their results. In more than 90 % of the cases, people averted the gaze from their game partner when they were lying independently of whether the game partner was human or synthetic. This finding is indeed surprising since it was quite obvious that the agent is not able to read the users' faces.

Turning to the addressee's gaze behavior gives a different picture. Whereas the speaker seems to be uninfluenced by the fact that one of his/her interaction partners is an agent, the addressee's gaze behavior shows a strong significant effect ($F(1,23)=23.97$, $p<0.05$) between the two conditions (i) agent (as interlocutor) and (ii) human (as interlocutor). Being spoken to by the agent grabs the user's attention significantly more than being spoken to by another human interaction partner.

The general patterns of gaze behavior adhere to the literature in that speakers look less at the interlocutor than addressees. Nevertheless, the average gazing time towards the speaker or the addressee is rather low compared to findings by [1]. As noted before, the PDA interface binds a lot of attention. Since the same conditions hold for the human users and the synthetic agents, the experiment should nevertheless enable a fair comparison of human-human and agent-human conversations.

Table 2. Gaze behavior of speaker towards addressee

Gaze Behavior	Agent	Human	Result
Total	9.33	8.75	F(1,23)=0.77
begin of utterance	3.25	3.08	F(1,23)=0.23
end of utterance	7.33	7.33	F(1,23)=0.00

Table 3. Gaze behavior of addressee towards speaker

Gaze Behavior	Agent	Human	Result
Total	31.75	20.17	F(1,23)=23.87
begin of utterance	24.58	17.08	F(1,23)=15.56
end of utterance	21.5	13.67	F(1,23)=10.98

As mentioned in the introduction, some interesting effects can be found at utterance boundaries. Therefore, we analysed the gaze behavior of speaker and addressee at the beginning and end of utterances, again for the two conditions agent and human (see Table 2 and 3). The speaker looks less to the addressee at the beginning and more at the end of an utterances independent on the condition agent or human and thus adheres again to the effects found in the literature [9]. In contrast to the speaker, the addressee tends to look less to the speaker at the end of an utterance. This effect has also been observed for both conditions. Unsurprisingly, there is a significant effect concerning the amount of gaze behaviors in the two conditions for both the beginning of the utterance (F(1,23)=15.56) as well as the end of the utterance (F(1,23)=10.98). The addressees follow a pattern of gaze behavior that is typical of human-human conversation, but the agent is attracting more attention than the other human user.

5   Discussion

The analysis of the users' gaze behavior in the multiuser setting revealed two effects. In general, users adhere to patterns of gaze behaviors for speaker and addressee that are also reported for dyadic human-human interactions. But they look significantly more often (1.6 times) to the agent when it is talking to them.

One explanation might be that users feel more comfortable to look at a synthetic agent than at a real person - especially when they have not met the other player before. That is to say, it could be less threatening or less embarrassing to concentrate on the agent, a more or less neutral technical artifact than on an unknown human. When looking at our data, it turned out, however, that only one of the six pairs for which the video recordings have already been annotated did not know each other before the game. We therefore consider shyness towards the other human interaction partner as a rather unlikely reason. Furthermore, shyness would not explain why the effect could only be observed in the user-as-addressee condition.

Another explanation for the longer looking time might be the users' hope to find deceptive cues in the agent's face. If we consider the reaction to the other human player as a baseline, the human addressees were indeed staring at the talking agent. Generally, staring at someone is either a sign of not understanding or interpreted as a threat. Maybe, people need longer to read faces of artificial agents while they restricted themselves to a short glance in the case of human game players.

A more plausible explanation of the user's strong attention towards the agent is the novelty effect of the exceptional conversational partner. None of the participants had encountered an embodied conversational agent in an application yet. All of the participants had already seen agents as manifestations of a new interface metaphor in their courses – and especially the agent employed in Gamble – but they had not interacted themselves with an agent so far. To counter this effect, subjects were shown a three minute video of the interaction during recruiting. To familiarize with the agent and the game, they played for five minutes before the experiment started. Moreover, every couple played two rounds of the game. Thus, when the second round started, every subject had already interacted for 17 Minutes. Even though the participants got some time to familiarize with the agent, the sensation of interacting with a synthetic agent might have persisted for a longer time. Furthermore, the size of the agent that has been projected on the wall might also have increased the user's attention. We suppose that the effect did not occur in the user-as-speaker condition since the agent did not make use of very sophisticated listener behaviors.

An analysis of the address forms employed by the users for the agent leads to interesting observations regarding the relationship between user and agent. Although users were expected to use the PDA interface to interact with the agent when making or responding to announcements, they occasionally addressed the agent directly, for instance, by uttering *Ähh, ich glaub's dir nicht*[3]. The user directly addresses the agent using the familiar *dir*. Far more frequent are utterances where the users talk about the agent, e.g., *Vielleicht glaubt sie's dir ja*[4] using the third person singular *sie*. Taking into account utterances containing personal pronouns and disregarding neutral game-relevant utterances, such as *Glaube ich*[5], 62% of the utterances were classified as talking-about and 38% as talking-to events. Talking about someone who is actually present during the interaction is usually considered as a gross violation of politeness in human face-to-face communication. Such a behavior is, however, typical of conversations involving babies and pets. Bergmann [3] presents categories of utterances found in talks about pets which include explanations of behavior and commenting on behavior. Both categories are also frequently found in talking about the agent which once more stresses the point that users try to make sense of this technical artifact interacting with them.

6   Conclusion

In this paper, we reported on an experiment we conducted to investigate to what extent humans regard synthetic agents as genuine conversational partners. In particular, we analyzed gaze behaviors in human-agent conversations as an important indicator of

---

[3] I don't believe you.
[4] Perhaps she believes you.
[5] I believe it.

conversational attention. Unlike earlier studies, we focus on gaze behaviors in multi-party scenarios consisting of human and synthetic interlocutors.

On the one hand, we were able to confirm a number of findings about attentive behaviors in human-human conversation. For instance, our subjects spent more time looking at an individual when listening to it than when talking to it - no matter whether the individual was a human or a synthetic agent. Furthermore, the addressee type (human vs. synthetic) did not have any impact on the duration of the speaker's gaze behaviors towards the addressee. Even though the game was in principle playable without paying any notice to the agent's nonverbal behaviors, the users considered it as worthy of being attended to. Surprisingly was the observation that people avoided gaze contact with the agent when they were lying.

While the users' behaviors in the user-as-speaker condition were consistent with findings for human-human conversation, we noticed differences for the user-as-addressee condition. People spent more time looking at an agent that is addressing them than at a human speaker. Maintaining gaze for an extended period of time is usually considered as rude and impolite. The fact that humans do not conform to social norms of politeness when addressing an agent seems to indicate that they do not regard the agent as an equal conversational partner, but rather as a (somewhat astonishing) artefact that is able to communicate. This attitude towards the agent was also confirmed by the way the users addressed the agent verbally.

In contrast to dyadic agent-user interactions, the multiparty setting allows for meta-communication with the other human interaction partner about what is going on. A rich source for such analysis are the comments which have been disregarded in the current paper but will be examined in the future.

To refine the agent's model of gaze behaviors, our future work will concentrate on an analysis of the human-human interactions in the scenario whereby we will pay special attention to the verbal and situative context. In particular, we are interested in studying the gaze behaviors of people that deliberately convey wrong emotions.

Acknowledgement

The work described in this paper was partially funded by by the EU Network of Excellence Humaine. We are grateful to Catherine Pelachaud, Maurizio Mancini, and Björn Hartmann for supporting our work with the Greta Agent.

References

1. M. Argyle and M. Cook. *Gaze and Mutual Gaze*. Cambridge University Press, Cambridge, 1976.
2. J. N. Bailenson, J. Blasovich, A. C. Beall, and J. M. Loomis. Interpersonal distance in immersive virtual environments. *Personality and Social Psychology Bulletin*, 29(7):819–833, 2003.
3. Jörg R. Bergmann. Haustiere als kommunikative Ressourcen. *Soziale Welt: Zeitschrift für sozialwissenschaftliche Forschung und Praxis, Sonderband: Kultur und Alltag*, 8:299–312, 1988.

4. BLAG.   Berliner Lexikon der Alltagsgesten.   *http://www.ims.uni-stuttgart.de/projekte/ nite/BLAG/*, last visited: 09.12.2004.
5. A. Colburn, M. Cohen, and S. Drucker. The role of eye gaze in avatar mediated conversational interfaces, 2000.
6. Paul Ekman. *Telling Lies — Clues to Deceit in the Marketplace, Politics, and Marriage.* Norton and Co. Ltd., New York, 3rd edition, 1992.
7. Maia Garau, Mel Slater, Simon Bee, and Martina Angela Sasse. The impact of eye gaze on communication using humanoid avatars. In *CHI '01: Proceedings of the SIGCHI conference on Human factors in computing systems*, pages 309–316, New York, NY, USA, 2001. ACM Press.
8. B. Hartmann, M. Mancini, and C. Pelachaud. Formational parameters and adaptive prototype instantiation for mpeg-4 compliant gesture synthesis. In *CASA 2002*, pages 111–119, 2002.
9. A. Kendon. Some functions of gaze direction in social interaction. *Acta Psychologica*, 32:1–25, 1967.
10. Michael Kipp. Anvil - a generic annotation tool for multimodal dialogue. In *Proceedings of the 7th European Conference on Speech Communication and Technology (Eurospeech)*, pages 1367–1370, Aalborg, September 2001.
11. Sooha Park Lee, Jeremy B. Badler, and Norman I. Badler. Eyes alive. In *SIGGRAPH '02: Proceedings of the 29th annual conference on Computer graphics and interactive techniques*, pages 637–644, New York, NY, USA, 2002. ACM Press.
12. Y.I. Nakano, G. Reinstein, T. Stocky, and J. Cassell. Towards a model of face-to-face grounding. In *Proceedings of the Annual Meeting of the Association for Computational Linguistics (ACL 2003)*, pages 553–561, 2003.
13. C. Pelachaud and I. Poggi. Subtleties of facial expressions in embodied agents. *Journal of Visualization and Computer Animation*, 31:301–312, 2002.
14. M. Rehm and E. André. Catch me if you can: Exploring lying agents in social settings. In *Proceedings of Conference on Autonomous Agents and Multi-Agent Systems (AAMAS)*. ACM Press, 2005.
15. Candace L. Sidner, Cory D. Kidd, Christopher Lee, and Neal Lesh. Where to look: a study of human-robot engagement. In *IUI '04: Proceedings of the 9th international conference on Intelligent user interface*, pages 78–84, New York, NY, USA, 2004. ACM Press.
16. Roel Vertegaal, Robert Slagter, Gerrit van der Veer, and Anton Nijholt. Eye gaze patterns in conversations: there is more to conversational agents than meets the eyes. In *CHI '01: Proceedings of the SIGCHI conference on Human factors in computing systems*, pages 301–308, New York, NY, USA, 2001. ACM Press.
17. Vinoba Vinayagamoorthy, Maia Garau, Anthony Steed, and Mel Slater. An eye gaze model for dyadic interaction in an immersive virtual environment: Practice and experience. *Comput. Graph. Forum*, 23(1):1–12, 2004.

Hierarchical Motion Controllers for Real-Time Autonomous Virtual Humans

Marcelo Kallmann[1] and Stacy Marsella[2]

[1] Institute for Creative Technologies**,
University of Southern California
kallmann@usc.edu
[2] Information Sciences Institute,
University of Southern California
marsella@isi.edu

Abstract. Continuous and synchronized whole-body motions are essential for achieving believable autonomous virtual humans in interactive
applications.

We present a new motion control architecture based on generic controllers that can be hierarchically interconnected and reused in real-time.
The hierarchical organization implies that leaf controllers are motion generators while the other nodes are connectors, performing operations such
as interpolation, blending, and precise scheduling of children controllers.

We also describe how the system can correctly handle the synchronization of gestures with speech in order to achieve believable conversational
characters. For that purpose, different types of controllers implement a
generic model of the different phases of a gesture.

1 Introduction

Interactive virtual humans [1] are software artifacts that look and act like humans
but are embedded in a virtual world where they interact with humans much like
humans interact with each other. To cohabit a virtual world with a human, a
virtual human needs to perform a range of behaviors. It must be able to look
and move around its environment, pick-up objects and engage in conversation
with a human.

To support human-like interactions, these behaviors must be performed continuously in realistic and meaningful ways. Specifically, we want these behaviors
to play a similar role in the virtual human's interaction with humans as they do
in human-human interaction. For example, people's nonverbal behaviors perform
a variety of roles during conversational interactions. Gestures can emphasize or
qualify what is being said. They can also substitute for words, for example by
conveying greetings, goodbyes, insults, spatial relations or physical properties of
objects. They also convey attitudes and reactions to events. The manner of gestures in particular reveals affective information. Gestures also serve to regulate

---

** The first author is now affiliated with the University of California, Merced.

T. Panayiotopoulos et al. (Eds.): IVA 2005, LNCS 3661, pp. 253–265, 2005.
© Springer-Verlag Berlin Heidelberg 2005

dialog interaction. For example, a speaker can relinquish a dialog turn with a gesture that metaphorically offers the turn to the next speaker, using an upward facing palm, or can seize the turn with a vertical hand with palm facing the speaker, essentially a "stopping" gesture. This expressiveness is not unique to gestures. Gaze behavior plays a similarly rich set of roles in human interactions.

There are several basic challenges that must be addressed in creating a virtual human body that can realize such behaviors. Because the virtual human is interacting with a human within a virtual world, it must be prepared to react to unexpected events either created by the human or by the virtual world itself. As such, body motions must be interruptable. Similarly, it must be prepared to adjust to the physical constraints implied by the virtual world itself. The virtual human may also be doing more than one thing at a time, for example, walking, gesturing and talking at the same time.

Further, virtual human's behaviors typically involve multiple parts of the body being in motion. Visually realistic gaze behavior, for example, often requires the careful coordination of a range of motions, including eye movements, head/neck movements, twisting of the joints in the torso as well whole-body stepping movements as necessary. Furthermore, gaze may also have to be coordinated and synchronized with other body movements and communication channels, e.g. with the phonemes and visemes of speech.

It is our experience that these requirements need behavioral flexibility. The virtual human body must be prepared to compose and synchronize multiple behaviors both sequentially and simultaneously, in a continuous fashion that allows it to be embedded and interacting with humans in the virtual world. Alternatives, such as long duration carefully crafted full body motions may look better but over-reliance on them restricts the behavioral responses of the virtual human and causes breakdowns in interactions with humans.

Indeed, a blend of animation approaches is required to achieve both flexibility and realism. The ability to point and look at an unexpected event arbitrarily located in the virtual world is a key capability in a virtual human. Procedural approaches for realizing this capability (e.g. using Inverse Kinematics [2]) are flexible and can exhibit sufficient realism, especially given that the human's attention is divided between the virtual human and the object that is being attended to. On the other hand, revealing a dejected affective state by the virtual human looking downward might be more effectively realized by crafted animations or motion captured sequences [3].

Because of the important role the virtual human's "physical" behavior plays as well as the challenges posed in realizing those behaviors, a key aspect of any virtual human is the animation algorithms and their coordination that constitute its "body". To address these concerns, we propose a motion control architecture based on generic controllers that can be hierarchically interconnected in real-time in order to achieve continuous motion respecting given constraints.

The approach is inspired by neuroscience evidence that complex motor behavior might be obtained through the combination of motor primitives [4]. Primitive controllers in our system are motion generators that can be built with arbitrary animation algorithms, such as keyframe interpolation or procedural animation. Primitive controllers can then be connected to higher level controllers performing different kinds of operations, such as scheduling, blending and interpolation.

In particular we show how our system handles the synchronization of motion segments with speech. The problem is formulated as a scheduling problem where motion controllers are sequenced and blended with gaps filled by interpolation, according to given timing constraints.

2   Related Work

A wide range of computer animation techniques have been proposed in the literature [2]. In particular for interactive virtual humans, different motion generation techniques are available: walking [5] [6] [7], reaching and object manipulation [8] [9] [10], Inverse Kinematics [11] [12] and keyframe interpolation of designed or motion captured [3] keyframes.

We focus on this work on the integration of such different animation techniques in a single animation platform. This involves building abstractions encapsulating the output of motion controllers which can then be blended, resulting in seamless transitions between the different controllers. Such integration has been already employed in some sense in previous systems [13] [14] [15]. In particular, the *AgentLib* system [15] [16] encapsulates controllers as specialized actions, which can then be blended for achieving smooth transitions. There are some new animation packages available in the web that seem to address similar issues, however no precise information about the employed techniques were found.

Our approach builds on these previous models by adding the capability of hierarchically organizing the motion flow between controllers. This allows the creation of controllers which are in fact modifying and/or controlling children motion controllers. For example, an open-door controller would control two children controllers (walking and reaching) for achieving the needed coordination for opening the door. In the end, the open-door controller is seen as any other motion controller and can be further processed and sequenced with other controllers. In our architecture, complex object interactions [17] can thus be seen as a standard motion controller. This notion of hierarchical organization has been already used in previous systems [18], however in the context of dynamical simulation and not with the goal of synchronized scheduling and blending as in our work.

The architecture is specially well suited for handling the speech-gesture synchronizations required in conversational characters [19] [20] [21]. We show how two controllers (a scheduler and an interpolator) are able to synchronize predesigned gesture motions in order to achieve perfect synchronization with speech.

3   Conversational Characters Requirements

We list here some of the particular requirements for synchronizing motion controllers with speech that have helped motivate our approach.

Meaning of Motion. The dynamic and spatial qualities of motions convey meaning in different subtle ways. In some cases this quality can most readily be preserved with carefully designed motions, built by skilled artists or via motion capture. On the other hand, some motions such as deictics/pointing can usually be synthesized with different Inverse Kinematics techniques [11] [12]. In our framework, generic motion controllers are used independent of the underlying motion generation technique.

Gesture Structure. Gestures have a structure comprised of several phases [22]. A preparatory phase brings the hand/arm into position to perform the gesture. The stroke phase is the main part of the gesture and largely carries its meaning. This phase is closely synchronized to the corresponding speech. There is also a relaxation phase where the gesture ends with the hand being in a resting pose. Between those phases, there may also be hold phases where the arm and hand are more or less stationary (see Fig. 1). The appropriate temporal manipulation of these phases is an important means to manipulate the expressive, affective quality of the motion as well as control the synchronization of gesture, speech and social interaction.

Continuous Gesturing. People regularly perform one gesture right after another. In such cases, the gesture does not go to a fully relaxed position but rather relaxes into a "gesture space" (roughly in front of the speaker), ready to perform another gesture. We call this continuous gesturing. Many factors influence the likelihood of such gesturing, including personality, cultural differences, situational and relational factors, and the arousal of the speaker. We see the ability to do such gestures as an important means to convey these factors. From the standpoint of the animation system, this suggests that there must be some means to compose, and if necessary procedurally adapt, the motions that comprise the gestures in order to achieve fluid, realistic motion over the multiple gestures.

Full Body Motion. The virtual human will only look realistic if the full body moves in a synchronized way. In the case of human gestures, gestures may involve motion of not only the hand and arm, but also the rest of the body. In fact, gestures that only involve the arm and hands often look robotic, or unexpressive. This is especially true of gestures that have strong dynamics and large spatial extent, both of which are an effective ways to convey arousal. It is also critical that the gesture be closely synchronized with the head and gaze motion. Shifts in the temporal relation between gestures and gaze/head movement can alter the interpretation of the gesture.

Synchronization. Motions must be able to be synchronized with external events. In the case study considered here, external events are timings for speech synchronization.

4   Motion Engine Architecture

The motion engine architecture is a C++ class library allowing the creation and interconnection of arbitrary skeletons (i.e. characters) and motion controllers.

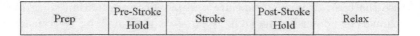

Prep	Pre-Stroke Hold	Stroke	Post-Stroke Hold	Relax

Fig. 1. The considered phases of a gesture

A controller is a generic self-contained object that maintains the description of the skeleton joints being controlled and as well the respective joint values of the generated motion at a given time. Joint values can then be sent to a skeleton or connected to other controllers for further processing. Generic methods are available for querying and evaluating controllers at any given (monotone) time. The specific motion generation algorithms are not relevant for using the controllers.

4.1 Character Representation

A character is represented as an articulated figure composed of hierarchical joints. Each joint rotation is parameterized differently and contains individually placed joint limits according to its anatomical properties.

The local rotations of joints are always represented in quaternion format [2]. However, different parameterizations can be defined for each joint. For joints with 3 degrees of freedom (DOFs), the swing and twist decomposition is usually preferred [23]. These joints have a local frame with the z-axis lying along the main axis of the corresponding limb. The swing rotation axis is always perpendicular to the z-axis and the twist rotation that follows is simply a rotation around the z-axis. The swing motion is therefore a rotation around a vector lying in the x-y plane and is represented as a 2D axis-angle $\mathbf{s} = (x, y)$, where $\mathbf{s}$ is the rotation axis and $\|\mathbf{s}\|$ is the rotation angle. Such representation allows straightforward use of spherical ellipses for meaningfully bounding the swing motion [23], which is very important for developing procedural controllers, for example based on Inverse Kinematics (IK) [11]. The twist rotation is bounded with minimum and maximum values.

Joints with 2 DOFs are either parameterized with a swing axis-angle, or with 2 Euler angles. For instance, the elbow and knee joints need to be parameterized with flexion and twist Euler angles while the wrist and ankle joints are better parameterized with a swing axis-angle and its ellipsoidal limits. As twist rotations, Euler angles are bounded with minimum and maximum values. Similarly, the remaining joints of the character are parameterized with Euler angles, swings, twists, or with quaternions as appropriate.

4.2 Channels

Each controller specifies the preferred type of parameterization in each controlled joint. For instance, controllers based on keyframe interpolation only need to interpolate joint values and therefore quaternion parametrization with no joint limits is usually the best choice. Procedural controllers however will prefer other parameterizations and with joint limits.

We use the term *channel* to specify one piece of information controlling a joint. Channels can describe one DOF, such as "x-rotation", or "y-translation", but they can also describe a 3-DOF rotation with a quaternion or a 2-DOF swing rotation. The used channels are therefore described as an ordered list in the following format:

$$C = ((j_1, c_1), ..., (j_n, c_n)),\qquad(1)$$

where j_i is the joint identifier, and c_i is a descriptor of the used parameterization for that joint, $0 \le i \le n$. Given the channels description C, a buffer containing joint values for C is denoted as:

$$B_C = (v_1, ..., v_m),\qquad(2)$$

where v_j is the jth channel value, $0 \le j \le m$, according to the channels description C ($n \le m$). For example if C describes a linkage with 1 swing rotation, and 1 Euler angle, we will have $m = 3$, which is the number of values required according to C. Note that, as controllers may choose different parameterizations for a same joint, joint values can always be converted to a same quaternion format when needed (e.g. to be blended).

4.3   Connections

Each controller defines the channels C to be used, and has an evaluation function that generates and stores the joint values for a given time t in buffer B_C. Usually t must be evaluated monotonically, but some controllers (as keyframe interpolators) allow evaluation at arbitrary times.

Controllers can be mainly of two types. Source controllers generate motion while connector controllers receive as input motion from source controllers, and perform further operations such as interpolation, blending, filtering, scheduling, etc. Connectors can also be connected to other connectors, achieving arbitrary hierarchical configurations. At any time, any controller can be connected to a skeleton for final visualization of the motion in the character. Fig. 2 exemplifies possible connections. In the figure, controller A affects the joints of the right arm and the resulting arm motion can be blended with another motion coming from controller B; the blending operations are decided by controller C.

Connections require a matching of joint identifiers and parameterization types. Each channels description C maintains a hash table with all pairs (j_i, c_i) (as in equation 1). These pairs are composed of integer identifiers and therefore simple and compact hashing functions can be used. When a controller with buffer B_{C_1} is mapped to another controller with buffer B_{C_2}, each channel in C_1 is searched for a matching channel in C_2. Relying on hash table allows a linear time matching algorithm. After the matching is done, a *mapping list* is obtained and tells exactly where in B_{C_2} each entry in B_{C_1} should be mapped to. Non-mapped channels are detected and can be treated as needed (e.g. ignored). The same mapping process is used to map controllers to skeletons, with the difference that the mapping is done directly to the joints of the skeleton. Controllers have a generic apply method that will send the current values in their buffer either to the buffer of another mapped controller or to any skeleton attached.

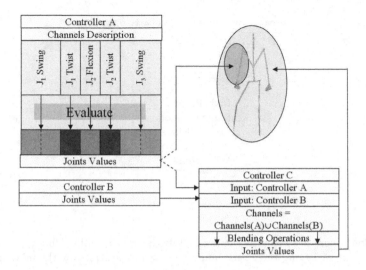

Fig. 2. Example of connections. When controller A is evaluated at a given time, it will fill its buffer with the joint values resultant from the evaluation. Controller A can be connected directly to a skeleton, or alternatively, connected to controller C for a blending operation with controller B.

5   Controllers for Scheduling Synchronized Gestures

Besides the fact that motion controllers are self-contained objects, they also contain higher level semantic information about the generated motions. For example parameters such as minimum and maximum allowed time warping factors, point of emphasis, etc, are available and are used for making decisions in the scheduling process.

We focus now on the problem of composing controllers for matching timing constraints for a conversational character. The problem is specified with annotated text telling the exact times when each motion should have its point of emphasis played. The timing annotation is specified with a text-to-speech synthesis system.

Motions are *played* with a keyframe-interpolator controller and synchronized with scheduler and controller-interpolator controllers. Composing these controllers is the role of a *body planner* that determines in real time a schedule of controllers to be played (see Fig. 3). The composition planning process is an extension of existing approaches [20] that takes into account the extra parameters introduced by the system. We present now each of the used controllers.

5.1   Keyframe Interpolator

The implemented keyframe interpolator controller basically interpolates joint values in quaternion format without considering joint limits, as the input key postures are supposed to be correct.

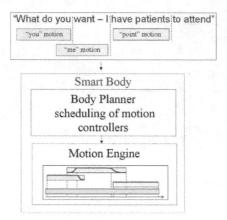

Fig. 3. Controllers are composed and scheduled in real time by a body planner, and the final result satisfying the given timing constraints is *played* by the motion engine

In general, commercial modeling packages store joint rotations with Euler angles, and we have created plug-ins that convert and export them directly in quaternion representation. In that way, the interpolator can directly apply spherical linear interpolation between keys without conversions and few other optimizations are possible, as for instance a quaternion does not require trigonometric functions when converted to a rotation matrix, which is the final representation needed by the graphics cards.

Exported motions are annotated with the local time of their emphasis points, and furthermore contain minimum and maximum time warping factors for allowing different operations when fitting the motions in the final solution schedule. For that purpose, we have developed an interactive application that is able to load the exported motions and annotate them with such parameters (see Section 7).

5.2   Scheduler

The scheduler (Fig. 4) is the main controller used for synchronizing children controllers. It keeps a stack of controllers, which are evaluated at any given time t in an ordered fashion, from the bottom of the stack to the top of the stack.

When inserted in the scheduler, several parameters are available for defining the evaluation behavior of the overall schedule, as for example the blending periods for ease-in and ease-out transitions. When a controller is evaluated, if the evaluation time falls inside a blending interval, the values resulted from the evaluation are blended with the current values in the scheduler buffer, and the result is put back in the same buffer. Therefore the final behavior is a pairwise blending sequence from the bottom of the stack to the top of the stack, equivalent to a layering mechanism.

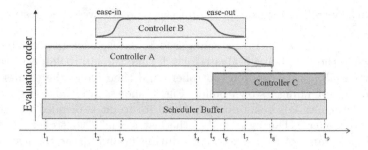

Fig. 4. Scheduler

Additional parameters are available, for example to extend a controller duration by repeating its last frame during a desired time interval, after the controller
completion. Early commencement of a controller can similarly be obtained.

Note that the scheduler also specifies start and end times to activate controllers and therefore the blending may only occur between controllers which
are active at the same given time. In general, blending occurs mainly between
pairs of adjacent controllers in the timeline. Even if other behaviors can be
achieved, the main purpose of the scheduler is to compose a motion sequence
of arbitrary length, with blends producing seamless transitions between controllers. The architecture also allows a same controller to be scheduled several
times (even blending with itself), and to schedule other scheduler-controllers,
achieving arbitrary hierarchical configurations.

5.3   Interpolator

A specific interpolator-controller was designed for blending the output motions of
two children controllers according to a user specified blending curve (see Fig. 5).
The blending curve allows designers to explore different kinds of effects and is
represented as a piecewise cubic spline editable via control points.

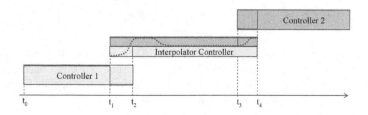

Fig. 5. The interpolator controller blends the results of controller 1 and controller 2
according to a user-specified blending curve

The interpolator can be configured in different ways. It can be used for in-
terpolating between the last frame of one controller and the first frame of the

subsequent controller, for example to fill the holds between the gesture phases shown in Fig. 1.

The interpolator can also be configured to interpolate the results of controllers while they are being evaluated. Each time the interpolator is evaluated, it will first evaluate its children controllers and then blend the results in each of the buffers for filling its own buffer. Fig. 5 shows an example where during t_1 and t_2 controller 1 is being evaluated and its result is blended with the first frame of controller 2. During t_2 and t_3 the last frame of controller 1 is blended with the first frame of controller 2, and during t_3 and t_4 the the last frame of controller 1 is blended with the result of the controller 2 evaluation. Note that such interpolator can have an arbitrary length, affecting the time duration between t_2 and t_3. The blending curve can be easily scaled as needed in order to fit arbitrary lengths.

6 Final Gesture Implementation

The gesture model depicted in Fig. 1 is finally implemented by combining the presented controllers. For each given gesture with a time constraint for its point of emphasis (see Fig. 3), the three keyframe-interpolator controllers designed for the gesture's *prep*, *stroke* and *relax* phases are sequenced in a scheduler. They are placed so as to respect the timings of the emphasis points of the *stroke* phases.

However depending on the required times, additional adjustments have to be made. Usually the motions are not long enough to provide a continuous motion, i.e., there might be empty spaces in the schedule timeline. In this case, empty spaces are filled with interpolators, which will produce motion for the "hold phases" (see Fig. 6).

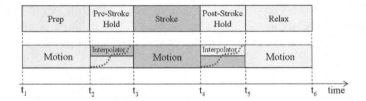

Fig. 6. Scheduling the phases of a gesture with several controllers. Keyframe animation motion controllers can vary their length with local time warping, and interpolator controllers can have arbitrary length. The gesture planner is responsible for finding the best schedule for respecting given timing constraints.

In the case the speech is faster than the disponible motions, there will be no time for holds and the keyframe-interpolator controllers might even be required to be time-warped for producing faster motions respecting the needed timings. In really fast speech cases the controllers of the *prep* and *relax* phases can even be removed from the scheduler. These cases give an idea of the decisions made

(a)   (b)   (c)   (d)

Fig. 7. Several postures from a talking doctor character protecting a clinic: a) "you are the threat...", b) "do you see that patient over there...", c) "we need to protect these people...", d) "what are you waiting for..."

by the body planner depicted in Fig. 3 and illustrates the several possibilities that can be handled by our system.

Fig. 7 shows some snapshots of our experiments with a conversational doctor character. During these experiments, the presented controllers have shown to be well suited for composing gesture motions under time constraints and at the same time providing a continuous full-body motion.

7 Current System

Our current Motion Engine system is under test in a larger project and consists of a stand-alone C++ library and a few applications for editing and testing the created controllers. Fig. 8 shows a snapshot of the main tool used for specifying controllers. We have also written a few Maya mel scripts for exporting motions and characters created by skilled animators.

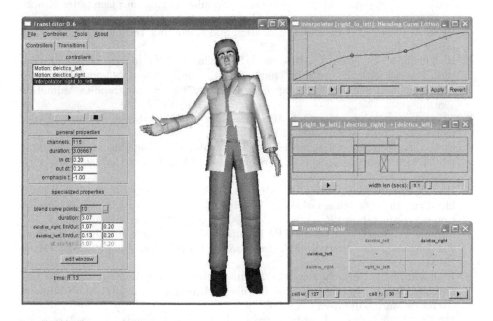

Fig. 8. Example of some windows used for editing and testing the several parameters of the interpolator controller

8   Conclusions

This paper presents an animation system based on the hierarchical organization of generic motion controllers, which can be interconnected and connected to characters arbitrarily in real-time. The approach is similar to the organization of 3D scenes in modern scene graphs, where nodes can be of several types (shapes, engines, transformations, etc).

We believe that such generic organization is of main importance for achieving complex motion for autonomous virtual humans, and we show how contŕollers can be scheduled in order to synchronize gestures for conversational characters.

As future work we intend to include additional channels for sensing the environment and for synchronization between concurrent controllers commanding different parts of the body. A challenge would be to develop algorithms for the emergence of complex controllers from given primitive ones [4].

Acknowledgments. The project or effort described here has been sponsored by the U.S. Army Research, Development, and Engineering Command (RDECOM). Statements and opinions expressed do not necessarily reflect the position or the policy of the United States Government, and no official endorsement should be inferred.

References

1. Badler, N.I., Phillips, C.B., Webber, B.L.: Simulating Humans: Computer Graphics, Animation and Control. Oxford University Press (1993)
2. Watt, A., Watt, M.: Advanced Animation and Rendering Techniques. ACM Press (1992)
3. Bodenheimer, B., Rose, C., Rosenthal, S., Pella, J.: The process of motion capture: Dealing with the data. In Thalmann, D., van de Panne, M., eds.: Computer Animation and Simulation '97, Springer NY (1997) 3–18 Eurographics Animation Workshop.
4. Thoroughman, K.A., Shadmehr, R.: Learning of action through combination of motor primitives. Nature **407** (2000) 742–747
5. Boulic, R., Magnenat-Thalmann, N., Thalmann, D.: A global human walking model with real-time kinematic personification. The Visual Computer **6** (1990) 344–358
6. Park, S.I., Shin, H.J., Shin, S.Y.: On-line locomotion generation based on motion blending. In: Proceedings of the ACM SIGGRAPH/Eurographics symposium on Computer animation (SCA), New York, NY, USA, ACM Press (2002) 105–111
7. Multon, F., France, L., Cani, M.P., Debunne, G.: Computer animation of human walking: a survey. Journal of Visualization and Computer Animation **10** (1999) 39–54
8. Kallmann, M.: Scalable solutions for interactive virtual humans that can manipulate objects. In: Artificial Intelligence and Interactive Digital Entertainment (AIIDE), Marina del Rey, CA (2005)
9. Liu, Y., Badler, N.I.: Real-time reach planning for animated characters using hardware acceleration. In: Proceedings of Computer Animation and Social Agents (CASA'03). (2003) 86–93

10. Kuffner, J.J., Latombe, J.C.: Interactive manipulation planning for animated characters. In: Proceedings of Pacific Graphics'00, Hong Kong (2000) poster paper.
11. Baerlocher, P.: Inverse Kinematics Techniques for the Interactive Posture Control of Articulated Figures. PhD thesis, Swiss Federal Institute of Technology, EPFL (2001) Thesis number 2383.
12. Tolani, D., Badler, N.: Real-time inverse kinematics of the human arm. Presence **5** (1996) 393–401
13. Granieri, J.P., Crabtree, J., Badler, N.I.: Production and playback of human figure motion for visual simulation. ACM Transactions on Modeling and Computer Simulation **5** (1995) 222–241
14. Perlin, K., Goldberg, A.: Improv: A system for scripting interactive actors in virtual worlds. In: Proceedings of SIGGRAPH 96, New Orleans, LA (1996) 205–216
15. Boulic, R., Bécheiraz, P., Emering, L., Thalmann, D.: Integration of motion control techniques for virtual human and avatar real-time animation. In: Proceedings of the ACM International Symposium on Virtual Reality Software and Technology (VRST'97), Switzerland (1997) 111–118
16. Emering, L., Boulic, R., Molet, T., Thalmann, D.: Versatile tuning of humanoid agent activity. Computer Graphics Forum **19** (2000) 231–242
17. Kallmann, M.: Interaction with 3-d objects. In Magnenat-Thalmann, N., Thalmann, D., eds.: Handbook of Virtual Humans. first edn. John Wiley & Sons (2004) 303–322
18. Faloutsos, P., van de Panne, M., Terzopoulos, D.: Composable controllers for physics-based character animation. In: SIGGRAPH '01: Proceedings of the 28th annual conference on Computer graphics and interactive techniques, New York, NY, USA, ACM Press (2001) 251–260
19. Kopp, S., Wachsmuth, I.: Synthesizing multimodal utterances for conversational agents. Computer Animation and Virtual Worlds **15** (2004) 39–52
20. Cassell, J., Vilhjálmsson, H.H., Bickmore, T.W.: Beat: the behavior expression animation toolkit. In: Proceedings of SIGGRAPH. (2001) 477–486
21. Carolis, B.D., Pelachaud, C., Poggi, I., de Rosis, F.: Behavior planning for a reflexive agent. In: Proceedings of the International Joint Conference on Artificial Intelligence (IJCAI), Seattle (2001)
22. McNeill, D.: Hand and mind: What gestures reveal about thought. The university of Chicago Press (1992)
23. Grassia, S.: Practical parameterization of rotations using the exponential map. Journal of Graphics Tools **3** (1998) 29–48

Modeling Dynamic Perceptual Attention in Complex Virtual Environments

Youngjun Kim, Martin van Velsen, and Randall W. Hill Jr.

Institute for Creative Technologies, 13274 Fiji Way, Suite 600,
Marina del Ray, CA 90292, USA
{yjkim, vvelsen, hill}@ict.usc.edu

Abstract. An important characteristic of a virtual human is the ability to direct its perceptual attention to entities and areas in a virtual environment in a manner that appears believable and serves a functional purpose. In this paper, we describe a perceptual attention model that mediates top-down and bottom-up attention processes of virtual humans in order for the virtual human to efficiently select important information with limited sensory capability within complex virtual environments.

1 Introduction

In a landscape of ever increasing rendering and animation capabilities there has been an accompanying drive for realistic interaction with intelligent virtual humans. An important characteristic of a virtual human is the ability to direct its perceptual attention to objects and locations in a virtual environment in a manner that appears plausible as an overt behavior and also serves a functional purpose. Not only must virtual humans pay attention to objects related to the tasks they are performing, but they must also be able to cope with sudden events that demand attention. It is often the case that the amount of information in the virtual environment far exceeds the processing abilities of the virtual human. In fact, only a small fraction of sensory information can be fully processed and assimilated into the cognitive model. This situation has been exacerbated as the fidelity of the graphical information in virtual scenes has increased—there is a growing lag in the ability of virtual humans to cope with the amount of environmental data presented to them. Fully simulated virtual humans experience similar cognitive loads as humans, especially in complex, shared virtual environments. One might even expect our digital counterparts to make the same mistakes as we do and might reject incorrect behavior however logical it is considering the circumstances. A large amount of interaction is negotiated through a common experience and understanding of our physical environment. If artificial intelligence progresses to the point where an agent can make human-like decisions, it will still need to make these decisions based on what it perceives to be its environment. Greater power in rendering capabilities expressed in polygons per second can enhance our own visual experience but might not be beneficial to an agent and can even downgrade its performance. A solution to this dilemma can be found in the human realm. Spatial cognition and especially spatial attention has allowed

T. Panayiotopoulos et al. (Eds.): IVA 2005, LNCS 3661, pp. 266–277, 2005.
© Springer-Verlag Berlin Heidelberg 2005

humans to make sense of the sensory stimuli that greets us when wake up in the morning.

Computational models of perceptual attention generally fall into one of two camps: top-down and bottom-up. Biologically inspired computational models [4,9] typically focus on the bottom-up aspects of attention, while most virtual humans [1,2,3,5,13,15] implement a top-down form of attention. Bottom-up attention models only consider the image information (e.g, color, intensity, orientation, and motion) without taking into consideration saliency based on tasks or goals. As a result, the outcome of a purely bottom-up model will not consistently match the behavior of real humans in certain situations. Models like Itti's [9] can predict the bottom-up salience of features in an image at any point in time, but such a model is not sufficient to predict where to actually look. Humans are generally task-oriented, and it is safe to say that a great deal of one's time is spent looking at objects related to the current task.

Modeling perceptual attention as a purely top-down process, however, is also not sufficient for implementing a virtual human. A purely top-down model does not take into account the fact that virtual humans need to react to perceptual stimuli vying for attention. For instance, Chopra-Khullar and Badler [2] built one of the most extensive models to date, a psychologically motivated framework for generating the visual attending behaviors of an animated human figure. Their implementation generates believable animation behaviors for a virtual human performing a fairly scripted set of tasks, but it is not clear how the model would fare in a much more dynamic environment where the need to react to events in the world is much higher than the virtual world they describe. Top-down systems typically handle reaction to perceptual stimuli in an ad hoc manner by encoding special rules to catch certain conditions in the environment. The problem with this approach is that it does not provide a principled way of integrating the ever-present bottom-up perceptual stimuli with top-down control of attention.

In this paper, we present a computational model of perceptual attention for virtual humans. This model extends a prior model of perceptual resolution [6,7] based on psychological theories of human perception. This model allows virtual humans to dynamically interact with objects and other individuals, balancing the demands of goal-directed behavior with those of attending to novel stimuli. This model has been implemented and tested with the MRE Project [8]. Based on the findings with spatial cognition in the MRE environment a self-contained software representation was designed termed ASCE (Agent Spatial Cognition Environment) that serves as a rapidly configurable sandbox for experimentation and testing with models of perceptual attention and spatial cognition.

2 Modeling Perception in Virtual Humans

Our virtual humans are implemented in the immersive environment called the Mission Rehearsal Exercise (MRE) [8] and in the Agent Special Cognition Environment (ASCE). The virtual humans' behavior in MRE is not scripted; rather, it is driven by a set of general, domain-independent capabilities. The virtual humans perceive events in the scenario, by interacting with the simulator, reason about the tasks they are performing, and they control the bodies and faces of the PeopleShop™ animated bodies to which they have been assigned.

ASCE allows virtual humans to dynamically interact with objects and other individuals, balancing the demands of goal-directed behavior with those of attending to novel stimuli. Using ASCE we can extend the semi 3-dimensional representation into a full spatial model by taking the inverse of our entity model that represents the available space for navigation.

We have developed a model of perceptual resolution based on psychological theories of human perception [6,7] for virtual humans in MRE and ASCE. Hill's model predicts the level of details at which an agent will perceive objects and their properties in the virtual world. He applied his model to synthetic helicopter pilots in simulated military exercise. We extended the model to simulate many of the limitations of human perception, both visual and auditory.

2.1 Visual Perception

As a human has a visual field that extends to around 95 degrees from the center, we limited the virtual human's visual field of view to 190 horizontal degrees and 90 vertical degrees so that the virtual human only gets updates that he is currently sensing through the field of view (FOV). When the virtual human senses the objects in the FOV, it first processes how salient each object is in the respect of size, distance, and color. We consider the computational model [11] to compute the visual salience of each object that is measured by observing individual visual attributes (e.g., size, shape, and color). After computing the visual saliencies of the perceived objects, we applied a sigmoid function as a utility function that reduces the degree of salience of an object in the respect of angle disparities between the virtual human and the object.

2.2 Auditory Perception

Human behavior is very often influenced by auditory inputs that appear to have automatic access to the eye control system via the lower levels. To model auditory perception, we estimate the sound pressure levels of objects in the environment and compute their individual and cumulative effects on each listener based on the distances and directions of the sources. This enables the virtual humans to perceive auditory events involving objects not in the visual field of view. For example, when a virtual human hears a vehicle is approaching from behind, he can choose to look over his shoulder to see who is coming. Another effect of modeling aural perception is that some sound events can mask others. A helicopter flying overhead can make it impossible to hear someone speaking in normal tones a few feet away. The noise could then prompt the virtual human to shout and could also prompt the addressee to cup his ear to indicate that he cannot hear.

Given a set of visually or aurally perceived objects, the agent's perceptual model updates the attributes of objects that fall in the limited sensory range. At any point in time, the virtual human must recognize which object is the most salient among those objects and draw his focus of attention on the object. The next section describes our approach to computing the salience of the objects in the field of view and the subsequent behaviors associated with shifting the agent's gaze.

3   Computational Model of Perceptual Attention

To compute object salience and to control gaze behaviors, we have developed a model called Dynamic Perceptual Attention (DPA). We adopt the decision-theoretic perspective to control gaze behaviors since some neurophysiology studies [18,19,20] show that neurons doing saccadic fixations consider the expected reward and the probability of a reward before reacting to the certain stimuli. Internally, DPA combines entities selected by bottom-up and top-down perceptual processes with a decision-theoretic perspective and then selects the most salient entity. Remember that this entity can be an area in the case of olfactory stimuli. Externally, DPA controls an embodied agent's gaze not only to exhibit its current focus of attention but also to update beliefs (e.g., position) of the selected object. That is, the embodied agent dynamically decides where to look, which entity to look for, and how long to attend to the entity.

3.1   Decision Theoretic Control

One of the consequences of modeling perception with limited sensory inputs is that it creates uncertainty on each perceived object. For instance, if an object that is being tracked moves out of an agent's field of view, the perceptual attention model increases the uncertainty level of the target information of the object that a virtual human tries to observe.

The information flow of the DPA module is shown in figure 1. Top-down and bottom-up processes give provide information to the DPA module in the form of tuples that are composed of the following components composed as follows:

$$tuple_i = \langle objP_i, objC_i, objDGI_i, objCGI_i, k_i \rangle$$

where, $objP_i$:   priority of the tuple$_i$
   $objC_i$:   concern of the tuple$_i$
   $objDGI_i$: desired goal information of the tuple$_i$
   $objCGI_i$: current goal information of the tuple$_i$
   k_i: constant for the tuple$_i$

The priority attribute, $objP$, is used to indicate the absolute importance of an object, whereas the concern attribute, $objC$, is used to indicate a conflict between the desired goal information ($objDGI$) and the current certainty of information ($objCGI$). For instance, even if a person is given a high priority task, he may not be concerned about monitoring objects associated with the task if the task is going well, resulting in less frequent observations. If the task goes differently what is predicted, he will increase his concern for the task, resulting in more frequent observations.

By considering both attributes (i.e., priority and concern), our virtual humans compute the benefits of attending to objects. Information certainty is one of factors that help the virtual human decide which object it has to focus on. To deal with certainties of the perceived objects, we have chosen to take a decision theoretic approach to computing the perceptual costs and benefits of shifting the focus of perceptual attention of the perceived objects. In the next two sections, we will describe how to compute the perceptual costs and benefits of shifting the focus of

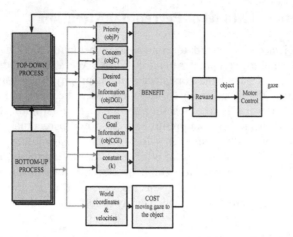

Fig. 1. The Information flow of the DPA module

perceptual attention. The expected cost is computed by calculating the perceptual cost of shifting the gaze to the selected object. The expected benefit is computed by considering the value of having acquiring accurate information about the selected object. Once a decision has been made, DPA shifts the virtual human's gaze to focus his perceptual attention on the object that has the highest reward.

3.2 Computing the Benefit

To compute the benefit of focusing perceptual attention on an object requires the estimated values of object-based information certainty. We consider object-based information certainty as a key factor in computing the benefit of shifting the focus of attention to the object. The term, *object-based information certainty*, is used here to describe the level of information certainty of an object rendered in the agent's mental image of a virtual world. Humans determine the desired goal information certainty of perceived objects (*objDGI*) based on their subjective preferences or prediction and then make efforts to maintain the current certainty of information (*objCGI*) within a certain specific range of objDGIs, that is defined as the information certainty tolerance boundary (*ICTB*) in our model).

Information certainty is dynamic both in space and time and requires stochastic functions of time and space to describe its dynamics. If the current certainty of information (*objCGI*) is out of *ICTB*, we activate one of two kinds of NEEDs: the NEED for observation or the NEED for inhibition. The NEED for observation is activated if objCGI goes below $ICTB_{lower}$. The NEED of inhibition is activated as objCGI goes over $ICTB_{upper}$. According to Klein's account of the behavior of *inhibition* and *observation* comes from the concept, the *inhibition of return* [12], too much information can be a bad thing. , which is the process by which the currently attended location or information is prevented from being attended to again and is a crucial element of attentional deployment of humans. By modeling the inhibition of return, perceptual attention will not permanently focus on the most active salient information but will increase the chances of diverting perceptual attention to less salient information.

The orthogonal process model between information certainty and the NEEDs of observation and inhibition is shown in figure 2.

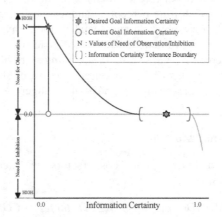

Fig. 2. The interrelation of Information Certainty and Need

The desired goal information certainty (objDGI) is determined by the priority attribute (objP). The information certainty tolerance boundary is set by the concern attribute (objC). The higher the concern attribute is, the narrower the length of the boundary is. The current goal information certainty of the target object (objCGI) is set by top-down and bottom-up processes. If a virtual human cannot retrieve any information certainty of the target from top-down and bottom-up processes, it sets objCGI as 0. After the values for objCGI and information certainty tolerance boundary are set, the virtual human computes the NEED for observation or for inhibition on each tuple as follows:

$$
\mathrm{NEED(tuple}_i) = \begin{cases} -1.0 \times objP_i \times \exp^{\alpha} & \text{if objCGI}_i > \mathrm{ICTB}_{upper} \\ 0 & \text{if } \mathrm{ICTB}_{lower} \leq \mathrm{objCGI}_i \leq \mathrm{ICTB}_{upper} \\ objP_i \times \exp^{\beta} & \text{if objCGI}_i < \mathrm{ICTB}_{lower} \end{cases}
$$

where, $\alpha = \mathrm{objCGI}_i - \mathrm{ICTB}_{upper}$ and $\beta = \mathrm{ICTB}_{lower} - \mathrm{objCGI}_i$

The NEED tuple$_i$ is used as a force that produces a benefit of diverting perceptual attention into tuple$_i$. The benefit is computed as follows:

$$
BENEFIT(tuple_i) = \frac{NEED(tuple_i)^2}{2}.
$$

Once *BENEFIT(tuple$_i$)* is computed, it will used with *COST(tuple$_i$)* as the factor to compute *REWARD(tuple$_i$)* with *COST(tuple$_i$)*.

3.3 Computing the Cost

Even if the benefit of drawing attention to one object is higher than the benefits of attending to others, the virtual human should not automatically select that object as the best one since the cost of shifting the focus of attention must also be considered.

To compute the cost of shifting perceptual attention from one object to another, we consider two sets of factors: physical and social factors. Physical factors include the degrees of head and eye movements and distance efficiency. Social factors indicate the relative costs of perceptual gaze shifts in social interaction. For instance, it may be rude to look away when someone is speaking (high cost of shift), yet it may be very important to attend to an unexpected or potentially dangerous event (high cost not to shift).

3.4 Shifting Perceptual Attention

With the benefit and two sets of cost factors of each tuple, we compute $REWARD(tuple_i)$ as follows:

$$REWARD(tuple_i) = BENEFIT(tuple_i) - COST(tuple_i).$$

After calculating REWARD(tuple) of all tuples, the virtual human selects a tuple that has the highest REWARD. If the selected tuple is holding the current focus of perceptual attention, the virtual human will keep focus on it. If not, it will divert its perceptual attention into the tuple having the highest REWARD.

The duration of a gaze at an object affects the information certainty level. While a virtual human gazes at an object (i.e., overt monitoring), the objCGI increases. Likewise, while the object is monitored only in the virtual human's memory and projection (i.e., covert monitoring), objCGI decreases. Covert monitoring will cause the certainty of information to decay over time.

4   Perceptual Attention Within the MRE Scenario

We implemented dynamic perceptual attention with virtual humans in the immersive environment called the Mission Rehearsal Exercise (MRE) [8].

In MRE, there are three embodied conversational virtual humans – the sergeant (SGT), the mother, and the medic – and a human participant (lieutenant) in an accident site where an Army vehicle has crashed into a civilian car, injuring a boy. The participant then takes on the task of directing the troops to rescue the boy by interacting with virtual humans. While the rescue task is proceeding, the mom perceives that the troops are moving out of the accident site. In despair, she stands up and cries out for help. Unfortunately, our virtual humans – the sergeant and the medic – are not aware of the mom's outcry, but the human participant is. The system may handle this bottom-up form of attention capture in an ad hoc manner by encoding special rules to catch certain condition in the environment. However, this approach does not provide a principled way of integrating the ever-present bottom-up perceptual stimuli with top-down control of attention.

Traum and Rickel [15] presented an attention layer in a state-of-art model of multi-party dialogue in MRE, which is organized as a set of dialogue management layers. Their attention model is not fully implemented and only (visual) give attention is currently fully modeled. Our aim in this section is to extend their attention layer by addressing the issue of dynamic perceptual attention (DPA). We controlled the sergeant's gaze movements with DPA.

Let's assume that the mom cries out for help while the sergeant is interacting with the medic to talk about the boy's health status. The sergeant's auditory perception computes how loud the mom's outcry is. If the outcry is audible, auditory perception assigns the priority in proportion to the loudness of the sound. Since the sergeant has never expected the auditory input, he will get the certain level of NEED of the auditory input. The auditory perception generates a tuple for the mom's outcry as follows:

$$\neg(mom\_outcry) = <objP=0.7, objC=0.0, objDGI=0.8, objCGI=0.0>$$

The task reasoner gives a tuple for the task of interacting with the medic as follows:

$$(get\_info\_boy\_health\_status)=<objP=0.9, objC=0.0, objDGI=0.7, objCGI=0.5>$$

The figures for this situation are shown in the figure 3.

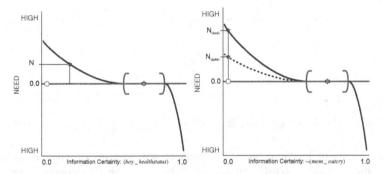

Fig. 3. Information Certainties and NEEDs of (boy_health_status) and $\neg(mom\_outcry)$

When DPA computes the REWARD of each tuple, the bottom-up auditory stimuli, the mom's outcry, gets the highest REWARD and then the sergeant diverts his attention from the medic to the auditory stimuli. This shift of attention will make the sergeant to recognize that the mom is crying out for help and update the tuple for the auditory stimuli as follows:

$$\neg(mom\_outcry) = <objP=0.7, objC=0.0, objDGI=0.1, objCGI=0.0>$$

The recognition of the mom's outcry for help makes the sergeant to interact with the mom so that the sergeant gets what makes her upset. As the result of this recognition, a new tuple is given as follows:

$$(get\_information\_from\_mom)=<objP=0.7, objC=0.0, objDGI=0.7, objCGI=0.0>$$

The figures for this situation are shown in the figure 4.

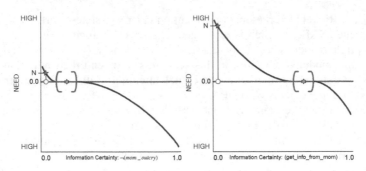

Fig. 4. Information Certainties and NEEDs of ¬(*mom _ outcry*) and (get_info_from_mom)

The tuple for (get_information_from_mom) now gets the sergeant's focus of attention. While getting information from mom, the sergeant gets certain level of information certainty on (get_info_from_mom).

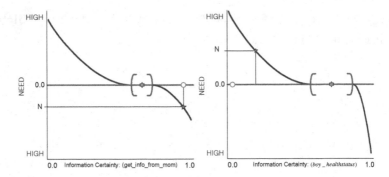

Fig. 5. Information Certainties and NEEDs of ¬(*mom _ outcry*) and (get_info_from_mom)

If the sergeant understands what she wants, he should think of what he should do to soothe the mom. While thinking, the sergeant updates the tuple, (get_info_from_mom) and gets the tuple, (boy_health_status), as the next focus of attention. The figures for this situation are shown in the figure 5. The sergeant will divert his attention to the medic to update the current state of the medic. As the result of thinking, the sergeant decides to say something to the mom such as "it's ok, we are staying right now with you. See, we've got the medevac coming right now." This speech event will make the sergeant to divert the sergeant's focus of attention to the mom and then the sergeant speaks the utterance as mentioned above. After getting the mom's proper reaction, the sergeant then shifts his focus of attention back to the medic.

This example illustrates the importance of gaze in acquiring perceptual information and monitoring task performance while embedded in the social context of conversation. Our aim is to have the sergeant's behavior seem appropriate within this context, both in terms of behaving human-like and using perceptual gaze to mediate between costs and benefits of information updating actions.

5 Modeling a Virtual Environment with ASCE

Any artificial environment where synthetic human-like characters represent digital life should also contain an artificial form of the complete range of sensory stimuli.

Within ASCE, where the environment is represented in a discrete fashion, all sensory sensations from the agent's perspective are experienced through interacting with volumetric sensory entities with varying complexity. In order to facilitate spatial perception, we developed a unified sensory oriented environment representation. ASCE's runtime simulation component analyzes the world geometry and extracts a volumetric representation. In essence, every object is fitted with a bounding volume with associated salience information, creating a stimulus entity. Doing so transforms the geometric model into an existence model, rich with sensory data. This new model can also be seen as a 3-dimensional representation of a saliency map [9]. Only cubic shapes are used for bounding volumes, much like the approached used by Noser et al [10] and Zhang et al [17]. Human perception spans the full spectrum of sensory experiences, from tactile sensations to olfactory stimulations. A volumetric approach provides a computational model that is faster to analyze and maintain than working with the original geometry [17]. Another rationale for this approach is that humans, unlike most robotic and agent implementations, do not consider all details of an entity relevant for interaction. When entering a room filled with objects with the purpose of sitting down at a desk for instance, it is not important what the logo in a trashcan is, it is only important to know its general dimensions and relative placement to avoid colliding with it. ASCE can represent and process any kind of stimuli provided that they are represented as a volume with cubic dimensions [14], out of the entire range of stimuli we will focus here on two of them to show how they are represented and used. One of the improvements over previous approaches [16,7] of data models for artificial sensors is that the inverse of our entity model represents the available space for navigation, which we termed the opportunity space. This allows for higher navigation fidelity than implementations within MRE. A further enhancement is obtained by using spatial attention to only refine those entities that were specifically paid attention to. Doing so removes the limitation of having to use a maximum observation radius [10] in which to calculate volumetric information.

6 Discussion and Future Work

One of critical questions is how to evaluate and validate that this model is better than other models. To be frank, it is not easy for us to evaluate our model since each model has its unique purpose. One of the distinctions between the work described in this paper and other models of perceptual attention is the purpose of the model. In many of the systems we reviewed, the purpose of perceptual attention was to make the virtual humans behave as though they were attending to the surroundings and tasks in a natural way. In contrast, our goal is also to develop virtual humans that can perform tasks, react to contingencies, interact with other agents, both virtual and human, plan, and make decisions about what to do next or at some future time [6,7]. To accomplish this, we have found that perceptual attention is a critically important mechanism for restricting the sensory information being processed by the perception module and controlling virtual humans to exhibit goal-directed and reactive behaviors. While the model of perceptual attention presented in this paper handles many aspects of behavior generation (e.g., gaze movement), there is another factor in the broader scope of attention: social attention. In a social situation, perceptual attention may interact with social attention since social factors may also change the relative costs of perceptual attention shifts. For instance, it may be very rude to look away when someone is speaking (high cost of shift), yet it may be very important to attend to an unexpected or potentially dangerous event (high benefit to shift). With high utility on either end, the choice may be difficult and moreover potentially very costly either way. By integrating an efficient social attention model with this model, we believe that the model will provide a large potential for generating more socialized behaviors. For the future work, we will focus on validating our model with the real human data retrieved from the experiment [21] by testing our virtual humans in the same environment.

Acknowledgment

The project or effort described here has been sponsored by the U.S. Army Research, Development, and Engineering Command (RDECOM). Statements and opinions expressed do not necessarily reflect the position or the policy of the United States Government, and no official endorsement should be inferred.

References

1. Cassell, J., H. Vilhjalmsson: Fully Conversational Avatars: Making Communicative Behaviors" Autonomous Agents and Multi-Agent Systems, Vol. 2. Kluwer Academic Publishers (1999) 45-64
2. Chopra-Khullar, S., Badler, N.: Where to Look? Automating Attending Behaviors of Visual Human Characters. Autonomous Agents and Multi-Agent Systems. (2001)
3. Conde, T., Thalmann, D.: An Artificial Life Environment for Autonomous Virtual Agents with multi-sensorial and multi-perceptive features. Computer Animation and Virtual Worlds , Volume 15, Issue 3-4, John Wiley (2004)
4. Courty, N., Marchand, E., Arnaldi, B.: A New Application for Saliency Maps: Synthetic Vision of Autonomous Actors. IEEE Int. Conf. on Image Processing, ICIP'03, Barcelona, Spain, Sep. (2003)
5. Gillies, M., Neil, D.: Eye Movements and Attention for Behavioural Animation. The Journal of Visualization and Computer Animation. (2002)
6. Hill, R.: Modeling Attention in Virtual Humans. Proceedings of the 8th Conference on Computer Generated Forces and Behavioral Representation, SISO, Orlando, Fla. (1999)
7. Hill, R.: Perceptual Attention in Virtual Humans: Toward Realistic and Believable Gaze Behaviors. Proceedings of the AAAI Fall Symposium on Simulating Human Agents, pp.46-52, AAAI Press, Menlo Park, Calif., (2000)
8. Hill, R., Gratch, J., Marsella, S., Rickel, J., Swartout, W., Traum, D.: Virtual Humans in the Mission Rehearsal Exercise System. Künstliche Intelligenz (KI Journal). Special issue on Embodied Conversational Agents (2003)

9. Itti, L., Koch, C.: Computational Modeling of Visual Attention. Nature Reviews Neuroscience, Vol. 2, No. 3, pp. 194-203, Mar (2001)
10. Noser, H. and Thalmann, D.: Synthetic vision and audition for digital actors, in Proceedings of Eurographics 1995, 1995
11. Nothegger, C., Winter, S., Raubal, M.: Selection of Salient Features for Route Directions. Spatial Cognition and Computation 4(2): 113-136 (2004)
12. Klein, R.: Inhibition of return. Trends in Cognitive Sciences, 4, 138–147. (2000)
13. Rickel, J., Johnson, L.: Animated Agents for Procedural Training in Virtual Reality: Perception, Cognition, and Motor Control. Applied Artificial Intelligence (1999)
14. Samet H.: The Quadtree and Related Hierarchical Data Structures, ACM Computing Surveys (CSUR), v.16 n.2, p.187-260, June (1984)
15. Traum, D., Rickel, J.: Embodied Agents for Multi-party Dialogue in Immersive Virtual Worlds. AAMAS'02, July 15-19, Bologna, Italy (2002)
16. Young, R. M., Riedl, M.: Towards an Architecture for Intelligent Control of Narrative in Interactive Virtual Worlds, In the Proceedings of the International Conference on Intelligent User Interfaces, January, 2003
17. Zhang, H., Wyvill, B.: Behavioural Simulation in Voxel Space. Computer Animation '97, June 04 - 07, Geneva, SWITZERLAND (1997)
18. Platt, M. L., Glimcher, P. W.: Neural Correlates of Decision Variables in Parietal Cortex. Nature 400, 233-238 (1999)
19. Glimcher, P. W.: The Neurobiology of Visual-saccadic Decision Making. Annu. Rev. Neurosci. 26, 133-179 (2003)
20. Dorris, M. C., Glimcher, P. W.: Activity in Posterior Parietal Cortex is correlated with the Subjective Desireability of an Action. Neuron 44, 365-378 (2004)
21. Rizzo, AA, Buckwalter, JG., Bowerly, T., van der Zaag, C., Humphrey L, Neumann, U., Chua, C., van Rooyen, A., Sisemore, D.,: The virtual classroom: A virtual environment for the assessment and rehabilitation of attention deficits. Cyberpsychol. Behav. 3:483-500 (2000)

An Objective Character Believability Evaluation Procedure for Multi-agent Story Generation Systems

Mark O. Riedl[1] and R. Michael Young[2]

[1] Institute for Creative Technologies, University of Southern California,
13274 Fiji Way, Los Angeles, CA 90292 USA
riedl@ict.usc.edu
[2] Department of Computer Science, North Carolina State University,
Raleigh, NC 27695 USA
young@csc.ncsu.edu

Abstract. The ability to generate narrative is of importance to computer systems that wish to use story effectively for entertainment, training, or education. One of the focuses of intelligent virtual agent research in general and story generation research in particular is how to make agents/characters more lifelike and compelling. However, one question that invariably comes up is: Is the generated story good? An easier question to tackle is whether a reader/viewer of a generated story perceives certain essential attributes such as causal coherence and character believability. Character believability is the perception that story world characters are acting according to their own beliefs, desires, and intentions. We present a novel procedure for objectively evaluating stories generated for multiple agents/characters with regard to character intentionality – an important aspect of character believability. The process transforms generated stories into a standardized model of story comprehension and then indirectly compares that representation to reader/viewer mental perceptions about the story. The procedure is illustrated by evaluating a narrative planning system, Fabulist.

1 Introduction

Narrative as entertainment, in the form of oral, written, or visual stories, plays a central role in our social and leisure lives. Narrative is also used in education and training contexts to motivate and illustrate. The prevalence of narrative in our lives is partly due to what is called *narrative intelligence* which refers to the ability – human or computer – to organize experiences into narrative. Computational systems that reason about narrative intelligence are able to interact with human users in a natural way because they understand collaborative contexts as emerging narrative and are able to express themselves through storytelling. The standard approach to incorporating storytelling into a computer system, however, is to script a story at design time. That is, the system designers determine ahead of time what the story should be and hard-code the story into the system. An alternative approach is to generate stories either dynamically or on a per-session basis (one story per time the system is engaged by a user). A system that can generate stories is capable of adapting stories to the user's preferences and abilities, has expanded "replay value" and is capable of interacting with the user in ways that were not initially envisioned by the system designers.

T. Panayiotopoulos et al. (Eds.): IVA 2005, LNCS 3661, pp. 278–291, 2005.
© Springer-Verlag Berlin Heidelberg 2005

A story generation system is any computer application that creates a written, spo-ken, or visual presentation of a story – a sequence of actions performed by multiple characters. There have been many approaches to generating story: autonomous agents (e.g. [1] and [2; 3]); authorial planning (e.g. [4] and [5; 6]); models of creativ-ity (e.g. [7]); models of dramatic tension (e.g. [8]); reactive selection of scene-like elements (e.g. [9; 10] to the extent that the drama will continue without active user participation). In some cases, the story emerges from real-time interaction between agents/characters. In other cases, a story is deliberately laid out by a single authoring agent and presented visually or as natural language. Regardless, one major drive of intelligent agent research is making agents – characters – more lifelike and believable.

For storytelling to be successful – to have an emotional or educational impact on the audience – a story must (a) be understandable and (b) believable in the sense that the audience is willing to suspend their disbelief. We argue that one property of story that affects both is *character believability*. Character believability refers to the nu-merous elements that allow a character to achieve the "illusion of life," including but limited to personality, emotion, intentionality, and physiology and physiological movement [11]. One important aspect of character believability is *character inten-tionality*. Character intentionality refers to the way in which the choice of actions and behaviors that a character makes appears natural (and possibly rational) to external observers. Character intentionality addresses the relationship of actions and behaviors to an agent's beliefs, desires, intentions as well as internal and external motivation.

The technical approach to automated story generation has implications for charac-ter believability and story coherence. There is a continuum between a strong auton-omy approach and a strong story approach [9]. The strong story approach advocates centralized control of character behaviors. In general, centralized control, in the form of a single authoring agent that decides on the actions for all story world characters, is advantageous because the authoring agent can approach the story from a global per-spective, choosing character actions in such a way that causal relationships are estab-lished [6]. Central control can be advantageous for character believability as well, helping to coordinate character actions in a way that eliminates the appearance of "schizophrenia" [12]. However, the more centralized control of character behaviors, the more likely it is that the characters will not be perceived by the reader/viewer as acting upon their own beliefs, desired, and intentions. This is particularly true of plan-based automated story generation systems in which the story planner is primarily concerned with establishing causal coherence of the story structure. In this case, character actions are chosen because of the effects they achieve and not necessarily based on whether it is believable for a character to perform an action.

Once the capability for story generation exists and stories are generated, evaluation becomes important. Evaluation of stories created by automated story generation sys-tems often relies on subjective assessment. However, subjective assessment can be tangled up in many factors such as quality of natural language, subject interest in the topic of the story, novelty, and so on. An objective evaluation can be performed based on metrics such as story length or complexity of character roles (e.g. [3]) under the assumption that these metrics correlate to better stories. Other metrics may exist as well. Narrative has an impact on an audience; we believe that to understand the success of a narrative on an audience, one must measure the degree to which the reader/viewer perceives character intentionality since character is an integral part of

Once there was a Czar who had three lovely daughters. One day the three daughters went walking in the woods. They were enjoying themselves so much that they forgot the time and stayed too long. A dragon kidnapped the three daughters. As they were being dragged off, they cried for help. Three heroes heard the cries and set off to rescue the daughters. The heroes came and fought the dragon and rescued the maidens. Then the heroes returned the daughters to their palace. When the Czar heard of the rescue, he rewarded the heroes.

Fig. 1. An example story [14]

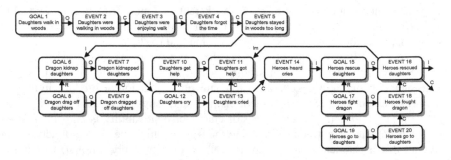

Fig. 2. A portion of the QUEST model for the story in Figure 1 [14]

story. A reader/viewer forms a mental model of the narrative structure and the characters in the narrative over time as the narrative unfolds and queries that mental model in order to actively predict outcomes and rationalize character actions [13]. The QUEST model of question-answering in the context of stories [14] provides a technique for devising a model of story comprehension for a story that can be indirectly compared to the mental model held in a subject's mind.

2 The QUEST Model of Question-Answering

The QUEST model [14] accounts for the goodness-of-answer (GOA) judgments for questions asked about passages of prose. One application of the QUEST model is to show that people build cognitive representations of stories they read that capture certain relationships between events in a story and the perceived goals of the characters in the story [14]. A reader's cognitive representation of the story is queried when the reader answers questions about the story. The types of questions supported by the QUEST model are: why, how, when, enablement, and consequence. For example, the story in Figure 1 has the corresponding QUEST knowledge structure shown in Figure 2. There are two types of nodes in the QUEST knowledge structure: event nodes, which correspond to occurrences in the story world, and goal nodes, which correspond to goals that characters have. The links between nodes capture the different types of relationships between events and character goals.

- Consequence (C): The terminal event node is a consequence of the initiating event node.
- Reason (R): The initiating goal node is the reason for the terminal event node.

– Initiate (I): The initiating event node initiates the terminal goal node.
– Outcome (O): The terminal event node is the outcome of the initiating goal node.
– Implies (Im): The initiating event node implies the terminal event node.

Graesser et al. illustrate the QUEST model of question answering with the following question pertaining to the story in Figure 1: "Why did the daughters stay in the woods too long" (node 5)? There are many possible answers, some of which are:

A. Because the daughters forgot the time (node 4).
B. Because the dragon kidnapped the daughters (node 7).
C. Because the daughters were walking in the woods (node 2).
D. Because the heroes fought the dragon (node 18).

Both the question and each possible answer correspond to nodes in the knowledge structure. The QUEST model defines arc search procedures for each type of question (e.g. why, how, when, enablement, and consequence). The arc search procedures, starting at the queried node, distinguish between legal answer nodes and illegal answer nodes. That is, only nodes reachable by the arc search procedures are legal answer nodes. Answers (A) and (C) are legal answers. Of those two, (A) is preferred by the QUEST model because the corresponding node has a smaller structural distance from the queried node. The legality of answers and the weight of structural distance correspond to GOA judgments of human story readers.

3 Evaluation Procedure

To evaluate the character believability of a story generation system, we describe a procedure involving two conditions: a control condition and a test condition. The assumption is that a story generation system has been augmented or improved with regard to character believability. The control condition consists of a story generated by the story generation system without enhancement and/or augmentation while the test condition consists of a story generated by the same story generation system, but with enhancement. Given that the QUEST model of question-answering in the context of stories is empirically validated and that human narrative intelligence is relatively the same across subjects, the procedure for evaluating story generation systems is to compare an instance of a QUEST model of a specific generated story to subject comprehension of narrative structure for that story. In QUEST, "why" questions inquire about character goals, intentions, and motivations. The general idea behind the process described here is that a better story generation system (presumably the test condition) will result in stories whose structures better support human perception of character intentionality. The better the structure of the generated story, the better a QUEST representation of that story will predict reader/viewer question-answering. The procedure is as follows:

1. Generate control and test condition stories. Given two versions of a story generation system, generate a story from each. The two stories should be as similar as possible for evaluation to be possible. We assume that the story generation system will produce similar stories if given nearly identical initialization parameters but the test condition story will have elements and/or structure in the story that the control condition does not. Therefore, if there is a significant increase in the measure of understanding of character intentionality in the final results, then the enhancement to the story generation system does in fact improve the perception of character believability. Ideally, this will be achieved by initializing both systems with identical or nearly identical input parameters so as to avoid experimenter bias. It may not always be possible to use identical input parameters if the internal knowledge representations between versions of story generator are significantly different. In this case, one must control for the possibility that improvements are gained through different or increased knowledge.

2. Generate QUEST Knowledge Structures for each story. A QUEST Knowledge Structure (QKS) is an instantiation of a QUEST model for a particular story. This can be accomplished by hand or automatically. If done by hand, experimenter bias must be controlled for. To automatically generate a QKS from a story structure generated by a story generation system, there must be some formalized relationship between the data structures output by the story generation system and QUEST knowledge structures in general. For example, the results of [15] indicate a significant correlation between causal dependency plans and QKSs and validate the correlation experimentally.

3. Generate question-answer pairs. For each QKS, question-answer pairs can be composed from every possible combination of nodes in the QKS, as in [14]. It is important to compose both reasonable and nonsensical question-answer pairs. The study should focus on the "why" question-answer pairs since "why" questions emphasize understanding about intentional character actions. An example of a question-answer pair that can be generated from the QKS in Figure 2 is:

Q: Why did the heroes go to the daughters and dragon (node 20)?
A: Because the heroes heard the daughters cry (node 14).

Each question-answer pair will be rated by a subject on a Likert-type scale. The fact that there will be many question-answer pairs that occur in only one condition is not important since the analysis determines the degree to which subjects' mental models match a QKS within one condition and then compares that aggregate measure to the same from the other condition.

4. Use QUEST to identify "good" and "poor" question-answer pairs. QUEST specifies legal graph traversal routines which can be used to identify legal answers to questions. That is, if a legal graph traversal starting at the question node can find the answer node for a question-answer pair, then the question-answer pair is "good." This is a rough prediction of whether a subject's goodness-of-answer (GOA) rating of the question-answer pair will be favorable or not. For "why" questions, the arc search procedure searches for answer nodes by following forward reason arcs, backward initiate arcs, and backward outcome arcs [14]. The assumption is that the better a generated story supports human perception of character intentionality, the better the QKS for the story will predict subject GOA ratings.

5. Run subjects. Split subjects equally between the control and test conditions. The subjects make GOA judgments for the question-answer pairs, determining whether the answer seems like a reasonable response to the question. For each question-answer pair, there should be a Likert-type scale. For example, a four-point Likert-type scale has "Very bad answer", "Somewhat bad answer", "Somewhat good answer", and "Very good answer". Note that leaving out a middle ground ratings (e.g. "Neither agree nor disagree") forces a subject to commit to a positive or negative ranking, which is important because of the binary categorization of question-answer pairs. If the story is well-structured, subjects should rank question-answer pairs high when QUEST identifies the pairing as good and low when QUEST identifies the pairing as poor. Score the subject responses with numerical values. For example, "Very bad answer" gets a score of 1 and "Very good answer" gets a value of 4.

6. Compile and compare results. For each condition, find the between-subject mean for each question-answer pair. That is, the mean response value for question-answer pair X is n. For each condition, break the question-answer pairs into "good" and "poor" sets and find the mean response for each set. This gives you a 2-by-2 matrix of results: Mean response for "good" question-answer pairs versus mean response for "poor" question-answer pairs, and control condition versus test condition. For example, see Table 1. Favorable results are when:

- The mean GOA rating for "good" question-answer pairs for the test condition is statistically higher than the mean GOA rating for "good" question-answer pairs for the control condition.
- The mean GOA rating for "poor" question-answer pairs for the test condition is statistically lower than the mean GOA rating for "poor" question-answer pairs for the control condition.

4 Example – Story Planning

We illustrate our evaluation technique by evaluating previous research on a story generation system based on partial order planning. The story generation system is called Fabulist [6] and utilizes an Intent-driven Partial Order Causal Link (IPOCL) planner [5; 6] that is an enhancement of a more conventional Partial Order Causal Link (POCL) planner, specialized to narrative generation.

Young [16] suggests that planning has many benefits as a model of narrative. First of all, plans are comprised of partially ordered steps. If the plan steps represent actions that are performed by characters in the story world, then a plan makes a good model of a story fabula – the chronological enumeration of events that occur in the story world between the time the story begins and the time the story ends. Secondly, planners such as UCPOP [17] construct plans based on causal dependencies. Causal dependency planning ensures that all character actions are part of a causal chain of events that lead to the outcome of the story, resulting in a coherent story structure.

The causal dependencies between character actions and the story outcome ensure coherent story structure, but also pose a problem for character believability. Specifically, causal dependency planners attempt to find a sequence of operations that achieve a particular goal. In the case of a story planner, character actions are not chosen because they are the natural (e.g. believable) thing for a character to do at a particular time, but because they establish causal relationships that are necessary for plan soundness. Conventional planners do not reason explicitly about character intentionality and, consequently, their story plans are not guaranteed to possess this property. For example, the Universe story generation system [4] uses a hierarchical planner to piece together plot fragments into a story plan. Plot fragments are decomposed into character actions. Universe, however, selects plot fragments (and consequently character actions) to be in the story plan only when they establish causal conditions necessary to achieve the story outcome.

Our enhanced narrative planner, IPOCL, reasons about possible character intentions in order to construct narrative plans that not only have causal coherence but also motivate the actions that story world characters have.   The hypothesis is that our narrative planner will generate better structured narratives that facilitate reader/viewer perception of character believability (or at least character intentionality).

4.1 Fabulist

Fabulist [6] is a story generation system that uses a causal dependency planner to create a story involving multiple characters that are possibly antagonistic toward each other. The causal dependency planner accepts a description of the initial state of the story world, a partial description of the outcome that should result from the events of the story, and a library of actions that characters can perform. The output of the planner is a story plan where the operations of the plan are actions performed by story world characters.

The causal dependency planner used by Fabulist is a special planner designed for story generation called the Intent-driven Partial Order Causal Link (IPOCL) planner [5; 6] (although in the control condition of our evaluation, a conventional POCL planner will take its place for comparison purposes). In addition to the narrative planner, Fabulist also has a discourse planner and a media realizer that are configured in a pipeline. The narrative planner generates a narrative plan which describes all the events that will happen in the story world between the time the story begins and the time the story ends. The discourse planner takes the narrative plan as input and generates a narration of the story. The discourse plan consists of the communicative actions required to tell the story to an audience. Fabulist uses an unmodified version of the Longbow discourse planner [18]. The media realizer takes the discourse plan as input and generates natural language. Fabulist currently uses a simple template-matching routine to generate surface-level text, although a more sophisticated system such as that in [19] could be used instead.

The IPOCL planning algorithm addresses the limitations of conventional causal dependency planners when applied to story generation. Specifically, conventional planners make certain assumptions that are not valid in the domain of story planning.

- The planner is creating a plan for a single agent.
- The goal of the planning problem is the desired world state of the agent.

In contrast, a single planner that is creating a story plan must create a plan for multiple agents (story world characters). In addition, the goal of the planning problem represents the *outcome* of the story as intended by the human author. That is, the outcome is not necessarily intended by any character and most likely not intended by all characters. If the outcome is intended by all story world characters, then the characters will appear to collaborate to bring about the outcome. However, it is more likely that many characters do not share the same goals and may even have conflicting goals.

The IPOCL algorithm addresses the mismatch between conventional planning and story planning by decoupling the characters' intentions from the author's intentions. IPOCL does not assume that the story world characters intend the outcome (goal state) of the story. Instead, IPOCL (1) searches for the intentions that each character might have and (2) motivates through story events why those characters have the intentions that they do. At stake is the perception that a character has goals, that those goals are formed in reaction to stimuli, and that the character is acting to achieve those goals.

IPOCL is based on conventional causal dependency planners such as UCPOP [17]. However, IPOCL story plans contain richer structural representation because it includes character intentions that are distinct from the story goal and, consequently, tend to be longer than conventional plans. That is, given the same initialization parameters, IPOCL and a conventional planner would generate different plans. But does the IPOCL story plan support audience perception of character intentionality better than one generated by a conventional planner? We apply our objective evaluation procedure to determine this.

4.2 Method

To determine whether subjects perceived character intentionality in stories generated by Fabulist, we used two versions of Fabulist to generate two similar narratives. Subjects were separated randomly into groups, asked to read one of the stories, and rate the goodness of answer of question/answer pairs relating to the story they read. One version of Fabulist had a story planner component implementing the IPOCL algorithm, while the other used a conventional causal dependency planner. Both versions of Fabulist had identical discourse planner components based on the Longbow planner [18], and identical template-based text realizer components. Both versions of Fabulist were initialized with identical parameters.

A QUEST knowledge structure (QKS) – a representation of the cognitive structures held in the mind of a reader of a story – is a directed acyclic graph of events and goals. As such, QKSs are similar to plans, which are also directed acyclic graphs of events and goals. Christian and Young [15] define a procedure by which a simple yet functional QKS can be derived from a plan. They demonstrate that the QKS generated from a plan significantly predicts the goodness-of-answer judgments for "why" and "how" questions when arc search procedure was considered without structural distance[1].

Both the test condition story and the control condition story are generated from the same set of inputs. The stories differ due to the fact that the test condition story planner reasons about character intentions distinct from the outcome and introduces additional motivating actions into the story to provide explanation for why characters act. The story in the control condition has 10 events and is shown in Figure 3, while the story in the test condition has 13 events and is shown in Figure 4. Figures 5 and 6 show QKS representations of the control condition story and test condition story, respectively. The narrative plans from which the QKSs are derived are not shown here; see [6] for more details. Note that there are significant similarities between the

---

[1] An additional study by the authors (not reported) determined that QKSs derived from IPOCL plans significantly predict GOA judgments when structural distance is ignored ($p < 0.0005$).

There is a woman named Jasmine. There is a king named Mamoud. This is a story about how King Mamoud becomes married to Jasmine. There is a magic genie. This is also a story about how the genie dies.

There is a magic lamp. There is a dragon. The dragon has the magic lamp. The genie is confined within the magic lamp.

There is a brave knight named Aladdin. Aladdin travels from the castle to the mountains. Aladdin slays the dragon. The dragon is dead. Aladdin takes the magic lamp from the dead body of the dragon. Aladdin travels from the mountains to the castle. Aladdin hands the magic lamp to King Mamoud. The genie is in the magic lamp. King Mamoud rubs the magic lamp and summons the genie out of it. The genie is not confined within the magic lamp. The genie casts a spell on Jasmine making her fall in love with King Mamoud. Jasmine is madly in love with King Mamoud. Aladdin slays the genie. King Mamoud is not married. Jasmine is very beautiful. King Mamoud sees Jasmine and instantly falls in love with her. King Mamoud and Jasmine wed in an extravagant ceremony.

The genie is dead. King Mamoud and Jasmine are married. The end.

Fig. 3. Text of story in control condition

There is a woman named Jasmine. There is a king named Mamoud. This is a story about how King Mamoud becomes married to Jasmine. There is a magic genie. This is also a story about how the genie dies.

There is a magic lamp. There is a dragon. The dragon has the magic lamp. The genie is confined within the magic lamp.

King Mamoud is not married. Jasmine is very beautiful. King Mamoud sees Jasmine and instantly falls in love with her. King Mamoud wants to marry Jasmine. There is a brave knight named Aladdin. Aladdin is loyal to the death to King Mamoud. King Mamoud orders Aladdin to get the magic lamp for him. Aladdin wants King Mamoud to have the magic lamp. Aladdin travels from the castle to the mountains. Aladdin slays the dragon. The dragon is dead. Aladdin takes the magic lamp from the dead body of the dragon. Aladdin travels from the mountains to the castle. Aladdin hands the magic lamp to King Mamoud. The genie is in the magic lamp. King Mamoud rubs the magic lamp and summons the genie out of it. The genie is not confined within the magic lamp. King Mamoud controls the genie with the magic lamp. King Mamoud uses the magic lamp to command the genie to make Jasmine love him. The genie wants Jasmine to be in love with King Mamoud. The genie casts a spell on Jasmine making her fall in love with King Mamoud. Jasmine is madly in love with King Mamoud. Jasmine wants to marry King Mamoud. The genie has a frightening appearance. The genie appears threatening to Aladdin. Aladdin wants the genie to die. Aladdin slays the genie. King Mamoud and Jasmine wed in an extravagant ceremony.

The genie is dead. King Mamoud and Jasmine are married. The end.

Fig. 4. Text of story in test condition

two stories, making a comparison study possible. Specifically, the set of events in the test condition story is a superset of the events in the control condition story.

There is one distinct action ordering difference between the two fabula plans: the event where the King falls in love with Jasmine is temporally constrained to occur first in the test condition story but is under-constrained in the control condition story and happens to fall late in the story. Had it come earlier in the control condition, some subjects may have *inferred* a relationship between the king falling in love and Aladdin's actions even though there is no actual relationship in the QKS. However, the ordering of this particular action does not affect the QKS representation because QUEST does not capture the temporal relationship between events beyond what is needed for causal coherence. From this, we conclude that the ordering will only have an insignificant impact on the results of the comparison between subjects' mental models and the QKS for the story.

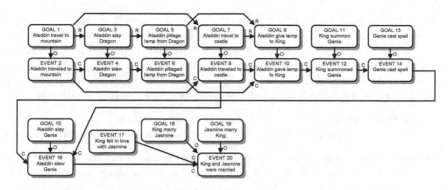

Fig. 5. QKS for the story in the control condition

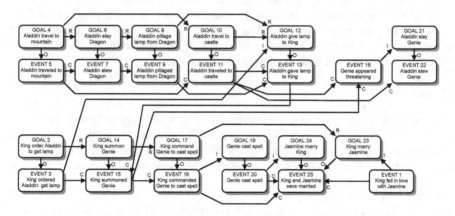

Fig. 6. QKS for the story in the test condition

The evaluation was set up as a questionnaire in which subjects read a story and then make goodness-of-answer (GOA) judgments about pairs of question and answers. A question-answer pair has a "why" question about an intentional action performed by a character in the story and a possible answer. For example, the question, "Why did Aladdin slay the dragon?" might be paired with the answer, "Because King Mamoud ordered Aladdin to get the magic lamp for him." The subjects were asked to rate the goodness of the answer for the given question on a four-point Likert scale ranging from "Very bad answer" to "Very good answer." The subjects were shown examples of a question-answer pairs before the rating task began, but were not otherwise given a definition of "good" or "poor" or trained to make the judgment. Subjects rated the GOA of a question-answer pair for every combination of goal nodes in a QKS for the story. Subjects were asked to read the story text completely at least once before proceeding to the ratings task and were allowed to refer back to the original text at any time during the rating task. The control condition questionnaire had 52 question-answer pairs while the test condition questionnaire had 82 question-answer pairs due to the increased story plan length. The question-answer pairs in each condition were evaluated by QUEST. "Why" questions were classified as "good" or "poor" based on the arc search procedure following forward reason arcs, backward initiate arcs, and backward outcome arcs [14] applied to the QKS derived from the story plan for the particular condition. The aim was to determine if there was a statistically significant difference in subjects' mean agreement with the relevant QKS between conditions. An example of a question-answer pair that is likely to be judged as "good" in the test condition but judged ambiguously in the control condition is:

Q: Why did Aladdin travel from the castle to the mountains?
A: Because King Mamoud wanted to rub the magic lamp and summon the genie.

In the test condition story, the story explicitly motivates Aladdin's sequence of actions involving traveling into the mountains and slaying the dragon – Aladdin is ordered to get the King the magic lamp. In the control condition the reason for Aladdin's sequence is left unmotivated and some readers will infer the answer to be a justifiable reason (especially in hindsight) while others will not.

Thirty-two undergraduate students in the Computer Science program at North Carolina State University participated in the study. All subjects were enrolled in the course, *Game Design and Development*, and were compensated for their time with five extra credit points on their final grade in the course.

4.3   Results

Each question-answer pair in each questionnaire was assigned a "good" rating or a "poor" rating based on the QUEST prediction. The results of subjects' answers to questionnaire answers are compiled into Table 1. The numbers are the mean GOA ratings for each category and each condition. The numbers in parentheses are standard deviations for the results.

A standard one-tailed t-test was used to compare the mean GOA rating of "good" question-answer pairs in the test condition to the mean GOA rating of "good" question-answer pairs in

Table 1. Results for character intentionality evaluation

	Mean GOA for "good" Q/A pairs (std. dev.)	Mean GOA for "poor" Q/A pairs (std. dev.)
Test condition	3.1976 (0.1741)	1.1898 (0.1406)
Control condition	2.9912 (0.4587)	1.269 (0.1802)

the control condition. The result of the t-test with 15 degrees of freedom yields $t = 1.6827$ ($p < 0.0585$). Subjects in the test condition had significantly higher GOA ratings for "good" question-answer pairs than subjects in the control condition.

A standard one-tailed t-test was used to compare the mean GOA rating of "poor" question-answer pairs in the test condition to the mean GOA rating of "poor" question-answer pairs in the control condition. The result of the t-test with 15 degrees of freedom yields $t = 1.8743$ ($p < 0.05$). Subjects in the test condition had significantly lower GOA ratings for "poor" question-answer pairs than subjects in the control condition.

Favorable results were achieved for each relevant comparison. From this we can conclude that the story in the test condition supported reader comprehension of character intentionality better than the story in the control condition. It is reasonable to infer that the improvement of the test condition over the control condition is due to enhancements to the automated story generation capability.

4.4 Discussion

There is a large degree of commonality between the two stories generated in the study, suggesting that the additional content in the IPOCL (test condition) plan had an impact on subject comprehension of character intentionality. Since subjects in the test condition are more in agreement with the QUEST model than subjects in the control condition, we conclude that stories generated by a story planner implementing the IPOCL planning algorithm support a reader's comprehension of character intentionality better than stories generated by a story planner implementing a conventional POCL planner. However, there were limitations to our study that must be taken into consideration. These limitations are largely due to our use of a novel evaluation technique and consequently the inability to foresee difficulties. We present them here as lessons learned during the application of the evaluation methodology.

The standard deviation for the control condition and "good" question-answer pairs was high. Further analysis reveals that subjects are likely to judge a question-answer pair as "good" if there is lack of evidence against the possibility that the character action might have been intentional. We speculate that reader/viewers simultaneously consider multiple hypotheses explaining character behavior until they are disproved. Regardless of the content of any communicative act, one will always be able to provide a more or less plausible explanation of the meaning [20].

One independent variable we failed to control for was story length and complexity. It is possible that the effects we measured were a result of story length and complexity instead of improved story structure generated by the story generation system. We believe this to be unlikely, but future evaluations should add to the control condition story hand-written filler sentences that do not impact character believability so that it matches the length and complexity of the test condition.

A second limitation to the evaluation, as we have already noted, was the lack of control for partial ordering of actions in the control condition. Since the story planners used for the evaluation were least-commitment planners, they did not commit to a total ordering of actions unless necessary. A total order was artificially imposed on partially-ordered action sequences so that the plans could be rendered into natural language. To be thorough we would have had to consider different total orderings to determine if ordering had an effect on reader comprehension of character intentionality. The QUEST model remains the same for all possible, legal orderings since it factors out temporal considerations that are not relevant to causality. This leads us to conclude that different orderings would not significantly impact our results. In fact, having the King fall in love with the princess sooner will likely have resulted in a wider range of GOA judgments to some question-answer pairs, making the standard deviation in the control condition higher and the difference in means with the test condition larger.

A final limitation to our evaluation of Fabulist is related to our simplistic domain modeling of discourse generation. The Longbow discourse planner [18] is a very powerful tool for discourse generation. However, we used a simplified model of discourse structures that caused explicit statements of character intention to be rendered into the story text for the test condition. That is, subjects in the test condition were told how the characters formed their intentions. We believe that our results would be the same if these explicit statements were excluded because human readers are very good at inferring intentions from observations of actions. However, to be complete, we would have to control for such artifacts from discourse generation.

5 Conclusions

The ability to computationally generate stories can result in computer systems that interact with humans in a more natural way. To date story generation systems have used autonomous multi-agent technologies and single authoring agent approaches. Regardless of the technology, automated story generation continues to improve, particularly within the bounds of character believability. It is useful, therefore, to be able to evaluate the degree to which enhancements to story generation technology improves the quality and character believability of generated stories. Instead of using subjective measures, we present a process for objectively assessing the degree of enhancement to character intentionality – one important aspect of character believability – in generated stories. The process relies on the fact that a reader/viewer's perception of character intentionality can be compared to a QUEST representation of the story because QUEST is a validated model of human question-answering in the context of stories. We present the evaluation process and illustrate it by describing how it was applied to the evaluation of the Fabulist story generation system.

Acknowledgements

This work has been supported by NSF CAREER award 0092586. Statements and opinions expressed do not necessarily reflect the position or the policy of the United States Government, and no official endorsement should be inferred.

References

1. Meehan, J.R.: *The Metanovel: Writing Stories by Computer*. Ph.D. Dissertation, Yale University (1976).
2. Cavazza, M., Charles, F., &Mead, S.: Planning characters' behaviour in interactive storytelling. *Journal of Visualization and Computer Animation*, vol. 13 (2002) 121-131.
3. Charles, F. & Cavazza, M.: Exploring the scalability of character-based storytelling. *Proceedings of the 3rd International Joint Conference on Autonomous Agents and Multi Agent Systems* (2004).
4. Lebowitz, M.: Story-telling as planning and learning. *Poetics*, vol. 14 (1985) 483-502.
5. Riedl, M.O. & Young, R.M.: An intent-driven planner for multi-agent story generation. *Proceedings of the 3rd International Joint Conference on Autonomous Agents and Multi-Agent Systems* (2003).
6. Riedl, M.O.: *Narrative Planning: Balancing Plot and Character*. Ph.D. Dissertation. North Carolina State University (2004).

7. Turner, S.R.: *The Creative Process: A Computer Model of Storytelling*. Hillsdale, NJ: Lawrence Erlbaum Associates (1994).
8. Szilas, N.: IDtension: A narrative engine for interactive drama. *Proceedings of the 1st International Conference on Technologies for Interactive Digital Storytelling and Entertainment* (2003).
9. Mateas, M.: *Interactive Art, Drama, and Artificial Intelligence*. Ph.D. Disssertation, Carnegie Mellon University (2002).
10. Mateas, M. & Stern, A.: Integrating plot, character, and natural language processing in the interactive drama Façade. *Proceedings of the 1st International Conference on Technologies for Interactive Digital Storytelling and Entertainment* (2003).
11. Bates, J.: The role of emotion in believable agents. *Communications of the ACM*, vol. 37 (1994).
12. Sengers, P.: Narrative and schizophrenia in artificial agents. In M. Mateas and P. Sengers (Eds.) *Narrative Intelligence*. John Benjamins, Amsterdam (2003).
13. Gerrig, R.J.: *Experiencing Narrative Worlds: On the Psychological Activities of Reading*. Yale University Press, New Haven (1993).
14. Graesser, A.C., Lang, K.L., & Roberts, R.M.: Question answering in the context of stories. *Journal of Experimental Psychology: General*, vol. 120 (1991).
15. Christian, D.B. & Young, R.M.: Comparing cognitive and computational models of narrative structure. *Proceedings of the 19th National Conference on Artificial Intelligence* (2004).
16. Young, R.M.: Notes on the use of planning structures in the creation of interactive plot. In: M. Mateas and P. Sengers (Eds.): *Narrative Intelligence: Papers from the 1999 Fall Symposium*. American Association for Artificial Intelligence, Menlo Park CA (1999).
17. Penberthy, J.S. & Weld, D.: UCPOP: A sound, complete, partial-order planner for ADL. *Proceedings of the 3rd International Conference on Knowledge Representation and Reasoning* (1992).
18. Young, R.M., Moore, J.D., & Pollack, M.E.: Towards a principled representation of discourse plans. *Proceedings of the 16th Conference of the Cognitive Science Society* (1994).
19. Callaway, C.B. & Lester, J.C.: Narrative prose generation. *Artificial Intelligence*, vol. 139 (2002).
20. Sadock, J.M.: Comments on Vanderveken and on Cohen and Levesque. In: P.R. Cohen, J. Morgan, and M.E. Pollack (Eds.): *Intentions in Communication*. The MIT Press, Cambridge MA (1990) 257-270.

Proactive Mediation in Plan-Based Narrative Environments

Justin Harris and R. Michael Young

North Carolina State University,
Department of Computer Science,
{jtharris, young}@csc.ncsu.edu

Abstract. In interactive plan-based narrative environments, user's actions must be monitored to ensure that conditions necessary for the execution of narrative plans are not compromised. In the Mimesis system, management of user actions is performed on a reactionary basis by a process called mediation. In this paper, we describe an extension to this approach, proactive mediation, which calculates responses to user input in an anticipatory manner. A proactive mediation module accepts as input a plan describing the actions being performed by the user (generated by a plan recognition system) and identifies portions of that plan that jeopardize the causal structure of the overall narrative. Once these portions are identified, proactive mediation generates modifications to the narrative plan structure that avoid the unwanted interaction between user and story. This extension to the original mediation algorithm provides more responses to a user's actions and generates responses that are tailored to the user's actions.

1 Introduction

Recently, a number of interactive applications, including computer games, training simulations, and intelligent tutoring software involve a human user interacting with one or more embedded agents acting in a virtual environment. These applications often require the agents, in concert with the user, to perform coordinated sequences of novel actions structured as an unfolding story or narrative. One approach used to address the coordination of the actions within these story-based systems is the use of a centralized planning system, in which a single planner defines the actions of all agents in a narrative plan [1,2,3].

If the user in such plan-based systems is allowed a significant amount of autonomy, careful attention must be paid to guarantee that she does not alter the environment such that those actions specified by the planning system cannot be performed. A previously defined process called reactive mediation [4] addresses this issue by pre-determining responses to destructive user behavior. One noteworthy limitation of reactive mediation is that user behavior is examined on a per action basis. That is, mediation responses are taken only at the point where the harmful action is performed. While preserving the validity of the plan's causal structure, this approach fails to take into account the larger

T. Panayiotopoulos et al. (Eds.): IVA 2005, LNCS 3661, pp. 292–304, 2005.
© Springer-Verlag Berlin Heidelberg 2005

context of the user's actions. Often, a user performs a *sequence* of actions leading to some desired result, in which one or more of those actions may be harmful to the global plan.

In this paper, an extension to reactive mediation, a process called *proactive mediation*, is described. Rather than examining single user actions, the proactive mediation module examines a proposed plan (provided by an external plan recognition component) that the user is performing in the context of a larger story. Having knowledge about hypothetical future actions that the user may execute allows the proactive mediation module to generate a wider variety of responses to potential harmful user activity, as well as to shape those responses to better integrate with the overall course of the narrative.

2   Background

Generating responses to unanticipated change in an environment has been addressed by a number of research efforts. Firby's Reactive Action Packages define various action sequences that a robot can perform for a given task in case of failure [5]. Gordon and Iuppa [6] introduce storyline adaptation strategies which define the ways that a story can change in response to unanticipated user action at choice points in a story. Steve, an animated pedagogical agent, monitors user activity and appropriately responds if a user interrupts the current task being demonstrated [7]. While these approaches deal with the generation of responses to unexpected behavior as it arises, none of these systems exploit expectations about likely future events to alter the unfolding action.

In contrast, work by Magerko and Laird [8] incorporates hypothesized future user behavior in the Interactive Drama Architecture (IDA) system. IDA uses a rule-based user model to predict world state changes between predefined plot points in a narrative. Their model is used to determine if a user's expected actions are likely to satisfy the preconditions of any plot points and to adapt their execution environment accordingly to further advance the story. While their approach detects and reacts to anticipated inconsistencies in the story, the system responds to expected user actions only at the end of the simulation created by their rule-base. In contrast, the process we define below uses an explicit plan representation to describe hypothesized user behavior. This representation not only allows for planning responses to user actions, but also identifies specific harmful actions and the conditions they require for execution. The resulting system can preemptively alter the world state and the actions the system will execute in order to prevent the user from performing some harmful action.

The following section contains a brief overview of Mimesis, the system in which our approach is implemented. For a more detailed description, see [3].

2.1   Mimesis Architecture

The Mimesis system architecture is a distributed, service-oriented approach to the generation and execution of interactive narratives within virtual environments. Components of the system communicate via XML across the internet to reason about high-level narrative structure.

Two of these components are central to the discussion here: a story planning system based on the Longbow planning system [9] and the component that serves as the virtual world interface between a user and the rest of Mimesis. This component, called the MWorld, contains logic for translating declarative descriptions of the narrative produced by the planning system into function calls that execute directly in the user's virtual environment.

The planning component of Mimesis is used to generate the story structure executed by the characters within the story world. Before an interactive session begins, the planning system builds a story plan which represents the actions of all the agents in the story world, including those of the user. Longbow plan structures are similar to those used in partial-order, causal link and HTN-style planning systems [10,11]. The plans contain annotations that explicitly mark the temporal relationships between all actions in the story plan, defining a partial order indicating the steps' order of execution. Other annotations, called causal links, mark all causal relationships between the actions in the plan as well. A causal link connects plan steps s_1 and s_2 via condition e, written $s_1 \rightarrow^e s_2$ when s_1 establishes the condition e needed by subsequent action s_2 to execute.

Once the planning system has generated a plan for a story, a scheduler component called the execution manager translates the plan structure into a directed acyclic graph (DAG) representing the temporal dependencies between the steps in the plan. As steps in the DAG are ready to execute, the manager sends commands to the MWorld invoking the corresponding function calls. The MWorld provides updates to the execution manager regarding the status of each function's execution; as each function call completes, the manager updates the temporal dependencies within the execution DAG and sends commands to execute the next set of plan actions.

2.2   Reactive Mediation

As described above, Mimesis drives the action within its story world based on the structure of a plan produced by a narrative planner. Plan execution is complicated, however, because users are relatively unconstrained with respect to the actions that they can perform in the world as the plan is being executed. The plans used by Mimesis are dependent upon user actions, both because some user actions are required for the plans to progress and because the consequences of user actions may inadvertently interfere with the world state on which the plan structure depends. As users issue commands for their characters to perform actions within the story world, these actions must be checked against the narrative plan to determine how they fit with the plan's structure. This process, called *reactive mediation*, is described in detail in [4]. We provide a summary of the process below as background for the extension to mediation that is the main contribution of this paper.

Characterizing User Actions. As the user performs an action, Mimesis must characterize the act with respect to the story's requirements; actions that the story is depending upon must be identified in order for the story to progress, while actions that interfere with the story's structure must be identified so that the damage that they might cause to the narrative can be avoided or minimized. By comparing each action executed by the user to the structure of the story world plan, Mimesis automatically characterizes user actions into one of three categories: constituent, consistent, and exceptional.

A *constituent* action is one that maps directly to a step in the story world plan. The action's type, arguments and temporal and causal structure all match the corresponding constraints on a step specified for user execution.

A *consistent* action is one that is not constituent and whose effects do not alter the virtual world in a way that interferes with the successful execution of the story world plan. Specifically, an action a is consistent just when it is not constituent and, for each of its effects e, there is no causal link in the story world plan that spans the point in time where a is being executed and that is labeled $\neg e$. In practice, most user actions fall into this category.

An *exceptional* action is neither constituent nor consistent, that is, at least one of the effects of the action threatens a causal link in the narrative plan. Formally, action a with effect $\neg e$ threatens causal link $s_1 \rightarrow^e s_2$ when a is performed after s_1 and before s_2. Exceptional actions, if allowed to execute, break the causal dependencies on which a story plan is based, making the plan impossible to execute.

Responding to Exceptional Actions. When exceptional actions are initiated by the user, their execution changes the state of the story world in such a way that the story plan is no longer executable. In order to prevent this consequence, the Mimesis execution manager monitors each command sent by the user to the virtual world, characterizing it immediately as consistent, constituent or exceptional. When an exception is detected, the system determines an appropriate response before the user's command is queued for execution. The Mimesis execution manager responds to each exception either by preventing the exception's threatening effect to be established or by adjusting the narrative such that the action's performance poses no threat. These outcomes are achieved by *accommodation* or *intervention*, described briefly below.

When an exceptional action is accommodated, it is allowed to execute, and the remaining plan is restructured so that no causal links are threatened. This restructuring can often be slight, such as selecting a different character to perform a task. However, in certain cases, the revised narrative plan may be substantially different from the original, requiring significant computation on the part of the planner. Further discussion of this re-planning process is beyond the scope of this paper.

When an exceptional action is handled by intervention, an alternative action is executed in its place. This alternative action, instantiated from a set of pre-defined failure modes, is similar in appearance and function to the exceptional action, but has a different set of preconditions and effects.

Policy Tables. The process of revising plans and finding suitable failure modes is complex, and cannot reliably execute in an acceptable amount of time if performed when the exception occurs. In order to provide satisfactory response time when an exception does occur, accommodations and interventions are generated in advance, and held in the *mediation policy table*.

After generating a narrative plan but prior to its execution, Mimesis examines the plan's causal structure and identifies which user actions can cause exceptions at every point in the plan where a user may act. For every possible exception, a queue of appropriate responses (interventions and accommodations) is computed. This action/response queue pair is inserted as an entry into a mediation policy table, along with the interval in the narrative plan during when the action can be performed. The queue of responses is sorted by a heuristic function which determines a qualitative measure of the responses' effectiveness.

3   Extending Mediation

One significant limitation of reactive mediation is that it responds to user activity at the last possible moment. While this approach localizes the point in a story where a user's agency may need to be restricted, intervention and accommodation at the point of an exception can be problematic. Consider a scenario in which the user executes a long series of actions that clearly lead to an exceptional action, for instance, besieging the castle of a story's central character, capturing him and then attempting to kill him. If the system allows the user to spend the time and resources to capture the nobleman, but then intervenes repeatedly as the user swings his sword, the user will not only be frustrated with his apparent inability to hit his target but also with the failure of the system to have guided the story more effectively. The user has put in significant effort in pursuit of a particular course of action, and yet the system has done nothing to deter the user until the action sequence's very end.

This problem is addressed by proactive mediation, which preemptively restructures the narrative plan to better account for anticipated user activity. Rather than monitoring the user's activity only as it occurs, a proactive mediator also examines the user's anticipated plan of action provided by an external plan recognition component (e.g., [12,13]). Steps in the user's anticipated plan[1] are characterized as constituent, consistent, or exceptional, just as individual actions are categorized under reactive mediation. Proactive mediation extends the notions of intervention and accommodation to avoid threats from exceptional steps that have not yet occurred. While the basic objectives of reactive and proactive mediation are the same, a proactive mediator's knowledge of expected future steps is utilized to allow a wider range of responses to user activity.

3.1   Proactive Mediation Input

As described above, Mimesis uses a plan representation to describe story events in a virtual environment. Proactive mediation uses the same plan representation

---

[1] Here, it is appropriate to make the distinction between a step and an action. A step refers to a data structure which describes an event in the virtual world. A plan contains a set of steps, whose referent events,, at the time of planning, have not yet occurred. An action refers to an event which is occurring at the present time, regardless of whether or not it is described in a plan.

to describe likely future event sequences that the user may perform. This plan is supplied by a plan recognition component which, upon recognizing a user's plan, submits it to the proactive mediator. A plan is defined formally below.

Plan: A plan is a tuple $< S, B, O, L >$ where S is the set of steps, B is the set of binding constraints on the steps in S, O is the set of ordering constraints between steps in S, and L is the set of causal links between steps in S. The proactive mediator takes as input a *narrative* plan, a *recognized* plan and an *operator library*, defined formally below:

Narrative plan: A narrative plan is a plan $N :< S_N, B_N, O_N, L_N >$ generated by the Mimesis system which describes all of the steps to be performed by the characters in a story, including those of the user. We say that a step s is a narrative step just when $s \in S_N$.

Recognized plan: A recognized plan is a plan $R :< S_R, B_R, O_R, L_R >$ that is proposed by a plan recognition system. This plan hypothesizes the sequence of steps that the user intends to perform, and that the user expects to occur. We say that a step s is a recognized step just when $s \in S_R$.

Operator library: An operator library is a collection of operators characterizing the actions available for the given story world domain, instantiated as steps. An operator is a tuple $< P, E >$ where P is a set of preconditions that must hold true before the step is executed, and E is a set of effects that are true after the step is executed. Each step in either the narrative plan or the recognized plan can be a system step (any action executed by system resources, characters, etc) or a user step (one initiated by the user and performed by the user's character) and is identified by a unique ID. The set of system steps is denoted S_{SYS}, where $S_{SYS} \in (S_N \cup S_R)$. The set of user steps is denoted S_{USER}, where $S_{USER} \in (S_N \cup S_R)$.

3.2 Generating the Mediated Plan and Identifying Steps

The first step in the proactive mediation process is the creation of a working plan that encapsulates the actions of both input plans. This new plan, called the *mediated plan*, is formed by merging the narrative and recognized plans in the following manner. To simplify the current discussion, a step in the narrative plan and a step in the recognized plan whose IDs are identical are assumed to refer to the same event. The mediated plan is thus a tuple $M =< S_M, B_M, O_M, L_M >$ where $S_M = S_R \cup S_N$, $B_M = B_R \cup B_N$, $O_M = O_R \cup O_N$ and $L_M = L_R \cup L_N$.

Once the mediated plan is created, the steps in the recognized plan are then categorized as *inclusive* or *exclusive*. Inclusive steps occur in both plans (i.e., N and R), while exclusive steps only occur in the recognized plan. Inclusive steps may be either user steps or system steps, while exclusive steps are assumed to be only performed by the user. That is, it is assumed that the user will not plan for system steps to occur which are not actually part of the narrative plan.

A step s is an inclusive step just when $s \in S_R \cap S_N$. The set of inclusive steps is denoted S_{IN}. A step s is an exclusive step just when $s \in S_R$ and $s \notin S_N$. The set of exclusive steps is denoted S_{EXL}.

User steps can be constituent, consistent, or exceptional, just as user actions. The definitions of these steps are similar to their action counterparts, with the understanding that the steps refer to future events. The one deviation is the definition of an exceptional step, which can be described as a potential exceptional action given the ordering constraints of the mediated plan. All inclusive steps that are performed by the user are identified as constituent, and all exclusive steps are identified as either consistent or exceptional.

Constituent Step: A step s is constituent just when $s \in S_{IN} \cap S_{USER}$.

Exceptional Step: A step s with effect $\neg e$ is exceptional just when **a)** $s \in S_{USER}$, **b)** $\exists s_1 \rightarrow^e s_2 \in L_N$, and **c)** s is not required to come before s_1 or after s_2, based on the transitive closure of the ordering constraints within O_M. The set of exceptional steps is denoted S_{EXP}.

Consistent Step: A step s is consistent just when $s \in S_{EXL} - S_{EXP}$.

3.3 Handling Exceptional Steps

Once the steps in the mediated plan have been characterized, the mediator then determines how to respond to each exceptional step. We say that an exceptional step is avoided when the mediator alters the narrative plan in a manner that deals with the harmful effects of the exceptional step. For each exceptional step $s_x \in S_M$ with effect $\neg e$ that threatens some causal link $s_1 \rightarrow^e s_2 \in L_M$, s_x can be avoided by:

- *Proactive Intervention*: Stopping the user from performing step s_x in the mediated plan.
- *Proactive Accommodation*: Eliminating the need for the causal link $s_1 \rightarrow^e s_2$ in the mediated plan.
- *Proactive Reordering*: Enforcing orderings such that s_x cannot occur between s_1 and s_2.

Proactive Intervention. The purpose of intervention is to prevent the exception's threatening condition from being established. Reactive intervention achieves this by replacing the execution of the exceptional action with the execution one of its failure modes that does not have the threatening condition as an effect. This solution is also possible under proactive intervention. However, since an exception considered by the proactive mediator has not yet occurred, additional action can be taken by the system to make one or more preconditions of the exception false, thus making the action itself un-executable. This can be achieved by executing a system step which makes a condition false, or by removing a step that causally leads to the exception.

Proactive intervention prevents the user from performing some exceptional step s_x in question. This can be done by stopping the execution of s_x itself, or any step that *contributes* to s_x.

A step s_1 contributes to s_x just when $\exists s_1 \rightarrow^e s_x \in L_M$ or some other step s_2 contributes to s_x and $\exists s_1 \rightarrow^e s_2 \in L_M$. The execution of each contributory or exceptional step s in the mediated plan can be avoided via intervention by one of the following measures:

Substitution: Prevent the exceptional step from establishing the threatening condition by replacing s with one of its failure modes s^*. If s is contributory, s^* must be selected so that at least one of the conditions established by s and used in a contributory causal link is not asserted by s^*. If s is exceptional, the effects of the failure mode must not threaten any causal link in the narrative plan. If the substituted failure mode has any preconditions which are not in the original step, those preconditions are considered open, and appropriate flaws are added to the plan. Fixing these flaws requires additional plan construction in order to make the resulting plan complete.

Aversion: Prevent the execution of s by making one or more preconditions of s false at the point immediately prior to its execution. This is achieved by inserting a system step s_i, called an inversion step, into the plan. Step s_i has an effect $\neg f$, where f is a precondition of s. Additional ordering constraints are added such that s_i must come before s, and s_i must come after all steps which establish f, including the original source of the causal link. If the resulting plan's ordering constraints are inconsistent, aversion using s_i cannot be performed.

Although the inversion step s_i is ordered before s, there is no guarantee that the condition $\neg f$ will be established before s is executed by the user. A race condition exists between the system's execution of s_i and the user's execution of s; if s appears early in the recognized plan, or if a long sequence of steps is required to establish $\neg f$, then s could be executed first. This race condition is avoided by the system "instantaneously" executing the aversion steps, unconstrained by rules in the virtual world such as animation times or physics . For instance, the system can programmatically shut and lock a door without requiring that a character perform the act. This approach will work, however, only if a) the user does not already know the status of any aversion effects, and b) the user cannot directly observe the state changing from these actions.

Disablement: Remove a contributory inclusive step s from the mediated plan. This prevents s from establishing causal links which contribute to an exceptional step. Once s has been removed (along with all causal links, variable bindings and step orderings relating to s), conditions in the narrative plan that were satisfied by s are no longer satisfied, and some re-planning will be required to reestablish those conditions.

Proactive Accommodation. Proactive accommodation allows the user to perform the exceptional step s_x; in response, the system re-plans the narrative to reestablish any causal links threatened by s_x's effects. In this regard, there is no difference between proactive accommodation and reactive accommodation, and the basic mechanism does not differ between the two. The fundamental difference between proactive accommodation and reactive accommodation is that proactive accommodation can alter the narrative steps which occur prior to s_1. By modifying steps prior to s_1, proactive accommodation can eliminate extraneous steps from being executed to establish the original causal link, resulting in a narrative plan that is potentially more coherent. Further, plans generated with proactive accommodation can use effects of exclusive steps in the recognized plan to satisfy any open preconditions, potentially giving the user a stronger sense of participation in the story line.

Proactive Reordering. Proactive Reordering introduces additional orderings to the narrative plan that make it temporally impossible for s_x to be executed between s_1 and s_2. Conceptually, there are two ways to enforce this: add the ordering $s_x < s_1$, or add the ordering $s_2 < s_x$. Both of these options effectively reorder the steps to prevent s_x from being executed between s_1 and s_2, but neither option is particularly viable.

If the ordering $s_x < s_1$ is introduced into the mediated plan, Mimesis would wait for the user to perform s_x before executing s_1. This rigid requirement can easily stall the entire narrative if the plan recognition component proposed an inaccurate plan, or if the user simply changed her mind about performing s_x.

Enforcing the ordering $s_2 < s_x$ can be problematic as well, for the simple reason that s_x is to be performed by the user. Stopping the user from executing s_x if attempted before s_2 is already accomplished by reactive intervention.

There is a case, however, in which system steps can be reordered such that s_x can only be executed after s_2. If $\exists s_c \in S_{IN} \cap S_{SYS}$ and s_c is ordered before s_x, adding the ordering $s_2 < s_c$, implicitly ensures that s_x cannot occur before s_2 (assuming that the ordering is consistent with the mediated plan).

3.4   Re-planning

A number of mediation strategies described above involve removing elements of the mediated plan and filling in the resulting gaps with alternative plan structure. The re-planning process used to fill in the missing plan structure is similar to the plan generation process we use, with one notable difference: no ordering link $s_n < s_e$ can be added to the plan, where s_n is a narrative step and s_e is an exclusive user performed step. This restriction is in place because the system has no direct control over when s_e will be performed, since its execution is left up to the user. As a result, s_e's execution cannot be guaranteed to follow that ordering. Ordering links and causal links are, however, allowed from exclusive steps to narrative steps, which can act to further involve the user in the narrative by effectively making exclusive actions inclusive.

3.5   Mediation Algorithm

A single mediated plan can potentially contain multiple exceptions, which must all be avoided before the plan can become the active storyline and begin execution. The mediation algorithm used to avoid all of the exceptions is similar in many respects to our planning algorithm, which can be characterized as a *refinement search* through a plan space graph [14]. A node in the graph represents a partial plan, and a node's children are refinements of a specific flaw in the parent. Similarly, the mediation algorithm is a refinement search through a

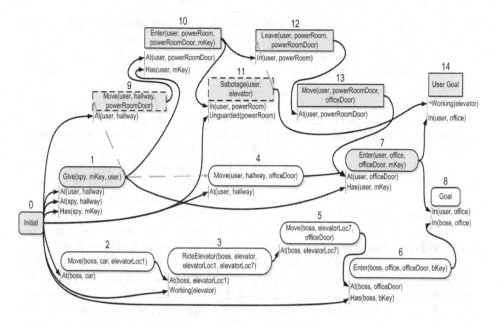

Fig. 1. An example of a merged plan, with all steps identified: the rounded nodes indicate narrative steps, the gray nodes indicate recognized steps, the box nodes indicate exclusive steps, and the dashed nodes indicate exceptional steps. Solid arrows represent causal links, dashed arrows represent ordering constraints.

mediation space graph, where a node represents a plan and its corresponding policy table, and a node's children are responses to a specific exception. Search through this mediation space is guided by an author-defined heuristic, which is used to qualitatively evaluate each plan/policy table pair. This heuristic could be derived from the same planning heuristic used to generate the original story plan, so that proactive responses that coincide with the author's intended story are favored.

While expanding the mediation space tree, choosing an exception to avoid is not completely arbitrary. Avoiding an earlier exception can (in the case of intervention) implicitly avoid any exceptions that are causally dependent on the former, so only candidate exceptions that have no contributory exceptions are chosen.

4   Example

The following is an example of a mediated plan just after the narrative plan and recognized plan have been merged and the steps identified. The original narrative plan describes the events in a single chapter of a larger story, in which a secret agent played by the user is attempting to acquire secret documents by posing as an employee of a corporation. The chapter ends with the user being caught in her boss's office looking for the documents. The scenario begins with the user being given a master key to the building by a collaborator on the inside (*spy*), and then walking to her boss's office and using the master key to enter. At the same time, the boss arrives in his car, takes the elevator to the seventh floor, and then enters his office. This narrative corresponds to steps 0-8 in the merged plan depicted in Figure 1.

The clever user, knowing that the boss rides the elevator every morning, decides to sabotage the elevator so that she will not be caught. This threatens the narrative plan, as the goal of this portion of the story is for the user to be caught. Specifically, *Move* (Step 9) is identified as exceptional because one of its effects, ¬*At*(*user, hallway*), threatens the causal link between the *InitialState* (Step 0) and *Move* (Step 4). Similarly, *Sabotage* (Step 11) is identified as exceptional because one of its effects, ¬*Working*(*elevator*), threatens the causal link between the *InitialState* (Step 0) and *RideElevator* (Step 3).

The first exceptional step, *Move* (Step 9), must be allowed to execute, because no failure modes have been defined for *Move*, and no inversion steps exists which can move the user to a different location (she must do this on her own). The only viable option is accommodation, which in this case can remove *Move* (Step 4) and all associated causal links and ordering constraints. This does not introduce any new flaws to plan because *Move* (Step 13) also establishes the condition *At*(*user, officeDoor*) which was originally established by *Move* (Step 4).

Substitution can be used to stop the user from sabotaging the elevator, by replacing *Sabotage* (Step 11) with a failure mode, or by replacing any exclusive contributory step (Steps 9 or 10) with a failure mode. Performing a substitution on the *Sabotage* step is handled by reactive mediation (since that single action is exceptional), and in this world no failure modes have been defined for the *Move* operator. The *Enter* operator, however, does have a failure mode defined, which is called *JammedDoor*. This failure mode results in the door not opening and the user not being in the power room.

Aversion can also be used to mediate this plan by inserting a *Move* step followed by an inversion step: *StandWatch*, which moves the seventh floor's security guard to watch over the power room. This has an effect of ¬*Unguarded*(*powerRoom*), which prevents the user's character from sabotaging the elevator. Note that the animations for walking the security guard to the power room do not need to play out if the user is not in the area (the action is not observable). The system can simply make the effects of the step true, in effect"warping" the guard to his new post.

The third form of intervention, disablement, can be applied to *Give* (Step 1), because it is the only inclusive step that contributes to *Sabotage* (Step 11). After removing the step from the mediated plan, two preconditions are left open (in Steps 10 and 7). Some additional planning is required to reestablish *Has*(*user, ?key*-7) with the additional constraint that *Has*(*user, ?key*-10) is not reestablished. In this particular world, the spy has a second key which only opens the boss's door, so one alternate plan replaces *Give* (Step 1) with a different *Give*, in which this second key is given to the user.

Accommodation allows the user to sabotage the elevator, planning around the *Working(elevator)* causal link between the *InitialState* (Step 0) and *RideElevator* (Step 3). Alternate plans can include a repairman fixing the elevator, or the boss taking the stairs instead.

The *Sabotage* step can also be allowed if it occurs after the boss is on the seventh floor. This can be achieved by adding the ordering constraint 3 < 1 to the plan, which waits for the boss to be on the seventh floor before the spy gives the user the master key.

5   Conclusions

In many interactive environments, a human user is permitted to manipulate the environment in a variety of ways. In a plan-based narrative environment, this manipulation may disrupt the actions of other agents or even the actions that the system intends the user to perform. Proactive mediation expands upon reactive mediation to generate a variety of responses to a user's proposed sequence of actions in the environment. Having a hypothesis about future user actions allows proactive mediation to generate a broader range of responses to user actions that can be temporally distributed over the course of a plan.

There are, however, additional factors to consider in evaluating our approach. Proactive mediation relies on effective plan recognition and can be sensitive to the frequency of change in input from the plan recognition component. In addition, planning is computationally complex; in cases where many proactive responses require re-planning, there is no guarantee that an appropriate response can be generated within a reasonable amount of time. However, our preliminary consideration indicates that plans containing potential exceptions occur relatively rarely compared to the number of actions a user is, in practice, likely to perform at any given moment within a story. Most user actions are consistent or constituent; it is the effects of exceptions on the coherence of the story rather than their frequency that motivates the need to address them. While computation performed by proactive mediation can be costly in some cases, the approach we outline is readily implemented as an anytime algorithm: should proactive mediation fail to generate a response in time to address an exception, reactive mediation can still be used. Similarly, should reactive mediation fail to generate an accommodation in time, intervention (which typically amounts to a straightforward look-up) can be invoked.

Finally, restructuring the narrative plan may result in system-controlled agents performing actions that are not clearly motivated. Our current work includes integration of the proactive mediation component with an intent-driven planner [15] that generates plans where agents' actions can be understood in terms of their own beliefs, desires, and intentions.

Acknowledgments

This work has been supported by National Science Foundation CAREER award 0092586 and by Microsoft Research's University Grants Program.

References

1. Cavazza, M., Charles, F., Mead, S.: Planning characters' behaviour in interactive storytelling. The Journal of Visualization and Computer Animation **13** (2002) 121–131
2. Mateas, M., Stern, A.: Architecture, authorial idioms and early observations of the interactive drama façade. Technical Report CMU-CS-02-198, Carnegie Mellon University (2002)
3. Young, R.M., Riedl, M., Branly, M., Martin, R., Saretto, C.: An architecture for integrating plan-based behavior generation with interactive game environments. Journal of Game Development **1** (2004) 52–70
4. Riedl, M., Saretto, C., Young, R.M.: Managing interaction between users and agents in a multi-agent storytelling environment. In: Proceedings of the Second International Conference on Autonomous Agents and Multiagent Systems. (2003) 741–748
5. Firby, R.J.: Adaptive Execution in Complex Dynamic Worlds. PhD thesis, Yale University (1989)
6. Gordon, A.S., Iuppa, N.V.: Experience management using storyline adaptation strategies. In: Proceedings of Technologies for Interactive Digital Storytelling and Entertainment Conference. (2003) 19–30
7. Rickel, J., Johnson, W.: Animated agents for procedural training in virtual reality: Perception, cognition, and motor control. Applied Artificial Intelligence **13** (1999) 343–382
8. Magerko, B., Laird, J.: Mediating the tension between plot and interaction. In: AAAI Workshop Series: Challenges in Game AI. (2004) 108–112
9. Young, R.M., Pollak, M., Moore, J.: Decomposition and causality in partial-order planning. In: Proceedings of the Second AI Planning and Scheduling Conference. (1994) 188–193
10. Penberthy, J.S., Weld, D.S.: UCPOP: A sound, complete, partial order planner for ADL. In Nebel, B., Rich, C., Swartout, W., eds.: KR'92. Principles of Knowledge Representation and Reasoning: Proceedings of the Third International Conference, San Mateo, California, Morgan Kaufmann (1992) 103–114
11. Sacerdoti, E.: The nonlinear nature of plans. In: Advance Papers of the Fourth International Joint Conference on Artificial Intelligence. (1975) 206–214
12. Albrect, D., Zuckerman, I., Nicholson, A.: Baysian models for keyhole plan recognition in an adventure game. User Modeling and User-Adapted Interaction **8** (1998) 5–47
13. Fagan, M., Cunningham, P.: Case-based plan recognition in computer games. In: Proceedings of the 5th International Conference on Case-Based Reasoning. (2003) 161–170
14. Kambhampati, S., Knoblock, C.A., Yang, Q.: Planning as refinement search: A unified framework for evaluating design tradeoffs in partial-order planning. Artificial Intelligence **76** (1995) 167–238
15. Riedl, M., Young, R.M.: An intent-driven planner for multi-agent story generation. In: Proceedings of the 3rd Autonomous Agents and Multiagent Systems Conference. (2004) 186 – 193

FearNot! - An Experiment in Emergent Narrative

R.S. Aylett[1], S. Louchart[2], J. Dias[3], A. Paiva[3], and M.Vala[3]

[1] MACS, Heriot-Watt University, Riccarton, Edinburgh EH10 4AS
ruth@macs.hw.ac.uk
[2] Centre for Virtual Environments, University of Salford, Salford M5 4WT
s.louchart@salford,ac.uk
[3] Instituto Superior Tecnico and INESC-ID, Av. Prof. Cavaco Silva, IST, Taguspark,
Porto Salvo, Portugal
ana.paiva@inesc-id.pt, joao.dias@gaips.inesc-id.pt
marco.vala@tagus.ist.utl.pt

Abstract. We discuss the experience of constructing the application FearNot!
(Fun with Empathic Agents Reaching Novel Outcomes in Teaching), an application of virtual drama to anti-bullying education inspired by Forum Theatre.
An appraisal-driven agent architecture is presented as a mechanism for generating an emergent, that is, unscripted, narrative. A small-scale evaluation is discussed and the lessons learned are described.

1 Introduction

Virtual Storytelling (VS) has recently become an active research field in AI with enthusiastic researchers, active working groups and a growing community [6,12, 13, 15,
16, 18]. Although the VS community is now well established there are still many fundamental differences between approaches and frameworks and no generally agreed
theoretical framework has as yet been established.

The concept of *Emergent narrative* [1, 2, 3,11] addresses the narrative paradox [3]
observed in graphically represented VS. It revolves around the conflict between pre-
authored narrative structures – especially plot - and the freedom a VE offers a user in
physical movement and interaction, integral to a feeling of physical presence and immersion. The overall project could be described as the creation of a graphical system
involving participating users in a highly flexible real-time environment where authorial activities are minimised and the distinction between authoring–time and presenta-
tion-time is substantially removed. Authorial activities would be limited to the set up
of the story – in particular to the creation of characters and their milieu - and to providing the users with the necessary background information needed for them to play a
significant part in the unfolding of the story. There would be no pre-determined end to
the story or event time line, the development of the story would be handed to both the
user and the Intelligent Agents and depend entirely on the interactions between themselves and their environment. The role of the author would thus be limited to the one
of elaborating a high-level plot: this would be necessarily hypothetical in nature, since
though it would be possible to have an idea of what the different characters could do,
there would be no certainty that they would behave as expected.

T. Panayiotopoulos et al. (Eds.): IVA 2005, LNCS 3661, pp. 305–316, 2005.
© Springer-Verlag Berlin Heidelberg 2005

The richness of characters and world together with advanced user interaction modalities needed to make this a reality are formidable, and as an initial step towards the overall concept, we describe here a much smaller-scale application of the ideas of emergent narrative in the demonstrator FearNot! – created as part of the EU-funded project VICTEC – Virtual ICT with Empathic Characters.

2 FearNot!

VICTEC, involving five partners in the UK, Germany and Portugal, sought to apply virtual dramas acted out by 3D graphically-embodied characters to what is known generically in the UK as Personal and Social Education (PSE) (or more recently as Personal, Social and Health Education – PSHE). This covers topics such as education against bullying and racism, on drugs, including smoking and alcohol, and sex education. A common thread in these topics is that knowledge in and of itself is not sufficient to meet the pedagogical objectives, since attitudes and emotions are at least as important to producing desired rather than undesired behaviour. For this reason, techniques such as small-group discussion, role-play and dramatic performance by Theatre-in-Education TiE) groups may be used.

A motivation for the project was to try to create some of the impact of dramatic performance through virtual dramas. The specific topic selected was anti-bullying education. Effective though theatrical performance is in this domain, it is necessarily collective, and in any group it is very likely that some individuals will be victims of bullying by some other in the group and thus will be inhibited in their participation. Thus a virtual drama application that could be used by the individual seemed to have a possible use.

The aim of the FearNot! (Fun with Empathic Agents Reaching Novel outcomes in Teaching) demonstrator was to allow children to explore what happens in bullying in an unthreatening environment in which they took responsibility for what happened to a victim, without themselves feeling victimized. The creation of an empathic relationship between child and character was seen as the mechanism through which this sense of responsibility would be achieved, so that the child user would really care what happened to the victimized character. The child was asked to act as an 'invisible friend', and to give advice which would influence the behaviour of the victim without undermining its autonomy of action and the child's ability to believe in it as a character with an independent inner life.

The interactional structure of FearNot! was inspired by the Forum Theatre approach developed by Brazilian dramatist Augusto Boal [5] in order to incorporate theatre into the development of political activism. In this dramatic form, an audience is split into groups, with each group taking responsibility for one of the characters in the drama. Between episodes of dramatic enactment, each group meets the actor, who stays in role, and negotiates with them what they should do next in the drama, respecting the constraints of their role and character. This structure of dramatic episodes divided by periods in which advice can be given to a character has been adopted for FearNot! as shown schematically in Figure 1.

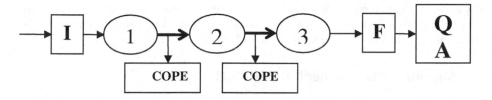

Fig. 1. Interactional structure of FearNot!

The session starts with an introduction to the school and the characters (I) and then a dramatic episode follows (1) in which a bullying incident occurs (see Figure 2 for an example). The victim then asks the child for advice in dealing with this, and the child suggests a coping behaviour (COPE). This structure is repeated – currently twice – and a simple educational message (F) is displayed, followed by an online question-naire (QA) assessing how far the child can out itself in the shoes of the characters he or she has just seen.

The exploratory nature of the application is due to the lack of any 'magic wand' solution to the problem of bullying. Even the generally agreed educational message "Don't suffer in silence, tell someone you trust" is not guaranteed to work, though making a new friend and telling them is one of the more successful strategies. Some advice is controversial – parents often tell children to 'hit back' when faced by physi-cal bullying, while teachers are universally opposed to violent responses. In fact 'hit-ting back' is statistically not often successful, but since it is memorable when it does succeed it is quite possibly over-reported [17].

Fig. 2. A bullying incident

To retain the empathic link between child and victim, it is clearly helpful if the child feels the victim is taking the advice seriously. This is incompatible with a scripted approach, and indeed the use of a scripted version of the application in a large evaluation in June 2004, while demonstrating that children did indeed empathise with the characters, raised the criticism that the victim was not responsive to the ad-vice given [9]. In this early version of FearNot!, only the third episode was influenced by either of the two pieces of advice given. If one of these was to 'tell someone' then the victim was shown as improving their situation in the final episode, and if not, the third episode showed the situation was as bad as ever.

3   Narrative Management in FearNot!

Given there are around 7 different pieces of coping advice a child could give, and the order in which they are given before the second or third episode would also have to be taken into account, a branching narrative of the type used successfully in MRE [7] or Carmen's Bright IDEAS [12] seems infeasible. Thus an emergent narrative approach, in which action is driven by the characters themselves, is a natural solution to making the victim responsive to the advice the child gives.

At the same time, the repetitive nature of bullying, and the fact that it is naturally episodic, does not require too much from the emergent mechanism in terms of dramatic complexity or length. The Forum Theatre approach taken also means that the emergent mechanism does not have to take user actions directly into account. There were several good reasons for putting the child in the role of spectator during each dramatic episode. We have already mentioned the need to offer distance for children who are being bullied in real life; in addition the fact that child users would be able to hurt the virtual characters without being physically hurt themselves would have created a real imbalance in roles. 'God-like' intervention is not feasible in the real world either, and in any case the educational aim was to promote reflection, not to create a 'bash the bully' game.

The choice of an emergent narrative mechanism did not however remove the need for a narrative manager. Unlike a Forum Theatre production in which the action is temporally contiguous, it was always envisaged that each episode would be freestanding and could be thought of as happening over an extended period of weeks. Thus a choice has to be made about where each new episode is located and which characters are involved in it, as well as any other initial conditions. For example, it was envisaged that if the advice was to 'tell a teacher' or 'tell a parent'., then this would happen off-stage to avoid the difficult issues involved in representing teachers and parents as (possibly less than perfect) story characters. The initializing of episodes also allows a pedagogical influence to be exerted in terms of the situations and characters to be considered, which could be used for example to tailor FearNot! to specific schools. In addition, there has to be some method of determining when an episode has finished once there is no script encoding this information.

For these reasons, a Stage Manager agent was included in FearNot!, [15] with a series of levels of control, from determining every character action (used in the scripted version, and also in both versions for the introduction segment), to the ability to intervene in one-off fashion (used to end episodes), to merely setting up scene and characters and merely monitoring what happens.

4   An Affectively-Driven Architecture for Characters

If what happens in an episode is to be driven directly by character interaction, then a key aspect of the system must be the agent architecture. With an emergent narrative

mechanism, it is the ability of characters to autonomously select actions – their action-selection mechanism – that determines the narrative. Figure 3 shows the affectively-driven agent architecture.

Each agent in the world (the character) perceives the environment, through a set of
sensors (allowing the perception of events, objects, etc. in the world) and acts on the
environment though its effectors, allowing different actions to be performed (for example, a bully may hit the victim and the victim may cry). Upon receiving a percept
(for example, be the presence of another agent or an object, or even an action from
another agent) the agent appraises its significance and triggers the appropriate emotions. Additionally, if a goal has become active, it will add a new intention to achieve
the active goal.

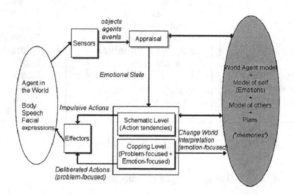

Fig. 3. Affectively-driven agent architecture

The appraisal process feeds the resulting emotional state into action-selection at
two different levels: that of action-tendencies and that of coping behaviour [10]. For
example, if the victim character starts to cry when bullied, it is not because s/he has a
goal that involves crying – this is an innate reaction to a particular distressed emotional state and the inability to fight back.

On the other hand, other actions, such as begging the bully to stop, do result from
the internal goals of the agent and are planned.

This second layer defines two kinds of coping: problem-focused coping, involving
planning and acting to achieve goals; and emotion-focused coping in which the character's interpretation of the environment is altered. For example, an agent that feels
distressed by being unable to achieve a given goal, may lower the goal's importance
as a way of reducing its distress. In this way, emotions will not only influence the
agents' reactive behavior, but also guide the planning process, since emotional focused coping changes the agent's interpretation of its plans. The continuous partially-
ordered planner used in FearNot! selects the intention associated with the currently
most intense emotion from the intention structure. This becomes the target goal for
the planner to achieve. The planner then either removes a flaw or executes an action.
The resulting plan is stored with the intention and can be pursued later.

5 Appraisal

The emotional component of the architecture applies a subset of the appraisal rules from the taxonomic definitions of Ortony, Clore and Collins (OCC) [14] which can be seen as a subjective evaluation of a given stimulus according to the character's goals, standards and beliefs. Figure 4 shows three examples of such rules, which generate the majority of OCC emotion types: *Well Being* emotions, *Attraction* emotions, *Fortune of Others* emotions and *Attribution* emotions, and are similar to those of [19].

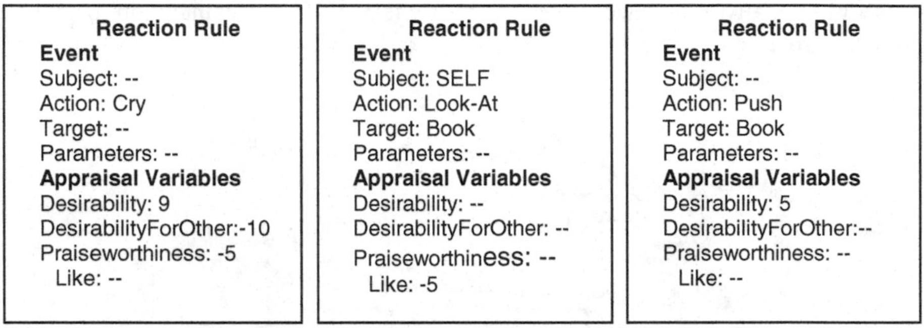

Reaction Rule	Reaction Rule	Reaction Rule
Event	**Event**	**Event**
Subject: --	Subject: SELF	Subject: --
Action: Cry	Action: Look-At	Action: Push
Target: --	Target: Book	Target: Book
Parameters: --	Parameters: --	Parameters: --
Appraisal Variables	**Appraisal Variables**	**Appraisal Variables**
Desirability: 9	Desirability: --	Desirability: 5
DesirabilityForOther:-10	DesirabilityForOther: --	DesirabilityForOther:--
Praiseworthiness: -5	Praiseworthiness: --	Praiseworthiness: --
Like: --	Like: -5	Like: --

Fig. 4. Three examples of emotion appraisal rules

Table 1. Types of links between goals

Goal link	Description
SufficientTo	If goal A has a sufficient link to goal B then achieving A will also achieve B.
NecessaryTo	If goal A has a necessary link to goal B, then, in order to achieve B, one must achieve A
FacilitativeTo	If goal A has a facilitative link to goal B with value c, achieving A will raise the likelihood of achieving B by a factor of c.
InhibitoryTo	If goal A has a inhibitory link to goal B with value c, achieving A will lower the likelihood of achieving B by a factor of c.

Two of the OCC-defined goal types - *active-pursuit* goals and *interest* goals – are used. *Active-pursuit* goals are those the characters plan to achieve directly, such as physically attacking a victim. *Interest* goals are those a character has but does not actively pursue, such as avoiding getting hurt. Unlike the *active-pursuit* goal, the *inter-*

est goal does not have any pre-conditions, success or failure conditions since it does not become active or inactive. Instead it has a protection-constraint parameter, modeling those conditions that the character wishes to maintain. To allow the system to build a goal hierarchy, both goal types may possess several goal links as seen in Table 1.

The prospect-based emotions hope and fear are not however dealt with through domain-specific rules (as in [19], Hope and fear are related to goal achievement or not, so a similar approach to [8] was taken which takes advantage of explicitly storing the agent plan state and intentions. Prospect based reactions can then be automatically obtained from the plans and goals active in the agent memory.

6 Creating a Story

In this section we examine an example of an emergent narrative in order to show how the components already discussed fit together.

In the first episode, the Stage Manager locates John, the victim in the classroom studying and has Luke enter. Luke does not like John and so when he sees John he starts insulting him (reactive action tendency). As a result, John has an active pursuit goal of fighting back that is triggered when he is insulted by other characters. He tries to build a plan in order to fight back. However all the actions that John considers have some likelihood of getting hit back. When such an action is selected, a threat to John's interest goal of not getting hurt is detected and John feels frightened. Because he has a fearful nature (part of the personality profile for a victim), his fear is much stronger than the hope of succeeding in fighting back and so he gives up the goal and does not do anything.

Fig. 5. In the classroom   **Fig. 6.** User interaction

At the same time, Luke notices the book on the table and generates a bullying opportunity. He makes a plan to push John's books to the floor. Figure 5 shows a snapshot of this situation. Luke feels confident of his plan, so he starts walking towards the book with a happy face (the hope emotion is mapped to a happy facial expression). On the other hand John feels very distressed at being insulted and disappointed by not being able to fight back. Luke moves towards the books and pushes them away. This event matches an emotional reaction generating the emotion *gloat*, which triggers an action tendency. Luke performs a *tease* language action that corresponds to saying something like: "Come and get them you Muppet!" When the victim realizes that the books are on the floor he activates the goal of picking them, and thus walks towards them and picks them up. When the bully sees John picking up the books he decides to push him. Once more this is achieved by an active pursuit goal that becomes active in that situation. So Luke goes behind John and pushes him.

The result of pushing John is uncertain: in the real world it is decided by physics, and in the virtual world by a probability set in the 3D visualization. Thus sometimes a character may fall, and in others, not. If John falls, he appraises this event as very undesirable and activates an action tendency to start crying. At the same time, Luke appraises the same event as very desirable and starts gloating John by saying something in the lines of "What a wimp, I've hardly touched you". When John cries, Luke finds it very blameworthy and thus threatens him to stop crying and to not tell anyone. If John does not fall, Luke will not mock him. Instead, the victim may feel angry and asks Luke why is he always picking on him. Luke responds negatively to the question by insulting John even more. Figure 6 shows a snapshot of the interaction mode in which the child user talks with the character victim and advises him/her on what to do next. The user types whatever he wants in the lower text box on the right and by pressing the OK button the written utterance is sent to the agent. The agent receives the utterance and converts it to a language action using a template-based language system [2]. When the interaction mode is first displayed, John arrives in the library crying, but he realizes that the user has entered the set as for any ordinary character (in fact the agent victim does not distinguishes the user from other synthetic agents) and activates the goal of asking for help which makes him perform an *askforhelp* speech act. If the user then suggests fighting back, this has the effect of raising the importance of the goal, so that the next time John meets Luke the fear generated by the possibility of getting hurt is not strong enough to make him give up the goal. Thus user interaction changes the behaviour of the victim by indirect influence rather than because the victim does exactly what he is told. However if John tries pushing Luke and it does not succeed, then he will not accept a further suggestion to hit back since the experience of being hurt as a result again alters his emotional state, this time in the direction of greater fearfulness.

7 Small-Scale Evaluation

A small-scale evaluation was carried out with eleven children randomly chosen from the third and fourth grade in a Portuguese school. The physical bullying story just described was used and each child participated individually. After the initial introduction and the first episode, each child was asked to write anything in order to help the victim. The victim had already asked for help, but the children did not always realize that they could really write something. All the interactions with the victim were saved in log files with a unique code for each child. At the end of the trial/interaction each child completed the same agent questionnaire that had been used in the large-scale evaluation of the scripted version of FearNot! [9]. One additional question was introduced relating to the dialog between child and victim, This could not have been used with the scripted version since dialog was handled by menu selection in that version. It asks the child if the victim understood the conversation (by giving appropriate responses to the child's inputs).

Also differently from the scripted version, the emergent version has no sound at all. This is a disadvantage as the episodes may not seem so engaging, making the understanding of the story more difficult. Moreover, the lack of sound in the character dialogs requires the children to read the utterances written on the screen, which is more difficult than simply hearing them. Some children had difficulties reading utterances and in a few cases, they took so long to read a line that it disappeared before it was all read. In those few situations the researchers briefly explained what had been said. In terms of empathy with the characters, very similar results were obtained as with the scripted version: children disliked the bully and felt sad for the victim. However noticeably better results were obtained for aspects relating to the responsiveness of the characters as seen in Table 2. The first two questions refer to the conversation and dialogue between the characters.

Table 2. Responses to questions about character responsiveness

	Scripted version	Emergent Version
Conversations: did the conversations seem real? (yes-1;no-5)	2.4	1.9
Were the conversations (interesting-1; boring-5)	2	1.64
Did the victim understand the conversation? (yes-1; no-5)		1.36
Did the victim follow the advice? (yes-1; no-5)	2.3	1.7
Did you help the victim? (helped a lot-1; no- 5)	1.8	1.27

Since the episodes displayed are physical bullying episodes which contain few dialogue lines and the dialogues in the emergent version are very similar to the scripted version, the different results can be explained by the influence of the interaction with the character. The conversation with the victim makes the children look at the characters as more believable. For instance when the victim accepts the fight back strategy, it seems more real to see him threatening the bully on the next episode than to behave as in the first episode.

8   Lessons Learned

The first lesson of the work reported here is that a substantial amount of effort is required to produce an essentially bottom-up system. Because interaction between characters is the driving force for the development of narrative, the whole agent architecture and the surrounding framework allowing agents to interact with each other have to be completely in place before any real testing of the narrative produced can be carried out. This is very different from a top-down approach in which a subset of facilities can typically be made available early and then elaborated. In particular, if emergent narrative is to be presented graphically, the graphic visualization must support full agent autonomy, including movement in the environment and the execution of animations. Due to the way in which the graphical world had been designed in Wild-Tangent, autonomous characters were able to walk through furniture rather than around it, and in the absence of a viable implementation for local sensing in the WildTangent 3D world, waypoints had to be defined to support very simple path-planning.

In addition, when the character is itself able to decide what action to carry out, the animation that represents it in the graphical world must be visually correct, and this requires the character to position itself so that this is true. For example, if a push animation is designed such that the victim is pushed from behind, then it will only look correct visually if the character carrying it out is indeed standing behind the victim. In order that the character can check this before executing the animation, it was necessary to design spatially-specific execution points for animations, and include the necessary motion planning for a character to move to the correct execution point.

A further issue in the graphical environment is how to deal with dramatic cinematography when the actions and movement of characters are being decided on the fly. Camera position and lighting effects can make a great deal of difference to the dramatic impact of a scene on the user, and the scripted version was noticeably more competent in those respects. Once characters have autonomy, then the intelligence embedded in camera and lighting agents has also to be increased.

Speech output raises particular problem too in an unscripted environment. The template-based language system developed for FearNot! seems perfectly capable of generating the range of utterances needed for inter-character dialogue, and also coped – rather better than had been feared, and in both English and Portuguese – with character-child dialogue. However, given the robotic nature of text-to-speech synthesis systems, it was decided at an early stage to stick to text output on the screen rather than destroy the believability of the characters. Recorded speech would have been suitably expressive, but the amount of recording needed for the generative language system was prohibitive. Good quality unit-selection based speech systems are commercially available, but they currently require the load into memory of a very large database – incompatible with the resources available when running interactive graphics – and moreover have been designed for adult voices only and the equable tones of the telephone help system, not the angry or miserable child characters of FearNot!

A methodological point was raised by the use of this approach in an educational application. To what extent is the necessarily somewhat unpredictable outcome of episodes in conflict with the pedagogical objectives? It is possible for example for the Stage Manager to bring characters together with a view to bullying taking place and for none to happen. This is like the real world, but an educational application is more constrained than the real world. The use of the Stage Manager allows the degree of emergent narrative to be constrained if desired, and it may be that the amount of narrative variability that is acceptable will depend on the exact application chosen.

9   Related Work and Conclusions

In a project covering as much ground as this one, many pieces of previous work had an influence. We have already cited earlier work using an OCC approach such as [19] , while the use of an emotion-driven planner and of expressive behaviour for dramatic purposes can be seen in [8] [9] and [12]. Like most other researchers in this field we must also acknowledge the seminal work of the OZ project and in particular its emphasis on believability [4]. However, apart from the novelty of the application domain – no previous autonomous agent application has targeted anti-bullying education – the emergent narrative experiment was also truly novel in our view. Much other interesting story-telling work is going on, but no other group seems as yet to have attempted an unscripted approach in this way. Variation in story outcome has been generated for example by [6] but this is derived from pre-built goal-trees which interact in different ways for an initial random positioning of characters in an environment rather than generatively as in this case. Façade [13] is a beautifully designed story environment, but its conception of beats is closer to that of universal plans and produces a very large authoring task that may not be sustainable for an educational environment. VICTEC and Façade differ in their narrative approaches, the stories in VICTEC being created form rather than articulated around the user actions, as it is the case in Façade. The Mimesis environment [18] is a very interesting application of planning, but is aimed at authoring and not at unscripted drama as is [16]. As we have discussed in the previous section, many issues have arisen from the emergent narrative work carried out in FearNot! and further research is required to deal with these. However we believe that we have shown there is an interesting role for this approach to unscripted narrative, and that there may be applications such as this in which an open-ended and somewhat unpredictable narrative has much to offer.

References

1. Aylett, R (2000) Emergent Narrative, Social Immersion and "Storification"; Proceedings Narrative andLearning Environments Conference NILE00 Edinburgh, Scotland.
2. Louchart S, Romano D, Aylett R, Pickering J (2004) Speaking and acting - Interacting language and action for an expressive character. Proceedings for the AISB workshop Leeds Uk 2004
3. Aylett R, Louchart S. (2003) Towards a narrative theory of VR. Virtual Reality Journal, special issue on storytelling. To appear 2003.
4. Bates, J. (1994). The Role of Emotion in Believable Agents *Communications of the ACM* 37, 7 122—125
5. Boal, Augusto. (1979) The Theatre of the Oppressed. Urizen Books, 1979
6. Cavazza, M, F. Charles, S.J. Mead, Character-Based Interactive Storytelling, IEEE Intelligent Systems, July/August 2002, pp 17-24
7. Gratch J., Marsella S., (2001). Tears and Fears: Modeling emotions and emotional behaviors in synthetic agents, Proc. of Autonomous Agents 2001, Montreal, ACM Press. 278-285. 2001.
8. Gratch.J (2000) Emile: Marshalling passions in training and education. In *Autonomous Agents 2000*. ACM Press, 2000.

9. Hall, L; Woods, S; Dautenhahn, K; Sobral, D; Paiva, A; Wolke, D. and Newall, L. (2004) Designing empathic agents: Adults vs Kids.In: James C. Lester, Rosa Maria Vicari, Fábio Paraguaçu (Eds.): *Intelligent Tutoring Systems, 7th International Conference, ITS 2004,* (604-613) LNCS 3220 Springer
10. Lazarus, R. (1991) *Emotion and Adaptation.* Oxford University Press, 1991.
11. Louchart S, & Aylett R.S (2002) Narrative theories and emergent interactive narrative; Proceedings NILE02 Edinburgh, Scotland pp 1-8
12. Marsella, S; Johnson, L.W. & LaBore, C. (2000) Interactive Pedagogical Drama Proceedings, Autonomous Agents 2000
13. Mateas, M., & Stern, A. (2000). Towards integrating plot and character for interactive drama. In Working notes of the Social Intelligent Agents: The Human in the Loop Symposium. AAAI Fall Symposium Series. Menlo Park, CA: AAAI Press. A shorter version of this paper appears in K. Dautenhahn (Ed.), Socially Intelligent Agents: The Human in the Loop. Kluwer. 2002.
14. Ortony, G. Clore, and A. Collins. (1988) *The Cognitive Structure of Emotions.* Cambridge University Press, New York, reprinted 1994 edition, 1988.
15. D. Sobral, I. Machado, and A. Paiva. Managing authorship in plot conduction. In *Virtual Storytelling: Using Virtual Reality Technologies for Storytelling.* Springer,2003.
16. Szilas.N, 2003. *Idtension, a narrative engine for Interactive drama,* Proceedings TIDSE. 2003.
17. D. Wolke, S. Woods, H. Schultz, and K. Stanford. Bullying and victimization of primary school children in soth england and south germany: Prevalence andschool factors. British Journal pf Psychology, 92, 2001.
18. Young, R.M. (2001) An Overview of the Mimesis Architecture: Integrating intelligent narrative Control into an existing gaming environment. Working notes of the AAAI Spring Symposium on Artificial Intelligence and Interactive Entertainment, A*AAI Press 2001
19. Martinho C.: *"Emotions in Motion: short time development of believable pathematic agents in intelligent virtual environments",* Universidade Técnica de Lisboa, Instituto Superior Técnico, Lisboa, Master Thesis, 1999.

Intelligent Virtual Agents in Collaborative Scenarios

Rui Prada and Ana Paiva

IST-Technical University of Lisbon,
Avenida Prof. Cavaco Silva - Taguspark,
2780-990 Porto Salvo, Portugal
rui.prada@tagus.ist.utl.pt
ana.paiva@inesc-id.pt

Abstract. Today, many interactive games and virtual communities engage several users and intelligent virtual agents (IVAs) all interacting in the same virtual environment, which additionally, may present collaborative tasks to the participants. The success of the interactions relies on the ability of the agents to meet the user's expectations, thus, showing a coherent and believable set of behaviours. For this reason, in scenarios where users and IVAs interact as a group, it is very important that the interactions follow a believable group dynamics. Focusing on this problem, we have developed a model that supports the dynamics of a group of IVAs, inspired by theories of group dynamics developed in human social psychological sciences. The dynamics is driven by a characterization of the different types of interactions that may occur in the group. The model was implemented in a computer game that engage the user with a group of four IVAs in the resolution of collaborative tasks. This game was used in an evaluation experiment which showed that the model had a positive effect on the users' social engagement in the group, namely on their trust and identification with the group.

1 Introduction

Intelligent Virtual Agents (IVAs) are commonly used in interactive games and virtual communities as a way to enhance the interaction experience of users. However, this positive effect will only be achieved if the agents are able to show coherent and believable behaviours.

Furthermore, some of these interactive systems present tasks to the participants that must be solved, collaboratively, in group. For example, in computer role-playing games several players form groups of adventures that undertake the challenges and quests of the game's world. However, in such collaborative scenarios the role of the IVAs is usually very restricted as they do not take an active part on the group. If they do participate in the group users frequently have strong control over the them, which, consequently, reduces their autonomy. For example, in the "Star Wars: Knights of the Old Republic"[6], the user starts the adventure with one character, but as the game evolves other characters join the player's quest and s/he will end up controlling simultaneously

T. Panayiotopoulos et al. (Eds.): IVA 2005, LNCS 3661, pp. 317–328, 2005.
© Springer-Verlag Berlin Heidelberg 2005

an entire party of several characters. This fact decreases the players' perception of the synthetic members as individuals and increases the distance between the player and her/his character, which makes the users' interaction experience in the group less interesting.

We believe that the main reason because the IVAs do not successfully participate in the group with users is due to their lack of social skills to engage in the group social interactions. Research on IVAs has not been particularly focusing on this problem. It is usually centered on the interactions between a single user and a single character [5] [13] or on the interactions of the IVASs among themselves [17] [15] without considering the user within the group and without a common collaborative task.

In addition, we argue that it is not enough to endow the agents with social skills that allow them to behave in a coherent manner from an individual perspective, but it is also necessary that the agents are able to use their social skills to engage in a believable group dynamics. Thus, their behaviours should be coherent with the group composition, context and structure. In multi-agent systems (a related field of IVAs) we can find some work related to the simulation of group dynamics[14], however, it is usually centered on the issues of the efficiency of the group rather than the socio-emotional dimension of the group and the believability of the group interactions in relation to the user.

The goal of the work present here, is to enhance the role of IVAs in collaborative scenarios making them part of the group. To do that we have developed a model for the dynamics of the group, inspired in theories developed in human social psychological sciences. The model defines the knowledge that each individual agent should build about the others and the group and how this knowledge drives their interactions in the group.

The model was implemented in the behaviour of IVAs that collaborate with the user in the resolution of tasks within a collaborative game. The game was used in an experiment conducted to assess the influence of the model on the users interaction experience, which showed that the model had a positive effect on the users' social engagement with the group, namely their trust and identification with the group.

This paper describes the model for the synthetic group dynamics and the game and study developed to evaluate its effects on user's interaction with a group of IVAs.

2   The Test Case: *Perfect Circle*

Perfect Circle[1] is a game that engages the user in a collaborative task with a group of four autonomous synthetic characters. It takes the user into a fantasy world where certain gemstones contain the essence and power of the gods. In this world, certain men, the Alchemists, dedicate their lives to the study of the gemstones' powers and are looking for a special one that merges the power of all

---

[1] This game can be downloaded from *http://web.tagus.ist.utl.pt/ rui.prada/perfect-circle/*.

the seven essences (ruby, topaz, citrine, emerald, sapphire, amethyst and iolite), known as the Rainbow Pearl.

The user plays the role of one Alchemist that has joined a group of other four Alchemists to undertake the quest for the rainbow pearl, which they believe to be hidden in one of the elemental planes. These planes are reached through magic portals that can be activated by the powers of a given combination of gems. The goal of the group is to progressively gather the necessary gems needed to open one portal in order to proceed to the next one (see figure 1).

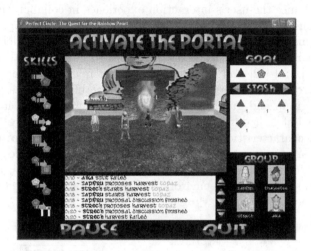

Fig. 1. The group of Alchemists is trying to activate one of the portals to move further in the planes

Each of the members of the group have different skills, which allows them to gather gemstones from the ground and manipulate them in order to change their shape, size and essence.

Furthermore, every member in the group is engaged in the same goal, thus trying to solve the same task. However, there are many ways to reach a solution, and if each of the characters follows its own, the group may never solve the task. Thus, characters have to coordinate their actions in order to follow a similar strategy in the search for the correct stones to activate the portal.

For this reason, every action that is performed in the group concerning the resolution of the task is discussed by the group beforehand. The discussion protocol has three different steps:

1. First, one character declares that s/he wants to take a certain action (e.g. *"I think that it will be best if I merge these two sapphires"*).
2. The other characters respond to the proposal by agreeing or disagreeing with it.
3. Then, based on the opinions expressed by the group, the character decides to proceed with the execution of the action or to withdraw the proposal.

The group interactions are not restricted to the execution of the task. Each member can, at any time, engage in social-emotional interactions by encouraging or discouraging the other members of the group. Note that the user can perform, through her/his character, exactly the same type of actions in the group that the autonomous members do.

3   A Model for the Group Dynamics

In order to enhance the user's interaction experience in collaborative scenarios, such as the game described in the previous section, we have developed a model to support the dynamics of groups of IVAs, the SGD Model. The model was inspired on several theories of group dynamics developed in human social psychological sciences [7], [4] and [12] and is based in the principle that each IVA must be aware of the group and its members and should be able to build a proper social model of the group and guide its behaviour in the group with it. The model is characterized at four different levels: (1) **the individual level** that defines the individual characteristics of each group member; (2) **the group level** that defines the group and its underlying structure; (3) **the interactions level** that defines the different classes of interactions and their dynamics; and (4) **the context level** that defines the environment and the nature of the tasks that the group should perform.

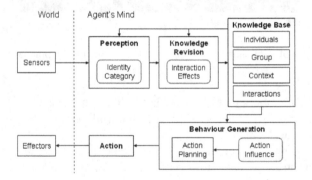

Fig. 2. The SGD Model in the agents' mind

These four levels describe on one hand the knowledge that the agents should build and on the other the dynamics of their behaviour. This dynamics relies on the agents' perception of the group state, the group interactions and their capability to classify these interactions into one of the classes defined in the model (interactions level). For example, agents must be able to recognize if the actions of the other members facilitate or not the resolution of the group tasks. Thus, the dynamics of the model is achieved through these three different processes (see figure 2):

1. **Classification of the Interactions:** First, the agent classifies the actions in the group into categories of interaction with specific semantics. For example, in this process the agent interprets if certain actions are helpful for the group of not. This process uses the information on the four levels of the agent's knowledge, specially on the interaction level, that defines the possible categories of interaction, and in the context level that defines how should the actions of the group be interpreted.
2. **Propagation of the Interaction Effects:** Then, based on the identified category, the interactions produce some changes on the knowledge, in particular on the individual and group level. For example, the interaction may change the social relations established between the members that it engages.
3. **Influence of the Agent's Actions:** Finally, the agent's perception of the group and its members influences the actions that it performs in the group. For example, if the agent is not motivated it will not try to solve the group's tasks.

3.1   The Individual Level

In the individual level each agent is modelled as a unique entity, having a name that identifies it in the group, a set of abilities that define the actions that it can perform in the environment which are related to the task (e.g. change the shape of one gem) and a personality. The personality is defined using two of the dimensions proposed in the Five Factor Model [11]: *Extraversion* that is related to the dominant initiative of the agent and, thus, will influence the agent's frequency of interaction; and *Agreeableness* that is related to the socio-emotional orientation of the agent so it defines the type of socio-emotional interactions that the agent will favour (e.g. more agreeable members will encourage the others more often).

3.2   The Group Level

The group level contains knowledge related to the group's composition (e.g. set of members), identity and structure. The identity defines a way to distinguish the group in the environment (e.g. a unique name), thus allowing its members to recognize and refer to it. The group structure emerges from the social relations established between the members and can be defined in two different dimensions:

1. **Structure of power:** that emerges from the members' social influence relations. These relations define relations of power, they quantify the capacity of one agent to influence the behaviour of another. The influence is defined as the difference of power that one individual can exert on another and the power that the other is able to mobilize to resist [9].
2. **Sociometric structure:** that emerges from the members' social attraction relations. These relations are related to like (positive attraction) and dislike (negative attraction) attitudes. They are unidirectional and not necessarily reciprocal, thus, if one agent A has a positive attraction for agent B this does not necessarily mean that agent B has a positive attraction for agent A.

The social relations are directed from one agent, the *source*, to another, the *target*, and are assessed by a *value* which can be positive, zero or negative.

In addition to the relations that agents build with each other, agents also build a relation with every group that they belong to. This relation captures the member's attitude towards the group and supports the notion of membership. It categorizes the member in the group in two different levels:

1. **Motivation in the Group:** defines the level of engagement of the agent in the group's interactions and tasks.
2. **Position in the Group:** reflects the agent's relative significance in the group that defines how important are its contributions and how well are they accepted by the group. For example, actions performed by agents that have more social influence on the group members have stronger effects on the group process. The position of an agent in the group depends on the overall social influence that the agent may exert on the others, on the attraction that the others have for the agent and on the agent's relative expertise in the group.

3.3   The Context Level

The context level defines the knowledge that the agent builds concerning the environment where it performs and the nature of the group's tasks. One of these definitions is the task model, that allows the agent to interpret the group interactions in terms of their effects on the the task and, therefore, allows the agent to classify them in the instrumental categories. For example, if the group needs a squared ruby to open one portal, then any action that generates a squared ruby will be interpreted as a positive move for the group.

Additionally, the context may define some social norms that will guide the agent in the interpretation of the social-emotional interactions. These social norms define the acceptable behaviours and the misconducted interactions. For example, if one agent reiterates the importance of merging two sapphires right after the failure to perform such merge attempted by another member, this may be considered not polite and, thus, be interpreted as a negative socio-emotional interaction.

3.4   The Interactions Level

The interaction level describes the knowledge that the agent builds concerning the group interactions: their classification and dynamics. The dynamics reflects, on one hand, the changes that the group interactions induce on the agent's perception on the group (*interaction effects*) and, therefore, on the knowledge the it builds about the group, and on the other hand, the rules that drive the behaviour of the agent (*action influence*).

The central notion is the concept of interaction with the group, which is related to the agents' execution of actions. An interaction is characterized by: (1) the set of *performers* that are responsible for the occurrence of the interaction;

(2) the set of *supporters* that agree with the interaction and support it, but are not directly involved in its execution; (3) a set of *targets* that are affected by the interaction; and (4) the interaction's *strength* in the group, which determines its relative importance in the group and, therefore, determines the strength of the effects of the interaction in the group. This *strength* depends on the position in the group of the members that are responsible for its execution or have supported it. For example, if one member has a low position in the group and performs well one of the actions that are relevant for the group then it will gain a small amount of influence. However, if one influent member has agreed with the action, thus, supporting it, the amount of influence gained will be higher.

The Classification of the Interactions. In order to model the dynamics of the group process we have classified the several possible group interactions into different categories. This categorization is then embedded in the knowledge that the agent has a priori and will support the agent's process of perception and identification of the interactions.

This classification is more than just the classification of the actions themselves. It depends on the actions' results, on the context of the execution, and also on the agents' perception of the group. Thus, for example, the same action can be perceived as a positive interaction to the group by one agent but negative in the view of another.

The classification, was based on the categories that Bales proposed on his IPA system [4]. Bales argued that members in a group are simultaneously handling two different kind of problems: those related with the group task and those related to the socio-emotional relations of its members. Based on this, in the model, the members interactions are divided into two major categories: the *instrumental interactions* that are related to the group task and the *socio-emotional interactions* that are related to the group social relations. In addition, the interactions can be classified as positive, if they convey positive reactions on the others, or negative, if they convey negative reactions.

The *socio-emotional* interactions fall into four categories:

1. **Agree [positive]:** this class of interactions show the support and agreement of one agent towards one of the interactions of another agent consequently raising the importance of that interaction in the group.
2. **Encourage [positive]:** this class of interactions represent one agent's efforts to encourage another agent and facilitate its social condition.
3. **Disagree [negative]:** this class of interactions show disagreement of one agent towards one of the interactions of another agent, consequently decreasing the importance of that interaction in the group.
4. **Discourage [negative]:** this class of interactions represent one agent's hostility towards another agent and its efforts to discourage it.

In addition, we defined four categories of instrumental interactions, that are:

1. **Facilitate Problem [positive]:** this class of interactions represent the interactions made by one agent that solves one of the group problems or ease its resolution.

2. **Obstruct Problem [negative]:** this class of interactions represent the interactions made by one agent that complicates one of the group problems or render its resolution impossible.
3. **Gain Competence [positive]:** this class of interactions make one agent more capable of solving one problem. This includes, for example, the learning of new capabilities, or the acquisition of information and resources.
4. **Loose Competence [negative]:** this class of interactions make one agent less capable of solving one problem. For example, by forgetting information or loosing the control of resources.

The Dynamics of the Interactions. The interactions constitute the mechanism that create the dynamics in the group. Such dynamics is supported by the classification presented on the previous section and is modelled through a set of rules that follow the ideas found in the social psychological theories of group dynamics. For example, we use ideas from the theory of social power by French and Raven [9] and Heider's balance theory [10].

These rules define, on one hand, how the agent's and the group's state influence its behaviour and the occurrence of each kind of interaction, and on the other, how the occurrence of each type of interaction influences the agent's and group's state.

First of all, the interactions of one member in the group depend on its individual characterization as well as her/his perception of the group state. Thus, the member will interact in a completely different way according to different group situations, such as for example, in groups with different elements or with different emergent structures. To model this we defined a set of rules that describe the conditions that are more favourable for the occurrence of each type of interaction:

1. In general the frequency of the interactions depends on the agent's *motivation*, *group position* and *personality* [16] [12] [1]. Thus, highly motivated agents engage in more interactions, as well as agents with a good group *position* or high *extraversion*. On the other hand, agents not motivated, with a low *position* in the group, or with low levels of *extraversion* will engage in few interactions or even not interact at all.
2. The agent's personality also defines some of the agent tendencies for the *social emotional interactions* [1]. Thus, agents with high levels of *agreeableness* will engage more frequently in positive *socio-emotional interactions* while agents with low *agreeableness* will favour the negative *socio-emotional interactions*. For example, if an agent fails to perform and important action in the group, it will probably be encouraged to try again and not to give up by the members that are very agreeable, while the disagreeable members will probably discourage her/him.
3. Furthermore, the agent's skills influence the occurrence of the *instrumental interactions*. Thus, more skillful agents will engage in more *instrumental interactions* than non skillful agents [12].

4. Moreover, agents with higher *position* in the group are usually the targets of more positive *socio-emotional interactions* while the agents with lower *position* are the targets of more *negative socio-emotional* interactions [12][2].
5. In addition, when one agent is considering to engage in a *socio-emotional interaction* its social relations with the target are very important. Members with higher *social influence* on the agent and/or members for which the agent has a positive *social attraction* will be more often targets of positive *socio-emotional interactions*, otherwise they will be more often targets of negative *socio-emotional interactions*. Thus, agents will encourage those they like or those that have high influence over them.

Furthermore, when agents get the perception of the execution of one interaction, they react to it according to the classification that they internally give to the interaction. These reactions are translated into changes on the perceived state of the group. These changes follow the set of rules described below:

1. The *positive instrumental interactions* will increase its performers *social influence* on the members of group, by means of expert and information power [9], as well as its own *motivation*. Which means that any member that demonstrates expertise, solves one of the group's problems or obtains resources that are useful to its resolution, will gain influence over the others. On the other hand members that obstruct the problem or loose competence, will loose influence on the group and become less motivated.
2. *Socio-emotional interactions* by their turn are associated with changes in the *social attraction* relations. One agent changes its attraction towards another agent positively if it is target of positive *socio-emotional interactions* by that agent and negatively otherwise. The encourage interaction has the additional effect to increase the target's *motivation* in the group.
3. Agents also react to *socio-emotional interactions* when they are not explicitly the targets of the interaction. Following Heider's balance theory [10], if one agent observes a positive *socio-emotional interaction* on an agent that it feels positively attracted to, then its attraction for the performer will increase. If the agent performed a negative *socio-emotional interaction* then the observer's attraction for the performer would decrease.

The intensity of the interactions' effects described on the previous rules depends directly on the strength of the interaction in the group, which depends of the position in the group of its performers. For example, encourage interactions performed by members with a better position in the group will increment more the target's motivation.

4   Evaluation

We have conducted an experiment with the Perfect Circle game, in order to evaluate the effects of the SGD Model on users that interact with groups of

---

[2] Note that an agent has an high group position if it has high influence over the others and/or if the others have an high social attraction for it.

synthetic characters. The experiment was conducted with 24 university students, 20 male and 4 female, using two main control conditions:

1. **Use of the SGD Model:** we built two different versions of the game: one where the characters followed the SGD Model and other where they did not. When the characters did not use the model they were not able to engage in socio-emotional interactions, except Agree and Disagree (without any socio-emotional connotation). In addition, their frequency of interaction was always constant and the decision to proceed with a proposed action was not weighted by the members' group position, it was a simply majority rule.

2. **The Group Initial Structure:** subjects can start the game in a group with non neutral initial social relations of attraction and influence, which means that the initial group can have different levels of cohesion. Such levels may be very high or very low. We have considered two different scenarios: one where the group has neutral social relations and another where the members of the group dislike each other, which, takes the group cohesion to very low levels. Note that this condition can only be applied when the game is run with the believable group dynamics component.

Following the work of Allen et al.[2] we have decided to measure the users' interaction experience by measuring the users' trust and identification with the group. Allen et al. have conducted an experiment to measure the satisfaction of the members of a group that performed their tasks through computer-mediated interactions. They argue that, since trust and identification have a strong relationship with group satisfaction [8] [3], using their measures is a good approach to assess the user's satisfaction in the group.

During the experiment we divided the subjects into three different groups with 8 elements each. Each group played the game with a different condition: (C1) the first group played the game without the SGD Model; (C2) the second played with the SGD Model and with the group at neutral cohesion levels; (C3) and the third played with the SGD Model but with the group at low levels of cohesion.

Subjects played the game for an hour and afterwards had half an hour to answer a questionnaire, similar to the one used by Allen et al.[2].

We have analyzed the questionnaire results using the Kruskal-Wallis non-parametric test which computed the mean-ranks shown in figure 3.

The chart on figure 3 shows a comparison of the group trust and group identification measured on the three control conditions. As one can see, there is a clear difference on the levels of trust and identification observed on the subjects that played with the SGD Model and those who played without the SGD Model. Trust and identification were higher when the synthetic characters followed a believable group dynamics. There is also some difference between the identification of the subjects with the group on condition C2 and condition C3, which we believe is due to the fact that in the first case the group socio-emotional interactions were mostly positive, what may be less believable than a group where the socio-emotional interactions are both positive and negative, as the second case. However, we need further evaluation on this issue.

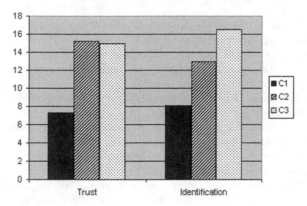

Fig. 3. Kruskal-Wallis test mean-ranks results. The Asymp. Significance for Trust was 0,039 and for Identification was 0,051.

5 Conclusions

In this paper we argued that usually IVAs do not take an active role in collaborative scenarios with users because they do not have the desired social skills to engage in the group interactions.

Thus, to enhance the participation of the agents in the group, we have proposed a model that supports their group behaviour, which was inspired by theories of group dynamics developed in human social psychological sciences. This model defines the dynamics of the group based on a characterization of the different types of interactions that may occur in the group. This characterization addresses socio-emotional interactions as well as task related interactions.

The model was implemented in the behaviour of IVAs that collaborate with the user within the context of a computer game (*Perfect Circle*). This game was used in an evaluation experiment that showed that the model had a positive effect on the users' social engagement in the group, namely on their trust and identification with the group.

References

1. S. Acton.   Great ideas in personality - theory and research.   *(online)* *http://www.personalityresearch.org/bigfive.html*, last access on Jan 2005.
2. K. Allen, R. Bergin, and K. Pickar. Exploring trust, group satisfaction, and performance in geographically dispersed and co-located university technology commercialization teams. In *Proceedings of the NCIIA 8th Annual Meeting: Education that Works*, March 18-20, 2004.
3. J. Ang and P. H. Soh. User information satisfaction, job satisfaction and computer background: An exploratory study. *Information and Management*, 32:255–266, 1997.
4. R. F. Bales. *Interaction Process Analysis*. The University of Chicago Press, Chicago, 1950.

5. T. Bickmore and J. Cassell. Relational agents: A model and implementation of building user trust. In *Proceedings of the Conference on Human Factors in Computing Systems - CHI'2001*, Seattle, USA, 2001. ACM Press.

6. Bioware.   Star   wars: Knights   of   the   old   republic.   *(online)* *http://www.lucasarts.com/products/swkotor/*, 2003.

7. D. Cartwright and A. Zander. *Group Dynamics: Research and Theory.* Harper and Row, New York, 1968.

8. J. W. Driscoll. Trust and participation in organizational decision making as predictors of satisfaction. *Academy of Management Journal*, 21:44–56, 1978.

9. J. R. P. French and B. H. Raven. *Group Dynamics: Research and Theory*, chapter Bases of Social Power. Harper and Row, New York, 1968.

10. F. Heider. *The Psychology of Interpersonal Relations.* Wiley, New York, 1958.

11. R. McCrae and P. Costa. *The five factor model of personality: Theoretical perspectives*, chapter Toward a new generation of personality theories: Theoretical contexts for the five factor model, pages 51–87. Guilford, New York, 1996.

12. J. E. McGrath. *Groups: Interaction and Performance.* Prentice Hall, Englewood Cliffs, New Jersey, 1984.

13. S. Pasquariello and C. Pelachaud. Greta: A simple facial animation engine. In *Sixth Online World Conference on Soft Computing in Industrial Appications*, 2001.

14. M. Prietula and K. Carley. Computational organization theory: Autonomous agents and emergent behaviour. *Journal of Organizational Computing*, 4(1):41–83, 1994.

15. M. Schmitt and T. Rist. Avatar arena: Virtual group-dynamics in multi-character negotiation scenarios. In *4th International Workshop on Intelligent Virtual Agents*, page 358, 2003.

16. M. E. Shaw. *Group Dynamics: the Psychology of Small Group Behaviour.* McGraw-Hill, New York, 1981.

17. B. Tomlinson and B. Blumberg. Social synthetic characters. *Computer Graphics*, 26(2), May 2002.

A Conversational Agent as Museum Guide – Design and Evaluation of a Real-World Application

Stefan Kopp[1], Lars Gesellensetter[2], Nicole C. Krämer[3], and Ipke Wachsmuth[1]

[1] A.I. Group, University of Bielefeld, P.O. Box 100132, 33501 Bielefeld, Germany
{skopp, ipke}@techfak.uni-bielefeld.de
[2] IPD, University of Karlsruhe, Adenauerring 20a, 76128 Karlsruhe, Germany
lars@ipd.info.uni-karlsruhe.de
[3] Dept. of Psychology, University of Cologne, Bernhard-Feilchenfeld-Str. 11,
50969 Köln, Germany
nicole.kraemer@uni-koeln.de

Abstract. This paper describes an application of the conversational agent *Max* in a real-world setting. The agent is employed as guide in a public computer museum, where he engages with visitors in natural face-to-face communication, provides them with information about the museum or the exhibition, and conducts natural small talk conversations. The design of the system is described with a focus on how the conversational behavior is achieved. Logfiles from interactions between Max and museum visitors were analyzed for the kinds of dialogue people are willing to have with Max. Results indicate that Max engages people in interactions where they are likely to use human-like communication strategies, suggesting the attribution of sociality to the agent.

1 Introduction

Embodied conversational agents (ECAs) begin to show impressive human-like capabilities of natural face-to-face dialogue. Agents of this kind have been successfully developed for various target applications. Yet, it is noteworthy that they are normally designed for specific settings and have rarely made the step out of their laboratories into real-world settings. One problematic consequence of this is that we still have little data on how such agents do in real-world settings and which factors influence acceptance and success in such scenarios. But, to make ECAs ultimately a useful and successful application, we need to make them capable of interacting with naïve, uninformed humans in everyday situations.

Originally started out as platform for studying the generation of natural multimodal behavior, we have extended the agent *Max* in following projects to a conversational assistant in Virtual Reality construction tasks [13] or to a virtual receptionist that welcomes people in the hallway of our lab [12]. In January 2004, we have brought Max to an application in the *Heinz Nixdorf MuseumsForum* (HNF), a public computer museum in Paderborn (Germany), thus venturing the step from a lab-inhabiting research prototype to a system being confronted daily with real humans in a real-world setting. In this setting (shown in Figure 1), Max is visualized in human-like size on a static screen, standing face-to-face to visitors of the museum. The agent is equipped with camera-based visual perception and can notice visitors that are passing by. Acting as a

T. Panayiotopoulos et al. (Eds.): IVA 2005, LNCS 3661, pp. 329–343, 2005.
© Springer-Verlag Berlin Heidelberg 2005

museum guide, Max's primary task is to engage visitors in conversations in which he provides them in comprehensible and interesting ways with information about the museum, the exhibition, or other topics of interest. Visitors can give natural language input to the system using a keyboard, whereas Max will respond with a synthetic German voice and appropriate nonverbal behaviors like manual gestures, facial expressions, gaze, or locomotion. In doing so, he should be as natural and believable as possible a communication partner, being entertaining and fun to talk with. He should not give talks in a teacher-like manner, but tailor his explanations to contextual factors like the visitor's interests and respond to questions, interruptions, or topic shifts. To create the impression of an enjoyable, cooperative interaction partner, the agent should also be capable of coherent small talk which helps reduce the social distance between the interlocutors [3].

Fig. 1. Max interacting with visitors in the Heinz-Nixdorf-MuseumsForum

After discussing related work in the next section, we start to describe the design of our system by explaining shortly the overall architectural layout in Sect. 3. In Sect. 4, we then focus on how Max's conversational capabilities are achieved. Finally, we have studied the communications that take place between Max and the visitors. Some anecdotal evidence on Max's capabilities to engage visitors in communicative episodes in the hallway setting was already reported in [12]. Now we were interested in the kind of dialogues that the museum visitors—unbiased people with various backgrounds, normally not used to interact with an ECA—are willing to have with Max and whether these bear some resemblance with human-human dialogues. We describe results of our first studies in the last section of this paper.

2   Related Work

Systems capable of spoken dialogue, either text-based or in natural language, have been around for quite a period of time and the approaches differ in many respects, from the modeling of linguistic structure and meaning to their efficiency, robustness, or coverage of domains. Already Weizenbaum's virtual psychotherapist Eliza [24], although not even trying to understand its 'patients', often managed to make them feel taken care of, thus demonstrating the effects achievable with rule-based, adeptly modeled small talk. During the last years, this genre of conversational agents revived as so-called chatterbots on the web, still making use of the 'Eliza-effect'. To name the most elaborated one, ALICE [23] utilizes a knowledge base containing 40.000 input-response rules concerning general categories, augmented with knowledge modules for special domains like Artificial Intelligence. This approach was also employed in other domains, e.g., to simulate co-present agents in a virtual gallery [7].

With enhancement of virtual agent technology and a growing awareness of the fact that a dialogue contribution is usually an ensemble of verbal and nonverbal behaviors, ECAs have become prominent. Some ECAs take a deep generation approach to generation, like the real estate agent REA [4] that was capable of understanding speech and gesture and of planning multimodal utterances from propositional representations of meaning. Keeping a model of interpersonal distance to the user, REA used small talk to reduce this distance if she noticed a lack of closeness to the client [3]. Systems like BEAT [5] or Greta [20] have addressed the generation of complex multimodal behavior from aspects like information structure, semantic-pragmatic aspects, or certainty and affect. Other ECAs have been designed based on more practical approaches aiming at robustness, efficiency or coverage of multiple, yet shallowly modeled domains. For example, MACK [6] could give directions to visitors of the MIT Media Lab based on a repository of user queries and system responses. August [9] was a talking head that has been used for six months as an information kiosk at the Stockholm Cultural Center. The system replied to spoken utterances by predefined answers in synthetic speech, facial expression, head movement, and thought balloons. Similar systems have been proposed as virtual museum guides, e.g. in [25]. The virtual H.C. Andersen system [2] uses spoken and gestural interaction to entertain children and educate them about life and work of HCA. Conversational skill is modeled by fairy tale templates and topic-centered mini-dialogues, while paying attention to the rhapsodic nature of non-task-oriented conversation and conversational coherence. These main tenets have been confirmed in user tests.

3   System Architecture

To comply with the requirements in the HNF setting, we have designed the overall architecture of the system as shown in Fig. 2. It resembles what has been proposed as reference architecture for ECAs [4], but is based on more cognitively motivated tenets [18]. As the agent should be able to conduct natural language interactions, constraints on linguistic content (in understanding as well as in producing utterances) should be as weak as possible. Thus, a keyboard was used as input device, avoiding problems that arise from speech recognition in noisy environments. Note also that this restricts Max to dialogues with only one visitor at a time. Nevertheless, camera-based perception provides the agent with constant visual information about the space in front of the keyboard as well as a greater view at the exhibition area. Real-time capable, standard image processing techniques are employed to scan the video data for skin-colored areas, find regions that probably correspond to faces, and track them over time. That way Max is able to detect the presence of multiple persons and to discriminate between them as long as no overlaps of face regions in the image occur. All speech and visual input are sent to a perception module that utilizes sensory buffers, ultra-short term memories, to compensate for recognition drop-outs and to integrate both kinds of data. It thus detects changes that take place in the scene and distributes them in the form of events, e.g., `person-13-entered` or `person-22-speaks`, to both reactive and deliberative processing.

Reactive processing is realized by the behavior generation component, which is generally in charge of realizing the behaviors that are requested by the other components. On the one hand, this includes feedback-driven reactive behaviors. For example, it hosts a behavior that, based on incoming positioning events, immediately triggers the agent's motor control to perform all eye and head movements needed to track the current interlocutor by gaze. Such reactive behaviors can be activated, deactivated or set to other stimulus objects at any time. Other behaviors concern the agent's secondary actions like eye blink and breathing. On the other hand, the behavior generation component must accomplish the realization of all utterances Max is to make. This includes the synthesis of prosodic speech and the animation of emotional facial expressions, lip-sync speech, and coverbal gestures, as well as scheduling and executing all verbal and nonverbal behaviors in synchrony. This task is realized using our *Articulated Communicator Engine*, a framework for building and animating multimodal virtual agents [14].

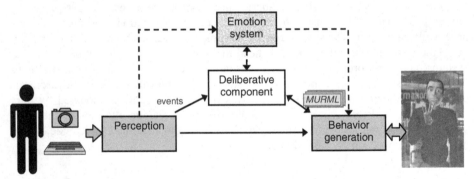

Fig. 2. Overview of the system architecture

Deliberative processing of events takes place in a central deliberative component (the white box in Fig. 2). This component determines when and how the agent acts, either driven by internal goals and intentions or in response to incoming events, which, in turn, may originate either externally (user input, persons that have newly entered or left the agent's visual field) or internally (changing emotions, assertion of a new goal etc.). It maintains a dynamic spatial memory that contains all objects and persons in the agent's environmental context. This enables Max to directly refer to objects in its real-world surrounding, for example, to point at a robot placed next to the screen when mentioning it. How the deliberative component produces conversational behavior is described in Sect. 4.

Finally, Max is equipped with an emotion system that continuously runs a dynamic simulation to model the agent's emotional state. The emotional state is available anytime both in continuous terms of valence and arousal as well as a categorized emotion, e.g. happy, sad or angry, along with an intensity value (see [1]). The continuous values modulate subtle aspects of the agent's behaviors, namely, the pitch and speech rate of his voice and the rates of breathing and eye blink. The weighted emotion category is mapped to Max's facial expression and is sent to the agent's deliberative processes, thus making him cognitively "aware" of his own emotional state and subjecting it to his further deliberations. The emotion system, in turn, receives input from both the perception (e.g., seeing a person immediately causes positive stimulus) and the deliberative component. For example, obscene or politically incorrect wordings ("no-words") in the user input leads to negative impulses on Max's emotional system (see [1]). Since subsequent stimuli in the same direction accumulate in the emotion system, repeated insults will put the agent in an extremely bad mood, which in turn can eventually result in Max leaving the scene, an effect introduced to de-escalate rude visitor behavior.

4 Generating Conversational Behavior

The deliberative component carries out the three basic steps in creating conversational behavior: interpreting an incoming event, deciding how to react dependant on current context, and producing the appropriate response. Fig. 3 shows the flow of processing in this component, exposing separate processing stages for these steps and the knowledge structures they draw upon. On the one hand, the agent has static (long-term) knowledge that encompasses former dialogue episodes with visitors, informs his capabilities of dialogue management, and lays down his general competencies in interpreting natural language input and generating behaviors for a certain communicative function. On the other hand, there is evolving dynamic knowledge that provides the context in which interpretation, dialogue management, and behavior generation are carried out. A discourse model contains a history of the last utterances as well as up-to-date context information: The currently perceived persons and the active participant (interaction level); the holder of the turn, the goals the dialogue is pursuing and who brought them up, i.e. who has the initiative (discourse level); the current topic and contexts, the rhetorical structure, and the grounding status of information (content level). A user model contains all information that is gained throughout the dialogue. This includes information about the user (name, age, place of residence, etc.), his preferences and interests (determined by topics the user selected or rejected), and his previous behavior (cooperativeness, satisfaction, etc.). Lastly, a system model comprises the agent's world knowledge as well as current goals and intentions (for details see [8]). These structures enable Max's to act proactively in dialogue, e.g., to take over the initiative, rather than being purely responsive as classical chatterbots are.

All processes in the deliberative components are carried out by a BDI interpreter, which incessantly pursues multiple plans (*intentions*) to achieve goals (*desires*) in the context of up-to-date world knowledge (*beliefs*). We use an extended version of JAM [10]. Most of the plans implement condition-action rules, one of the underlying mechanisms with which Max's conversational knowledge is modeled. Such rules can

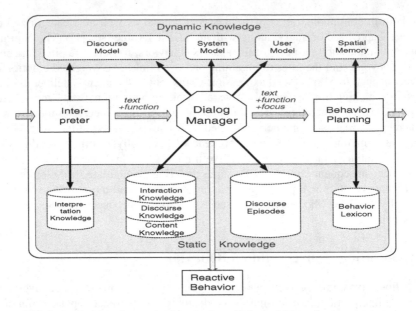

Fig. 3. An interior view at the functioning of Max's deliberative component

test either the user input (text, semantic or pragmatic aspects) or the content of dynamic knowledge bases (beliefs, discourse or user model); their actions can alter the dynamic knowledge structures, raise internal goals and thus invoke corresponding plans, or trigger the generation of an utterance (stating words, semantic-pragmatic aspects, and markup of the central part). All rules are defined in an XML-based specification language that builds on and extends the AIML language from the ALICE system [23]. These XML descriptions were turned automatically into JAM plans (via XSL transformations) and added to the plan library of the BDI system.

4.1 Dialogue Acts and Conversational Functions

In general, our approach to modeling conversational behavior assumes a *dialogue act* to be the basic unit of interaction, comparable to but more specific than Poggi & Pelachaud's [20] communicative act. Every user input as well as every response by the agent is considered to consist of one or more dialogue acts. Following Cassell et al. [4] and building on speech act theory, we consider each dialogue act as goal-directed action performed in context, and we distinguish between the overt behaviors and the functional aspects these behaviors fulfill. That is, every dialogue act fulfills a *communicative function*. It can thereby be effective on different levels of dialogue (cf. [22]), of which we distinguish the following three: the *interaction* level, the *discourse* level, and the *content* level. Actions at the interaction level can take place anytime and concern the establishment and maintenance of a conversation (greeting/farewell). Within an interaction, actions at the discourse level manage the topic and flow of conversation (e.g., the suggestion of a new topic to talk about). At the content level, information about the current topic is conveyed.

A communicative function, which explicates the functional aspects of a dialogue act with respect to these levels, consists of the following independent components:

- *performative*: the action that the dialogue act performs, reflecting part of the speaker's intention—to provide or require (askFor) information
- *reference level*: which level the act refers to—content, discourse, or course of interaction
- *content*: the information that further specifies the performative, e.g., which information the speaker asks for or which interactional signal she emits.

These aspects are collapsed into one single communicative function of the form `<performative>.<reference level>.<content> [arguments]`. Further details can be added either as a forth component or as the optional arguments (in brackets). The resulting function covers, from left to right, a spectrum from pragmatic to semantic aspects of the dialogue act. This allows for grouping the functions, e.g., `provide.content` comprises all propositional contributions regardless of the semantic information they convey. In our current system, about 200 communicative functions are distinguished, including for example

`provide.interaction.greeting`	(e.g. "Hi there!")
`askFor.content.name`	(e.g. "What's your name?")
`askFor.discourse.topic.sports`	(e.g. "Let's talk about sports.")

4.2 Interpretation

Starting out from textual user input, the first stage in deliberative processing is interpretation (see Fig. 3). Its task is to derive the intended communicative function and to pass it along with the original text on to the dialogue manager. A regular parser would constantly fail in the museum setting where mistyped or ungrammatical input is not unusual. We thus opted for simple but robust text analysis techniques that neglect most of syntactic well-formedness. Incoming input is interpreted by dedicated JAM plans in two steps. First, general semantic concepts are identified (negation, agreement, pos./neg. adjective, references) by simple pattern matching rules. To deal with negated expressions, different patterns are matched sequentially. For example, the utterance "I won't agree" contains a negation ("won't") and a signal for agreement ("agree"), therefore resulting in a disagreement. The second step determines the communicative function, again, using dedicated rules whose preconditions match actual words, the occurrence of semantic concepts, or entries of the discourse or user model. Ordering rules by decreasing generality, a general rule can be corrected by a more specialized one. When none of the rules matches, i.e. no function could be recognized, only the text is being passed on and Max can still revert to small-talk behavior using, e.g., commonplace phrases.

Currently, Max has 138 interpretation rules. To demonstrate how they work in detail, we give here two examples of rules—for sake of clarity in the original XML format—that interpret user input for its communicative function. The first example is a rule that checks in its condition part (`match`) for keywords, specified as regular expressions with an asterisk, and `asserts` in its action part a modifier `farewell`. A modifier constitutes an intermediate representation of communicative aspects, which are then further processed by subsequent rules. Note that this rule does not make any assumptions about the performative or reference level.

```
<rule name="interprete.type1.farewell">
  <match>
    <keywords>bye,cu,cya,exit,quit,ciao,ade,adios,hasta*,auf
    wieder*,tschoe,tschues*,tschau,und weg,so long,machs
    gut,bis bald,bis dann,bis spaeter,wiedersehen</keywords>
  </match>
  <assert>
    <convfunction modifier="farewell" filter="yes"/>
</assert> </rule>
```

The second example shows a rule that inspects semantic-pragmatic aspects of the current as well as the former dialogue act, notably, whether the utterance this input is in response to was a request for confirmation and whether the semantics of this input has been analysed by previous rules to be undecided. In this case, the rule will assert to Max's beliefs a communicative function meaning that the visitor has provided information indicating that he is undecided regarding the previous question of Max:

```
<rule name="interprete.type4.provide.content.indecision">
  <match>
    <allof>
      <convfunction ref="lastReply" type="askFor.content.
                                          confirmation"/>
      <convfunction modifier="undecided"/>
    </allof>
  </match>
  <assert>
    <convfunction type="provide.content.indecision"/>
</assert> </rule>
```

4.3 Dialogue Management

The tasks of the dialogue manager amount to updating the dynamic knowledge bases, controlling reactive behaviors, and—most importantly—creating appropriate utterances. While a simple rule-based approach seems appropriate to model robust small talk, the agent must also be able to conduct longer, coherent dialogues, calling for a more plan-based approach and a profound modeling of the respective domains. We have combined these two approaches employing the BDI interpreter that affords both kinds of processing. A skeleton of JAM plans realize the agent's general, domain-independent dialogue skills like negotiating initiative or structuring a presentation. These plans are adjoined by a larger number of small JAM plans that implement condition-action rules like the ones shown above. These rules define the agent's domain-dependant conversational and presentational knowledge, e.g., the dialogue goals that can be pursued, the possible presentation contents, or the interpretation of input. As currently set up in the museum, Max is equipped with 876 skeleton plans and roughly 1.200 rule plans of conversational and presentational knowledge. At run-time, the BDI interpreter scores all plans dependant on their utility and applicability in context. The most adequate plan is then selected for execution.

Max's conversational behavior is laid down through this collection of JAM plans, which can be differentiated according to the level of dialogue they act upon. The plans at the *interaction level* state how Max can start/end a dialogue and how to react to various input events (e.g., when the user starts or finishes typing). If there is no ongoing conversation, newly perceived persons are greeted and encouraged to start an interaction. If an interaction is concluded, the gained knowledge (models of the discourse and its participants) is compressed into a dialogue episode and stored in long term memory. In future discourses the system draws upon these episodes to answer questions like "How many people were here today?" or to derive user-related answers: If a user states a favorite movie, the system looks up whether it has been stated before, possibly resulting in the response "Seems to be a rather popular movie".

The *discourse layer* deals with mechanisms of turn-taking, topic shift, and initiative. The user can take the turn by starting to type, causing Max to stop speaking as soon as possible and to yield the turn. As the system performs a mixed-initiative dialogue, it needs to know about the user's wish to take the initiative, how to deal with conflicts, and how to establish initiative at all. Initiative is modeled as the raising of obligatory dialogue goals. The system is aware of these goals (discourse model) and disposes of plans for initiating, holding, resuming and releasing them. Dedicated rules analyse the input communicative function, e.g., to determine if the user wants to seize control over discourse and what goal she wants to pursue.

From the point of view of the system, initiative is the key for maximizing the coherence of the dialogue. If Max has the goal of coming to know the interlocutor's name, he will try to seize control over dialogue and to ask for the name. If the user refuses to answer but brings up another topic to talk about, Max will accept this "intermezzo", giving away the initiative temporarily but will re-seize it and return to his goal at the earliest time possible. This is one instance where a rule-based, merely responsive approach to dialogue would break down. Max can handle these cases by utilizing longer-term plans and the notion of desires to influence plan execution in the BDI framework: the agent's own desire for initiative increases when it is available and neither of the participants is about to take it. He then seizes control when a threshold is reached. Instead of being only reactive to user input, Max is thus able to keep up the conversation himself and to conduct a coherent dialogue.

The *content layer* comprises general conversational knowledge that comprises a dictionary of given names, a lexicon of "no-words" according to the museum's policies, and 608 rules that state how to react to keywords or keyphrases in a given context, forming Max's small talk capabilities. This also encompasses rules for a guessing animal game where Max asks questions to find out an animal that a visitor has in mind based on discriminating features. In addition, the content layer contains plans that form Max's presentation knowledge. This knowledge is chunked into units that are categorized (e.g., 'technically detailed', 'anecdotal') and organized according to the rhetorical relations between one another (e.g., 'elaborates', 'explains'). Three top-level units (introduction, overview, summary) form the skeleton of a presentation. The remaining units form a tree with the overview unit on top. After giving an overview, the ongoing presentation can be influenced by the user as well as the system. Upon finishing a unit, Max offers the user possible units to elaborate. Explained units are noted in the discourse model. If the user is reluctant to select a unit or a certain unit might be of interest to the user, Max may also proceed with this unit himself. Such evidence comes from the user model and is gained either explicitly in previous dialogue or is inferred when the user rejects or interrupts the presentation of a unit of a certain type. In general, Max knows all possible dialogue goals of a certain domain, their preconditions, and the dialogue acts to open, maintain and drop them. When taking the initiative, Max can thus select one of these goals and initiate a presentation, small talk, or a guessing game himself.

4.5 Behavior Planning

Behavior planning receives the words, the communicative function of the dialogue act, and the focus of the utterance to produce, and it is always informed about the current emotional state. It adds to the utterance nonverbal behaviors that support the given communicative function. Behaviors are drawn from a lexicon containing XML-based specifications in MURML [14]. At the moment, 54 different behaviors are modeled.

The mapping of communicative functions onto nonverbal behaviors is not easy, nor clearly definable for all cases. One reason for this that behaviors like hand gestures or facial expressions may serve fundamentally different semiotic functions. Additionally, there is barely a one-to-one mapping as multiple behaviors can often realize one function, just as one behavior can fulfill several functions [4]. To account for most of the flexibility and complexity of this mapping, the indexing of nonverbal behaviors in our lexicon can address single parts of the hierarchical structure of a communicative function. For examples, defined mappings are

```
provide.interaction.greeting    → hand wave
provide.discourse.agreement     → head nod
provide.content.ironical        → eye blink
provide.content                 → raise hand
*.content.number-two            → handshape two fingers stretched
```

The functions' hierarchical structure allows to suitably represent the functions of more general behaviors, like the quite generic, yet frequent metaphorical gesture of simply raising a hand in front of the body (example four). Omitting the content part of the function (provide.content), our mapping assumes that this gesture signals that some content is being brought up, independent of the content itself. That is, while this gesture focuses on pragmatic aspects, it can be chosen to accompany words and other nonverbal behaviors that probably inform better about the content itself. On the other hand, a nonverbal behavior can serve a semiotic function of conveying a certain meaning, regardless of pragmatic aspects like whether this meaning is part of a request or an inform type dialogue act. Using an asterisk symbol as shown in the last example, the symbolic gesture for the number of two, single aspects of the function can be left open for such behaviors. In result, Max can choose this gesture whenever he needs to refer to this meaning, in statements as well as in questions.

When augmenting a dialogue act with nonverbal behaviors, the generation component picks behaviors whose functions cover most of the semantic-pragmatic aspects of the dialogue act (trying to increase informativeness). Yet, there will often be too large a number of possible behaviors. As in other systems [5], this conflict is resolved partly based on information about the scope of each behavior (the occupied modality) and partly by random choice. Behavior planning also allocates the bodily resources and can thus take account of the current movement and body context. For example, a greeting gesture that can potentially be made with either hand is performed with, say, the left hand if this hand has been mobilized before and has not returned to its rest position yet. Drawing upon the spatial memory, behavior planning also refines deictic gestures by translating symbolic references like camera into world coordinates.

5 Evaluation of Max´s Communicative Effects

We wanted to see (1) if Max's conversational capabilities suffice to have coherent, fluent interactions with the visitors to the museum, and (2) whether the dialogues bear some resemblance with human-human dialogues, i.e. if Max is perceived and treated as human-like communication partner. Recent findings demonstrate remarkable effects of an agent on the user's (social) behavior: An embodied agent may lead people to show increased impression management and socially desirable behaviors [21,15]; may influence the user's mood [16] or affect the user's task performance (social facilitation/inhibition [21,17]). Also, agents have proven to affect the communication of the human user: When interacting with ECAs, people are more inclined to use natural language than when interacting with text- or audio-based systems [17,15], children accommodate their speech to that of the virtual character [19], and people engage in small talk with a virtual character and take its social role into account [11]. Yet, none of these studies has been conducted in a real-world setting.

Study 1
A first screening was done after the first seven weeks of Max's employment in the Nixdorf Museum (15 January through 6 April, 2004). Statistics is based on logfiles, which were recorded from dialogues between Max and visitors to the museum. During this period, Max on average had 29.7 conversations daily (SD=14), where "conversation" was defined to be the discourse between an individual visitor saying hello and good bye to Max. Altogether there were 2259 conversations, i.e. logfiles screened. On the average, there were 22.60 (SD=37.8) visitor inputs recorded per conversation, totalling to 50,423 inputs recorded in the observation period. The high standard deviation (SD) reveals a great variation in the length of the dialogues, with extremely short interactions as well as long ones of more than 40 visitor inputs. The data were further evaluated with respect to the successful recognition of communicative functions, that is, whether Max could associate a visitor's want with an input. A rough screening among these further pertained to whether visitors would approach Max politely or whether they would employ insulting, obscene, or "politically incorrect" wordings. Finally, we looked at how often visitors would play the guessing game with Max.

We found that Max was able to recognize a communicative function in 32,332 (i.e. 63%) cases. Note that this is the absolute number of classifications, including possibly incorrect ones. We can thus only conclude that in at most two-thirds of all cases Max conducted sensible dialogue with visitors. In the other one-third, however, Max did not turn speechless but simulated small talk behavior by employing commonplace phrases. Among those cases where a communicative function was recognized, with overlaps possible, a total of 993 (1.9%) inputs were classified by Max as polite ("please", "thanks"), 806 (1.6%) as insulting, and 711 (1.4%) as obscene or politically incorrect, with 1430 (2.8%) no-words altogether. In 181 instances (about 3 times a day), accumulated negative emotions resulted in Max leaving the scene "very annoyed". The guessing animal game was played in 315 instances, whereby 148 visitors played the game once, 34 twice, and 26 three or more times. A qualitative conclusion from these findings is that Max apparently "ties in" visitors of the museum with diverse kinds of social interaction. Thus we conducted a second study to investigate in what ways and to what extent Max is able to engage visitors in social interactions.

Study 2

We analysed the content of user utterances to find out whether people use human-like communication strategies (greetings, farewells, commonplace phrases) when interacting with Max. Specifically, we wanted to know if they use utterances that indicate the attribution of sociality to the agent, e.g., by asking questions that only make sense when directed to a human. We analysed logfiles of one week in March 2005 (15th through 22nd) containing 205 dialogues. The number of utterances, words, words per utterance, and specific words such as "I/me" or "you" were counted and compared for agent and user. The content of user utterances was evaluated by means of psychological content analysis and following criteria of qualitative empirical approaches: using one third of the logfiles, a scheme was developed that comprised categories and corresponding values as shown in Table 1. Two coders coded the complete material and counted the frequencies of categories and values, with multiple selections possible. We chose this method since a solid theoretical foundation and a thorough understanding of the kinds of social interactions one could expect to take place between Max and the visitors is currently lacking. We thus developed the categories data-driven instead of deduced from theory. In order to achieve a maximum of inter-coder reliability, the coders jointly coded parts of the material and discussed unclear choices.

The quantitative analysis showed that the agent is more active than the user is. While the user makes 3665 utterances during the 205 dialogues (on average 17.88 utterances per conversation), the agent has 5195 turns (25.22 utterances per conversation). Not only does the agent use more words in total (42802 in all dialogues vs. 9775 of the user; 207.78 in average per conversation vs. 47.68 for the user), but he also uses more words per utterance (7.84 vs. 2.52 of the user). Thus, the agent in average seemed to produce more elaborate sentences than the user does, which may be a consequence of the use of a keyboard as input device. Against this background, it is also plausible that the users utters less pronouns such as "I/me" (user: 0.15 per utterance; agent: 0.43 per utterance) and "you" (user: 0.26 per utterance; agent: 0.56 per utterance). These results might be due to the particular dialogue structure that is, for some part, determined by the agent's questions and proposals (e.g., the guessing game leaves the user stating "yes" or "no"). On the other hand, the content analysis revealed that 1316 (35.9 %) of the user utterances are proactive (see Table 1). Concerning human-like strategies of beginning/ending conversations, it turned out that especially greeting is popular when confronted with Max (used in 57.6% of dialogues). This may be triggered by the greeting of the agent. But, given that the user can end the conversation by simply stepping away from the system, it is remarkable that at least 29.8% of the people said goodbye to Max. This tendency to use human-like communicative structures is supported by the fact that commonplace phrases—small talk questions like "How are you?"—were uttered 154 times (4.2% of utterances).

As with all publicly available agents or chatterbots, we observed flaming (406 utterances; 11.1%) and implicit testing of intelligence and interactivity (303; 8.3%). The latter happens via questions (146; 4%), obviously wrong answers (61; 1.7%), answers in foreign languages (30; 0.82%), or utterances to test the system (66; 1.8%). However, direct user feedback to the agent is more frequently positive (51) than negative (32). Most elucidating with regard to whether interacting with Max has social aspects are the questions addressed to him: There were mere comprehension questions (139; 18.6% of questions), questions to test the system (146; 19.6%), questions about

Table 1. Contents of user utterances and their frequencies

Category & corresponding values	Examples (translated to English)	N
Proactivity		
Proactive utterance		1316 (36%)
Reactive utterance		1259 (34%)
Greeting		
Informal greeting	Hi, hello	114
Formal greeting	Good morning!	4
No greeting		87
Farewell		
Informal farewell	Bye	56
Formal farewell	Farewell	5
No farewell		144
Flaming		**406** (11%)
Abuse, name-calling	Son of a bitch	198
Pornographic utterances	Do you like to ****?	19
Random keystrokes		114
Senseless utterances	http.http, dupa	75
Feedback to agent		**83** (2%)
Positive feedback	I like you; You are cool	51
Negative feedback	I hate you; Your topics are boring	32
Questions		**746** (20%)
Anthropomorphic questions	Can you dance? Are you in love?	132
Questions concerning the system	Who has built you?	109
Questions concerning the museum	Where are the restrooms?	17
Commonplace phrases	How are you?	154
Questions to test the system	How's the weather?	146
Checking comprehension	Pardon?	139
Other questions		49
Answers		**1096** (30%)
Inconspicuous answer		831
Apparently wrong answers	[name] Michael Jackson, [age] 125	61
Refusal to answer	I do not talk about private matters	8
Proactive utterances about oneself	I have to go now	76
Answers in foreign language		30
Utterances to test the system	You are Michael Jackson	66
Laughter		24
Request to do something		**108** (3%)
General request to say something	Talk to me!	10
Specific request to say something	Tell me about the museum!	13
Request to stop talking	Shut up!	24
Request for action	Go away! Come back!	61

the system (109; 14.6%), the museum (17; 2.3%), or something else (49; 6.6%). The vast amount of questions are social, either since they are borrowed from human small talk habits (commonplace phrases; 154; 20.6%) or because they directly concern social or human-like concepts (132; 17.7%). Thus, more than one-third of the questions presuppose that treating Max like a human is appropriate—or try to test this very assumption. Likewise, the answers of the visitors (30% of all utterances) show that people seem to be willing to get involved in dialogue with the agent: 75.8% of them were expedient and inconspicuous, whereas only a small number gave obviously false information or aimed at testing the system. Thus, users seem to engage in interacting with Max and try to be cooperative in answering his questions.

6 Conclusion

Current ECAs have for the most part stayed within the boundaries of their lab environments and there is only little data on whether conversational virtual agents can be successfully employed in real-world applications. We have developed our agent Max to apply him as a guide to the HNF computer museum, where he has been interacting with visitors and providing them with information daily since January 2004 (more than one and a half years by now). To comply with the requirements for human-like, yet robust conversational behavior, our design adopts the rule-based approach to dialogue modeling but extends it in several ways. It takes account of the semantic-pragmatic and context-dependent aspects of dialogue acts, it combines rule application with longer-term, plan-based behavior, and it drives the generation of not just text output but fully multimodal behavior.

The field studies that we have conducted to see if Max, based on this design, is accepted by the visitors as a conversation partner and if he succeeds in engaging them in social interactions yielded promising evidence. Judging from the logfiles, people are likely to use human-like communication strategies (greeting, farewell, small talk elements, insults), are cooperative in answering his questions, and try to fasten down the degree of Max's human-likeness and intelligence. This indicates the attribution of sociality to the agent. Our studies also provide clues to how the design should be enhanced. For example, we realized from many anthropomorphic questions that Max should be capable of flirting behavior as he is tested in this respect quite frequently. The studies will also serve as pre-test for a more experimentally controlled study on Max's social effects and subtle user reactions, which would also include analyses of video data.

Acknowledgement

This work was partially supported by the *Heinz Nixdorf MuseumsForum* (Paderborn).

References

1. C. Becker, S. Kopp, I. Wachsmuth: Simulating the Emotion Dynamics of a Multimodal Conversational Agent. Affective Dialogue Systems (2004)
2. N.O. Bernsen, L. Dybkjær: Domain-Oriented Conversation with H.C. Andersen. Affective Dialogue Systems (2004)
3. T. Bickmore, J. Cassell: 'How about this weather?' Social Dialog with Embodied Conversational Agents. Proc. of AAAI Symposium on Socially Intelligent Agents (2000)

4. J. Cassell, T. Bickmore, L. Campbell, H. Vilhjalmsson, H. Yan: Human Conversation as a System Framework: Designing Embodied Conversational Agents. In: Cassell et al. (eds.) Embodied Conversational Agents, MIT Press (2000)
5. J. Cassell, H. Vilhjalmsson, T. Bickmore: BEAT: The Behavior Expression Animation Toolkit. Proc. of SIGGRAPH 2001, Los Angeles, CA (2001)
6. J. Cassell, T. Stocky, T. Bickmore, Y. Gao, Y. Nakano, K. Ryokai, D. Tversky, C. Vaucelle, H. Vilhjalmsson: MACK: Media lab Autonomous Conversational Kiosk. Proc. of Imagina '02, Monte Carlo (2002)
7. M. Gerhard, D.J. Moore, D.J. Hobbs: Embodiment and copresence in collaborative interfaces. Int. J. Hum.-Comput. Stud. 61(4): 453-480 (2004)
8. L. Gesellensetter: Planbasiertes Dialogsystem für einen multimodalen Agenten mit Präsentationsfähigkeit. (Plan-based dialog system for a multimodal presentation agent) Masters Thesis, University of Bielefeld (2004)
9. J. Gustafson, N. Lindberg, M. Lundeberg: The August Spoken Dialogue System. Proc. of Eurospeech '99, Budapest, Hungary (1999)
10. M.J. Huber : JAM : A BDI-Theoretic Mobile Agent Architecture. Proc. Autonomous Agents'99, Seattle (1999)
11. K. Isbister, B. Hayes-Roth: Social Implications of Using Synthetic Characters. IJCAI-97 Workshop on Animated Interface Agents: Making them Intelligent, Nagoya (1998), 19-20
12. B. Jung, S. Kopp: FlurMax: An Interactive Virtual Agent for Entertaining Visitors in a Hallway. In T. Rist et al. (eds.): Intelligent Virtual Agents, Springer (2003), 23-26
13. S. Kopp, B. Jung, N. Lessmann, I. Wachsmuth: Max-A Multimodal Assistant in Virtual Reality Construction. KI-Künstliche Intelligenz 4/03: 11-17 (2003)
14. S. Kopp, I. Wachsmuth: Synthesizing Multimodal Utterances for Conversational Agents. Computer Animation and Virtual Worlds 15(1): 39-52 (2004)
15. N.C. Krämer, G. Bente, J. Piesk: The ghost in the machine. The influence of Embodied Conversational Agents on user expectations and user behaviour in a TV/VCR application. In: G. Bieber & T. Kirste (eds): IMC Workshop 2003, Assistance, Mobility, Applications. Rostock (2003) 121-128
16. N.C. Krämer, B. Tietz, G. Bente: Effects of embodied interface agents and their gestural activity. In: T. Rist et al. (eds.): Intelligent Virtual Agents. Springer (2003) 292-300
17. N.C. Krämer, J. Nitschke: Ausgabemodalitäten im Vergleich: Verändern sie das Eingabeverhalten der Benutzer? (Output modalities compared: Do they change the input behavior of users?) In: R. Marzi et al. (eds.): Bedienen & Verstehen. 4. Berliner Werkstatt Mensch-Maschine-Systeme. VDI-Verlag, Düsseldorf (2002) 231-248
18. N. Leßmann, I. Wachsmuth: A Cognitively Motivated Architecture for an Anthropomorphic Artificial Communicator. Proc. of ICCM-5, Bamberg (2003)
19. S. Oviatt, C. Darves, R. Coulston: Toward adaptive Conversational interfaces: Modeling speech convergence with animated personas. ACM Trans. on CHI, 3 (2004) 300-328
20. C. Pelachaud, I. Poggi: Multimodal Communication between synthetic Agents. Proc. of Advanced Visual Interfaces, L'Aquila, Italy (1998)
21. R. Rickenberg, B. Reeves: The effects of animated characters on anxiety, task performance, and evaluations of user interfaces. Letters of CHI 2000 (2000), 49-56
22. D.R. Traum, J. Rickel: Embodied Agents for Multi-party Dialogue in Immersive Virtual Worlds. Proc. of AAMAS'02 (2002)
23. R.S. Wallace: The Anatomy of A.L.I.C.E. Tech.report, ALICE AI Foundation (2000)
24. J. Weizenbaum: ELIZA: a computer program for the study of natural language communication between men and machines. Communications of the ACM, vol.9 (1996)
25. X. Yuan, Y.S. Chee: Embodied Tour Guide in an Interactive Virtual Art Gallery. International Conference on Cyberworlds (2003)

Using Ontology to Establish Social Context and Support Social Reasoning

Edward Chao-Chun Kao[1], Paul Hsueh-Min Chang[2], Yu-Hung Chien[2], and Von-Wun Soo[1,2,3]

AI laboratory in
[1] Institute of Information and System Applications
[2] Department of Computer Science,
National Tsing Hua University,
101 Section 2, Guangfu Road, 300 Hsinchu, Taiwan
[3] Department of Computer Science, National University of Kaohsiung,
700, Kaohsiung University Road, 811 Kaohsiung, Taiwan
{edkao, pchang, sot, soo}@cs.nthu.edu.tw

Abstract. Believable agents are required to express human-like characteristics. While most recent research focus on graphics and plan execution, few concentrate on the issue of flexible interactions by reasoning about social relations. This paper integrates the idea of social constraints with social ontology to provide a machine readable framework as a standard model which can support social reasoning for generic BDI agents. A scenario is illustrated to show how social reasoning can be attained even in different social context.

1 Introduction

Believable agents are expected to perform human-like behaviors in a virtual environment, so that they may create "the illusion of life" [2] during interaction with users, and furthermore make users immersed in the virtual reality. Such systems are designed to achieve certain purposes, such as health intervention [16], social simulation [5], and digital entertainment [18]. Believable agents are required to achieve their goals as other types of agents do, but simply achieving their goals is insufficient to show believable behaviors. From ordinary agents to believable agents, a few pieces are missing. Many research efforts in believable agents interpret the missing parts as vivid graphics [17], interactive plan execution [7], and emotional responses about incoming events [15]. However, the social aspect of believable agents is often ignored. A real human may generate additional goals according to his current status, mostly his social background, to form a story of his own, whether these potential goals are fulfilled or not. While interacting with another person, a human would follow established regulations between them, either in the level of individuals or institutions, to determine their ways to communicate. Since recent research in believable agents usually involves multiple agents, these agents are supposed to form an artificial society of a certain scale, according to the size of presenting scenarios. A human without any social relations to others is not likely to exist in real world, and thus an agent without proper social links would have reduced believability in the virtual soci-

T. Panayiotopoulos et al. (Eds.): IVA 2005, LNCS 3661, pp. 344–357, 2005.
© Springer-Verlag Berlin Heidelberg 2005

ety and may eventually let users realize the separation between agents and organizations that designers intend to construct in the first place.

While scenario designers can carefully design a planned scenario according to the social background of each agent, this scenario is not explicitly grounded in social relations among agents with a complete social model. Difficulties arise when the scenario become longer because agent interactions may become too complicated to manually or even automatically taken care of as social context among agents are unclear.

This paper proposes a social model, which comprises two parts: a social ontology as a machine readable framework to describe interrelations of social relations, and a set of social constraints to further define each instance of social relations. The model allows agents to infer social context they hold, and then to detect direct and potential conflicts between different social constraints, so that it can provide enough information for socially intelligent agents in the decision making process.

The rest of this paper is organized as follows. Section 2 describes the related work, motivations, and technical background. In section 3, we introduce an ontology for social model. Section 5 proposes an illustration using our formulations. We conclude in section 6. For the sake of clarity, in the rest of this paper, we recognize all relations as directed links, and we use two main characters, namely Sot and Julie, to describe relations in various social contexts.

2   Background

2.1   Related Work

Gratch [13] introduced the idea of socially situated planning with an implementation of social control program. An explicit social reasoning layer with a model of social context is implemented to alter agent's planning process. As explicit social rules and reasoning mechanisms are introduced, they would confine actions in instantiated plans. As a result, agents can have different responses according to the outcome of social reasoning, and this social reasoning layer is independent from the general planning, which makes social reasoning a modular component. Nevertheless, an agent would not realize how social relations affect the opponent's responses, and what differences can be made by changing their social relations. Therefore an agent is unable to change the relations with other agents to achieve their goals, such as making friends with others so that others may be willing to cooperate.

Cavedon and Sonenberg [8] analyzed social context as social roles. Each social role has a set of related goals, and roles are relational, such as supervisor-student or author-coauthor. An agent enacting one role would inherit defined goals, and have influence over the other agent that enacts the corresponding role. While this framework showed the foundation for agents to collaborate, it is often too strict to interpret social context as merely social goals. Though they attempted to adopt the term Social Commitment [6][20][21] to express social influence of higher level, social commitments were still seen as goals in this framework. Besides, the interrelations between different social relations remained undiscussed. For example, if Sot is a student of AI lab, and AI lab is located in National Tsing Hua University (NTHU) in Taiwan, then

Sot is definitely a student in NTHU. Another example is, if Julie and Sot are both Edward's teammates, then they will also be each other's teammate. More expressivity is required to represent the examples shown above.

2.2 Introduction to Ontology and OWL

To describe the nature of social context in a more precise way, we adapt the formulation of ontology. The term ontology refers to the methodology of describing the world as classes of known entities and how they are related. Traditional relations in ontology between two classes comprise the hierarchy of classes and relations between instances of classes, and thus suit perfectly to describe social relations. On the other hand, global relations defined by Institutional rules fall outside the ordinary expressivity of ontologies, and it would become confusing if we cannot present both types of social context within a single framework. Fortunately, Institutional relations can still be described in ontology with a little workaround, as is described in the next section.

To encode the ontology into a machine readable format, we choose W3C's Web Ontology Language (OWL) [19], the standard for creating ontologies on the Semantic Web and providing a foundation for knowledge-based agents. OWL basically provides two categories of predefined elements, which are classes and properties. Classes are the basis of taxonomy, as every individual in OWL must be a member of at least a class. All individuals belonging to a class also belong to any superclass of the current class. A property, serving as a directed link from an instance of the domain class to that of the range class, defines the relation between instances.

While there is a variety of software [4][14] that support creation of OWL ontologies, OWL consists of three branches with ascending levels of expressivity, which are OWL Lite, OWL DL, and OWL Full. We adopt OWL DL to describe our social context, as it strikes a balance between expressivity and efficiency. OWL DL is based on Description Logic, and it has an appropriate set of predefined elements (e.g. disjointness, union, intersection, complement of classes, and reflexivity, transitivity of properties) with several reasoners available. Social relations of the examples shown in the end of section 2.1 can be elegantly described as, (1) Sot is an instance belonging to AI lab, and AI lab is a subclass of NTHU; (2) Sot, Julie, and Edward are all instances belonging to the same team. Nevertheless, the social influence on a student or a teammate would require further elaboration.

3 Composition of Social Models

We recognize background settings as a set of different ontologies, describing different aspects of related concepts for agents to follow. See [9] for further discussion, including an example of physical ontology, which defines physical rules, simple objects, and artifacts for special purposes, and describes relations among them. While other aspects of concepts may be constructed in a similar vein, social concepts, however, are different from others because of the complicated nature of social relations itself. For example, the effect of ignite can be formulated simply as associating the target instance with the concept Fire, but we cannot simply formulate the effect of making friends as only associating the social relation between two agents to the concept Friendship, because:

1. While "ignite" can be defined as a primitive action or a fixed action sequence (e.g. pick up a match, light it up, and move it under the target object), "making friends", or a *social action*, may involve different interactions from two agents and give rise to different primitive actions only when it is performed. To define a social action in the same way as defining a *physical action* such as "ignite" would be less believable and less convincing, as we cannot make friends to everyone in the exactly same fashion.

2. The effects of friendship are more than merely a status and cannot be defined uniformly. As everything on fire would emit heat and light, friendship may not have the same characteristics on every relation between different believable agents, e.g. Edward may pat his friend Sot when Sot is upset, but he may not do it to Julie, even if Julie is also his friend and upset; on the other hand, Jessica may comfort and listen to any of her friends when they are upset. To explicitly model each possible interaction between every individual agent would be very time consuming and not applicable in a large agent society. Therefore, the internal architecture of social agents should include mechanisms to cope with social context so that complete ability of social reasoning may be achieved, and the responsibility of the external social model is to provide higher-order information, which is in terms of *social constraints* in this paper, rather than changing agent states directly.

Due to spatial limits, this paper only focuses on social constraints. More discussions about social actions can be found in [11].

3.1 The Nature of Social Context

We defined two types of social context that are related to agents in the level of individuals and the institutional level respectively. By *social relations*, we mean the relation with another agent that an agent would establish, modify, or terminate. While how agents accomplish these actions is outside the scope of this paper, it is still clear to say that, any social relation is purely personal (constraining only two individuals). An example of social relations is friendship. Sot can make friends with Julie by establishing a social relation of friendship between him and Julie, while Julie needs not to establish a relation of friendship to Sot. Here we argue that none but both of them are responsible for supervising this relation, since they are the only ones able to take social actions directly toward this relation. While Vicky may be aware of their relation and become jealous because of their relation, Vicky has no authority to supervise this relation directly.

On the other hand, internal rules of an institution may impose global relations to specific roles inside the institution. An agent enacting such a role is subject to some obligations or action constraints with respecting to other roles, or more precisely, any agents that enact those roles. Such a global relation is defined as an *Institutional rule*, which differs from similar terms in [1]. For example, in an imaginary feudal-flavored society, a bandit is forbidden to marry a noble (role-bandit has a forbidden-to-marry rule to role-noble, while the detail content of rules and relations would be defined later). As a result, Sot the Bandit is forbidden to marry Julie the Noble, Vicky the Noble or any other Nobles while they are still enacting their roles. Different from violating social relations, violating Institutional relations brings punishment from the rest of this Institutional group (rather than from the opponent). An example of punishment is becoming an outcast in that society.

3.2 Schema of the Social Concepts

Our system prototype named AI-RPG intakes a concept model that follows OWL-based schema to interpret the virtual environment to agents. In other words, any object in AI-RPG is an instance of an existing class in the concept model. Fig. 1 depicts the schema of social model described in section 3.1, where rectangles represent classes, and elliptic squares represent properties.

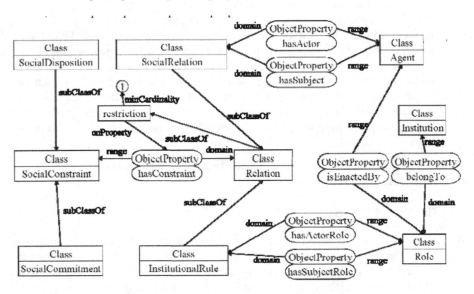

Fig. 1. OWL-based schema of the Social Model

The class Relation, while it serves as a linking word between two entities, it is constituted by two subclasses which represent individual relations as SocialRelation, and global relations as InstitutionalRelation. This schema also defines that Relation brings the effect of having social constraints from Actor (or ActorRole) towards Subject (or SubjectRole). From another view, Relation emerges from aggregation of social constraints, and social constraints affect both behaviors and mental states of agents. Before we further define social constraints, we would need one of generic goal-oriented agent architectures to exemplify what states can be affected by social constraints. Here we choose the well-known BDI model as our example architecture, but the social model can be integrated with other types of agent architectures as long as they have internal states similar to desires and intentions.

3.3 BDI Agent Architecture as Example

Current BDI model [12] is derived from philosophical formulation of resource-bounded planning [3] to reduce the complexity required to form plans from means-end reasoning, and it consists of three major states: beliefs, desires, and intention. A BDI agent firstly generates its desires, which correspond to potential goals, according to its beliefs. Next, it chooses one of its desires as its intention, which indicates its current goal to achieve. After it decides its intention, planning techniques or scripted behaviors associated with that goal is introduced to generate detail actions to execute.

Social constraints serve as the generating functions of desires and intentions induced by social context. A social disposition will create and change the desirability of certain goals when the state of beliefs conforms to its conditions. On the other hand, social commitments can filter out contradictory desires by using conflict detection on the discharging conditions.

3.4 Definitions of Social Constraints

Intensive research of social commitments has been made to facilitate multi-agent systems, and we recognize social commitments as one important type of social constraints.

From Singh's work [21], a social commitment can be defined as below.

Definition 1 (Social commitment): A social commitment is a four-place relation C (a_1, a_2, G, p): agent a_1 has a social commitment towards agent a_2, where a_1 is the actor, a_2 the subject (which are the debtor and creditor respectively in Singh's notations), G the context group, and p the proposition as the discharging condition of this commitment. A proposition is 0-order iff it refers to anything but a commitment, and is (i+1)-order iff the highest order commitment it refers to is i-order. A social commitment is i-order iff the order of its discharging condition is i.

Though Singh defined six types of operators to manipulate social commitments, here we only discuss how agent can comprehend social context, so we leave operators alone except Create () and Cancel(), which represent to create/cancel a commitment according to the content in the brackets, and thus they are necessary for conditional commitments to take place.

The effect of social commitments is strict, and an agent would suffer penalty from context group G by not acting as committed. On the other hand, we propose another type of social constraints that is in a more loose form, which is represented as social dispositions.

Definition 2 (Social Disposition): A social disposition is represented as D (a_1, a_2, G, p) has exactly the same structure and meaning as a social commitment, except a social disposition modify an agent's desires, while a social commitment functions on an agent's intention. Since a social disposition shapes an agent's desire toward other agent(s), it can only be undone by a_1 itself or rejected by a_2, and its context group G is strictly defined as the union of a_1 and a_2.

While social dispositions resembles to precommitments [20], there is difference in their very nature. A precommitment allocate resources to achieve rational behaviors without deliberation, and thus its effect still remains in the intention level. On the other hand, a social disposition is induced to simulate social effects on generating additional desires, and hence would participate in deliberation and cannot be reduced into commitments.

To maintain consistency between social context and other concept models, the discharging condition p in a social commitment or a social disposition should be represented in the form of ontology instances.

Definition 3 (Ontological Proposition): Three types of atomic propositions exist in our view, which are Concept (individual), Property (Subject, Object), and Action (Actor, Target). Any of them can be represented as a triple in OWL. A composite proposition is the conjunction of two or more atomic propositions.

The meaning of constraint orders is exemplified as follows. Sot and Julie are two members in the AI lab. As Sot and Julie are friends, Sot would have a social commitment, which proposition is buying a lunchbox for his friend Julie, since Julie is busy writing her thesis. This example is shown as assertion 1:

$$\text{Diet\_Friend1 (Sot, Julie)} = \text{C (Sot, Julie, AI\_lab, p), where} \tag{1}$$
$$p = (\text{buy (Sot, lunchbox1)} \wedge \text{hasOwnership (Julie, lunchbox1))}$$

Nevertheless, such a 0-order commitment is a one-shot commitment, which would be discharged and vanish after Sot actually buys a lunchbox. Afterward he would let Julie starve to death, even they are still friends. What Sot is more likely to commit, is to buy a lunchbox for Julie whenever he discovers that Julie is hungry. This is a 1st-order social commitment, which is shown in assertion 2:

$$\text{Diet\_Friend2 (Sot, Julie)} = \text{C (Sot, Julie, AI\_lab, p), where} \tag{2}$$
$$p = (\text{isHungry (Julie)} \Rightarrow \text{create (Diet\_Friend1 (Sot, Julie)))}$$

To model their friendship in a more believable fashion, social dispositions should be used instead of social commitments, because Sot only desires to buy Julie a lunchbox whenever she is hungry, but may not intend to do so every time, as no commitment has been made between them. His disposition toward Julie can only be modified by himself and Julie, which confines the context group of this disposition. In the case that Sot follows this disposition to buy Julie a lunchbox, a 0-order social commitment in assertion (1) would be formed. This situation is elaborated as:

$$\text{Diet\_Friend3 (Sot, Julie)} = \text{D (Sot, Julie, (Sot, Julie), p), where} \tag{3}$$
$$p = (\text{Belief (Sot, isHungry (Julie))} \Rightarrow \text{create (Diet\_Friend1 (Sot, Julie)))}$$

3.5 Conflict Detection

While much work has been done to convert commitments into communication protocols such as finite state machines [10], few have addressed the issue of conflicts between different commitments, which concern us most. As high-order social constraints contain other commitments recursively in their propositions with specific conditions, they would be outside the expressivity of description logics in OWL, and become incomprehensible to the inference engine, since logical operators "OR" and "NOT" do not exist in description logics. Currently we need to define specific subclasses of predefined constraints to satisfy needs in our scenario, and additional algorithms are used to analyze their content.

Continuing from assertion (3) in section 3.4, let Sot has a new friend, Vicky. Vicky does not like Julie, so she asks Sot not to buy any lunchboxes for Julie in front of all members in AI lab. By saying so, Vicky actually wants Sot to make a social commitment to her, which is

$$\text{Unfriendly\_Agreement1 (Sot, Vicky)} = C \text{ (Sot, Vicky, AI\_lab, p), where} \qquad (4)$$
$$p = \neg(\text{Diet\_Friend1 (Sot, Julie)})$$

However, according to Diet_Friend3, Diet_Friend1 would come to Sot's mind only when he realizes Julie is hungry. In this case, this unfriendly agreement does not conflict directly with Diet_Friend3, and two social constraints can coexist although a potential conflict can be easily perceived.

To detect conflicts between different social constraints, firstly we need to define two types of meta-relations exist between two propositions. S () represents a social constraint in definition 4 and 5:

Definition 4 (Direct conflict): If $C1 = S (a_1, a_2, G, p_1)$, $C2 = S (a_1, a_2, G, p_2)$, where $\neg p_1 \subset p_2$ and p_1 and p_2 are both 0-order social constraints, then C1 and C2 have a direct conflict.

Definition 5 (Potential conflict): When the order of C1 differs from that of C2, they may have different Degrees of Consistency (DOC) to avoid potential constraint conflicts. An algorithm is defined to detect various potential conflicts in first-person (here is a_1) perspective.

```
Algorithm CD1 (p₁, p₂)
    initialize DOC ← 0
    detect_Conflict (p₁, p₂):
        if (order (p₁) == order (p₂) == 0):
            if (!(p₁ ∧ p₂)): /* p₁ conflicts directly with p₂ */
                return <True, DOC>
            else:
                return False
        else:
            Sort p₁ and p₂ in descending order, that order(p₁) ≥ order(p₂)
            if (∃conditions in p₁ or p₂):
                DOC ← DOC + Number of Conditions
                Remove all conditions in p₁ and p₂
            if (∃p' ∈ social constraints which is referred inside p₁):
                p'' ← discharging condition of p'
                p₁ ← p''
            detect_Conflict (p₁, p₂)
```

Fig. 2. Algorithm 1: Conflict detection in first-person perspective

This algorithm increase DOC according to the number of conditions, and orders it finds in both propositions. The higher of DOC, the less possible it is to have a conflict. DOC == 0 implies a direct conflict, which is the most serious case. With this algorithm, determining whether p_1 conflicts with p_2 would become feasible. This algorithm firstly sorts out and records all conditions in two social constraints, then determines if two propositions conflict directly with the simple operation $p_1 \wedge p_2$ due to the definition of composite proposition in definition 3.

3.6 The Meanings of Conflicts

The Conflict Between Two Social Dispositions
While social dispositions represent loose constraints as agent's social attitudes, it is possible that direct conflicts do exist among them, and there is no urgent need to resolve these conflicts, as they may not finally become one's intentions. Such conflicts only mean different social attitudes exist and are grounded in different social relations.

The Conflict Between Two Social Commitments
When a potential conflict exists between two commitments, the agent will have a chance to fail one of them, causing the blame from the context group. The value of DOC serves as a rough indicator about the chance to keep both commitments without failing either of them (for example, this agent can discharge a commitment quickly, and then discharge another before the conflict actually occurs).

The Conflict Between Two Desires
An agent would always try to find the maximum utility of consistent set of desires and turn it as the set of intentions. When there are inconsistent desires, the agent should filter out inappropriate desires with lower utility values. Any desires remain not transited to intentions may fade to exist, and lose its appraised utility.

The Conflict Between a Desire and a Social Commitment
If a conflict exists between a desire and a social commitment, this desire can still become an intention by the choice of agent, whether this conflict is potential or direct. However, in the case of potential conflict, the agent should be aware of the fact that its intention and following plans could be interrupted at any time once the commitment is triggered, whereas in the case of direct conflict, adopting such a desire implies immediate change of intention and replanning.

4 Deliberation Process of a Social BDI Agent

In Fig. 3, the simplified deliberation process of a social BDI agent is shown as an event-driven workflow. To concentrate on the deliberate process itself, other irrelevant flows are either omitted or simplified. The number in each component indicates the order of steps. The algorithm of conflict detection is frequently used in step 1, 3, 4, and 6 to detect inconsistency between different couples of instances. . All conflicted instances are reserved until select intentions. According to the types of instance, the conflicts have different meanings. The functions of each component are explained as follows:

1. Select: Activate social dispositions corresponding to the received event, and detect conflicts between each activated disposition.
2. Generate Desires: According to the activated dispositions, multiple instances of desires would be generated.

3. Unify Desires: Merge new desires with the old ones and detect conflicts among them. An agent would always try to find the consistent set of desires with maximum utility. Conflicted desires may still be reserved.
4. Select: Activate social commitments corresponding to the received event, and detect conflicts between each activated commitments.
5. Generate Intentions: According to current desires and activated commitments, new intentions will be generated.
6. Select Intentions: New intentions and the old ones are merged, and conflict detection algorithm is performed to identify conflicted intentions. Finally, only a set of consistent intentions would be chosen to execute.
7. Planning: Plan the intention and send out actual actions, which is outside the scope of this paper.

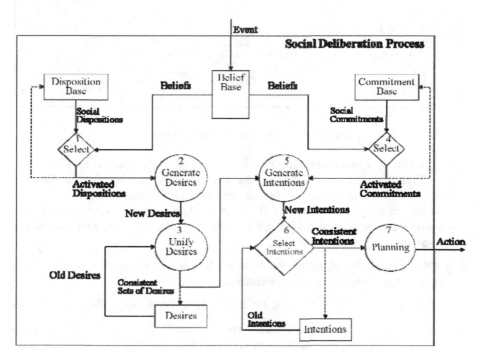

Fig. 3. The deliberation process of a social BDI agent

5 Illustration: A Bandit and a Princess

This section presents a short scenario about how an agent can reason in the social context. The hexagons in Fig. 4 represent social commitments, whereas the octagons stand as social dispositions.

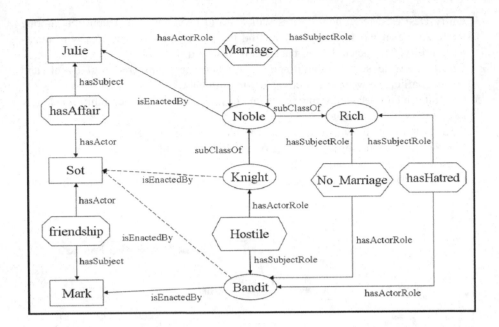

Fig. 4. Social Model for the feudal mini-society

Sot and his best friend Mark are two members of a group of notorious bandits, the Cursed Vipers, and they followed other bandits to pillage the rich. Sot and Mark are friends, and Sot had an affair with Julie, so much that he wanted to marry her.

One day, he happened to discover that Julie is actually a princess (incoming event), and his deliberation process is illustrated according to the workflow given in the previous section:

1. Sot's original belief about he and Julie are lovers is a social disposition to make him love Julie, which can be represented as

$$\text{hasAffair (Sot, Julie)} = D \text{ (Sot, Julie, (Sot, Julie), love (Sot, Julie))} \qquad (5)$$

2. By knowing Julie is a noble princess (which is also rich, via the subClassOf property), Sot the Bandit's social disposition to hate Julie the Rich activates.

$$\text{hasHatred (Bandit, Rich)} = D \text{ (Bandit, CursedVipers, CursedVipers, p), where} \qquad (6)$$
$$p = (\text{Belief (Bandit, Rich)} \Rightarrow \text{create (hate (Bandit, Rich))))}$$

Given beliefs that
●   isEnactedBy (Bandit, Sot)
●   isEnactedBy (Noble, Julie)
Hate (Sot, Julie) is then created.

3. These two social dispositions do not conflict (as we all know love != ¬hate) and coexisted to cause Sot has two desires, which are Love and Hate. These two desires transited to his intention.

4. Sot loved Julie so much, that he committed to marry Julie, which is

$$\text{Pledge1} = C \text{ (Sot, Julie, (Sot, Julie), p), where} \qquad (7)$$
$$p = (\text{Love (Sot, Julie)} \Rightarrow \text{marry (Sot, Julie)}))$$

5. However, by knowing Julie is a noble, his commitment as a member of Cursed Vipers activated, which is not marrying the Rich,

$$\text{No\_Marriage (Bandit, Rich)} = C \text{ (Bandit, CursedVipers, CursedVipers, p),} \qquad (8)$$
$$\text{where p} = (\text{Belief (Bandit, Rich (Person))}) \Rightarrow \text{create}$$
$$C \text{ (Bandit, CursedVipers, CursedVipers, } \neg\text{marry (Bandit, Person)}))$$

Given the same beliefs in assertion (6), Sot faced to fulfill his commitment,

$$\text{create } C \text{ (Sot, CursedVipers, CursedVipers, } \neg\text{marry (Sot, Julie))}$$

6. As a result, he has four new intentions now, which are love (Sot, Julie), hate (Sot, Julie), marry (Sot, Julie) and create (C (Sot, CursedVipers, CursedVipers, ¬marry (Sot, Julie)).
7. However, his new social commitment C (Sot, Julie, Cursed Vipers, ¬marry (Sot, Julie)) has a potential conflict with his intention marry (Sot, Julie), with DOC == 1. Assume Sot values Julie over the Cursed Vipers, he chooses to marry (Sot, Julie), love (Sot, Julie) and hate (Sot, Julie) (because he is still a bandit in the Cursed Vipers).
8. As a result, Sot loves and hates Julie at the same time, and he still puts it into action to marry her at the risk of violating an institutional rule.

On the other hand, Sot can join in the Order of Ares as a knight, and previous mental states in Sot would change according to his situated role, as he is allowed (and instructed) to marry another noble. Besides, he would become hostile to the Cursed Vipers, including Mark, who is his best friend, since eliminating bandits is one of the Knight's duties. The social model provides interrelations according to their situation. As scenario designers adds new institutional roles, relations to the social model by using OWL editors, and setups predefined social commitments, Sot can have more possibilities to change his future.

6 Conclusion and Future Work

This paper presents a social model that captures social context in scenarios. The model includes an ontology schema of relations between entities in the artificial society. An agent, given a BDI-based architecture, can find how to exhibit socially acceptable behavior by reasoning about the social commitments and social dispositions that come with the relation between agents. The agent can also detect the conflicts among relations with different agents and decide to take an action to make best of the situation. Moreover, confliction detection enables the agent to choose whether or not to accept a social relation or to enact a role because the agent can evaluate the consequences of taking a social commitment or disposition. NPC agents endowed with such social intelligence have the potential to form a virtual society and thus enhance the long-term believability of the scenario.

This paper addresses the conceptual modeling of social relations and institutional rules, which are to be incorporated with other schemas to generate concrete scenarios, such as schemas for communicative acts and content language to model agent communications, social actions, and modeling other agents, which are listed in our future work. In addition, elaborated algorithms may be needed to record DOC in a more systematic way for reference in the deliberation process of believable agents.

Acknowledgement

This research is supported by National Science Council of ROC under grants NSC 93-2213-E-007-061. We would like to give our thanks to Joseph Chen in Logitech for his equipment support. We are also indebted to the anonymous reviewers for their helpful comments, which have improved this paper considerably.

References

1. Artikis , A., Pitt , J., Sergot M. J. Animated specifications of computational societies. In Proceedings of the first international joint conference on Autonomous Agents and Multi-agent Systems (AAMAS02), Bologna (2002) 1053-1061
2. Bates, J. The role of emotion in believable agents. Communications of the ACM, 37(7), (1994) 122-125
3. Bratman, M. E., Israel, D., E. Pollack, M. E.: Plans and Resource-bounded Practical Reasoning. Computational Intelligence, 4(4): 349-355 (1988)
4. Carroll, J. J., Dickinson, I., Dollin, C., Reynolds, D., Seaborne, A., Wilkinson, K.: Jena: Implementing the Semantic Web Recommendations. Proceedings of the 13th International World Wide Web Conference. ACM Press, New York (2004) 74-83
5. Carley, K. M., Fridsma, D., Casman, E., Altman, N., Chang, J., Kaminsky, B., Nave, D., Yahja, A.: BioWar: scalable multi-agent social and epidemiological simulation of bioterrorism events. In Proceedings of North American Association for Computational Social and Organizational Science (NAACSOS) Conference, Pittsburgh, PA, USA (2003)
6. Castelfranchi, C.: Commitments: from individual intentions to groups and organizations. Proceedings of International Conference on Multi-Agent Systems (ICMAS) (1995)
7. Cavazza, M., Charles, F., Mead, S., J.: Characters in search of an author: AI-based virtual storytelling. In Proceedings of the 1st International Conference on Virtual Storytelling. Springer-Verlag, Avignon, France, (2001) 145-154
8. Cavedon, L., and Sonenberg, L. On social commitment, roles and preferred goals. In Proceedings of the 3rd International Conference on Multi Agent Systems (ICMAS). IEEE Computer Society, Paris, France, July 3-7 (1998) 80-87
9. Chang, P. H.-M., Chen, K.-T., Chien, Y.-H., Kao, E., Soo, V.-W.: From Reality to Mind: A Cognitive Middle Layer of Environment Concepts for Believable Agents. In Weyns, D., Parunak, H. V. D., Michel, F. (eds): Environments for Multi-Agent Systems. Lecture Notes in Artificial Intelligence, Vol. 3374. Springer-Verlag, Berlin Heidelberg New York (2005) 57-73
10. Chopra, A. K., Singh, M. P.: Nonmonotonic Commitment Machines. Proceedings of the International Workshop on Agent Communication Languages and Conversation Policies (ACL), Melbourne (2003)
11. Conte, R., Castelfranchi, C.: Cognitive and Social Action. UCL Press, London (1995)

12. Georgeff, M. P., Pell, B., Pollack, M. E., Tambe, M., Wooldridge, M.: The Belief-Desire-Intention model of agency. In Proceedings of the 5th International Workshop on Intelligent Agents V, Agent Theories, Architectures, and Languages (ATAL), Springer-Verlag, Paris, France, July 4-7 (1998) 1-10
13. Gratch, J.: Socially situated planning. In AAAI Fall Symposium on Socially Intelligent Agents: The Human in the Loop, North Falmouth, MA, November (2000)
14. Knublauch, H., Musen, M. A., Rector, A. L.: Editing Description Logic Ontologies with Prot´eg´e OWL Plugin. Proceedings of the 2004 International Workshop on Description Logics, Whistler, British Columbia, Canada (2004)
15. Marsella S., Gratch, J.: Modeling coping behavior in virtual humans: don't worry, be happy. In Proceedings of Autonomous Agents and Multi-Agent Systems (AAMAS03). ACM, Melbourne, Victoria, Australia, July 14-18 (2003) 313-320
16. Marsella S., Johnson, W. L., LaBore, C: Interactive Pedagogical Drama for Health Interventions. Proceedings of the Eleventh International Conference on Artificial Intelligence in Education. Australia (2003)
17. Mateas, M.: An Oz-centric review of interactive drama and believable agents. Artificial Intelligence Today, Springer-Verlag, (1999) 297-328
18. Molyneux, P.: Postmortem: Lionhead Studios' Black & White. Game Developer Magazine. June (2001)
19. Smith, M. K., Welty, C., McGuinnes, D. L (eds).: OWL Web Ontology Language Guide. W3C Recommendation. http://www.w3.org/TR/owl-guide/ (2004)
20. Singh, M. P.: On the Commitments and Precommitments of Limited Agents. IJCAI Workshop on Theoretical and Practical Design of Rational Agents, Sydney, Australia (1991)
21. Singh, M. P.: An ontology for commitments in multiagent systems: toward a unification of normative concepts. Artificial Intelligence and Law, 7(1): 97-113 (1999)

Integrating Social Skills in Task-Oriented 3D IVA*

Fran Grimaldo[1], Miguel Lozano[2], Fernando Barber[2], and Juan M. Orduña[2]

[1] Institute of Robotics, University of Valencia,
Pol. de la Coma, s/n (Paterna) Valencia, Spain
fran.grimaldo@robotica.uv.es
[2] Computer Science Department, University of Valencia,
Dr. Moliner 50, (Burjassot) Valencia, Spain
{miguel.lozano, fernando.barber, juan.orduna}@uv.es

Abstract. This paper presents a set of mechanisms oriented to incorporate social information into the decision taking of task-oriented 3DIVA. The aim of this approach is to integrate collaborative skills in different character's roles (seller/buyer, worker, pedestrian, etc.) in order to enhance its behavioral animation. The collective intelligence expected in this kind of multi-character domains (e.g. storytelling, urban simulation, interactive games, etc.) requires agents able to dialogue/interact with other characters, to autonomously group/ungroup (according to their goals), or to distribute tasks and coordinate their execution for solving possible conflicts. The social model implemented follows the definitions for collaborative agents, since agents use communicative acts to cooperate. In this context, collaboration derives mainly from two points: team formation (grouping for 3DIVA) and task coordination (reducing dependences between agent activities). Finally, we show the results obtained in 3D multi-character simulations (resource competition), created to verify the social behavior introduced.

1 Introduction and Related Work

Artificial worlds inhabited by 3D Intelligent Virtual Agents (3DIVA) can be considered as Multi-Agent Systems [10] where a number of actors deal with a finite number of shared resources. They are applications where collective intelligence arises as the result of the interaction established between characters that cannot avoid the social aspects of the behavioral animation problem.

3DIVA spectrum comprises a huge range of actors with different features. We basically identify two trends. On one side, we find reactive agents; from the classical *boids* introduced by Reynolds [18] up to more sophisticated crowds [20]. They can animate crowd behavior, normally reduced to movement generation and reactive actions, since individuals are so simple that their operation is quite limited. On the other side, deliberative agents, such as Jack [19] or Steve [9], can execute complicated tasks but they are not really designed to autonomously

---

* Supported by the Spanish MCYT under TIC-2003-08154-C06-04.

T. Panayiotopoulos et al. (Eds.): IVA 2005, LNCS 3661, pp. 358–370, 2005.
© Springer-Verlag Berlin Heidelberg 2005

collaborate with their peers. Somewhere in between, interactive storytelling and other group simulation scenarios tend to reproduce a global approach in which interactions and communications are normally script driven [17] or predefined by the "author" [6]. Therefore, virtual worlds lack characters intelligent enough to autonomously animate conversations (e.g. manage non expected meetings between two characters).

The simulation of a number of task-oriented agents (devoted to accomplish some tasks/goals in the environment) easily falls in conflictive domains even though the goals are compatible [10]. Obstruction situations then appear when characters compete for the use of shared resources (3D objects). Bearing this in mind, we identify the need to integrate social mechanisms in order to enrich the agent-centered decision making.

Three main problems appear when dealing with inhabited Intelligent Virtual Environments (IVE): communication, coordination and cooperation. Regarding to the first one, two capital Agent Communication Languages (ACL) have been developed; KQML and FIPA ACL. Both define communication between agents as an asynchronous exchange of messages, known as speech-acts. For instance, 3D BDI actors in [11] use FIPA ACL for the internal control of the agent. Unfortunately, interaction does not take place between 3D actors inside the virtual world but between the internal modules that constitute an individual. On the other side, Benford has a system that allows communication inside a crowd [2]. However, the process is controlled by an specific *Third Party Object* and the basic scenario is then formed by three objects.

Different formalisms can be used in order to achieve multi-agent coordination: tuple centers (which follow a blackboard model that do not reflect the peer-to-peer communication we are interested in), interaction protocols and ACL semantics. Nevertheless, all of them have their weaknesses when dealing with complex situations [3]. For example, Multiagent Planning Language (MAPL) [4] uses speech-acts to synchronize planned tasks. As the control over each resource is assigned to a unique agent, the model supports communication and coordination but it does not cooperate nor compete for common resources (as 3DIVA requires). Another example of coordination mechanisms intended for assisting in scheduling activities is Generalized Partial Global Planning (GPGP) [8]. In this approach, static tree structures describing the operational procedure are shared between the characters which merge the meta-plans and figure out the better action order to maximize global utility. As stated in [10], this solution has a limitation in the number of agents trying to make a coherent global plan and it is not very good at facing not planned situations which are quite common in dynamic and unpredictable environments (e.g. unexpected meetings between characters).

Collaborative planning has been deployed in several different domains. In SharedPlans [13], agents must have previously agreed about a common high-level team model and also about certain procedures (e.g. to assign agents and subgroups to subactions) to complete partial actions and plans, thus performing the group decision making. In STEAM architecture [21], oppositely, team formation and conflict resolution are governed by a leader. Besides, once role allocation is done, team members are supposed to perform their tasks independently. Nevertheless, this ideal situation is not commonly found in shared worlds where actors interfere while executing their actions. Lastly, virtual platoons in the RETSINA system [12] support multi-agent collaboration, thanks to the use of a planner that has all communicative acts predefined inside Hierarchical Task Networks (similar to storytelling approaches). Communication is then used to synchronize tasks and punctually manage conflicts but there is no conversational animation designed to get information and create an internal representation of the other agent that can be considered for future decisions.

mVITAL [1] and SimHuman [23] appear as two close systems in the literature of virtual humans but they are not focused on collaborative 3DIVA. The system presented in this paper, though, follows the Co-X definitions for agent interactions [22] and it exhibits Collaboration. That is, it uses both Conversation (direct peer-peer communication) and Cooperation (joint intent on the part of the individual agents) to face topics such as organizational techniques (grouping), task distribution, coordination, conflict resolution, etc.

The next section reviews the general requirements needed by task-oriented agents in order to extend their planning modules with social skills. We focus on two collaborative mechanisms: teamwork and task coordination. The solutions implemented for these two issues are the subject matter of section 3. Section 4 shows the first results obtained in 3D multi-character environments where resource competition is used to verify the social mechanisms introduced. Finally, we state our conclusions and future work.

2   Requirements for Social 3DIVA

Complex IVE (e.g. urban domains) need the instantiation of autonomous 3D actors performing different *client/server* roles; for instance: virtual waiters in a crowded bar, assistants in a virtual museum, and obviously the corresponding customers. This kind of characters face situations that require the animation of dialogues as well as the ability to develop relationships and use them in a proactive way.

We emphasize three different interaction situations while simulating this type of social roles: *resource competition, grouping between actors* (i.e. create and destroy groups to fulfill certain objectives) and *joint task execution* (e.g. carry heavy objects by two actors). To resolve them, agents need to embed a planning system able to recognize the lack of information and to manage communication in an autonomous way. This article is focused on the team formation protocol that the characters use to create groups as well as the task coordination mechanism implemented to reduce conflicts when competing for shared objects. *Joint task execution* is out of the scope of this paper.

2.1   Grouping Between Actors

The Joint Intentions Theory [7] states that a team is created when each agent commits to a goal and receives notification about the commitment of the remaining individuals. However, the theory does not consider important aspects such as how actors arrive at this point, that is, how a team objective is acquired. Systems doing team work have generally avoided this problem by settling the teams beforehand and giving the agents the awareness of being part of the group [13,12]. This persistent definition of teams, though, is unsuitable in some 3D simulations, where characters can change their roles and make temporary associations to better fulfill parts of their global goal (e.g. ephemeral associations in [5]). In these scenarios, groups can be dynamically formed and disintegrated (i.e. new agents join the group while some others decide to leave).

For example, a 3D construction domain could be inhabited by a number of foremen and laborers that work together to build a virtual space. Sociability can appear when several virtual laborers are assigned the same objective (e.g. make concrete) by different foremen. Initially, they might be unaware of that common assignment, therefore, there would not be a formed team and agents will act independently. But, as soon as they realize their common goal, they will jointly commit to it and resource competition between the partners of the group will consequently be relaxed. That is, one agent's planning process must consider the other members of the group.

To animate this behavior, independent characters first need to detect when their operation is being affected or interrupted by the actions of other individuals [1]. Once this communication need is identified (i.e. a precondition has been violated), the agents can manage the situation by: a) initiate a conversation, b) exchange their individual goals, c) detect compatibility between them, and d), decide whether to be part of a group or to leave it. In the next section we will present the team formation protocol defined to implement these aspects.

2.2   Task Coordination

As mentioned before, resource competition is managed through the use of a task coordination mechanism. Despite the fact that some scenarios tend to reproduce task-independent actors, this constitutes a strong simplification which will directly affect the quality of the resulting animation. Actions being performed by task-oriented agents can be dependent, in these situations, their execution will affect the operation of other 3D actors and will generate coordination problems. Hence, coordination can be defined as *managing dependences between activities* [16].

Basically, coordination mechanisms are based on an information gathering stage, followed by the processing of the data previously exchanged. To minimize the normal dependency problems in multi-activity simulations with shared resources, the participants should complete the perceived state with the activities already planned by other characters. In this manner, the embedded planning formalism will be more informed to select a proper task that reduces interference (e.g. one barman will attend other customers while the desired bottle is

---

[1] In STRIPS-based planners, this can be achieved by regularly checking the preconditions of the current task.

being used by another barman).Task coordination within a group will require an internal publication of the ongoing tasks, so that, members of a team can avoid interfering or disturbing their mates (see sections 3.3 and 4).

We have designed another way to avoid the dependences between the activities of two agents: to partition the goal set, so agents try to accomplish different independent subgoals. Unfortunately, identifying the independence of subgoals may be as difficult as the planning process itself and it is not generally affordable for a 3D agent. Therefore, we have defined an estimator to help task coordination attending to the objects involved in the set of facts that define the final goal. This heuristic obtains a good partitioning although it is not guaranteed that the subgoals are independent.

Goal Partitioning: We say two facts f_1 and f_2 are related ($f_1 \sim f_2$) if both refer to a common object (see equation 1^2). Therefore, the partition of a set of facts (S) will be given by the quotient set of this relation: $S/\sim$.

$$f_1 \sim f_2 \quad iff \quad \exists o : (f_1(o, o') \vee f_1(o', o)) \wedge ((f_2(o, o'') \vee f_2(o'', o)) \tag{1}$$

Using this definition each agent can divide his goal in a set of "near independent" subgoals. The aim of this approach is to relax the dependencies between activities being performed by the actors. According to this, when two agents compete for the use of some shared objects, they use goal partitioning and try to select independent subgoals (see section 4).

3 Social Model

Agents presented in [15] suffer from autonomous communication modules to coordinate their actuation or exchange information with their partners. Thus, the behavioral consistency of the multi-agent animations can be poor. According to this, we have extended the previous agent centered architecture in order to allow social characters to work together in a common scenario.

Our multi-agent animation system follows a distributed architecture. This modular structure separates the graphics engine and its semantic database (Unreal Tournament) from the deliberative agents. These are in charge of controlling the actuation of the 3D actor inside the virtual world thanks to the use of an heuristic planner. The collaborative features developed for our characters and presented in this paper are based on a communication model [14] in which the environment acts as a transmission channel (similarly to the air in the real world). Therefore, communication can be considered as an action carried out throughout the world; that allows us to design message filters depending on distance to other agents, presence of walls, etc. Opposite to blackboard systems, the environment directly delivers the ACL structured messages between the agents, which animate the conversation.

The social model embedded is composed by three mechanisms: a Conversational Task Controller, which permits agents to handle conversations with their

---

^{2} This definition is for facts of arity 2, but it can be easily extended to any fact.

peers (point 3.1); a team formation protocol, that assess the convenience of being part of a group (point 3.2); and a task coordination mechanism, in charge of reducing conflicts while competing for shared resources (point 3.3).

3.1 Conversational Task Controller

The Task Controller governs the agent activity at anytime and it decides what to do depending on the agent and world states. This Finite State Machine (FSM) incorporates several states to control conversations between characters, hence, it is able to animate the behavior of 3D actors with social skills. As shown in figure 1, after having reached a comfortable position to speak (REACH AGENT brings the conversers near), agents will alternatively TALK and LISTEN. These two states allow the agents to generate the typical query/response interchange to gather information. This FSM can only manage one conversation at the same time, thus, agents already part of a dialogue will deny another proposal of interaction.

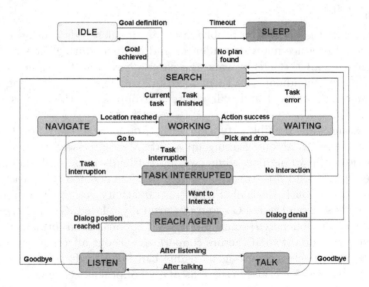

Fig. 1. Conversational Task Controller

One important aspect is when to start a conversation. The need of communication is generated when an action fails due to the interference of another agent (e.g. an actor takes an object that another character wanted to pick). This situation is resolved by conversing with the character who interfered in the success of the execution. Within this dialogue, the agents will communicate their current occupation (i.e. send their current STRIPS task, for example, *move Chair_1 from Bedroom to Kitchen*) so that task coordination can be applied further on, as we will explain in point 3.3.

3.2   Team Formation

The aim of grouping is to reduce interagent interference and to enhance the quality of the behavioral animation. Whereas non interfering agents do not normally need to agree to reach their goals, others interrupting their operation will need to consider the possibility of temporarily creating a group to better fulfill their tasks and achieve their goals. This evaluation will be done through a team formation protocol which is based on a goal checking between agents. Say agent A and B have goals composed by a set of facts $(G_A = \{f_i\}, G_B = \{f_j\})$, then, three different types of situations are distinguished:

- A couple of agents have *fully related* goals when they share the same set of facts $(G_A = G_B)$ or when the facts of one of them are a subset of the facts of the other one $(G_A \subset G_B$ or $G_A \supset G_B)$.
- The goals are *partially related* when the intersection is not complete and there are still some facts solely ascribed to one agent $(G_A \cap G_B \neq \phi)$.
- The goals are *non related* when there is no intersection between the goals $(G_A \cap G_B = \phi)$.

Fully related goals can be problematic, as the close relationship of the objectives could produce many dependences and conflicts during the simultaneous execution (e.g. all the agents want the same objects at the same time). According to this, candidates to form a group will use goal matching in their team formation protocol and will create a group when their goals are fully related.

For instance, one possible extension of the *funny dinner-date* problem [6] can consist on some 3D actors cleaning up a flat. More precisely, the owner could want to clean the whole flat, while two more friends would only help in some tasks (see figure 2). In this scenario, agent A can join agent B to dust the kitchen and agent C to polish the hall. However, transitivity cannot be applied when forming groups. Even though G_A and G_B are fully related, G_B and G_C are non related, as a consequence, B joins A but not C. Thus, team formation protocol is limited to decide if two 3D actors cooperate, without affecting previous commitments. Nevertheless, multi-agent teams can be reproduced due to the fact that characters can separately create as many couples as needed.

The ability to coordinate groups is a key point to produce consistent and lifelike simulations. We consider cooperation as an internal intentional posture of the agents, therefore, while being part of a team, they will continuously communicate their intentions [3] to their mates in order to facilitate task coordination. Knowing at all times the current actions of the teammates will prevent constant obstruction between characters.

Finally, characters should also be able to leave their teams, that is, they have to communicate their departure of the group when necessary. This occurs when their goal is no longer fully related with the objectives of the community (e.g. a foreman orders a laborer to change his personal goal).

---

[3] Their current task is used to consider the actual intention.

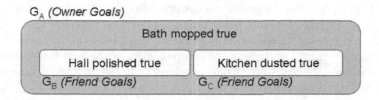

G_A *(Owner Goals)*

Bath mopped true

| Hall polished true | Kitchen dusted true |

G_B *(Friend Goals)* G_C *(Friend Goals)*

Fig. 2. Example of the goals of three agents cleaning up a flat. Intersection relationships between their goals impede to apply transitivity in the team formation protocol.

3.3   Coordinated Task-Oriented agents

Task-oriented agents can coordinate their operation if they know the intentions of their surrounding mates. The information about the ongoing actions that other characters intend to complete can be used to manage the constraints imposed by them. In order to represent the operation of external agents, 3D actors need an extended memory model that, aside from the perceived state of the environment, holds a set of communicative beliefs (*c_beliefs*) acquired through the conversations established with other cohabitants of the virtual world (see figure 3).

A *c_belief* corresponds to a task being executed at this moment by another character. Two aspects appear when working with *c_beliefs*:

– Whether to trust another character about his current task is an important issue, because it could lead the actor to an incongruent mental state. Due to the reactive nature of our planning formalism, an actor should not think, for example, that one partner will successfully open a door while a second

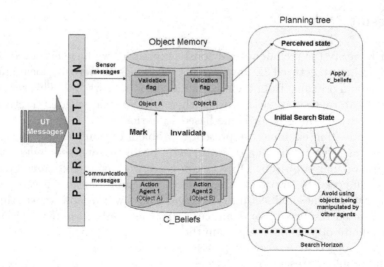

Fig. 3. Coordination model

one is going to close the same door; since he does not know their timing. In this way, all the operators being communicated by external agents will not become a *c_belief* in the memory. Instead, after receiving a communication message, the agent will check the compatibility of the new information with the *c_beliefs* already stored. This checking is based on the resources, which will be locked when an agent has a *c_belief* above them (see *Mark* signal in figure 3). Therefore, when an agent tries to match a new operator, if it uses a locked resource, it will be considered incompatible and it will be discarded. Hence, the actor trusts the first agent who notified his intents and avoids conflicts that might happen with later *c_beliefs*.

– When to remove a *c_belief* from the memory is another problem. However, as characters are continuously perceiving the state of the world, they can contrast the sensorized information against the preconditions of the current *c_beliefs* and delete them when they are not true (*Invalidate* signal in figure 3).

This new information, stored inside the memory, can be used by the planning formalisms of the agent to generate coordinated plans. As previously exposed, characters are benevolent and their intention is to let the others finish their previous commitments. Following this premise, the miniMin-HSP planner used by our 3DIVA [15] will now start the search from a future virtual state resulted from applying the *c_beliefs* over the current perceived state (this mental execution uses the *add* and *delete* lists of the STRIPS definition for the the external ongoing actions).In this manner, it constructs a prospective situation that skips actual dependences. Additionally, each *c_belief* will lock the objects being used by other agents thereby forbidding to jeopardize the success of the tasks previously initiated (see figure 3).

4 Results

In order to verify the techniques previously explained, we have executed several simulations in a structured 3D environment where agents perceive local information (in a room domain) from their synthetic vision sensors [14]. This simulation framework can reproduce social worlds where 3DIVA deal with interactive situations (e.g. urban, building or home-based scenarios).

As a motivating example, we present a problem of multi-character resource allocation (inspired by the *funny dinner-date* problem), where agents compete for the use of shared objects. Objects can be moved using the *move* operator, which is composed by two tasks: *pick object* and *drop object*. These operators are similar to the ones defined in the classical blocks world, however, in this case we have limited resources. For example, a table can only have one object on it and not infinite objects (as happens in the classical problem), and also an agent may have an object *occupied* (i.e. picked) so no one else can use it.

In the problem presented in figure 4, the characters have to organize a flat composed of four rooms. Snapshot 4a shows a situation with three agents in where: *Agent_1* wants to put all the books in room number 4; *Agent_2* desires to move each plant to room 3; and finally, *Agent_3* has the two previous objectives as well as stacking the boxes together (this goal is partitioned into three independent subgoals). At first, agents are unaware of the others' goals but they will gather data during the simulation thanks to the dialogues established between them when an interruption occurs. This is the case of 4*b*, where *Agent_1* wanted to move away the plant that was on top of the books but *Agent_2* takes it first. In this situation, since goals are clearly independent they reject to form a group and continue their actuation but knowing the new information about the current task that has been exchanged. Nevertheless, agents with fully related goals will create groups, this is the result of the competition for the book between *Agent_1* and *Agent_3* in 4*c*. While they are a group, task coordination is continuously applied. According to this, as *Agent_1* informs his partner about his current task when he moves the book to room 4 in snapshot 4*d*, *Agent_3* can change to another subgoal and avoid interferences (e.g. pile boxes up instead of trying to pick the book as well).

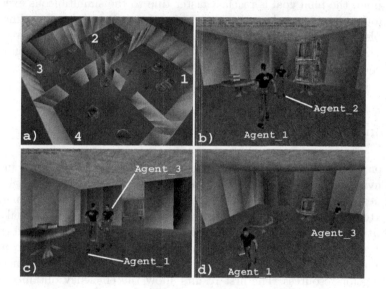

Fig. 4. Snapshots of Team formation and Task Coordination within a 3D IVE

As stated in [10], cooperation can be measured by three indicators: survival, performance improvement and conflict resolution. According to this, we have executed some simulations over a 3D blocks world scenario where four agents try to perform a common goal. The survival indicator has no sense in this problem as all agents achieve their goals. We have estimated performance improvement by the amount of executed tasks (TE) and the number of planner invocations (PC). Finally, conflict resolution is estimated by the number of plan interruptions (PI). Table 1 resumes the results obtained.

Table 1. 3D blocks world problem results with and without collaboration

Agent	PC		PI		TE	
	Simple	Collaborative	Simple	Collaborative	Simple	Collaborative
A	14	13	4	5	10	8
B	9	5	3	2	6	3
C	15	9	4	2	11	7
D	15	6	7	2	8	4

PC = Planner Calls, PI = Plans Interrupted, TE = Task executed

Although one single character successfully allocates all the resources in 14 steps, non-communicative individuals need the execution of 35 tasks. The execution of many more tasks than the optimal number needed to complete a goal implies that the simulation will be less realistic. With communicative actors, multi-agent performance can be enhanced as they lower this number down to 22 non-conflictive tasks. Despite the fact that the total number of tasks is not optimal, the final goal is reached faster due to the simultaneous execution. On the other hand, social agents need to invoke their planner less times than the simple ones (see column PC), whose plans are interrupted more frequently (see column PI). To sum up, the new way of planning reduces the number of interferences and produces a coordinated set of tasks whose execution can be overlapped.

5   Conclusions and Future Work

In this paper we have described a system able to introduce social skills in multi-agent environments. These abilities appear derive from the use of collaborative techniques based on message passing (communication) and the implementation of an extended model of memory that stores the operation of external agents (cooperation). The social model presented is composed by the team formation protocol and the task coordination mechanism that allows 3DIVA to manage dependences, resolve conflicts and enhance the behavioral performance when competing for resources. The first results show the efficiency obtained thanks to the use of goal partitioning and the application of communicative beliefs (c_beliefs) to generate coordinated plans. Besides, action interferences are clearly reduced when characters can create groups to achieve a common set of goals.

There is still work in progress in order to evaluate our agent model in more complex scenarios and roles. For example, *joint task execution* (i.e. operators carried out by more than one agent) needs plenty of communication between the individuals that perform the actions. Currently, dialogs are fully dependent on the planning in the sense that 3D actors interact solely with the objective of gathering information to better fulfill their goals. However, a greater number of dialogues have to be implemented over the Conversational Task Controller so that characters can animate different conversations.

Acknowledgments

We would like to thank all the support and help received from Norman Badler and Jan Allbeck during the stay in the Center for Human Modeling and Simulation in the University of Pennsylvania.

References

1. G. Anastassakis, T. Panayiotopoulos and T. Ritchings. Virtual Agent Societies with the mVITAL Intelligent Agent System. In *Proc. of the 3rd International Workshop on Intelligent Virtual Agents*, 2001.
2. S. Benford, C. Greenhalgh and D. Lloyd. Crowded collaborative virtual environments. In *Proc. of the SIGCHI conference on human factors in computing systems*, 1997.
3. F. Bergenty and A. Ricci. Three approaches to the coordination of multi-agent systems. In *Proc. of ACM Symposim on Applied computing*, pages 367-372, 2002.
4. M. Brenner. A multiagent planning language. In *Proc. of ICAPS'03 Workshop on PDDL*, 2003.
5. T. Bouron and A. Collinot. SAM: a model to design computational social agents. In *Proc. of the 10th European Conference on AI (ECAI'92)*, pages 239-243, 1992.
6. M. Cavazza, F. Charles and S.J, Mead. Planning characters' behaviour in interactive storytelling. *The Journal of Visualization and Computer Animation*, pages 121-131, 2002.
7. P. Cohen and H. Levesque. TeamWork. On *Nous, Special Issue on Cognitive Science and AI*, 1991.
8. K. S. Decker and V. R. Lesser. Designing a Family of Coordination Algorithms. On *Readings in Agents*, Huhns and Singh editors, 1997.
9. C. Elliot, J. Rickel and J. Lester. Lifelike pedagogical agents and affective computing: An exploratory synthesis. *Artificial Intelligence Today* Springer, 1999.
10. J. Ferber. *Multi-Agent Systems: An Introduction to Distributed Artificial Intelligence*. Addison Wesley Longman, 1999.
11. C. Geiger and M. Latzel. Prototyping of complex plan based behaviour for 3D actors. In *Proc. of the 4th International Conference on Autonomous Agents*, 2000.
12. J. A. Giampapa and K. Sycara. Team-Oriented Agent Coordination in the RETSINA Multi-Agent System. On *Tech. Report CMU-RI-TR-02-34*, Robotics Institute-Carnegie Mellon University, December 2002.
13. B. Grosz and S. Kraus. Planning and Acting Together. On *AI Magazine*, 1999.
14. M. Lozano, R. Lucia, F. Barber, F. Grimaldo, A. Lucas and A.F. Bisquerra. An Efficient Synthetic Vision System for 3D Multi-Character Systems. In *Proc. of the 4th International Workshop of Intelligent Agents (IVA03)*, September 2003.
15. M. Lozano, F. Grimaldo and F. Barber. Integrating miniMin-HSP agents in a dynamic simulation framework. In *Proc. of the 3rd Hellenic Conference on Artificial Intelligence*, May 2004.
16. T. W. Malone and Kevin Crowston. The interdisciplinary Study of Coordination. *ACM Computing Surveys* , 26(1): 87-119, 1994.
17. C. O'Sullivan et al. Crowd and group simulation with levels of detail for geometry. In *Proc. of the 3rd Irish Workshop on Computer Graphics*, Eurographics Ireland, 2002.

18. C. Reynolds. Steering behaviors for autonomous characters. In *Games developer conference*, 1999.
19. J. Shi, T.J. Smith, J.P. Granieri and N.I. Badler. Smart Avatars in JackMOO. *VR'99: Proceedings of the IEEE Virtual Reality*, 1999.
20. M. Sung, M. Gleicher and S. Chenney. Scalable behavior for crowd simulation. *Computer Graphics Forum*, 23(3), Eurographics 2004.
21. M. Tambe. Towards Flexible TeamWork. On *Journal of Artificial Intelligence Research*, 7: 83-124, 1997.
22. H. Van Dyke Parunak, M. Fleishcher, S. Brueckner and J. Odell. Co-x: Defining what agents do together. In *Workshop on Teamwork and Coalition Formation, AAMAS*, 2002.
23. S. Vosinakis and T. Panayiotopoulos. SimHuman: A platform for real time Virtual Agents planning capabilities. In *Proc. of the 3rd International Workshop on Intelligent Virtual Agents*, 2001.

Emergent Affective and Personality Model

Mei Yii Lim, Ruth Aylett, and Christian Martyn Jones

School of Mathematical and Computer Sciences,
Heriot Watt University,
Edinburgh, EH14 4AS, Scotland
{myl, ruth, cmj}@macs.hw.ac.uk

Abstract. The Emergent Affective and Personality model is a body-mind model of emotions for a mobile tour guide agent. This research is inspired by work in Psychology, Brain Research, Personality, Narrative, Mobile Computing and Artificial Intelligence. The main goal is to build an 'intelligent guide with attitude'. This paper presents a review of related work, the affective model and the future work to be carried out.

1 Introduction

Research interest on interactive characters has increased significantly in recent years. Artificial intelligence researchers have long wished to build creatures whom you'd like to make a companion or a social pet. The better that computational agents can meet our human cognitive and social needs, the more familiar and natural they are, the more effectively they can be used as tools [1]. Humans are social animals, therefore, our computational systems should be able to engage our social abilities, which means that emotions and personality are vital for computer agents.

Emotions represent an important source of information, filtering relevant data from noisy sources and provide a global management over other cognitive capabilities and processes, important when operating in complex real environments [2]. Emotions play a critical role in rational decision-making, in perception, in human interaction and in human intelligence [3]. Even animators felt that the most significant quality in characters is appropriately timed and clearly expressed emotion [4]. Famous Bugs Bunny animator, Chuck Jones said that it is the oddity, the quirk, that gives personality to a character and it is personality that gives life.

Hence, the current focus of character development research is on the design of motivational structures, emotional and personality traits and behavior controls systems for characters to perform in context-specific environments with well-defined goals and social tasks [5, 6]. Adaptation capability is another important criterion for virtual characters in order to survive in the dynamic environment where strong measure of unpredictability exist.

Having this awareness, the Emergent Affective and Personality Model, designed based on the 'Psi' theory [7] integrates perception, motivation, action-selection, planning and memory access to create a tour guide agent that can

T. Panayiotopoulos et al. (Eds.): IVA 2005, LNCS 3661, pp. 371–380, 2005.
© Springer-Verlag Berlin Heidelberg 2005

respond to various circumstances and user action appropriately. It is an integrated body-mind model of emotions where the higher cognitive-level accounts result from lower-level processing.

The main aim of this research is the creation of an 'agent with attitude' to provide adaptive guidance and engaging interaction. The guide agent is being implemented on a PDA, taking advantage of the current mobile technologies such as wireless hotspots and Global Positioning System for position tracking. It is an outdoor tourist guidance application. Detailed explanation of the system can be found in [8] and is not given here as the focus of this paper is on the affective model.

In addition to the development of a believable agent, the use of different personality guide agents to narrate the story is necessary due to the fact that there usually exist multiple interpretations of the same historical event, depending on the storyteller's perspective [9]. The guide will tell stories based on his or her past experiences taking into consideration the user's interest. The guide's long-term memory holds declarative memories that can be divided into emotional memory and semantic memory.

2   Related Work

There has been a series of effort for making artifacts with their own emotional structure. Most of these projects focus either on the cognitive aspect of emotion adopting appraisal theories, or on the neurophysiological aspect. Very few attempts have been carried out to bridge the gap between these two aspects where models such as perception, motivation, learning, action-selection, planning and memory access are integrated.

The Oz project [10, 11, 12, 13] aimed at producing agents with a broad set of capabilities, including goal-directed and reactive behavior, emotional state, social knowledge and some natural language abilities. Individual *Woggles* had specific habits and interests which were shown as different personalities. Social relations between the agents directly influenced their emotional system and vice versa. However, Oz focused on building specific, unique believable characters, where the goal is an artistic abstraction of reality, not biologically plausible behavior.

Cañamero [14] proposed an architecture that relies on both motivations and emotions to perform behavior selection. This model was implemented in *Abbots and Enemies* through a microworld, Gridland, a two-dimensional toroidal grid containing resources. This model allows activation of several emotions at the same time where the emotions run in parallel with the motivational control system and influence the creatures perception of both the external world and their own body. The main problem of this architecture is that it was totally hand-coded.

Breazeal [15] built a robot called *Kismet* that has the ability to express nine emotions through its facial expressions. Its design is focused on feed forward operation of motivation and is within the framework of a kind of reflex model.

Duration and intensity of certain types of interactions that the designer had in mind are the main factors that affect its drive states.

On the other hand, Velásquez's robot, *Yuppy* [16], utilized feed backward operation of emotion. It is a biologically plausible computational framework for Emotion-Based Control, integrating an emotional system with models of perception, motivation, behavior and motor control. Previous emotional experiences are fed back to the behavior system forming an emotional memory, which affects action selection strategy when it re-encounters similar situations. However, *Yuppy* capabilities are prespecified and it does not show emotional responses to a novel object or situation.

AlphaWolf [17], offers a computational model that captures a subset of the social behavior of wild wolves, involving models of learning, emotion and development. The emotion model is based on the Pleasure-Arousal-Dominance model presented by Mehrabian and Russell [18]. The wolves are able to form an association with other wolves. The wolves' emotions lead to formation of context-specific emotional memories based on the "somatic marker hypothesis" presented by Damasio [19], which affects how they will interact in the future. This research emphasises social learning and offers initial steps toward a computational system with social abilities.

In addition, [7, 20, 21, 22] try to create a body-mind link for virtual agents. The 'Psi' agents [7, 20, 21] framework focuses on emotional modulation of perception, action-selection, planning and memory access. Emotions are not defined as explicit states but rather emerge from modulation of information processing and action selection. They become apparent when the agents interact with the environment and display expressive behavior, resulting in a configuration that resemble emotional episodes in biological agents. Dörner's agents react to the environment by forming memories, expectations and immediate evaluations. They possess a number of modulators that lie within a range of intensities. These modulators together with built-in motivators produce complex behavior that can be interpreted as being emotional.

[22] integrates a connectionist cognitive model of emotional processing called SESAME [23] with a synthetic force model, SOF-Soar architecture [24] for training in a battlefield simulation. The intention of this project is to investigate improved realism in generating complex human-like behavior by integrating behavior moderators with higher cognitive processes. The appraisal system provides information to, while the response system accepts information from, the connectionist emotions model. Emotional states can be viewed as arising from a combination of pleasure/pain, arousal, clarity/confusion components and by changing these connection strengths, different personalities result.

All these works aim at the creation of believable, emotional or social agents, which serve as sources of inspiration to our research. Basically, our research attempts to create a biologically plausible agent, bridging the gap between the lower- and higher-level processes, taking into consideration various factors such as perception, motivation, action-selection, planning, and memory access.

3   Emergent Affective and Personality Model

The Emergent Affective Model, presented in Fig. 1 takes advantage of the interesting characteristics of the previous work. Its design takes the 'Psi' model as basis but with the addition of emotional memory.

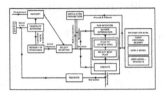

Fig. 1. The Emergent Affective and Personality Model

In this architecture, motivation is represented by needs and aims of the user as well as the guide's, emotions are reflected by the modulating parameters, their causes and influences, while cognition is represented by information processes in GENERATE INTENTION, SELECT INTENTION, RUN INTENTION and PERCEPT as well as in the memory of intentions and other environmental factors. The guide has a need to maintain its level of competence (the degree of capability of coping with differing perspectives) and a need to keep user attention high by adjusting its behavior appropriately to the level of uncertainty (the degree of predictability of the environment).

Functionally, the agent perceives the environment continuously and generates intentions based on the external information and needs, that is, the guide reads the user inputs, system feedback and the GPS information continuously, then, generates a goal, let's say a story topic based on this information. These intentions together with its built-in motivators - level of competence and level of uncertainty are stored in a memory of intentions. The user's response, for example, the degree to which he or she agrees with the guide's argument, contributes to the guide's competence level, while the accuracy of the GPS reading contributes to the level of uncertainty.

Next, depending on the importance of the need and the urgency for realization, one of the active intentions is selected. For intention execution, the guide decides autonomously whether to explore for more information, to design a plan using the available information or to run an existing plan. The decision is made based on the value of the built-in motivators and modulators such as arousal level (speed of information processing), resolution level (carefulness and attentiveness of behavior) and selection threshold (how easy is it for another motive to take over) or in another word, the agent's current emotional state.

An agent with a higher arousal level will process information more quickly than a lower arousal level agent. A careful agent will pay more attention to various circumstances and perform a more detailed planning before the execution of an intention compared to an agent with lower resolution level. While an agent with a higher selection threshold will hold to its current intention more firmly than a lower selection threshold agent. Interaction between these modulators and built-in motivators results in complex emotional state. There is no direct mapping of the high-level emotion labels to the different values of the modulators. In other words, the resulting emotions are in the eye of the beholder.

Let's take a look at some examples. In an uncertain environment (GPS accuracy is low) and a low level of competence (user is in disagreement with the guide's perspective), it is reasonable to react quickly, concentrate on the respective task and forbid time consuming memory search. Therefore, the guides arousal level and selection threshold should be high while its resolution level should be low in which case, we may diagnose that the guide is experiencing anxiety. In this situation, the agent tends to give a more general story of the current site without details. On the other hand, when its level of competence is high and the environment is stable, it may experience a high, but not too high level of arousal and selection threshold, with a medium resolution level. This time, the agent may be said to experience pride and hence, it is not easy for another goal to take over. It will perform some planning and provide a more elaborated story on the current subject.

By doing so, it adapts its behavior according to its internal states and the environmental circumstances. Each execution of intention will produce a feedback into the system and recovery will be performed when necessary.

3.1 Emotional Memory

Recent studies in neurology provide evidence that memory files contain not only data or information but emotions as well [25]. Memory files thus consist of the information about an event and the emotions we experience at the time when the event occurs. It is the emotional arousal, not the importance of the imformation that organises memory [26]. The stronger the emotional factor, the longer the memory remains due to the fact that emotional arousal has a key role in the enhancement of memories for significant information [27]. However, the correlation between emotional arousal intensity and memory strength is not necessarily linear.

It has also long been known that emotionally arousing events are more likely to be later recollected than similar, neutral events [28]. Those memories are part of what makes up our personality, controls our behaviors and often produces our mood.

Adopting this idea, the guide possesses a long-term memory that is made up of declarative memories, both semantic and emotional memories. Semantic memory is memory for facts, including location-related information and the user profile while emotional memory is memory for experienced events and episodes. The guide's emotional memories will be generated through simulation of past experiences. Additionally, the guide's current memory holds information about recent processing.

Emotional information can be categorised into two dimensions: arousal, that is, how exciting or calming an experience is and valence, that is, whether an experience causes a positive or a negative impact [29]. Consequently, the guide's emotional memory holds not only information about when, what and how an event happened, but also an 'arousal' tag and a 'valence' tag.

The inclusion of 'arousal' tag is analogous to the *Emotional Tagging* concept, according to which the activation of the amygdala in emotionally arousing events marks the experience as important and aids in enhancing synaptic plasticity in other brain regions [30]. While the amygdala plays an important role in emotional memory enhancement [31, 32, 33], [34] identified two distinct regions of brain activity specifically related to emotional memory retrieval - the anterior temporal cortex and the left amygdala. In contrast, the prefrontal-cortex and hippocampus are involve in enhancement of valence information [29]. The 'valence' tag serves as basis of the guide's level of competence.

When interacting with the user, the agent will be engaged in meaningful reconstruction of its own past [1], at the same time presenting facts about the site of attraction. This recollective experience is related to the evocation of previously experienced emotions through the activation of the emotion tags. These values combine with the built-in motivators values to trigger the resolution level and selection threshold, resulting in re-experiencing of emotions, though there might be a slight variation due to the input from the user.

Therefore, the activation of the emotion tags is directly related to the story being told and it affects the agent's current emotional state. It may also lead to activation of other relevant story about the agent's current experiences. The user provides feedback to the agent from time to time using the graphical user interface throughout the tour or when the agent explicitly asks some questions that require user's input.

The user's responses form positive and negative stimuli to the agent. Based on these responses, the guide will make assumptions about the user's interest. This information will be stored in the information base for later use. For example, a high level of competence may decrease the arousal level and lead to a higher resolution level and a lower selection threshold value.

In terms of storytelling, this will mean that when the user adopts the guide's perspective by agreeing, the agent's level of competence increases which leads to a more detailed explanation about the subject or related subjects. Similarly, when the user disagrees, the agent's level of competences decreases and the agent tends to focus on only the important points of the subject without much elaboration. That is, the emotion elicited determines the information retrieved and how it is retrieved.

3.2   Personality

As mentioned earlier, personality plays an important role in this application. Based on a brief survey of tour guides experiences, we found that factors like role, interest, experience, type of tour, guide's belief, guide's personality and visitors group can affect the presentation of information.

The surveys were performed by direct participation in indoor tours around museums and outdoor tours such as English Heritage Castle tours, the Edinburgh Underground Tour, the York City Haunted Tour, audio tours, etc. The number of participants in indoor tours falls in the range from 5 to 15 while the number of participants in outdoor tours is from 10 to 25. Besides that, short informal interviews were also carried out with some of the tour guides concerning their experiences and the factors they take into account for story generation.

Most guides tend to incorporate belief and past experiences, whether his/her own or others while narrating a story. Different guides have different presentation styles and some guides are more chatty than others. They usually welcome interaction in order to get clues about the visitors' interest. Visitors' age, origin, race, group size, etc. also contribute to the type of story told. Indoor tours are usually more continuous while outdoor tours involve more idling moments due to walking from one place to another.

Similarly, the virtual guide's personality will affect the way they behave and the story presentation. The story content on the other hand, will reflect the guide's ideology or perspective about a particular historical event. Besides that, it also manifests the guide's personal life experiences.

In our model, rather than assigning different traits to the guide, personality emerges from varying the weight of each modulator which ranges from 0 to 1. Different combinations of weights will result in different personality guides and when combined with the emerging emotions can produce a vast range of expressions. Fig. 2 gives an illustration of how variation of the modulators' weight can lead to different personality guides.

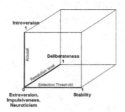

Fig. 2. Personality cube

The personality of the guide is reflected by the way it tackles interaction circumstances which map nicely to a personality traits model. The modulators are mapped onto the temperament dimensions defined by [35], however, with a slight modification where 'Psychoticism' is replaced by the Impulsivity-Deliberateness dimensions of [36] which better describe the resolution level. Arousal level corresponds to the Extraversion-Introversion dimension while selection threshold represents the Neuroticism-Stability dimension.

Let's take the selection threshold dimension for explanation. If a guide is given a selection threshold weight of 0.1, this will mean that it is almost impossible for the guide to achieve a goal as it is very easy for another motive to take over. The guide will be neurotic as it changes its goal most of the time without actually carrying out the plan to achieve it. As the weight increases, it becomes more and more difficult for the competing motives to exert control. When the value reaches 1, the agent is stable and will always hold to its current dominant goal.

4   Future Work

Having designed the Emergent Affective and Personality model, the next step of this research is to proceed with the development. Since the model integrates many components, construction will be performed in a rapid prototyping manner. Initially, skeleton framework for basic functionality will be set up, before complexity is added for each component in an incremental manner.

Evaluation is essential throughout and at the end of development phase to ensure a functional model as well as to allow refinement. Furthermore, it will be interesting if the agent is able to tag its interaction with the user so that it can pick up the point at which it left off in the next interaction.

Acknowledgements

Work supported by the European Union's Sixth Framework Programme, in the IST (Information Society Technologies) Thematic Priotity IST-2002-2.3.1.6 Multimodal Interfaces, HUMAINE (Human-Machine Interaction Network on Emotion) [37] (Contract no. 507422). The authors are solely responsible for the content of this publication. It does not represent the opinion of the European Community and the European Community is not responsible for any use that might be made of data appearing therein.

References

[1] Dautenhahn, K.: The art of designing socially intelligent agents – science, fiction and the human in the loop (1998)
[2] Oliveira, E., Sarmento, L.: Emotional advantage for adaptability and autonomy. In: Proceeding of 2nd International join Conference on Autonomous Agents and Multiagents Systems, Melbourne, ACM 2003 (2003)
[3] Picard, R.W.: Affective Computing. MIT Press (1997)
[4] Bates, J.: The role of emotions in believable agents. Communications of the ACM **37** (1994) 122–125
[5] Doyle, P., Isbister, K.: Touring machines: Guide agents for sharing stories about digital places (1999)
[6] Lester, J.C., Rickel, J.: Animated pedagogical agents: Face-to-face interaction in interactive learning environments. International Journal of Articial Intelligence in Education (2000)
[7] Dörner, D., Hille, K.: Articial souls: Motivated emotional robots. In: Proceedings of the International Conference on Systems, Man and Cybernetics. (1995) 3828–3832

[8] Lim, M.Y., Aylett, R., Jones, C.M.: Empathic interaction with a virtual guide. In: Proceeding of the Joint Symposium on Virtual Social Agents, AISB'05:Social Intelligence and Interaction in Animals, Robots and Agents, Hatfield, UK (2005) 122–129

[9] Tozzi, V.: Past reality and multiple interpretations in historical investigation. Stud Social Political Thought 2 (2000)

[10] Reilly, W.S., Bates, J.: Building emotional agents. Technical Report CMU-CS-92-143, School of Computer Science, Carnegie Mellon University, Pittsburgh, PA, USA (1992)

[11] Bates, J.: The nature of characters in interactive worlds and the oz project (1992)

[12] Bates, J., Loyall, A.B., Reilly, W.S.: An architecture for action, emotion, and social behavior. Lecture Notes in Computer Science **830** (1994) 55–69

[13] Mateas, M.: An oz-centric review of interactive drama and believable agents (1997)

[14] Cañamero, D.: Modeling motivations and emotions as a basis for intelligent behavior. In Johnson, W.L., Hayes-Roth, B., eds.: Proceedings of the 1st International Conference on Autonomous Agents, New York, ACM Press (1997) 148–155

[15] (Ferrell), C.B.: A motivational system for regulating human-robot interaction. In: Proceeding of AAAI 98, Madison, WI (1998)

[16] Velásquez, J.: A computational framework for emotion-based control. In: Proceeding of the Grounding Emotions in Adaptive Systems Workshop, SAB '98, Zurich, Switzerland (1998)

[17] Tomlinson, B., Blumberg, B.: *AlphaWolf*: Social learning, emotion and development in autonomous virtual agents (2002)

[18] Merahbian, A., Russell, J.: An Approach to Environmental Psychology. MIT Press, Cambridge, MA (1974)

[19] Damasio, A.R.: Descartes' Error: Emotion, Reason, and the Human Brain. G.P. Putnam, New York (1994)

[20] Bartl, C., Dörner, D.: Comparing the behavior of psi with human behavior in the biolab game. In Ritter, F.E., Young, R.M., eds.: Proceedings of the Second International Conference on Cognitive Modeling, Nottingham, Nottingham University Press (1998)

[21] Dörner, D.: The mathematics of emotions. In Frank Detje, D.D., Schaub, H., eds.: Proceedings of the Fifth International Conference on Cognitive Modeling, Bamberg, Germany (2003) 75–79

[22] Randolph M. Hones, Amy E. Henninger, E.C.: Interfacing emotional behavior moderators with intelligent synthetic forces. In: Proceeding of the 11th CGF-BR Conference, Orlando, FL (2002)

[23] Chown, E.: Consolidation and Learning: A Connectionist Model of Human Credit Assignment. PhD thesis, University of Michigan (1993)

[24] G. Taylor, F.K., Nielsen, P.: Special operations forces ifors. In: Proceeding of the 10th Conference on Computer Generated Forces and Behavioral Representation, Norfolk, VA (2001) 301–306

[25] Carver, J.M.: Emotional memory management: Positive control over your memory. Burn Survivors Throughout the World Inc. (2005) http://www.burnsurvivorsttw.org/articles/memory.html.

[26] Memory, A.: The role of emotion in memory. About Memory: Learning about Memory for Permanent Memory Improvement (2005) http://www.memory-key.com/NatureofMemory/emotion.htm.

[27] Winograd, E., Neisser, U.: Affect amd Accuracy in Recall. Cambridge University Press, Cambridge, UK (1992)

[28] Riesberg, D., Heuer, F.: Remembering the details of emotional events. Affect and Accuracy in Recall: Studies of 'Flashbulb' Memories (1992) 162–190

[29] Kensinger, E.A., Corkin, S.: Two routes to emotional memory: Distinct neural processes for valence and arousal. PNAS **101** (2004) 3310–3315

[30] Richter-Levin, G., Akirav, I.: Emotional tagging of memory formation - in the search for neural mechanisms. Brain Research Reviews **43** (2003) 247–256

[31] Cahill, L., Haier, R.J., Fallon, J., Alkire, M.T., Tang, C., Keator, D., Wu, J., McGaugh, J.L.: Amygdala activity at encoding correlated with long-term, free recall of emotional information. In: Proceeding of the National Academy of Science. Volume 93., USA (1996) 8016–8021

[32] Hamann, S.B., Ely, T.D., Grafton, D.T., Kilts, C.D.: Amygdala activity related to enhanced memory for pleasant and aversive stimuli. National Neuroscience **2** (1999) 289–293

[33] Canli, T., Zhao, Z., Brewer, J., Gabrieli, J.D., Cahill, L.: Event-related activation of the human amygdala associates with later memory for individual emotional experience. Journal of Neuroscience **20** (2000) 1–5

[34] R. J. Dolan, R. Lane, P.C., Fletcher, P.: Dissociable temporal lobe activations during emotional episodic memory retrieval. NeuroImage **11** (2000) 203–209

[35] Eysenck, H.J., Eysenck, M.: Personality and Individual Differences: A Natural Science Approach. Plenum Press, New York (1985)

[36] Buss, A.H., Plomin, R.: A temperament theory of personality development. Wiley, New York (1975)

[37] HUMAINE: Human-machine interaction network on emotion.   (2004) http://emotion-research.net.

Judging Laura: Perceived Qualities of a Mediated Human Versus an Embodied Agent

Renate ten Ham[1], Mariët Theune[1], Ard Heuvelman[2], and Ria Verleur[2]

[1] Department of Computer Science
{theune, hamrh}@cs.utwente.nl
[2] Department of Behavioral Sciences,
University of Twente, P.O. Box 217, 7500 AE, Enschede, The Netherlands
{a.heuvelman, r.verleur}@utwente.nl

Abstract. Increasingly, embodied agents take over tasks which are traditionally performed by humans. But how do users perceive these embodied agents? In this paper, we describe an experiment in which we compared a real person and a virtual character giving route instructions. The voice, the outfit and the gestures were kept (close to) identical for both cases. The participants judged them, among other things, on trustworthiness, personality and presentation style. In contrast to the outcome of earlier investigations, in most categories the agent scored better or comparable to the human guide. This suggests that embodied agents are suitable to take the place of humans in information-giving applications, provided that natural sounding speech and natural looking nonverbal behaviors can be achieved.

1 Introduction

In order to make human-computer interaction similar to face-to-face communication between humans, an increasing number of interfaces are being equipped with human-looking virtual characters that can use natural language and display nonverbal behaviors. These characters are referred to using different terms, including 'synthetic personae' (McBreen et al., 2000), 'embodied conversational agents' (Cassell et al., 2000), and 'animated interface agents' (Dehn & van Mulken, 2000). For brevity, in this paper we will refer to them as 'embodied agents' or simply as 'agents'.

It is generally assumed that for an agent to be optimally engaging and effective, it has to be as lifelike as possible. Several studies showed that when an embodied agent seems more human in its appearance and behavior, more human qualities are accredited to it. King & Ohya (1996) carried out an experiment with stimuli varying from simple geometric shapes to lifelike human forms, which were rated on agency and intelligence. One of their conclusions was that a human-like appearance and 'subtle behavioral displays' - such as eye blinking - have a great effect on the user's appraisal of these capabilities. Embodied agents can offer intelligence, personality and emotion and therefore communication properties that help to make us feel understood and appreciated (Nijholt, 2004). Users have been shown to like embodied agents and find them engaging (Takeuchi & Naito, 1995; Koda & Maes, 1996).

T. Panayiotopoulos et al. (Eds.): IVA 2005, LNCS 3661, pp. 381–393, 2005.
© Springer-Verlag Berlin Heidelberg 2005

Increasingly, agents are used for tasks that are traditionally performed by humans, such as providing information, explaining or answering questions as an instructor or a teacher. More and more companies use an agent on their website, or use an agent to give information in their office building. Cassell et al. (2002) observed that "users' behaviors appeared natural, as though they were interacting with another person" when using MACK (Media lab Autonomous Conversational Kiosk), an embodied agent answering questions about and giving directions to the MIT Media Lab's research groups, projects and people. With respect to educational applications, Lester et al. (1999) state that "... because of their strong visual presence and clarity of communication, explanatory lifelike avatars offer significant potential for playing a central role in next-generation learning environments." But how do users feel, when they get information from an agent instead of a real person? Reeves and Nass (1996) have shown that people respond to computers and other media like they respond to people, treating them as social actors and attributing them with personality. But how will people judge the personality of an embodied agent, compared with the personality of a real person? Will they have the same emotional response to agent and person, and will they trust information given by the agent as much as information given by the person?

This study provides an exploratory investigation into these questions. An experiment was performed in order to compare an embodied agent and a video recording of a real person on, among other things, trustworthiness, personality, presentation style and user's emotional response. In our experiment we focused on the effect of human versus synthetic appearance rather than on behavior.

2 Related Work

Most embodied agent evaluations have focused on comparing interfaces with or without an embodied agent, and on comparing agents with different visual appearances.

Koda & Maes (1996) compared agents in a poker game that were embodied as a smiley, a dog, a cartoon face, a realistic face (a photo of a real person), or not at all. They found that the embodied agents were considered more likeable and engaging than the disembodied agent. The realistic face was found slightly more likeable and engaging than the other faces, but not significantly so.

Sproull et al. (1996) compared the use of a realistic 3D talking head (stern or neutral looking) with a textual interface in a career counseling application. Their subjects responded in a more social way to the talking heads than to the text-only interface. On the other hand, subjects perceived the personality of both versions of the talking head as less positive than that of the text-only interface. As suggested by Dehn & van Mulken (2000) the latter result may have been influenced by the voice of the talking heads, which lacked inflection and thus did not sound entirely natural.

McBreen et al. (2000) compared the following agent embodiments: a photo of a real person with or without lip movement, a 3D talking head, and a video of a real person. They also compared a disembodied condition, where the agent was represented by a voice only. The same (human) speech soundtrack was used in all cases. Overall, the videos were rated best for likeability (friendliness, competence, naturalness) and several other aspects. The talking heads were rated worst on almost all fronts. However, this might be explained by the fact that the talking face had minimal facial expressions.

Beun et al. (2003) compared a photorealistic 2D talking head, a cartoon character, and an agent represented by only a text balloon, measuring two variables: anthropomorphism (in terms of the agent being helpful, sensible, etc.) and memory performance (subjects had to remember two stories told by the agents). The realistic face scored highest on anthropomorphism. For both embodied agents, memory performance was better than for the disembodied agent.

3 Experiment

The question we try to answer in our experiment is how users perceive an embodied agent as compared to a real person, in the context of an information presentation task. Here, we focus on the user's subjective experience rather than on objective measures such as memory performance. The presentation task chosen for our experiment is that of route description. This is a task where embodiment is quite appropriate: in real life, verbal route descriptions are most often presented in a face-to-face situation, and the speaker typically displays nonverbal behavior (mainly in the form of gestures) while giving the description. This makes route description a suitable task for our experiment.

Applications that involve an embodied agent giving route descriptions include virtual receptionists (e.g., Cyberella, Rist et al., 2002) and virtual guides in real or virtual environments (Cassell et al., 2002; Kopp et al, 2004; Theune et al., 2005). In general, such applications are not aimed at achieving maximal efficiency but rather at giving the user a lifelike experience.

3.1 Design

There were two conditions in our experiment. The participants were initially presented with a route description that was either given by a human guide, recorded on video (condition 1) or by an embodied agent (condition 2). We adhered to methodological standards by making the human guide and the agent guide as similar to each other as possible, only varying the dimension under investigation: i.e., the synthetic versus human appearance of the guide. How we achieved this is discussed in section 3.4.

For both versions of the guide we used the name Laura: the actual name of the human guide. After the participants had watched the route description by the human or the agent guide, they were asked several series of questions, measuring among other things their emotional response and their perception of the guide's personality. Then they were shown a movie with the same route description, but this time presented by the version of the guide they had not seen yet. After this second movie, when the participants had seen both agent and human guide, they were asked their opinion about the quality of the agent, and they had to indicate which version of the guide they preferred.

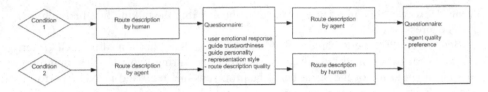

Fig. 1. Graphical representation of the research design

A few limitations of this experimental design are the following. First, arguably the most important property of agents is their ability to interact with users. In our experiment, however, we used an agent for a non-interactive task: presenting route information. We opted for one-way communication so that all participants would get the same information in the same way, thus restricting the variation to the dimension we were interested in. Second, we used a video recording rather than a 'live' person to compare the agent with. However, watching a video is not fully comparable to being face-to-face with another person. For example, Burgoon et al. (2002) found that mediated interaction (video conferencing) in a decision-making task scored much lower than face-to-face interaction on social judgments such as involvement, trust and sociability. On the other hand, this effect of mediation can be expected to be smaller in situations where there is no actual interaction, as in our experiment. People are used to seeing mediated people presenting information, for example newsreaders on television. And an embodied agent is in any case mediated: people need a computer to interact with it. This means that to keep the experimental conditions as similar as possible, the human guide in our experiment had to be mediated too.

3.2 Dependent Variables

After having seen the route description given by either the agent or the human guide, the participants in the experiment answered several questions. In this section we explain how these questions were grouped, and how reliable these groupings are. All questions were measured on a nine-point scale, except the question about preference.

User emotional response was measured using the Self-Assessment Manikin (SAM), a visual scale which represents the user's emotional response to a stimulus, with respect to the dimensions valence (pleasant or unpleasant), arousal, and dominance (Lang, 1985). SAM reflects each dimension with a graphic character arrayed along a continuous nine-point scale. For valence, SAM ranges from a smiling happy figure to an unhappy figure (see Figure 2). For arousal, SAM ranges from an excited figure to a sleepy figure. Finally, the dominance scale goes from a very small figure to a very big figure.

Guide trustworthiness was measured in terms of seven items: expertise, believability, realism, reliability, friendliness, sympathy, and dominance.

Guide personality was measured using Cattell's 16PF, Personality Factors. These 16 factors represent the most important personality factors according to Cattell & Cattell

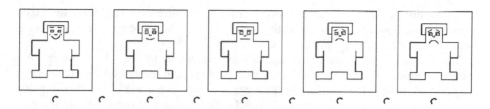

Fig. 2. The SAM scale for valence

(1995). The 16 factors are: warmth, reasoning, emotional stability, dominance, liveliness, rule-consciousness, social boldness, sensitivity, vigilance, abstractness, privateness, apprehension, openness to change, self reliance, perfectionism and tension.

Presentation style regards the way the guide presented the route. This reliable index (α=0,78) was formed by twelve nine point scale items: good-bad, pleasant-unpleasant, polite-impolite, natural-artificial, flowing-clumsy, relaxed-tense, energetic-lethargic, dynamic-static, accurate-inaccurate, calm-excited, exuberant-apathetic, and interested-uninterested.

Route description quality measured the way participants felt about the route description itself. This index was comprised of eight nine point scale items: concise-tedious, simple-complex, easy-difficult, interesting-boring, structured-unstructured, useful-useless, clear-unclear, and comprehensible-incomprehensible. This index is reliable: α = 0.80.

Agent quality consists of six items measuring how participants felt about the quality of the embodied agent: good-bad, modern-old fashioned, realistic-unrealistic, advanced-outdated, usable-unusable, innovative-traditional.

Preference was determined using one simple question: "Which of the two do you prefer: virtual person (agent) or real person (video)?"

3.3 Participants

Participants in the experiment were 78 undergraduate students from different faculties in our university. They were all following a course in Media Psychology and were rewarded with bonus points to participate. Participants were randomly assigned to one of the conditions, with age and gender approximately balanced across conditions. The average age of the participants was 21; 60 % of the participants were female.

3.4 Material

For the agent we used the Living Actor™ technology from Cantoche.[1] We wanted to make the agent as human-like as possible, so we selected an agent that looked realistic rather than cartoon-like and had a large repertoire of gestures. The agent that best met these requirements happened to be female, the Cantoche character 'Julie'. We wanted to reduce the differences between the agent and the human guide as much as possible, so that synthetic versus human appearance (the dimension under investigation) was

---

[1] www.cantoche.com

the only dimension on which the two guides were different. Therefore we asked someone who looked like the agent to play the role of the human guide, and dressed her in exactly the same clothes as the agent.

The movies of the route presentations were created as follows. First, we made a video recording of the human guide as she spontaneously described the route. Then we scripted the agent to simulate the gestures that had been made by the human guide as closely as possible, e.g., pointing left and right. Because of limitations in the gesture repertoire of the agent, this simulation deviated in a few respects from the original recording. Therefore we made a final recording of the human guide as she was describing the route, this time mimicking the agent. The human actor was not asked to imitate the agent in every behavioral detail, only at the more global level of gestures. The use of different gestures would have made the presentations of the guides too dissimilar to allow for a reliable comparison, but we considered the smaller unconscious movements such as blinking and head movements as part of what made the human guide appear human and the agent guide synthetic.

Finally, we added the speech of the human guide to the agent, synchronized the agent's gestures and lip movements with the speech, and created a white background for both movies. This resulted in two route description movies by guides that used exactly the same speech, had roughly the same appearance, and used the same gestures. Also, both guides had a neutral facial expression. Only the more subtle nonverbal behaviors such as blinking, head movements and small posture shifts were different between the guides. Overall, they acted and looked similar, the main difference being that one guide was human and the other an embodied agent (see Figure 3).

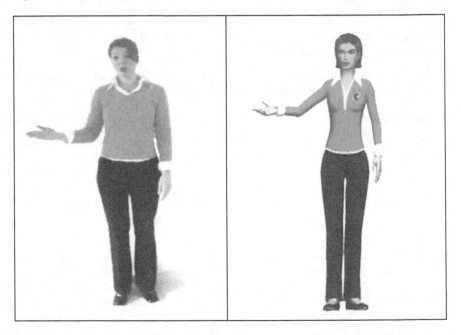

Fig. 3. The human guide (left) and the agent (right)

3.5 Procedure

The experiment was performed in a Web environment. After a short instruction, the participants started the questionnaire on their computer. The movies with the route presentations were integrated in the questionnaire. The participants could not see the movies twice, nor could they go back to see or change their previous answers.

Depending on the group they were assigned to, participants would start with watching a movie with either the agent or the human guide presenting the route. Both movies started with the guide introducing herself: "Hi, I'm Laura." She would then thank them for their cooperation and explain she was going to give them a route description. This way the participants could get used to the voice and the appearance of the guide.

4 Results

With the exception of user emotional response, which was measured using SAM (see section 3.2), and preference, where the participants had to indicate whether they preferred the human or the agent guide, a nine-point scale was used for all questions. The ends of the scale correspond to contrastive attributes such as good-bad, pleasant-unpleasant etc. In the results given below, the high end of each scale corresponds to the positive attribute, and the low end to the negative attribute in the pair. For most pairs, e.g., good-bad, it is clear which attribute is positive and which is negative. However, for some pairs, e.g., calm-excited, we had to judge which attribute would be considered most positive given the task performed by the guide. In the tables below, the attribute we judged to be more positive is always listed first.

We used the SPSS program (T tests) to compare the mean of the scores on all dimensions as described in paragraph 3.2. This test compares the mean of each item or index for both conditions. The F-value indicates the difference between the two conditions. Differences where $p < .05$ will be treated as significant.

User emotional response
On this dimension, there were no significant differences between both groups (see Table 1).

Table 1. Separate items for user emotional response (* $p < .05$)

	Agent	Human	Significance (2-tailed)
Valence	4.37	4.83	.09
Arousal	6.68	6.13	.19
Dominance	4.97	5.45	.21

Guide trustworthiness
The participants felt that the agent was more competent than the human guide (F = 0.98, p<0.05). The scores on the other items did not differ significantly between human guide and agent. Reliability of the guide was rated exactly the same for both guides.

Guide personality
The agent was seen as more relaxed than the human guide (F = 1.07, p<0.01), more self assured (F = 0.73, p<0.05) and less traditional (F = 1.40, p<0.01). Participants

who saw the agent remarked that they found it likable, but businesslike. On the other hand, several participants who saw the person said that they couldn't really judge personality based on the short presentation. This comment did not occur for the agent.

Presentation style
Table 2 shows all the separate items from this index. The presentation style of the agent was seen as significantly more relaxed, dynamic and interested than the presentation style of the human guide. Overall, there was a significant main effect with regard to the presentation style index ($F = 0.39$, $p<0.05$), such that participants found the presentation style of the agent better than the style of the human guide. A few of the remarks are: "very humanlike" and "neutral, but very accurate and polite". The real person was found "too boring" and "pretended".

Table 2. Separate items for presentation style (* $p<.05$)

	Agent	Human
Good-bad	4.79	4.70
Pleasant-unpleasant	4.92	4.70
Polite-impolite	6.39	6.23
Natural – artificial	5.47	4.88
Flowing – clumsy	5.82	5.28
Relaxed – tense	6.05	5.35*
Energetic – lethargic	5.29	4.75
Dynamic – static	4.47	3.36*
Accurate – inaccurate	6.42	3.38
Exuberant – apathetic	4.26	4.03
Calm – excited	3.16	3.13
Interested - uninterested	5.53	4.83*

Route description quality
There was a significant main effect with regard to this index ($F = 0.50$, $p<0.05$), such that participants found the route description better when it was presented by the agent. As Table 3 shows, the agent scored higher on every single item, although only one item is significant: the route description given by the agent was considered significantly less boring than the description given by the human guide.

Table 3. Separate items for route description quality (* $p<.01$)

	Agent	Human
Concise - tedious	4.05	3.30
Simple - complex	3.82	3.33
Easy - difficult	3.97	3.58
Interesting - boring	3.95	3.00*
Structured - unstructured	5.92	5.55
Useful - useless	4.45	4.08
Clear - unclear	5.34	5.00
Comprehensible - incomprehensible	5.63	5.28

Agent quality

After the participants had answered the previous questions (which they answered for either the human or the agent guide, i.e., the only guide they had seen so far), they were shown the version of the guide they had not yet seen. Then, when it was certain that all participants had seen the agent guide, they were asked to rate its quality.

Table 4 shows the results, split between participants who had first seen the agent (and had rated its personality, etc.) and participants who had first seen the real person (and had rated its personality, etc.). We can see that participants who first saw the real person, and then the agent, regarded the agent as less realistic ($F = 0{,}92$, $p<0{,}05$) and less advanced ($F = 0{,}89$, $p<0{,}05$) than the participants who saw the agent first.

Table 4. Separate items for agent quality index, split between participant groups (* p<.05)

	Agent first	Human first
Good - bad	6.05	6.08
Modern - old-fashioned	5.95	6.00
Realistic - unrealistic	6.18	5.20*
Advanced - outdated	6.03	5.03*
Usable - unusable	6.24	5.53
Innovative - traditional	5.16	5.35

Table 5 shows the overall scores, averaging over both groups. In general, we can see that the agent is regarded as fairly modern, realistic and usable.

Table 5. Separate items for agent quality index

	Overall score
Good - bad	6.06
Modern - old-fashioned	5.97
Realistic - unrealistic	5.68
Advanced - outdated	5.51
Usable - unusable	5.87
Innovative - traditional	5.26

Preference

About half (52%) of the participants preferred the real person; the other half preferred the agent. The most mentioned reason for choosing the agent is that people felt less distracted. Several participants indicated that curiosity about age, profession, or what she is wearing will distract when working with a human guide. When working with an agent they could concentrate more on the message instead of the guide. Participants who chose the real person commented mostly that the real guide was "more personal" or "more intimate". Or just said that they liked a real person better. It seems as though subjects preferring the agent had a clearer motivation to do so than subjects preferring the human guide.

Previous experience
Participants who didn't have any previous experience with embodied agents found the agent to be more believable ($F = 1.38$, $p<0.05$), and its presentation style more relaxed ($F = 1.05$, $p<0.05$), flowing ($F = 1.19$, $p<0.05$) and exuberant ($F = 1.12$, $p<0.05$) than participants who had no prior experience with embodied agents.

5 Discussion

In previous experiments, videos or photos of real persons were generally preferred over 2D or 3D agent embodiments (e.g., Koda & Maes, 1996; McBreen et al., 2000). Remarkably, in our experiment the findings are reversed: overall, the embodied agent received more positive ratings than the video recording of the human guide. There are several factors that may help explain these results. First of all, the agent was of good quality (as confirmed by the participants' ratings), having a realistic appearance, a natural human voice,[2] and quite natural movements that included not only gestures but also more subtle behaviors such as blinking, head movements and posture shifts. All in all, despite being an animation, the agent appeared fairly realistic and this may have led to more positive judgments than were found in previous experiments.

Another factor that may have caused a preference for the agent is that the participants in our experiment were young people, who are generally open to new technology and may appreciate a novelty, like a virtual character, more than a well-known phenomenon like a real person. With an older age group, the outcomes might well have been different. A comparison between an older group of participants and the original group of students might make clear if age is of influence on the results.

At the same time, there are also some factors that may have negatively influenced the scores of the human guide. One of these is the fact that in the final version of our recording, she was acting instead of behaving spontaneously. She had to recreate her earlier spontaneous description, this time keeping in mind which gestures the agent could and could not make. For this reason she may have come across as less self-assured and less relaxed, and thus also as less competent. The participants may also have had higher expectations of the human guide than of the virtual guide: when people see a real person explaining a route, they may expect more spontaneous gestures than were actually performed by the actress. This could have caused the participants to judge the route description by the human as relatively static and boring. On the other hand, one of the participants remarked: "I can imagine an agent explaining something in a very boring way". An agent will give a steady, always similar performance, and people expect this to happen. This may explain as well why the real person was found to be more static and boring. In addition, the combination of a hu-

---

[2] We used the same voice for both human and agent in order to reduce the differences between the two conditions, and to avoid possible negative effects of a synthetic voice (cf. Sproull et al. 1996). However, some subjects (in particular those having previous experience with embodied agents), commented that they found the combination of a human voice with a synthetic agent somewhat unnatural. So, the use of a natural voice might as well have been an advantage as a disadvantage.

man voice and appearance with artificial behavior (as in some sense the human guide was mimicking the artificial agent) may have been perceived as inconsistent. As shown by Isbister & Nass (2000), people tend to dislike inconsistency within agents. However, our agent was also inconsistent in the sense that it coupled an artificial appearance and behavior with a human voice (i.e., the voice of the human guide). Some participants remarked that they found this unnatural, although this did not lead to a more negative judgement.

Most participants who reported previous experience with embodied agents, referred to computer games. The characters in computer games have much more advanced graphics and animation than the agent used in our experiment, and this probably explains why this group of participants was significantly less positive about agent quality than the group who had no experience with embodied agents at all. Also remarkable is that participants who saw the agent first rated the quality of the agent significantly higher than participants who saw the human guide first. The explanation for this may be that people who watched the agent first focused more on the information it presented, whereas people who watched the agent second were already familiar with the information, and therefore had more attention to spare for the inherent properties qualities of the agent.

An interesting factor is also the time people spend with the embodied agent. One might expect that if people get the time to get used to how an agent presents the information, they might be able to focus even more on the message instead of the presenter. In our experiment people were confronted with only very short movies; but if there is extended usage, the differences in perception will probably be more pronounced. Of course with respect to the use of ECA's in applications it is also very relevant to find out how 'syntheticness' influences task performance; in fact we have investigated this too, but we will report on that in another paper.

6 Conclusions and Further Research

The question we tried to answer in our experiment is how users perceived an embodied agent as compared to a real person. We carried out an experiment with 78 participants who either received a route description from a human on video, or from an embodied agent. The equal scores on emotional response to, and trustworthiness of, the agent and the real person indicate that agents have strong potential as a guide, tutor or advisor. A striking result was that the comparison in presentation style turned out in favor of the agent rather than the human guide. The quality of the route description given by the agent was also perceived more positive on every dimension. Even though these results may have been partially influenced by the set-up of our experiment (with the human guide acting not entirely spontaneously), this is encouraging news for developers of interface agents. The fact that agent and human scored about the same on personality is encouraging as well. An important caveat is that to be comparable with a human guide, the agent has to sound natural and display human-like nonverbal behaviors. Especially in fully interactive situations, which go beyond pure information presentation as in our experiment, achieving this still presents an important challenge.

We see several options for further research. For instance, repeating the experiment with a male agent or with an older age group might very well produce different outcomes. Also, as mentioned above, speech and interaction are a very important part of the communication between humans and agents. Further research on the influence of these factors will help to determine how people perceive agents.

Acknowledgements

We thank Cantoche for allowing us to use their agents, and Jan Oosterhuis for technical support in setting up the experiment. We also thank Zsófia Ruttkay and three anonymous referees for their useful comments on the first version of this paper. This work was carried out in the context of the ANGELICA project, sponsored by NWO (Netherlands Organization for Scientific Research).

References

Beun, R.J., de Vos, E., & Witteman, C. Embodied conversational agents: effects on memory performance and anthropomorphisation. Proc. IVA (2003), 315-319.

Burgoon, J.K., Bonito, J.A., Ramirez, A., Dunbar, N.E., Kam, K., & Fischer, J. Testing the interactivity principle: Effects of mediation, propinquity, and verbal and nonverbal modalities in interpersonal interaction. J. of Communication special issue: Research on the Relationship between Verbal and Nonverbal Communication: Emerging Integrations (2002), 657-677.

Cassell, J., Sullivan, J., Prevost, S., & Churchill, E. Embodied Conversational Agents. MIT Press (2000).

Cattell, R.B. & Cattell, H.E.P. Personality structure and the new fifth edition of the 16PF. Educational and Psychological Measurement, (1995), 6, 926-937.

Dehn, J., & van Mulken, S. The impact of animated interface agents: A review of empirical research. Int. J. Human-Computer Studies (2000), 52, 1-2.

Isbister, K. & Nass, C. Consistency of personality in interactive characters: Verbal cues, nonverbal cues and user characteristics. Int. J. of Human Computer Studies 53 (2000), 251-267.

King, W.J. & Ohya, J. The representation of agents: Anthropomorphism, agency and intelligence. CHI ' 96 Conference Companion, Vancouver, B.C., (1996), 289-290.

Koda, T. & Maes, P. Agents with faces: The effect of personification. Proc. IEEE Robot-Human Communication (1996).

Kopp, S., Tepper, P. & Cassell, J. Towards integrated microplanning of language and iconic gesture for multimodal output. Proc. of the International Conference on Multimodal Interfaces (ICMI), 2004.

Lang, P.J. The Cognitive Psychophysiology of Emotion: Anxiety and the Anxiety Disorders. Hillsdale, N.J.: Lawrence Erlbaum (1985).

Lester, J. Zettlemoyer, L, Gregoire, J., & Bares, W. Explanatory lifelike avatars: Performing user centered tasks in 3D learning environments. Proc. Autonomous Agents'99, ACM Press (1999).

McBreen, H., Shade, P., Jack, M., & Wyard, P. Experimental assessment of the effectiveness of synthetic personae for multi-modal E-retail applications. Proc. 4th Int. Conf. on Autonomous Agents (2000), 39-45.

Nijholt, A. Where computers disappear, virtual humans appear. Computers and Graphics 28 (2004).

Reeves, B. & Nass, C. The Media Equation: How People Treat Computers, Television, and New Media like Real People and Places. Cambridge University Press, New York (1996).

Rist, T., Baldes, S., Gebhard, P., Kipp, M., Klesen, M., Rist, P., & Schmitt, M. CrossTalk: An interactive installation with animated presentation agents. Proc. of COSIGN'02 (2002).

Sproull, L., Subramani, R., Kiesler, S., Walker, J., & Waters, K. When the interface is a face. Human-Computer Interaction, 11 (1996), 97-124. (Reprinted in B. Friedman, (1997) Human values and the design of technology, CLSI, Publications.)

Takeuchi, A., & Naito, T. Situated facial displays: Towards social interaction. Proc. SIGCHI conference on Human factors in computing systems (1995), 450-455.

Theune, M., Heylen, D. & Nijholt, A. Generating embodied information presentations. In O. Stock and M. Zancanaro (eds.), Multimodal Intelligent Information Presentation, Kluwer Academic Publishers (2005), 47-70.

The Significance of Textures for Affective Interfaces

Paula M. Ellis and Joanna J. Bryson

Department of Computer Science, University of Bath, Bath BA2 7AY, United Kingdom
paulini13@hotmail.com, J.J.Bryson@bath.ac.uk

Abstract. This paper reports experiments demonstrating that the extent to which subjects ascribe emotions to VR faces is highly dependent on textures applied to the face. We demonstrate this for both a photo-realistic vs. non-photo-realistic texture pair and for a male vs. female texture pair. In both cases, experiments were conducted over the Internet on still frames taken from a well-controlled VR emotion modelling system. Given the enormous extent to which textures determine emotion recognition, we consider this a critical area for future research in affective virtual agents.

1 Introduction

There is much disagreement in the academic world regarding facial representation of emotion [6, 34]. There is also little available research regarding the success of virtual agents in effectively displaying their emotions to users. Haddad and Klobas [15] suggest that "character-agent visual representation" may influence the effectiveness of information delivery. Predinger and Ishizuka [23] argue that there is an ongoing debate of how to make agents more 'life-like', whether this is achieved by employing photo-realistic or more cartoon-like faces. As Predinger and Ishizuka suggest, it is the cartoon-like characters that tend to be more readily available in the entertainment/video game sector. They argue that users have higher expectations for the performance of the more realistic characters as opposed to the cartoon-like ones. Realistic characters take the risk that users may notice minor discrepancies in their actions that they might not notice in less realistic characters. Haddad and Klobas [15] go on to present evidence that in academic fields outside of the character-agent concern, the feeling also goes that less realistic is better. Graphic designers suggest that more cartoon-like animated characters more effectively convey information. Yet most VR literature points toward the supposed advantage of photo-realistic faces.

This paper reports our preliminary efforts to determine whether it is better to use photo-realistic or non-photo-realistic textures on VR faces designed to communicate emotion. While we do not yet have enough exemplar faces to determine that issue conclusively, we have shown highly significant results in the recognized emotion ascribed to identical models with different textures. This is true both for our photo-realistic vs. non-photo-realistic texture pair and for a male *vs.* female texture pair.

2 Background and Related Research

Our main aim is to discover on which type of facial skin texture an emotion can be most easily recognised. Past research appears inconclusive and contradictory in its findings.

T. Panayiotopoulos et al. (Eds.): IVA 2005, LNCS 3661, pp. 394–404, 2005.
© Springer-Verlag Berlin Heidelberg 2005

Although Fabri et al. [9] found that participants were 78.6% successful at recognising the correct emotion on photographs but only 62.2% successful with the virtual heads, on closer inspection of their data it can be seen that fear and disgust had much lower scores for the virtual heads than for the other expressions and without these anomalies the results may have shown no significant difference. Much past research, however, has been concerned with how effective virtual faces have been in assisting the system they are attached to in conveying particular information. Very little research has concentrated on whether or not these faces can actually convey particular facial expressions to a recognisable degree.

2.1 What Is Emotion?

Ferh and Russell [10, p. 177] observed that "everyone knows what emotion is until asked to give a definition" and Shaver et al. [25, p. 117] argue that "despite an enormous increase in research...there is still no widely accepted definition of emotion." Izard [18], who reviewed the available literature on emotion in 1969, discovered that "the area of emotional experience...is one of the most confused and ill defined in psychology." In fact Gaggioli et al. [14] have suggested that there are over 90 different definitions of emotion in existence in the scientific literature. Humans convey emotions to each other in many ways, through voice, body language and facial expression. As Cassell [3] explains "we make complex representational gestures with our hands, gaze away and towards each other...and use the pitch and melody of our voices" to communicate emotion. Cassell goes on to explain that non-verbal behaviours play an important role in the design of Embodied Conversational Agents, such as gesture, eye gaze and facial display.

Davis [6] suggests that there is a need to consider five 'basic' facial expressions of emotion. These are fear, anger, disgust, sadness, and happiness. Other authors too, such as Ekman et al. [8], have argued for the existence of basic emotions, but it seems that the main problem is that there is huge difficulty in establishing a way to truly reference each of the emotions that humans can recognise. It is true that as more research is carried out, experimenters are faced with the problem that although most people can recognise and identify various emotions, they are all so very subjective in their identification. This may be due to a number of factors, such as the ability of people to read body language and not just facial expressions. In summary there is huge disagreement in the academic field as to what emotion actually is, and how it is represented by the human body. This will pose problems for any researcher wishing to test or measure emotions in some way, as it is so hard to establish controls.

Collier [4, p.68] suggests that "one of the most persistent controversies among researchers ... has revolved around the issue of whether facial expressions are learned or innate." Fox [12] argues for three main perspectives that can help to explain the need for humans to recognise facial emotional expressions. He explains the biological, behavioural and cognitive arguments for the need to recognise expressions of emotion. The need to recognise the emotion another person is displaying is clearly an essential tool for life. It has been found that infants as young as 3.5 months old are able to recognise different emotions just by looking at still images of faces, supporting the argument that there is an evolutionary or behavioural advantage to emotion recognition [19]. Fox et al.

[11, p. 61] suggest that humans are "hard-wired for facial recognition, especially for the recognition of anger or threat." Their experiment has shown that babies as young as five months old, can discriminate between the facial expressions of fear and anger. Another study by Hansen and Hansen [16] found that adult humans have the ability to spot an angry face in a crowd faster than a happy face [13, p. 94].

2.2 Emotional Expression in Virtual Agents

There has as yet been little work in the evaluation of animated virtual characters and their faces. One of the first virtual humans to be created was the 'Boeing Man'. This was a three dimensional model, used to aid engineers in the building of cockpits. It was made using a collection of three-dimensional line segments, with articulated joints. There was only limited facial detail and no varying of the facial expression [21]. Massaro et al. [20] carried out an evaluation of a talking head named 'Baldi', which was constructed of polygons and approximately 900 surfaces joined together. Massaro et al. aimed to discover how informative certain properties of the Baldis's was. The experiments concluded that participants were 94%, 95% and 73% correct at identifying happy, angry and sad faces, as demonstrated by Baldi.

Vinayagamoorthy et al. [32] found evidence that users in a virtual environment respond well to "humanoid representations of other users" in the environment. They aimed to test the importance of behavioural realism in avatars and virtual humans in virtual environments. Vinayagamoorthy et al. asked, should the behaviour of avatars mimic real life and to what extent? They also aimed to explore the optimum level of visual realism needed to make a character believable in a virtual environment. They reference the work of Strippgen [27], who has suggested that participants will expect more visually realistic avatars to behave "in a manner that portrays greater human like qualities." In their study Vinayagamoorthy et al. [32] used a realistic avatar and a cartoonish avatar, which were modelled onto virtual faces that gave either realistic or non-realistic eye gaze. They found that the less realistic the avatar, the less effect the realism of eye movement had on the effectiveness of avatar communication. Others have supported these findings, suggesting that the employment of apparently human agents has only served to raise the users expectations of its performance, placing more pressure on the system to perform as 'humanly' as possible [24]. Takeuchi [29] suggested that when more realistic faces are used, the user will spend more time trying to interpret its expression that actually engaging in the task. De Rosis et al. [7] present a 3D embodied agent known as 'Greta'. They argue that "the more a character aims at being realistic... the more complex its implementation becomes."

Fabri et al. [9] developed a study that aimed to show whether photo-realistic or animated facial expressions could be understood more easily. The photo-realistic expressions were represented using photographs and the more animated cartoon facial expressions were displayed using virtual heads. Seven different facial expressions were represented by each of the two facial forms, in four variations of expression. Software was used to present each of the 56 facial images to participants in a random order and this software also recorded the emotion that each face was assigned by the participants. Mann-Whitney statistical analysis was carried out on the data and the findings suggest that realistic photographs are easier to interpret than the expressions of the virtual heads. Participants were 78.6% successful at recognising the correct emotion on the photographs but only 62.2% successful with the virtual heads. However, on closer inspection of the data it can be seen that fear and disgust had much lower scores for the virtual heads than for the other expressions and without these anomalies it may be possible that results would have shown no significant difference.

Ward et al. [33] carried out an investigation monitoring the facial movements of participants engaged in a web-based task. Participants were asked to complete an online test that contains one surprise event and FaceStation 1.2, facial tracking software was used to track their faces as they completed the task. The captured data from this was then transferred to create the movements of a virtual face. 'Judges' were asked to observe the footage of the real faces completing the tasks and of the virtual faces that had been created by the tracking software [33]. With respect to the reactions of both types of face judges considered the movements of the virtual and real faces to be in agreement for 7 out of the 15 pairs of faces. In their conclusion Ward et al. 2003, suggest that the failure of the facial tracking software is to blame for the results. However, in presenting their work, Ward et al. suggested that participants in some cases seemed to be recognizing emotions in the virtual faces constructed by the facial tracking system that they had failed to notice on the films of real human faces [2]. This report, in addition to some similar experiences with demonstrating the DER [31, see below] in different texture conditions, lead to the present research.

3   Experiment 1

Our experiments use the Dynamic Emotional Representation (DER) facial representation model, developed by Tanguy et al. [31], to create faces representing emotions. Pairs of skin textures are tested showing various degrees of various emotions in experiments conducted over the Internet. Note that the values for varying degrees of 'intensity' are a somewhat arbitrary amount that is only relevant to the piece of software used for these experiments. However, they were entirely consistent across textures, which is what matters for the significance of our results.

3.1   Equipment and Stimuli

Tanguy et al. [31], present a facial animation platform with an integrated Dynamic Emotional Representation. The design of the DER is based on the Sloman [26] model of emotion representation, describing three-layer architecture to emotion. The face is animated using the Parke and Waters [22] abstract model for the facial mesh [30]. Tanguy et al. [31] explain that the DER is designed to "enforce consistency in the production of emotional facial displays," providing, a "rich, real time representation of emotions... without their automatic generation." The DER interface can be used to produce various facial expressions on the various skin textures that are available, such as a photo-realistic male face and a more cartoon-like male face. These skin textures are used to generate the facial images for the experiments. The DER package contains a user interface that allows users to select various facial skins and to view in real time

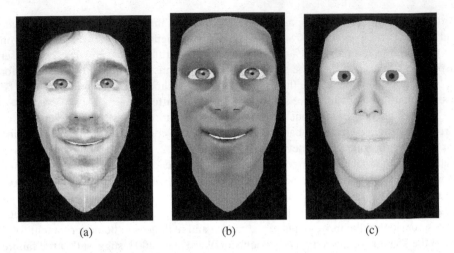

(a)   (b)   (c)

Fig. 1. Virtual faces as created by the DER. (a) Photo-realistic male face, used in both experiments. (b) Non-photo-realistic face, used in Experiment 1. (c) Photo-realistic female face, used in Experiment 2.

the changes of the facial components as an emotion is selected. The required facial skin texture is displayed to the user by using the interface to open the required file. Once a facial skin texture has been loaded, the user can select the 'Present of Textures' button that removes the photo-realistic skin texture from the face and displays a more simple animated or cartoon-like face. The textures used in our study can be seen in Fig. 1. Some of the related controls can be seen in Fig. 2.

The DER has been set to produce facial representations of the following expressions: 'Happy', 'Sad', 'Angry', 'Surprised' and 'Disgusted'. Past studies have shown that people often have trouble correctly distinguishing between various expressions. Hara and Kobayashi [17] found participants identifying emotions on a robot face would often confuse expressions of fear with surprise and disgust. Fabri et al. [9] also found that disgust was generally harder to identify on virtual heads. It is with this in mind that expressions of disgust are disregarded for this particular experiment.

For this experiment 24 still facial images were created. 12 still images are required for both facial types; the photo-realistic one (known as 'PR') and the cartoon-like one (known as 'An'). The user interface to the DER allows the user to select the desired emotion by clicking on a button labelled with the desired expression. When the button is clicked the skin displays the emotion and then returns to a neutral expression. It is important to check that various other settings are standardised for each face before aiming to capture a still image. As the DER, by it's very nature, creates dynamic facial images, it is important that all other expression intensity values except the one being created are set to '0', or this will affect the way an expression is produced. See Figure 1.

It should be noted at this point that *intensity* in this context is an arbitrary amount because there is no way to measure the intensity of a facial expression. It is still useful however because the intensity measure serves as a way to express the difference between various emotions and to check that others are displayed to the same degree as

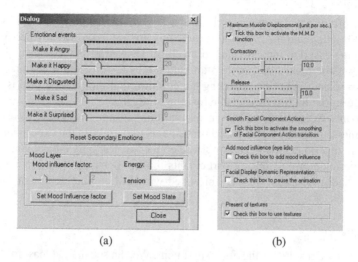

(a)   (b)

Fig. 2. (a) Shows the box that allows the user to select emotions and demonstrates how the intensity for all expressions other than happy are set to 0. (b) Shows an example of how the tick boxes and settings can be set up.

another. The purpose of other settings is irrelevant to this study, but as each facial still is captured, it is critical to ensure that the settings for 'release' and 'contraction' are set to the same amount for every face. It is also essential to ensure that the various 'tick boxes' are in the same status for every face. See Figure 2.

As mentioned above, 24 faces are produced. Both facial skin textures are captured displaying the four expressions: Happy, Sad, Angry and Surprised. These expressions are displayed in the intensities 10%, 30% and 50%. As each face is produced, screen shots are taken and then imported into a suitable package such as Microsoft Paint. The facial image can then be saved in jpg format ready to be called by the PHP code.

3.2 Design and Method

The experiment uses a repeated measures, forced response design, where all participants are exposed to the Dependent Variable being the various representations of facial expression. The forced responses participants must choose from are: 'happy', 'sad', 'angry', 'surprised' or 'unsure'. A similar methodology was used by Breazeal [1], who used a forced-choice design during evaluation of Kismet, a robot head. There participants were given the choice of ten labels and were asked to assign these to a number of still images of Kismet performing various facial expressions. Calder (2001) also used a forced choice design when evaluating animated humanoid heads. The repeated measures design also eliminates the possibly that any differences in results are caused by differences between participants, as all participants are exposed to all changes in the dependent variable [5].

In our study, faces are displayed to participants in a random order as generated by the PHP script, and no one face can be displayed more than once to each participant.

Participants are directed to the experiment home page. Here they are able to read the experiment briefing and instructions. Participants are not asked for any personal information, but are asked to indicate the most truthful answer as they complete the experiment. When participants click on the start button they are directed to the first face, and prompted to select the button reflecting the emotion that they feel the face is showing. Answers are stored in the correct table for later analysis.

Participants were collected via an on-line chat forum frequented by the experimenter. A message on the forum asked participants to partake in the experiment, and informed them that no personal data would be collected. The only ethical considerations for this experiment are to inform participants that no personal data will be collected from them and ensure that they are provided with full contact details of the experimenter.

3.3   Results

Table 1 shows the results for the first experiment. We can see that, at least for these two exemplars, it is significantly easier ($\chi^2(1, N = 90) = 20.57$), $p < .001$) to correctly identify the emotion for the face with the photo-realistic texture than for the animated-style one. Note that there is no significant difference for the happy or surprised conditions, but all the variance results from the sad and angry conditions, both of which favour the photo-realistic face. No general conclusions about recognizing specific emotions can necessarily be drawn from this data, given the fact that the emotion exemplars and what it means to be at 10, 20 or 30% of them have been set by hand by Tanguy and have not yet been thoroughly tested. However, to first approximation they do seem to be reasonably good models and well matched.

Table 1. Total number and percentage of correct assignments for each group of expression

	Texture Type				
	Photo-Realistic		Non-Photo-Realistic		
Correct	correct	percent	correct	percent	Significance
Expression	of 90	correct	of 90	correct	
Happy	86	95.6%	85	94.4%	N/S
Sad	59	65.6%	31	34.4%	$* * *\chi^2(1, N = 90) = 17.42, p < .001$
Angry	53	58.9%	24	26.7%	$* * *\chi^2(1, N = 90) = 19.09, p = .001$
Surprised	42	46.7%	40	44.4%	N/S
Totals	240	66.7%	180	50%	$* * *\chi^2(1, N = 90) = 20.57, p < .001$

Regardless of the validity of the between-emotion measurements, the between-face measurements clearly show a significant, texture-dependent effect.

4   Experiment 2

As a first step to creating additional stimuli, we used one of the author's face to create a female photo-realistic face. Because the framework underlying the face is still identical to the previous experiment, the result was somewhat androgynous. Out of interest, we decided to conduct a second experiment comparing the male and female textures.

4.1   Equipment, Stimuli, Design and Method

The equipment and stimuli were all largely as before, except for the different texture, which can be seen in Figure 1 as well.

The apparatus in this case consists of a simple piece of HTML and PHP code similar to that used in the main experiments and four sets of male and female faces showing the same intensity of the same expression. This code creates four basic web pages that display one pairing of a male and female face showing the identical expression, at a time. Participants are asked to select a single radio button, to log which face they believe is showing the stronger emotion. The page title says "Experiment on Emotions in Faces." The text under the two (happy) stimuli reads "Please Select an option from the list below to indicate which face you believe looks more Happy. If you think there is no difference please select the 'No difference' button." The options are 'Male', 'Female' or 'No difference'. The participants for this experiment were again collected via an online forum, though less effort was made to recruit since, at the time, this experiment seemed less central to our study.

4.2   Results

In experiment 2, we again see that assessed expression difference for two different textures is highly significant, although in this case which face is perceived as more emotional depends on the particular emotion expressed. Although there is a weakly significant trend toward ascribing more emotional expression to the female face, what we see is a strong gender effect in line with previous psychological results: participants are more sensitive to anger in the male face but to sadness and surprise in the female face. The strength of the significance of these results is particularly stunning given the fact that the female texture is not overtly female (e.g. is not wearing significant makeup) and, as mentioned earlier, is placed on a 'male' facial mesh identical to that of the male stimuli. However, it was labelled as 'female' in the answer key, which may in itself introduce some bias [24]. In future work we would like to re-run this experiment labelling the faces simply 'a' and 'b'.

Table 2. Participants' assesment of the relative intensity of emotional expression with male vs. female textures. Note that, in fact, the underlying facial structure and intensity of expression were identical in all cases, so the expected choice should be no difference.

Expression	Male	Female	No Difference	Significance
	\multicolumn{4}{c}{Total number of each answer assigned by participants}			
Happy	4	9	10	N/ S
Sad	1	21	1	$***\chi^2(2, N = 23) = 42.17, p < .001$
Angry	18	2	3	$***\chi^2(2, N = 23) = 31.43, p < .001$
Surprised	3	12	8	$*\chi^2(2, N = 23) = 7.9, p < .05$
Total	26	44	22	$**\chi^2(2, N = 23) = 13.43, p < .01$

5   Discussion and Future Work

As we said from the outset, these results can only be seen as preliminary pilot work in so far as they represent the issues of photorealism vs. caricature or male vs. female stimuli. In particular with the photorealism issue, our non-photo-realistic texture is not particularly caricature-like. It is basically androgynous and lacks the highly caricatured, exaggerated features, such as big bushy eyebrows, a large nose or an over-exaggerated smile one expects in cartoon-like faces. The default texture for the DER's frame is mainly made of pink pixels, with a white line that represents teeth and blue eyes. Although there are definite areas that represent bone structure above the eyes and around the checks, in general when looking at this facial representation, one is looking at a large amount of pink pixels. As these pixels move over a virtual bone structure to simulate the wrinkles formed by a smile, for example, the observer has trouble noticing such a movement as pixels of one colour are just moving around the facial texture. If more obvious features were added in then it is possible the facial texture would be much easier to interpret.

At the time these experiments were first conducted, we suggested also that the eyes were not sufficiently expressive. Collier [4] suggested that when conversing, humans spend most of their time looking at one another's eyes. Sullivan and Kirkpatrick [28] also observed the areas of the face that we watch when conversing with each other. They found that for expressions of happiness, sadness and surprise, more time is spent looking at the mouth but the eyes are important when observing expressions of anger. The point to be made here is that clearly various parts components of the face are important when reading facial expressions. It is possible that the way the DER and facial textures work to portray facial emotions is not close enough to that of a real human face. This is in fact an area that has since been developed by Tanguy, and is still under development.

As for our own work, it is obviously essential to begin working with more mesh frameworks and a vastly greater number of texture stimuli in order to explore both the questions we have opened up. It would also be more useful to log more information about the participants, such as sex, age, cultural background and even ethnicity, to see whether these characteristics play a role.

Nevertheless, even these preliminary results give a clear warning to those working on developing virtual affective interfaces. The extent to which their emotional interface will be perceived as such is heavily determined by the texture they choose to apply to their characters.

6   Conclusions

We have shown that textures overlying the framework of a VR face have an enormous impact on how emotions are perceived on that face. In a series of experiments all using the same emotional expressions and the same mesh framework underlying the texture, we have shown highly significant differences in whether the intended emotion is perceived (on photo-realistic vs. non-photo-realistic textures) and even on the extent to which an expression is being displayed on side-by-side comparisons (on male vs. female textures). We recommend a great deal of further research is necessary in this area, as such significant differences from texture could have an enormous impact on the utility of any affective display.

Acknowledgements

Thanks to Emmanuel Tanguy and Robin Hodges for their assistance in running this project, and to our very helpful reviewers. This work was funded in part by The Engineering and Physical Sciences Research Council (EPSRC) Grant GR/S79299/01.

References

[1] Cynthia Breazeal. Emotion and sociable humanoid robots. *International Journal of Human Computer Interaction*, 59:119–155, 2003.

[2] Joanna Bryson. Personal communication, based on data presented at *HCI 2003 by Ward, Bell & Marsden*, 2004.

[3] Justine Cassell. Nudge nudge wink wink: Elements of face-to-face conversation for embodied conversational agents. In Justine Cassell, Joseph Sullivan, Scott Prevost, and Elizabeth Churchill, editors, *Embodied Conversational Agents*, pages 1–27. MIT Press, London, 2000.

[4] Gary Collier. *Emotional Expression*. Lawrence Erlbaum Associates, London, 1985.

[5] Hugh Coolican. *Research Methods and Statistics in Psychology*. Hodder & Stoughton, London, second edition, 1994.

[6] Darryl N. Davis. Agents, emergence, emotion and representation. In *IECON '00: 26th Annual Conference of the IEEE Industrial Electronics Society*, volume 4, pages 2577–2582. IEEE, October 2000.

[7] Fiorella De Rosis, Catherine Pelachaud, Isabella Poggi, Valeria Carofiglio, and Berardina De Carolis. From greta's mind to her face: Modelling the dynamics of affective states in a conversational agent. *International Journal of Human Computer Studies*, 59:81–118, 2003.

[8] Paul Ekman, Wallace Friesen, and Phoebe Ellsworth. *Emotion in the Human Face: Guidelines for Research and an Integration of Findings*. Pergamon Press, New York, 1972.

[9] M. Fabri, D. J. Moore, and D. J. Hobbs. Expressive agents: Non-verbal communication in collaborative virtual environments. In *Proceedings of AAMAS 2002 Workshop: Embodied Conversational Agents: Let's Specify And Evaluate Them!*, pages 402–409, July 2002.

[10] B. Ferh and J. A. Russell. Concept of emotion viewed from a prototype perspective. *Journal of Experimental Psychology: General*, 113:464–486, 1984.

[11] Elaine Fox, Victoria Lester, Riccardo Russo, R. J. Bowles, Alessio Pichler, and Kevin Dutton. Facial expression of emotion: Are angry faces detected more efficiently? *Cognition and Emotion*, 14(1):61–92, 2000.

[12] Jeremy Fox. Factors of emotion recognition in faces: Three perspectives. *Journal of Young Investigators*, (3), March 2004.

[13] Alan J. Fridlund. The behaviour, ecology and sociality of human faces. In Margaret S. Clark, editor, *Emotion*, pages 175–212. Sage, London, 1992.

[14] A. Gaggioli, F. Mantovani, G. Castelnuovo, B. Wiederhold, and G. Riva. Avatars in clinical psychology: A framework for the clinical use of virtual humans. *CyberPsychology and Behavior*, 6(2):117–125, 2003.

[15] Hanadi Haddad and Jane Klobas. Expressive agents: Non-verbal communication in collaborative virtual environments. In *Proceedings of AAMAS 2002 Workshop: Embodied Conversational Agents: Let's Specify And Evaluate Them!*, July 2002.

[16] C. H. Hansen and R. D. Hansen. Finding the face in the crowd: An anger superiority effect. *Journal of Personality and Social Psychology*, 54:917–924, 1988.

[17] Fumio Hara and Hiroshi Kobayashi. A face robot able to recognise and produce facial expression. In *IEEE International Conference on Intelligent Robots and Systems (IROS'96)*, Osaka, 1996.

[18] C. E. Izard. The emotions and emotion constructs in personality and culture research. In R. B. Cattell, editor, *Handbook of Modern Personality Theory*. Aldine Press, Chicago, 1969.

[19] R Kahana-Kalman and A. S. Walker-Andrews. The role of person familiarity in young infants perception of emotional expressions. *Child Development*, 72:352–369, 2001.

[20] Dominic. W. Massaro, Michael. M. Cohen, Jonas Beskow, and Cole Ronald. A. Developing and evaluating conversational agents. In Justine Cassell, Joseph Sullivan, Scott Prevost, and Elizabeth Churchill, editors, *Embodied Conversational Agents*, pages 287–317. MIT Press, London, 2000.

[21] Frederic I. Parke. Computer graphic models for the human face. In *Proceedings of the IEEE Computer Society's Third International Computer Software and Applications Conference (COMPSAC'79)*, pages 724–727, Chicago, November 1979.

[22] Frederic I. Parke and Keith Waters. *Computer Facial Animation*. A. K. Peters Ltd., 1996.

[23] Helmut Predinger and Mitsuru Ishizuka, editors. *Life-Like Characters: Tools, Affective Functions and Applications*. Springer, Berlin, 1998.

[24] B. Reeves and C. Naas. *The Media Equation: How People Treat Computers, Television and New Media Like Real People and Press*. Cambridge University Press, 1996.

[25] Phillip R. Shaver, Shelley Wu, and Judith C. Schwartz. Cross cultural similarities and differences in emotion and it's representation: A prototype approach. In Margaret S. Clark, editor, *Emotion*, pages 175–212. Sage, London, 1992.

[26] Aaron Sloman. Beyond shallow models of emotions. *Cognitive Processing*, 2(1):177–198, 2001.

[27] Simone Strippgen. INSIGHT: A virtual laboratory for design, test and evaluation of autonomous agents. In Richard N. Zobel and Dietmar P. F. Möller, editors, *Twelfth European Simulation Multiconference: Simulation — Past, Present and Future*, Manchester, UK, June 1998.

[28] L. A. Sullivan and S. W. Kirkpatrick. Facial interpretation and component consistency. *Genetic, Social and General Psychology Monographs*, 122(4):389–404, 1996.

[29] A. Takeuchi. Situated facial displays: Towards social interaction. In *Proceedings of CHI '94*, pages 450–454. ACM Press, 1994.

[30] Emmanuel Tanguy. An abstract muscle model for facial animations. Dissertation about a year project carried out during the third year of a computer science degree in the Univeristy of Sheffield., May 2001.

[31] Emmanuel A. R. Tanguy, Philip J. Willis, and Joanna J. Bryson. A layered Dynamic Emotion Representation for the creation of complex facial animation. In Thomas Rist, Ruth Aylett, Daniel Ballin, and Jeff Rickel, editors, *Intelligent Virtual Agents*, pages 101–105. Springer, September 2003.

[32] V. Vinayagamoorthy, M. Garau, Steed, and M. Slater. An eye gaze model for dyadic interaction in an immerse virtual environment: Practice and experience. *Computer Graphics Forum*, 23(1):1–11, 2004.

[33] Robert Ward, Dennise Bell, and Phil Marsden. A exploration of facial expression tracking in affective HCI. In Eamonn O'Neill, Philippe Palanque, and Peter Johnson, editors, *People and Computers XVII — Designing for Society (HCI '03)*, pages 383–399, Bath, September 2003. Springer.

[34] Michelle S. M. Yik and James A. Russell. Interpretation of faces: Cross-cultural study of a prediction from Fridlund's theory. *Cognition and Emotion*, 13(1):93–104, 1999.

Levels of Representation in the Annotation of Emotion for the Specification of Expressivity in ECAs

Jean-Claude Martin[1], Sarkis Abrilian[1], Laurence Devillers[1],
Myriam Lamolle[2], Maurizio Mancini[2], and Catherine Pelachaud[2]

[1] LIMSI-CNRS, BP 133, 91403 Orsay Cedex, France
{martin, sarkis, devil}@limsi.fr
[2] LINC, IUT de Montreuil, Université Paris 8, France
{m.lamolle, mancini, c.pelachaud}@iut.univ-paris8.fr

Abstract. In this paper we present a two-steps approach towards the creation of affective Embodied Conversational Agents (ECAs): annotation of a real-life non-acted emotional corpus and animation by copy-synthesis. The basis of our approach is to study how coders perceive and annotate at several levels the emotions observed in a corpus of emotionally rich TV video interviews. We use their annotations to specify the expressive behavior of an agent at several levels. We explain how such an approach can be useful for providing knowledge as input for the specification of non-basic patterns of emotional behaviors to be displayed by the ECA (e.g. which perceptual cues and levels of annotation are required for enabling the proper recognition of the emotions).

1 Introduction

Embodied Conversational Agents (ECAs) use a wide range of modalities such as speech, gestures, and facial expressions. This rich set of modalities can provide the user with different non-verbal behaviors depending on the current application requirements. Yet, the definition of the dynamics of these various modalities still remains to be done. For example, emotional behavior and expressivity of animated agents play a central role for the user, e.g. in Story-telling systems. But how to define the dynamics of each modality and their combination during emotional behavior? At which temporal and abstraction levels? How to make sure that the emotional behavior of the ECAs will be perceived by the user and benefits not only from basic acted emotions but rather from the richness of real life emotional behavior?

The externalization of nonverbal behaviors plays an important role in the perception of emotions. To model different ECA's behaviors we have decided to take such a stand point: to model what is visible; that is to consider the signals and how they are displayed and perceived. We do not model the processes that were made to arrive to the display of such and such signals; we simply model the externalization part. We are interested in understanding and modeling how a given emotion would be both perceived and expressed quantitatively and qualitatively.

To achieve such a goal we took a two-steps approach: 1) annotate perception of emotion at multiple levels in TV interview videos, 2) animate by copy synthesis. In the first phase we annotate manually a video corpus at several dimensions which are

T. Panayiotopoulos et al. (Eds.): IVA 2005, LNCS 3661, pp. 405–417, 2005.
© Springer-Verlag Berlin Heidelberg 2005

relevant to the perception of emotion. Annotation of communicative behavior in social settings in extremely complex due to the large amount of variables acting in the communication process. Several annotation schemes of gesture [23], [29], [5], face [19], gaze [37], emotion [18], [39] exist. These schemes are extremely rich in the data they encode and complex to use. When we have developed our annotation scheme, we had in mind the aim our study. Thus our annotation scheme encodes multimodal behaviors observed during emotionally rich behaviors and combinations of emotions as they are observed in natural data. Our annotation scheme encodes not only the signals being displayed but also their temporal evolution. Our second phase of study consists of animating an ECA. The ECA system takes as input the annotation made in the first phase and computes the face and gesture animation of the ECA.

Our expectation from this work is manifold. On one hand we aim at studying which perceptual cues are used and combined to perceive a given emotion. The use of an ECA allows one to turn on and off given signals. By studying what subjects perceive from the synthesized animation, we can circumscribe which cues are the most salient to convey a given emotion. On the other hand, the copy synthesis method allows us to refine both our annotation scheme and animation model, in particular in relation to the modeling of ECA expressivity.

2   State of the Art

There has been a lot of psychological researches on emotion and nonverbal communication of facial and vocal expressions of acted basic emotions: anger, disgust, fear, joy, sadness, surprise [18], and also on expressive body movements [15], [30], [4], [43]. Yet, these studies were based mostly on acted basic emotions. Annotation of non acted communicative multimodal behaviors in TV videos has also been addressed but without a focus on emotion [25] or without the use of any annotation tool. Thus, real-life multimodal corpora are indeed very few despite the general agreement that it is necessary to collect audio-visual databases that highlight naturalistic expressions of emotions [16]. Results from the literature in Psychology are very useful for the specification of Embodied Conversational Agents, but yet provide few details, nor do they study variations about the contextual factors of multimodal emotional behavior. Very few researchers have been using context specific multimodal corpora for the specification of an ECA [25]. In [7], the multimodal behaviors of subjects describing a house were annotated and used for informing the generation grammar of the REA agent.

An overview of recent ECA implementations can be found in [8] and [38]. Several models have been proposed for agent's behavior selection and agent's behavior animation. Work in behavior selection has mostly been concerned with semantic aspects of human gesturing, often following McNeill's method of classification [29]. Cassell et al. select suitable non-verbal behaviors to accompany user-supplied text based on a linguistic analysis [9]. More recently, this group has generated iconic gestures from a parametric model grounded in video corpus analysis [40]. Noot and Ruttkay address the need for inter-subject variability in GESTYLE [31], which chooses between atomic behaviors based on 'style dictionaries'. Gesture animation is concerned with realistic movement generation of arms and hands. Animation systems often introduce a custom representation language to describe gestures [21], [26]. EMOTE [10] implements a model of adapting agent gestures to add expressivity. In the field of affective ECAs, most of the work done so far in animating agents from recorded data use acted data. The majority of the works in this research area uses either motion capture data [6], [17], [27], or videos [42], [33]. We differentiate our approach from them as we use a corpus of real emotions. Our aim is not only to reproduce multimodal behaviors with an ECA but rather to study the coordination between modalities during emotional behaviors, in particular in the case of complex emotions.

3 Example Description

In this section we describe shortly an example for illustrating our approach. More details are provided in the following sections. The frame provided in figure 2 left is from a video sample of a TV interview from the EmoTV corpus [1]. The woman is reacting to a recent trial in which her father was kept in jail. As revealed by the manual annotation of this video by three coders, the behavior displayed by this woman is perceived as a complex combination of anger and despair with temporal variation within the video clip. Furthermore, this emotional behavior is perceived in speech and in several visual modalities (head, eyes, torso, and gestures). Several levels of annotation are coded in EmoTV using the Anvil tool [24] (figure 1): some information regards the whole video (called the `global level'); while some other information is related to emotional segments (the `local' level); at the lowest level, there is detailed time-based annotation of multimodal behaviors including movement quality.

We use the annotated emotion labels as well as the description of the movement quality as input to our ECA system called Greta. We have transcribed the speech of the woman and use this transcription as a starting point. This input is enhanced with tags that drive the animation of the ECA. We follow an analysis-synthesis loop approach to refine the animation of the ECA. The annotation of the video segment is rewritten to follow the ECA specification language, APML [14]. In the example of figure 2 the annotated emotion is `anger' for the first half part of the segment and then it fades into `despair' for the rest of the segment. Finally from the global level annotation, we define the agent's behavioral profile. At this point, given the APML text and the agent's behavioral profile, the system computes the animation of the agent.

4 Annotation and Modeling Emotional Behaviors

The annotation and the modeling of emotional behaviors require representing the multiple levels of abstraction and the temporality involved in the emotional process: the emotion itself and the corresponding multimodal behaviors.

4.1 Emotion Labels

Three types of emotion annotations are generally used in research on emotion: appraisal dimensions, abstract dimensions and most commonly verbal categories. These verbal categories include both *primary* labels (anger, fear, joy, sadness, etc. [18]) and

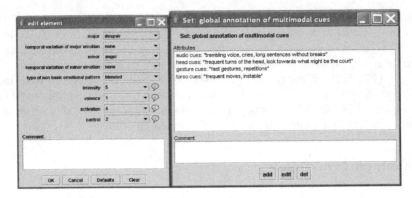

(a) Annotation at the global level of a whole video: emotion labels and dimensions (*left*), free text multimodal cues (*right*)

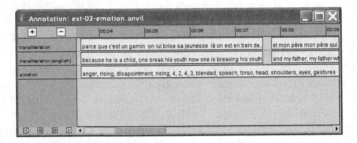

(b) Annotation at the local level of a non-basic emotion segment by one of the coders with a combination of 2 categorical labels (anger and disappointment), classical dimensions (intensity, valence, activation, control) and emotionally relevant modalities

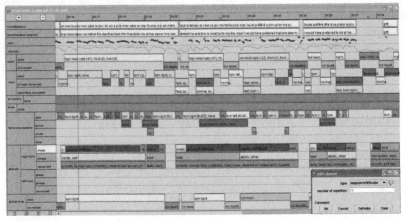

(c) Lowest level of annotation: time-based annotation of behaviors in several modalities including movement quality

Fig. 1. Multilevel annotation of emotional behavior in the EmoTV corpus

Fig. 2. A frame from a video of a real-life emotional behavior displaying a blend of anger and despair (left). A first simulation with the Greta system (right).

secondary labels for social emotions (e.g. love, submission). Plutchik [35] also combined primary emotions to produce other labels for *intermediate* emotions. For example, love is a combination of joy and acceptance, whereas submission is a combination of acceptance and fear. The number of labels required for annotating real-life emotions might be very high when compared to basic emotions. Actually, most of the emotion modeling studies have used a minimal set of labels to be tractable [3]. Instead of using these limited number of categories, some researchers define emotions using continuous abstract dimensions: Activation-Evaluation [16], or Intensity-Evaluation [13]. But, these dimensions do not allow precise emotion representation. For example, it is impossible to distinguish between Fear and Anger. Finally, the appraisal model is useful for describing the perception / production of emotion. The major advance in this theory is the detailed specification of appraisal dimensions that are assumed to be used in evaluating emotion-antecedent events (pleasantness, novelty, etc) [39].

4.2 Expressive Behavior

We define a behavior as a pair (meaning, signal). These pairs can be elaborated based on video corpus analysis [36]. To a given meaning may be associated different sets of signals. For example, the meaning *emphasis* (of a word) may co-occur with a raise eyebrow, or a head nod, or a combination of both signals. Vice versa, a same signal may be used to convey different meanings; e.g. a raise eyebrow may be a sign of surprise, of emphasis, or even of suggestion. A third element characterizes a behavior: the manner of execution of the behavior; we call this parameter the expressivity of the behavior. The second element of the pair, the signal, is described *statically*: a facial expression at its apex, the shape of a gesture at the stroke phase. The expressivity parameter refers to the *dynamic* variation of the behavior along this static description, for e.g., the temporal duration and strength of the behavior.

To define the expressivity parameters we looked in the literature of perception studies to see which parameters were investigated [43], [20]. Six dimensions representing behavior expressivity are defined. The expressivity dimensions have been designed for communicative behaviors only. Each dimension acts differently for each modality. For the face, the expressivity dimensions act mainly on the intensity of the muscular contraction and its temporal course (how fast a muscle contracts). On the other hand, for an arm gesture, expressivity works at the level of the phases of the gesture: for example the preparation phase, the stroke, the hold as well as on the way two gestures are co-articulated. We consider six dimensions of expressivity [22]:

- *Overall activation*: amount of activity (e.g., passive/static or animated/engaged). This parameter influences the number of behaviors happening during speech. For example, as this parameter increases, the number of head movements per time will also increase.
- *Spatial extent*: amplitude of movements. This parameter determines the quantity of physical displacement involved in the expression (e.g., amplitude of a raise eyebrow and or arms opening).
- *Temporal extent*: duration of movements (e.g., quick versus sustained actions). This temporal parameter modifies the speed of execution of expressions/gestures. Low values will produce very quick movements while higher values will produce slower ones.
- *Fluidity*: smoothness and continuity of movement (e.g., smooth, graceful versus sudden, jerky); articulation between consecutive expressions/gestures. Fluidity determines the way in which consecutive expressions/gestures are performed. Higher fluidity allows direct interpolation between target keyframes of consecutive movements instead of moving the arms or the face back to the initial rest position.
- *Power*: dynamic properties of the movement (e.g., weak/relaxed versus strong/tense). Higher (lower) values will increase (decrease) the acceleration of the muscles, making movements become more (less) powerful. High values correspond to short time needed to reach the target while lower values produce slower movements.
- *Repetitivity*: this factor allows the repetition of the same expression/gesture several times.

5 Multi-level Annotation of Non-basic Emotions

In order to model realistic emotional behavior, literature can be completed by the collection and annotation of audio-visual data. The EmoTV corpus features 50 videos samples of TV interviews with emotional behaviors [1]. The main difficult point in defining the coding scheme for annotating and representing such emotional behaviors is to find the useful levels of description in term of granularity and temporality. The goal of the EmoTV corpus is to provide knowledge on the coordination between modalities during non-acted emotionally rich behaviors. It does not aim at providing detailed data on each individual modality. The specificities of the multi-level coding scheme used for EmoTV are thus: to enable the annotation of both emotion labels and abstract dimensions in order to study their redundancy and complementarity, the definition of non-basic emotional patterns, the use of two labels for labeling a single emotional behavior, the emotional context including some appraisal-based dimensions, a coarse temporal description of intensity variation in each segment, a global description of perceived signs of emotion in the different modalities, and a more detailed description of multimodal behaviors in each segment [2].

In order to find an appropriate list of emotional labels, different strategies can be used [11], [13]. In EmoTV, two annotators labeled the emotion they perceived in each emotional segment, each time selecting one label of their choice (free choice). This resulted in 176 fine-grain labels (after a normalization phase) which were classified into the following set of 14 broader categories: anger, despair, disgust, doubt, exaltation, fear, irritation, joy, neutral, pain, sadness, serenity, surprise and worry. We have kept several levels of granularity. The coarse-grained level is composed of the 6 well-known Ekman classes [18] plus the *neutral* and *other* classes. The EmoTV coding scheme also features two classical abstract dimensions [12]: activation (passive, normal, active) and valence (negative, neutral, positive). The intensity (low, normal, high) and control dimensions (controlled, normal, and uncontrolled) have also been added since they provide relevant information for the study of real-life emotions. Furthermore, for each segment coarse temporal descriptors for intensity variation are used as they are well-known for their relevance to animation dynamics.

Regarding the annotation of multimodal behaviors, the speech transliteration including non-verbal events markers was done using the Linguistic Data Consortium (LDC)[1] transliteration norm. Prosodic and spectral cues are automatically extracted. In the videos only the upper body of people is visible. The coding scheme contains tracks for each visible modality: torso, head, shoulders, arms, facial expressions, gestures and global body. Torso, head and shoulders contain a description of the pose, and of the movement. Pose and movement annotations thus alternate. Head pose contains a primary position attribute (adapted from the FACS coding scheme): front, turned left / right, tilt left / right, upward / downward, forward / backward. A secondary position is available for representing combinations of positions (e.g. head to the right and down). Head primary movement observed between the start and the end pose is annotated with the same set of values as the primary position attribute. A secondary movement enables the combination of several movements. (e.g. head nod while turning the head). As for gesture annotation, we have kept some classical attributes [25] but also focused on repetitive and manipulator gestures which occur frequently in the EmoTV corpus. Our coding scheme enables the annotation of structural phases of gestures [29]: preparation (bringing arm and hand into stroke position), stroke (the most energetic part of the gesture), sequence of stroke (a number of successive strokes), hold (a phase of stillness just before or just after the stroke), and retract (movement back to rest position). We have selected the following set of values for the gesture function: *Manipulator*: contact with body or object; *Beat*: synchronized with the emphasis of the speech; *Deictic*: arm or hand is used to point at an existing or imaginary object; *Representational*: represents attributes, actions, relationships about objects and characters; *Emblem*: movement with a precise, culturally defined meaning. Representational gestures and emblems revealed to be very few in our corpus after a first annotation phase. Movement quality is also annotated for torso, head, shoulders, gestures, global pose and movement. The attributes of movement quality that we selected as relevant in our corpus are: the number of repetitions, the fluidity (smooth, normal, jerky), the strength (soft, normal, hard), the speed (slow, normal, fast), the spatial expansion (contracted, normal, and expanded).

---

[1] http://www.ldc.upenn.edu/

6 Multi-level Specification of Emotions and Behaviors in ECAs

We have developed a system that generates the behaviors of a talking ECA. Our system considers several elements to compute the final animation of the agent: what the agent aims at communicating as well as a description of the agent's baseline behavior.

To determine speech-accompanying non-verbal behaviors the system relies on a taxonomy of communicative functions proposed by Isabella Poggi [37]. A communicative function is defined as a pair (meaning, signal) where meaning corresponds to the communicative value the agent wants to communicate and signal to the behavior used to convey this meaning. In this taxonomy, communicative functions are classified based on the type of information they convey. We consider the communicative functions that provide information about speaker's beliefs, intentions, affective state and meta-cognitive information about speaker's mental state. To control the agent we are using a representation language, called `Affective Presentation Markup Language' (APML) where the tags of this language are the communicative functions [14]. We have added an *exprFactor* variable that specifies with which expressivity is displayed a given communicative act. An example of a text an agent says (in bold) enhanced with communicative functions information is:

```
<performative type="criticize">
<rheme affect="anger" exprFactor="1.3">
They have taken my father
<boundary type="HL"/>
the day they took him
<boundary type="LH"/>
they took
<emphasis x-pitch-accent="Lstar" deictic= "self3"> me
...
```

To allow for the generation of a specific expressive ECA, we associate to each agent a *behavioral profile* which specifies the agent's modality hierarchy[2] (range of the modalities over which the agent is the most expressive) [41], the agent's predispositions (how expressive each modality is (e.g. an agent may be more expressive with its face than with its gesture)) and the global expressivity (global characteristics of the agent's behavior defined by the six dimensions described in Section 4.2). The behavioral profile represents somehow the 'baseline' (Batliner, personal communication) of an agent; that is how an agent behaves in a 'neutral' way.

The *exprFactor* attribute specifies how the global expressivity of the behavioral profile should be "modulated" in order to obtain *local expressivity* that is the expressivity values that have to be used in that part of the APML text. The animation system scans the APML file and determines the local expressivity of each tag, plus the set of multimodal signals that have to be used to convey the meaning of the tag. The behavioral engine scans the input file and determines the local expressivity of each tag. It also determines the (eventually multimodal) signals that have to be used to convey the meaning of a given tag. The engine reads the physical description of these signals (for

---

[2] In case several modalities have the same preferential level, we consider that agent's nonverbal behavior to express a communicative act is visible through several modalities.

example, the position of the arms and hand shape, the facial expression) from a database and instantiates them according to the local expressivity values. This instantiation can be seen as a modification of the qualitative aspects of the signal as explained in 4.2. Given the same APML tags as input, different behavioral profiles will correspond to different selection of modalities, signals and their respective expressivity values. Consequently agents defined by different behavioral profiles will react differently to the same APML file.

7 From Corpus Annotation to Emotional ECAs

Figure 3 describes our approach for using the corpus annotations for the specification of the ECA. The input of our simulation is a manual specification designed from studying both the video and the corpus annotations. These specifications feed in the ECA system at two levels: 1) the text the agent has to say tagged with APML [34], and 2) the behavioral profile of the agent.

The system instantiates the communicative functions into the appropriate signals. The output of the system is the audio and the animation files that drive the facial model. The APML tags, corresponding to the meaning of a given communicative function, are converted into their corresponding facial, gesture and gaze signals. At first the system has to select which behaviors are the most appropriate to select for a particular communicative act and a given agent. There are two selection phases [28]: the modality selection and the signals pre-selection. The first selection corresponds to determining which modality the agent uses; the second selection consists in ordering the set of possible behaviors having an equivalent meaning. This ordering takes into account the expressivity of the agent. Finally, we proceed with the animation generation for the agent.

8 Conclusion and Future Directions

In this paper we presented a methodology based on the manual annotation of a video corpus to create expressive ECAs via an analytical approach: we have proposed a representation scheme and a computational model for such an agent and explained how the multi-level annotation of expressivity in TV interviews is compatible with the multi-level specifications of our ECA. Our approach is at an exploratory stage and does not currently include the computation of statistics over a large amount of videos. Yet, it did enable us to identify the relevant levels of representation for studying the complex relations between emotions and multimodal behaviors in non acted and non basic emotions.

We will apply this protocol on our selection of videos. We will use in the ECA specification the hybrid scheme used for annotating each segment with two labels in order to consider non basic emotional patterns (our ECA is currently using only one emotional label at a time). A fuzzy logic model for computing facial expressions of complex emotion is currently being implemented in the ECA system [32].

The annotation of our EmoTV videos along several annotation dimensions is ongoing. The average annotation time is 15 minutes per clip for the annotation of

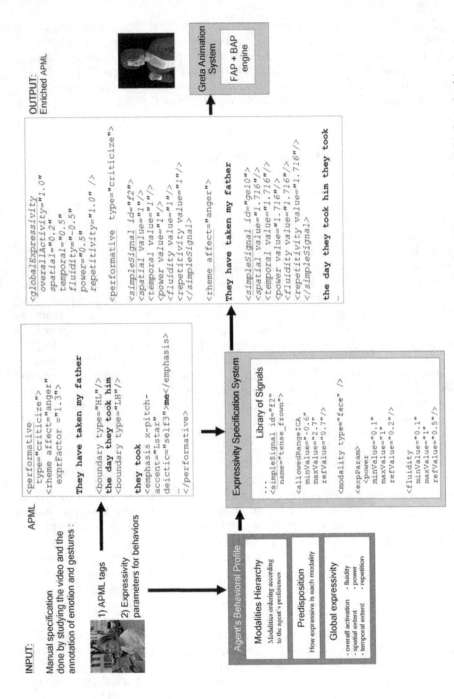

Fig. 3. Use of multiple levels of annotations of emotion in a video (*left*) for the specification of the expressive ECA Greta (*right*)

emotion and 1 hour for the annotation of the multimodal behaviors (the average clip duration is 14 seconds). This annotation cost might decrease in the future as the coders will learn how to use the coding scheme more efficiently. We will also investigate the possibility to use image processing to decrease annotation time, although this might be quite difficult given the video quality of TV clips and the variability of the outdoor environments seen in many interviews.

The procedure will be validated via perceptual tests for evaluating if the contextual cues, the emotion and the multimodal behaviors are perceptually equivalent in the original video and in the simulation of the corresponding behaviors by the ECA, thus revealing how much such a technique is successful. These perceptual tests will also help finding out if differences of quality and of level of details between the real and the simulated multimodal behaviors have an impact on the perception of emotion. Another application of these tests that we foresee is the possibility to refine our ECA system. Indeed having to reproduce complex real behaviors allows us to refine our behavioral engine; we will apply the methodology *learning by imitation*.

Complex emotions do not happen solely in TV interviews. They are very common in everyday conversation. Display rules, lies, and social context often lead to the combination of the emotions as the ones we observed in our corpus. We thus believe that the methodology that we have described in this paper might be useful with other videotaped monologues than TV interviews.

Acknowledgments. This work has been partially supported by the Network of Excellence Humaine (Human-Machine Interaction Network on Emotion) IST-2002-2.3.1.6 / Contract no. 507422 (http://emotion-research.net/). We are very grateful to Bjoern Hartmann for implementing the expressive behavior module and to Vincent Maya for his help.

References

1. Abrilian, S., Devillers, L., Buisine, S., Martin, J.-C.: EmoTV1: Annotation of Real-life Emotions for the Specification of Multimodal Affective Interfaces. HCI International (2005a) Las Vegas, USA
2. Abrilian, S., Martin, J.-C., Devillers, L.: A Corpus-Based Approach for the Modeling of Multimodal Emotional Behaviors for the Specification of Embodied Agents. HCI International (2005b) Las Vegas, USA
3. Batliner, A., Fisher, K., Huber, R., Spilker, J., Noth, E.: Desperately seeking emotions or: Actors, wizards, and human beings. Speech Emotion (2000) 195-200
4. Boone, R. T., Cunningham, J. G.: Children's decoding of emotion in expressive body movement: The development of cue attunement. Developmental Psychology 34 5 (1998)
5. Calbris, G.: The semiotics of French gestures. University Press Bloomington Indiana (1990)
6. Cao, Y., Faloutsos, P., Kohler, E., Pighin, F.: Real-time Speech Motion Synthesis from Recorded Motions. ACM SIGGRAPH/Eurographics Symposium on Computer Animation (2004)
7. Cassell, J., Stone, M., Hao, Y.: Coordination and context-dependence in the generation of embodied conversation. INLG (2000) 171-178

8. Cassell, J., Sullivan, J., Prevost, S., Churchill, E.: Embodied Conversational Agents. MIT Press (2000)
9. Cassell, J., Vilhjàlmsson, H., Bickmore, T.: BEAT: the Behavior Expression Animation Toolkit. 28th annual conference on Computer graphics and interactive techniques (2001) 477-486
10. Chi, D., Costa, M., Zhao, L., Badler, N.: The EMOTE model for effort and shape. 27th annual conference on Computer graphics and interactive techniques (2000) 173-182
11. Cowie, R.: Emotion recognition in human-computer interaction. IEEE Signal processing Magazine 18 (2001)
12. Cowie, R., Douglas-Cowie, E., Savvidou, S., McMahon, E., Sawey, M., Schröder, M.: 'FEELTRACE': An Instrument for Recording Perceived Emotion in Real Time. ISCA Workshop on Speech & Emotion. (2000)
13. Craggs, R., Wood, M. M.: A categorical annotation scheme for emotion in the linguistic content. Affective Dialogue Systems (ADS'2004) (2004)
14. De Carolis, B., Pelachaud, C., Poggi, I., Steedman, M.: APML, a Markup Language for Believable Behavior Generation. Life-like characters. Tools, affective functions and applications. Springer (2004)
15. DeMeijer, M.: The contribution of general features of body movement to the attribution of emotions. Journal of Nonverbal Behavior 13 (1989)
16. Douglas-Cowie, E., Campbell, N., Cowie, R., Roach, P.: Emotional speech; Towards a new generation of databases. Speech Communication 40 (2003)
17. Egges, A., Kshirsagar, S., Magnenat-Thalmann, N.: Imparting Individuality to Virtual Humans. First International Workshop on Virtual Reality Rehabilitation (2002) Lausanne, Switzerland
18. Ekman, P.: Basic emotions. Handbook of Cognition & Emotion. John Wiley (1999)
19. Ekman, P., Friesen, W. V.: Manual for the facial action coding system. Consulting Psychology Press Palo Alto, CA (1978)
20. Gallaher, P.: Individual differences in nonverbal behavior: Dimensions of style. Journal of Personality and Social Psychology 63 (1992)
21. Hartmann, B., Mancini, M., Pelachaud, C.: Formational Parameters and Adaptive Prototype Instantiation for MPEG-4 Compliant Gesture Synthesis. Computer Animation (2002)
22. Hartmann, B., Mancini, M., Pelachaud, C.: Implementing Expressive Gesture Synthesis for Embodied Conversational Agents. Gesture Workshop (2005) Vannes
23. Kendon, A.: Human gesture. Tools, Language and Intelligence. Cambridge University Press (1993)
24. Kipp, M.: Anvil - A Generic Annotation Tool for Multimodal Dialogue. Eurospeech'2001 (2001)
25. Kipp, M.: Gesture Generation by Imitation. From Human Behavior to Computer Character Animation. Boca Raton, Dissertation.com Florida (2004)
26. Kopp, S., Wachsmuth, I.: A knowledge-based approach for lifelike gesture animation. 14th European Conference on Artificial Intelligence (ECAI) (2000)
27. Kshirsagar, S., Molet, T., Magnant-Thalmann, N.: Principal components of expressive speech animation. Computer Graphics International (2001) 38-44
28. Maya, V., Lamolle, M., Pelachaud, C.: Influences on Embodied Conversational Agent's Expressivity: Toward an Individualization of the ECAs. AISB 2004 convention. Symposium on Language, Speech and Gesture for Expressive Characters (2004) 75-85
29. McNeill, D.: Hand and mind - what gestures reveal about thoughts. University of Chicago Press (1992)
30. Newlove, J.: Laban for actors and dancers. Routledge New York (1993)

31. Noot, H., Ruttkay, Z.: Gesture in Style. Gesture-Based Communication in Human-Computer Interaction - GW 2003. Springer (2004)
32. Ochs, M., Niewiadomski, R., Pelachaud, C., Sadek, D.: Intelligent Expressions of Emotions. 1st International Conference on Affective Computing and Intelligent Interaction (ACII'2005) (submitted) Beijing, China
33. Pandzic, I. S.: Facial Motion Cloning. Elsevier Graphical Models Journal 65 6 (2003)
34. Pelachaud, C., Carofiglio, V., De Carolis, B., De Rosis, F., Poggi, I.: Embodied Contextual Agent in Information Delivering Application. First International Joint Conference on "Autonomous Agent and Multiagent Systems" (AAMAS) (2002) Bologna, Italy 758-765
35. Plutchik, R.: The psychology and Biology of Emotion. Harper Collins College New York (1994)
36. Poggi, I.: Mind Markers. 5th International Pragmatics Conference (1996) Mexico City
37. Poggi, I., Pelachaud, C., deRosis, F.: Eye communication in a conversational 3D synthetic agent. AI Communications. Special Issue on Behavior Planning for Life-Like Characters and Avatars. 13 3 (2000)
38. Prendinger, H., Ishizuka, M.: Life-like characters. Tools, affective functions and applications. Springer (2004)
39. Scherer, K. R.: Emotion. Introduction to Social Psychology: A European perspective. Oxford: Blackwell (2000)
40. Tepper, P., Kopp, S., Cassell, J.: Content in Context: Generating Language and Iconic Gesture without a Gestionary. Workshop on Balanced Perception and Action in ECAs at Automous Agents and Multiagent Systems (AAMAS) (2004) New York, NY
41. Theune, M., Heylen, D., Nijholt , A.: Generating Embodied Information Presentations. Multimodal Intelligent Information Presentation. Kluwer Academic Publishers (2004)
42. Tsapatsoulis, N., Raouzaiou, A., Kollias, S., Cowie, R., Douglas-Cowie, E.: Emotion Recognition and Synthesis based on MPEG-4 FAPs. MPEG-4 Facial Animation. John Wiley & Sons (2002)
43. Wallbott, H. G.: Bodily expression of emotion. European Journal of Social Psychology 28 (1998)

Extended Behavior Networks and Agent Personality: Investigating the Design of Character Stereotypes in the Game Unreal Tournament

Hugo da Silva Corrêa Pinto and Luis Otávio Alvares

Instituto de Informática – Universidade Federal do Rio Grande do Sul (UFRGS)
Caixa Postal 15.064 – 91.501-970 – Porto Alegre – RS – Brazil
{hsspinto, alvares}@inf.ufrgs.br

Abstract. The Extended Behavior Network (EBN) is an architecture and action selection mechanism to design agents capable of selecting sets of concurrent actions in dynamic and continuous environments. It allows one to specify context-dependent motivations and build agents modularly, and has achieved good results in the Robocup and in the 3D action game Unreal Tournament. PHISH-Nets, another behavior network model capable of selecting just single actions, was applied to character modeling, with promising results. We investigate how EBNs fare on agent personality modeling via the design and analysis of 5 stereotypes in Unreal Tournament. We discuss three ways to build character personas and situate our work within other approaches. We conclude that EBNs provide a straightforward way to develop and experiment with different personalities, being interesting for building agents with simple personas and for character prototyping.

1 Introduction

The personality of an agent is largely characterized by its motivations and goals and how it behaves to achieve these goals. These motivations may be many and conflicting, and usually an agent has many ways of satisfying them. If the agent is situated in a dynamic domain, we have to develop a good enough action selection policy for the agent, regardless of its personality, in order to enable the agent to fulfill its goals.

Behavior Networks[1] were proposed as an action selection mechanism to choose good actions in complex and dynamic environments. They gracefully treat conflicts among the goals, are fast, robust, reactive and favor actions that contribute to more than one goal.

PHISH-Nets[2], an extension of the original behavior network[1], was proposed as an architecture to develop personalities for characters in an interactive domain, based on the Bad Wolf and Three Little Pigs tale. The main limitations of the mechanism were that it could select just one action at a time, used boolean conditions and supported only context-independent goals.

Extended Behavior Networks (EBN)[3] are another extension of [1]. They use real-valued propositions and are able to specify situation-dependent goals. Action selection is done concurrently, so more than one action may be selected

T. Panayiotopoulos et al. (Eds.): IVA 2005, LNCS 3661, pp. 418–429, 2005.
© Springer-Verlag Berlin Heidelberg 2005

simultaneously. They have been applied with good results in the Robocup [4] [5] and in the game Unreal Tournament[6]. These works focused on validating the extended behavior network model and on assessing agent performance. To date, we are unaware of any application of EBNs to personality modeling, even though it is applicable to a larger domain than PHISH-Nets.

In this work we investigate the design of five stereotypical personalities for agents in the game Unreal Tournament [7]: The Veteran, The Novice, The Coward, The Berserker and The Samurai. Unreal Tournament is a 3D action game where warriors fight each other in an arena.

In the remaining of this paper we present an overview of extended behavior networks, followed by a description of the game environment and the designing and experimenting of each agent warrior stereotype. Next, we discuss ways to design agent personalities using EBNs based on the stereotypes presented and situate our contribution within a body of related work. We conclude by pointing the easiness of personality design with EBNs, the applicability and scope of our approach, and our next research steps.

2 Extended Behavior Networks

An extended behavior network can be viewed as a set of linked modules and goals that mutually inhibit and excite each other via activation spreading, starting at the goals and flowing to the modules. The modules with higher activation and executability that do not use the same resources are selected for execution at each step. In the next subsections we examine in detail the structure of the network and the action selection algorithm.

2.1 Structure

An extended behavior network is defined by a set of behavior modules (M), a set of goals (G), a set of sensors (S), a set of resources (R), and a set of control parameters (C). Figure 2.1 shows the specification of part of a behavior network used in our experiments, and figure 2.2 the network built from this specification.

A goal i is defined by a proposition that must be met (Gi), a strength value (Sti) and a disjunction of propositions that provide the context for that goal, called the relevance condition (Li). The strength provides the static, context-independent importance of the goal and the relevance condition provides the dynamic, context-dependent one.

The use of two kinds of conditions in the goals enables us to express goals that become more or less important, depending on the situation the agent is in.

A context independent goal is modeled leaving it without relevance conditions. Goal *EnemyHurt* in figure 2.1 is an example of such a goal. Note that a goal without relevance conditions amounts to a goal that is always relevant, i.e., its relevance is always maximal.

Each behavior module is specified by a conditions list, an effects list, an action and a resources list. The first list is a conjunction of real valued propositions that represent the needed conditions for the module to execute. The effects list is a conjunction of propositions (each possibly negated) whose values are the values that we expect them to have after the module's action execution. The resources list is made of pairs (resource, amount), each indicating the expected amount of a resource an agent uses to perform the action.

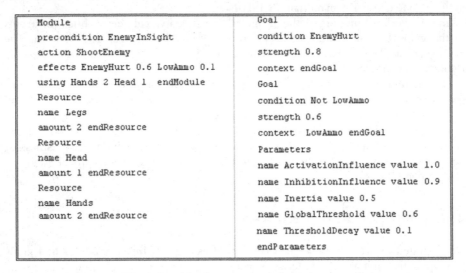

```
Module                                      Goal
precondition EnemyInSight                   condition EnemyHurt
action ShootEnemy                           strength 0.8
effects EnemyHurt 0.6 LowAmmo 0.1           context endGoal
using Hands 2 Head 1  endModule             Goal
Resource                                    condition Not LowAmmo
name Legs                                   strength 0.6
amount 2 endResource                        context  LowAmmo endGoal
Resource                                    Parameters
name Head                                   name ActivationInfluence value 1.0
amount 1 endResource                        name InhibitionInfluence value 0.9
Resource                                    name Inertia value 0.5
name Hands                                  name GlobalThreshold value 0.6
amount 2 endResource                        name ThresholdDecay value 0.1
                                            endParameters
```

Fig. 1. Specification of a simple behavior network

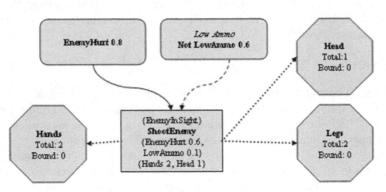

Fig. 2. Simple Behavior Network Diagram. The goals are represented by round cornered rectangles, the behaviors by sharp cornered rectangles and the resource nodes by octagons. Straight lines represent predecessor links, dashed lines conflict links and pointed lines resource links.

Goals and modules are linked with two kinds of links. Predecessor links go from a module or goal B to a module A, for each proposition in the condition list of B that is in the effects list of A, such that the proposition has the same sign (true + or false -) in both ends of the link. The link from goal *EnemyHurt* to module *ShootEnemy* in figure 2 is an example. Conflict links go from a module or goal B to a module A, for each proposition in the condition list of B that is in the effects list of A, such that the proposition has opposite signs at each end of the link. In figure 2, the link from *Not*

LowAmmo to *ShootEnemy* is a conflict link. Conflict links take energy away from their targets and predecessor links input energy to their targets. This way a module or goal tries to inhibit modules whose execution would undo some of its conditions and attempts to bring into execution modules whose actions would satisfy any of its conditions.

Each resource is represented by a resource node and defined by a function $f(s)$ that specifies the expected amount of the resource available in each situation s. In addition to $f(s)$, each node has a variable *bound* that keeps track of the amount of bound resources and a resource activation threshold $\theta_{Res} \in (0..\theta]$, where θ is the global activation threshold. In figure 2 we see that the expected used amount of each resource is constant for all situations. This is not surprising as our agent has the same number of body parts available in any situation (the game does not account for limb loss or similar gruesome events).

The modules are linked to the resource nodes through resource links. For each resource type in the resources list of a module there is a link from the module to the corresponding resource node.

The control parameters are used to fine tune the network and have values in the range [0, 1]. The activation influence parameter γ controls the activation from predecessor links. Inhibition influence, δ, the negative activation from conflict links. The inertia β, the global threshold θ and the threshold decay $\Delta\theta$ have their straightforward meanings. Their function will become clearer in the next subsection.

2.2 Action Selection Algorithm

The modules to be executed at each cycle are selected in the following way:

1) The activation a of each module is calculated.

2) The executability e of each module is calculated using some triangular norm operation over its condition list.

3) The execution-value $h(a,e)$ is calculated by multiplying a and e. Note that this value combines the utility of executing a behavior (activation) and the probability of executing it successfully (executability). This way even modules with conditions not much satisfied may execute if they have high activation.

4) For each resource used by a module, starting by the last non-available resource, the module checks if it has exceeded the resource threshold and if there is enough of that resource for its execution. If so, it binds the resource.

5) If a module has bound all of its needed resources it executes and resets the resources thresholds to the value of the global threshold.

6) Each module unbinds the resources it used.

The thresholds of the resources linearly decay over time, ensuring that eventually a behavior will be able to bind its needed resources and that the most active behavior gets priority.

The formulae of Figure 3 detail the activation spreading process.

Formula (1) shows the activation that goes from a goal i to a module k through a predecessor link at instant t. Function f is a triangular norm that combines the strength and the dynamic relevance of a goal. The term ex_j is the value of the effect proposition that is the target of a link.

$$a_{kg_i}^t{}' = \gamma \cdot f(\iota_{g_i}, r_{g_i}^t) \cdot ex_j \tag{1}$$

$$a_{kg_i}^t{}'' = -\delta \cdot f(\iota_{g_i}, r_{g_i}^t) \cdot ex_j, \tag{2}$$

$$a_{kg_i}^t{}''' = \gamma \cdot \sigma(a_{succ\,g_i}^{t-1}) \cdot ex_j \cdot (1 - \tau(p_{succ}, s)), \tag{3}$$

$$a_{kg_i}^t{}'''' = -\delta \cdot \sigma(a_{conf\,g_i}^{t-1}) \cdot ex_j \cdot \tau(p_{conf}, s), \tag{4}$$

$$a_{kg_i}^t = abs\,\max(a_{kg_i}^t{}', a_{kg_i}^t{}'', a_{kg_i}^t{}''', a_{kg_i}^t{}''''). \tag{5}$$

$$a_k^t = \beta a_k^{t-1} + \sum_i a_{kg_i}^t \tag{6}$$

Fig. 3. Activation Spreading Formulae. Reproduced from [4]

Formula (2) shows the activation that goes from a goal i to a module k through a conflict link at an instant t.

Formula (3) shows the activation spreading from a module $succ$ to a module k at an instant t through a predecessor link. p_{succ} is the proposition of the successor module and a_{succ} the activation of the successor module. $\tau\left(p_{succ}, s\right)$ is the value of p_{succ} in situation s. We see that the activation spreading increases as the proposition at the start of a predecessor link becomes less satisfied. Thus, we can see unsatisfied conditions as increasingly demanding sub-goals of the network. Function σ, shown below, is used to make the behavior modules strong attractors [8] with a high probability. This reduces unnecessary behavior switches, as small changes in the percepts will be less likely to disrupt an ongoing behavior.

$$\sigma(x) = (1 + e^{\kappa(\mu - x)})^{-1} \tag{7}$$

Formula (4) describes the activation spread from a module through a conflict link. a_{conf} and p_{conf} stand for the activation and proposition of the module that is the source of the conflict link, respectively.

Formula (6) shows that the activation of a module k at an instant t is its activation in the previous time step t-1 weighted by the inertia constant β plus the sum of the activations retained of each goal i.

Formula (5) shows that a module retains just the activation of greatest absolute value from each goal. It amounts to keeping only the strongest path from a module to each goal.

3 Experiments

We designed agents with different personalities for Unreal Tournament, a 3D action game. In the game mode we used, DeathMatch, agents are warriors who must exterminate their rivals in a battle arena. Agents have many weapons available, each with certain properties (beat, pierce or explode) and several items to use. The action repertory is large (run, walk, turn, crawl, shoot, change weapons, jump, strafe, pickup item and use item among others) and an agent may carry out more than one action simultaneously, such as dodging while shooting. The scenarios are three-dimensional continuous spaces and the action happens in real-time, so the agent has to decide quickly what to do.

Five stereotypes come to mind in this scenario: The Veteran, The Novice, The Coward, The Samurai and The Berserker. The following subsections detail the requirements and design of each character.

3.1 The Veteran

The Veteran is calm and rational, trying to maximize all its goals in the long run. He has great self-control and persistence and wants to kill as many enemies as possible, but never at the expense of his life. These requirements are very similar to the requirements for an agent that wants to maximize its score over a series of games. This was the case of the agent presented at [6], so we use it as a basis for the Veteran. Figure 4 shows the Behavior Network and global parameters for this character.

The overall behavior of the agent could be described as follows: It started exploring the level and kept wandering until it found an enemy (*Explore*). Upon finding an enemy it started shooting (*ShootEnemy*) and approached the enemy (*GoToEnemy*). When it reached the enemy it switched weapons and used the more powerful weapon Hammer (*FinalizeWithHammer*). After the enemy died, it stopped shooting (*StopShoot*) and started wandering again. When shot repeatedly it kept shooting and after a while stopped going to the enemy and started dodging subsequent shots. If the enemy stopped shooting it would go towards it again. When the agent was hurt in combat, if it knew the location of a medkit (*GoToKnownMedkit* had a high truth value), it would go to it and restore its health after a while. If when approaching the enemy the agent became with very low health, if there was a reachable medical kit (*MedKitReachable*) the agent would stop going to the enemy and go to the medkit, while keeping shooting unless it was close to the enemy, in which case it attempted a killing with the hammer (*FinalizeWithHammer*).

We see that this behavior matches the personality of an archetypical combat veteran: The agent is persistent when killing, heals itself when it is safe to do so and has the endurance to keep fighting even when being shot back, without panicking.

3.2 The Novice

The Novice aspires to be like the veteran, has similar values, but still lacks the endurance and discipline to act properly. He is impulsive and frequently does not take the best action for a circumstance. To achieve this lower discipline and greater impulsiveness we investigated lowering two global parameters, the inertia β and the global threshold θ.

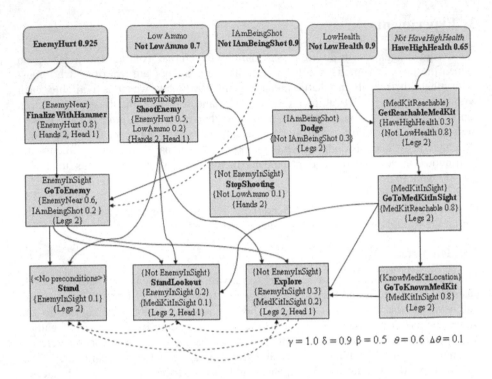

Fig. 4. Veteran's Behavior Network

We lowered the inertia to 0.1. This way the agent would be too reactive. The agent, when shot, immediately attempted to dodge. If there was a medkit nearby and it needed it, it would stop chasing the enemy and get it. Immediately dodging is not very good because dodging is not guaranteed to succeed, so an agent should dodge to avoid bursts of shots, but not single ones.

To augment the number of mistakes of the novice, we lowered the global threshold. This way we decreased the quality of action selection, as many modules surpassed the threshold simultaneously, and among modules that are over the threshold no one has priority over others. Now, often the agent shot the enemy even when it was very near and could be hammered. For the extremely low value of 0.1, the agent also often just stood still(*Stand*) instead of exploring the level(*Explore*).

The best parameters we found to bring forth the character of the Novice were $\gamma = 1.0$, $\delta = 0.9$, $\beta = 0.1$, $\theta = 0.25$ and $\Delta\theta = 0.1$.

3.3 The Coward

The Coward's main goal is getting out of the combat alive and unhurt, so he will avoid confrontation and will prioritize maintaining and restoring its health.

To bring forth the Coward working on the global parameters would be of little use, as he is as persistent as the Veteran and we have no reason to believe him to make decisions less thoughtfully. Instead, we worked on the goal strengths. We lowered *EnemyHurt* and raised *HaveHighHealth*. We left the global constants untouched.

The behavior of the coward could be thus described: It started exploring the level until he found an enemy. With an enemy in sight he started shooting .When shot back, if the enemy missed him, he would start dodging after a little while, for all subsequent shots. If actually hit he would go get the medkit immediately if there was one reachable. If there was none he would keep dodging and fighting until it had a low health. When it happened he would flee combat and go restore its health, even if he had to go all the way to a far known medkit.

We see that even though the agent is far more concerned with its health and could not be described as brave anymore a key point of its specification is missing: its active avoidance of engagement. We implemented a new module for the network: *GoAwayFromEnemy*. With this module added, when the Coward spotted an enemy, he would go away from him while shooting. Figure 5 shows the full network of the Coward character. Note that adding a new behavior was a simple modular operation, dispensing adjustments.

3.4 The Samurai

The Samurai is cold, persistent and aggressive. To die in battle is his highest honor, and he likes fair matches. Killing his opponent is his stronger goal and he will try to achieve it even at the expense of his life. When in a fight with an enemy it won't stop to attack another agent, nor will be stopped by pain or danger.

To transform the Veteran into a Samurai we worked on the goals strengths. We set *EnemyHurt* to 1.0, *NotIAmBeignShot* to 0.6, *NotLowHealth* to 0.5 and *HaveHighHealth* to 0.4. With these strengths the agent will always approach the enemy instead of dodging bullets and will not stop to get medkits if in a fight. We verified that whenever he found an enemy it went towards it shooting and then attacked with the hammer (FinalizeWithHammer) if the enemy had not died yet. If there was no enemy in sight the Samurai would go after medkits to restore its health. For a gamer the Samurai displayed the exact behavior we desired: He was never disturbed by pain (low health) or danger (shoots) in his pursuit of an enemy and employed good tactics (shooting from afar and hammering when near).

3.5 The Berserker

The Berserker is aggressive, undisciplined and non-persistent. Once in the arena he will attack fiercely its opponents, in a mad frenzy. He is insensitive to pain, and most times will not stop attacking to heal itself or even to dodge bullets.

To bring into being the mad berserker we started from the Samurai. We lowered even more its sensibility to pain by decreasing the importance of goal *LowHealth* and to bring forth his frenzy we diminished both its inertia and its global threshold. Lowering β made the agent very reactive and lowering θ made the agent take insane actions, such as shooting instead of hammering at close quarters.

The overall behavior of the berserker was as intended – he would not stop to dodge or heal while in combat and he fought madly, hammering and shooting everything that went into his path.

4 Discussion

We illustrated three approaches to develop agent personality: changing the global parameters, changing the goal strengths and changing the network topology itself.

Changing the global parameters allowed us to control two key personality characteristics: Thoughtfulness (through the activation threshold θ) and persistence (through the inertia β).

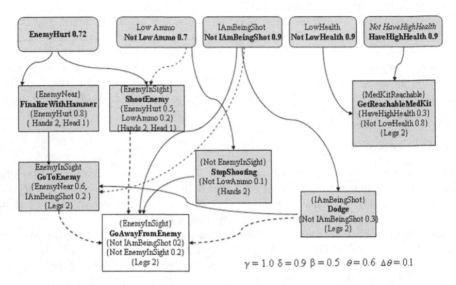

Fig. 4. Part of the Coward Behavior Network. We have displayed only modules directly connected to a goal for clarity.

A high activation threshold θ lead to better action selection as only actions that had a high activation could execute, that is, it required on average more activation spreading cycles to decide what to do next and also required higher executability for the modules. For an external observer it amounts to a thoughtful behavior, as an agent does mostly what seems effective and proper to its goals. We saw a thoughtful behavior typical of an experienced soldier in the Veteran and the thoughtless behavior of a newbie in the Novice.

A high β leads to a persistent behavior: An agent only changes its behavior if there is a large or long change in its sensory information. This was the case of the Veteran taking some time to start dodging bullets. A single shot was not enough to make he interrupt his course of action. Symmetrically, the Novice changed actions due to slight changes in its sensors.

The predecessor link activation constant γ, the conflict link activation constant δ and the threshold decrease $\Delta\theta$ were not used to design agent personality.

Changing the goal strengths was our first try when changing the global constants could not lead to the desired behavior. This is somewhat harder because the strength of a goal must be set in relation to the other goals of the agent. Altering the goal strengths is the default way to alter deep personality characteristics, the very motivations and values of a character. This was the solution needed to implement both the Samurai and the Coward.

Finally for some cases we may have to add a whole new module. Adding a module to a behavior network is a straightforward operation – the network itself takes care of its integration, with the automatic creation of predecessor and conflict links. It may be a time consuming option due to subtleties that may arise in the actual implementation of the module, if one does not exists yet. If we have a library of behavior modules, then this option is also easy.

Summing all up, we could make the reverse question: how do we build agents with different personalities from scratch? First we define the agent's goals and their relative importance. Next we assemble a set of modules capable of achieving these goals. Next we tune the global parameters to achieve the subtleties of the personality. Having one working agent, making other with radically different personalities is simple, as we have seen.

5 Related Work

The design of agents with personality has a long tradition. Sophisticated models, with a focus on agent personality and interaction, have been developed over the last decade and the present. Usually they address the question "What is the best way to design an agent with personality and emotional traits capable of carrying out sophisticated interactions with humans and other agents?" They have shown promising results in the domains where applied, such as embodied conversational characters [9] and interactive drama [10].

Our work answers a different question: "Given that I have to design several complex agents capable of having good performance (or scores) in a real-time continuous and complex game environment in a short time span, how may I make them with different personalities?" This precludes solutions that require long processing or very complex design and favors solutions that produce a fast acceptable result. Sophisticated interaction with humans are not a concern as the interactions are quite simple and do not involve mood detection, gesture recognition or the exchange of roles.

The only previous application of behavior networks to character design that we are aware of is [2]. In this work, a behavior network model called PHISH-Nets was used to design the Big Bad Wolf and the Three Little Pigs of the famous kids tale in a simple discreet 3D environment. There was no pressure for the actions to be carried in real time. Most experiments investigated how the agent handled action failures and its capacity to improvise. Despite its interesting results for character modeling we could not use this model to answer our question, unless it was drastically modified, as for complex real-time games we need to select several actions concurrently and deal with continuous quantities.

Blumberg's [11] [12] work on synthetic characters, particularly the architecture described in [11], seems potentially fit to address the problem we pointed. It integrates learning capabilities and allows deeper emotional modeling, being more sophisticated and complicate.

Other architectures have been proposed to the modern game environment domain. Of immediate interest is an implementation of the Cog-Aff architecture [13] that used an anytime planner [14], A-UMCP. It was deployed in the Unreal Tournament domain, though for the game mode Capture the Flag. Although the Cog-Aff architecture explicitly takes into account agent personality into its design, it was not mentioned in this work [15].

The Excalibur architecture [16] is also proposed as a generic architecture for autonomous agents in complex game environments. Its distinctive feature is its ability to incorporate resources in its planning process in a sophisticated manner. Though one can easily think of ways of incorporating personality modeling into this framework we are unaware of works with this approach.

Finally we may cite the applications of the Soar architecture to computer games [17]. Soar stands in a different stratum: It is a sophisticated cognitive architecture aimed at human-level intelligence, with a considerable learning curve. Usually the foci of these works revolved around cognitive plausibility and depth of the agent models. Soar seems a good choice when one's focus is fidelity and depth but overkill for creating agents with simple personas.

6 Conclusion

It is relatively easy to build agents with different personalities using extended behavior networks when we consider other approaches. To build a seminal agent one starts by setting goals that reflect the character values and motivations. Next, one proceeds by assembling a set of modules capable of achieving those goals (modules that have the goal conditions as effects). Finally, by adjusting the goal strengths and global parameters one builds very different agent personalities for agents with similar capabilities.

Extended Behavior Networks are an interesting technique for building agents with similar capabilities and different personalities when we retain the focus on agent performance.

The main limitation is that the personalities built are static and simple, enabling only stereotypical personalities to come about. To be more realistic, an agent should be able to display different personas based on its mood or its emotions.

This work presented the first results of using extended behavior networks to design agent personality. Our next step is making quantitative measures of the believability of each of these personas, using ratings of human players.

References

1. Maes, P. How to do The Right Thing. Connection Science Journal, Vol. 1, No. 3., 1989.
2. Rhodes, Bradley. PHISH-Nets: Planning Heuristically in Situated Hybrid Networks . MSc Thesis. MIT. 1996.
3. Dörer, K. Concurrent Behavior Selection in Extended Behavior Networks. Team Description for RoboCup2000, Melbourne. 2000.
4. Dörer, K. Extended Behavior Networks for the Magma Freiburg Team. In RoboCup-99 Team Descriptions for the Simulation League. Linkoping University Press, 1999. p. 79-83.

5. Müller, K. Roboterfußball: Multiagentensystem CS Freiburg, Diplomarbeit. Univ. Freiburg, Germany. Feb 2001.
6. Pinto, Hugo; Alvares, L. O. C Applying Extended Behavior Networks to 3D Action Games. In: Brazilian Simposium on Games and Digital Entertainment - W Jogos, 2004, Curitiba. SBGames 2004 - Proceedings of W Jogos, 2004.
7. Unreal Tournament http://www.unrealtournament.com 28/03/2005.
8. Goetz, P. Attractors in Recurrent Behavior Networks. Phd Thesis. University of New York.Buffalo.1997.
9. Cassell, J. et al. Human Conversation as a System Framework: Designing Embodied Conversational Agents, in Cassell, J. et al. (eds.), Embodied Conversational Agents, pp. 29-63. Cambridge, MA: MIT Press.2000.
10. Rayes-Roth, B. Improvisational puppets, actors, and avatars, Proceedings of Computer Games Conference, 1996
11. Isla, D., Burke, R., Blumberg, B.et.al. "A Layered Brain Architecture for Synthetic Characters," in the Proceedings of the International Joint Conference on Artificial Intelligence (IJCAI), pp.1051-1058, Seattle, WA, August 2001.
12. Kline, C. and Blumberg, B. The Art and Science of Synthetic Character Design. In Proceedings of the AISB1999 Symposium on AI and Creativity in Entertainment and Visual Art, Edinburgh, Scotland. 1999
13. Scheutz, M. and Sloman, A. A Framework for Comparing Agent Architectures. In Proceedings UKCI'02, UK Workshop on Computational Intelligence, Birmingham, UK. 2002.
14. Zilberstein, S. Using Anytime Algorithms in Intelligent Systems. AI Magazine, 17(3):73-83, 1996.
15. Hawes, Nick. An Anytime Planning Agent For Computer Game Worlds. In Proceedings, Workshop on Agents in Computer Games at The 3rd International Conference on Computers and Games (CG'02), July 27th 2002. Pages 1--14.
16. Nareyek, A. Beyond the Plan-Length Criterion. In Nareyek, A. (ed.), Local Search for Planning and Scheduling, Springer LNAI 2148, 55-78. 2001.
17. Magerko, B. Laird, J. et al, AI Characters and Directors for Interactive Computer Games. In Proceedings of the 2004 Innovative Applications of Artificial Intelligence Conference, San Jose, CA, July 2004. AAAI Press.

Direct Manipulation Like Tools for Designing Intelligent Virtual Agents*

Marco Gillies[1], Dale Robeterson[2], and Daniel Ballin[2]

[1] Department of Computer Science, University College London, London, UK
[2] BT plc, Adastral Park, Ipswich IP5 3RE, UK
m.gillies@cs.ucl.ac.uk
{dale.e2.robertson, daniel.ballin}@bt.com

Abstract. If intelligent virtual agents are to become widely adopted it is vital that they can be designed using the user friendly graphical tools that are used in other areas of graphics. However, extending this sort of tool to autonomous, interactive behaviour, an area with more in common with artificial intelligence, is not trivial. This paper discusses the issues involved in creating user-friendly design tools for IVAs and proposes an extension of the direct manipulation methodology to IVAs. It also presents an initial implementation of this methodology.

As computer graphics techniques progress from research result to wide popular adoption, a key step is the development of easy-to-use tools. A well known example in the last decade has been the development of HTML handling tools from simple text editors to graphical tools. These tools radically change the way in which graphical content is produced. They remove the need for programming ability and the concern with syntactic detail that is required by textual tools. They shift the focus to the purely graphical/artistic factors that are really central to graphics production. They allow professional artists (designers) to express themselves to the best of their abilities. They also enable amateurs access to the technology, enabling end-user content-creation and also content creation by non-artistic professionals such as educationalists or scientists. They remove the need for a programmer to be involved in the production process, thus putting more of the process in the hands of the artists or designer. Thus the development of easy to use tools is vital to any aspect of graphics research.

One of the most interesting and active areas of research in the graphics field in recent years has been in intelligent virtual agents. The distinguishing feature of intelligent agents is that they have proactive behaviour, and they respond autonomously to their environment. In research terms they lie on the boundary between graphics and artificial intelligence. They are used many in applications such as multi-user on-line worlds, computer games, health and therapy systems, interactive education environments and e-commerce[1]. IVAs can exhibit many types of behaviour, we focus on Non-Verbal Communication (NVC), and in particular posture and gestures, which are important expressive elements in social

* This work has been supported by BT plc, and the EU FET PRESENCIA project IST-2001-37927.

T. Panayiotopoulos et al. (Eds.): IVA 2005, LNCS 3661, pp. 430–441, 2005.
© Springer-Verlag Berlin Heidelberg 2005

interaction. Providing user-friendly tools for IVAs would greatly increase the ease of production of interactive graphical environments, reduce the cost and potentially increase the quality of the IVAs' behaviour by allowing more direct artistic input. Allowing end users to edit IVAs' behaviour would also be highly beneficial. This is particularly true of on-line environments where each user is represented by an IVA, called an avatar, with autonomous beheaviour as suggested by Vilhjálmsson and Cassell[2]. In existing multi-user virtual environments users are keen to personalize the appearance of their avatars[3], it is therefore likely that they would want to be able to personalize the behaviour as well, if user friendly tools were available.

IVAs have important features that affect design tools and make creating these tools an important research challenge. Most importantly they have autonomous behaviour. A character in an animated film will have their animation entirely specified beforehand by an human animator. By contrast, an IVA will generate new animation (or select existing animations) in real time based on its internal state and events in its environment. We will refer to this generation or choice of animation as the agent's *behaviour.* The major challenge in creating design tools for autonomous behaviour is that it depends on the state of the enviroment, what we will call context, and therefore this context must be taken account of whenever the behaviour is edited. The context can contain many features, the location of the IVA, the behaviour of other IVAs, or the behaviour of human participants in the environment (maybe captured through position tracking). The context therefore consists of large quantities of heterogeneous information, however, we assume that this can be reduced to a number of discrete and continuous variables. This reduction could be done by a number of pre-processing steps on the inputs. As we are dealing with NVC we mostly use information about social context, for example, whether the IVA is talking to an authority figure, or whether the topic of discussion is political. In this paper we assume the an IVA's behaviour is controlled by a fixed set of algorithms, which take a context and a set of parameters and use this to generate animation. The parameters of the IVA define its individual behaviour, how different IVAs behave differently in the same context. Parameters in our system mostly deal with how context maps onto behaviour, or onto intermediary internal states, for example, a parameter might be an IVA's tendency to become excited when discussing politics or its tendency to gesture when excited. We assume in this work that the design tools change only the parameters, while the algorithms remain the same. The conclusion will describe future approaches to editing the algorithms themselves.

Direct manipulation has been one of the most successful human computer interaction paradigms, particularly in graphics. The most important features of the paradigm is that it allows uses to edit the final visible result, rather than the, possibly difficult to understand, internal parameters. It seems particularly applicable to the animated behaviour of IVAs. However, traditional applications of Direct Manipulation rely on the ability to view the entire result at once, however, this is not possible for IVAs due to the highly context dependent nature of their behaviour. This paper presents tools that maintain the benefits of direct

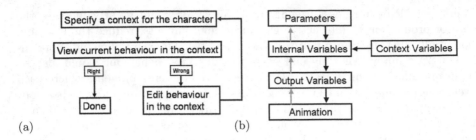

Fig. 1. (a)An overview of the proposed interaction style for editing IVA behaviour. (b) an overview of the behaviour generation process. The black arrows show the behaviour generation process and the grey arrows show the inference process that determines parameters from animation.

manipulation. We propose an interaction style illustrated in figure 1(a). User may successively view the behaviour of the IVA in different contexts. The users set up the various variables that define the context and views the current behaviour within that context. They can then edit this behaviour if it is not correct and then pass on to the next context until the results are largely correct. Each edit made to the behaviour provides a new constraint on the parameters of the behaviour generation system. These constraints allow the user to successively refine the behaviour with each context viewed.

Our direct-manipulation like interface aims to allow end users to edit the behaviour of the IVA rather than its internal parameters. This could be achieved by allowing the users to directly animate the IVA, with a traditional 3D animation interface. This would given very exact control of the IVA's behaviour, and allow a great deal of nuance. We discuss this type of interface in section 2.2. However, this approach has a number of disadvantages, 3D animation can be very difficult for untrained end users. Also, the behaviour of an IVA is also often composed of a number of discrete possible actions (e.g. crossing arms, nodding, waving), rather than a continuous range of behaviour. Direct animation is unsuited to this sort of discrete action space, simply choosing actions from a list is a simpler interface. We therefore also provide an interface, aimed at untrained users and discrete action spaces, that provides buttons to select actions, described in section 2.1.

1   Related Work

This work builds on a long tradition of character animation. The lower level aspects focus on body animation in which there has been a lot of success with techniques that manipulate pre-existing motion data, for example that of Gleicher [4,5], Lee and Shin[6] or Popović and Witkin[7]. However, the more important contributions deal with higher level aspects of behaviour control. This is a field that brings together artificial intelligence and graphics to simulate character behaviour. Research in this area was started by Reynolds[8] whose work on simulating birds' flocking behaviour has been very influential. Further important contributions include the work of Badler *et al.* on animated humans[9]; Tu and Terzopolous' work on simulating fishes[10]; Blumberg and Galyean's "Silas T. Dog"[11] and Perlin and Goldberg's "IMPROV" system[12]. We mostly deal with non-verbal communication, which is a major sub-field of behaviour simulation with a long research history including the work of Cassell and her group[13,14,2]; Pelachaud and Poggi[15] and Guye-Vuilléme *et al.*[16]. The two types of behaviour we are using are gesture which has been studied by Cassell *et al.*[13] and posture which has been studied by Cassell *et al.*[14] and by Bécheiraz and Thalmann[17].

Most of the work described above deals with the algorithms for simulating behaviour rather than tools for designing behaviour. Of the work on tools, most has focused on using markup languages to specify IVA behaviour, for example the APML language[18]. However, though markup languages are an important step towards making it easier to specify IVA behaviour they are a long way from the usability of graphical tools. There have also been tools for designing the content of behaviour, for example designing gestures[16], however, these tools do not address the autonomous aspects, i.e. how to decide which behaviour to perform in a given context. Del Bimbo and Vicario[19] have worked on specifying IVA behaviour by example. Pyandath and Marsella[20] use a linear inference system to infer parameters of a Partially Observable Markov Decision Process used for multi-agent systems. This inference system is similar to ours, however, they do not discuss user interfaces. In the field of robotics Scerri and Ydrén[21] have produced user friendly tools for specifying robot behaviour. They use a multi-layered approach, with programming tools to design the main sections of the behaviour and graphical tools to customise the behaviour. They were working with soccer playing robots and used a graphical tool based on a coach's tactical diagrams to customise their behaviour. Their multi-layered approach has influenced much of the discussion below. Our own approach to specifying IVA behaviour has been influenced by work on direct manipulation tools for editing other graphical objects, for example the work on free form deformations by Hsu, Hughes and Kaufman[22] and Gain[23].

2   The Interface

This section describes the two user interfaces we have implemented, one based on specifying actions from a set, and the other based on directly animating the IVA's pose. This section also gives examples of their use. The remaining sections will then describe how the interfaces are implemented.

2.1   The Action Based Interface

The simpler of the two interfaces allows the user to specify an animation by selecting a number of actions. Action can either be discrete (you are either doing them or you are not, e.g. crossing your arms) or continuous (you can do them to

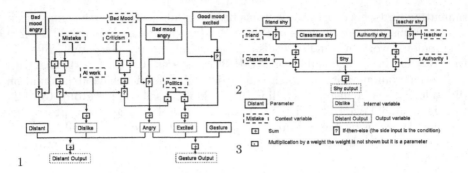

Fig. 2. The relationships between parameters and variables used in our examples (1) action based specification (2) direct animation (3) a key for the diagrams

a greater or lesser degree, e.g. leaning backward). The interface contains button which can select discrete actions and sliders to vary the degree of continuous actions. The user interface is shown in figure 3. The user first sets the context for a behaviour, which is itself expressed as discrete or continuous variables that are edited by buttons and sliders. The user may then view the resulting animation and if they are unhappy with it they may go to an editing screen to change the animation. When they are happy with this they submit the animation, which is then solved for to updated the parameters of the IVA.

Figure 3 gives an example of a sequence of edits. The example is based on editing gestures which tend to be discrete and therefore suited to action based editing. The behavioural control used is shown in figure 2. In it two types of behaviour are defined, *gesture* (beat gestures, which often acompany speech) and *distant* (more hostile gestures). These behaviours depend on a number of contextual paramters: whether the IVA is at work, in a bad mood, discussing politics, has made a mistake, or been criticised. These are used to generated a number of derived parameters which are used to calculate the behaviour parameters. These are: general tendencies to be distant or to gesture, how angry the IVA is, how excited the IVA is and whether it dislikes the person it is talking to.

2.2   The Direct Animation Interface

The other method for specifying behaviour is to directly animate the IVA. This leaves the IVA in a particular posture that must be solved for (currently direct animation is only supported on postures not full animations, extending it would not be too difficult). The user interface used for direct editing is similar to the previous example but the user directly edits the IVA's posture by clicking and dragging on its body rather than using buttons and sliders. Figure 4 shows an example that deals with head and torso posture. The space of these postures is more continuous than gestures and has far fewer degrees of freedom, making it more suited to direct animation. Figure 2 shows how behaviour is generated in this example. In this example there are three types of behaviour distant (turning head or body away), close (the distictive "head cock" posture with the head to the side) and shy (hunched over postures). Only the shy behaviour is shown but the other two have identical dependencies. The example is based on school children's relationships having two types of relationship, classmates (of which friends are a special case) and authority figures (of which teachers are a special case). Each of the three behaviour types can be exhibited differently with each type of relationship. There is also a general tendency to a behaviour type in all contexts, called the "shy".

3   Behaviour Generation

The Demeanour architecture is used to generate behaviour for an IVA[24,25], figure 1(b) shows the behaviour generation method. The basic components of the behaviour system are parameters and context variables, which can be combined together to form internal variables, and finally output variables that are used to animation the IVA. There are two mains ways of combining parameters and variables. The first is by addition and multiplication, which is often used to combine context variables with weighting parameters. For reasons described below we only allow parameters and variables that depend on parameters to be multiplied by variables that do not depend on parameters (a variable depends on a parameter if the parameter's value is used to calculate the variable's value, directly or indirectly). Variables and parameters can also be combined by if-then-else rules that set the value of a variable to that of one of two parameters or variables depending on the value of a boolean condition variable, which can be a context variable but not a parameter:

$$x = x_1 \text{ if } x_c = a$$
$$= x_2 \quad \text{otherwise}$$

Some of the variables produced are outputs that are passed to the animation system. The animated behaviour is generated using a set of basic pieces of motion. Each basic motion has a corresponding output variable that is used as a weight, with which to interpolate the motions, using a quaternion weighted sum technique similar to Johnson's[26]. Many motions can be continuously interpolated, for example leaning forward, however, others are more all-or-nothing, for example it makes no sense to cross your arms 50%. Therefore some motions are classed as discrete and can only have weights of 0 or 1. In this case the corresponding variable is thresholded so that values over 0.5 give a weight of 1.

4   Inferring Parameters from Behavior

The main technical requirement for this user interface is the ability to use a number of examples of behaviour to generate constraints which are then solved for a suitable set of parameter values for the IVA's behaviour. To be more exact, each example is a tuple $< a_i, c_i >$ containing a context for behaviour c_i and an animation specified by the user a_i, which is the behaviour of the IVA in that context. The output of the method is a set of parameters. Each example tuple provides a constraint on the possible values of the parameters. We must solve for these constraints using a method that makes it simple to add new constriants, as the editing methods is iterative users will continually be solving and adding new constraints. The method must also be fast enough to solve in real time, if the tools is to be usable. This is simplified by the fact that the parameters and variables are combined together using linear summation, meaning that all relationships between variables, and therefore constraints are linear. This allows us to use Linear Programming[27] to solve for the constriants. Linear programming mimimizes a linear expression subject to to a number of linear equality and inequality constraints:

$$\sum c_i x_i \text{ subject to } \sum d_i y_i = 0$$
$$\sum e_i z_i \geq 0$$

where the x, y, z are variables and the c, d, e are constant coefficients. We form constraints from the characters behaviour and internal parameters as described in the next sections. We then minimize the sum of all parameters values using a simplex linear programming method[27]. This minimization solves for the parameters while keeping their values as low as possible (to avoid extreme behaviour).

4.1   Constraints from Action Specifications

As described in section 2.1, the action based interface allows user to specify the IVA's behaviour using buttons and sliders which provide weights for each action (0 or 1 in the case of discrete actions). When a animation is submitted these weights are used to form linear constraints. For a continuous motion the weight of the motion (w_i) should be equal to the corresponding output variable (v_i) so we add the constraint $v_i - w_i = 0$. In the case of discrete actions we are less certain: if the w_i is 0 we know that v_i is less than 0.5, otherwise it is greater, so we add an inequality constraint:

$$v_i - 0.5 \leq 0 \text{ if } w_i = 0$$
$$\geq 0 \quad w_i = 1$$

4.2   Constraints from Direct Animation

At a high level any posture produced by Demeanour is a weighted sum over the various possible postures as described in section 3:

$$p = \sum w_i p_i$$

As the value of the posture p is known the above formula can be added as a constraint on the values of the weights w_i. A posture is represented as a 3-DOF rotation for each joint of the IVA, so three constraints added for each joint. The weights are then used to add constraints on the output variables as above.

4.3   Constraints from Internal Variables

With this initial set of constraint we then start to form new constraint based on internal variables and parameters. Any variable will depend on other variables and parameters. If the variable only depends on context variables and not parameters it has a constant value in a given context so it is a *known* (k_i) variable in the current constraint. Parameters and variables that depend on parameters are *unknowns*(u_i). We must form constraints on all unknowns. We start with the constraints that are given by the animations, each of these contain at least one output variable. Each variable v may take one of 4 forms. If it is a parameter it is an unknown and no further constraints are added. If it is a constraint variable it is a known and has a constant value (this is not allowed for an output variable). If it depends on other variables and parameters by addition and multiplication we add a linear constraint. To ensure that it is soluble we ensure that in each multiplication, only one term is an unknown. Thus the equation for the variable is of the form:

$$v = \sum_i (u_j \prod_j k_j)$$

We can evaluate all knowns to calculate the coefficients of each unknown and rearrange to get a constraint:

$$\sum_i c_i u_i + c_0 - v = 0$$

If the variable depends on other variables by an if-then-else rule the condition variable is a known so we can evaluate it and know which the variable v_i that v depends on, we can just add a constraint $v - v_i = 0$. The newly added constraints will have introduced new variables, and we recursively add new constraints for these until we are only left with knowns and parameters, at which point we perform the minimization as described above.

5   Conclusion and Further Work

As described in the introduction this paper has provided three contributions:

1. It has highlighted an important problem for future research, building user friendly tools for designing IVA behaviour.
2. It has proposed an adaptation of direct manipulation editing as a methodology for solving this problem.
3. It has described an implementation of this methodology.

This is roughly the order of importance in which we rank these contributions. We have little doubt that tools for IVA design is an important area that deserves more research. The methodology we propose is a highly valuable one which we consider the most promising. Our own opinion is that different methods will be useful for different types of behaviour. Finally our implementation has shown

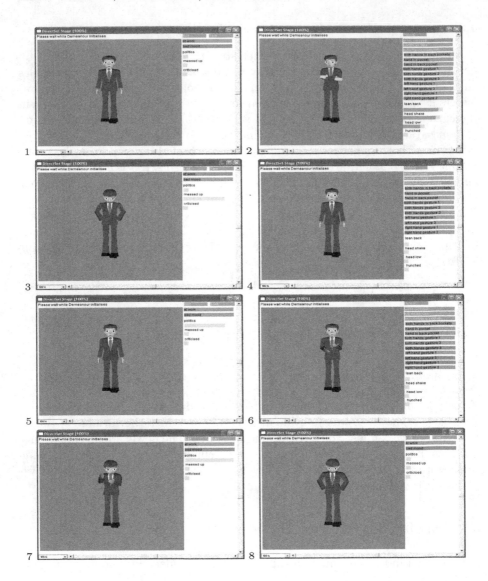

Fig. 3. A sequence of edits using the tool from the action based specification example. The the user initially specifies context (in this case that the IVA is in a bad mood). The initial behaviour (image 1) is neutral as there have been no edits (for clarity, in these examples neutral behaviour is merely a constant rest posture). The user then specifies some distant behaviour and submits it (2). The system has set the general Distant parameter so the IVA produces distant behaviour in a new context (3). The user removes this behaviour to specify a neutral context (4), thus reducing the contexts in which distant behaviour is produced, so in the next context (a political discussion) neutral behaviour is generated (5). The user adds gesturing and submits (6). The final two images show results after these edits, the IVA in a bad mood discussing politics produces both gesturing and distant behaviour (7). The final image has the same context as the original edit, showing that the same type of behaviour (distant) is successfully reproduced, but that the exact behaviour is different (8).)

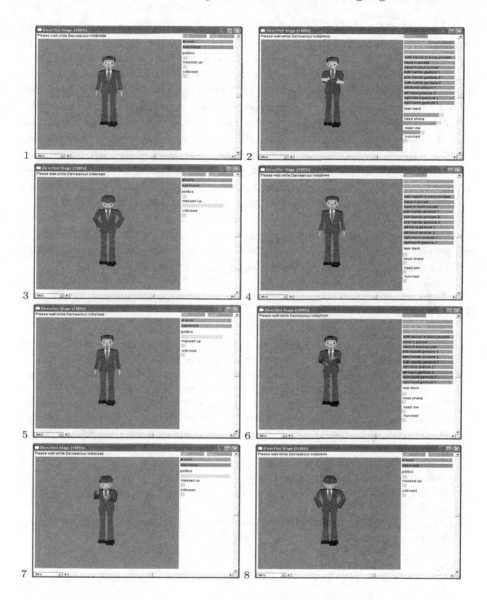

Fig. 4. A sequence of edits of the direct animation. The user initially chooses a "teacher" context (image 1) and creates a hunched over, shy posture (2). The system initially infers a general tendency to shyness (the "shy" parameter) and so displays the same behaviour in a classmate context (3). The user edits this posture back to a neutral one (4) and the system infers that the shy behaviour only occurs in authority contexts (the "authority shy" parameter). The user then adds a "head cock" in the "friend" context to add more close behaviour in that context (5, 6). The final two images show the resulting behaviour in different contexts. The system has generalized the shy behaviour from the "teacher" context to all "authority" contexts as shown in image 7, however, it is not displayed in a neutral context (8).

that the type of user interface we have described is possible in practice and has provided an important first step for research in this area. It is only a first step and more research is needed. It is important to extend our work to other types of behaviour, such as facial animation or speech. These extensions are likely to raise important new issues. Another issue is that our implementation only deals with setting the parameters of a behaviour system, we would also like to build tools that allow users to add new parameters and change the behaviour algorithms used. It is likely that this will require a different type of interface. One approach would be to use a machine learning method that is able to learn more than just parameters from behaviour. In fact a companion paper to this[28] describes initial experiments using reinforcement learning. Another approach is to divide the creation process into a number of stages, a more structural stage that defines the algorithms and one that defines parameters. Each stage could have its own interfaces. This has the benefit that each stage could have an interfaces that is well suited to it. Also, there is a natural division between experts who would perform the first stage and end users who could perform the second.

References

1. Schroeder, R., ed.: The Social Life of Avatars, Presence and Interaction in Shared Virtual Worlds. Computer Supported Cooperative work. Springer (2002)
2. Vilhjálmsson, H.H., Cassell, J.: Bodychat: Autonomous communicative behaviors in avatars. In: second ACM international conference on autonomous agents. (1998)
3. Cheng, L., Farnham, S., Stone, L.: Lessons learned: Building and deploying virtual environments. In Schroeder, R., ed.: The Social Life of Avatars, Presence and Interaction in Shared Virtual Worlds. Computer Supported Cooperative work. Springer (2002)
4. Gleicher, M.: Motion editing with space time constraints. In: symposium on interactive 3D graphics. (1997) 139–148
5. Gleicher, M.: Comparing constraint-based motion editing methods. Graphical Models (2001) 107–134
6. Lee, J., Shin, S.Y.: A hierarchical approach to interactive motion editing for human-like figures. In: ACM SIGGRAPH. (1999) 39–48
7. Popović, Z., Witkin, A.: Physically based motion transformation. In: ACM SIGGRAPH. (1999) 11–20
8. Reynolds, C.W.: Flocks, herds, and schools: A distributed behavioral model. In: ACM SIGGRAPH. (1987) 25–33
9. Badler, N., Philips, C., Webber, B., eds.: Simulating Humans: Computer Graphics, Animation and Control. Oxford University Press (1993)
10. Tu, X., Terzopoulos, D.: Artificial fishes: Physics, locomotion, perception, behavior. In: ACM SIGGRAPH. (1994) 43–49
11. Blumberg, B., Galyean, T.: Multi-level direction of autonomous creatures for real-time virtual environments. In: ACM SIGGRAPH. (1995) 47–54
12. Perlin, K., Goldberg, A.: Improv: A system for scripting interactive actors in virtual worlds. In: Proceedings of SIGGRAPH 96. Computer Graphics Proceedings, Annual Conference Series, New Orleans, Louisiana, ACM SIGGRAPH / Addison Wesley (1996) 205–216

13. Cassell, J., Bickmore, T., Campbell, L., Chang, K., Vilhjálmsson, H., Yan, H.: Embodiment in conversational interfaces: Rea. In: ACM SIGCHI, ACM Press (1999) 520–527
14. Cassell, J., Nakano, Y., Bickmore, T., Sidner, C., Rich, C.: Non-verbal cues for discourse structure. In: 41st Annual Meeting of the Association of Computational Linguistics, Toulouse, France (2001) 106–115
15. Pelachaud, C., Poggi, I.: Subtleties of facial expressions in embodied agents. Journal of Visualization and Computer Animation. **13** (2002) 287–300
16. Guye-Vuilléme, A., T.K.Capin, I.S.Pandzic, Magnenat-Thalmann, N., D.Thalmann: Non-verbal communication interface for collaborative virtual environments. The Virtual Reality Journal **4** (1999) 49–59
17. Bécheiraz, P., Thalmann, D.: A model of nonverbal communication and interpersonal relationship between virtual actors. In: Proceedings of the Computer Animation '96, IEEE Computer Society Press (1996) 58–67
18. DeCarolis, B., Pelachaud, C., Poggi, I., Steedman, M.: Apml, a markup language for believable behaviour generation. In Prendiger, H., Ishizuka, M., eds.: Life-like characters: tools, affective functions and applications. Springer (2004) 65–87
19. Del Bimbo, A., Vicario, E.: Specification by-example of virtual agents' behavior. IEEE transactions on visualtization and Computer Graphics **1** (1995) 350–360
20. Pynadath, D.V., Marsella, S.C.: Fitting and compilation of multiagent models through piecewise linear functions. In: the International Conference on Autonomous Agents and Multi Agent Systems. (2004) 1197–1204
21. Scerri, P., Ydrén, J.: End user specification of robocup teams. In: RoboCup-99: Robot Soccer World Cup III. Lecture Notes in Computer Science. Springer-Verlag (2000)
22. Hsu, W.M., Hughes, J.F., Kaufman, H.: Direct manipulation of free-form deformations. In: Proceedings of the 19th ACM SIGGRAPH annual conference on Computer graphics and interactive techniques, ACM Press (1992) 177–184
23. Gain, J.: Enhancing spatial deformation for virtual sculpting. PhD thesis, University of Cambridge Computer Laboratory (2000)
24. Gillies, M., Ballin, D.: Integrating autonomous behavior and user control for believable agents. In: Third international joint conference on Autonomous Agents and Multi-Agent Systems, Columbia University, New York City (2004)
25. Gillies, M., Crabtree, B., Ballin, D.: Expressive characters and a text chat interface. In Olivier, P., Aylett, R., eds.: AISB workshop on Language, Speech and Gesture for Expressive Characters, University of Leeds (2004)
26. Johnson, M.P.: Exploiting Quaternions to Support Expressive Interactive Character Motion. PhD thesis, MIT Media Lab (2003)
27. Press, W.H., Flannery, B.P., Teukolsky, S.A., Vetterling, W.T.: Numerical Recipes in C. Cambridge University Press (1992)
28. Friedman, D., Gillies, M.: Teaching characters how to use body language. In: Intelligent Virtual Agents. (2005) This volume.

Social Communicative Effects of a Virtual Program Guide

Nicole C. Krämer

Department of Psychology, University of Cologne, Bernhard-Feilchenfeld-Str. 11,
50969 Köln, Germany
nicole.kraemer@uni-koeln.de
http://www.uni-koeln.de/phil-fak/psych/diff/dafmitarb.htm

Abstract. Embodied interface agents are considered to be a promising interface
metaphor of the future since they are widely expected to facilitate HCI and trigger natural communication. Although first evaluations indicate that virtual
characters have various strong effects, it is still unknown if and how embodied
conversational agents affect the way in which users communicate with the technological system. An experimental study was conducted to analyze if users interact differently when confronted with different kinds of interfaces (GUI,
speech output, embodied interface agent) of a TV-VCR-System. 65 participants
were asked to solve different tasks choosing either natural speech or remote
control as input devices. Results show that a system is significantly more often
addressed by natural speech when an embodied interface agent is visible. Additional qualitative analyses of the semantic content of all 943 speech acts indicate that users seem to have a more human-like attitude and behavior towards
the system when it is represented by an anthropomorphic agent.

1 Introduction

Embodied interface agents are considered to be the interface of the future since they
are supposed to ease human-computer-interaction [1, 2]. The expected relief is due to
the fact that the anthropomorphic, i.e. human-like characters interact on the basis of
rules that are similar to a human-like face-to-face-interaction. This should facilitate
interaction since people are accustomed to this form of interaction - even novices or
the elderly should be able to handle computers and electronic devices easily. DeLaere,
Lundgren and Howe [3] term this the "dialog partner" metaphor and state:
"...interface designs which incorporate elements that evoke or simulate human social
interaction should result in more natural and infomative user-system communications" (p. 44). But empirical results demonstrating the general effects and specific
benefits concerning communicative reactions of the user are still scarce.

In particular, embodied interface agents have not yet been shown to actually ease
the communication process between human beings and machines, e.g., by inviting
intuitive interaction. The study that will be presented here contributes to this area by
analyzing how people react to different kinds of interfaces. It focuses on possible
advantages and drawbacks of the virtual characters in terms of their ability to affect
the users´ input behavior. In addition to these applied research aspects, basic research

T. Panayiotopoulos et al. (Eds.): IVA 2005, LNCS 3661, pp. 442–453, 2005.
© Springer-Verlag Berlin Heidelberg 2005

issues are considered by discussing and investigating the question whether interactions between user and interface agent reveal social attitudes [4, 5].

Effects of embodied interface agents can be termed 'social' if a participant's emotional, cognitive, or behavioral reactions are similar to reactions shown during interactions with other human beings. A number of studies show that those – actually inappropriate - reactions really do occur, sometimes even without the appearance of a human-like character. Even technological systems such as computers can evoke social reactions [5]. Various studies [6, 7, 8] indicate that in interactions with computers a) politeness phrases are employed, b) principles of person perception and gender stereotypes apply, and c) liking is triggered in a similar way as within human relationships (computer that 'flatter' and give positive feedback are evaluated more positive). Consequently, Nass et al. [8] postulate that a "rich human presentation" in the sense of e.g. embodied interface agents is not necessary to evoke social reactions. However, both their theoretical assumptions and additional empirical results suggest that these social processes can be intensified by human-like attributes (e.g. speech) [8, 9]. In fact, various studies indicate that social reactions are particularly strong in the presence of a human-like agent. It has for instance been shown that a face attracts attention [10] and automatically leads to attributions of emotion and intention [11] – even to such an extent that the original task is neglected. Further studies indicate that systems including an embodied interface agent are perceived as more credible and bring about increased feelings of trust [12, 13]. Similarly, it has been shown that virtual faces evoke cooperative behavior [4].

Additionally, there is evidence that even subtle social phenomena such as *impression management* [see e.g. 14] are prevalent in human computer interaction. When a human-like face is present, participants aim at leaving a favourable impression by e.g. choosing a socially desirable TV program (documentary about Albert Einstein compared to James Bond movie) [15] or by presenting themselves in a socially desirable way [13].

Merely a few studies have targeted communication processes. Here, agents have proven to affect the communication of the human user: Children accommodate their speech structure to that of the animated character they are conversing with [16] and logfiles of dialogues with a virtual bartender show that when people engage in small talk with the virtual character they take its social role into account [17].

Summing up it can be stated that concerning social effects some aspects have been investigated rather extensively. However, the communication process between user and computer or agent has so far been largely neglected. There are studies on the effects of natural language interfaces pointing to the fact that the language used with a computer differs from the language used between humans [18]. But analogous studies comparing effects of anthropomorphic agents, natural language output and text-based interfaces have not been presented. Specifically, attention should be devoted to whether agents actually do induce more natural interactions. The study presented here tries to answer this question by comparing the reactions and input behaviors of users when interacting with interface agents compared to when interacting with conventional and less anthropomorphic interfaces. Additionally, the study wants to make a contribution to a basic research area by increasing knowledge about the kind and quality of social reactions embodied interface agents evoke.

2 Method

In the study presented here we wanted to test if users react and behave differently when confronted with different interfaces. We were particularly interested in whether users employ more and particular forms of natural speech when faced by a human-like figure. The system used in this experimental study was developed by a joint interdisciplinary research group in the project EMBASSI (Multimodal Assistance for Infotainment and Service Infrastructures, see www.embassi.de) that was funded by the German Ministry of Education and Research (BMB+F). The combined TV-VCR-system assists in choosing a programme as well as in initializing the automated recording. It can be operated either by commands based on natural speech or by a remote control directing a cursor on the graphical user interface (GUI). Subjects were instructed to choose a programme from a list of today´s and tomorrow´s programmes that were displayed on the screen. The recording could be initiated either by remote control (in equivalence to a graphical user interface a button had to be pressed via cursor) or by natural speech (e.g. by saying "James Bond", which was one of the programmes). 65 subjects each had to carry out three tasks: in task 1 and 3 participants were asked to choose from today´s and tomorrow´s programme offer and initialize the recording, whereas in task 2 they were asked to arrange for the recording of a specified programme (a talk-show). During all tasks subjects were free to use natural speech commands or remote control and even were allowed to change the input device within a task (see dependent variables).

The study was conducted at Sony in Stuttgart-Wangen. The experimenter explained how to operate the system and the GUI navigation. Also, in order to increase recognition rates, usage of speech input was practised using two examples. Additionally, subjects were encouraged to try again if recognition failed during the experiment. Due to the system being a research prototype recognition actually failed in several cases, but subjects then patiently repeated their action.

2.1 Independent Variables

Output modalities, i.e. appearance of the interface, were varied. Three different interfaces were presented: GUI only (feedback was given by text on the screen stating e.g. "recording was arranged successfully"), GUI combined with natural speech output (via speech synthesis information about system state was given) or GUI including an embodied interface agent presenting the information via lipsynchronized speech (see figure 1).

Subjects were devided in four groups: Group 1 was asked to carry out the first two tasks with the help of the GUI only condition. Group 2 was confronted with the speech output condition, and group 3 received the embodied interface condition. In order to additionally gather data about which interface was preferred, group 4 was instructed to freely choose any kind of interface for each of the three tasks. Also, people in condition 1 to 3 were told to choose any output modality for the third task. Since interactions with the embodied interface agent were preferred [see 11], this resulted in 91 of the altogether 195 interactions/tasks between human and system being carried out with the embodied interface agent, 49 interactions with speech output and 55 interactions within the GUI only condition.

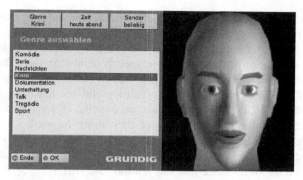

Fig. 1. GUI (by Grundig) including embodied interface agent (by Computer Graphics Centre ZGDV, Darmstadt)

2.2 Dependent Variables

Numerous different variables, such as speed of task solving, steps taken, and liking of the interface were assessed and results were reported elsewhere [19]. Results show that the embodied interface agent is evaluated rather positive, but ratings do not differ from those for speech and text condition. Performance in terms of speed of task solving and number of steps taken also did not prove to be significantly different when comparing conditions. Here, two other dependent variables will be analyzed and presented: a) Behavior of the subjects with regard to the selection of either natural speech commands or using remote control, b) the quality of the users´ utterances. Based on guidelines for qualitative psychological analyses [20], a category scheme was developed to classify the statements according to specific aspects. Since our research question was especially focused on structures and contents pointing to the personalisation and social aspects inherent in the commands, we were not able to use existing schemes or deduce one from theory. Instead, the categories were developed data-driven using one third of the material. All statements were coded using the scheme and occurrence was quantified. Additionally, the frequency of specific words used in social contexts (like "thank you", "you") was assessed.

2.3 Participants

In terms of profession, education, and technical/computer experience the sample was quite heterogenous. 29 male and 36 female participants were distributed equally to the conditions. Average age was 39,29 (sd = 15,50, minimum 12, maximum 72).

3 Results

3.1 Input Behavior of Users

Input behavior can be regarded as dependent on output modality (see figure 2): The more human-like features were presented, the more natural speech input the participants used. These differences can also be confirmed in statistical analyses (Anova). Especially in task 2 the differences are significant (F = 5,09; df = 62; p = ,009). A post-hoc test (Scheffé) shows that during the interaction with the embodied interface agent significantly more speech inputs are made than in the GUI condition (se = ,95; p = ,014). Results are even more distinct for the averaged values of all tasks: Generally, the embodied interface agent evokes more speech input than does the graphical user interface (F = 7,24; df = 191; p = ,001; post-hoc-Scheffé: se = ,73; p = ,001). Differences between GUI and speech output condition did not reach significance. When interacting with the GUI, participants make an average of 1,98 speech inputs per interaction, when listening to speech output they bring forward 3,33 utterances and when confronted with an embodied interface agent, they produce 4,73 speech acts. Results cannot simply be attributed to the fact that interactions with the embodied interface agent took longer since this was not the case [19].

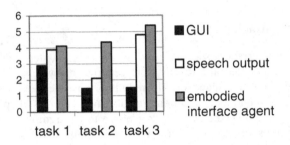

Fig. 2. Average number of speech inputs for three conditions in three tasks

3.2 Semantic Analyses of the Utterances

Based on the result that embodied interface agents triggered more speech input behavior we analysed *what* the participants said exactly. Would the embodied interface condition and other conditions also differ with regard to the semantics of the utterances? To investigate this we at first assessed the frequency of certain words that usually are only used in social contexts, i.e., with a human addressee. Furthermore, we developed a category system that allowed the categorisation of utterances according to specific qualities.

Frequency of Specific Words. For the quantitative analysis of specific words we chose pronouns and specific words such as "thank you" that usually indicate some sort of social relationship. Chosen were *thank you/thanks, please, you, we* and *I*. As can be seen in table 1, the majority of these words were used more frequently when confronted with the embodied interface agents – not only when considering the absolute number, but also when related to the number of interactions and number of utterances which both have been higher in the embodied interface condition (the related value has been calculated in equivalence to a percentage value). In nearly all cases the words are more frequently uttered when confronted with the human-like figure (see table 1). There is a consistent pattern that these words a) are never or rarely used when the interface is text-based, b) appear more often when the interface addresses the user by speech, but c) are most frequent when confronted with the anthropomorphic interface agent. This pattern is especially distinct with "thanks/thank you", while it does not apply to "I". On the whole it is obvious that the system is more directly addressed and treated more "politely" when represented by a human-like face whereas nearly no such social behaviors are induced by a text-based interface. This hints to the anthropomorphic system being perceived as a social entity.

Table 1. Absolute and relative quantity of specific words indicating a social relationship

		GUI	Speech output	ECA
	Number of interactions	55	49	91
	Number of utterances	168	220	555
Thanks/	N	0	1	7
Thank you	Related to interactions	0	2.04	7.69
	Related to utterances	0	0.46	1.26
please	N	37	54	159
	Related to interactions	67.27	110.2	174.76
	Related to utterances	22	24.55	28.65
you	N	0	2	6
	Related to interactions	0	4.08	6.59
	Related to utterances	0	0.91	1.08
we	N	0	1	5
	Related to interactions	0	2.04	5.49
	Related to utterances	0	0.46	0.9
I	N	11	14	29
	Related to interactions	20	28.57	31.87
	Related to utterances	6.55	6.36	5.23

Quality of Utterances. Based on the transcribed utterances an extensive category system was developed that enabled a qualitative and - later on - quantitative analysis of the material. One third of the material was used to develop a coding scheme [20]. Then all utterances were coded by two raters who were unaware of the conditions. In order to achieve a high interrater-reliability, the raters jointly coded a part of the material and discussed difficult choices. When specific utterances applied to more than one category, two or more codes were given. The category system is presented in the following.

Instruction to initialize a recording
- Personalized addressation ("record James Bond")
- Unpersonalized addressation ("James Bond, to be recorded")
- phrased as request ("I would like to...")

Requests (e.g. to show a genre or station)
- Personalized ("show me.." "could you show..")
- Unpersonalized ("Channel xy")
- phrased as request ("I would like to...")
- utterances to activate the system ("hello", "just do it")

Questions
- Information seeking ("what is being shown on channel xy?")
- Clarifying questions; interrogative reaction to an action/utterance of the system

Repetition when system does not react or understand
- Exact repetition
- Repetition with slight change

Reactions/utterances that indicate the user´s assumption of a human-like interactive relation
- Explaining comment, when system indicates to not understand ("I just thanked you")
- Correcting utterances ("I did not want that")
- Resignation; user indicates disappointment and surrender
- Comforting of the system after error message ("it´s ok", "don´t cry")
- Request to wait when input is demanded ("just a moment", "wait")
- Other special remarks ("I didn´t either" when system indicates that it did not understand)

Evaluating utterances addressed to the system
- Positive evaluations/utterances; praising of the system (e.g. "great")
- Negative evaluations/utterances (e.g. "terrible")
- Obviously ironic evaluating utterances (e.g. "just wonderful")

Evaluating utterances about the system
- Negative remarks ("this system is annoying")
- Neutral utterances about the system (e.g. about the functioning)

Politeness phrases
- Greetings and Goodbye ("Good evening", "Bye")
- Phrasing implying politeness ("Could you kindly...", "I would like to..")

Other
- Addressing the system with a name ("little one")
- Back channeling ("o.k.", "mmh, yes")
- Thinking aloud/talking to oneself (e.g. "Oh, I first have to press the button")

For every interaction it was coded if at least one utterance of the specific category was present or not. We chose the Chi^2-Test as an appropriate method to analyze differences between conditions. The test was conducted for each category to test for differences between interfaces. For three of the categories significant differences were found. In the following tables the frequencies merely for those three categories with significant differences are presented.

There was a difference for requests that were formulated in a personalized way (see table 2). When users were confronted with an embodied interface agent the number of personalized requests was greater than expected (Chi = 7.44; df = 2; p = .024). While in 12 interactions with embodied interface agents participants use personalized requests, in GUI and speech condition personalized requests are uttered merely once.

These results point to the possibility that users tend to perceive the embodied interface agent as a social entity that is more appropriately addressed in a personalized way.

Additional differences between conditions could be observed with regard to the categories "exact repetition of instruction/request" and "slightly changed repetition of instruction/request".

Table 2. Actual and expected values for the category "personalized request" (Chi=7.44; p=.024)

		GUI	Speech	ECA	total
No personalized request	N	33	41	67	141
	N (exp.)	30.9	38.2	71.9	141
Personalized request	N	1	1	12	14
	N (exp.)	3.1	3.8	7.1	14
total	N	34	42	79	155
	N (exp.)	34	42	79	155

N = actual number; N (exp.) = expected number

Table 3. Actual and expected values for the category "exact repetition" (Chi = 7.6; p = .022)

		GUI	Speech	ECA	Total
No exact repetition	N	24	27	36	87
	N (exp.)	19.1	23.6	44.3	87
Exact repetition	N	10	15	45	68
	N (exp.)	14.9	18.4	34.7	68
total	N	34	42	79	155
	N (exp.)	34	42	79	155

N = actual number; N (exp.) = expected number

As shown in table 3 an exact repetition of the request or instruction is more likely when the system is represented by an anthropomorphic agent (Chi = 7.6; df = 2; p = .022). Also, slightly changed repetitions are more frequent in this condition (Chi = 6.34; df = 2; p = .042; see table 4).

Table 4. Actual and expected values for the category "slightly changed repetition" (Chi = 6.34; p = .042)

		GUI	Speech	ECA	total
No slighltly changed rep.	N	21	27	34	82
	N (exp.)	18.0	22.2	41.8	82
Slightly changed repetition	N	13	15	45	73
	N (exp.)	16.0	19.8	37.2	73
Total	N	34	42	79	155
	N (exp.)	34	42	79	155

N = actual number; N (exp.) = expected number

The latter results may point to the fact that participants in the embodied interface condition felt that they were required to engage in further communication. This might have been due to the demand characteristics of a face "asking" for further interaction. Additionally, this effect could have been intensified by the fact that the face did not show an immediate reaction. The users were therefore probably unsure whether the system had really understood the request.

There were no significant differences for the remaining categories, partly because of the small sample. Nevertheless, a number of specific utterances that were only observable when participants were confronted with the anthropomorphic agent were quite remarkable. E.g., in the condition of the embodied interface agent three utterances of resignation occurred. Such a behavior was neither observed in the speech output condition nor in the text condition. The pattern is similar regarding correcting comments ("I did not want it this way") that are uttered in five interactions with the embodied interface agent. They occur once in the speech output condition but not at all in the text condition. This also indicates that participants had the impression that a system that was represented by a face would be more responsive to the utterance of interactive, reciprocal commands than the 'non-social', conventional conditions. Results even suggest that the human-like face triggers forms of social behavior that would only be regarded appropriate when interacting with a human being, not with a machine: For instance, some participants in the embodied interface agent condition personally greeted the interface. They ended the interaction with a 'goodbye', personally addressed system with a name ("little one"), or even comforted the agent when it reported the failing of an action. Additionally, utterances can be found that hint to unusual attributions for failed actions: One participant stated "You do not like me, do you?" when the system repeatedly reported a failure.

Summing up it can be stated that qualitative and quantitative analyses consistently show that embodied interface agents induce a significant change in how people interact with technological systems – compared not only to text but also to speech based interfaces. With regard to some aspects the communication even becomes rather human-like, e.g. regarding politeness phrases or expressing empathic sympathy.

4 Discussion

Results confirm that one of the expected profits [2] of embodied interface agents is actually observable: When confronted with a human-like character participants felt free to address it by natural speech. While it may have been awkward to address a merely text based interface it was obviously less a problem when a human face was visible. Thus, the advantage of anthropomorphic interfaces in terms of triggering users´ natural speech input is clearly observable. Even guidelines can be derived from this result: If an interface designer wants the user to engage in natural speech to a greater extent he should consider to put up a human-like face.

Also, clearly social reactions were observed: With an agent present the quality of utterances changed. The system was addressed in a more personalized way. In the embodied interface agent condition the frequency of the pronoun "you" as well as the amount of personalized requests was increased. This can be taken as indicating that the system was perceived as a social entity. Further, users engaged more frequently in reciprocal communication attempts such as correcting comments or resignation utterances. This not only indicates that the users have increased expectations about what the system is going to understand but that they even are more tempted to communicate their state.

Concerning the design of interfaces these tendencies might become a practical disadvantage or problem. Triggered by embodied interface agents the employed vocubulary increases and more unexpected phrases are used. Although this might be a future advantage, problems arise for present technologies. As has been proposed [21] realistic human faces lead to expectations that can not yet be met. Here, users are invited to use complex phrases and vocabulary that cannot be recognized and analyzed. Thus, when inserting an embodied interface agent the designer must at least be prepared for this phenomenon. One chance to overcome potential problems could be to point out the actual capabilities in a tutorial before first usage. But it can be doubted whether this would be sufficient. The experience we made during the study gives evidence against it: Although we pointed out by both instruction and exercising speech input that the system only has limited abilities in recognising speech, still participants especially in the embodied interface agent condition worded their wishes more freely.

Another practical problem arises when during the system's processing time the face does not show an immediate reaction of understanding or misunderstanding or at least indicates that the user has to wait for further feedback. Our result of people frequently repeating their input when interacting with an agent points to the danger of presenting a face that sometimes does not react immediately. Even for virtual faces Watzlawick's statement that you cannot not communicate seems to be true. So the designer has to take into account that users will always perceive the system to be communicating once there is a face visible and that it will be confusing when nothing is happening.

Concerning the question whether embodied interface agents evoke social reactions, it can be summed up that significant changes were observable with regard to different behavioral aspects. So participants used more natural speech input, more frequently addressed the system in a personalized way, attempted to engage in reciprocal communication and even informed the system about personal states – when the agent was visible. These findings once again confirm that when interacting with agents users show behavior that merely is appropriate in human face-to-face interaction. But in addition to the previous findings, our results verify that this also applies to the communication process respectively to the input behavior of the user.

Nevertheless, it remains an open questions whether the users' reactions will endure or if this is a phenomenon merely observable in laboratory studies where participants are confronted with new technologies for just half an hour. When embodied interface agents appear in our living rooms the effects might disappear. A process similar to the early days of television could happen: Some users at first did their hair on a Saturday evening when the newscaster came to their home but after some time they got used to the fact that the face on the screen did not see them. In order to answer the question if the effects will wear off we have to conduct field studies and observe users during a longer period of usage. Thus, in order to make valid predictions about effects and advantages of embodied interface agents we are not only reliant on more studies e.g. about task appropriateness or adaptation to user groups, but also have to plan studies that provide higher external validity e.g. by conducting them in a more natural setting.

Acknowledgements

The study was funded by the German Ministry of Education and Research (BMB+F) within the project EMBASSI (Multimodal Assistance for Infotainment and Service Infrastructures).

References

1. Cassell, J., Bickmore, T., Billinghurst, M., Campbell, L., Chang, K., Vilhjálmsson, H. & Yan, H.: Embodiment in conversational interfaces: Rea. CHI´99 Conference Proceedings, Association for Computing Machinery (1999), 520-527
2. Cassell, J., Bickmore, T., Campbell, L., Vilhjálmsson, H. & Yan, H.: Human conversation as a system framework: Designing embodied conversational agents. In: Cassell, J., Sullivan, J., Prevost, S. & Churchill, E. (eds.): Embodied conversational agents, Cambridge, MIT Press (2000) 29-63
3. DeLaere, K. H., Lundgren, D. C. & Howe, S. R.: The electronic mirror: Human-Computer interaction and change in self-appraisals. Computers in Human Behavior, 14, 2 (1998) 43-59
4. Parise, S., Kiesler, S., Sproull, L. & Waters, K.: Cooperating with life-like interface agents. Computers in Human Behavior, 15 (1999) 123-142
5. Reeves, B. & Nass, C. I.: The media equation: How people treat computers, television, and new media like real people and places, Cambridge University Press, New York (1996)
6. Fogg, B. J. & Nass, C.: Silicon sycophants: the effects of computers that flatter. International Journal of Human-Computer Studies, 46, 5 (1997) 551-561
7. Nass, C., Moon, Y., Morkes, J., Kim, E-Y. & Fogg, B. J.: Computers are social actors: A review of current research. In: B. Friedman (ed.), Moral and ethical issues in human-computer interaction, CSLI Press, Stanford, CA (1997) 137-162
8. Nass, C., Steuer, J. & Tauber, E. R.: Computers are Social Actors. In: Adelson, B. Dumais, S. & Olson, J. (eds.): Human Factors in Computing Systems: CHI´94 Conference Proceedings, ACM Press (1994) 72-78
9. Nass, C. & Moon, Y.: Machines and Mindlessness: Social responses to computers. Journal of Social Issues, 60, 1 (2000) 81-103
10. Dehn, D. M. & van Mulken, S:. The impact of animated interface agents: a review of empirical research. International Journal of Human-Computer Studies, 52 (2000), 1-22
11. Takeuchi, A. & Naito, T.: Situated facial displays: towards social interaction. In: Katz, I., Mack, R., Marks, L., Rosson, M. B. & Nielsen, J. (eds.): Human factors in computing Systems: CHI´95 Conference Proceedings, ACM Press, New York (1995) 450-455
12. Rickenberg, R. & Reeves, B.: The effects of animated characters on anxiety, task performance, and evaluations of user interfaces. Letters of CHI (2000) 49-56
13. Sproull, L., Subramani, M., Kiesler, S. Walker, J. H. & Waters, K.: When the interface is a face. Human Computer Interaction, 11, 2 (1996) 97-124
14. Leary, M. R.: Self presentation. Impression management and interpersonal behavior, Brown & Benchmark Publishers, Madison, Wis. (1995)
15. Krämer, N. C., Bente, G. & Piesk, J.: The ghost in the machine. The influence of Embodied Conversational Agents on user expectations and user behaviour in a TV/VCR application. In: Bieber, G. & Kirste, T. (eds): IMC Workshop 2003, Assistance, Mobility, Applications. IRB Verlag, Stuttgart, 121-128
16. Oviatt, S., Darves, C. & Coulston, R.: Toward adaptive Conversational interfaces: Modeling speech convergence with animated personas. ACM Transactions on Computer-Human Interaction, 3 (2004) 300-328
17. Isbister, K. & Hayes-Roth, B.: Social Implications of Using Synthetic Characters. In: Proceedings of the IJCAI-97 Workshop on Animated Interface Agents: Making them Intelligent, Nagoya (1998), 19-20. Available: http://www.ksl.stanford.edu/KSL_ Abstracts/KSL-98-01.html [29.4.2005].

18. Jönsson, A. & Dahlbäck, N.: Talking to a Computer is not Like Talking to Your Best Friend. Proceedings of The First Scandinivian Conference on Artificial Intelligence 1988, Tromsø, Norway (1988)
19. Krämer, N. C. & Nitschke, J.: Ausgabemodalitäten im Vergleich: Verändern sie das Eingabeverhalten der Benutzer? In: Marzi, R., Karavezyris, V., Erbe, H. H. & Timpe, K.-P. (eds.): Bedienen und Verstehen. 4. Berliner Werkstatt Mensch-Maschine-Systeme, VDI-Verlag, Düsseldorf (2002) 231-248
20. Mayring, P.: Qualitative Inhaltsanalyse. Grundlagen und Techniken, Deutscher Studien Verlag, Weinheim (2000)
21. Parke, F. I.: Techniques of facial animation. In: Magnenat-Thalmann, N. & Thalmann, D. (eds.): New trends in animation and visualization, John Wiley & Sons, Chichster (1991), 229-241

Maintaining the Identity of Dynamically Embodied Agents

Alan Martin[1], Gregory M.P. O'Hare[1], Brian R. Duffy[2],
Bianca Schön[1], and John F. Bradley[1]

[1] University College Dublin, Belfield, Dublin 4, Ireland
[2] Institut Eurécom, Sophia-Antipolis, France
{alan.martin, gregory.ohare, bianca.schoen, john.bradley}@ucd.ie
Brian.Duffy@eurecom.fr
http://chameleon.ucd.ie

Abstract. Virtual agents are traditionally constrained in their embodiment, as they are restricted to one form of body. We propose allowing them to change their embodiment in order to expand their capabilities. This presents users with a number of difficulties in maintaining the identity of the agents, but these can be overcome by using identity cues, certain features that remain constant across embodiment forms. This paper outlines an experiment that examines these identity cues, and shows that they can be used to help address this identity problem.

1 Introduction

Over the last number of years, extensive research has been carried out into the area of autonomous agents. These are software entities characterised by the attributes of autonomy, social ability, reactivity and pro-activity [1]. A number of features of agent technologies, including their autonomy, their ability to reason based upon limited knowledge and their ability to react to changes in the environment, make them suitable for use within virtual environments. Agents within virtual environments are referred to as *virtual agents*, where they normally control a graphical representation of themselves, called an *avatar*.

A number of different systems have sought to incorporate agents within virtual environments. These include the MAVE system, developed by Cobel, Harbison & Cook [2,3], which seeks to place virtual agents within a web based VRML environment. Also, André and Rist have developed MIAU, a system that animates characters based upon either a behaviour component or a response to user interaction [4].

Traditionally an agent's avatar is constrained to a single form, including in the above systems. This has a number of limitations on the agent's capabilities, as the capabilities are defined by the form of the avatar. We advocate a different system, the agent is capable of mutating its embodiment in order to expand upon its capabilities. The agent's embodiment is then dynamic and can change in order to take advantage of different capability sets. However, this freedom does present a number of difficulties, particularly in relation to the agent's identity.

T. Panayiotopoulos et al. (Eds.): IVA 2005, LNCS 3661, pp. 454–465, 2005.
© Springer-Verlag Berlin Heidelberg 2005

We define an agent's *identity* to be that which causes the agent to remain the same within the mind of the user. Maintenance of identity, despite the ability to change form, is vital, as the user must be capable of identifying the agent being dealt with, even if its appearance has changed significantly. In order to achieve this, we propose a system whereby agents are equipped with a number of *identity cues*. These are distinctive features that are common to all of the possible forms of the agent.

In this paper we examine the influence of these cues in maintaining the agent's identity. Section 2 introduces Agent Chameleons, a system for the provision of expanded capabilities through migration and mutation. Section 3 discusses embodiment and suggests how the embodiment could be capable of change. Section 4 looks at identity and how it can be maintained with dynamic embodiment. Section 5 then explains the experimental methodology used to examine this notion, with the results detailed in Sect. 6.

2 Agent Chameleons

This research forms part of the the Agent Chameleons project [5,6,7,8], in which we endeavour to create the next generation of virtual agents, autonomic entities that can seamlessly migrate, mutate and evolve between and within virtual information spaces. The Agent Chameleon can be seen as a digital *spirit*, capable of occupying a variety of different platforms, such as a physical entity (a robot), a virtual environment, or a mobile device such as a PDA.

The key concepts of migration and mutation underpin these agents, allowing them to react to environmental change. Agent Chameleons are capable of migrating to a wide variety of devices and information spaces as required, in order to utilise the features and capabilities of each. For instance an agent could migrate to a real world robot in order to achieve a physical manifestation and influence physical reality, to a PDA in order to travel with the user, or to a virtual environment in order to improve its abilities for interacting with the user.

Additionally, the agents are capable of mutating their form. This is particulary relevant within virtual environments, where the form of an agent is not constrained as it is in the real world, and is capable of changing to suit the task at hand.

We propose a system in which such agents are controlled by a *Belief-Desire-Intention* (BDI) architecture [9,10,11]. Specifically, the agents' deliberative mechanism is based upon Agent Factory [12,13,14,15]. Agent Factory provides a cohesive framework for the development and deployment of agent-oriented applications, delivering extensive support for the creation of BDI agents. The Agent Factory Run-Time Environment supports the deployment of agent-oriented applications across a large number of platforms. Agent Chameleons expands upon this by providing these agents with the ability to operate within a number of platforms and devices, and to migrate between them. The system also allows the agents to mutate their form when located within virtual environments.

It should be noted that a number of other virtual agent systems exist that also embrace BDI based reasoning. These include the VITAL system developed by Anastassakis et al. [16], systems developed by Torres et al. [17] and Huang et al. [18], the Avatar Arena system developed by Rist el al. [19] and PsychSim, a system for the control of synthetic characters used to educate children in how to recognise and deal with bullying [20].

3   Embodiment

The relationship between the mind and the body has been a psychological and philosophical problem for many years. For example, Descartes [21] argued that the mind and the body are distinct entities and can interact independently of one another. Within the Artificial Intelligence (AI) community, this question has also arisen. Popularised by Brooks [22], the predominant view is that while the mind and body can be seen as different components, they are not necessarily separable. The embodiment of the intelligent system is crucial, as it is through this embodiment that a system interacts with the world.

Within virtual environments an agent's (or a user's) embodiment has been defined as the provision of an appropriate body image for the representation of that agent to other agents and users, as well as to itself [23]. Normally, a virtual agent is embodied through an *avatar*, a graphical representation of the agent within the virtual environment. The use of embodiment within a virtual environments is crucial for the user to develop a sense of presence within the world. *Presence* refers to the subjective experience of being in one place or environment, even when one is physically situated in another [24]. Gerhard et al. state that the use of avatars to embody users within multi-user virtual environments encourages a sense of presence in those users [25]. It also helps users to understand the persona of the other users, and facilitates social encounters with those users. Gerhard et al. go on to state the the form of the avatar has an influence over the level of presence felt. They carry out experiments comparing user reactions to different types of avatars, concluding that realistic or cartoon-like avatars are better at inducing presence than abstract shapes.

Within Agent Chameleons, agents are not constrained to one particular environment. They are capable of *migration*, moving between various different platforms, such as a robot, a mobile device such as a PDA, or a virtual environment. Within all of these environments the agents are considered to be embodied. We define the *embodiment* of the Agent Chameleon to be its strong provision of environmental context, both individual and social. The agents have an embodiment within all environments, provided by the robot that they are controlling, or their representation within the virtual world. Within virtual environments, this embodiment is achieved by the provision of an avatar for the agent.

We define a *body-form* as a body that an agent can choose to adopt. Body-forms include the form of any robots that the agents can occupy, as well as the agent's choices of representation within a virtual environment, on a desktop or on a mobile device. Agents have traditionally been confined to a single form of avatar, a single body-form. This research proposes a contrasting approach, our vision is of a system whereby an agent can mutate between various different body-forms, depending upon its task. The choice of body-form limits the agent's capabilities as each has its own associated sets of capabilities. For example, the body-form of a robot is equipped with that robot's sensory and motor capabilities.

As the body-form is limited by the abilities provided by the environment that the agent is occupying, it must be provided by that environment. Within virtual environments, Agent Chameleons are provided with a library of different body-forms that they can adopt. Each of these body-forms also presents its own set of capabilities to the agent. For instance, a representation as a face may allow an agent to express certain facial expressions whereas a representation as a car will not. The ability to change body-form, therefore, enables the agent to expand its capability set by selecting the most appropriate body-form to its task.

In this way the concept of body-form is distinct from the traditional notion of a *body*, the physical instantiation of an individual. As agents are capable of switching between body-forms, rather than a fixed one-mind-one-body relationship the agent has a one-mind-many-body-forms one, and can decide which of the body-forms is most suitable to its task. We refer this ability to change embodiments as *dynamic embodiment*, and to the act of changing body-form as *mutation*. More details on the architecture that supports dynamic embodiment can be found in [8].

4   Identity

Identity is not a simple concept, and indeed the definition of identity, as it is used in both common speech and academic research, has expanded and changed over the years. Fearon, in an examination of this changing definition of identity, claims that it is currently seen as being either

> "(a) a social category, defined by membership rules and (alleged) characteristics attributes or expected behaviours, or (b) socially distinguishing features that a person takes a special pride in or views as unchangeable but socially consequential (or (a) and (b) at once)." [26]

One important point to realise is that identity is primarily a social concept. As de Levita [27] noted, we present identity to others and have their identity presented to us. The question that defines identity is not, therefore, "Who am I?" but "Who am I in the eyes of others?".

With the ability to change the body-form, the issue of identity becomes important. If the agent can change its form, how can the notion of that agent be maintained? This maintenance of identity is vital if the agent is to operate successfully. Users must know who an agent is, regardless of its adopted bodyform, if they are to develop a relationship with an agent and use it effectively. In order to achieve this, some understanding of the how humans perceive such identity is crucial.

We define an agent's *identity* to be that which causes an agent to remain the same within the mind of the user. It is what remains constant for the agent,

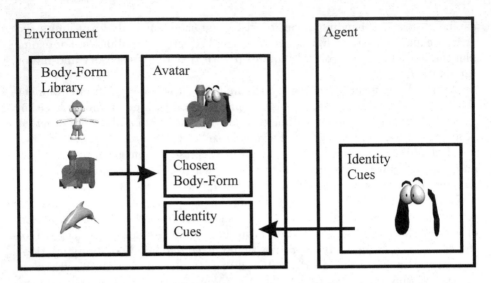

Fig. 1. The relationship between body-form and identity

regardless of its chosen body-form. It should be noted that the identity of the agent is primarily a perception of the user. This identity must be preserved across all body-forms that the agent can choose to adopt. In order to achieve this an agent has a number of features, called its *identity cues*, that remain constant across all body-forms, whenever possible. These identity cues help form the identity of the agent for the user.

The relationship between the the identity and the embodiment is outlined in Fig. 1. The body-form is a feature of the environment, as the environment defines the types of body-forms that are possible. On the other hand, identity and identity cues are features of the agent. Each agent has their own unique set of identity cues. When an agent is located within a virtual environment, the combination of its chosen body-form and identity cues is called the agent's *avatar*. The avatar is the agent's embodiment within the virtual world.

There are a number of different factors that can be used as identity cues, including visual factors such as the colour scheme, markings on the body, or particular features such as a specific style of eyes. Other possible identity cues include the type of character that the body-form represents (human, dog, insect) and non-visual factors such as the tone of voice used or the behaviour of the agent. The sense of identity applies not only to virtual environments, but to other platforms that the agents can occupy; other platforms such as robots or PDA's should attempt to use the same identity cues.

Despite the importance of understanding what underpins identity perception, the question of how a dynamic embodiment affects how one identifies an individual has, so far, remained unaddressed. In order to attempt to rectify this, we carried out an experiment that looks into the influence of identity cues on the identity of a dynamically embodied agent.

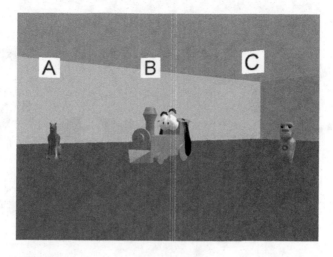

Fig. 2. Screen shot of the experimental environment

5   Experimental Method

To investigate how identity cues can affect the users perception of a virtual agent's identity, and to look at which identity cues are more suitable, we devised a laboratory experiment. A random sample of volunteers were placed within a virtual environment and shown a virtual character. They were able to move around within the world and examine the character. This character was then replaced by three new characters, each with a different level of similarity to the original character. An example of this experimental setup is shown in Fig. 2. Participants were asked to rate "the degree you feel that each of these characters would be recognisable as the original character", giving each a score between 0 and 7. This was repeated a number of times within the experiment.

As this experiment is a preliminary investigation it was limited to characters located within a virtual environment. Additionally, the identity cues were limited to visual factors. A number of these cues were examined, specifically when:

– characters share a common feature, such as a hat or glasses.
– characters share a common colour scheme.
– characters share a common set of markings.
– characters are of the same class of objects, for example characters are both human, or are both dogs.

While this is not an exhaustive set of the possible identity cues, it is adequate for this initial investigation.

For each set of characters in the experiment, each of the three characters shared only one identity cue with the original character. Additionally there were a number of characters that had no similarity to the original character that were used as controls. The test was carried out seven times for each participant, in a

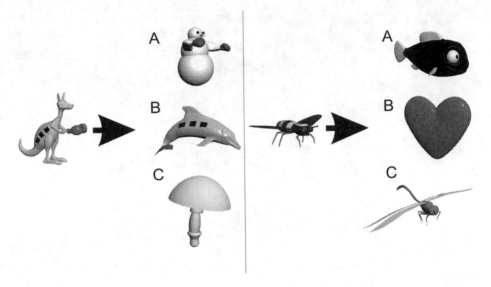

Fig. 3. Two sets of sample characters from the experiment

prescribed order. Each identity cue was repeated an identical number of times throughout these tests. Two examples of the character combinations are shown in Fig. 3. In the first (the kangaroo) where A has a common feature (i.e. boxing gloves), B has the same markings and C is a control. In the second (the wasp) A maintains colour, B is a control and C is the same class of character.

Participants were also asked some demographic questions, such as their age and gender, as well as being asked to rate their familiarity with both technology in general and computer games in particular.

6   Results

The experiment was carried out with a random sample of 31 individuals, 13 males and 18 females, aged between 8 and 50, with an average age of 23. The majority of participants were third-level students. The average score, out of 7, for the question of "receptiveness to technology" was 4.90, and the average score, again out of 7, for the question of "familiarity to computer games" was 3.83.

Analysis of the results suggest that the mean similarity score, for each of the identity cues, is as shown in Fig. 4. In order to ascertain that this represents a statistically valid difference between the different identity cues, an Analysis of Variance (ANOVA) was employed. The ANOVA is a standard method of identifying a statistically significant difference between means. A one-way ANOVA (repeated measures) was carried out on the main independent variable, the similarity score. The results, as shown in Table 1, reveal a significant difference between conditions ($F(4, 84) = 38.97; p < 0.001; MSE = 0.45$). Post-hoc analysis

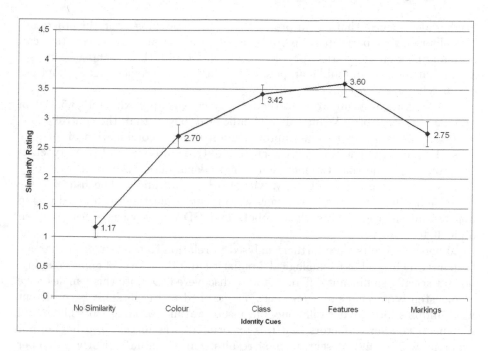

Fig. 4. The mean similarity score for each of the identity cues, with standard error indicated

Table 1. ANOVA Summary Table

Source	df	SS	MS	F	p-value
Identity Cues	4	69.93	17.48	38.97	0.00
Error	84	37.68	0.45		
Total	88	107.61			

suggested that, with a significance level of $p < 0.001$, the four different identity cues were significantly different from the control case. Thus we can claim that the inclusion of identity cues affects the user's perception of the character's identity. Additionally, with a significance level of $p < 0.05$, the use of common features is significantly better than the use of colours and of common markings.

A few observations need to be made about these results. Considering the results for colour, the choice of colour used clearly has an influence. When the colours used were black and yellow (the wasp's colours, as is Fig. 3) a much higher rating was observed, with a mean score of 3.68, on the other hand when a less vivid green and blue combination was used, the rating was much lower, having a mean score of only 0.97, below that of the control characters.

There are a number of possible reason why this is the case. Research into human colour perception suggests that colour preference is learned rather than innate, and is influenced by a number of factors such as age, gender and culture.

Studies also suggest that colour preference varies depending upon the object being coloured, with participants more open to colour variation in objects that can normally be seen in a variety of colours [28,29]. Despite these complications, we argue that colour can still be an powerful identity cue, provided an appropriate colour scheme is chosen.

The maximum mean score for the identity cues is approximately 3.5, out of a maximum score of 7. While this is significantly better than the control cases, it is possible that this can be improved upon using a combination of identity cues. This experiment was, by design, limited to purely visual identity cues; one would imagine that the inclusion of non-visual cues, such as the auditory factors or behavioural consistency, will also have an affect. The use of these non-visual will also become important when identity must be maintained within non-virtual environments such as robots and PDA's, as visual cues are then difficult to maintain.

When the results were further analysed in relation to the gender of the participants, their level of technological familiarity and their level of games playing, no statistically significant differences were discovered. Despite this females have a consistently lower mean than males, as graphed in Fig. 5. This is consistent with findings into gender differences in visuo-spatial reasoning [30]. There still remains a number of factors that this experiment was unable to examine. For example, will a child present different results than an adult? Clearly a number of further experiments must be carried out in order to evaluate some of these factors.

7   Conclusions and Future Work

When virtual agents are equipped with dynamic embodiment, that is the ability to mutate their form, they are afforded the ability to take advantage of an expanded set of capabilities. However, this presents problems with the agent's identity, specifically how this can be maintained in the mind of the user.

Maintaining visual identity cues that transcend such avatar transmogrification is of paramount importance. This paper has explored this very issue and has formulated and conducted experiments that offer an understanding of visual enablers for the maintenance of agent identity. From the statistical analysis of our experimental data, it can be concluded that the use of identity cues does indeed provide a valid method of maintaining an agent's identity when its embodiment is dynamic. Furthermore, it has been shown that the use of common features produces a higher level of identity than the use of common colours and markings. The Agent Chameleons must be equipped with these identity cues in order to aid the user in their identification of the agent when it mutates within the virtual environment and when it migrates from the virtual to the physical, such as to a robot or a PDA.

This work raises a number of questions that are yet to be answered. These include how other identity cues affect the result. The effect of behaviour and other non-visual cues, such as auditory cues, and the combination of identity

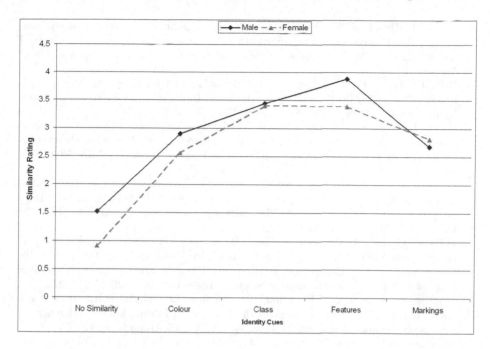

Fig. 5. The mean similarity score for males and females

cues also needs to be examined. Furthermore, questions are raised regarding the choice of colours that can be used for an identity cue, specifically what choices are appropriate and which are not. More experiments must be carried out in order to answer these questions.

Acknowledgements

The work undertaken as part of the Agent Chameleons project, a collaborative project between the Department of Computer Science, University College Dublin (UCD) and Media Lab Europe (MLE), Dublin. We gratefully acknowledge the financial support of the Higher Education Authority (HEA) Ireland and the Irish Research Council for Science, Engineering and Technology: funded by the National Development Plan. Gregory O'Hare gratefully acknowledges the support of Science Foundation Ireland under Grant No. 03/IN.3/1361.

References

1. Wooldridge, M., Jennings, N.R.: Intelligent agents: Theory and practice. Knowledge Engineering Review **10** (1994)
2. Cobel, J., Cook, D.J.: Virtual environments: An agent-based approach. In: Proceedings of the AAAI Spring Symposium on Agents with Adjustable Autonomy. (1999)

3. Cobel, J., Harbison, K.: MAVE: A multi-agent architecture for virtual environments. In: Proceedings of the Eleventh International Conference on Industrial and Engineering Applications of Artificial Intelligence and Expert Systems. (1998) 577–583
4. Rist, T., André, E., Baldes, S.: A flexible platform for building applications with life-like characters. In: Proceedings of the Eight International Conference on Intelligent User Interfaces - IUI 2003, Miami, Florida, USA (2003)
5. Duffy, B.R., O'Hare, G.M.P., Martin, A.N., Bradley, J.F., Schön, B.: Agent chameleons: Agent minds and bodies. In: Proceedings of the Sixteenth International Conference on Computer Animation and Social Agents - CASA 2003, New Jersey, USA (2003)
6. O'Hare, G.M.P., Duffy, B.R.: Agent chameleons: Migration and mutation within and between real and virtual spaces. In: Proceedings of the Society for the Study of Artificial Intelligence and the Simulation of Behaviour (SSAISB) - AISB'02 Conference, London, England (2002)
7. O'Hare, G.M.P., Duffy, B.R., Schön, B., Martin, A., Bradley, J.F.: Agent chameleons: Virtual agents real intelligence. In: Proceedings of the Fourth International Working Conference on Intelligent Virtual Agents - IVA 2003. Volume 2792 of Lecture Notes in Computer Science., Irsee, Germany (2003) 218–225
8. Martin, A., O'Hare, G.M.P., Schön, B., Bradley, J.F., Duffy, B.R.: Intentional embodied agents. In: Proceedings of the Eighteenth International Conference on Computer Animation and Social Agents - CASA 2005, Hong Kong (2005)
9. Bratman, M.E.: What is intention? In Cohen, P.R., Morgan, J., Pollack, M.E., eds.: Intentions in Communication. MIT Press (1990) 15–32
10. Cohen, P.R., Levesque, H.J.: Intention is choice with commitment. Artificial Intelligence **42** (1990) 213–261
11. Rao, A.S., Georgeff, M.P.: Modeling rational agents within a BDI-architecture. In: Proceedings of the Second International Conference on Principles of Knowledge Representation and Reasoning - KR 91, San Mateo, CA, USA, Morgan Kaufmann (1991)
12. Collier, R., O'Hare, G.M.P., Lowen, T., Rooney, C.: Beyond prototyping in the factory of agents. In: Proceedings of the Third Central and Eastern European Conference on Multi-Agent Systems - CEEMAS'03, Prague, Czech Republic (2003)
13. Collier, R., Rooney, C., O'Hare, G.M.P.: A UML-based software engineering methodology for Agent Factory. In: Proceedings of the Sixteenth International Conference on Software Engineering and Knowledge Engineering - SEKE 2004, Alberta, Canada (2004)
14. Collier, R.W.: Agent Factory: A Framework for the Engineering of Agent-Oriented Applications. Phd thesis, University College Dublin, Ireland (2001)
15. Ross, R., Collier, R., O'Hare, G.M.P.: AF-APL - bridging principles & practice in agent oriented languages. In: Proceedings of the First International Workshop on Programming Multiagent Systems, Languages and Tools - PROMAS 2004, New York, USA (2004)
16. Anastassakis, G., Ritchings, T., Panayiotopoulos, T.: Multi-agent systems as intelligent virtual environments. In: Proceedings of Advances in Artificial Intelligence, Joint German/Austrian Conference on AI - KI 2001. Volume 2174 of Lecture Notes in Computer Science., Springer (2001)
17. Torres, J.A., Nedel, L.P., Bordini, R.H.: Using the BDI architecture to produce autonomous characters in virtual worlds. In: Proceedings of the Fourth International Working Conference on Intelligent Virtual Agents - IVA 2003, Irsee, Germany (2003) 197–201

18. Huang, Z., Eliëns, A., Visser, C.: Programmibility of intelligent agent avatars. In: Proceedings of Agent'01 Workshop on Embodied Agents, Montreal, Canada (2001)
19. Rist, T., Schmitt, M., Pelachaud, C., Bilvi, M.: Towards a simulation of conversations with expressive embodied speakers and listeners. In: Proceedings of the Sixteenth International Conference on Computer Animation and Social Agents - CASA 2003, New Jersey, USA (2003)
20. Marsella, S.C., Pynadath, D.V., Read, S.J.: PsychSim: Agent-based modeling of social interaction and influence. In: Proceedings of the International Conference on Cognitive Modeling - ICCM 2004, Pittsburg, Pensylvania, USA (2004)
21. Descartes, R.: Discourse on Method and Meditations. New York Library of Liberal Arts (1960) Edited and Translated by L. F. Lafleur from original French, first published 1637.
22. Brooks, R.A.: Intelligence without reason. In: Proceedings of the Twelfth International Joint Conference on Artificial Intelligence - IJCAI 91, San Mateo, CA, USA (1991) 569–595
23. Benford, S., Bowers, J., Fahlén, L.E., Greenhalgh, C., Snowdon, D.: User embodiment in collaborative virtual environments. In: Proceedings of CHI 1995. (1995)
24. Witmer, B.G., Singer, M.J.: Measuring presence in virtual environments: A presence questionnaire. Presence: Teleoperators and Virtual Environments **7** (1998) 255–240
25. Gerhard, M., Moore, D.J., Hobbs, D.J.: An experimental study of the effect of presence in collaborative virtual environments. In Earnshaw, R., Vince, J., eds.: Intelligent Agents for Mobile and Virtual Media. Springer (2002) 113–123
26. Fearon, J.D.: What is identity (as we now use the word)? Mimeo, Stanford University (1999)
27. de Levita, D.: The Concept of Identity. Mouton & Co. (1965) Translated by Ian Finaly from original Dutch.
28. Burchett, K.E.: Color harmony. Color Research and Application **27** (2002) 28–31
29. Taft, C.: Color meaning and context: Comparisons of semantic ratings of colors on samples and objects. Color Research and Application **22** (1997) 40–50
30. Vecchi, T., Girelli, L.: Gender differences in visuo-spatial prcessing: The importance of distinguishing between passive storage and active manipulation. Acta Psychologicia **99** (1998) 1–16

The Behavior Oriented Design of an Unreal Tournament Character

Samuel J. Partington and Joanna J. Bryson

Department of Computer Science, University of Bath, Bath BA2 7AY, United Kingdom
sam@samsolutions.co.uk
J.J.Bryson@bath.ac.uk

Abstract. This paper presents a case study for using a relatively recently developed methodology, Behavior Oriented Design, to develop an Intelligent Virtual Agent (IVA). Our usability study was conducted in Unreal Tournament using the game Capture The Flag. The final agent displays reasonably competent behavior: she is able to pursue multiple goals simultaneously and produce well-ordered behavior.

1 Introduction

This paper presents a case study of the application of a recently-established methodology for developing complex humanoid agents to the problem of building a game agent. The methodology is Behavior Oriented Design [7, 8]. The game is Unreal Tournament [12], using the Gamebots interface [13].

We begin this paper with some background description of both the game and the development methodology. Then we describe the development of the robot, highlighting the elaboration of its action-selection network as the agent becomes more complex. This strategy is taken because it is fairly intuitive, since action selection determines the priorities of an agent. However, Behavior Oriented Design is at least as much about building the behavior objects that actually control the agent's actions, perception and memory as it is about the problem of action selection. The final section goes into detail about the trickier elements of building behavior for this agent, and shows how these problems interact with the problem of action selection.

2 Background

2.1 The Game

This case was conducted using the Capture the Flag game-mode of Unreal Tournament (UT). Unreal Tournament [12] is a First-Person Shooter (FPS) game. As the name suggests, the viewpoint adopted by the player in FPS games is that of the character he or she is controlling: the player sees the world through the character's eyes. The single-player version of Unreal Tournament pits the human player against computer-controlled players ('bots') in kill-or-be-killed deathmatches spread over a wide range of expansive

T. Panayiotopoulos et al. (Eds.): IVA 2005, LNCS 3661, pp. 466–477, 2005.
© Springer-Verlag Berlin Heidelberg 2005

3D environments. In Capture-the-Flag mode, two teams (or possibly two single players) compete against each other. Each team has a base in which their flag is located. The object of the game is to obtain your opponents' flag (done by running into it), and return with it to your own flag. This counts as a flag capture. Once a specified number of captures have been achieved, the game is won. If the opposing team captures your flag, you must recover it before you can make a successful capture, as returning to your base with the enemies' flag achieves nothing if your own team's flag is not there. Once a player has captured a flag, s/he may be forced to drop it by being killed (using the usual UT weaponry). The flag then lies on the ground waiting for someone (of either team) to pick it up. If you pick up your own flag dropped by an escaping enemy, it returns to your base instantly. Teams in CTF may be composed of human players alone, or of a mixture of human and computer players.

2.2 The Methodology

Behavior-Oriented Design (BOD) is a methodology for complex agent construction. It derives from the traditions of both Behavior-Based AI [2, 4, 6] and Object-Oriented Design (OOD) [3, 10, 16] the notion of strong modular decomposition. Each module (encoded as a class in an OO language) is semi-autonomous. The purpose of a module is to produce and control expressed behavior, but they also encapsulate whatever memory and perception is necessary for that behavior, and and whatever additional methods are necessary for maintaining the state of the memory or processing the perception and control.

Modular systems require some form of coordination between the modules to guarantee overall coherence for the agent and to arbitrate in cases where behavior modules would express conflicting actions (e.g. those that require going in two directions at once.) BOD uses Parallel-rooted Slip-stack Hierarchical (POSH) dynamic plans[1] encoded in a script file to do this arbitration.

BOD is an iterative development methodology. The iterations begin with an initial decomposition for the agent:

1. Specify at a high level what the agent is intended to do.
2. Describe likely activities in terms of sequences of actions. These sequences are the the basis of the initial dynamic plans.
3. Identify an initial list of sensory and action primitives from the previous list of actions.
4. Identify the state necessary to enable the described primitives and drives. Cluster related state elements and their dependent primitives into specifications for behaviors. This is the basis of the behavior library.
5. Identify and prioritize goals or drives that the agent may need to attend to. This describes the initial roots for the dynamic plan hierarchy (described below).
6. Select a first behavior to implement.

---

[1] Dynamic plans were historically referred to as 'reactive plans', because they responded rapidly to the environment. Unfortunately, this has lead some people to believe (falsely) that agents that use them are not *pro*-active. Since our agents all have their own goals and motivations, we have adopted this new nomenclature.

Getting the decomposition right the first time is neither critical nor expected — the iterative process will involve refactoring this decomposition. The lists compiled during this process should be kept, since they are an important part of the documentation of the agent.

The heart of the BOD methodology is an iterative development process:

1. Select a part of the specification to implement next.
2. Extend the agent with that implementation:
   - code behaviors and dynamic plans, and
   - test and debug that code.
3. Revise the current specification.

BOD's iterative development cycle can be thought of as sort of a hand-cranked version of the Expectation Maximization (EM) algorithm [11]. The first step is to elaborate the current model, then the second is to revise the model to find the new optimum representation. Of course, regardless of the optimizing process, the agent will continue to grow in complexity. But if that growth is carefully monitored, guided and pruned, then the resulting agent will be more elegant, easier to maintain, and easier to further adapt.

2.3   BOD Action Selection

Dynamic plans support action selection. At any given time step, most agents have a number of actions which could potentially be expressed, at least some of which cannot be expressed simultaneously, for example sitting and walking. In architectures without centralized action selection, such as the Subsumption Architecture [4] or the Agent Network Architecture (ANA) [15], the developer must fully characterize *for each action* how to determine when it should be expressed. This task grows in complexity with the number of new behaviors. For engineers, it is generally easier to describe the desired behavior in terms of sequences of events.

Of course, action-selection sequences can seldom be specified precisely in advance, due to the non-determinism of environments, including the unreliability of the agent's own sensing or actuation. Several types of events may interrupt the completion of an intended action sequence. These events fall into two categories:

1. some combination of alarms, requests or opportunities may make pursuing a different plan more relevant, and
2. some combination of opportunities or difficulties may require the current 'sequence' to be reordered.

Thus the problems of action selection can be broken into three categories: things that need to be checked regularly, things that only need to be checked in a particular context, and things that do not strictly need to be checked at all.

BOD uses dynamic plans to perform action selection through behavior arbitration. BOD dynamic plans provide three types of plan elements corresponding (respectively) to the three categories of action selection mentoned above. A *drive collection* provides the main loop of the action selection, continuously monitoring which drive should be attended to currently. A *competence* checks for context-specific behaviors, and action patterns encode true sequences.

There is a great deal more to be said about POSH action selection — most significantly the importance of prioritizing the elements of a competence in a way such that they converge. Some of this will be elaborated below. There are also many more details of the BOD development methodology, such as heuristics for determining when the complexity of a plan should be offloaded to a behavior, and *vis versa*. These details have been previously published [7, 8, 9]. We have also previously published extensive comparisons between BOD and related architectures [7, 9, 17].

The purpose of the present paper is to provide a case study of applying these rules. This serves both to clarify previous publications through an additional example, and also to illustrate the application of BOD to the important real-time domain of computer games. The code for this paper was written using the Kwong [14] python-based implementation of POSH, known as pyPOSH.

3   The Bot in Action

This section presents a number of scenarios demonstrating the actions of the bot we created (the *bodbot*) and relates these back to the plan files created. These scenerios are ordered to show iterations of the development cycle, thus they show bots capable of increasingly complex behaviour. BOD agents are generally referred to by the name of their POSH scripts, because the script determines an individual agent's priorities. Thus quite different agents can use the same BOD behaviour library — indeed, testing old scripts after elaborating the behavior library is part of the BOD iterative development cycle.

The section's purpose is threefold:

- To demonstrate the development of the plan files.
- To illustrate how the actions of the bot are guided by the plan file it uses.
- To give examples of the bodbot's actions, and thus provide a starting-point for the discussion of the development process.

The actions of the bot are illustrated by a series of commentary-style descriptions which are interleaved with brief analysis and samples of plan code. For brevity, only particularly noteworthy parts of the bots' runs are described. The first plan is illustrated by the actions of a male bot on the red team and remainder by the actions of a female bot on the blue team.

3.1   Walking to Navigation Points

We started from a bot based upon *poshbotfollow.lap*, the plan created by Kwong [14] for his "poshbot". *poshbotfollow.lap* had the bot wandering around and following any players he saw. Our initial plan removed the player-following element, replacing it with one which attempted to follow navpoints (navigation-points, aka pathnodes):

> *Yes, the bodbot has just this moment spawned into the play-area. He's wasting no time running off that ledge and towards the tunnel, seems to be having a bit of trouble on the corners, though: he's paying more attention to that wall than*

it really deserves... no, here he goes off again. Looks like he's missed that vital turning though, seems more interested in the walls of the tunnel again, no wait, he's coming back, takes the turning, now he's looking around again, trying to decide where to go. He's finally decided and now he emerges from the tunnel.

The important part of this plan is the competence below. (The top level of the plan hierarchy (the *Drive Collection*) only contains two drives at this point and thus almost always fires this competence as the other is only triggered when the bot walks into something.)

$$\textbf{get-to-enemy-base} \; \Rightarrow \; \left\langle \begin{array}{c} \text{(at-enemy-base)} \Rightarrow goal \\ \text{(reachable-nav-point)} \Rightarrow \text{walk-to-nav-point} \\ () \Rightarrow \text{wander-around} \end{array} \right\rangle \qquad (1)$$

A *competence* is essentially a focused set of productions, each associated with a priority as well as a trigger, and a habituation factor (described later.) The first (highest priority) element of this competence is its goal — triggering it causes the competence to terminate. The second element is intended to find the base, and the third to generate wandering behavior until the second element's trigger can be achieved.

When the bot starts up, he can see a navigation point specified as reachable (the *reachable-nav-point* trigger returns true) and so he runs off the ledge (only a short drop) to get to it. On the occasion of his trouble in the tunnel, the problem is that because of the curve of the tunnel he can no longer see any navpoints. For this reason the lowest-priority element takes over (an empty trigger means that it always fires if no higher-priority element can). This element triggers the *wander-around* competence, which causes the bot to walk around near (and into!) the walls as described. For brevity, this competence is not given here.

3.2   A Greater Awareness of Flags

And here comes the blue bodbot now. She's looking around, wondering where to go next. And now she's off, running towards the tunnel...

The "looking around" at the beginning comes from a modification to the *get-to-enemy-base* competence, whose elements are now the following (the second is new):

$$\textbf{get-to-enemy-base} \; \Rightarrow \; \left\langle \begin{array}{c} \text{(at-enemy-base)} \Rightarrow goal \\ \text{(reachable-nav-point)} \Rightarrow \text{walk-to-nav-point} \\ () ::10 \Rightarrow \text{rotate} \\ () \Rightarrow \text{wander-around} \end{array} \right\rangle \qquad (2)$$

Although two of the elements have triggers that succeed by default, the retries limit (*10*) on *find-nav-point* means that the lowest-priority element does sometimes get a chance to fire. In the example given above, however, the rotating leads to a position where the bot can see a reachable navpoint, and thus the first non-goal element fires.

The bodbot emerges from the tunnel, she's almost at the enemy base now, the prize in her sights. Yes, I think she's going to make it! She makes a clear run for the red flag and grabs it! Nice work there, but can she capitalise on this early success? Remember, she's still got to take it home.

To understand the bot's next actions (running to the enemy flag), we need to consider the, now extended, top-level Drive Collection, **life**:

$$
\left\langle\!\!\left\langle
\begin{array}{l}
\text{(our-flag-on-ground)} \Rightarrow \text{go-to-own-flag} \\
\text{(enemy-flag-on-ground)} \Rightarrow \text{go-to-enemy-flag} \\
\text{(see-enemy-with-our-flag)} \Rightarrow \text{attack-enemy-with-flag} \\
\text{(enemy-flag-reachable) (have-en.-flag } \bot \text{))} \Rightarrow \text{go-to-enemy-flag} \\
\text{(hit-object) (rotating } \bot \text{))} \Rightarrow \text{avoid} \\
\text{(have-enemy-flag)} \Rightarrow \text{go-to-own-base} \\
\Rightarrow \text{get-to-enemy-base}
\end{array}
\right\rangle\!\!\right\rangle
\tag{3}
$$

Life of course has no goal and should in theory never end, but otherwise a drive collection is much like a competence, except that its elements are checked on every iteration of the action selection in case a different drive element should take priority. Before elaborating the drive collection, the main element firing had been *to-enemy-base*. Now, once the bot approaches the enemy flag, however, the trigger *enemy-flag-reachable* returns true and *go-to-enemy-flag* is fired instead.

Wait a minute, John, there seems to be some sort of upset at the other end of the arena! Yes, the bodbot's quest for glory has left her own flag dangerously unguarded and the red player has stolen it!

To demonstrate a situation more similar to genuine Capture the Flag games, I intervened at this point and, playing as the red player, stole the blue flag.

The bodbot's leaving the tunnel now Clive, she's surely going to notice that thief any second now...
Too right, John, the bodbot rounds on the red player, running towards him and shooting and ... it's a success! He's been tagged, and he drops the blue flag to the ground where the bodbot grabs it, restoring it to its rightful place! Yes, nothing can stop her now! She's running back to her own flag, she's made it now, the blue team scores!!

In an attempt to get the blue player to notice me (and since I cannot win whilst the other team has my own flag), I returned to the blue player's base. The bodbot then noticed that I had her team's flag. Doing so meant that her current action of going home was interrupted as the *attack-enemy-with-flag* Drive Collection element fired instead (it has a higher priority) and the bot began to attack me.

Upon being tagged (killed), the red player drops the blue flag he has been carrying and the bodbot's current undertaking is again interrupted, as the *go-to-own-flag* element now fires (it has an even higher priority). Picking up one's own flag returns it instantly to the base, and the bodbot scores when returning to her own flag while carrying the red one. The bot only moves towards her own flag as the list of navpoints leads there: at this stage there is no specific drive to run directly there once it is reachable.

Well, that certainly was impressive. The bodbot seems to have had enough though, she's not going anywhere! This is remarkable, she's just standing there! What it she thinking?!

This final segment illustrates a problem: the expiry of out-dated state the bot holds. In this case, the instance of the *PositionsInfo* class held out-dated information about the enemy flag, claiming that it was reachable from the bot's current location (as that had the been the case until the bot scored and the red flag was returned to the red base). The bot therefore attempted to send a command to make it run directly to the enemy flag. This was not possible from its current location, and so nothing happened.

Out of date state is one of the reasons reactive AI proponents used to avoid all memory whatsoever, but such a strategy is pointless when an agent needs to learn and perform complicated tasks. Under BOD, the correct thing to do is to redesign the system on the next iteration to fix the bug.

3.3   Responding to Attack

This final scenario introduces a number of new elements, the most important being the bot's ability to respond when it is attacked.

> *For those of you who've just joined us, we're seeing a fine run by the blue bod-bot, she's just grabbed the red flag! But where are the defence? Well, someone's trying to shoot her but not doing a very good job of it, that shot landed just in front of her. The bodbot's off again now, and ouch! That goo-explosion's got to hurt.*

The assailant was a bot controlled by me. The goowand fires blobs of goo which stick to walls and floors and remain there for a few seconds before exploding.

> *Not one to let that sort of behaviour go unnoticed, she's looking around for the assailant, she's spotted him now and begins to shoot... ooh, right in the stomach! Keen not to throw that lead away though, she's now heading back to her own base. Obviously doesn't want another surprise attack, she's keeping firmly focussed on that attacker as she runs back through the tunnels.*

The response to attack comes as a result of the following new Drive Collection element:

$$\text{(damaged)(armed-\&-ammo)(responding-to-attack } \bot) \Rightarrow \text{respond-to-attack} \qquad (4)$$

This element has a higher priority than go-home, the drive element previously being attended to, and so the *respond-to-attack* competence is triggered. Note again this is substantially different from a normal dynamic plan — the last conjunct should not be necessary, the response to attack should be continuous under philosophies such as subsumption architecture. However, in this 'real world', actions not only have duration, but can only be sent to the game engine once in a while, so the robot has to maintain state to ensures he doesn't flood the game engine.

In some cases, the bot will receive details of the assailant when receiving a message from Gamebots about damage inflicted. For example, if the bot actually sees the shot being fired. This was not the case in this example, however, and so *respond-to-attack* triggers the following competence:

$$\textbf{find-attacker} \text{ (:: 3sec) } \Rightarrow \left\langle \begin{array}{c} \text{(see-enemy)} \Rightarrow \text{respond-to-visible-attacker} \\ \text{::1} \Rightarrow \text{big-rotate} \end{array} \right\rangle \qquad (5)$$

This competence is the reason the bot looks around for the attacker: the *big-rotate* element causes the bot to spin. Note the limit on retries here: the bot shouldn't keep on turning around as it may never be able to see the attacker. Further, this competence has no goal, but automatically times out after 3 seconds even if it is responding, to allow some other drive to take over the situation. In this case though, the search was successful, leading to the *see-enemy* sense returning true and the *respond-to-visible-attacker* element running. It is this element which makes the bot shoot the attacker. So the first element in this competence is actually somewhat redundant.

Finding an attacker results in variables being set telling the bot to keep looking at the attacker whilst performing other actions. In practice, this means that when running, the bot instead sends a command to *strafe*. Strafing is running in one direction while facing another.

> *Into the home strait now, she turns around for the final sprint, she's nearly there, yes ... she scores! Now she's going back to try another capture, it could be a high-scoring game, folks!*

The Drive Collection used for this scenario contains three unexciting but nevertheless very important elements: those which expire state. For example, the reason that the bot now goes back for another capture rather than just standing around as before is the following element:

$$freq\ :20\text{sec} \Rightarrow \text{expire-the-reachable-info} \qquad (6)$$

The expiry elements are the highest priority in the Drive Collection. However, their limits on frequency mean that other elements get plenty of chance to run.

4   The Development Process

The previous section focussed a great deal on action selection. This is a natural consequence of the fact that the dynamic plan scripts essentially determine the goals and motivations for an agent by ordering its priorities. However, there would be nothing to order if it weren't for the behaviour modules which provide the primitive action and maintain the agent's internal state / memory.

4.1   Behaviour Modules

The bot's expressed behaviour is generated by four primary modules, each of which is stored as a separate Python class:

- Movement: state to do with positions of objects, bases and the bot himself.
- Status: contains state regarding health level, weapons held and so on.
- Combat: state about who is attacking the bot, what enemies are around and what teammates are around.
- AndyBehaviour: primitives developed for the 'poshbot'.

Our bot makes much use of code from 'the poshbot', an Unreal Tournament agent designed by Kwong [14] as part of the development of pyPOSH. Although this meant that the behaviour decomposition was not as logical as it could be (many of these primitives would be logically suited to the <u>movement</u> module instead), we felt that such a distinction between the simple behaviour of the original bot and the more advanced behaviour of the bot I developed was useful.

There were also three behaviours dedicated primarily to maintaining internal state. These were made individual behaviours because their state was utilised by more than one of the other behaviours, so could not be seen as an attribute of just one of them.

- Bot_Agent – general information from the Gamebots interface, also inherited from Kwong.
- CombatInfoClass – holds state relating to combat (for example, details of the player holding the bot's flag), and is used by both the <u>Movement</u> and <u>Combat</u> behaviours.
- PositionsInfo – holds state relating to the position of the bot and position of the game objects (e.g. flags and navigation-points), and is used by <u>Movement</u>, <u>Status</u> and <u>Combat</u>.

Like the primitive-complexity *vs.* plan-complexity tradeoff, there is also a trade-off between plan-complexity and the amount of state required. Bryson [7, section 6.5] gives the example of an insect which could either have two plan elements for hitting something on its left side or its right, or have some state indicating which side it hit something on, and a single plan element whose primitive uses this state to decide whether to move left or right. The complexity of the information the bodbot required — and the need for persistence of data — meant that the need for extra state usually prevailed in this case.

4.2   The Primitives

This section illustrates part of the development process by presenting an example of a sensory primitive. In total, I coded 20 actions and 23 senses, and re-used the 5 actions and 9 senses of the poshbot ([14]). The sense shown in this section, *reachable-nav-point*, was chosen with a view to demonstrating interesting features of the bot, such as its use of state, the trade-offs between plans and behaviours and so on. For ease of explanation, I have broken it up into sections:

```
# returns True if there's a reachable nav point
# in the bot's list which we're not already at
def reachable_nav_point(self):
    # setup location tuple
    if not self.bot.botinfo.has_key("Location"):
        # if we don't know where we are, treat it as
        # (0,0,0) as that will just mean we go to the
        # nav point even if we're close by
        (SX, SY, SZ) = (0, 0, 0)
    else:
        (SX, SY, SZ) = utilityfns.location_string_to_tuple(
                            self.bot.botinfo["Location"])
```

As part of this sense, we must already determine whether we are already close to the navpoint we are aiming for. Our location is stored in the *botinfo* dictionary. However, this is stored as a string and thus must be converted into a tuple (in this case, a triple) for comparison, hence the call to *utilityfns.location_string_to_tuple*. This line also provides an example of Python's ability to perform multiple-assignment.

If the location is not available, we can treat the bot as being at *(0,0,0)*. This might mean that we are actually close to a navpoint but do not realise it, but it is worth taking this minor risk rather than doing nothing.

```
# is there already a navpoint we're aiming for?
# how near we must be to be thought of as at the nav point
DistanceTolerance = 30
if self.PosInfo.ChosenNavPoint != None:
    (NX, NY, NZ) = self.PosInfo.ChosenNavPoint
    if utilityfns.find_distance((NX, NY), (SX, SY)) >
                                      DistanceTolerance:
        return True
    else:  # set this NP as visited
        self.PosInfo.VisitedNavPoints.append((NX, NY, NZ))
        self.PosInfo.ChosenNavPoint = None
```

It may be that the bot has already chosen a navigation point to aim for (*self.PosInfo.-ChosenNavPoint*) and is currently heading there. In this case, we test whether the bot has already got there. This uses another utility function, *find_distance*. If the bot is not already there, then we need do nothing more – the bot has a location to head for so we can simply return. However, if the bot is there then we add the point to our list of visited navpoints and clear the variable stating where we are heading for. We do not return from the function but rather continue execution to find a new navpoint.

This extract of code is an interesting one as it is an example of something which could be accomplished either in a primitive (as here) or by making the plan file more complicated (i.e. adding a sense to check whether we are at the place we're heading and an action to clear it if we are.) There is no overwhelming advantage to either method, it is more a matter of personal preference. The trade-off this demonstrates (between complexity of plans and complexity of primitives) is an important one, however.

```
# now look at the list of
# navpoints the bot can see
if self.bot.nav_points == None or
                          len(self.bot.nav_points) == 0:
    return False
```

If the bot cannot see any navpoints then the sense obviously fails.

```
else:
    # nav_points is a list of tuples.  Each tuple
    # contains an ID and a dictionary of
    # attributes as defined in the API
    # Search for reachable nav points
    PossibleNPs = self.get_reachable_nav_points(
```

```
                self.bot.nav_points.items(),
            DistanceTolerance, (SX, SY, SZ))
```

The *get_reachable_nav_points* function takes a list of navpoints and returns a list of all those which are specified as "reachable" and which the bot is more than *Distance-Tolerance* units away from[2].

```
    # now work through this list of NavPoints
    # until we find one that we haven't been to
    # or the one we've been to least often
    if len(PossibleNPs) == 0:
        return False # nothing found
    else:
        self.PosInfo.ChosenNavPoint =
            self.get_least_visited_navpoint(PossibleNPs)
        return True
```

The function now searches this returned list (unless it is empty) and finds the one visited least often. This is accomplished by the *get_least_visited_navpoint* function which searches the list in *self.PosInfo.VisitedNavPoints*.

self.PosInfo.ChosenNavPoint is set to this least-visited navpoint. This variable then used by the *walk-to-nav-point* action primitive to actually make the agent run to this navpoint.

5   Conclusion

The final agent was one of the most complex BOD agents yet published (see further Partington [17]).

We found that BOD offered the following key advantages:

– More focussed development. Because an Action Selection mechanism was provided it did not need to be coded.
– An ease in constructing goal parallelism. This allowed both for higher-priority drives to interrupt lower-priority ones, and two goals to be pursued at once.
– The ability to set frequencies for pursuing goals and retries limits for attempting actions. This made fine-tuning of the agent's action selection relatively easy.

A number of minor problems with both pyPOSH and the methodology were discovered, some of which have already been addressed in the course of this project. Others will need to be addressed as future work. In particular, it would be useful to have a full-blown interactive development environment for debugging POSH plans.

Some problems in agent development are still just hard, particularly navigation and debugging the Gamebots interface itself. There is no way around needing to make elaborate modules for these sorts of problems. However, the fact that they *are* modules, and can be treated distinct from other problems, did at least simplify their construction. In general, we strongly recommend the BOD methodology.

---

[2] "Units" refers to Unreal Tournament distance units, discussed in the Gamebots API.

References

[1] Ronald C. Arkin. *Behavior-Based Robotics*. MIT Press, Cambridge, MA, 1998.

[2] Christian Balkenius. *Natural Intelligence in Artificial Creatures*. PhD thesis, Lund University Cognitive Studies, 1995.

[3] Kent Beck. *Extreme Programming Explained: Embrace Change*. Addison-Wesley, Reading, MA, 2000.

[4] Rodney A. Brooks. A robust layered control system for a mobile robot. *IEEE Journal of Robotics and Automation*, RA-2:14–23, April 1986.

[5] Rodney A. Brooks. Intelligence without representation. *Artificial Intelligence*, 47:139–159, 1991.

[6] Joanna J. Bryson. Cross-paradigm analysis of autonomous agent architecture. *Journal of Experimental and Theoretical Artificial Intelligence*, 12(2):165–190, 2000.

[7] Joanna J. Bryson. *Intelligence by Design: Principles of Modularity and Coordination for Engineering Complex Adaptive Agents*. PhD thesis, MIT, Department of EECS, Cambridge, MA, June 2001. AI Technical Report 2001-003.

[8] Joanna J. Bryson. The behavior-oriented design of modular agent intelligence. In R. Kowalszyk, Jörg P. Müller, H. Tianfield, and R. Unland, editors, *Agent Technologies, Infrastructures, Tools, and Applications for e-Services*, pages 61–76. Springer, 2003.

[9] Joanna J. Bryson and Lynn Andrea Stein. Architectures and idioms: Making progress in agent design. In C. Castelfranchi and Y. Lespérance, editors, *The Seventh International Workshop on Agent Theories, Architectures, and Languages (ATAL2000)*. Springer, 2001.

[10] Peter Coad, David North, and Mark Mayfield. *Object Models: Strategies, Patterns and Applications*. Prentice Hall, 2nd edition, 1997.

[11] A. P. Dempster, N. M. Laird, and D. B. Rubin. Maximum likelihood from incomplete data via the EM algorithm. *Journal of the Royal Statistical Society series B*, 39:1–38, 1977.

[12] Epic Games. Unreal tournament, 2004. http://www.unrealtournament.com/utgoty/, Accessed 2 November 2004.

[13] G. A. Kaminka, M. M. Veloso, S. Schaffer, C. Sollitto, R. Adobbati, Marshall, A. N., A. Scholer, and S. Tejada. GameBots: A flexible test bed for multiagent team research. *Communications of the ACM*, 45(1):43–45, 2002.

[14] Andy Kwong. A framework for reactive intelligence through agile component-based behaviors. Master's thesis, University of Bath, 2003. Department of Computer Science.

[15] Pattie Maes. Situated agents can have goals. In Pattie Maes, editor, *Designing Autonomous Agents : Theory and Practice from Biology to Engineering and back*, pages 49–70. MIT Press, Cambridge, MA, 1990.

[16] David Lorge Parnas, Paul C. Clements, and David M. Weiss. The modular structure of complex systems. *IEEE Transactions on Software Engineering*, SE-11(3):259–266, March 1985.

[17] Samuel J. Partington. A critical analysis of behaviour-oriented design (BOD), based on experiences in using it to create an unreal tournament capture-the-flag (CTF) team, *expected* 2005. Undergraduate Dissertation, University of Bath.

MyTutor: A Personal Tutoring Agent

Berardina De Carolis

Dipartimento di Informatica – Università di Bari Italy
decarolis@di.uniba.it

Abstract. Recently, Italian Universities promoted interventions in order to improve tutoring and orientation services for students during their course of studies. The main aim of this directive was to support each student with personalized solution to their problems. In this paper we present MyTutor, an Embodied Conversational Agents (ECA) that can be consulted on the student personal device and has the main aim to assist him/her during their studies by providing suggestions regarding the student problems. The paper discusses the design and technical issues involved in developing the architecture of this agent and the plan for evaluation.

1 Introduction

In the last five years, Italian Universities promoted an intervention in order to improve tutoring and orientation services for students during their course of studies [9]. The main aim of this directive was to propose to each student personalized solution to their orientation problems.

Student orientation at the University level means a set of integrated interventions that aim at following the student during the entire course of study, giving him personalized suggestions about different topics, helping him/her to take decisions.

At the Department of Computer Science at the University of Bari, a human tutor has the main goals of assisting and orienting the students focusing on:

- suggestions about orientation choices,
- personalization of the study curricula,
- removal of obstacles during the course of study,
- identification of appropriate and interesting research fields for the thesis,
- suggestions on how to make students more participative in their formative process.

Tutors are defined among available professors by the Department Council and, at the first year, each student is assigned to a tutor that follows him/her during the entire course of study. However, we noticed that this service was not fully exploited by students and we started to investigate about the reasons related to this phenomenon.

In order to assess the motivations of this behavior, we made a user study consisting in a questionnaire (150 subjects in total). The questionnaire was aiming at understanding which was the user expectation about the tutor role and at assessing why students were not using this orientation service.

Analyzing the results of questions about this last issue, it came out that main reasons were related to the difficulty sometime to find the tutor available were needed

T. Panayiotopoulos et al. (Eds.): IVA 2005, LNCS 3661, pp. 478–488, 2005.
© Springer-Verlag Berlin Heidelberg 2005

(professors teach, do research, are involved in meeting, etc.) and to the shyness of some student that are afraid to ask questions about their problems to professors.

For this reason, we decided to develop MyTutor, an Embodied Conversational Agent (ECA) acting as a personal tutor during the entire course of study.

In this relational role, ECAs offer to people the possibility to relate with computer media at a social level [14] and, therefore, they have potential as facilitators for this type of interventions.

According to research and evaluation studies in the field of intelligent interfaces, embodied conversational agents (ECA) [8,10] have shown to be a good interaction metaphor when acting in the role of counselors [11], personal trainer [1], healthy living advisor [5].

However, even if these agents have shown to have a good impact on settling an emphatic relation with the user [4, 1], involving them in a more deep and intimate interaction, it is difficult to communicate with these agents whenever needed (i.e. when the user is not in not in front of a computer but he/she has the need to get suggestions and advices). DESIA, the work of Johnson et al. [10], is a step in this direction. This agent present in *Carmen's Bright IDEAS* has been adapted for running successfully on a handheld device.

Following this idea and taking into account the motivations for developing MyTutor, we extended the Mind-Body architecture, developed in the context of the MagiCster project [5], in order to make it run on a PC as well as on the student personal device with the main aim to assist the student in orientation interventions and providing solution to his/her problem. Even if in this paper we focus on MyTutor application, the proposed architecture is general enough to be applied to other domains.

The paper discusses the design and technical issues involved in developing this agent on a handheld computer. Students can carry the handheld device with them during their daily activities and ask for their tutor intervention.   The paper is structured as follows: Section 1 gives an overview of the System. Section 2 shows how this architecture has been used to implement MyTutor; in particular, we describe the results of the user study and how its results have been used to implement the tutoring strategies. Finally, conclusions and future work directions have been discussed in Section 3.

2   System Architecture Overview

As mentioned in the Introduction, MyTutor is based on the architectural schema developed in the context of the MagiCster project.

In Magicster, the ECA was intended as an entity made up of two main components, a '*Mind*' and a '*Body*', interfaced by a I/O language, so as to overcome integration problems and to allow their independence and modularity. During the interaction, the Agent's Mind had the purpose of deciding what to communicate, by considering the dialogue history, the conversational context and its own current cognitive state.

The output of the mind module was an APML (Affective Presentation Markup Language) specification of the meaning to be communicated [3]. The Body had the purpose to interpret and render it at the surface level, according to the available communicative channels: different bodies may have different expressive capabilities and therefore may use different channels.

This approach was mainly driven by the the definition of *communicative function* in Poggi et al. [13]. In their theory, a communicative function is a (**meaning**, **signal**) pair, where the **meaning** item corresponds to the communicative value of the **signal** item. For instance, a smile can be the signal of a "joy" emotion.

Therefore, the Mind should convey only the meaning(s) associated with the act to be communicated and the Body should interpret these meaning and, according to the interaction context, render them into an expressive behaviour.

In the first version of the architecture, the APML interpretation process was embedded in the Body Player [3]. But, since the Agent's believability is strictly related to features such as its personality and role and the cultural and social context, abstracting, in the behaviour specification phase, the way in which the Body will render that meaning enforces adaptivity to these features. For instance, context-dependent meaning-signal tables might be defined for adapting the Agent behaviour to cultural differences [6].

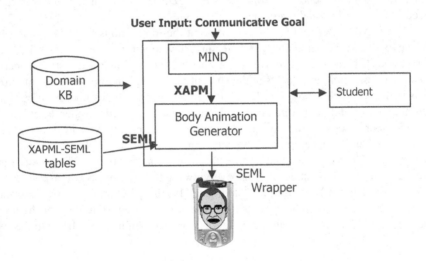

Fig. 1. Mind-Body Architecture

Moreover, since the agent has been conceived so as to be a *student companion* and has to accessible whenever the student needs it, we cannot make the hypothesis that there will be always a network connection. In order to support, MyTutor consultation on and off line on the student personal device, we adapted the ECA architecture so that the ECA player is completely managed on the mobile device. However, mobile devices places limitations on the functionality of the ECA, since their computational and display capabilities are limited; For this reason we had to adapt the Body Animation Generator and implement it with a technology that was simple enough to be handled also on small mobile devices. Let's see now how the architecture shown in Figure 1 has been adapted for this purpose.

2.1 Agent's Mind

The task of this module is to generate an **XAPML** (eXtended APML) specification representing the Agent's move at the meaning level. Planning is a difficult task, moreover MyTutor has to be consulted on and off-line, then it is not feasible to have a planner running on an handheld computer.

For this reason, when a communicative goals is posted to the system, derived by the interpretation of the user input, the Agent's Mind selects from the Plan Library the appropriate 'recipe' schema or a combination of schemas that allows to satisfy that goal. The result is a specification of meanings to be communicated written in XAPML.

XAPML is an extension of APML, it includes the following information that were not present in the first version:

- besides the specification of what the agent has to communicate it is possibile to specify the agent information **background** (access to more details, visualization of relevant domain objects, etc.);

- the *focus* attribute of the <performative> tag allows to establish which is the comunicative focus and to update the student model with information about what has been communicated to the student;

- the *voice* attribute has been added since, in case the student interact through its handheld device, the voice output has to generated on the server side and then passed to the client for being played together with the body animation.

These recipes have been designed on the basis of the results of the proposed questionnaire. Figure 2 shows results illustrating the interests and expectations of first year students.

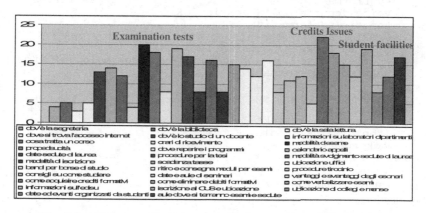

Fig. 2. Results of the questionnaire of first year students (labels are in Italian)

Analysing these results, major interests concern information about modalities for *accessing student facilities, setting an examination test, get credits* and *recover from formative debits*. According to this result, we developed XAPML schemas for answering to these families of questions and for getting more detailed answers once selected a topic question.

The following is a plan made up of two *recipes* for answering to the main question: *"how to set an exam* and *find useful material"*:

```
<XAPML-recipe goal="suggestion-how-to">
<agent>
      <performative      type="inform"      affect="happy-for"
      voice="happy.mp3"> I'm happy for </performative>
      <performative   type="inform"   voice="decision.mp3">
      your decision of [topic] </performative>
      <performative                            type="suggest"
      voice="suggestion.mp3">These    are    my    sugges-
      tions:</performative>
      [FORALL suggestion-i DO
            <performative type="suggest" focus="suggestion-
            i"   voice="[ordinal]_sugg.mp3">[ordinal],   you
            should [suggestion-i]</performative>
      ]
      </agent>
      <background>
      [FORALL suggestion-i DO
      [IF detail
            <object type="link" label="More details on
            [suggestion-i]">[URI-suggestion-i]</object>
      ]
            ]
      </background>
</XAPML-recipe>
<XAPML-recipe goal="find-material">
      <agent>
            <performative type="suggest" voice="material.mp3">
            You  can  consult  the  on-line  course  of  [topic]
            </performative>
            <performative                            type="inform"
            voice="course.mp3"><deitic=[URI-
            topic]</performative>
            <performative   type="suggest"   voice="joy.mp3">   I
            will be happy </performative>
            <performative   type="suggest"   voice="help.mp3">to
            help you</performative>

      </agent>
      <background>
            <object type="link" label="On-line course of
            [topic]">[URI-topic]</object>
      </background>
</XAPML-recipe>
```

These schemas are applied by the Mind in order to generate the XAPML instantiated specification.

In the previous example, square parenthesis represent instructions to the XAPML generator that will substitute them with the appropriate text by manipulating information in the Domain Knowledge Base and the voice files will be generated on the Mind side by a Text To Speech (TTS).

The following is an example of instantiated output generated for the first schema of the plan shown before:

```
<XAPML>
<agent>
      <performative    type="inform"    affect="happy-for"
voice="happy.mp3"> I'm happy for </performative>
      <performative    type="inform"    voice="decision.mp3">
your decision of setting an exam</performative>
      <performative                      type="suggest"
voice="suggestion.mp3">These     are     my     sugges-
tions:</performative>
      <performative    type="suggest"    focus="contact-
professor" voice="first_sugg.mp3">First, you should con-
tact the professor responsible for the exam you want to
set.</performative>
      <performative    type="suggest"    focus="contact-
professor"  voice="second_sugg.mp3">Second,  you   should
subscribe for the exam in the student list present on the
Department Web Site.</performative>
..
</agent>

<background>
      <object type="link" label="More details on subscribe
for the exam">http://www.di.uniba.it/esami.php</object>
</background>
</XAPML>
```

This transformation is executed on the server side and not on the handheld computer where, as we will see later on, only instantiated XAPML specification are interpreted and rendered at a surface level.

2.2 Agent's Body

When the student download the agent from the Department Web Site she can choose its Body that is strictly related to the way the agent is able to express meanings.

Since our main aim was not to develop a new ECA player but to test the validity of our approach we developed only two types of bodies (Figure 3): a face (male professor and a young female professor assistant) and a character (a funny ball).

Each ECA conveys the same meanings using signals that are typical of its body. For instance the two faces will use as signal channels those typical of a face (eye, eyebrow, mouth, gaze, etc.) while the funny ball, that can be used for instance in tutoring contexts suitable for children, will use movements, colors and changes in its dimensions as communicative channels.

The XAPML specification is not directly interpreted by the player that is the same for all the different bodies. This is possible since the proposed architecture decouples meanings from signals. Each body has a conditional meaning-signal table that allows to appropriately translate an XAPML tag into a Signal Expression Markup Language (SEML).

SEML tags define the expressions that can be performed on each channel of the Body.   Table 1 specifies how a body's <act> can be specified in SEML along the appropriate channels for the *face* [7,12] and the *ball*.

Table 1. SEML signals expression for two different bodies

Face Body	Funny Ball
<play channel="eye" value=" " />	<play channel="shape" value=""/>
<play channel="eyebrow" value=" "/>	<play channel="color" value=""/>
<play channel="mouth" value=" "/>	<play channel="size" value=""/>
<play channel="gaze" value=""/>	<play channel="look" value=""/>
<play channel="voice" value=" "/>	<play channel="sound" value=""/>
<play channel="text" value=""/>	<play channel="text" value=" "/>

An example of SEML output for both the "professor" and the "funny ball" bodies, deriving from a transformation of a XAPML performative, is shown in Table 2.

The first row shows the XAPML input, the second one the SEML specification for the two bodies and the third one their rendering by the player. In this example, the face body will show a typical human-like expression of *sorry-for*, while the funny-ball will express it by changing its shape (deflated) and color (grey instead of its normal bright colors).

Table 2. Example of transformation from **XAPML** to **SEML**

XAPML:
<performative type="inform" affect="sorry-for" voice="sorry.mp3">
I'm sorry for </performative>

The professor:
```
<act>
 <play channel="mouth" value="serious"/>
 <play                    channel="voice"
value="sorry.mp3"/>
 <play channel="text" value="I'm sorry!"/>
</act>
```

The funny ball:
```
<act>
 <play channel="shape" value="deflated"/>
 <play channel="color" value="grey"/>
 <play channel="size" value="1"/>
 <play channel="sound" value="cry.mp3"/>
 <play channel="text" value="I'm sorry!"/>
</act>
```

The Body Player, in My Tutor application, will then read which combination of signal to play and translate it into Flash composition and animation setting up a Scene.

This double translation allow to be independent from the technology used by the player since the translation of signal into specifications that can be played by the used technology is made by the SEML-PLAYER Wrapper Module.

2.3 Implementation Issues

MyTutor is implemented in Macromedia Flash using ActionScript and the .NET Compact Framework using Visual Basic.

The interaction may be performed on or off-line; when the user is on-line, the computation of the MIND output is performed server side and the rendering on the handheld (client-side). In this case, when the user connects to the server and asks for specific information the related communicative goal is passed to the system that computes and sends back the XAPML specification of the communication, the mp3 file corresponding to the voice output generated by a TTS on the server side and the set of frames needed for that animation if not yet available on the client side.

On the client side, MyTutor composes and plays a combination of animation and sound resources loaded onto the Pocket PC.

As in *DESIA*, with whom this system has a lot of similarities from the implementation point of view, we store the different animations for each body channel. A *scene* is a collection of sequences of animation frames that are composed in real time as needed according to the SEML specification. Obviously, one SEML specification is then translated into a sequence of frames that are synchronized with the mp3 files by the SEML-Wrapper Module.

3 An Example of Interaction

Once the user download MyTutor player a stereotype is assigned to him/her according to the year of course or specialization level. At the moment, we handle the stereotypes for modeling interests and background knowledge of first, second and third year students.

The stereotype is also used to select a set of basic XAPML recipes that can be used to match the user goals. Together with these recipes, the related mp3 files that have been generated by the server, are also transferred on the user platform.

From that moment the agent can be consulted off and on-line. In the first case the agent can use only the animation and the XAPML recipes available on the client, in the second case suggestions and answers are generated by the server on request and transferred on the user device for interpretation and rendering. After the agent initialization, the user stereotype becomes the user profile and is updated according to the user interaction with the agent. This can be used for adapting the information to the student situation but also for storing what the user wants to know and the system was not able to communicate due to lack of resources.

In this case, when the user will be physically in the Department or will connect to the Mind module through the internet the system will be able to download the needed resources and answer to the user requests.

MyTutor dialogs are mainly informative, however due to the nature of the system we plan to add plan for motivating the student and show empathy.

Figure 3 is an example that shows a simple interaction in which the student ask for something that the Agent do not know and, after having shown that it is sorry for this inconvenient, MyTutor suggest to look on the Department web site performing a deictic gaze. When the user input his/her move or look for details in a different page,

Fig. 3. A simple example of interaction, in Italian

it is always possible to go back and talk to the agent by selecting the icon on the bottom status bar of the handheld application.

As mentioned in the Introduction, we plan to evaluate the system in order to assess whether the number of requested intervention, compared to the one requested to the human one, increases and the provided suggestions match the user expectation and involve more the students in their formative process.

This is possible by analyzing after each semester, if students agree, their profile, measuring in this way the frequency of use of MyTutor, the frequency of question categories and the type of new questions asked by the students.

The study will also try to assess the student attitudes toward the Agent in terms of how much the presence of an embodied agent improved the effectiveness and engagement of interaction. This will be evaluated through the use of a questionnaire aiming at understanding how much the student liked the character and how much they found helpful MyTutor suggestions.

Finally, another possible evaluation concern the impact of the chosen body on the two previous evaluated issues.

4   Conclusions

MyTutor is an animated agent designed to support students along their course of study by providing orientation suggestions and information useful to solve their problems.

The agent can be consulted on a handheld device. For this reason we decided to use an extension of the Mind-Body architecture already used in the context of the MagiCster project. In particular, the Mind, running on the server side, decide what to say and generates, through the use of plan "recipes", a specification (in XAPML) of the meaning to be communicated by the Body that can be used to generate the agent behavior on the handheld computer (client side).

Since the architecture can support the use of different "bodies", that can express meanings using different signals according to their available channels, a meaning-signal table specify how a specific body has to convey particular meanings. This is represented through the use of another markup language SEML that specify which combination of signal to employ in correspondence of each XAPML tag. Then, the

SEML specification is interpreted by a Wrapper, developed in Flash for MyTutor application, that is responsible for the synchronization and the rendering of the agent animations.

We are aware that MyTutor agent animations are very simple, but this was a first step in order to test how the architecture could support this kind of interaction.

While waiting for the first evaluation results, we are developing a better set of animation for MyTutor body.

Acknowledgments

I wish to thank Patrizia Suma for her contribution on the implementation of the system and Fiorella de Rosis and other MagiCster partners for their contribution on the ideas at the basis of the Mind-Body architecture that has been extended for achieving the results shown in this paper.

References

1. Bickmore, T. 2003. Relational Agents: Effecting Change through Human-Computer Relationships. PhD Thesis, Media Arts & Sciences, Massachusetts Institute of Technology.
2. Cassell, J., Sullivan, J., Prevost, S., & Churchill, E., eds. Embodied Conversational Agents. Cambridge, MA: MIT Press.
3. Berardina De Carolis, Catherine Pelachaud, Isabella Poggi, Mark Steedman. APML, a Markup Language for Believable Behavior Generation. In H Prendinger and M Ishizuka (Eds): "Life-like Characters. Tools, Affective Functions and Applications". Springer, 2003.
4. F. de Rosis, A. Cavalluzzi, I. Mazzotta and N. Novielli.Can embodied conversational agents induce empathy in users? AISB'05 "Virtual Social Characters Symposium". Hatfield, April 2005.
5. F de Rosis, B De Carolis, V Carofiglio and S Pizzutilo: Shallow and inner forms of emotional intelligence in advisory dialog simulation. In H Prendinger and M Ishizuka (Eds): "Life-like Characters. Tools, Affective Functions and Applications". Springer, 2003.
6. de ROSIS, F., PELACHAUD, C. & POGGI, I.. Transcultural believability in embodied agents: a matter of consistent adaptation. In R.Trappl & S.Payr (eds.) Agent Culture: Designing virtual characters for a multi-cultural world. Dordrecht: Kluwer Academic Publishers, in press.
7. P. Ekman. Facial expression of emotion. American Psychologist, 48, 384-392.
8. Gratch, J., Rickel, J., Andre, J., Badler, N., Cassell, J., Petajan, E. "Creating Interactive Virtual Humans:Some Assembly Required", IEEE Intelligent Systems, July/August 2002, pp. 54-63.
9. http://informatica.uniba.it/info_comuni/tutorato.htm
10. W. Lewis Johnson, Catherine LaBore, and Yuan-Chun Chiu. A Pedagogical Agent for Psychosocial Intervention on a Handheld Computer. AAAI Fall Symposium on Dialogue Systems for Health Communication. October 22-24 2004.
11. Marsella, S.C., Johnson, W.L., & LaBore, C.M. 2003. Interactive pedagogical drama for health interventions. In U. Hoppe et al. eds., Artificial Intelligence in Education: Shaping the Future of Learning through Intelligent Technologies, 341-348. Amsterdam: IOS Press.

12. C Pelachaud, V. Carofiglio, B De Carolis, F de Rosis and I Poggi: Embodied Contextual Agents for Information Delivery Applications. Proceedings of AAMAS'02, Bologna.
13. I.Poggi, C. Pelachaud, and F. de Rosis. Eye communication in a conversational 3D synthetic agent. Special Issue on Behavior Planning for Life-Like Characters and Avatars of AI Communications. 2000.
14. Reeves, B. and Nass, C. 1996. The Media Equation. New York: Cambridge University Press.

Using Facial Expressions Depicting Emotions in a Human-Computer Interface Intended for People with Autism

O. Grynszpan[1], J.-C. Martin[1], and J. Nadel[2]

[1] LIMSI-CNRS, BP 133, 91403 Orsay Cedex, France
[2] CNRS UMR 7593, Hôpital Salpêtrière, 47 Bd de l'Hôpital, F-75013 Paris, France
{ouriel, martin}@limsi.fr, jnadel@ext.jussieu.fr

Abstract. Autism is a disorder altering verbal and non-verbal communication. People with high functioning autism, who have normal or above normal IQ scores, tend to have difficulties with facial expressions during social interactions. Researchers in multidisciplinary fields provide experimental evidence of the usefulness of computer education for autism. Yet, few software based on facial expressions have been experimentally evaluated. Our multidisciplinary research team aims at defining design guidelines for software dedicated to autism. In an experimental protocol, we have compared learning in two domains: dialogue understanding and spatial planning, an area in which people with autism are expected to be more skilful. Subjects' performances were assessed in each learning domain during two evaluation sessions, which occurred before and after a training period. Eight teenagers with high functioning autism attended a workshop once a week, during 13 weeks. The training exercise in dialogue understanding displayed a written dialogue, along with three assertions about the dialogue, only one of which was correct. Three training sessions were dedicated to testing a modality where every reply in the dialogue was bound with a 3-D image of the character's facial expression. Each reply of the dialogue was successively displayed and pronounced by a synthetic voice, while the corresponding facial expression was displayed. The user could then click on any reply to see the associated facial expression. Facial expressions depicted six possible emotions: happiness, sadness, fear, surprise, laughter, anger. Dialogues would contain pragmatic subtleties. We wanted to test the impact of emotional facial expressions on dialogue disambiguation, by comparing subjects' performances with and without facial expressions. The influence of pictorial style was also tested by comparing realistic with cartoon like facial expressions. Three dependent variables were computed for performance analysis: the number of incorrect trials, the number of correct scenarios and the mean duration of correct scenarios. First results indicate a significant progression in the social dialogue understanding domain after the overall training period. The influence of the emotional facial expressions modality is still being examined at the time of writing.

T. Panayiotopoulos et al. (Eds.): IVA 2005, LNCS 3661, p. 489, 2005.
© Springer-Verlag Berlin Heidelberg 2005

A Survey of Computational Emotion Research

Donglei Zhang[1,2], Cungen Cao[1], Xi Yong[1,2], Haitao Wang[1,2], and Yu Pan[1,2]

[1] Key Lab of Intelligent Information Processing, Institute of Computing Technology,
Chinese Academy of Sciences, 100080, Beijing, China
[2] Graduate School of Chinese Academy of Sciences, 100039, Beijing, China
{dlzhang, cgcao, yongxi, htwang}@ict.ac.cn,
guiziliu_panyu@sina.com

Abstract. Emotion reserch covers a multi-disciplinary domain. In the past three decades, a number of theoretical models and computer applications have been proposed from different perspectives. There are models of appraisal theory, such as OCC and Frijda's model, as well as computational systems such as Affective Reasoner, EMA and Cathexis, to make agents believable and human-like. This paper conducts a comprehensive analysis of those state-of-the-art based on the following six criteria, each of which we believe represents a critical aspect in a computational emotion system.

Emotion Type Set. Each emotion model is explicitly or implicitly associated with a set of emotion types, each of which needs a clear characterization. Different models may distinguish different types clearly from others, but it should explain as many as possible, which reflects the adaptability for different emotions.

Emotion Simultaneity. According to psychology research, emotion is not a single and exclusive phenomenon. More than one emotion can arise simultaneously within one emotion experiencer. The ability to handle this feature is important for compatibility.

Role-Orientedness. Human in society have one or more special positions, which are distinguished as social roles. People with different roles may explain and respond to the same event differently, relying on which different emotions arise.

Emotion Situatedness. Most emotions may have an abstract definition or charac-terization. However, such definitions can not be used directly in real-world applications for the gap between abstract characterizations and actual circumstances. A practical system needs the ability to map daily emotional situations into general emotional rules.

Distributed Emotion. People do not live isolated in society. An individual will interact or have various relations with other people at times, thus will influence the emotion response each other by speech and behavior, even by one's own attitude and emotion state. A broad model may deal with these factors and represent the emotions of the group.

Behavior Display. Following emotions, an individual may express some responses. Moreover, for a given emotional agent in the system, emotions, together with the agent's goals, may play a key role for the action selection of this agent.

T. Panayiotopoulos et al. (Eds.): IVA 2005, LNCS 3661, p. 490, 2005.
© Springer-Verlag Berlin Heidelberg 2005

A Study on Generating and Matching Facial Control Point Using Radial Basis Function

Lee Hyun Cheol[1], Eun Seok Kim[1], Hee Young Choi[2], and Hur Gi Taek[1]

[1] Department of Digital Contents, Dongshin University,
252, Daehodong, Naju, Jeonnam, 520-714 Republic of Korea
{hclee, eskim, gthur}@dsu.ac.kr
[2] Dept. of Computer and Information Science, Chonnam National University,
300, Youngbong, Bukgu, Kwangju, Republic of Korea
hychoi@sunny.chonnam.ac.kr

1 Introduction

3D face animation has been applied widely through virtual reality, MPEG-4 image compression, teleconference, advertisement, and game. Especially, it has developed to a point where it can express 3D face in real time thanks to a development of hardware and software. General 3D face modeling generates 3D face model and matches face model by using vertex points on 3D mesh as control points or generating random control points to match the image corresponding to each individual's face form. However, since this type of work uses control point coordinates on a whole mesh, it takes a lot of time and effort to distort mesh form or to match the image corresponding to user's face form. Therefore, this study developed a method that generates 3D individual face model automatically using 2D full face image. In addition, this study provided a face control point generating and matching method using FFPs(Facial Feature Points) information extracting method using RBF from 3D face mesh.

2 Generating Facial Control Points Using Radial Basis Function

This study made a special study on effective method that generates 3D individual face model automatically using 2D full face image. Using FFPs extracting method that uses RBF from 3D face mesh, face control point generating and matching method were suggested. Likewise, this study suggested 3D face model generating method activated by inputting one full face image and control point generating and matching method using RBF allowing users to express exact face model according to an each individual's face form easily and intuitively.

T. Panayiotopoulos et al. (Eds.): IVA 2005, LNCS 3661, p. 491, 2005.
© Springer-Verlag Berlin Heidelberg 2005

A Platform Independent Architecture for Virtual Characters and Avatars*

M. Gillies[1], V. Vinayagamoorthy[1], D. Robeterson[2], and A. Steed[1]

[1] Department of Computer Science, University College London, London, UK
[2] BT plc, Adastral Park, Ipswich IP5 3RE, UK
{m.gillies, v.vinayagamoorthy, a.steed}@cs.ucl.ac.uk
dale.e2.robertson@bt.com

We have developed a Platform Independent Architecture for Virtual Characters and Avatars (PIAVCA), a character animation system that aims to be independent of any underlying graphics framework and so be easily portable. PIAVCA supports body animation based on a skeletal representation and facial animation based on morph targets.

An important features of PIAVCA is the "Motion Abstraction", a single abstract data type that represents any form of animation of a character. Different implementations of the abstraction can provide very different sources of animation, for example motion capture data, procedural animation or real time tracking data. The abstraction itself is very simple, each motion has a number of "tracks" each of which has a value that varies over time, which could be stored (in the case of motion capture data) but it could also be computed on the fly. It can represent both body animation and facial animation, where each track corresponds to a morph target. However, the real power of the motion abstraction is that is becomes possible to implement transformation on animations without knowing what the source of the animation is, or even without knowing whether it is a body or face animation. We have implemented a number of transformations on single motions (e.g. scaling, altering the speed, looping) and on multiple animations (e.g. smooth transitioning, interpolated motions, performing different motions on different parts of the body, randomly scheduling multiple motions). All these transformations are themselves implementations of the motion abstraction, making it possible to pass the result of one transformation to another one. This simple mechanism allows a new method of creating complex motions by composing multiple stages of transformations. The motion abstraction also makes PIAVCA highly extensible as new transformations or sources of animation merely have to implement the motion abstraction in order to be completely interoperable with existing ones.

PIAVCA also contains a number of other features that make it simple to use. It has a queue that makes it possible to smoothly sequence motions. It is also possible to play a number of "background motions" concurrently with other motions, for example, to provide variety and idling behaviour. PIAVCA has been used for a number of immersive virtual reality studies and we have developed a TCL-based framework for quickly creating experiemenal scenarios.

---

* This work has been supported by BT plc and European Union FET project PRESENCIA, IST-2001-37927.

T. Panayiotopoulos et al. (Eds.): IVA 2005, LNCS 3661, p. 492, 2005.
© Springer-Verlag Berlin Heidelberg 2005

GAL: Towards Large Simulations with Tens of Agents*

Cyril Brom, Ondřej Šerý, Tomáš Poch, and Pavel Šafrata

Charles University, Faculty of Mathematics and Physics,
Malostranské nám. 2/25, Prague, Czech Republic
brom@ksvi.mff.cuni.cz, ondrej.sery@seznam.cz

Abstract. Most of the current intelligent virtual agents (IVAs) either "live" in small, toy-like artificial worlds (*e.g.*, in a room, not in a village), or do exhibit only a small portion of human-like behaviour (*e.g.*, only object-grasping, walking or a few tasks). We think that there is a growing need of IVAs exhibiting a larger scale of behaviours in larger worlds, especially in virtual storytelling applications, and computer games. As an example, consider an artificial merchant riding on its donkey across a virtual kingdom in an adventure game. Furthermore, assume that there are tens of such persistent agents important for the course of the game.

During our previous work [1], we discovered that it was very hard to populate a large artificial world with tens of such IVAs because of limited computational and memory resources. We have identified four key aspects of long-lasting simulations:

1. Because of the requirement of an incremental design, they must be easily extensible. That means IVAs must be adaptive to newly added components.
2. There often exist only few places in the artificial world important at a given simulation time. The unimportant places do not need to be simulated precisely.
3. While some IVAs must "live" throughout the simulation (*e.g.*, the merchant), others can exist only for a particular period, and carry out only a specific task.
4. An IVA usually needs neither its own internal world representation, nor its own set of plans driving its behaviour. Memory resources can be often shared.

Considering these aspects, we have aimed at developing a design and programming framework GAL that can cope with large simulations running on a single PC. The GAL has two key features. First, it extends the technique of smart objects, unites it with the technique of role-passing, presenting the concept of *smart processes*. Smart processes are agents that can be placed anywhere in an artificial world and that can navigate IVAs. Second, GAL exploits the *level-of-detail technique* at the behavioural level. The simulation of details that a user cannot see is automatically simplified.

We are now implementing a prototype scenario in order to prove usefulness of GAL. More information is available at: http://mff.modry.cz/ive.

Reference

1. Bojar, O., Brom, C., Hladík, M., Toman, V.: The Project ENTs: Towards Modeling Human-like Artificial Agents. In *SOFSEM 2005 Communications* Slovak Republic (2005)

---

* This research is partially supported by the Program "Information Society" under the project 1ET10030051.

T. Panayiotopoulos et al. (Eds.): IVA 2005, LNCS 3661, pp. 493, 2005.
© Springer-Verlag Berlin Heidelberg 2005

Virtual Agents in a Simulation of an ISO-Company*

Cyril Brom[1] and Petr Kocáb[2]

[1] Charles University, Faculty of Mathematics and Physics,
Malostranské nám. 2/25, Prague 1, Czech Republic
[2] SoftDeC, spol. s r. o., U Průhonu 32, Prague 7, Czech Republic
{c.brom, p.kocab}@softdec.cz

Abstract. Most companies require a precise "process-oriented" description of actions, tasks and processes carried out by their employees. "Who does what and in which order?" – it is often asked. The description is a ground for quality management and for further evaluation and effectiveness optimalisation. Most business toolkits allow process modelling and some of them also process simulation, e.g. [3]. However, these simulations and their results are visualized by means of some diagrams or statistical analysis, and it is often hard for managers to cope with these techniques.

We aimed at exploiting intelligent virtual agents in business-process simulations in order to ease evaluation. We want to develop a toolkit for prototyping customisable virtual company inhabited by graphically embodied artificial employees carrying on exactly specified business-processes. The toolkit will also offer some analytical tools.

Specifications of business-processes are often given in some diagrams or "condition-action" natural sentences. For the purposes of a simulation, they must be "translated" into a formal description. Because an action selection model of virtual agents can be relatively simple, we aimed at "converting" ISO 9001 documentations (which are grounds for all ISO-certified companies) [4] into hierarchical reactive if-then rules and exploiting behavioural oriented design [2]. Every particular simulation will be instantiated with attributes of virtual employees and purchase orders. As 3D visualisation is not vital, a viewer will be based on an isometric "2½"D platform [1].

Contribution will be twofold. First, in addition to classical diagram-based simulations and statistical analysis, evaluation of processes by means of neat visualisation will be possible. Second, the simulations will serve well for presentational and educational purposes of managers.

References

1. Bojar, O., Brom, C., Hladík, M., Toman, V.: The Project ENTs: Towards Modeling Human-like Artificial Agents. In *SOFSEM 2005 Communications* Slovak Republic (2005)
2. Bryson, J.: The Behavior-Oriented Design of Modular Agent Intelligence. In: *Proc .of Agent Technologies, Infrastructures and Tools for E-Services*, LNCS 2592 (2003) 61-76
3. IDS Scheer AG: ARIS Design Platform, ARIS Simulation. www.ids-scheer.com
4. Int. Organisation for Standardisation: ISO 9001-4, Quality Systems. www.iso.org

---

* This research is partially supported by the Program "Information Society" under the project 1ET100300517, and by SoftDeC spol. s r. o. company, http://www.softdec.cz.

Appraisal for a Character-Based Story-World

Stefan Rank[1] and Paolo Petta[1,2]

[1] Austrian Research Institute for Artificial Intelligence,* Freyung 6/6, A-1010
Vienna, Austria
stefan.rank@ofai.at

[2] Dept.of Med.Cybernetics and AI, Centre for Brain Res., Med.Univ.of Vienna,
Freyung 6/2, A-1010 Vienna, Austria
paolo.petta@meduniwien.ac.at

Dramatic story-worlds, i.e., *simulations inhabited by software actors for enacting* (not necessarily explicitly anticipated) *dramatically interesting plots*, require situated software agents with emotional competences. The operationalisation of concepts from appraisal theories of emotion can contribute to providing flexible autonomous roleplayers for character-based approaches that reduce the required external macro-level control.

Situatedness and the analysis of the *social lifeworld* of characters [1] are the foundations of the *appraisal-based* agent architecture ActAffAct that generates simple cliché plots. Our approach views emotions as the links between actions that render a plot plausible. The subjective evaluative interpretation of changes in a character's environment according to its *concerns*, and the reactions entailed, provide causal and emotional connections that can lead to the unfolding of a story. Situatedness obviates the need to continuously control the agent on a low level, where structure results inherently from the needs of situated activity and routine functioning. The main problem, then, is the allocation of the agent's bounded resources to behaviour coordination.

For simple story-worlds, context-dependent interpretation of sensations and annotation of current behaviours allows to ease implementation of the appraisal process. Behaviour phases of different degrees of persistence and a preliminary implementation of regulation increase coherence of activity. Especially when triggered by coping, this meets our aim towards delivery of comprehensible and diversified plot links. First evaluations of a simulation of an environment inhabited by agents with the roles of narrative archetypes encourages the broader survey work and further pursuit of principled approaches for the integration of affective

---

* The Austrian Research Institute for Artificial Intelligence is supported by the Austrian Federal Ministry for Education, Science and Culture and by the Austrian Federal Ministry for Transport, Innovation and Technology. This research is carried out within the Network of Excellence Humaine (Contract No. 507422) that is funded by the European Union's Sixth Framework Programme with support from the Austrian Funds for Research and Technology Promotion for Industry (FFF 808818/2970 KA/SA). This publication reflects only the authors' views. The European Union is not liable for any use that may be made of the information contained herein.

T. Panayiotopoulos et al. (Eds.): IVA 2005, LNCS 3661, pp. 495–496, 2005.
© Springer-Verlag Berlin Heidelberg 2005

processes, deliberation, and situated action, being undertaken in the context of the European FP6 NoE Humaine (http://emotion-research.net).

Reference

1. S. Rank, P. Petta: Motivating Dramatic Interactions. In *Agents that Want and Like: Motivational and Emotional Roots of Cognition and Action, Proc. AISB05 Symposium*, April 12-15 2005, Univ. Hertfordshire, Hatfield, UK, pp.102–107, 2005.

Evolving Emotional Behaviour for Expressive Performance of Music

Eduardo Coutinho, Eduardo Reck Miranda, and Patricio da Silva

Future Music Lab - University of Plymouth,
206 Smeaton Building – Drake Circus – Plymouth PL4 8AA – United Kingdom
{eduardo.coutinho, eduardo.miranda,
patricio.dasilva} @plymouth.ac.uk

Abstract. Today computers can be programmed to compose music automatically, using techniques ranging from rule-based to evolutionary computation (e.g., genetic algorithms and cellular automata). However, we lack good techniques for programming the computer to play or interpret music with expression. Expression in music is largely associated with emotions. Therefore we are looking into the possibility of programming computer music systems with emotions. We are addressing this problem from an A-Life perspective combined with recent discoveries in the neurosciences with respect to emotion.

Antonio Damasio refers to the importance of emotions to assist an individual to maintain survival, as they seem to be an important mechanism for adaptation and decision-making. Specifically, environmental events of value should be susceptible to preferential perceptual processing, regarding their pleasant or unpleasant. This approach assumes the existence of neural pathways that facilitate survival. Stable emotional systems should then emerge from self-regulatory homeostatic processes.

We implemented a system consisting of an agent that inhabits an environment containing with a number of different objects. These objects cause different physiological reactions to the agent. The internal body state of the agent is defined by a set of internal drives and a set of physiological variables that vary as the agent interacts with the objects it encounters in the environment. The agent is controlled by a feed-forward neural network that integrates visual input with information about its internal states. The network learns through a reinforcement-learning algorithm, derivate from different body states, due to pleasant or unpleasant stimuli.

The playback of musical recordings in MIDI format is steered by the physiological variables of the agent in different phases of the adaptation process.

The behaviour of the system is coherent with Damasio's theory of background emotional system. It demonstrates that specific phenomena, such as body/world categorization and existence of a body map, can evolve from a simple rule: self-survival in the environment. Currently, we are in the process of defining a system of higher-level emotional states (or foreground system) that will operate in social contexts; i.e., with several agents in the environment reacting to objects and interacting with each other.

T. Panayiotopoulos et al. (Eds.): IVA 2005, LNCS 3661, p. 497, 2005.
© Springer-Verlag Berlin Heidelberg 2005

A Model of an Embodied Emotional Agent

Cyril Septseault and Alexis Nédélec

Centre Européen de Réalité Virtuelle (CERV),
25, rue Claude Chappe,
BP 38 F-29280 Plouzané France
{septseault, nedelec}@enib.fr

Abstract. We propose a model of embodied agent using SOAR rules engine to define believable behaviour of agents equipped with emotions, motivations, and episodical memory. The aim of our work is to create tools for simulation of virtual human with a believable behaviour which can be used in virtual environment for group meetings training or games.

This work comes from a research project on relational groups of collaborative and emotional agents called GRACE [1]. It is focused on the simulation of the behaviour of an autonomous character evolving in a virtual environment in which users can interact by controlling avatar. One of the goals of this project is to have a believable group's behaviour by modelling individual behaviour of characters. To improve believability, the modeling of an agent must take into account an emotional module which will introduce a skew into the decision, but also will allow to communicate in a nonverbal way between agents.

The design of the model is done in an incremental way. The basic model will make it possible to select an action among a list of possible actions, and to apply it. Then to obtain a believable behavior one must eliminate the not-relevant actions according to the goals of the agent. Next by associating capacities of anticipation, we will allow it to envisage the consequences of its actions and thus to eliminate those which will have harmful results compared to these goals. The addition of an emotional state will allow to improve the evaluation of the anticipated situations. Taking into account the episodical memory will make it possible to remind the emotional impact of actions carried out in a similar situation. The attentional process will make possible for our model of agent to filter in a more significant way the actions suggested. And finally taking into account the motivations of the agent will make it possible to add and modify goals dynamically during simulation.

---

[1] Groupe Relationnel d'Agents Collaboratifs et Emotionnels.

T. Panayiotopoulos et al. (Eds.): IVA 2005, LNCS 3661, p. 498, 2005.
© Springer-Verlag Berlin Heidelberg 2005

Agent Assistance for 3D World Navigation

Bianca Schön, Gregory M.P. O'Hare, Brian R. Duffy, Alan Martin,
and John F. Bradley

University College Dublin, Department of Computer Science,
Belfield, Dublin 4, Ireland
{bianca.schoen, gregory.ohare, brian.duffy, alan.martin,
john.bradley}@ucd.ie
http://chameleon.ucd.ie

This paper presents mechanisms and approaches to assist user navigation and exploration within 3-dimensional worlds. Specifically, we advocate the deployment of an agent based approach for dynamic system assistance and intervention. An algorithm has been developed, that produces a performance measure, which is employed by the intelligent agent to activate system interventions. We outline the importance of providing discrete navigational cues to users in order to increase their sense of immersion and their overall satisfaction while working within the 3D world. We present HADES - the **H**ome of the **Ad**aptive **E**nvironmental **S**ystem, which is a 3-dimensional world within which the intelligent agent is immersed. The agent therefore has the ability to transform this 3D world into an intelligent environment. HADES reacts proactively to users' movements and offers navigational help indirectly. *Indirect* navigational support increases the user's satisfaction with his own performance and therefore endorses the user's sense of immersion.

The algorithm that determines the user's performance within the environment employs an area-based mask which includes the start and goal points. The quantity of the user's movement within the masked area is then compared to the quantity of his movement within the unmasked area. This value is then divided through time in seconds that the user spent inside the 3D world. After determining the user's performance, the agent then tries to offer indirect navigational support. Navigational support can either be tactile, like adjusting the keys' sensitivity or visually by blending out unimportant areas or repositioning intermediate goal points for a fraction of a second.

However, the underlying algorithm to acquire the performance value requires the agent to have previous knowledge about the users' tasks. Further work will compare each adaptivity measure, both separately and in combination. Additonally, the degree of offered support has to be determined.

Reference

1. Schön, B., O'Hare, G. M. P., Duffy, B. R., Martin, A. and Bradley, J. F.: An Agent-based Approach to Adaptive Navigational Support within 3D-Environments. Proceedings of the 2004 IEEE Conference on Cybernetics and Intelligent Systems - CIS 2004. Singapore (2004)

T. Panayiotopoulos et al. (Eds.): IVA 2005, LNCS 3661, p. 499, 2005.
© Springer-Verlag Berlin Heidelberg 2005

NeXuS: Delivering Perceptions to Situated Embodied Agents

Gregory M.P. O'Hare, John W. Stafford, and Abraham G. Campbell

Department of Computer Science, University College Dublin, Ireland
{Gregory.OHare, John.Stafford, Abey.Campbell} @ucd.ie

NeXuS[1] is a framework for the development of Augmented Reality (AR) applications that utilises perceptive intentional agents to create rich interactive environments where traditional boundaries between virtual and physical spaces may be overcome. The NeXuS framework demonstrates how behavioural realism can be achieved by placing such agents within an AR environment. Fig. 1 illustrates how a NeXuS *Teen* agent's perceived beliefs about its environment alters the state of its visual avatar. When a virtual light source located on a marker enters the line of sight of the *Teen's* avatar, the agent must change its avatar's position in the world to one that it deliberately reasons to be most appropriate for avoiding the light's 'glare'.

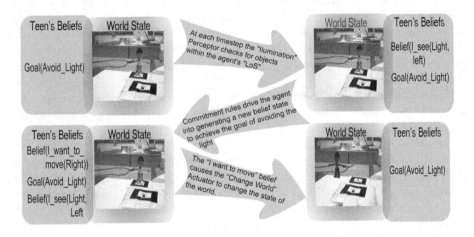

Fig. 1. Teen avoiding the light

Gregory O'Hare gratefully acknowledges the kind support of Science Foundation Ireland under Grant No. 03/IN.3/I361. For more information on NeXuS please visit http://nexus.ucd.ie.

Reference

1. G. M. P. O'Hare, A. G. Campbell, J. W. Stafford, and R. Lowe. Nexus: Behavioural realism in mixed reality scenarios through virtual sensing. In *Proceedings of Computer Animation and Social Agents (CASA 2005)*, October 2005.

T. Panayiotopoulos et al. (Eds.): IVA 2005, LNCS 3661, p. 500, 2005.
© Springer-Verlag Berlin Heidelberg 2005

Emotion in Artificial Intelligence and Artificial Life Research: Facing Problems

Jackeline Spinola de Freitas[1], Ricardo Gudwin, and João Queiroz[2]

School of Electrical and Computer Engineering - State University of Campinas,
PO Box 6101 – 13083-852 SP - Brazil
{jspinola, gudwin, queirozj}@dca.fee.unicamp.br

Abstract. In last decades, neuroscience and psychology research findings about emotion have been increasingly attracting the attention of many researchers in Computer Science and Artificial Intelligence (AI) areas. AI, interested in cognitive processes modeling and simulation, clearly see that emotion is a crucial element to model perception, learning, decision processes, memory, behavior and others functions. Currently, two Computer Science areas use emotion concepts on their research: Human-Computer Interaction and systems whose internal architecture is emotion-based.

Even considering current state-of-art projects, theoretical aspects of emotion to be employed in computational systems projects are scarcely discussed. Our research intends to discuss these problems and propose tentative directions to solve them.

First, (ii) the lack of a well defined scientific framework to approach 'Artificial Emotion', with few advanced attempts been published suggesting one.

Besides that, a close look at some projects provides a non-exhausted list of (ii) important questions they might face to achieve trustworthy results. They can be grouped in two types, theoretical-conceptual or computational questions. Examples are: How to integrate emotion with other mechanisms, such as: sensory, learn, selection and communication? Can artificial emotion be an emergent property? What kind of data structure and computational mechanisms should be used to both capture and represent the complexity of emotion processes? What kind of experimental test allows to better explore emotion-based models? Moreover, an essential question to be answered is related to which extent supposed structural complexity involved in emotion phenomenon can be abstracted and modeled, not missing important brain structure interactions and not being too complex to impair computational representation.

Last, these facts mainly contribute to a third noticeable problem: (iii) lack of comparative analysis between projects and also within same project, with beneficial comparisons of emotion and non-emotion-based experiments.

Positively, overcome these challenges can be an important step to field progress goes beyond engineering applications and towards a more scientific discipline.

---

[1] Supported by CNPq – Brazil.
[2] Supported by FAPESP – Brazil.

T. Panayiotopoulos et al. (Eds.): IVA 2005, LNCS 3661, p. 501, 2005.
© Springer-Verlag Berlin Heidelberg 2005

A Synthetic Agent for Mentoring Novice Programmers Within a Desktop Computer Environment

Desmond Case, Bernadette Sharp, and Peter J. King

University College Northampton,
Boughton Green Road
desmond.case@northampton.ac.uk

Abstract. This research proposes the hypothesis that a synthetic animated agent can provide effective mentoring support for the novice in overcoming problems and pitfalls when learning a programming language for the very first time. Computer programming is a skills-based activity that involves problem solving within the constraints imposed by a computer environment. Numerous authorities have observed that novice programmers make the same mistakes and encounter the same problems when first programming language. The learner errors are usually from a fixed set of misconceptions that are easily corrected by experience and with simple guidance. This research investigates the viability of a synthetic animated agent to provide effective guidance to mentor novice programmers.

The primary pedagogical model that the mentor agent will use is based on the Scaffolding model, where a tutor provides temporary support to the learner and removes the support as it is no longer needed. The support will take many forms e.g. explanations, examples, direction, etc. but requires the learner to be active participants in producing work of their own. For the agent mentoring systems it is planned that the learner will continue to be lectured and tutored as normal with the mentoring agent to provide support in the practical, skills based activity of writing code. The agent will monitor the learner's development environment as they proceed with writing code, the animated agent would then impart guidance when the learner generates errors or unexpected results.

An innovative agent architecture is then proposed based on an analysis of the problem domain that will consist of a Beliefs-Desires-Intentions agent model, to control the animated agent interaction and interface with the programming environment, combined with a Case-Based Reasoning engine to process deep domain knowledge and guide the overall mentoring strategy.

The mentoring agent will operate alongside the development environment for the programming language, for this research Visual Basic and within the Microsoft Windows environment. Experimentation with a working agent system is planned to begin in the autumn of 2005 with cohorts of undergraduate programming novices.

T. Panayiotopoulos et al. (Eds.): IVA 2005, LNCS 3661, p. 502, 2005.
© Springer-Verlag Berlin Heidelberg 2005

vBroker: Agents Teaching Stock Market

Gábor Tatai, László Gulyás, László Laufer, and Márton Iványi

AITIA Inc, Infopark sétány 1. V. em,
H-1117, Budapest, Hungary
{tatus, gulya, laufer, mivanyi}@aitia.ai

Abstract. On our poster we give an overview of our project *vBroker*, an effort aimed at familiarizing the Hungarian public with the workings of the stock market. *vBroker* was a year-long service that consisted of an e-learning portal with material on financial markets, enhanced by the presence of an intelligent tutoring agent (an intelligent chatter robot connected to a specialized knowledge base and with responses based on emotional modeling of the user). In addition, the portal also hosted a virtual stock market based on multi-agent based simulation.

In *vBroker* the chatter robot is used in two functions. It helps website navigation and also serves as a tutoring agent. In its latter function, it can draw the user's attention to understudied topics, it is able to get engaged in conversations on the subject, and provides feedback about test results. In addition, the agent also serves as a virtual broker assisting the user in its effort of accumulating virtual wealth on the virtual stock market. This virtual broker can answer questions about the current trends and prices on the market and also provides feedback about the performance of the user's portfolio.

In contrast to the high number of online stock market games hosted by the Internet in the past, the *vBroker* participatory stock market applied real trading rules, realistic market institutions and infrastructure. Moreover, the simulated market was rooted in an 'artificial economy'. This was achieved by a heterogeneous multi-agent system, where human and artificial agents traded together. For example, artificial agents ensured market liquidity and realistic price movements, in addition to competing with human participants for greater wealth. We try to describe the *vBroker* portal as a whole, giving an overview of its main modules and discussing its e-learning module and its artificial stock market in more detail. In both parts we are focusing on the role of the tutoring agent, who is a mediator between the user and the e-learning material, and the user and the virtual stock market.

T. Panayiotopoulos et al. (Eds.): IVA 2005, LNCS 3661, p. 503, 2005.
© Springer-Verlag Berlin Heidelberg 2005

Emergence of Representational Structures in Virtual Agents

Argyris Arnellos and Spyros Vosinakis

Univ. of the Aegean, Dept of Product & Systems Design Engineering, 84100, Syros, Greece
{arar, spyrosv}@aegean.gr

Autonomy and human-like personality in general is a crucial property of a virtual agent. This paper introduces a framework of self-organised Peircean semiotic processes, which is used to demonstrate the emergence of grounded representational structures in a virtual agent interacting with the environment.

A completed semiosis consists of the three inferential procedures: *abduction*, *deduction* and *induction*, which drive the agent's logical argumentation. In the abductive phase, the agent observes the environment and describes the nature of a surprising phenomenon on the basis of its anticipations. An analogy between the surprising phenomenon and the agent's anticipations is attempted, in order to indicate a possible direction of a hypothesis explaining the phenomenon, and the formulation of this hypothesis takes place.

In the deductive phase the consequences of the hypothesis are examined. A possible direction is indicated based on the agent's anticipations, and the formulation of these consequences takes place. The, in a way, objective meaning, which results from the semantic processes, should be open to revision, which takes place in the inductive phase. The consequences of the hypothesis formulated in the deductive phase are observed in the context of the surprising phenomenon. In case of acceptance, the hypothesis can be used to account for similar surprising phenomena in the future.

An example is set up as an attempt for an application of the proposed framework. There is a simple environment with a number of entities: passive objects and agents. Each agent has its own abilities concerning perception and action, and objects have different qualities and values. The environment uses simple physics that allow collision detection and response that depends on the relevant size and motion of the objects. The agents are wandering around the environment, probably moving some objects due to collisions. Initially they have no representational structures regarding possible actions. The objective is to show that grounded representational structures will emerge through the random interaction of the agent with the environment.

The results of this example are that each agent in the environment creates its own categories of actions based on its experiences, and thus the emergent representational structures could be reused and adapted to other environments with similar physics. Furthermore, the frame-like structure of the semiotic elements allows the representational structure of an agent to be stored and corrected offline by a designer, e.g. to remove possible false hypotheses about actions.

T. Panayiotopoulos et al. (Eds.): IVA 2005, LNCS 3661, p. 504, 2005.
© Springer-Verlag Berlin Heidelberg 2005

Author Index

Lecture Notes in Artificial Intelligence (LNAI)

Vol. 3464: S.A. Brueckner, G.D.M. Serugendo, A. Karageorgos, R. Nagpal (Eds.), Engineering Self-Organising Systems. XIII, 299 pages. 2005.

Vol. 3452: F. Baader, A. Voronkov (Eds.), Logic for Programming, Artificial Intelligence, and Reasoning. XI, 562 pages. 2005.

Vol. 3451: M.-P. Gleizes, A. Omicini, F. Zambonelli (Eds.), Engineering Societies in the Agents World V. XIII, 349 pages. 2005.

Vol. 3446: T. Ishida, L. Gasser, H. Nakashima (Eds.), Massively Multi-Agent Systems I. XI, 349 pages. 2005.

Vol. 3445: G. Chollet, A. Esposito, M. Faundez-Zanuy, M. Marinaro (Eds.), Nonlinear Speech Modeling and Applications. XIII, 433 pages. 2005.

Vol. 3438: H. Christiansen, P.R. Skadhauge, J. Villadsen (Eds.), Constraint Solving and Language Processing. VIII, 205 pages. 2005.

Vol. 3430: S. Tsumoto, T. Yamaguchi, M. Numao, H. Motoda (Eds.), Active Mining. XII, 349 pages. 2005.

Vol. 3419: B. Faltings, A. Petcu, F. Fages, F. Rossi (Eds.), Constraint Satisfaction and Constraint Logic Programming. X, 217 pages. 2005.

Vol. 3416: M. Böhlen, J. Gamper, W. Polasek, M.A. Wimmer (Eds.), E-Government: Towards Electronic Democracy. XIII, 311 pages. 2005.

Vol. 3415: P. Davidsson, B. Logan, K. Takadama (Eds.), Multi-Agent and Multi-Agent-Based Simulation. X, 265 pages. 2005.

Vol. 3403: B. Ganter, R. Godin (Eds.), Formal Concept Analysis. XI, 419 pages. 2005.

Vol. 3398: D.-K. Baik (Ed.), Systems Modeling and Simulation: Theory and Applications. XIV, 733 pages. 2005.

Vol. 3397: T.G. Kim (Ed.), Artificial Intelligence and Simulation. XV, 711 pages. 2005.

Vol. 3396: R.M. van Eijk, M.-P. Huget, F. Dignum (Eds.), Agent Communication. X, 261 pages. 2005.

Vol. 3394: D. Kudenko, D. Kazakov, E. Alonso (Eds.), Adaptive Agents and Multi-Agent Systems II. VIII, 313 pages. 2005.

Vol. 3392: D. Seipel, M. Hanus, U. Geske, O. Bartenstein (Eds.), Applications of Declarative Programming and Knowledge Management. X, 309 pages. 2005.

Vol. 3374: D. Weyns, H. V.D. Parunak, F. Michel (Eds.), Environments for Multi-Agent Systems. X, 279 pages. 2005.

Vol. 3371: M.W. Barley, N. Kasabov (Eds.), Intelligent Agents and Multi-Agent Systems. X, 329 pages. 2005.

Vol. 3369: V. R. Benjamins, P. Casanovas, J. Breuker, A. Gangemi (Eds.), Law and the Semantic Web. XII, 249 pages. 2005.

Vol. 3366: I. Rahwan, P. Moraitis, C. Reed (Eds.), Argumentation in Multi-Agent Systems. XII, 263 pages. 2005.

Vol. 3359: G. Grieser, Y. Tanaka (Eds.), Intuitive Human Interfaces for Organizing and Accessing Intellectual Assets. XIV, 257 pages. 2005.

Vol. 3346: R.H. Bordini, M. Dastani, J. Dix, A.E.F. Seghrouchni (Eds.), Programming Multi-Agent Systems. XIV, 249 pages. 2005.

Vol. 3345: Y. Cai (Ed.), Ambient Intelligence for Scientific Discovery. XII, 311 pages. 2005.

Vol. 3343: C. Freksa, M. Knauff, B. Krieg-Brückner, B. Nebel, T. Barkowsky (Eds.), Spatial Cognition IV. XIII, 519 pages. 2005.

Vol. 3339: G.I. Webb, X. Yu (Eds.), AI 2004: Advances in Artificial Intelligence. XXII, 1272 pages. 2004.

Vol. 3336: D. Karagiannis, U. Reimer (Eds.), Practical Aspects of Knowledge Management. X, 523 pages. 2004.

Vol. 3327: Y. Shi, W. Xu, Z. Chen (Eds.), Data Mining and Knowledge Management. XIII, 263 pages. 2005.

Vol. 3315: C. Lemaître, C.A. Reyes, J.A. González (Eds.), Advances in Artificial Intelligence – IBERAMIA 2004. XX, 987 pages. 2004.

Vol. 3303: J.A. López, E. Benfenati, W. Dubitzky (Eds.), Knowledge Exploration in Life Science Informatics. X, 249 pages. 2004.

Vol. 3301: G. Kern-Isberner, W. Rödder, F. Kulmann (Eds.), Conditionals, Information, and Inference. XII, 219 pages. 2005.

Vol. 3276: D. Nardi, M. Riedmiller, C. Sammut, J. Santos-Victor (Eds.), RoboCup 2004: Robot Soccer World Cup VIII. XVIII, 678 pages. 2005.

Vol. 3275: P. Perner (Ed.), Advances in Data Mining. VIII, 173 pages. 2004.

Vol. 3265: R.E. Frederking, K.B. Taylor (Eds.), Machine Translation: From Real Users to Research. XI, 392 pages. 2004.

Vol. 3264: G. Paliouras, Y. Sakakibara (Eds.), Grammatical Inference: Algorithms and Applications. XI, 291 pages. 2004.

Vol. 3259: J. Dix, J. Leite (Eds.), Computational Logic in Multi-Agent Systems. XII, 251 pages. 2004.

Vol. 3257: E. Motta, N.R. Shadbolt, A. Stutt, N. Gibbins (Eds.), Engineering Knowledge in the Age of the Semantic Web. XVII, 517 pages. 2004.

Vol. 3249: B. Buchberger, J.A. Campbell (Eds.), Artificial Intelligence and Symbolic Computation. X, 285 pages. 2004.

Vol. 3248: K.-Y. Su, J. Tsujii, J.-H. Lee, O.Y. Kwong (Eds.), Natural Language Processing – IJCNLP 2004. XVIII, 817 pages. 2005.

Vol. 3245: E. Suzuki, S. Arikawa (Eds.), Discovery Science. XIV, 430 pages. 2004.

Vol. 3244: S. Ben-David, J. Case, A. Maruoka (Eds.), Algorithmic Learning Theory. XIV, 505 pages. 2004.

Vol. 3238: S. Biundo, T. Frühwirth, G. Palm (Eds.), KI 2004: Advances in Artificial Intelligence. XI, 467 pages. 2004.

Vol. 3230: J.L. Vicedo, P. Martínez-Barco, R. Muñoz, M. Saiz Noeda (Eds.), Advances in Natural Language Processing. XII, 488 pages. 2004.

Vol. 3229: J.J. Alferes, J. Leite (Eds.), Logics in Artificial Intelligence. XIV, 744 pages. 2004.

Vol. 3228: M.G. Hinchey, J.L. Rash, W.F. Truszkowski, C.A. Rouff (Eds.), Formal Approaches to Agent-Based Systems. VIII, 290 pages. 2004.